THE OLD TESTAMENT
IN ARCHAEOLOGY AND HISTORY

THE OLD TESTAMENT
IN ARCHAEOLOGY AND HISTORY

Jennie Ebeling, J. Edward Wright, Mark Elliott,
and Paul V. M. Flesher
Editors

BAYLOR UNIVERSITY PRESS

Unless otherwise stated, Scripture quotations are from the New Revised Standard Version Bible, copyright 1989, Division of Christian Education of the National Council of the Churches of Christ in the United States of America. Used by permission. All rights reserved.

Cover design: Daniel Benneworth-Gray
Cover image: In this relief from the Assyrian King Sennacherib's palace in Nineveh, Lachish's soldiers defend against an approaching battering ram by throwing torches from a tower. In the lower right, civilians attempt to leave the besieged city via the gate. Photo from Todd Bolen/bibleplaces.com.

The printed case ISBN is 9781481309271.

Library of Congress Cataloging-in-Publication Data

Names: Ebeling, Jennie R., editor. | Wright, J. Edward, editor. | Elliott, Mark Adam, 1956– editor. | Flesher, Paul Virgil McCracken, editor.
Title: The Old Testament in archaeology and history / Jennie Ebeling, J. Edward Wright, Mark Elliott, and Paul V.M. Flesher, editors.
Description: Waco, Texas : Baylor University Press, [2017] | "A century ago it was true that if you wanted to understand the ancient Israelites you had to read the Bible, the Old Testament. Today, if you want to understand the Old Testament, you need to study the history and archaeology of the ancient people of Israel"—Preface. | Includes bibliographical references and index.
Identifiers: LCCN 2017003708 (print) | LCCN 2017027764 (ebook) | ISBN 9781481307413 (ePub) | ISBN 9781481307420 (ebook-Mobi/Kindle) | ISBN 9781481307437 (web PDF) | ISBN 9781481307390 (hardback: alk. paper) | ISBN 9781481307406 (pbk. : alk. paper)
Subjects: LCSH: Bible—Antiquities. | Bible—Criticism, interpretation, etc.
Classification: LCC BS621 (ebook) | LCC BS62.O43 2017 (print) | DDC 221.9—dc23
LC record available at https://lccn.loc.gov/2017003708

To our students,
past, present, and future

CONTENTS

I
Archaeology, the Bible, and Epigraphy
Discovery, Techniques, and Development

PREFACE

Several years ago the editors began discussing how beginning students in college Bible courses and a public interested in biblical studies and the ancient Israelites actually studied the Bible. In particular, we wondered, how much did new archaeological discoveries and historical research impact their understanding of ancient Israel and its history? Were such students dependent on biblical scholarship that strictly privileged the biblical narrative? Did the public only encounter apologetic testimonies supported and presented by church and synagogue?

What we found was disappointing. Introductory textbooks, even at the college level, focus mostly on the biblical books and refer to archaeological knowledge only in passing—usually when there is a good picture. Old Testament textbooks depend on the biblical narrative rather than on archaeology for their organization. The situation for the general public is worse. From "biblical mysteries" TV programs more interested in viewership than accuracy to books propounding a variety of theologies and tendentious interpretations, we could not see how an interested and intelligent reader would get a solid understanding of the contributions made by the fields of archaeology, biblical studies, and ancient history to the understanding of ancient Israel. Finally, where serious works are available, they were not written to be accessible to beginning students.

A century ago it was true that if you wanted to understand the ancient Israelites, you had to read the Bible, the Old Testament. Today, if you want to understand the Old Testament, you need to study the history and archaeology of the ancient people of Israel.

The editors decided it was necessary to present ancient Israel's origins and history in a such way that students could understand the Israelites from all of the evidence, not just from a single collection of ancient writings. The study of ancient Israel should be multifaceted and not simply a study of the Bible. This book aims to address the needs of students and the public at large by showing how archaeological finds, including ancient texts and inscriptions from other countries and empires, help modern readers comprehend the political, social, and sometimes military dynamics that shaped the ancient Israelites and led their scribes to write the books now in the Bible.

The present book brings together biblical experts and active archaeologists to contribute their understanding of the present state of research and put together a picture of the origins and history of the people Israel, within the history of the ancient Near East. Despite the in-depth expertise of our authors, all of them composed their chapters for an audience without a deep knowledge of ancient Israel—for people seeking a better understanding rather than those who were already knowledgeable. Fourteen experts in different periods of ancient Israel's history contributed chapters, as did the editors. This achievement is a result of teamwork, for despite the seemingly natural conjunction of the Bible and the archaeology of ancient Israel, the two fields do not have a history of working together. True, archaeologists working in Israel were once accused of digging with a trowel in one hand and a Bible in the other. But few archaeologists were trained as biblical scholars. As William Dever identifies the distinction in chapter 5, the combination inherent in "biblical archaeology" before the 1970s was between archaeology and *theology*, not archaeology and *biblical studies*. Indeed, as Mark Elliott shows in chapter 2, biblical archaeologists like William F. Albright saw themselves as opponents of "higher criticism" and its related research into the biblical text. From the opposite perspective, few biblical scholars had the training and background to understand the details of archaeological investigation and were able to incorporate it into their research at the primary level. Textual scholars of course made use of the inscriptions archaeologists unearthed, but the excavations that discovered them? Not so much.

In this light, the teamwork and cooperation that this textbook represents was hard won. The editors thank the authors for working with us to help achieve the vision that guided this book. They put up with many editorial "suggestions" and requests for revision in particular areas. We appreciate the patience and diligence that all showed to us.

Baylor University Press and its director, Carey Newman, have shown a great deal of support and patience for this project. The BUP production team has shepherded this work through the publication project to its completion. The editors are pleased and thankful for the care and creativity that this book has received from BUP. Another institution deserving our thanks for its support of this work is BiblePlaces.com and especially Todd Bolen. BiblePlaces.com supplied most of the photographs in this book gratis. Thanks also go out to Norma Franklin, Jim West, and Pat Landy, who read drafts of many chapters and provided useful comments, and to Conor McCracken-Flesher, for doing the index.

Both Jennie Ebeling and Paul Flesher would like to thank the W. F. Albright Institute of Archaeological Research in Jerusalem for support provided during the final year of work on this project. The Albright appointed Jennie as the prestigious Annual Professor for 2015–2016, and it made Paul the Seymour Gitin Distinguished Professor during spring 2016. The libraries of the École Biblique et archéologique française de Jérusalem and the Israel Antiquities Authority in the Rockefeller Museum were also extremely helpful. Paul would also like to thank Dean Paula Lutz and the University of Wyoming for awarding him sabbatical leave for 2015–2016 (during which he worked to bring this project to conclusion) as well as the staff of the Interlibrary Loan Department of the University of Wyoming's Coe Library for their work in obtaining volumes not available on campus. Jennie would like to thank the Department of Archaeology and Art History at the University of Evansville as well as Alexandra Cutler.

Mark Elliott wants to thank all the other editors—Jennie Ebeling, Paul Flesher, and Ed Wright—for their valuable assistance in creating and developing the website *Bible and Interpretation* (www.bibleinterp.com). Ed Wright thanks the faculty, staff, students, and supporters of The Arizona Center for Judaic Studies for their interest in and support of this project over many years.

Finally, the editors would like to thank their spouses and children for their support and love during the long process of putting this book together. This volume is dedicated to our students—past, present, and future. Every day the students in our classes reveal their fascination for the ancient world as they seek insight into the choices people made when confronted with momentous (and not so momentous) events. Our past students inspired us to create this volume, and we hope it will guide the learning of our future students.

ARCHAEOLOGICAL AGES

Paleolithic Era	1,500,000–22,000 BP
Lower	1,500,000–250,000
Middle	250,000–50,000
Upper	50,000–12,000
Epipaleolithic Period	12,000 BP–8500 BCE
Neolithic Period	8500–4500 BCE
Pre-Pottery Neolithic	8500–5500
Pottery Neolithic	5500–4500
Chalcolithic Period	4500–3600 BCE
Early Bronze Age	3600–2400 BCE
EB I	3600–3000
EB II	3000–2750
EB III	2750–2400
Intermediate Bronze Age	2400–2000 BCE
Middle Bronze Age	2000–1550 BCE
MB I	2000–1900
MB II	1900–1650
MB III	1650–1550
Late Bronze Age	1550–1200 BCE
LB I	1550–1400
LB II	1400–1200
Iron Age	1200–586 BCE
Iron I	1200–1000
Iron II	1000–586
Iron IIA	1000–928
Iron IIB	928–722
Iron IIC	722–586
Neo-Babylonian Period	586–539 BCE
Persian Period	539–332 BCE
Hellenistic Period	332–63 BCE

Roman Period   63 BCE–330 CE
Byzantine Period   330–630 CE
Islamic Period   630–1918 CE
    Early Arab Period   630–1099
    Crusader Period   1099–1250
    Mamluk Period   1250–1517
    Ottoman Period   1517–1918
Modern Period   1918–present

HISTORICAL TIMELINE

Focus is primarily on kings and political figures, as well as key events, with
some mention of extrabiblical finds. All dates are BCE.

ca. 9400	Jericho inhabited
ca. 7000	Megiddo inhabited
ca. 4000	Beer Sheva inhabited
ca. 3500	Hazor inhabited (upper city)
1353–1336	Pharaoh Akhenaten
	Builds capital at Amarna
	Receives the Amarna letters
1292–1290	Pharaoh Ramesses I
1290–1279	Pharaoh Seti I
1279–1213	Pharaoh Ramesses II
ca. 1250	Exodus of the Israelites from Egypt
1213–1203	Pharaoh Merneptah
	Commemorates his invasion of Canaan in the Merneptah Stele. Claims to have defeated Ashkelon, Gezer, and Yanoam and a people known as Israel.
ca. 1250–1050	Major increase in small settlements in Canaan's Central Hill Country
ca. 1200–1000	Period of Israelite tribes and the Judges
	Judges: Ehud, Deborah, Gideon, Jephthah, Samson
1186–1155	Ramesses III
	Sea Peoples (including Philistines) attempt to invade Egypt. Ramesses drives them off and settles them on the Levant coast.
1185–1175	Sea Peoples (including Philistines) begin settling in cities along the Canaanite coast
1030–1010	Saul, king of Israel
1010–970	David, king of Israel
	Founds a united kingdom of Israel, bringing together all twelve/thirteen tribes

	Captures Jerusalem and makes it the capital
	Conquers Ammon, Edom, Aram, and Moab
970–931	Solomon, king of Israel
	Builds palace, fortifications, Millo (stepped-stone structure), and temple of Yahweh in Jerusalem
	Builds fortifications at Gezer, Hazor, Megiddo, and possibly other sites
	Solomon establishes a shipping trade out of Eilat into the Red Sea
931	Division of kingdom into Northern Kingdom of Israel and Southern Kingdom of Judah
931–911	Jeroboam I, king of Israel (Northern Kingdom)
	Creates independent Kingdom of Israel from ten tribes
	Establishes capital at Shechem
	Builds major shrines at Dan and Bethel
931–915	Rehoboam, king of Judah (Southern Kingdom)
926	Pharaoh Sheshonq I (Shishak) invades Israel and Judah
915–912	Abijah/Abijam, king of Judah
912–871	Asa, king of Judah
911–910	Nadab, king of Israel
910–887	Baasha, king of Israel
	Moves capital to Tirzah
887–886	Elah, king of Israel
886	Zimri, king of Israel
886–875	Omri, king of Israel
	Moves capital to Samaria
	Conquers Moab
875–852	Ahab, king of Israel
	Fortifies Gezer, Megiddo, and Hazor
	Builds second palace at Jezreel
871–849	Jehoshaphat, king of Judah
853	Ahab fights Shalmaneser III, King of Assyria, to a draw at Qarqar, as part of a coalition of eleven countries (Kurkh Monolith)
852–851	Ahaziah, king of Israel
851–842	Joram/Jehoram, king of Israel
	Defeated by Aram and loses northeastern lands
	House of David Stele at Tel Dan
842	King Mesha of Moab throws Israel's control off Moab (Mesha Stele)
849–84	Joram/Jehoram, king of Judah

842–814	Jehu, king of Israel
	Overthrows Joram (last of Omride Dynasty) and slays all relatives
	Jehu submits to Assyrian king Shalmaneser III as a vassal (Black Obelisk)
842–841	Ahaziah, king of Judah
841–835	Athaliah, queen of Judah
835–796	Joash/Jehoash, king of Judah
814–806	Joahaz, king of Israel
806–791	Joash/Jehoash, king of Israel
796–766	Amaziah, king of Judah
791–750	Jeroboam II, king of Israel
776–736	Uzziah/Azariah, king of Judah (became a leper in 750)
750–735	Jotham, king of Judah
750	Zechariah, king of Israel
749	Shallum, king of Israel
749–739	Menahem, king of Israel
745–727	Tiglath-Pileser III, king of Assyria
742	Menahem pays tribute to Tiglath-Pileser as a vassal
739–737	Pekahiah, king of Israel
737–732	Pekah, king of Israel
735–715	Ahaz/Jehoahaz I, king of Judah
	Assyrian vassal
735–733	Syro-Ephramite War
732	Tiglath-Pileser invades Galilee, Gilead, and the northern part of Israel; takes many Israelites captive; and resettles them in Assyria
732–722	Hoshea, king of Israel
727–722	Shalmanezer V, king of Assyria
722–705	Sargon II, king of Assyria
722	Fall of Samaria to Assyrians
	Vast numbers of Israelite citizens taken into exile by Assyrians; population reduced significantly
	Samaria, Aram, and Phoenicia absorbed into Assyrian Empire
	Judah, Philistia, Ammon, Moab, and Edom become vassal states
715–687	Hezekiah, king of Judah
	Expands and improved the fortifications of Jerusalem; has the Siloam tunnel excavated (Siloam Inscription)
	Tries to centralize worship at the Jerusalem temple and eliminate other worship sites

705–681	Sennacherib, king of Assyria
701	Sennacherib invades Judah, conquers Lachish, and besieges but does not conquer Jerusalem.
687–642	Manasseh, king of Judah
	Assyrian vassal
642–640	Amon, king of Judah
640–609	Josiah, king of Judah
	Centralizes worship in Jerusalem by destroying all hill shrines, temples, and other worship sites in Judah and southern Israel
	Killed when attacking Pharaoh Necho II and his army
622	Josiah remodels Jerusalem temple
609	Jehoahaz II/Shallum, king of Judah
608–598	Jehoiakim, king of Judah
605	Babylonian Empire conquers Assyrian Empire at Carchemish
598–597	Jehoiachin/Jeconiah, king of Judah
597	Babylonians under King Nebuchadnezzar sack Jerusalem
	Judah's royalty and most members of its nobility and middle and upper classes taken into exile and settled near Babylon.
597–586	Zedekiah, king of Judah
586	Babylonians under King Nebuchadnezzar destroy Jerusalem
	Take more Judahites into exile
	Ezekiel active in Babylonia
	Jeremiah active in Judah and Egypt
586–538	The Babylonian Exile
576–530	Cyrus the Great (Cyrus II), king of Persia
539	Persian Empire conquers Babylonian Empire
538	First Israelite return from Babylon to Jerusalem under Sheshbazzar
520	Second Israelite return to Jerusalem under governor Zerubbabel and priest Joshua/Jeshua
515	Jerusalem temple rebuilt
458	Third return to Jerusalem under Ezra
445	Fourth return to Jerusalem under Nehemiah
	Jerusalem walls rebuilt
333	King Alexander the Great of Macedon begins to conquer the Persian Empire, including Syria, Israel, and Egypt

ANCIENT JERUSALEM

When one reads the Bible's descriptions of Jerusalem during David and Solomon's time—the tenth century BCE—it is easy to imagine a large city. But Jerusalem in their time was actually quite small, just a sliver of a city along the ridge of a hill that had its highest point in the north and then dropped down toward the valley in the south. Jerusalem did not add substantially to its walls until several centuries later (see chapters 13, 15, and 17).

It was King Hezekiah who expanded and fortified Jerusalem after the fall of the Northern Kingdom of Israel to accommodate the many refugees who fled south into Judah. This apparently happened as he readied for the Assyrian Empire's invasion, which finally took place in 701 BCE. Jerusalem then retained this form until its destruction by the Babylonian Empire in 586 BCE (chapter 17).

When the exiled refugees and/or their descendants returned to Jerusalem in 539 BCE and later, there were only enough people to repopulate the city of David and Solomon (chapters 19–20).

Today, the cities of David, Solomon, Hezekiah, and the returning exiles are buried under more than two millennia of continuous human habitation. Archaeologists have unearthed some remains, including the occasional stretch of city wall. Jerusalem's "Old City" of today is not old at all but was built by Sultan Suleiman the Magnificent in the sixteenth century, between 1535 and 1542 CE. It is just over one-third of a square mile in size. The ancient cities during the First Temple Period were significantly smaller. Furthermore, Suleiman built his Jerusalem with most of it outside the ancient boundaries of Jerusalem, at least those prior to the end of the Persian Pleriod.

Below you will find three outline maps of Jerusalem. Map 1 features the walls of Suleiman's Jerusalem that appear today. Map 2 places the City of David and Solomon's expansions within the background of today's Old City. Map 3 shows Hezekiah's expanded Jerusalem in the same format. While Map 3 shows Jerusalem as it was from about 701 to 586 BCE, Map 2 shows it at two times: 940(?) to 701 BC, and after 539 BCE.

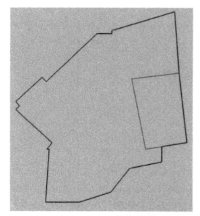

JERUSALEM MAP 1

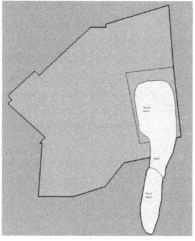

JERUSALEM MAP 2

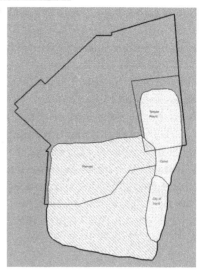

JERUSALEM MAP 3

LIST OF MAPS

All maps of territory were designed by Paul V. M. Flesher using ArcGIS software by Esri (Esri.com). They were constructed on a base map showing modern topographical imagery supplied by Esri and used with permission. All maps copyright © (2017) Esri. All map designs, except 7-1, 7-2, and 7-3: © Paul V. M. Flesher.

LIST OF FIGURES

The following list indicates credits and permissions. Unless noted otherwise, all photos (and Figure 9-1) © Todd Bolen/BiblePlaces.com. Tables (excluding Figure 14-2) are creations of respective chapter authors.

ABBREVIATIONS

ABD	David Noel Freedman, ed. *Anchor Bible Dictionary*. 6 vols. New York: Doubleday, 1992.
AD	Anno Domini, "Year of the Lord"
Amos	Amos
ANET	James B. Pritchard, ed. *Ancient Near Eastern Texts*. 3rd ed. Princeton: Princeton University Press, 1969.
AUSS	*Andrews University Seminary Studies*
BA	*Biblical Archaeologist* (forerunner of *NEA*)
BAR	*Biblical Archaeology Review*
BASOR	*Bulletin of the American Schools of Oriental Research*
BC	Before Christ
BCE	Before the Common Era
BibRev	*Bible Review*
BN	*Biblische Notizen*
BP	Before Present
^{14}C	Carbon-14
CAP	A. E. Cowley, ed. *Aramaic Papyri of the Fifth Century B.C.* Oxford: Clarendon, 1923.
CAT	Manfried Dietrich, Oswald Loretz, and Joaquín Sanmartín, eds. *The Cuneiform Alphabetic Texts from Ugarit, Ras Ibn Hani and Other Places*. 3rd enlarged ed. KTU3. AOAT 360/1. Münster: Ugarit Verlag, 2013.
CE	Common Era
CH	Chronicler's History
1 & 2 Chr	1 & 2 Chronicles
COS	William W. Hallo and K. Lawson Younger. *Context of Scripture*. 3 vols. Leiden: Brill, 2003.
Dan	Daniel
Deut	Deuteronomy
DH	Deuteronomistic History

EB	Early Bronze Age
Eccl	Ecclesiastes
Esth	Esther
Ex, Exod	Exodus
Ezek	Ezekiel
Gen	Genesis
Hag	Haggai
Harper Atlas	James B. Pritchard, ed. 1987. *Harper Atlas of the Bible.* New York: Harper & Row.
Hos	Hosea
Isa	Isaiah
JAOS	*Journal of the American Oriental Society*
JBL	*Journal of Biblical Literature*
Jer	Jeremiah
JJS	*Journal of Jewish Studies*
Jon	Jonah
Josh	Joshua
JSJ	*Journal for the Study of Judaism*
JSOT	*Journal for the Study of the Old Testament*
Judg	Judges
Lam	Lamentations
LB	Late Bronze Age
Lev	Leviticus
1 & 2 Macc	1 & 2 Maccabees
Mal	Malachi
MB	Middle Bronze Age
MCC	Modified Conventional Chronology
Mic	Micah
Nah	Nahum
NEA	*Near Eastern Archaeology* (successor to *BA*)
NEAEHL	Ephraim Stern, ed. *New Encyclopedia of Archaeological Excavations in the Holy Land.* 4 vols. New York: Simon & Schuster; Jerusalem: Israel Exploration Society and Carta, 1993. Vol. 5, 2008.
Neh	Nehemiah
Num	Numbers
Obad	Obadiah
PEF	Palestine Exploration Fund
PEQ	*Palestine Exploration Quarterly*
Prov	Proverbs
Ps, Pss	Psalms

1 & 2 Sam	1 & 2 Samuel
SBL	Society of Biblical Literature
Song	Song of Songs
SS	Supplement Series
TDOT	G. Johannes Botterweck and Helmer Ringgren, eds. *Theological Dictionary of the Old Testament*. 15 vols. Grand Rapids: William B. Eerdmans, 1974–2006.
UF	*Ugarit-Forschungen*
Zech	Zechariah
Zeph	Zephaniah

INTRODUCTION

The people known as **Israel** stand at the center of the Hebrew Bible—a collection of books Christians call the Old Testament.* The Bible describes their origins—how God rescued them from **Egypt** and made an "everlasting" **covenant** with them. It then relates their interactions with God over the following centuries. This set of stories, laws, and other writings became the foundation for three major religions: Judaism, Christianity, and Islam.

For many centuries, the only information about Israel came from the Hebrew Bible/Old Testament. Then, at the end of the nineteenth century, a new source of information about ancient Israel became available: **archaeology**. The remains of ancient Israel and its neighbors could be dug up from the ground at sites in the Holy Land, the Middle East, and the eastern Mediterranean. These discoveries provided knowledge that could be used to supplement and inform the study of the Bible. From its origins, archaeology in the Holy Land was subordinated to the Bible and became an important weapon in the fight of faith. In the aftermath of the Enlightenment, the Bible and its reliability had come under attack. To counter this, Protestant Christians used the new "science" of archaeology to provide support for the Bible's historical accuracy. This approach came to be known as biblical archaeology, and its fundamental goal was to use archaeological excavations and their finds to demonstrate the correctness of biblical accounts—that is, to prove that the Bible is historically accurate.

Today the idea of subordinating archaeology to biblical studies seems entirely wrongheaded, even backward, but it describes the conception and motivation of biblical archaeology up to the latter half of the twentieth century. As many biblical scholars have noted (see chapter 2), even the great archaeologist W. F. Albright—who is credited with founding the American branch of archaeological research in the Holy Land and did much to set such research on a sound footing—saw archaeology as demonstrating the accuracy of the Bible. As late as the 1960s, Albright held that archaeology confirmed Scripture.

---

* The first appearance of a glossary entry is indicated in **bold** type.

As J. Edward Wright (2002, 63) has observed, when Albright moved from excavation to explanation,

> Albright's reconstruction of biblical history and religion followed the existing biblical narratives almost literally. He noted that archaeological evidence confirmed repeatedly the basic reliability of biblical history.

Albright epitomized the practices and theological interpretations of biblical archaeology that had developed in the twentieth century. As chapters 3 and 4 lay out, archaeological finds were interpreted and presented as upholding biblical accuracy whenever possible. But despite Albright's accomplishments—and in part because of them—biblical archaeology's heyday was coming to an end.

The 1970s saw important changes in both the archaeology of ancient Israel and in the discipline of archaeology as practiced in Western universities. The decade's beginning saw two of biblical archaeology's foremost practitioners—G. Ernest Wright (1971) and Roland de Vaux (1970)—arguing that archaeology and theology needed to be practiced separately, each according to the independent standards of its own discipline. Only when results were complete within each field, they argued, could archaeology be used to address questions posed by theology (see chapter 5). In other words, the theological component inherent in biblical archaeology needed to be separated from the archaeological one, giving archaeological research into the Middle East's past independent standing.

At the same time, archaeology as a field began a transformation inspired by "New Archaeology"—now referred to as processual archaeology. These changes emphasized archaeology as a branch of anthropology and a part of that discipline's investigation of human culture. Archaeology's purpose was to study past human cultures through the remains they left behind. In this transformation, archaeology self-consciously reformulated itself along scientific lines. Rather than "just digging," it required explicit research questions with planned excavation projects to answer them. It worked to interpret **artifacts** as evidence of past societies and it studied them in comparison to similar human cultures, both past and present. Archaeology furthermore allied itself with other scientific disciplines—creating new specialties such as **archaeozoology** and **paleoethnobotany**.

New Archaeology quickly impacted archaeological practices in the land of Israel, as chapter 5 describes, where its new character led it to take on the name "Syro-Palestinian archaeology." By 1985, archaeological research into Israel's past and that of other peoples in the southern **Levant** had ceased to be a stepchild of biblical studies and operated as an independent field, pursuing its own research agendas guided by anthropological and scientific principles. Today, the archaeology of ancient Israel fits into the discipline of anthropology alongside the archaeology of other ancient cultures. Its professorial practitioners usually consider themselves anthropologists and publish in that discipline's journals, as well as in more specialized ones, where the analysis and debate over the archaeology of ancient Israel take place among, and according to the same standards as, the archaeology of other past societies and cultures around the world.

And that is where this textbook comes in. Despite its acceptance in archaeological circles, Syro-Palestinian archaeology has been slow to make inroads into biblical studies and its text-based approach to studying ancient Israel. Tens of thousands of students in universities and colleges across North America take courses on the Old Testament or ancient Israel—usually in religious studies or theology departments. But the results, discoveries, and insights of Syro-Palestinian archaeology have made surprisingly little impact on these courses' textbooks. Typical Old Testament introductory texts emphasize the biblical books and their analysis. In a few places, archaeological materials are brought in, but they remain subordinated to textual explication and rarely shape the pedagogy of even a single chapter. And although a few textbooks of other kinds explore archaeology alongside the Bible, too often they still seek to use archaeology to support Scripture's reliability.

In this light, the present textbook focuses on the history of ancient Israel. While the Old Testament immortalized the Israelites through its stories, laws, psalms, and prophecies, the people Israel were much more than the limited picture presented in those pages. They were more than the priests and prophets, the kings and judges who led Israel. Even though these leaders usually take center stage in the biblical books, we must recognize that they were the "1 percent." The rest of the Israelites were more like Ruth, Naomi, and Boaz—land holders, farmers, and day laborers in the agricultural economy. Archaeological excavations have the ability to reveal all levels of Israelite society: from the farming villages of the hill country to the cities of the Jezreel Valley—from the wine vats, olive presses, and pottery workshops to the palaces of Samaria. It can inform us about people's diet, their standard of health, their houses, and their level of wealth. It can uncover the society's economic structure and trade relations as well as their use of metal and technological sophistication. The biblical texts may provide hints on some of these matters, but it is the archaeological record that can provide solid evidence for them and for topics Scripture does not even suggest we broach.

Not even the language of the Hebrew Bible is complete. Although the average American adult has an active vocabulary of twenty thousand to thirty-five thousand words, the Hebrew Bible contains about only eight thousand different words. It is clear that much is missing. The Bible talks about combing one's hair but does not use the word for "comb." It speaks of knives and forks but never mentions spoons. It speaks of sewing but never of needles (Ullendorf 1971, 251–52). All these items, by the way, appear in the archaeological record.

It was thought for many centuries that to understand the ancient Israelites, you had to understand the Bible. It is now clear that to understand the Old Testament / Hebrew Bible, you must understand ancient Israel, and the only way to do that is to use all aspects of archaeological and textual data to reconstruct Israel's history.

That is what this book aims to accomplish. Its goal is to develop for its introductory readers a historical understanding of the ancient Israelites as they were, in all their achievements and failures. It will describe what events happened to the Israelites and what they were like—back then. The book is not interested in how the biblical material has been interpreted and reimagined by later Judaism, Christianity, and Islam in the centuries since it was composed. Thus, the integration in this book comes not between archaeology and theology—as it had in biblical archaeology—but between archaeological analysis of data from the ground and literary analysis of the Old Testament / Hebrew Bible. These provide the evidence for the history of ancient Israel.

The book's opening chapters lay out these two key categories. Chapter 1 explains how archaeology works, from planning and carrying out an excavation to the types of analyses archaeologists perform on their finds. It also looks at the geography of the ancient Middle East, the location where these archaeological excavations take place. Chapter 2 looks at the Old Testament / Hebrew Bible, describing its books, how we know what its text says, and how modern scholarship studies its literary and historical character. The next three chapters explore the development of archaeology in the Holy Land and the Middle East over the last two centuries, how it has changed in recent decades, as well as its future. In chapter 6, the book settles into its main task of laying out the history of ancient Israel, and the following chapters pursue that goal in a chronological fashion—more about those chapters in a moment. But first we must unpack what we mean by the two terms we have used in these opening pages: Old Testament and Hebrew Bible.

What Do We Call It?

The collection of books Christians call the Old Testament comprises a sacred, foundational document for two religions, Judaism and Christianity. But despite this commonality, each religion understands the collection differently and sees it as leading to the formation of their own religion, their own community of believers, and their own theology and practices. For the benefit of their community, both religions emphasize how the contents are relevant today, not just in hoary antiquity.

In Christianity, the name "Old Testament" indicates that, along with a second collection called the "New Testament," it is part of a larger sacred work Christians call the "Bible." This combination implies that the former can be understood only in conjunction with the latter. In Judaism, by contrast, this work is called the "TaNaK" (usually transcribed as "**Tanakh**"), which is a Hebrew acronym indicating the three collections of books out of which it was formed. "T" stands for the books of the **Torah**. "N" stands for the books of the **Neviim** (the "Prophets"), and "K" stands for **Ketuvim** (the "Writings"). When Jews use the word "Bible," they mean the Tanakh. Both Old Testament and Tanakh are sectarian titles and both usually imply an interpretation that conforms the relevant religion. By contrast, this book focuses on history, seeking the meaning of the books at the time they were composed.

Recognizing this problem, biblical scholars coined the designation "Hebrew Bible." They aimed to create a neutral term for the Tanakh/Old Testament, and the term became widely adopted for that purpose in the academic world. This identification has its own problems, not the least of which is the fact that the Hebrew Bible uses Aramaic as well as Hebrew. However, since this book's chapters are written by authors of differing religious, academic, and national backgrounds, the editors decided to allow each author to use the term(s) they preferred. We should also note that this book's title uses "Old Testament" because it is the most widely used designation in English.

The Academic Study of History

In and of itself, the past is unknown. We are not born knowing what happened before our birth, nor do we know about events at which we were not present—to state the obvious. We learn about past events from what people tell us, either orally or in writing, and from objects (to use a general, all-inclusive term) that were created in the past and still exist in our time. The academic study of history takes all the evidence that can be found and draws upon it to compose a reconstruction of the past, whether of past events or of the character and circumstances of past societies.

The academic discipline of history differs significantly from notions of history found in popular culture. It aims to reconstruct the past as accurately as possible and as neutrally as possible, based on evidence. Historians may not always achieve this aim, but that is the standard. Historical research uses all available evidence; it does not cherry-pick. It does not ignore inconvenient data. Historical research aims for a neutral and unbiased use of that evidence; it does not purposely slant its conclusions to suit a modern agenda. It seeks honest results and transparent explication of the research.

The practice of academic history takes place in three steps. The first step in the study of a past event or culture is to find as much information as possible.

To function at its best, the academic study of history draws upon evidence, lots of evidence. The more sources of data about the past event or society being studied, the more reliable its conclusions can be. The fewer sources of information we have, the more uncertain the reconstruction of the past. When dealing with the ancient world, unfortunately, there is often too little evidence. Many events are known from a single source—the exact opposite of what is needed for a successful and reliable historical reconstruction.

In the study of ancient Israel, as this book's title suggests, historical research can draw upon the Hebrew Bible / Old Testament and archaeological finds. Depending on what is being studied, both the Hebrew Bible and archaeology may reveal multiple sources of data. If the research question focuses on the laws of ancient Israel, for example, the Ten Commandments, the Covenant Code, the Priestly Code, and the Deuteronomic Code could be sources, as well as stories about the practice of laws, as seen in the books of Ruth and Kings. The law codes of many ancient societies have been discovered by archaeologists, such as the Code of Hammurabi, and they contain laws parallel to those found in Scripture. If the research topic concerns **Philistine** society, the excavations at Philistine sites would constitute evidence, along with the Egyptian records about contact with them as well as the biblical stories in the books of Judges, Samuel, and Kings about Israelite interaction with them. Investigations into diet draw from descriptions of food in the Old Testament and from the excavated remains of bones, grains, and cooking implements.

Once all the data have been gathered, the second step takes place. Here, a historian must examine and test each piece of evidence for reliability, evaluate its relevance, and assess its content. Written evidence, whether drawn from a biblical book or found in an archaeological excavation, is always composed from the author's perspective, knowledge, and ability. The historian must appraise those, examine the character of each source, gauge the accuracy and amount of its information, and then use and trust the piece of evidence accordingly. If the subject is a conflict, for instance, the side a writer favors will affect the way the writer presents information and draws conclusions. Or perhaps an author knows about an event only through an earlier source. The author's work then cannot be treated as an independent piece of evidence.

Archaeological finds pose a different challenge at this stage; they must be interpreted by the field's scientific and disciplinary principles. Indeed, archaeology's strength comes from its ability to discover objects from an ancient human context and work out their dating, their function, and what they reveal about the people who created and/or used them. See chapter 1 for further explanation.

Finally, in the third step of the academic approach to history, a historian studying an event takes all the sources into account and brings them together in a synthesis. The historian uses the results of the previous two steps and matches the different pieces of evidence that fit together. When several reliable items of information point to the same conclusion, that makes the historian's job easy. But, frequently, pieces of evidence differ—sometimes in major ways, sometimes in minor ways. Then historians must use their judgment, drawing on their determination of the reliability of each source, to create the most accurate reconstruction.

These three steps should not be seen as a simple progression that historians follow through once to arrive at their synthesis or reconstruction. Academic historians are always asking questions, both of the data and of their conclusions. The questions then inspire them to find answers, sending them back to step one to search for more evidence to answer them. Indeed, historians continually seek to understand a past event fully, repeatedly moving back and forth through the three steps until they are satisfied that all evidence has been found and plumbed and that the synthesis they created from it is the strongest and most accurate reconstruction possible.

When their research is complete, academic historians present their reconstructions to their peers, ultimately in a published form. Each presentation then undergoes evaluation by their peers, who assess it and respond to it in ways that can range from a withering critique to an appreciating confirmation of the overall synthesis. Some scholars may write their own reconstruction of the past from the same data. The goal is to develop a historical reconstruction that accounts for all the evidence and that resolves as many questions being asked by historians as possible. A solid synthesis of this type may guide understanding and interpretation of the period for decades, but it must also be remembered that the synthesis and assessment process never ends, since new data and new interpretations often emerge.

Two further observations are needed at this point. First, historical analysis does not artificially line up textual data on one side and group archaeological data on another side and then compare them. Each piece of evidence, whatever its type, stands independently and must be evaluated on its own merits. A research question may have dozens of relevant pieces of evidence, from the Bible and from archaeology. Analysis may find textual *and* archaeological data in favor of one interpretation, while other textual *and* archaeological data support another interpretation. The search for history does not pit text against archaeology but weighs all evidence together according to their relative merits.

Second, our simplified explanation of this book's goal should not be understood to imply that neither textual scholars nor archaeologists practice history. Nothing could be further from the truth. Both address historical questions regularly, and they often bring in data from the other field to help them out.

Unfortunately, this sometimes has the effect of subordinating one field to the other. At the introductory level of this textbook, however, the goal is to bring all the evidence for ancient Israel together and to treat each source equally, using them together to create the best reconstruction of ancient people of Israel, their history and culture, and how they changed through the centuries.

A Guide: What to Expect in This Book

As you might expect from a book featuring the evidence of archaeology and the Bible, the first two chapters provide an introduction to each type of data. This is preceded by an overview of the geography of the Middle East and the place of the land of Israel in it, for this is the location of both kinds of evidence.

Chapters 3 through 5 complete section 1 and trace the recent history of how the archaeological study of the Middle East and the land of Israel arose in the past two centuries or so. This leads to the advances in "digging up the past" that ultimately inspired the formation of what became known as biblical archaeology. This field, despite later criticism, made important and lasting contributions to archaeological practice in the Middle East, even though its theological presuppositions were later replaced by more theoretically sound foundations. This new approach to archaeological investigation enables this book's focus on history and historical evidence of all kinds, treated equivalently.

Chapter 6 begins the book's historical study of ancient Israel, drawing upon archaeological and biblical data. From here, the book is divided into four further sections. Sections 4 and 5, the book's second half, have a clear thematic unity: their chapters feature the People of Israel in the land of Israel, beginning with David's creation of the Israelite kingdom and continuing to its split into two smaller countries and then to their destruction and the exile of their inhabitants, followed by the return of some exiles and their reestablishment of the Israelite community in the land. Throughout these chapters, the historical reconstruction draws upon both biblical and archaeological information.

Sections 2 and 3 (chapters 6 through 12) are not so neat. At their start, neither the people of Israel nor the land of Israel exist. The first two chapters of this section (chapters 6 and 7) feature the land of **Canaan** before it became the land of Israel sometime after 1200 BCE. They begin with the appearance of human beings in the southern Levant and then quickly move to the two thousand years of Canaanite cities and culture during the Bronze Age—before anyone knew anything about the Israelites. These chapters draw solely from archaeological finds, since the Hebrew Bible contains only a small amount of material that is relevant to these time periods.

The next two chapters (8 and 9) address the biblical books of the Torah and feature the Hebrews—first through Abraham and his extended family and then a growing group of his descendants. At the beginning, they are not called Israelites or Hebrews but acquire that name in the course of their experiences. During these five books, the Israelites and their ancestors are nearly always traveling. The tales never describe putting down roots, not even in Genesis when Abraham and his descendants journey in Canaan or in Exodus, where, despite generations of forced labor in Egypt, the story is about leaving and then traveling for forty years. It should not be surprising that most of the discussion in these two chapters focuses mainly on the biblical tales, with little contributed from archaeology—since people on the move leave few long-lasting remains.

Chapters 10 through 12 examine in detail the appearance of the People of Israel in the land of Canaan, which will become the land of Israel. And here we have both types of evidence. The biblical books of Joshua and Judges tell of how the Israelites arrived in Canaan, took possession of it, and lived there. Archaeologically speaking, this is the Iron Age I, beginning at the end of the thirteenth century and the early twelfth century. At this time, archaeological evidence reveals a period of increasing population in the previously empty **Central Hill Country** of Canaan. This is essentially where the biblical books place the early presence of the Israelites and at roughly the same time. But because archaeology has discovered no written finds from this time, we cannot reliably name these settlers. Even though we cannot be sure of the origins of theses settlers, many scholars believe the proto-Israelites lived among them. But another group appears in Canaan at about the same time, one that settles in the lowlands along the southern coast: the Philistines. And it is the interaction of the Canaanites with these newcomers—the Philistines and the Israelites (as well as the newcomers with each other)—that sets the stage for the next segment of Israelite history.

The six chapters of section 4 then look at the rise of the Israelite kingdoms in the hill country, as they appear in the archaeology and as recorded in the books of Samuel, Kings, Chronicle, and many of the prophets. This begins in chapter 13 with David's establishment of the united monarchy and his son Solomon's continuation of it, a period of approximately seventy years. The kingdom David established split in two after Solomon's death, and chapters 14 and 15 describe the history of the northern country of Israel and the southern country of Judah over the next two centuries, respectively. This stable political period provides an opportunity to shift our attention in chapter 16 from the elite to the vast majority of working people who supplied the food and labor for the two countries.

The two and a half centuries beginning with David—which archaeologists identify as Early Iron Age II—were characterized by a lack of foreign domination in the land of Israel. This situation certainly eased the way for David's establishment of his monarchy and for the continuing independence of first one and then two countries in the land of Israel. During the earlier Late Bronze Age, by contrast, Canaan had been under the thumb of Egypt and only gradually escaped that control in Iron Age I. True, Solomon's son Rehoboam had to deal with an invasion by Pharaoh Shishak/Sheshonq as well as with Egyptian interference in his succession, but this seems to be Egypt's last incursion into the southern Levant for several centuries. Israel and Judah continued without threat from external empires until the **Mesopotamian** empire of **Assyria** appeared on the scene in the eighth century. This provides the focus of chapter 17, which looks at the increasing pressure on Israel from the Assyrian Empire until Israel's defeat in 720 BCE and then looks at Judah's response.

Since a major recurring theme of all the biblical books is Israel's relationship with God, we need to take a look at what we know about Israelite religion from the sources. This provides the main focus of chapter 18.

Section 5 contains the last two chapters, featuring the end of the historically oriented material in the Old Testament. Chapter 19 deals with the defeat, exile, and destruction of Judah and Jerusalem by the **Babylonian Empire**—an event that should have been the end of Israel. But the biblical books of Ezra and Nehemiah tell of a new start, when the **Persian Empire** permitted the exiles' descendants to return to the land of Israel and reestablish a community there. Chapter 20 brings the archaeological discoveries of this period to bear on the biblical materials.

And this is where the biblical "history" ends, although not the history of the people Israel. They remained under Persian rule until the coming of Alexander, when the Greek culture and Greek empires replaced that of Persia—first under the Egyptian-located Ptolemaic Empire and then under the Syrian-located Seleucid Empire. Then, beginning in 167 BCE, the Maccabees threw off Greek overlordship and established the last independent Kingdom of Israel before the modern era, and perhaps the largest. Even though this continued into King Herod's time (d. 4 BCE), this achievement failed to make it into either the Old Testament / Hebrew Bible or the New Testament.

How to Use This Book

Each chapter has been written by a different author—some are primarily experts in the Old Testament literature and others have their expertise in archaeology—and represents the author's expert analysis and judgment about content and presentation. That means that there will sometimes be interpretive differences between them. At times, different dates will be given for the same event; these should be seen not as mistakes but as deriving from differing evaluations of the available evidence. Given the ongoing debates in these fields, it would be impossible to arrive at and enforce unity; the editors did not even try. These divergencies are actually good, for they show readers that these are living and active fields and not old, accepted wisdom.

To keep footnotes at a minimum, citations are given by parentheses within the text by author, date, and page numbers. These works appear in the bibliography in the back of the book. Each chapter ends with a few suggestions for further reading, for students who would like to pursue the chapter's central topics in greater depth.

From chapter 6 onward, this book is organized in chronological order. Within each chapter, the order likewise is roughly chronological. For further chronological information about events, see the "Historical Timeline" in the front of the book. Since much of the discussion is based on Syro-Palestinian archaeology, which determines time by archaeological eras rather than year-by-year progression, a table of the "Archaeological Ages" appears in the book's front matter as well.

Most chapters feature a map or two to indicate towns, cities, and other sites mentioned within. Sites mentioned in chapters without maps usually appear in other maps. There is a gazetteer in the back that indicates the map on which a site first appears. Jerusalem maps appear separately at the front. There is also a glossary, which defines key terms whose first occurrence is **highlighted**.

Finally, a word about unprovenanced objects—archaeological excavations constitute careful, controlled, recorded, scientific investigations into the remains of the past. Any object found in this way is related both spatially and temporally to a host of other material items—from architectural remains and pottery to seeds and pollen, to bones, and so on. Archaeologists can then link the entire complex of items to the peoples who produced them and to the time when they lived. An object's context can often reveal more about the object than the object itself. Unfortunately, nonarchaeologists will sometimes dig into ancient sites looking for items that can be sold. These looters disturb the site, destroy items important to archaeology but worthless to them, and strew around their holes everything from human bones to remains of stone tools and rotted materials of fabric, wood, and basketry as well as pottery. "Valuable" objects taken in this way and stripped of their ancient context often make their way into Western hands, ending up in collections and even occasionally museum displays. Indiana Jones is a looter rather than an archaeologist.

Unprovenanced objects constitute a major problem for archaeologists and historians. Should they be used as evidence about ancient peoples? Much information about them that could have been gleaned in a controlled archaeological excavation is missing. However, if they display writing or a picture of some sort, they may reveal useful information—if they can be trusted. Many unprovenanced objects are modern fakes. Even if they are real, the exact location where they were dug up is usually unknown, and sometimes even their country of origin is unidentified. Modern scholarly societies, such as the American Schools of Oriental Research and the Society for Biblical Litera-ture, have policies that discourage use of such materials. However, often the temptation for scholars to use them is too great to overcome, especially if they contain writing. This is the case with the **Dead Sea Scrolls** (which are a mix of provenanced and unprovenanced texts and fragments) and more recently with the so-called James **Ossuary** and the Jehoash Inscription. In the present work, there are general references to unprovenanced objects (such as seals and bullae) and occasionally to specific items (such as the tablets from Al-Yahudu in Babylonia/Persia and related places discussed in chapters 19 and 20). In these cases, the authors see their fields as a whole engaging with this material; to leave it out would be seen as providing an incomplete explanation.

I

ARCHAEOLOGY, THE BIBLE, AND EPIGRAPHY

Discovery, Techniques, and Development

1

INTRODUCTION TO THE GEOGRAPHY AND ARCHAEOLOGY OF THE ANCIENT NEAR EAST

Gary P. Arbino

Every good story needs a setting. Whether Thucydides' Peloponnese, J. R. R. Tolkien's Middle Earth, Jane Austen's England, Mark Twain's Mississippi River, or even Stephen Hillenburg's Bikini Bottom, the specifics of time and place perform an integral narrative function. This is certainly true for the Hebrew Bible, since it narrates stories grounded within actual and often identifiable ancient settings. Biblical authors assumed their readers had detailed knowledge of the world of the text. Regular and specific use of place-names—**toponyms**—and constant references to geographic, environmental, cultural, and architectural aspects of the stories illustrate this. Comprehending these elements is integral to determining meaning in the texts, and it even plays an important function at the most foundational level of the text—the translation of words. For example, the common Hebrew word *har* can be translated as "hill" or "mountain," and the choice can be both a topographical and a narrative concern.

We in the twenty-first century—removed by time, space, and culture from the ancient contexts of the Hebrew Bible—require help in deciphering the ancient authors' information about setting. Two fields of study provide the modern reader access to these essential aspects of the Bible: geography (which illuminates the basic physical stage) and archaeology (which points the spotlight on more specific cultural and historical settings for the stories told).

Geography and the Hebrew Bible

Scarcely a chapter in the Hebrew Bible goes by without some mention or description of a locale or territory. Early in Genesis (Gen 11:31–12:10), readers are told that Abram traveled from Ur of the Chaldeans toward the land of Canaan. He resided for a time at Haran, then went on to the oak of Moreh at Shechem, subsequently pitched his tent in the hill country east of Bethel and west of Ai, and then moved toward the **Negev Desert**, into Egypt, and back to the Negev before settling. Here are specific settings, directions, and named locales—the basics of physical geography. Apparently, the intended readers understood where and what each of these was and how these references influenced and created meaning in the stories.

While the foundation of geography consists of names, places, and features on a map (cartography), the discipline is much broader. Geography encompasses the interplay between the many elements of the physical world (e.g., geology, topography, climate, ecology, and hydrology) that create a range of environmental and ecological niches—marked by specific flora and fauna— which humans have sought to exploit to preserve and improve their lives.

Because the Hebrew Bible narrates a past world, utilizing modern geographic data alone is not sufficient to aid our reconstructions of that world. The reader of the Hebrew Bible must turn to *historical geography* in order to comprehend the ancient text. This spatial, temporal, and cultural investigation synthesizes data from multiple fields of research, including physical geography, historical **philology**, toponymy, and archaeology (Rainey and Notley 2006, 9–24). The goal is to see beyond the modern world and understand the biblical text in light of ancient **human geography**—the interplay between people and their environment.

The biblical world was primarily an agricultural world in which people were fully dependent on the vicissitudes of nature for daily survival. Thus, the stories in the Hebrew Bible are very often the stories of humans responding to the divine because of environmental need. Most twenty-first-century urban readers cannot fully grasp the impact of the rainstorm called down by Samuel (1 Sam 12:16-18) or fully grasp the life-or-death nature of the decision to reject **Baal**—the god of fertility and rain and thus of life (1 Kgs 18)—and to accept instead that the Israelite God, Yhwh, was the true controller of the environment (Ps 135:7; Deut 27–28).

Historical geographers piece together ancient ecology from a variety of ancient sources. Artistic representations and references in ancient documents to plants, animals, physical situations, and toponyms are mined for information. Archaeological research, especially analysis of the remains of ancient plants (paleoethnobotany) and animals (archaeozoology), provides a bridge between the ancient and modern environments. Paleoethnobotanical study of charred beams and other wood remnants from ancient buildings enables archaeologists to determine much about ancient forests and forestry. Through careful statistical and scientific analysis, archaeozoology supplies data on the types of animals hunted or raised domestically for food, labor, and even cultural needs. For example, some have argued that the absence of pig bones in "Israelite" territories is a cultural and ethnic indicator, given the biblical prohibition on consumption of pork. Collection of microfaunal remains (such as rodents, birds, fish, mollusks, and even insects) and microfloral vestiges (seeds and burnt grains, animal dung, ancient pollen, and phytoliths [silica husks of plants]) sheds light on the ancient ecology, economic patterns, and even daily life and diet. This is the smaller scale of human geography; the interaction between people and their local ecology which is essential to understanding the agrarian daily life of many of the people and events mentioned in the biblical texts.

Geography and the Biblical World

The biblical narratives also entail a wider scope—the impact of geography upon societies and cultures. Whether ancient or modern, societies thrive where there is arable and defensible agricultural land with sufficient natural resources. Where these are lacking, people look beyond their borders to acquire additional natural resources through trade or conquest and, in some cases, migration. Thus, the geographic realities and environmental limitations of Egyptians, Assyrians, Babylonians, Persians, and others drove them into frequent economic, cultural, religious, and military interaction with the Israelites and the other people of the Levant. When faced with the geographic limitations of their own lands, Israelites also sought resources—natural, economic, political, and cultural—from the societies that surrounded them. Understanding the physical and human geography of the wider world clarifies much in the Hebrew Bible.

Most of the Hebrew Bible takes place in the southern Levant—home to Israel and **Judah**—a very small part of the biblical world. Enclosed by mountains to the north and desert to the east and south, this area along the southeast coast of the Mediterranean Sea extends about 150 miles along the coast and between 40 and 100 miles inland. Because the Bible maintains such a strong focus on this parcel of land—about two-thirds of the literature has its primary setting in the land of Israel—readers often do not realize the influence of the wider world on what they are reading.

FIGURE 1-1. *The Shephelah is the lowland region east of Lachish and west of the Judean Hills.*

As small as ancient Israel was, its geography ensured that it was often contested; it is the narrow land bridge between Africa, Europe, and Asia. This wider world of the Hebrew Bible—the Near East and Egypt—is largely encircled by five "seas" and defined by three river systems. Circling clockwise from the west are the Mediterranean Sea, Black Sea, Caspian Sea, "Lower Sea" (Persian Gulf), and Red Sea. Flowing southeast into the Persian Gulf are the Mesopotamian rivers (the Tigris and the Euphrates), while the third river—Egypt's Nile—flows north and empties into the Mediterranean. Human culture and population flourished along the banks of these three rivers from earliest times.

EGYPT

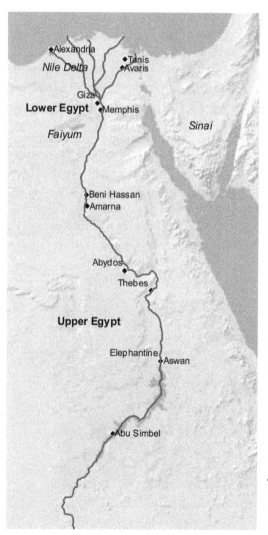

Although 1,200 miles of the 4,100-mile-long Nile River between the First and Sixth Cataracts belonged to the peoples of Nubia and Cush (Ethiopia), the northern 750-mile stretch—from Aswan to the Mediterranean—was controlled by Egypt from at least 3000 BCE. Egypt was the Nile, and its history, culture, and literature were strongly impacted by this environment.

The Nile's predictable annual flooding, between mid-August and late September—brought irrigation and rich alluvial soils to the land along the banks of the Nile Valley (called Upper

MAP 1-1. *Egypt is a long, thin fertile country surrounded by desert. Ninety percent or more of its population lives within twenty miles of the Nile River.*

Egypt) and to its delta (Lower Egypt). While Upper Egypt was a narrow band of lush terrain immediately along the river, never more than a few miles wide, Lower Egypt was a 120-by-120-mile triangle of verdant and partially swampy land. It is in Lower Egypt (Goshen) that the Israelites are said to have settled prior to the exodus and where the city of Pi-Rameses was built (Exod 1). Transport on the Nile was fast and efficient, allowing cargo and trade along the length of Egypt and out into the Mediterranean.

Resources in Egypt were predictable and plentiful. Egyptians enjoyed a steady and abundant supply of cereal crops, vegetables and fruit, papyrus (for paper) and flax (made into linen for clothing, ropes, and sails), as well as minerals, semi-precious stone, and prized granite. Exporting the surplus produced wealth. These geographic realities created an Egyptian world that was generally stable, predictable, and comfortable (at least for the elite). This worldview is seen in their religious and political systems. Although Egypt was a well-off society, the Levantine corridor to the northeast offered Egypt some needed resources and was essential as a military buffer zone against eastern invaders, necessitating continual attempts to control Judah and Israel. These struggles play out in the narratives extending from the book of Genesis through 2 Kings and throughout the prophetic oracles.

MESOPOTAMIA

At the heart of the circle of the five seas lies the **Fertile Crescent**. This long arch of land stretches from the Mediterranean Sea to the Persian Gulf, bounded by high mountains, part of a longer system that extends from Europe to China. In this arch, there is water, and it is relatively easy to grow crops.

At the eastern end of the Fertile Crescent—the eastern edge of the world of the Hebrew Bible—are the Zagros Mountains, with an average elevation of about 8,000 feet and some peaks soaring to over 14,000 feet. Nestled among these often-forested heights are numerous small valleys in which agriculture is possible within what is otherwise an arid mountain environment. From about 600 BCE on, this was the territory of the Persians, whose main ancient capital, Persepolis, was located in one of the southern mountain valleys (Marv-Dasht) about 5,300 feet above sea level.

Along the northern edge of the arch, from west to east, are the Taurus, Anti-Taurus, Pontus, and Kurdistan Mountains, with peaks rising to almost 17,000 feet. These stretch from modern central Turkey to western Iran and Armenia. In the center of these mountains lay the territory of Urartu, from which we get the name Ararat, whose mountains are famous from the Noah story (Gen 8:4). Access to the rich natural resources of these mountains was highly prized throughout the ancient world.

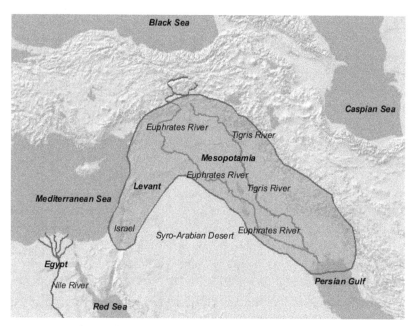

MAP 1-2. *The Fertile Crescent is a fertile area with large amounts of water from rivers and rainfall stretching from the Persian Gulf to the southern Levant. Some experts include the Nile River basin in this concept as well.*

Down the western edge of the crescent, a series of lower mountain chains stretches southward along the Mediterranean coast. The 4,000-mile-long fault system that produced the African Rift Valley splits these Levantine ranges into twin parallel chains with a deep north-south valley between them. This creates a series of north-south topographical strips marching from the coast to the east: coastal plain, western highlands, rift valley, eastern highlands, steppe, and desert. This is the territory of the ancient Israelites and their immediate neighbors.

Along the inside edge of the Fertile Crescent's mountains arcs a narrow band—30 to 150 miles wide—of arable **steppe**. Because of the atmospheric uplift provided by the mountains, these steppes receive enough rain (minimum 8 inches per year) to create the environment necessary for basic agriculture: the dry farming (without irrigation) of cereals—hence the name "Fertile Crescent." Toward the center of the arch, the steppe grades rapidly into increasingly dryer and less fertile lands surrounding the vast Syro-Arabian Desert.

Within the Fertile Crescent, there are really only two seasons: the predictable summer drought (late May to mid-September) and the months in which rainfall can occur (mid-October to April). Precipitation across the crescent is unpredictable and irregular and may come in the form of hail, downpours, light rain, or even snow.

Precipitation high in the Anti-Taurus Mountains replenishes the headwaters for the Tigris and Euphrates rivers. The easternmost river, the Tigris, is joined along its 1,150-mile course by four major tributaries cascading down from the Zagros. Further west and totaling more than 1,800 miles in length flows what the Bible often simply refers to as "the River," the Euphrates. Both rivers flooded annually, but the results were often violent and destructive or woefully inadequate, especially along the Tigris. About 120 miles north of the Persian Gulf, the two rivers converge to form one channel, the Shatt al-Arab. This empties into the gulf through a series of wide marshes, which provided plentiful fish and game. These rivers, especially the Euphrates, and their tributaries served as transportation arteries in the ancient Near Eastern world. Along the 1,100 miles between the mountains and the gulf, this wide, slow-moving waterway allowed almost year-round navigation, enabling communication, commerce, and conquest.

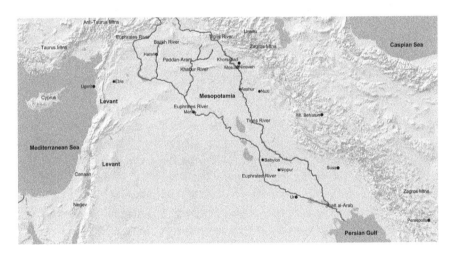

MAP 1-3. *As its name implies, Mesopotamia is the territory between the two rivers of the Tigris and Euphrates.*

The two major tributaries of the Euphrates—the Balikh and Khabur Rivers—flow southward through the rolling foothills of the Anti-Taurus and across the northern steppes. The Khabur River plain contained a vast swath of uncommonly rich agricultural steppe and plentiful rain. It is this region—called Aram-Naharaim in Genesis 24:10 and Paddan-Aram in Genesis 28:1-7—that is Abraham's ancestral homeland (Deut 26:5).

Between the Tigris and Euphrates, the land is known as Mesopotamia (Greek for "land between rivers"). This territory possessed the rivers and adequate soils but few other natural resources. Unlike on the northern steppes, rainfall is inadequate for dry farming in the south. This is one of the main distinctions between northern and southern Mesopotamia. From earliest times southern Mesopotamian cultivation has been characterized by the canal irrigation in the floodplains of the dryer parts of the Tigris and Euphrates that enabled a measure of agricultural stability. Traces of these ancient canals (noted in Ezekiel and Daniel) can still be seen in aerial photographs and satellite images.

Throughout the biblical period, northern and southern Mesopotamian cultures vied for control of their minimal available resources. In the south, Sumerian culture began in the fourth millennium BCE and was later supplanted by Akkad (ca. 2300 BCE), followed by numerous Babylonian entities. North, along the Tigris, the Assyrians were the dominant culture starting in the second millennium BCE. The lack of local natural resources pushed these societies to reach beyond their borders to gain control of commodities. Expansionist policies of Assyrians and Babylonians— as well as Egyptians—helped define the societies of Israel and Judah and had a major influence on Hebrew history, literature, and culture. Most notably, Assyria subjugated the Northern Kingdom of Israel in 722 BCE, and Babylon conquered Judah, destroying Jerusalem and its temple in 586 BCE.

LEVANT: NORTH

Phoenicians and **Arameans** inhabited the western edge of the Fertile Crescent in the northern Levant. The apex of the Levantine highlands is formed by the Lebanon Mountains. Rising toward ten thousand feet, these barren limestone peaks were capped by almost year-round snow—hence their name, which means "white." This chain was noted for its desirable forests of pine, cypress, oak, and especially the famous "cedars of Lebanon." These mountains plunge into the sea, leaving only a series of small, relatively isolated stretches of coastal plain. Exploiting the few small harbors and ports—such as Byblos, Beirut, and Sidon—as well as ports on the near-shore islands of Tyre and Arvad, the Phoenicians became the seafaring Mediterranean merchants for Mesopotamia, Egypt, and Israel.

East of the Lebanon Mountains, across the Valley of Lebanon (Josh 11:17; the **Beqaa**/Biqaʾ) climb the Anti-Lebanon Mountains. This chain's southern extension, Mount Hermon (Ps 29:6), rises to 9,263 feet, retains snow all year long in most years, and provides headwaters for the Jordan River. Northeast of Mount Hermon lies a large piedmont oasis and agricultural region called the *Ghouta*. In this oasis stands the ancient city of Damascus, whose strategic

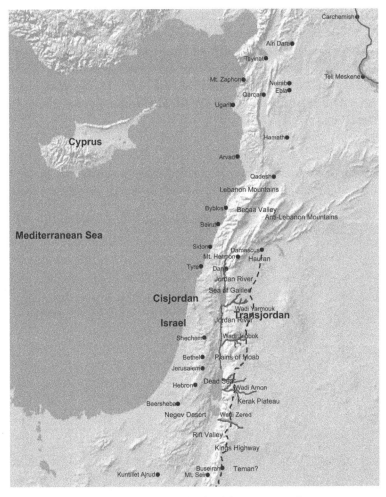

MAP 1-4. *The Levant consists of the lands of the eastern Mediterranean coast.*

location allowed the city, its territory (Aram), and its Aramean population to be key players in Israelite and **Judean** politics and culture. At times Damascus controlled much of the southern Levant from Philistia (2 Kgs 12:17) and perhaps **Edom** (2 Kgs 16:6) throughout the east side of the Jordan River (2 Kgs 10:32-33) and across Israelite and Judahite territory on the west. Aram plundered Jerusalem's temple (2 Kgs 12:17-18) and even attempted to remove its king (2 Kgs 16; Isa 7).

From the heights of the Lebanon Mountains, elevation declines significantly along the southern ranges. Here, too, the Rift Valley plunges. From headwaters near Mount Hermon, the 125-mile-long Jordan River flows through swampy Huleh Basin (ca. 230 feet above sea level), rapidly drops into the Sea of Galilee (ca. 700 feet below sea level), and finally empties into the Dead Sea (whose surface is about 1,400 feet below sea level, with its bottom another 1,000 feet below that). On either side of this deep valley rise the two highland regions featured in the Hebrew Bible—the **Transjordan** plateau to the east and the western hill country of the **Cisjordan** that became the home of the Israelites.

Levant: Transjordan

Fairly abundant natural resources coupled with control of the major trade route between Damascus and the Red Sea (the "King's Highway") made the

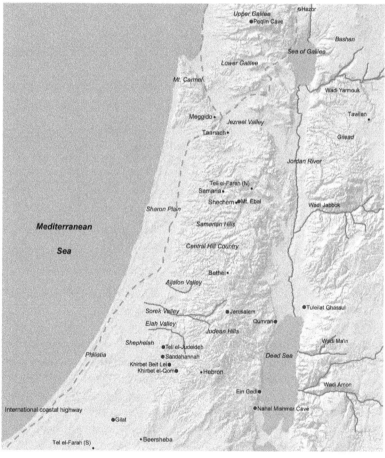

MAP 1-5. *The southern Levant was home to the Canaanites for more than two millennia during the Bronze Ages. This began to change around 1200 BCE when Israelite tribes and other groups, such as Philistines, settled in the region.*

Transjordan plateau a desirable region in which to settle. Arameans, **Ammonites**, **Moabites**, Edomites, and Israelites all vied for its control throughout the period covered by the Hebrew Bible.

The plateau averages between two thousand and four thousand feet in elevation and is characterized by five major subregions, known to readers of the Bible as Bashan, Gilead, Mishor, Moab, and Edom (Deut 2–3; Josh 13). Cutting through these are four large **wadis**: Yarmuk, Jabbok, Arnon, and Zered.

FIGURE 1-2. *Sea of Galilee viewed from the west.*

Northernmost and east of **Lake Kinneret** (Sea of Galilee) spreads the fertile plain of the Hauran (biblical Bashan). This well-watered steppe region of rich decomposed volcanic soil where extinct volcanic cones dot the landscape was noted for its good grazing and grain (Ps 22:12; Amos 4:1). Bashan was controlled through much of the biblical period by the kingdoms of Geshur and Maacah and later by Aram-Damascus. Thickly wooded with pine and oak forests and **maquis** (a dense growth of underbrush and scrub vegetation), the bountiful hill country of Gilead falls between the Wadi Yarmuk and the north extent of the Dead Sea. Although Israel often occupied much of Gilead, the eastern slope of the plateau—south of the Wadi Jabbok—was home to the Ammonites.

Moab controlled the narrow strip between the Dead Sea and the vast desert to the east from Gilead south to the Wadi Zered (el-Hesa). Sloping up from the Plains of Moab at the north end of the Dead Sea is the Mishor, a fertile steppe tableland often contested by Israelites, Moabites, and Ammonites and home to the biblical figure Ruth. The region was well suited to dry farming and **pastoralism** as well as tree farming and viticulture. South of the Wadi Arnon, Moab's Kerak Plateau was less productive and less populated.

From the Wadi Zered south, the uplands gain in elevation and are increasingly dominated by the red (Hebrew, *edom*) Nubian sandstone. Mount Seir—the watershed—reaches altitudes of over five thousand feet in Central Edom and was known as a steep and desolate mountain fortress (Obad 3–4) and an early home of the Israelite God (Judg 5:4). The ridge drops precipitously west into the Rift Valley (here called the **Arabah**), across which the Edomites sometimes expanded their control into southern Judah.

LEVANT: CISJORDAN (ISRAEL AND JUDAH)

The Cisjordan highlands are divided into four basic regions: Galilee, Central Hill Country, Judean Highlands, and the Negev. The designation of "from Dan to Beersheba" (1 Sam 3:20)—a distance of only about 150 miles—describes the traditional northern and southern boundaries of this region. Agricultural capacity, rainfall, and natural resources diminish to the south, requiring ingenious agriculture practices, especially in Judah, to achieve and maintain a functional economy.

Appearing in the sparsely settled western highlands during the Iron Age I (1200–1000 BCE), Israelite tribes changed the ecology of this region extensively (Borowski 1987, 15–20). They expanded cultivated lands by clearing the existing forests (Josh 17:14-18) and establishing extensive terracing systems that became the foundation for Israelite cultivation and are still in use today. On otherwise impractically steep slopes, **terraces** created level planting spaces that harvest runoff and control erosion. In the dryer southern highlands, a similar system was introduced—runoff farming. Because of inadequate rainfall, water **catchments** were created alongside terraces and fields by diverting rainwater runoff along walls or channels into basins or **cisterns**. This water could be used for drinking and flooding fields and terraces. In these ways the growing populations could augment the cereal crops with vegetables, nuts, and fruits, especially grapes, as well as provide drinking water during the long dry season. This allowed, when rainfall cooperated, for a measure of stability for the Israelites, otherwise lacking in many natural resources.

The Upper Galilee (with its highest point Mt. Meiron at 3,963 feet) and Lower Galilee (where Mt. Kemon reaches only 2,000 feet) form the northern extent of these highlands. Although the region averaged as much as forty inches of rain per year, its mountainous and thickly forested terrain made cultivation—and thus settlement—difficult; the Galilee is the setting for relatively few narratives in the Hebrew Bible (Judg 4–7; 1 Kgs 9:11-14).

The heart of the territory of the Northern Kingdom of Israel lay in the Central Hill Country. At the north end of these uplands is the Jezreel Valley, a swampy but rich agricultural gap in the highlands extending from the Mediterranean to the Rift Valley. Receiving more-than-adequate rainfall for

FIGURE 1-3. *Agricultural terraces were created for hillside farming to protect the soil from erosion and hold in precious moisture.*

dry-farming cultivation, it was and still is a major breadbasket for the region. Rising some 1,800 feet above the Jezreel floor juts the limestone promontory of Mount Carmel, which forms the northern extent of the Samarian highlands (the Central Hill Country). Stretching south, these low mountains reach their peaks in the summits of Mounts Ebal and Gerizim (2,849 and 2,621 feet, respectively). The well-watered, fertile valleys and foothills of this region produced olives, grapes, fruit, and other crops in relative abundance. Samaria, the Israelite capital, sat roughly equidistant between the Jezreel Valley and the Bethel Hills and midway between the Jordan River and the coast. The main shrines of Israel were placed near the southern border at Bethel and in the far north of Galilee at Dan.

Abundant agriculture, adequate natural resources, and access to the sea made for a strong economy. In its territory, Israel controlled the main western overland transportation artery between Mesopotamia and Egypt. Known as the "Way of the Sea" ("Via Maris"), this international coastal highway crossed the Rift Valley at the city of Hazor and the Jezreel at Megiddo, cut through a gap in the Carmel range, navigated the foothills along the swamp-prone coastal Sharon Plain, and then ran south to the Nile Delta.

Prosperity was common, especially in the eighth century, when Israel controlled the territory from Damascus to the Red Sea (2 Kgs 14:23-28). Israel's location and prosperity also made it a frequent target of the military aspirations of the smaller neighboring nations, including Judah, as well as the empires in Mesopotamia and Egypt.

Positioned on the Judean and Negev Highlands, the Southern Kingdom of Judah was not well situated—having few natural resources, marginal agriculture, and no major trade routes. This "backwater" status provides a window on Judah's history, its conflicts with Israel and other local entities, and its longevity among Levantine states in the face of Assyrian, Egyptian, and Babylonian aggression. It also affords insight into the mindset of the Hebrew Bible, which was written largely from a Judean perspective that focused on Jerusalem and its temple as divinely chosen yet positioned within a less-than-desirable environmental and geopolitical situation.

Reaching over 3,000 feet, the Judean Highlands comprise a rather uniform watershed incised with numerous westward spurs separated by deep and steep valleys, most often lacking any floodplain. Several of these—such as the Aijalon, Sorek, and Elah—form the main western routes from the coastal plain into the hill country. At the northern end of these hills, at about 2,400 feet, sits Judah's capital city and religious and cultural center, Jerusalem.

Precipitation in Judah's hills is characterized not so much by amounts, which can reach twenty-one inches per year, but "in the number of rainy days and in the intensity of rain per hour or per day" (Ashbel 1971, 185–86). Rain in Judah was limited to about fifty days annually, largely in January and February. Agriculture here was unpredictable and not as plentiful as in the highlands to the north but sufficient for orchards and vineyards. Cereal farming for this region was centered in the foothills on west flank of Judah—the **Shephelah**.

The Shephelah foothills transition gently over ten miles into the low, rolling topography of the coastal plain. Here, the international coastal highway bypassed Judah's territory, passing instead through Philistia. The Philistines controlled the coast, with its almost straight coastline and wide, sandy coastal plain stretching south to the Egyptian border at the Brook of Egypt (Wadi el-Arish). The Shephelah was prized as a border region. Over the millennia, Canaanites, Judahites, Israelites, Arameans, Egyptians, Philistines, Assyrians, Babylonians, and later Persians and Greeks all fought to control it.

Eastward from the watershed of the Judean Highlands toward the Rift Valley lies the wilderness of Judah, the **Jeshimon**. Long represented in the biblical materials as a place of desolation, the wilderness is a region cut by numerous valleys with thin soils and minimal precipitation—"badlands." Sloping steeply into the Jordan Valley, the elevation drops dramatically in only a few miles from about 2,400 feet above sea level to 1,400 feet below sea level at the Dead Sea.

Rising slowly from the coast, south of the Judean Hills, are the Negev Highlands, which drop sharply into the desolate Rift Valley, here known as the Arabah. Poor soils and minimal rainfall in the Negev allow for marginal dry farming and cultivation of cereals. Sheep and goat grazing better fit the ecology; this is the seminomadic lifestyle of the biblical patriarchs, whose range was centered in the Negev.

The world of the Hebrew Bible was diverse and complex. From the ecology of daily life to the sweep of regional geopolitics, ancient geographic realities played a crucial role in the history, culture, and even theology recorded within its pages.

Archaeology and the Hebrew Bible

Archaeology has long captured the public's imagination. The excitement of discovering lost civilizations like Egypt, Rome, Greece, and Israel has frequently been the stuff of adventure tales. The work of the archaeologist, while not usually quite so adventurous, is nonetheless essential to understanding and reconstructing ancient worlds. Certainly that is the case with the world of the Hebrew Bible. Archaeological investigation supplies important details regarding the ancient landscape and also background information about the characters themselves who populated it.

Broadly defined, archaeology is the systematic recovery and analysis of material evidence to support investigations and reconstructions of past human activity within past environmental, historical, and cultural contexts. Archaeologists excavate and examine all manner of materials left behind by humans, from the smallest seed to the largest city. While singular and sensational finds often attract the most popular attention, it is generally the multitude of more mundane discoveries that provide scholars with a wealth of information regarding the people and how they lived.

Archaeological History

Although even the ancient Mesopotamians engaged in a form of archaeology, the modern discipline really had its roots in the seventeenth century. Since then, archaeology in the Near East has tended to operate in two interconnected spheres. The first involves the excavation of an ancient site, while the second seeks to understand more large-scale human activity through local or regional surveys.

Aside from the "treasure hunting" of museums and wealthy patrons, Near Eastern archaeology's main interest early on was to connect the biblical text to places in the Levant. For centuries, religious pilgrims to the lands of the Bible conducted personal "surveys," making use of local traditions to identify biblical sites. In the eighteenth and especially nineteenth centuries, more rigorous and intentional surveys took place for both biblical and military purposes. It was largely the work of these historical geographers that gave us the foundation for the "Bible maps" as we have them today.

This focus on survey was replaced in the early twentieth century with an emphasis on the excavation of tells, which, thanks to the work of the nineteenth-century historical geographers, were often identified with ancient biblical names. The first systematic excavation in the Levant was undertaken by Flinders Petrie at **Tell** el-Hesi in 1890, and thousands of excavations have followed. The relationship between the biblical text and archaeology was (and remains) a methodological flashpoint, with some scholars arguing for a more text-based "biblical archaeology" and others seeking a non-text-based discipline. Today, most archaeologists follow a path between the two: a closely controlled integration of text and artifact (Maeir 2010b; Davis 2004b).

TEXTS AND EPIGRAPHY

Perhaps the most sensational archaeological finds have been those involving writing—found on a variety of materials: clay tablets, parchment, papyrus, vessels of ceramic, stone or metal, stone monuments, and **ostraca** (fragments of broken pottery used as "scrap paper"). While these comprise but a small portion of the **realia** uncovered by archaeologists, they provide important pegs upon which to hang geography and ancient history and offer a glimpse into the thought life of the ancient peoples. For example, the only way we are able to call something "Jerusalem" or "Israel" or a people "Egyptians" or "Canaanites" is because some inscription or document has been excavated and deciphered and linked to a specific geographic locale. Smaller finds such as coins and personal **seals** (scarabs, stamp, and cylinder seals) and seal impressions on **bullae** (clay tags used to seal documents) add to our knowledge of individuals and their situations. Finally, literary compositions (such as Mesopotamian and Egyptian texts, the famous Dead Sea Scrolls, and even the biblical text itself) allow access to the thoughts and worldviews of the ancient peoples. Deciphering and investigating these ancient writing is the work of the **epigrapher** and philologist. Beyond written artifacts, countless pictorial representations of events, people, and stories adorned media as diverse as large reliefs and tomb decoration to small seals and graffiti. These illustrate the geography, environment, history, culture, and even attire of the ancient world.

ARCHAEOLOGICAL METHOD

The vast majority of archaeological realia come from daily life—potsherds, building foundations, bones, mud-bricks, grinding stones, the occasional luxury item, and a myriad of other artifacts, both small and large. It is from this mountain of **"material culture"**—a term designating anything that humans produced, from buildings to dung—and the contexts from which it comes that archaeologists piece together the ancient world. In order to comprehend the usefulness and limitations of archaeology for understanding the ancient world, its history, and its texts—including the Hebrew Bible—it is important to understand how the data have been gathered.

At present, archaeology in the Near East strives to encompass a diverse set of disciplines in its research agendas, utilizing both excavation and survey work. While excavations center on a single site, surveys focus on broader regional issues.

ARCHAEOLOGICAL SURVEY

Since the 1970s, archaeological survey has become more sophisticated, and its goals have broadened. Technology (such as **GIS**, GPS, and various types of satellite imagery) has greatly increased the speed, precision, detail, and amount of data able to be recorded and synthesized, but survey methodology itself has remained much the same. At its most basic, an archaeological survey identifies an area to be surveyed, organizes it into a set of grids, and then has a trained team physically walk that grid pattern, mapping its features—especially extramural agricultural **installations** and tombs—and collecting material culture samples such as pottery **sherds**. Through the use of statistical analysis, archaeologists are then able to make general conclusions regarding human activity outside the walls of ancient settlements. This is especially helpful for regional demographic studies.

Understanding agricultural activity, including pastoralism, in the context of both environment and human settlement is essential for piecing together the human geography of an ancient city or region. The remains left behind by these activities—such as olive and grape presses, threshing

FIGURE 1-4. *St. Etienne's cave, dated to the Iron Age,*
with burial chamber and repository.

floors, terraces, grinding installations, agricultural outposts, irrigation systems, cisterns, and field walls—are usually ephemeral and covered by vegetation. These remains yield a wealth of information not otherwise attainable
through site excavation.

Several types of extramural burial practices were employed in the Levant.
The most common of these were cyst tombs designed for interring a single
body, and tombs designed for multiple individuals—cave and bench tombs
dug out of the limestone hillsides. In these, bodies were placed on benches
carved in the rock, and, when the flesh had decomposed, the bones were
placed in repositories within the tomb and mingled together with those of
other deceased family members. This fleshes out our understanding of the biblical phrase "sleeping with the ancestors," and it gives us a frame of reference
for the conceptions of death and Sheol (the underworld) in the Hebrew Bible.
Graves and tombs often contain well-preserved grave goods: local, common
pottery types, local and imported fine wares, and both mundane and luxury
goods; these illustrate a variety of cultural features.

EXCAVATION

Modern archaeological excavation is a multidisciplinary endeavor. In addition
to those trained as archaeologists, specialists from other disciplines are routinely employed. These include architects, conservators, epigraphers and phi-
lologists, **osteologists** and archeozoologists, paleobotanists, ceramicists, lab
specialists, data managers, and others. Of course there is a work crew—either
workers hired locally or, as is often the case, students and other volunteers who
participate in an on-site **field school** to gain archaeological experience. Each

FIGURE 1-5. *Student excavators at Jezreel.*

plays a part in the excavation, recording, analysis, and interpretation of the finds unearthed.

SITE SELECTION

Because excavation is expensive and time consuming, site selection is a critically important part of the archaeological enterprise. Although archaeologists excavate a number of different types of sites—from small single-occupation farmsteads, underwater structures, and sunken ships to multiuse tombs—most commonly, archaeologists excavate ancient cities and villages. The location of ancient settlements depended on a number of common factors. Access to water, arable land, and resources has always been a high priority, as was access to trade routes. Because of the desirability of these locations, defense was also a necessary component. Thus, the village or town would usually be situated on a hill, enabling the inhabitants to guard water sources, farmlands, trade routes, and territory. Over successive generations of use, these population centers would be destroyed—either through human or natural activity—and rebuilt numerous times. The result of these successive building activities is that the hill takes on the form of a "layer cake," with the oldest occupational layers, known as **strata**, resting on the original hill surface and the most recent strata at the top. The natural hill becomes a tell. Although the strata of a tell are far more complex than those of a layer cake, the analogy is useful. Slicing through these strata to reveal the successive phases of building activity on the site is the basic task of the archaeologist.

FIGURE 1-6. *Tell Dothan. A tell is an artificial mound formed over centuries and millennia on the ruins of successive settlements.*

Settlements in the Levant were generally very small by modern standards. Regional cities were twenty to forty acres; towns were usually between five and seven acres; and villages—the most common settlement type—rarely covered more than three acres. What this means for readers of the Hebrew

Bible is that when the text mentions a "city," it likely refers to fewer than 3,000 people. Thus, modern readers of the Hebrew Bible need to shrink their mental picture of a "city" or "town" and also realize that most of the population of Israel and Judah lived in villages with populations averaging about 250 people.

Towns in the ancient Near East usually had defensive perimeter walls made from large boulders with a mud-brick superstructure. Frequently ten or more feet wide and up to forty feet high with towers placed at strategic spots, these fortifications were built either as solid walls (commonly with a "saw tooth" or "offset/inset" pattern) or as a **casemate** wall system. A casemate is constructed of two parallel perimeter walls with perpendicular walls joining them at regular intervals, forming rectangular rooms between the walls and providing strength and stability to the wall system. This enabled the occupants of the city to utilize the rooms for storage or other uses or, in the event of a siege by an enemy, to backfill the spaces with rubble, creating one extremely wide solid wall. Against the outer face of the fortification wall and extending down the slope of the hill, city planners often constructed a **glacis**. These were made from a layering of soil and chalk and often were covered with stones. This solid, sloping mantel prevented erosion and made it difficult for attackers to converge at the base of the wall or to dig under it.

Access through the city wall was protected by a fortified gatehouse. In towns and cities, the gateway consisted of an entryway—often ten feet or wider and protected by double doors—leading through a central passageway. The passageway was flanked by small parallel chambers opening onto it from each side, forming a defensible structure encasing the entry and incorporated into the city wall. In addition to their defensive function, these gate structures were important elements of social and cultural space. They defined community, separating the outsider from the insider—as illustrated in the sacred areas uncovered in the gate complexes at Tell Dan and Bethsaida. Business also was often conducted in the gate (Ruth 4:1-2), justice was meted out in this space (Deut 21:18-21; 2 Sam 15:1-4), and community affairs were discussed (Prov 31:23).

Excavating inside the fortifications, archaeologists endeavor to locate the various sectors of the city or town, such as the domestic zone (where people lived) and the public or administrative quarter. In the larger cities, an upper city, or acropolis, occupied the highest section of the site and was sometimes surrounded by its own wall. Town planning at many sites included a peripheral ring of buildings adjacent to or separated by a roadway from the city wall. Within this belt, construction was often haphazard, creating a warren of interconnected structures with narrow alleyways between them. More regular grid plans were sometimes used (e.g., Beersheba), mostly in later periods.

The public or administrative zone, generally found near the gate complex, is evidenced by larger, monumental architecture. The types of structures in this zone include community food and storage facilities, administrative buildings, temples and religious structures, military facilities, and large-scale residences. These buildings are characterized not only by size but also by a higher quality of construction and by the finds uncovered within them.

Domestic buildings, such as the **four-room house**, occupy the bulk of space in most settlements. The size and design of these housing units, coupled with insights gained from **ethnoarchaeological** research, illustrates the basic household activities necessary for survival (food preparation and storage, textile and craft production, and child rearing) as well as the foundational social structure of the ancient Levant, known in the Bible as the *bet av* (Hebrew, "House of the Father"). This term identifies the multigenerational extended family living in one house or compound of houses (Gen 24:38; Stager 1985; Schloen 2001). This information then adds accuracy and depth toward understanding biblical texts that discuss the Israelite family and social structure (e.g., Deut 21:15-17; Prov 31; Judg 17, 18) as well as those in which the houses themselves play a role (e.g., Judg 11:29-40; 1 Kgs 17:17-24).

Some settlements contain "elite" zones that are marked by high-quality architecture and artifacts, while other towns may contain areas set aside for industrial use, such as pottery manufacture or oil and wine production. Tel Miqne-Ekron of the Philistines is an excellent example of most of these zones (fortifications, administrative, elite, industrial, and domestic) at one site.

EXCAVATION ESSENTIALS

There are three essential points to remember about archaeological work.

The first of these is so obvious that it is often overlooked by those utilizing archaeological data—archaeology is by nature *destructive*. Once an archaeologist has dug something up, no one can ever dig it up again. Archaeological excavation then, unlike other scientific investigation, is a series of nonrepeatable experiments performed on only a percentage of the site being excavated. In this regard it must be remembered that the excavated remains represent only a very small percentage of the materials that were present at a site in a given period in antiquity. This has crucial ramifications for both archaeological methodology and interpretation.

Second, archaeological results are only as good as the recording of data during excavation. As archaeologists dig downward, they are moving through, and destroying, a three-dimensional space, and thus they must vigilantly control both the horizontal and the vertical dimensions. Descriptions and measurements are made along x, y, and z axes, and careful observations regarding even small changes in soil color and **matrix** are recorded. The goal is to be able to re-create the original three-dimensional space as accurately as possible in order to determine the stratigraphy of the site—what features belong to which layers/strata, and how do these strata relate temporally and contextually to each other. Because of the nature of deposition on a tell, the general principle of stratigraphy is that the upper layers are successively later than those below them. Archaeologists number these strata starting at the top, delimiting major and minor phases of occupation.

Third, awareness and understanding of these *contexts* and the *relationships* that create them are essential. An artifact on display in a museum may be aesthetically pleasing and may provide art historical information, but what the archaeologist seeks is its original relationships to the materials around it. An excavated storage jar has little archaeological meaning on its own, but seen **in situ** (meaning "in its original location")—in relationship to the other vessels found in the same room, with that room understood as part of a larger building, and that building as part of a town—that storage jar becomes an interconnected piece of a larger world. Understanding the relationships between all of the excavated realia is crucial to the work of the archaeologist, and this guides excavation methodology.

FIGURE 1-7. *A bowl from the Middle Bronze period in situ at Tel Megiddo.*

EXCAVATION TECHNIQUE

To maintain control along the horizontal plain, sites to be excavated are mapped in a grid pattern, the individual units of which are called **squares**. Depending on the nature of the site, these squares may be large (ten-by-ten meters) or small (one-by-one meter); most excavators use a grid of five-by-five meters or six-by-six meters. This allows for control over both the site as a whole as well as materials within each square. Groups of squares, known as **fields** or "areas," are selected for excavation according to zones on the tell considered to have the most potential for providing the maximum amount of information. At times, a long rectangular trench, called a **sondage**, is excavated down the slope of the tell to allow a window into multiple strata in one view.

As part of the vertical control of the dig, excavators leave a section of each square unexcavated: a "wall" of material—usually one meter wide—remains standing between squares. These remnants, called **balks**, provide the archaeologist with a visual record of the various layers (e.g., a construction backfill or the debris of a destroyed building) and features (e.g., a wall, oven, floor, or street) that have been unearthed in the square. These untouched balks provide control evidence and so are extremely helpful for stratigraphic analysis. The vertical faces of the balks, called **sections**, are carefully cleaned, labeled, drawn, and photographed and are used to check the results of excavation both in the field and in later analysis.

Managing the horizontal aspect of digging requires that each square supervisor attempt to excavate all of the remains of a particular phase of ancient occupation at the same time before moving below it to the next. The goal is to excavate each **locus** (the general designation for a layer or feature; pl. loci) as completely as possible—even when it is found in several squares (such as a long wall or a building). Each locus is given a discrete number that identifies it and places it in context among the loci of its square and field. Squares within fields are often kept roughly "in phase" to gain a wider perspective.

To maintain phase within a square, excavators dig across the square as horizontally as practical given the nature of the material. They do not dig holes or pull partially unearthed artifacts out of their matrix, because this would destroy the relationships within the context. Elevations (in relation to sea level) are frequently taken; thus, there is a record of the top and bottom levels of each locus that provides their height or depth. As excavation proceeds horizontally and vertically into new layers, the soil matrix changes, and new features emerge. Such changes are often hard to see, and so a great deal of energy is expended on keeping the excavation area clean. Because of this, the most commonly used digging tool is a mason's trowel. Scraping with a trowel allows the excavator better control and minimizes loose dirt. It may seem odd, but archaeologists also spend a lot of time sweeping dirt. Even using a trowel, some of the smallest artifacts (e.g., seeds, bone fragments, jewelry) may be missed. To avoid this, excavated soil is often dry-sifted in the field. The amount and extent of this sifting is determined by the goals of the excavation and the type and location of the locus from which the soil came. Wet sifting—the **flotation** of botanical remains to separate them from their soil matrix—is also part of the processing of certain types of loci. As artifacts are unearthed, the locus from which they were dug is documented, registered and sometimes photographed to create a record of their context within the square.

Horizontal relationships between loci are carefully recorded on a daily **"top plan."** This bird's-eye view of each square creates a graphic representation of the various loci in the square and their elevations. These drawings are taken into the field and are modified throughout the day as excavation progresses. At the end of the season, this series of daily plans, along with photographs taken, provides a visual record of the horizontal excavation progression to go along with the vertical section drawings.

By the end of the excavation, each square will have produced a detailed record of the excavation. This includes the daily top plans, the section drawings and photographs, and the square supervisor's daily excavation notes, which consist of the design and plan for, and implementation of, each day's digging, relationships between loci, measurements, and other observations. Detailed information about each locus (its description, measurements, relationships, and the artifacts found within it) is recorded on a "Locus Sheet." Finally, the supervisor produces a summary of all the loci excavated in his or her square and all the stratigraphic and contextual relationships between them. These records are the primary and foundational documents for all subsequent analysis, interpretation, and publication.

With the advent of smaller computers and tablets, many excavations keep digital records in the field. While this can be a helpful innovation, what is important is not the technology of the record keeping but the quality of the information being recorded. This should also be said of the many technological advancements now being used in the field. With the increasing availability of laser technology, Total Stations are replacing visual surveying and GIS-based applications—such as **LiDAR** (Light Detection and Ranging)—and are providing faster and perhaps more detailed data recording, integration, retrieval, and visualization. Recent technological advances in cost-effective and mobile chemical and mineral analysis of the soil matrix enables an increasingly more comprehensive understanding of specific contexts and use patterns of loci. These new technologies are enabling excavators to create a more complete, accurate, and usable record of all aspects of the excavation.

PROCESSING AND ANALYSIS OF ARTIFACTS

Artifacts collected in the field through survey or excavation are processed and analyzed in the camp and/or by an off-site laboratory. Artifacts usually fall into one of five basic categories: pottery, organic samples, animal bones, epigraphic materials, and MCs (material culture artifacts not grouped in one of the other categories).

MCs are divided further according to material: ceramics (e.g., figurines, spindle whorls, **faience** items) and lithics (e.g., flint blades, grinding stones, stone vessels) usually require minimal initial processing. Objects composed of metal (e.g., agricultural implements, weapons, jewelry, vessels) or tools or crafts made from animal remains (e.g., bone, ivory, horn, hide) or botanical remains (e.g., wood, linen or papyrus) require more stabilization, attention, and processing. Specific analysis of the MCs is conducted along a variety of lines according to specific research agendas both within the scope of the excavation and from external researchers.

POTTERY TYPOLOGY

Found in almost every locus, the most ubiquitous artifacts uncovered are sherds of broken pottery. These sherds are placed in buckets (called "baskets") and carefully labeled by locus number and top and bottom levels of the specific part of the locus from which it was dug. As each basket is filled, the location from which it was taken is noted on the top plan.

The pottery in each basket is washed, dried in the sun, and then examined (known as "reading") to determine the type and nature of the sherds within it in an attempt to ascertain to what type of vessel they initially belonged. An experienced archaeologist can determine the form and relative age of a vessel from what are known as "diagnostic sherds"—small portions of a rim, or a piece of a base or a handle, or a small amount of decoration on a body sherd. Other aspects of pottery analysis provide additional insight into manufacture, origin, and use. Examining a pot's decoration (**slip**, paint, or **burnishing**), whether the ware is coarse or fine, and its firing tells us much about the technology of the potter and the intended use of the vessel. Statistical analysis of the relative numbers of different types, forms, and ages of pottery sherds yields information about the locus from which they were dug. For example, a locus with more serving or cooking vessels

FIGURE 1-8. *Teaching pottery identification and sorting at the Jezreel excavations.*

than storage vessels likely was part of a space used for food preparation rather than storage. Microscopic examination and trace-element analyses of the clays used in pottery excavated at a site can provide information regarding the place of manufacture of specific vessels, thereby indicating trade patterns.

Archaeological Dating

Pottery analysis not only illuminates the nature of individual loci but is also one of the main ways that the relative succession of strata at one site is dated and linked across sites.

RELATIVE CHRONOLOGY

In the ancient world, styles and forms of pottery tended to be somewhat locally standardized and changed gradually but discernibly over time in terms of technique, form, and decoration. This has enabled the creation of typologies for various pottery forms, such as lamps or bowls. A chronological aspect is added as archaeologists note shifts in pottery forms between the different strata at a site; lower layers contain only earlier forms, while layers above contain a larger percentage of later forms. In general principle, a locus cannot be dated earlier than the latest pottery (or artifact) found within it.

Because the same form of a vessel is often found at several different sites, the strata and relative stratigraphic sequences between the sites have been correlated. This permits archaeologists and art historians to create regional relative chronological and typological sequences of forms for Near Eastern, Egyptian, and other pottery from the ancient world. While these typologies continue to be refined and discussed, they form the foundation for dating the layers of any given site and across multiple sites.

ABSOLUTE DATING

Linking a relative dating sequence to specific years in the Western Julian/ Gregorian calendar system—called absolute dating—has been done commonly by connection to textual materials and aided by lab-based analysis of realia, usually organic finds. Western calendars traditionally have worked from the birth of Jesus in their schema. Thus, dates are BC (before Christ) and AD (Anno Domini—Latin, in the "Year of the Lord"). Recently, scholars have used more religiously neutral designations for the same time frame: BCE (Before the Common Era) and CE (Common Era).

Record keeping in the royal courts of the ancient world has left us relative chronologies of events and people. When an absolute date, obtained by science or other means, can be reliably assigned to a textual detail, the ancient chronology can be connected to modern dating systems. For example, when a solar eclipse mentioned in the Assyrian Eponym List (an annual list of officials and important events) was precisely dated by astronomers, the terms of the officials and the events on that list were dated and then cross-referenced to other texts across geography and time. Correlating absolute dates to a particular site and its strata can be seen in the example of Tel Miqne-Ekron. Evidence of a major change in both architecture and pottery types between Ekron's Strata IIA and IC permitted the excavators to connect this shift to an absolute date known from Assyrian texts, the 701 BCE Assyrian conquest of Ekron. Another major change in Ekron's realia was seen between artifacts from Strata VIII and VI. This shift corresponded to dateable Egyptian textual evidence concerning the influx of the Sea Peoples near the beginning of the twelfth century BCE. Such intersections between archaeological evidence and textual evidence were key factors in dating the overall stratigraphic sequence at Tel Miqne.

Comparing dated stratigraphic sequences between sites makes regional dating possible. If particular forms of pottery and other realia are found within a dateable stratum at one site, then the equivalent strata at other sites may be similarly dated. Absolute date ranges can then be assigned to the pottery series across a region. In addition, the presence or absence of special types of pottery—especially, imported wares dateable from other cultures—aids in the dating process. This correlation between pottery and dating has resulted in a temporal sequence by which archaeologists and historians reconstruct the chronology of the Levant. Most of the focus and creation of the Hebrew Bible falls within the Iron Age and Persian Period, with the events of the Torah set in the Bronze Ages (see archaeological ages chart).

While text-based dating is common, the application of advanced laboratory dating techniques on realia has been utilized. Perhaps the most well known, and misunderstood, is radiocarbon or carbon-14 dating (^{14}C). Radiocarbon dating measures the decay of carbon isotopes found in organic remains over time. When organic material—such as timbers, preserved cereals and fruits, and organic residue from the inside of sealed storage jars—is unearthed and properly prepared, ^{14}C analysis is possible. These laboratory findings are calibrated using known dates from other ancient materials—particularly dendrochronology, in which master sequences of annual tree rings have been plotted back as far as nine thousand years before the present (BP). These measurements produce probable date ranges for each sample.

Because any single sample measured provides only a date range (often as wide as ±100 years), archaeologists carefully take several short-lived organic samples from a series of sequential contexts (loci) and often send them to several labs. This enables a progression of calibrated sample date ranges that allows for more statistical precision. However, even high-precision ^{14}C dating results (±25 years) are often not precise enough to answer some of the more specific questions asked by historians of the Bible—for example, whether a building phase should be attributed to the late tenth-century Solomon or to a monarch of the early ninth century (Levy and Higham 2005). Pottery typology also lacks this level of precision.

Archaeological Results as Historical Evidence

We began this chapter by noting that every good story needs a setting. As we have seen, archaeologically informed depictions of ancient macroscale geographic, environmental, and geopolitical realities and trends allow a more nuanced visualization of ancient narrative settings. Archaeological analysis enables us to see more details—localized social, cultural, political, and economic realities, agrarian activities, urban and rural strategies, and how these changed through time. On occasion we may even catch a glimpse of a specific event mentioned in the texts themselves, usually those of a larger-scale nature where a noticeable shift in material culture is discernible, such as construction and destruction.

By setting the stage, archaeological evidence marks a boundary for the understanding of ancient texts, including the Hebrew Bible. Hyperliterary, tendentious, or theological interpretations that ignore or deny the real-world settings of the texts divorce themselves from the authors' intended meanings, and those that assume that the ancient authors portray a fictional world are simply not dealing with the evidence.

As detailed as the picture of the setting may become, clear-cut absolute archaeological verification for singular events will likely remain somewhat elusive. This is especially true as it relates to the more localized and small-scale occurrences regularly depicted in the ancient texts, including the Bible. Simply put, while archaeology illustrates daily life on a general level, and substantial shifts in material culture reveal aspects of large-scale events, local and particular incidents do not usually have a discernible impact on the archaeological record. Connecting textual events to stratigraphic remains requires very precise dating and correlation of several lines of evidence, something that is not generally possible even as the details continue to be refined and debated.

In spite of the inherent difficulties, archaeologists do seek to illuminate localized occurrences, often adopting the methodology of detectives. They gather, analyze, and classify the disparate pieces of evidence and then develop a theory of what happened. Some evidence, when properly interpreted and connected to the "case," can provide crucial information. Other lines of evidence reflect the circumstances surrounding the events and may even confirm or negate the theory. Evaluation and interpretation of all the data—epigraphic/textual and material culture—work to produce the most probable historical reconstruction of the event in rare cases, even near certainty.

This reliance on probability in historical reconstruction has resulted in considerable debate regarding the nature of historical reliability of ancient texts, especially the Bible. Often, a part of these discussions is archaeology's inability to assess the theological or ideological claims made by ancient Near Eastern texts. Archaeological realia simply cannot provide substantiation—according to empirical standards and probability—that an event was divinely enabled.

In the final analysis, however, archaeology does provide crucial and indispensable data for historians and interpreters of the biblical text. The responsible **exegete** will use archaeological research and reconstructions with an integrated understanding of both the strengths and the limits of archaeological investigation, realia, and conclusions.

Through the use of geographic and archaeological studies, the ancient settings for the stories, poems, laws, and oracles of the Hebrew Bible emerge from the shadows. These rich, colorful, and textured backgrounds and foregrounds provide the modern reader with a more nuanced and perhaps more accurate appreciation of these texts upon which so much of Western civilization is founded.

Suggestions for Further Reading

There are many good atlases for the study of the ancient world in general and ancient Israel in particular. The *Oxford Bible Atlas* is widely used in college courses, while *The Macmillan Bible Atlas* (1993) is just one of many that can be found on the shelves of college and university libraries. A recent publication is William Schlegel's *Satellite Bible Atlas*, which provides maps of biblical places and events drawn upon satellite imagery. The compendious work *The Sacred Bridge: Carta's Atlas of the Biblical World*, by A. Rainey and S. Notley (2006), is an excellent source of further geographical information.

The geographical study of lands relevant to the Hebrew Bible / Old Testament has been summarized by Denis Baly in his *The Geography of The Bible: A Study in Historical Geography* (abridged as *Basic Biblical Geography*). Yohanan Aharoni provides a different take on this topic in *The Land of the Bible: A Historical Geography*.

The ancient Near East and its history is a huge topic. Jack M. Sasson's *Civilizations of the Ancient Near East,* in four volumes, provides a solid overview of the variety of different countries and empires that rose and fell during that time, while A. Mazar's work *Archaeology of the Land of the Bible*, vol. 1, *10,000–586 B.C.E.*, and E. Stern's *Archaeology of the Land of the Bible*, vol. 2, *The Assyrian, Babylonian, and Persian Periods (732–332 B.C.E.)*, give a view of the history of the land of Israel.

There are seemingly innumerable sites that archaeologists have excavated in Israel and across the Near East. Encyclopedias provide a good introduction to many of them. For the ancient Near East generally, consult Eric Meyers, *The Oxford Encyclopedia of Archaeology in the Near East*, in five volumes (1997). For Israel in particular, see E. Stern, *The New Encyclopedia of Archaeological Excavations in the Holy Land*, in four volumes (1993). A fifth supplementary volume appeared in 2008, which updates many sites and adds new ones.

Several books have been written that provide an introduction to archaeology and its methods, especially as it is practiced in Israel and surrounding countries. Perhaps the most helpful in terms of basic questions and procedures is John Currid's *Doing Archaeology in the Land of the Bible*. Walter Rast's short book *Through the Ages in Palestinian Archaeology: An Introductory Handbook* provides an overview of periods of prehistory and history and the technological changes that featured in each.

2

INTRODUCTION TO THE OLD TESTAMENT
AND ITS CHARACTER AS HISTORICAL EVIDENCE

Mark Elliott, with Paul V. M. Flesher

Studying the Old Testament has its limitations. We have no direct evidence revealing how the Bible was composed or collected, and our understanding of its authors and editors as well as the dating of its books and their component parts comes from analysis rather than explicit description. Scholars can only surmise how accurately our present texts reflect the original compositions. The Old Testament was rewritten and reedited for centuries. No one from the seventh century BCE, the fourth century BCE, or even the first century BCE (or CE) thought it important to describe in full what books the collection would contain, how the process of selection developed, who made these decisions, and what arguments and agreements took place at momentous or secretive assemblies. So since we want to use the Bible as historical evidence, where does this lack of knowledge leave us? To answer the question, we must briefly remind ourselves what it means to do history according to academic standards, as we set forth in the Introduction. Then we will see how the Bible and its information can be fit into that approach.

When an event takes place—whether a significant event like a car driving into a telephone pole or a minor event like a conversation between two friends—how do we know what happened? Of course, one way to know was to have been present as a witness or a participant. Events at which we were not present can be only known in two ways. One of these is through an oral or written report, such listening to the description of a friend who had been there or by reading a newspaper story. (Oral statements are useful for contemporary and recent events, but for the biblical period, two thousand to three thousand years ago, they are unavailable.) The other is by inferring from evidence. For example, a damaged car or pole would indicate that an accident happened.

The academic study of past events—i.e., history—is not dissimilar to how we learn about the past in our everyday lives. It differs primarily in that it follows a stricter standard of reliability for its data. It does not just trust a report without question, but subjects both oral and written observations to testing— for truth, accuracy, perspective, bias and reliability. With this in mind, let's recall the three steps of doing history, as we set them out earlier.

First, the initial step in the academic study of the past—the historical method—is to gather as much information about an event as possible. The most reliable histories are ones that are written on the basis of lots of data. Less information can lead only to a less reliable reconstruction of the past. And of course, when dealing with the far past, there is often too little evidence. Many events are known from a single source—the exact opposite of what is needed for the academic study of history. Without evidence there is no knowledge of the past.

Second, information is not knowledge; data are not facts. Every piece of the gathered data must be examined and tested. An author always has a perspective, whether conscious or not, that shapes how they saw the event, what they thought was important about it, and what they put into their description. Historians must work the character of each source, in this sense, and then trust it (or not) accordingly. Mesha, the king of Moab, for example, writes in the Mesha Stela about his kingdom's confrontation with Israel from a perspective quite different from that recorded in the Israelite source in 2 Kings 3. The issue before the historian is not to choose one as accurate and the other as inaccurate, but to reconstruct the event so that it reflects both, in accordance with their evaluated reliability. Archaeological data must be evaluated according to its standards—as explained in chapter 1—before being brought into connection with other sources.

Third, an academic historian studying an event then takes all the data into account, trusting them in accordance to their level of reliability. She then reconstructs the event, constructing a portrayal in keeping with her best, most expert, judgment. Historians must use all the sources or indicate why some are left out and should indicate their best judgment about each one's reliability, indicating where the data support each other and describing how they balance the information when it is contradictory. The goal here is a neutral, dispassionate synthesis that accounts for all the data as opposed to a one-sided, tendentious portrayal serving a modern purpose. As part of this, they should also indicate the reliability of their own reconstruction and its different elements. When there is insufficient evidence to provide anything more than a guess at its reconstruction, they must acknowledge that as well.

This book is interested in understanding the history of ancient Israel, from its formation to the end of the events recounted in the Hebrew Bible. To reach that goal, the books of the Hebrew Bible are used as historical data. That means that as scholars, whether expert scholars or student scholars, we must ignore the fact that the two religions of Judaism and Christianity view these books as divinely inspired sacred texts. We must treat them as compositions of human beings and put them through the same methodology applied to other texts. If we do not, then we wind up creating some sort of sacred theology rather than academic history. Since the latter is this book's goal, then we must follow its methods.

To use the Hebrew Bible's books as historical data, we must evaluate them and their reliability, just as we must do to all other sources of historical evidence. That means we must address two questions. The first question is, how were the books of the Hebrew Bible composed? Who wrote them? Some books clearly come from a single author, such as Ruth. Other books are composite constructions, edited together from multiple sources. Some of these, like Ezra-Nehemiah, seem to have been put together at a single point in time from letters, decrees, lists, and even a memoir. Others were apparently reworked over generations and perhaps centuries, bringing together different sources and then reworked generations later, with new material being added.

The second question is, how do we moderns come to have these books? How did they get from the first millennium BCE to the third millennium CE? Unlike archaeological discoveries, the Bible is important not because it was found in a stratified excavation but because it was handed down through the centuries and millennia—the Dead Sea Scrolls notwithstanding. At each stage, human beings were actively involved in its transmission, from collecting the books together, to copying them and distributing those copies, to deciding they were sacred, and so on. Most people know that the main language of the Old Testament is Hebrew. But there is a small but significant amount of **Aramaic** as well: large sections of Daniel (2:4–7:28) and Ezra (4:8–6:18; 7:12–26) as well as two words in Genesis (31:47) and a verse in Jeremiah (10:11).

FIGURE 2-1. *The Isaiah Scroll is one of the Dead Sea Scrolls discovered near Khirbet Qumran. Since it was copied in the second century BCE or earlier, it is perhaps the oldest and largest biblical manuscript in existence.*

Ironically, however, one of our oldest and nearly complete manuscripts is the Greek translation called the **Septuagint**. One manuscript of this translation known as *Codex Vaticanus* comprises one of our oldest, nearly complete texts of the Old Testament and was written in the fourth century CE. All of that activity has implications for how we can use the biblical writings in our search for an understanding of ancient Israel.

To address these matters more fully, this chapter will approach them in reverse. It begins by introducing the books of the Hebrew Bible and then looks at the where the Hebrew Bible / Old Testament comes from and how it has been transmitted through the centuries. Finally, it will take a look at the first five books—known as the Torah—and use them as an example for how scholars of different centuries gradually came to see them as human compositions done at particular historical moments. The chapter ends by looking at how the archaeology of ancient Israel was brought into the analysis of the Hebrew Bible.

What Is the Hebrew Bible?

The English title "Bible" originates with the Greek word *biblia*, a plural word that simply means "books." The earliest use of *biblia* for sacred texts appears in 1 Maccabees 12:9, where the author refers to such writings as "holy books," *ta biblia ta hagia*. The term initially derived from the ancient city Byblos—in its singular form, *biblion*—which was a Phoenician city that served as a commercial center for the ancient papyrus trade. Papyrus was a predecessor of paper and was made from a reed grown in the Nile Delta, then beaten and pressed and made into a sheet or a scroll.

During the first millennium BCE, books took the form of scrolls. At that time, the books that became known as the Hebrew Bible existed in only scroll form—a long single piece of writing material written upon in columns. It was rolled up for storage and unrolled for reading. In Hebrew, the word for "scroll" is *megillah*, as the prophet Jeremiah said when he commanded Baruch: "Bring the scroll [*megillah*] that you read in the hearing of the people" (Jer 36:14). One book is called a *sefer*, and, when Daniel consults several sacred writings, he calls them "books," *sefarim* (Dan 9:2).

When the Christian Church decided to include the Jewish Bible as part of its own sacred texts, two things happened. First, the Christians separated its books from those written about Jesus or after Jesus. These two parts are known as "testaments," as in the Old Testament (the Hebrew Bible) and the New Testament (works about Jesus and his impact). The word "testament" comes from the Latin *testamentum*, which derives from the Greek *diathekea*, which in turn constitutes a translation of the Hebrew word *berit*, "covenant"— echoing the term used by Jews in Exodus, such as in the "Book of the Covenant" (Exod 24:7). For Christians, the New Testament indicated a change in the significance of the Hebrew Bible and God's relationship with Jews. They based this change upon a new interpretation of Jeremiah 31:30-32: "The days are surely coming, says the LORD, when I will make a new covenant with the house of Israel and the house of Judah." Christians understood their new religion as Jeremiah's "new covenant."

Second, during the first century CE, the **codex** was invented, and the early Christians adopted it as their preferred form of presenting these two testaments. A codex is a set of rectangular sheets of papyrus or parchment that were fastened together on one side—much like a modern book. By the fourth century, the codex had largely replaced scrolls across the Mediterranean world. Christianity adopted it quite early and helped popularize it. Jews retained scrolls as the preferred liturgical form for their sacred books, although they adopted the codex for most other uses.

CONTENTS OF HEBREW BIBLE

The earliest term in Judaism for the Hebrew Bible as a fixed collection of writings is *Miqra*, which is used widely in the earliest Jewish law code, known as the Mishnah and compiled around 200 CE. While this term continues to be used today, it has been joined by a second term, *Tanakh*, which was coined in the medieval period. It is an acronym for the three sections of the Hebrew Bible: Torah, *Neviim*, and *Ketuvim*.

The Tanakh's first division is called the Torah. The word's meaning is complicated. The term "Torah" is based on the Hebrew root meaning "to point or direct" and so can be translated as "instruction," "law," or even "pathway." The Septuagint renders Torah into Greek as *nomos*, "law." The first five books of the Tanakh are termed "Torah" and are considered God's revelation to Moses. Its earliest use appears as "The Torah of Moses" found in Joshua 8:31-32: "just as Moses the servant of the LORD had commanded the Israelites, as it is written in the book of the law [*torah*] of Moses. . . ." Other names include "The Book of Moses" (Ezra 6:18), "The Book of the Torah" (Neh 8:3), and "The Book of the Torah of God" (Neh 8:8, 18).

Our English name for Torah is **Pentateuch**, which is derived from the Greek *pentateuchos*, "five scrolls"—that is, the first five books from the Greek translation called the Septuagint. The English titles for those books—Genesis, Exodus, Leviticus, Numbers, and Deuteronomy—derive from the Greek. The titles attempt to describe the contents of the respective books in the Hebrew Bible.

The second division of the Bible is known as *Neviim*, "prophets" in English. The section is subdivided into Former Prophets and Latter Prophets—terms that refer to their order in the Tanakh and *not* the chronological position of their contents. The Former Prophets—Joshua, Judges, Samuel, and Kings—comprise books that are considered historical works that aim to depict past experiences of the people Israel, from the emergence of the Israelites in Canaan, through the kings of Israel and Judah, to the end of the Judean monarchy in Babylon. The books of the Latter Prophets contain oracles and revelations given to the named prophets by God. These include the major literary works of Isaiah, Jeremiah, and Ezekiel, as well as "The Twelve"—also known as the twelve books of the "minor prophets": Hosea, Joel, Amos, Obadiah, Jonah, Micah, Nahum, Habakkuk, Zephaniah, Haggai, Zechariah, and Malachi. The term "minor prophets" reflects the works' brevity rather than their importance.

The Tanakh's third and last division is *Ketuvim* (writings). If we were naming this section today, we might call it "miscellaneous," for it contains books of different genres: poems, songs, prayers, and psalms as well as wisdom and **apocalyptic literature** and historical narratives. The books are Psalms, Proverbs, Job, Lamentations, Song of Songs, Ecclesiastes, Esther, Daniel, Ruth, Chronicles, Ezra, Nehemiah, and 1 and 2 Chronicles. In most cases the authors are unknown, and these books were most likely produced between the fifth century and the second century BCE.

The Books of the Tanakh

The word **canon** is from *kanōn*, a Greek word meaning "reed" used for measuring. From the fourth century onward, Christianity used the term "canon" to refer to a "norm" or "list" of sacred books; thus, canon is the closed list of inspired writings. This is a Christian-specific term. Nowhere in the Hebrew Scriptures or rabbinic literature is the term "canon" used; instead they refer to "sacred writings" (*kitve haqodesh*), whose holiness renders impure the hands of anyone who handles them (Flesher and Chilton 2011, 316–18). Scholars have adapted the word "canon" to describe those books that a religious community considers authoritative and binding, and applied the concept to all faiths.

The number of books differs in the Jewish, Protestant, Catholic, and Orthodox versions of the Hebrew Bible / Old Testament, usually because different works were included. However, even when the same books were included, they were counted differently. Although the Jews used the Hebrew Bible in its original language, the Christians knew it primarily in Greek. When they created the Old Testament in the fourth century CE, they included other Greek works that the Hebrew Bible did not contain. So, although the Hebrew Bible contains twenty-four books (counting the Minor Prophets as one book), Catholicism's Old Testament canon contains forty-six books, while that of the Greek Orthodox holds forty-nine. Later, in the early 1600s, nascent Protestantism eliminated the books outside the Hebrew Bible, making their Old Testament the same as the Hebrew Bible. But since the Protestants count

FIGURE 2-2. BOOKS OF THE TANAKH
(= HEBREW BIBLE / PROTESTANT OLD TESTAMENT)

Torah				
Genesis	Exodus	Leviticus	Numbers	Deuteronomy
Neviim/Prophets				
Former Prophets				
Joshua	Judges	1 & 2 Samuel	1 & 2 Kings	
Latter Prophets				
Isaiah	Jeremiah	Ezekiel	The Twelve	
The Twelve (Minor Prophets)				
Hosea	Joel	Amos	Obadiah	Jonah
Micah	Nahum	Habakkuk	Zephaniah	Haggai
Zechariah	Malachi			
Ketuvim/Writings				
Psalms	Proverbs	Job	Song of Songs	Ruth
Lamentations	Ecclesiastes	Esther	Daniel	Ezra
Nehemiah	1 & 2 Chronicles			

the books differently from the Jews, their Old Testament is said to contain thirty-nine books. (For instance, the Christians count the Minor Prophets as twelve books.)

The books of the **Apocrypha**, which the Protestants removed from the Old Testament, are those that appear in the early Greek translation known as the Septuagint (see below) but not in the Hebrew Bible. These are Tobit, Judith, Wisdom of Solomon, Ecclesiasticus (known also as Sirach and the Wisdom of Ben Sira), Baruch, 1 and 2 Maccabees, 1 and 2 Esdras, and additions in Greek to the books of Esther and Daniel. The standing of these works has been debated since Jerome based his fourth-century CE Latin translation on the Hebrew Bible rather than the Septuagint. In Catholicism and Orthodoxy, these writings have been called the **Deuterocanonical** Books (i.e., "second canon"). Protestantism labeled them the Apocrypha, and this is the term most used in academic circles. While early Protestants like Martin Luther did not consider the works divinely inspired, they thought the Apocrypha useful and deserving of study. Judaism has no position on this question since this is a debate within Christianity. Today, editions of the Bible for college study usually print the Old Testament as defined by Protestantism and include the Apocrypha as a separate section.

Scholars have no evidence of the process of canonization that chose the books of the canon of the Hebrew Bible. Instead, ancient writings reveal moments when different works had apparently achieved a canonical status. For instance, when the priest and scribe Ezra read the Torah to the assembled Jews who had returned from the **Babylonian Exile** (Neh 8; roughly 480 BCE), this probably referred to the acceptance of the five books of the Torah. When Jesus ben Sira's grandson translated his grandfather's book the Wisdom of Ben Sira (Ecclesiasticus) into Greek in 132 BCE, he referred in the prologue to "the Law and the prophets and the other books of our ancestors." This indicates that, at this point, there are collections of holy books known as the Torah and as the Prophets, probably containing the books listed above. Some "other books of our ancestors" have achieved that status as well, pointing to some but not all of the books that would become known as the Writings. In the first century BCE, 2 Maccabees 2:13 speaks of the importance of a variety of books that include "books about the kings and prophets, and the writings of David, and letters of kings about votive offerings."

At the end of the first century CE, the historian Josephus stated that the Jews had twenty-two books that were "believed to be divine" (*Against Apion* 1.8). These included the five books of Moses, thirteen prophetic books, and four that "contain hymns to God, and precepts for the conduct of human life." The missing two books may well be Esther and Ecclesiastes—the final Hebrew Bible canon contains twenty-four books—which the rabbis were still debating when the Mishnah was compiled a century later in 200 CE (see M. Yadayim 3:5). Shortly after this time, these last two books were included.

The achievement of a fixed canon for the Hebrew Bible should not be downplayed. Many religious works were composed during these centuries. In addition, there was a widespread phenomenon from the third century BCE onward in both Judaism and early Christianity that interfered with it. This was the composition of books later designated as **Pseudepigrapha**. These books were written by Jews and Christians and falsely ascribed ("pseud-") to biblical figures, including Enoch, Daniel, Abraham, Noah, Moses, Baruch, and Jeremiah (as well as Christian figures like Paul, Peter, James, Mary, and John). Although widely acknowledged and read, few pseudepigraphical books entered the biblical canon.

Where Did the Hebrew Bible Come From?

Once a book was written in antiquity, it needed to be distributed. And once it achieved a holy status, that need increased. The only way to meet that need was to copy each book or collection of books by hand—a process that took weeks or even months to produce a single copy of a single book. And this time-consuming and expensive activity was not error-free. Copyists often made mistakes, and then when a later scribe copied an earlier manuscript, those mistakes would be faithfully included in the new manuscript, along with the later scribe's mistakes.

Since the advent of printing, scholars have developed a process for ascertaining the most accurate biblical text possible. This process is called **text criticism**, and generally speaking it takes all known manuscripts of the Old Testament and compares them, evaluating alternate readings in an effort to achieve the most ancient and accurate text of the Old Testament possible. In general, the older a manuscript, the more reliable it is assumed to be. However, even ancient manuscripts can contain mistakes, so their evidence must always be evaluated carefully. Manuscripts come from several key sources and languages. Let us discuss the most important.

THE MASORETIC TEXT

For more than a millennium, Jewish religious figures have recognized a single Hebrew text as the one authoritative text. This is the tenth-century CE **Masoretic Text** known as the Ben Asher text. Our oldest and most complete version is *Codex Leningradensis*, dated to 1008 CE. Another important witness is the *Aleppo Codex* from 930 CE. Unfortunately, it was damaged during riots in Aleppo, Syria, over the 1947 United Nations Resolution establishing the State of Israel. It is now incomplete.

The Masoretic Text is the result of a process of settling the reading of the Hebrew text and stabilizing that reading. This was done by Jewish scholars called **Masoretes**, who perhaps as early as the sixth century began working to standardize the **orthography** (i.e., spelling), sentence structure, and vocalization of the

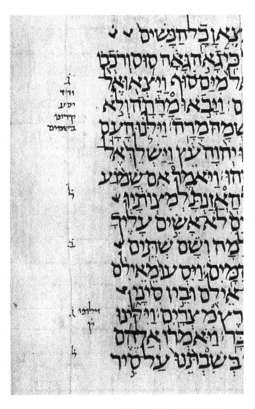

FIGURE 2-3. *Partial page from the* Codex Leningradensis, *the oldest complete manuscript of the Hebrew Bible.*

text of the Tanakh. There were schools of Masoretes in **Palestine** and Babylonia, but the most famous is the school located in the Galilean city of Tiberias between 780 and 930 CE.

To tackle the problem of orthography and sentence structure, the Masoretes developed a system that counted all verses, words, and letters in the text and noted the location of the verse, the word, and the letter in the center of the manuscript for the benefit of future copyists. This they recorded in marginal notes along with other information. When copyists followed this key, they were able to produce nearly error-free reproductions of the Tanakh.

Addressing the problem of vocalization was more involved. In antiquity, the Hebrew language was written without vowels. Readers had to memorize the different ways of adding vowels to a single set of consonants, a process called vocalization. There could be up to a dozen ways of vocalizing (i.e., pronouncing) a word of two or three letters. Readers had to make the right choice, based on the context of the word and their own knowledge. A wrong choice would alter a sentence's meaning or even render it incomprehensible.

The books of the Hebrew Bible were composed and transmitted in a consonantal text that contained no vowels or accents. The Masoretes developed a system of dots and other small signs that could be added under, over, and to the side of each consonant without altering its position. In that way, they could reproduce the consonantal text exactly while adding in the vocalization information to ensure the proper reading and understanding.

Despite the antiquity of our present Masoretic texts, they are over a thousand years removed from the earliest Hebrew texts discovered at **Qumran** near the Dead Sea and dating from the second or first centuries BCE (see more below). The Masoretic Text enabled the scribes that followed to preserve an accurate version of the Tanakh's text; it was only as accurate as the text they had. In the previous millennium, changes and errors had crept in, as in any other ancient text. Scribes' careful transmission of the Masoretic Text also preserved the errors it contained. Before discussing the Qumran materials, let us look at a possibly even older version of the biblical text, the translation known as the Septuagint.

Septuagint

The earliest translation of the Hebrew Bible, the Septuagint, was into Greek. The name Septuagint derives from the Greek word for "seventy"—**LXX** in Roman numerals, a designation that has become its official abbreviation. The number seventy comes from the Letter of Aristeas, which tells an idealized story of the translation process in which seventy-two [sic] Jewish experts traveled to Egypt to translate the Hebrew Torah into Greek.

Aristeas' tale goes like this. The king of Egypt, Ptolemy II (285–246 BCE), on the advice of the director of the great library of Alexandria, decided to add a Greek translation of the Jewish Law for that library. He requested the high priest Eliezer in Jerusalem to send scholars to undertake the translation. Eliezer sent six scribes from each of the twelve tribes, seventy-two in total. The distinguished translators were welcomed to Alexandria and entertained at a seven-day feast where they displayed their wisdom to the pharaoh. The translators were led to the island of Pharos, where they did their work. The completed translation was read to the Jewish population of Alexandria for their approval. They acknowledged it as sacred writ, and the priests and elders pronounced "a curse in accordance with their custom upon anyone who should make any alteration either by adding anything or changing in any way whatever any of the words which had been written or making any omission" (Letter of Aristeas 311).

Aristeas' account of a royal initiative for a Greek translation of the Hebrew Bible is mostly legendary. But it establishes the third century BCE as the time when the Torah was translated into Greek, possibly during the reign of Ptolemy II. It is more likely, however, that the translation was intended to meet the needs of the Greek-speaking communities of Jews living in Egypt. A Greek translation would give these Jews, who possessed little or no understanding of Hebrew, access to the biblical text.

The Septuagint faced the criticism of any translation: it does not accurately convey all the meaning of the original. Indeed it could not, because no two languages have a one-to-one correspondence of either words or meaning. This is particularly a problem for a sacred text such as the Torah, for those who consider it sacred believe it preserves the very words of God, and so the words, their order, and their meaning should all be preserved. Since the Greek rendering frequently could not achieve this, it received significant criticism.

The Letter of Aristeas, probably written by an Alexandrian Jew during the second century BCE, aimed to defend the Septuagint as authoritative. By having Ptolemy instigate the Torah's translation for the Alexandrian library, Aristeas gives it the highest Greek authority possible. That the translation's wording was agreed upon by seventy-two Jewish experts who were selected by the Jerusalem high priest—the highest Jewish authority at the time— makes it the product of great knowledge and wisdom from within Judaism. According to Aristeas, the translators "set to work comparing their several results and making them agree, and whatever they agreed upon was suitably copied out" (Letter of Aristeas 302). Aristeas uses his description of this process—remarkably similar to the way modern scholars of Bible translations work—to make clear that this large group of experts in language and Scripture agreed upon the accuracy of the Septuagint translation. Aristeas' message is clear—the translation was under the highest human authorities in both the Greek and the Jewish worlds and produced by a cadre of the best experts available. Before such an array, individual critiques could not stand.

The Letter of Aristeas did not persuade everyone, and criticism of the differences continued. The first-century Alexandrian Jew Philo Judeas wrote a second defense of the translation (*Vita Mosis* 2.25–55). In his version, the translators worked separately, isolated from each other. When they compared the translations, they found that miraculously all their versions were identical. Philo even termed them "prophets" to indicate that the Septuagint came not from human knowledge but from divine direction.

Some of the Septuagint's critics took a different approach; rather than defending the translation, they worked to "correct" it—changing or retranslating it to bring it more in line with the Hebrew text. The three most important of these were done by Aquila (a convert to Judaism), Theodotian, and Symmachus. Today, we have only a few fragments of their work, often as quotations in other authors' writings.

The designation Septuagint first referred to the translation of the Torah into Greek. Over the next two centuries, the remainder of the Hebrew Bible was translated into Greek. These were joined by other works in Greek that later became the Apocrypha. Although the Septuagint was produced by and for

FIGURE 2-4. *St. Catherine's Monastery. During the nineteenth century,
the* Codex Sinaiticus, *a Greek manuscript dating to the fourth century CE,
was discovered there. It contains approximately half the Old Testament
and the entire New Testament.*

Jews in Egypt, it spread to Greek-speaking Jews throughout the eastern Mediterranean. Jewish followers of Jesus outside Israel read it, and, by the second century CE, Christians were using the Septuagint as their Scriptures. Indeed, our most complete manuscripts of the Septuagint come from Christian communities. There are three main codices ("books," plural form of "codex")—*Codex Vaticanus, Codex Alexandrinus,* and *Codex Sinaiticus*—which date from the fourth century CE. A few Septuagint fragments appear among the Dead Sea Scrolls, dating to the second and first centuries BCE.

The Septuagint's importance lies in helping to establish an early text of the Hebrew Bible because it was translated as much as 1,200 years before the Masoretic Text. While we do not have manuscripts from its early period, those we possess are at least 500 years older than the Masoretic Text, and a few fragments bring our knowledge back more than 1,000 years earlier. To be sure, there is still the problem of translation, but it is a translation of a work 500–1,000 years older than the Masoretic Text.

THE SAMARITAN TORAH

The **Samaritans** are a Jewish sect that separated from Judaism sometime between the fifth and second centuries BCE. Samaritans claim they are the direct ancestors of Judaism and have preserved authentic Jewish traditions. Judaism regards them as descendants of the foreigners who were brought to Samaria by the Assyrians after the fall of the Northern Kingdom in 721 BCE, where they intermarried with the few remaining Jews. The Samaritans produced a version of the Torah in Hebrew no later than the second century BCE. The oldest extant copies of the Samaritan Torah date from the eleventh or twelfth century CE. The Samaritans regard the Abisha Scroll as their most revered copy of the Torah.

With the exception of a few key passages—the Samaritan Torah exalts the importance of Shechem and Mount Gerizim, their holy place, over Jerusalem—the Samaritan Torah constitutes a third reliable witness to the early text of the Torah. Its Hebrew text was once regarded as aligned with the Septuagint rather than the Masoretic Text, but now scholars recognize that the Samaritan Torah includes components of both versions.

THE DEAD SEA SCROLLS

In 1946 a few scrolls were discovered in a cave in the cliffs near Khirbet Qumran at the northwest side of the Dead Sea. In the ensuing years, more manuscripts and fragments were found, and these have come to be known collectively as the Dead Sea Scrolls. Most were written in Hebrew, with a few in Greek or Aramaic. These scrolls apparently belonged to the community of Essenes—described by Pliny and Josephus—who lived at Qumran in the first

FIGURE 2-5. *The Qumran settlement. The Dead Sea Scrolls were discovered in the caves near this site, and some were probably copied or composed here.*

centuries BCE and CE. The site was destroyed by the Romans during the Jewish Revolt of 66–70 CE.

The fragments and the few whole works of the Dead Sea Scrolls come from roughly 930 manuscripts. Nearly a quarter are biblical texts and constitute the earliest biblical texts in existence. Their dates range from the mid-third century BCE to early first century CE. Fragments of every book of the Hebrew Scriptures have been unearthed at Qumran except for Esther. The most common biblical texts are Psalms, Deuteronomy, and Isaiah—including one complete scroll. All books of the Torah are well represented with more than fifteen manuscripts each. The manuscripts at Qumran contain the oldest complete scroll of a book of the Hebrew Bible—namely, Isaiah. But the rest of the manuscripts are fragmentary—indeed, there are thousands of (mostly small) fragments—although most predate our earliest biblical texts by a thousand years. Unfortunately, in no sense has a complete Hebrew Bible been uncovered at Qumran.

Equally important as the biblical texts are the nonbiblical texts. Some of these manuscripts are specific to the Qumran community and describe its doctrines, community rules, theological views, and messianic beliefs. They include commentaries, theological treatises, monastic rules, and apocalyptic works predicating a cosmic war and the establishment of God's kingdom. There are also a number of apocryphal and pseudepigraphical writings previously known, but only in Greek and Latin translations. These texts are important because they provide scholars with information about Judaism prior to the fall of the Jewish state in 70 CE.

Until the discovery of the Dead Sea Scrolls, scholars relied on the Masoretic Text, the Septuagint, and the Samaritan Torah as authoritative sources for the Hebrew Bible's text. Since 1946, however, our understanding of the Hebrew text has been radically transformed by the biblical Dead Sea Scrolls.

By comparing existing Hebrew and Greek manuscripts with the scrolls and fragments at Qumran, scholars are able to understand in greater depth how biblical texts developed. Most of the biblical scrolls are written in the Aramaic script (which today we call Hebrew script), but some works continued to be written in the old Paleo-Hebrew script. Furthermore, some of the biblical scrolls and fragments at Qumran demonstrate extensive discrepancies and textual diversity with our latest Hebrew manuscripts. Paragraphs and sentences in scrolls identified as 1 Samuel are missing in the Masoretic Text. There were six Jeremiah scrolls discovered at Qumran, and two versions differ considerably from the Masoretic version. And there were many, many differences in wording and spelling in all biblical books.

After half a century of analysis, the conclusion is that the biblical works at Qumran do not bring us closer to a single, original text but bring us closer to three texts, at least for the Torah. To oversimplify, one set of fragments shares key similarities with the Masoretic Text, while another is closer to the Septuagint, and a third set parallels the Samaritan Torah. All three strands were already in play for centuries by the first century BCE, if not earlier. And finally, a few of these fragments reveal material not attested in any previously known biblical text. The text of the Hebrew Bible was thus already in flux in the first century BCE.

Targums

Although Qumran shows three text types in use among Jews during the first century BCE, Judaism in the next few centuries centralized on the text type that became the basis for the Masoretic Text. This became clear even as Hebrew gradually ceased to be the spoken language of the Jews of Judea and Galilee and their everyday language became Aramaic. They drew upon this "proto-Masoretic" text and translated it into Aramaic to use in worship and study. The term for these translations was **Targum**, a word that means "translation." Targum translations exist for every book of the Hebrew Bible except Ezra-Nehemiah and Daniel, both of which contain extensive Aramaic passages already.

A much-debated question is when these Targums began. Aramaic translations of Job and Leviticus appear at Qumran dated to the second century BCE. But the Targums proper date to the first century CE at the earliest. Targum Onqelos to the Pentateuch (Torah) and Targum Jonathan to the Prophets were first translated during the first or early second century CE, while the Palestinian Targums to the Pentateuch—for which we have the remains of more than forty versions, including the complete manuscript of Targum Neofiti—were first composed in Galilee in the late second century or early third century. The Writings Targums were probably composed some centuries later (Flesher and

Chilton 2011). Targums were widely used among Jews in the land of Israel, Syria, and Babylonia until the Middle Ages. For centuries, they were recited alongside the Hebrew Torah in synagogue services to ensure its understanding. Targums Onqelos and Jonathan continue to be published in Orthodox Jewish circles for study purposes even today.

VULGATE

The **Vulgate** ("common" in Latin) is the Latin translation of the Bible. The church in the western Mediterranean needed an accurate, definitive Latin translation of the Bible. Previous Latin translations had been poorly done. The Old Latin Bible manuscripts developed in the latter half of the second century were inconsistent and contained many variations. Pope Damasus I commissioned Jerome in 382 CE to make a revision of the Old Latin translations. At this time, Jerome was already a noted biblical scholar who also happened to be the pope's private secretary. He began his work in Rome and shortly thereafter went to Bethlehem, where he worked on this project for twenty-two years, from 383 to 405 CE. For a time Jerome worked from the Septuagint, but over time he realized the deficiencies of the Greek texts and decided that an accurate Latin translation of the Hebrew Bible must come from a Hebrew text. After abandoning the Septuagint, he turned to proto-Masoretic Hebrew texts to use as the basis for his Latin translation. Although he was criticized for producing a translation "tainted with Judaism," he defended his work, and it eventually was accepted by the Church and became the Latin Bible. His translation, known as the Vulgate, was finally accepted by Latin-speaking Christians in the eighth century. For text-critical study, the Vulgate's importance lies in its foundation upon the (proto-Masoretic) Hebrew and Aramaic texts instead of the Greek Septuagint.

THE IMPORTANCE OF PRINTING TO THE BIBLICAL TEXT

Before the rise of printing, the Bible in Christianity was the sole property of religious authorities; few outside the Church had access to it. With the publication of the Latin Bible in 1452–1455 by Johann Gutenberg (the first book to be printed), that privilege changed. Furthermore, at this time, the Renaissance—a rebirth of arts and letters—was in full bloom. Renaissance scholars, especially in Italy, argued there could be no understanding of ancient classic works without returning to the original texts in Hebrew, Greek, and Latin. The printing press answered the demand for widespread distribution of works from the ancient world. These documents moved from dusty monasteries, wealthy private collectors, and university libraries to a printed format that became available to a broad audience.

The printing of the Hebrew Bible was a major revolution in biblical scholarship. The text was now largely fixed and not dependent upon scribes laboriously copying manuscripts in order to study the biblical text or to serve the needs of the local churches. Furthermore, these ancient texts, especially the Bible, could be translated into current, local languages. This was a revolutionary act of another kind. Throughout sixteenth-century Europe, ordinary people could now read the Bible or listen to it read in their native languages. This inaugurated a new era of biblical literacy.

The first attempt to publish a portion of the Hebrew Bible took place in 1477 in Bologna, Italy. It was a commentary on the book of Psalms printed in three hundred copies. In 1482, Abraham b. Ḥayyim dei Tintori printed the first edition of the Torah. The edition contained vowel and accent signs and was accompanied by Targum Onqelos and the commentary composed by the famous rabbi known as Rashi.

In Soncino, a small town near Milan in Italy, Israel Nathan b. Samuel and his family established a printing house. Here, the first complete Bible was published in 1488. This Masoretic Hebrew Bible contained accents and vowels but no commentary. The firm published another edition from Brescia, Italy, in 1492–1494. This Bible was used by Martin Luther in his translation of the Old Testament into German. Early printed Hebrew Bibles reflected the available manuscripts, which varied in quality; there were limited opportunities for publishers to assemble and collate a large number of manuscripts for their printed editions. Errors in early Bibles arising from manuscripts or during the printing process were often reproduced in later editions. As many as twenty-four editions or parts of the Hebrew Bible were printed between 1477 and 1530.

Another important development was the assembling of polyglot editions that printed the biblical text in several different languages alongside the Masoretic Hebrew text. The most famous is the Complutensian Polyglot Bible. Cardinal Francisco Jiménes de Cisneros, an enthusiastic crusading Inquisitor General, began editing this massive project in 1502. Each page of Cisneros' Old Testament displayed the text in Latin, Greek, and Hebrew as well as the Aramaic Targum of Onqelos accompanied by its own Latin translation. The Complutensian Bible comprised six volumes and appeared in 1520. Although the Masoretic accents were missing and vowel markings were inconsistent, the Complutensian Bible was a major accomplishment of publishing.

In 1516, a Christian named Daniel Bomberg founded a printing house in Venice and produced a number of Hebrew works, including the all-important first and second Rabbinic Bibles. Over the decades, Bomberg published nearly two hundred Hebrew books, and, through him, Venice became known as the capital of Hebrew printing—a reputation that lasted well into the eighteenth century. It did not hurt Bomberg's reputation that he was wealthy and that his family was connected to the royal courts in Europe.

In 1517, Bomberg and an editor named Felix Pratensis published the first Rabbinic Bible (known in Hebrew as *Miqra'ot Gedalot*) in Venice. He published two editions of the Hebrew text: one for Jews, the other for Christians. Like the polyglot Bibles, the Rabbinic Bible contained Greek, Hebrew, and Latin versions of the Bible as well as Targums and rabbinic commentaries. Bomberg received Pope Leo X's blessing and a license prohibiting any other publisher from producing a similar Bible. The Rabbinic Bible's preface contained the following claim: "on this book the entire superstructure of Christianity rests." Obviously, a Hebrew-printed Bible blessed by the pope and edited by a converted Jew was not supported by potential Jewish buyers.

Eight years later, in 1525, the second edition of the Rabbinic Bible was published. The editor, Jacob ben Hayyim (a Jew at the time but who later converted to Christianity), wanted to correct the many inaccuracies concerning Masoretic notes contained in the first edition and appeal to a Jewish audience. With the printing of this edition, Bomberg highlighted that his printers and editors were devout Jews. This edition contained at least two biblical commentaries on every book and a more complete Masoretic Text. The 1525 edition of the Rabbinic Bible, known as the second Rabbinic Bible, became the standard work for the study of the Bible by Jewish and Christian scholars as well as the standard for all subsequent editions of the Hebrew Bible into the twentieth century.

Critical Study of the Torah

The traditional view of Christianity and Judaism is that Moses authored the Torah. Historically, Jews were taught that the Torah was revealed by God to Moses. Deuteronomy (31:9, 24-26) states that Moses writes "this *torah*" on a scroll, and this was taken to mean that "the Torah" had been recorded by Moses. Exodus 24:4 affirms that "Moses wrote down all the words of the LORD." Likewise, Deuteronomy 31:24 states, "When Moses had finished writing down in a book the words of this law to the very end . . ." Few contemporary scholars are persuaded that the Torah could have been written by Moses. For them, evidence in the text itself shows that the Torah is not a creation of one writer but a work of multiple authors and editors written over a period of centuries.

By the third century CE, anti-Christian philosophers such as Celsus and Porphyry noted problems in the Hebrew Bible and raised questions about Mosaic authorship. Rabbis also acknowledged peculiarities within the Torah, but, through their creative reinterpretations, they successfully reconciled these inconsistencies for centuries. In the eleventh century, Isaac

Ibn Yashush wrote that the Edomite kings' list in Genesis 36 must have been written long after Moses since those kings lived centuries after Moses' death. In the twelfth century, Ibn Ezra noted different sources in the Torah and problems in the book of Isaiah. He identified Torah passages that appeared to include later additions and could not have been written by Moses. Ibn Ezra identified Genesis 12:6 ("The Canaanites were then in the land") as troubling. Since Moses never entered the Holy Land and never knew a time when the Canaanites were not in the land, he instructed his readers by saying, "And he who understands will keep silent" (Friedman 1987, 19). In his fourteenth-century commentary on Ibn Ezra's work, Joseph Bonfils understood that Moses could not have written that verse and thought Joshua or another prophet wrote it. Other rabbis were aware of the discrepancies in the biblical text and sought to ameliorate them.

During the Renaissance and the Reformation, Christian scholars regarded the biblical text as inspired by God. They held to a dictation theory of inspiration where God used human authors as mere writing instruments to whom he dictated the text. The Torah was recognized as the work of Moses. So even as they pioneered early critical methods in their research—the study of grammar and the vocabularies of the original languages to understand the theological content—they had little difficulty in accepting the notion that Moses authored the entire Torah.

Isaac La Peyrère (1596–1676) insisted that there were men before Adam and that the Old Testament was focused on Jewish history rather than world history. He argued that neither Moses nor any other single individual wrote the Torah. He eventually was tried for heresy and spent time in prison. His work was read by Richard Simon (1638–1712), a priest who wrote what many regard as the first major critical approach to the Bible, *Historical Criticism of the Old Testament*. Here he stated, "Moses cannot be the author of all that exists in the books attributed to him." He noted that Moses died on the east side of the Jordan River and so never crossed into the land of Canaan. Yet the book of Deuteronomy begins, "These are the words that Moses spoke to all Israel beyond the Jordan—in the wilderness." The author of these verses wrote from the perspective of the west side of the Jordan, in the land of Canaan, a land Moses never in fact entered. Simon believed Moses may have written a few verses, but later writers created most of the text. Simon's works were censored and burned, and he was expelled from his order. In the seventeenth century, Thomas Hobbes (1588–1679) denied Moses wrote the majority of the Pentateuch. He focused on Deuteronomy 34:6, which indicated the tomb of Moses was unknown "to that day." Certainly, Moses could not have written such a passage. That verse and others convinced Hobbes to view the Bible as document produced by human hands like any other literary work.

Baruch Spinoza (1632–1677) played an invaluable role in the intellectual development of the European Enlightenment and the critical investigation of the Bible. Spinoza acknowledged Ibn Ezra's observations and suggested the possibility that the Torah was not produced in its entirety by Moses. Appropriate study of the Bible involved reading it like any other historical document. This approach must ask questions concerning authorship, the book's literary and linguistic attributes, how the book was preserved and transmitted, and the historical setting in which the text was composed. Spinoza pointed to the author of the Torah as speaking in the third person. Abraham is said to have visited the city of Dan (Gen 14:14), but the city of Dan received its name only later in Judges 18:29. Spinoza recognized that some of the Torah may have originated with Moses, but it was only many centuries after Moses' death that the Torah appeared as a completed work. Spinoza asserted that much of the Bible was created by the priest and scribe Ezra hundreds of years after Moses. Due to his insightful observations, Bible scholars regard Spinoza as the founder of modern biblical criticism.

Charles Houbigant (1686–1783) noted in the eighteenth century that the Hebrew text had been hopelessly corrupted. After studying a number of Hebrew manuscripts, he recommended over five thousand corrections, thus demonstrating Houbigant's understanding of the fragility of the sacred text. Another major leap in the critical investigation of the Hebrew Bible was the work of Jean Astruc (1684–1766), counselor and physician to Louis XV. His book *Conjectures sur la Genèse* (1753) was published anonymously. Astruc insisted that there were two documents in Genesis and that each author used different names for God: **Elohim** or **Yahweh**. The two sources were combined by Moses to create the book of Genesis. Furthermore, Astruc identified other additions and repetitions based on ten other fragments used by later copyists. Astruc's research laid the foundation for the modern investigation of the composition of the Torah and other biblical texts. Independent of Astruc, Henry Bernard Witter (1683–1715) noted that the parallel accounts of the creation story in Genesis 1:1–2:4 and 2:4–3:24 used different names for the deity: Elohim or Yahweh. These names could be used for analyzing the sources used by Moses.

Relying on Astruc and others, Johann Gottfried Eichhorn (1753–1827) expanded the study of the two sources, which we now term the Elohist and Yahwist. He employed a more rigorous analysis of these sources by focusing on the striking differences in the sources of Genesis regarding character, language, and content. His investigations led him to the conclusion that "most of the writings of the Hebrews have passed through several hands." He was a proponent of **higher criticism** that sought to apply to the Bible the same methods of study used in science and other historical inquiries of other ancient texts. Moreover, his publications on the Old Testament and New Testament exposed the study of biblical literature to a wider audience.

W. M. L. De Wette (1780–1849) "inaugurated a new era in critical Old Testament Scholarship" (Rogerson 1985, 28), and among his groundbreaking works he convincingly demonstrated that Deuteronomy was composed during the religious reform of King Josiah (640–609 BCE) hundreds of years after Moses. He maintained that the story about the finding of the "book of the Law" in the temple at the time of the reform of Josiah (2 Kgs 22:3-20) was a fiction and that this "book of the Law" was likely the book of Deuteronomy, composed during Josiah's reign. De Wette also seriously doubted the historicity of the books of Genesis through Numbers, concluding that these books, also, had been written in a later period. He argued against the dependability of Chronicles and questioned the depiction of Israelite religion in the early books of the Bible. His insights became the foundation of critical biblical scholarship in the nineteenth century.

John William Colenso (1814–1883), Anglican archbishop of Natal, was an advocate for social justice and political reform for the Zulu people. Colenso's book *The Pentateuch and Book of Joshua Critically Examined* (1862–1879) was over 3,500 pages long. Although some of Colenso's views now appear naive and in many cases were not original, he had a major impact on English critical scholarship. He denied the Mosaic authorship of the Pentateuch, disputed the accuracy of the exodus (especially the figure of six hundred thousand males wandering about in the Sinai), and claimed that the book of Deuteronomy was authored by Jeremiah. These views caused a firestorm among Anglicans, and he was repudiated by his church. John Rogerson states that Colenso's *The Pentateuch* was "the most remarkable achievement by a British scholar in the field of Old Testament criticism in the nineteenth century" (1985, 232). Other far-reaching theories developed by Heinrich Ewald (1803–1873), Abraham Kuenen (1828–1891), and Karl Graf (1815–1869) all contributed to the critical study of the biblical text. These scholars arranged the chronology of the sources of the Torah and identified a "Priestly source," thus demonstrating that there were three major sources from Genesis to Numbers. Deuteronomy was regarded as a separate source written hundreds of years after Moses. Critics continued to question the historical authenticity of the Torah. The Yahwist source was now envisioned as the earliest source in the biblical text. The religion of the early Hebrews was analyzed according to new scientific models, and this indicated that there was a slow evolutionary growth from a religion of primitive nature to prophetic monotheism, culminating in a form of priestly legalism. This scheme results from the view that the priestly laws were composed in the exile (586–538 BCE) or later.

The results of these centuries of research liberated European biblical scholars from traditional, orthodox claims about the formation of the law of Moses and encouraged later scholars to propose new theories about the composition of the Torah as well as the work of the authors and groups responsible for its creation. Modern biblical scholars cannot begin their work without mastering the critical analyses developed by their predecessors. Once biblical scholarship had been reinvented and reinvigorated in the nineteenth century, it became clear that there could be no turning back to the pious theories of biblical revelation, infallibility, authority, and inspiration at the expense of a critical examination of the biblical text.

JULIUS WELLHAUSEN AND THE DOCUMENTARY HYPOTHESIS

The classic synthesis of the major trends in nineteenth-century European study of the biblical text was created by Julius Wellhausen (1844–1918). Building on the work of previous scholars, Wellhausen developed the **Documentary Hypothesis**, which became the foundation for nearly all critical research on the Torah and the Bible in the twentieth century. Wellhausen's 1883 German work *Prolegomena zur Geschichte Israels*—translated into English as *Prolegomena to the History of Ancient Israel*—demonstrated the case that the Torah was composed of a number of primary literary sources that were woven together in the final version. He identified four main sources, or documents, that contained distinct points of view concerning religion, **cult** practices, politics, and the history of Israel's relationship with God as a covenant people. Using linguistic and literary criteria, Wellhausen identified differences in the geographical origins of the documents and chronology. He labeled the sources J, E, P, and D. Once they were identified, he worked to provide an absolute date for each one and saw that sources were not created by eyewitnesses but instead written centuries later than the events they purported to describe.

FIGURE 2-6. *Julius Wellhausen, the author of the Documentary Hypothesis.*

The oldest source in the Torah is the J source. According to the J source, the deity's name is Yahweh, which Wellhausen's native German spelled as Jahweh. English renders the same name as Yahweh. The J source's author is termed the Yahwist, and he probably did his work in ninth-century BCE Jerusalem. J is a collection of stories reflecting the early origins of humanity, the Israelite patriarchs, and events surrounding the exodus.

The tribe of Judah is featured prominently in the patriarchal stories, a feature that stems from its origins in Judah and Jerusalem. The author of J is focused on locating events and people in the southern part of the land of Israel. The J source is a largely continuous story that incorporates a number of ancient poems, stories, and songs into its narrative.

The second major source in Wellhausen's thesis is the E, or Elohist, source. It regularly calls God Elohim. The Elohist focused on the religious sites in the Northern Kingdom of the land of Israel and probably did his work in Samaria, the capital of Israel, in the eighth century BCE. Wellhausen believed E was a complete and continuous story running parallel with J. Yet E offers no primordial history, instead displaying an interest in prophetic activity. When the Northern Kingdom of Israel was destroyed by the Assyrians in 722 BCE, many refugees from the north fled to the south, bringing E and perhaps other written traditions with them. Over time, J and E were supplemented with other materials, edited together into a work now called JE.

P stands for the Priestly source, which originated with the Jerusalem temple priesthood. These priests reedited and supplemented other narratives. The writers of P use Elohim throughout Genesis, later changing to Yahweh in Exodus 6:2-3. This source emphasizes the cult and religious law, rules of sacrifice, keeping the Sabbath, the importance of circumcision, and dietary requirements. Like J and E, P contains traditions of the early history in Genesis, genealogies, stories about the patriarchs, and narratives from Exodus. Wellhausen argued that this P source was the last chapter of Israelite history. Much of P is located in the second half of Exodus, Leviticus, and Numbers.

The fourth source of the Torah is called the D, or Deuteronomistic, source, and its ideals are enshrined in the book of Deuteronomy. Wellhausen embraced De Wette's claims that Deuteronomy was composed as part of the religious reform program during the reign of Josiah (640–609 BCE) and had nothing to do with Mosaic authorship. Moreover, Deuteronomy was most likely the book "found" by Hilkiah the high priest (2 Kgs 22) in the temple in Jerusalem in 622 BCE. The cultic practices described in Deuteronomy reflect the features of the reforms enacted by King Josiah of Judah in the seventh century BCE. The work was composed by royal scribes and priests, but it was attributed to Moses in order to justify the work as an authoritative text to support Josiah's reforms of Israelite religion. Deuteronomy focused on the worship at "the place which Yahweh your god shall choose." This could mean only Jerusalem, the capital of Judah. Just like King Josiah, Deuteronomy demanded strict monotheism and the elimination of the "popular heathenish elements" that competed with Yahweh. Josiah and Deuteronomy opposed all forms of idolatry and demanded the destruction of the high places and other forms of non-Yahwistic worship throughout the land.

Wellhausen concluded that the Torah was not completed before the fifth century BCE and considered Moses uninvolved in any part of this multisource process. The priest Ezra, not Moses, instituted Judaism around the year 444 BCE through the public presentation of the Torah to the returned Jewish exiles (Neh 8). Furthermore, Wellhausen did not regard the patriarchal era as historical. The late date of Genesis precluded the possibility that the book contained any historical information related to the beginnings of ancient Israel.

Revisions to the Documentary Hypothesis

Wellhausen's scheme incurred many attacks in subsequent years. Numerous aspects of the Documentary Hypothesis have been disputed, but the broad outline of the theory still provides the foundation for most pentateuchal research. Even Wellhausen's severest critics recognized that the Torah was composed by different authors and that other books of the Bible have been rewritten and reedited several times. Scholars still debate a number of issues regarding the creation of the Torah and the rest of the biblical text: the number of authors, dates of composition, the relation of the biblical books to one another, why they were written, and what they actually impart to readers. However, no other detailed theory concerning the origins and composition of the Torah has found such a large consensus among modern biblical scholars. Nearly all scholars rule out the possibility of a single author.

The critical study of the biblical text in the nineteenth and early twentieth century was a European Protestant enterprise, and often Jewish scholars regarded this scholarship as anti-Judaic and even anti-Semitic. Following a tradition began by Wellhausen, many Christian scholars often portrayed rabbinic Judaism, as practiced from the first century CE to the twentieth century, as a dead, narrow, legalistic, degenerate, and a fossilized religion, preoccupied with the letter of the law, instead of its spirit. Wellhausen was hypercritical of rabbinic Judaism and openly formulated his opposition to Jewish law. He asserted that Judaism was but a ghost of ancient Israel and its prophets (Levenson 1993, 10–15). In 1903, Solomon Schechter, the president of the Jewish Theological Seminary, referred to higher criticism, the form of study championed by critical Protestant scholars, as "Higher Anti-Semitism." Wellhausen's negative critiques of Judaism corresponded with the rise of racism and anti-Semitism that was prevalent in Europe and especially in Germany in the late nineteenth century. An unfortunate consequence of critical scholarship in some circles was that a number of Christian scholars engaged in anti-Judaism, challenging Judaism's legitimacy and authenticity. Their scholarship often inferred that Christianity was superior to Judaism, a dead form of religion. For them Israelite religion's evolutionary apogee was to be found in the religion of Jesus.

Throughout the twentieth century, scholars raised serious reservations about many aspects of Wellhausen's theory. The dating of the sources was one of the most contentious issues, as biblical scholars presented a plethora of arguments regarding early or late dates for the various sources of the Torah. To bolster Wellhausen, some biblical scholars looked for illustrations in ancient literature of a document created by a school of scribes who pasted contrasting written sources together in one written record. However, they found few parallel examples of ancient religious documents created in the manner represented in Wellhausen's hypothesis.

Critics of the Documentary Hypothesis insisted that Wellhausen failed to recognize the ancient oral traditions that lie behind some of the Torah narratives. Hermann Gunkel developed a new method for studying the biblical text called **form criticism**, which examined the genres used in the biblical narratives, such as sagas, legends, and traditions. He maintained that the *Sitz im Leben* (situation in life) of oral traditions was the key to understanding the biblical narratives. Other academics, especially in the latter half of the twentieth century, claiming early origins for the elements of the Torah, pointed to a number of poetic forms identified as archaic Hebrew. Such poems appear in the Song of the Sea (Exod 15:1-18), the Song of Miriam (Exod 15:21), the Song of Moses (Deut 32), the Song of Deborah (Judg 5), and the Song of Hannah (1 Sam 2:1-10). Furthermore, ancient sources listed in the Bible, such as the Book of Jashar (Josh 10:12-14) and the Book of the Wars of Yahweh (Num 21:14), have not been preserved, but the citation of these sources indicates that the biblical authors and editors may have drawn on such written sources. Though the importance of oral traditions was acknowledged, modern scholars cannot verify their historical reliability, and they note the deleterious effects of the numerous generational revisions of these memories. Clearly, older oral traditions do not necessarily preserve historically accurate descriptions of Israel's past traditions.

Other opponents to Wellhausen detected that the Covenant Code (Exod 21–23), suzerain treaties (binding agreements between a king and his vassals, or a lesser king), and the oldest body of laws in the Pentateuch have analogues in ancient legal forms and treaty traditions found throughout the Near East. The **cuneiform** texts from ancient **Ugarit** (1300–1150 BCE) provide a wealth of information on Levantine culture, religion, and trade in the Late Bronze Age. These works were discovered only in 1928 and so were not available to Wellhausen. These texts provide insight into the "language, poetry, social structure, religious terminology and religious practice . . . and conceptualizations of the deity" (M. Smith 2001, 17). The **Ugaritic literature** provides a unique background for understanding the ancient Israelite religion. They "constitute the single greatest extra-biblical textual witness" and may indicate the ancient character of Israel's polytheistic nature. And a recent view supporting older scholarship insists the personal names found in Genesis 1–11 originate from the second millennium rather than the later periods of the Iron Age leading to the exilic era (Hess 2010). However, a number of scholars are not convinced of the historical value of the Torah. Many of the narratives in Genesis 1–12 are more easily explained as originating during the Babylonian Exile (587–539 BCE) than as oral traditions preserved by Abraham and his descendants passed down over hundreds of years until finally written down during the period of David or Solomon in the tenth century BCE.

Wellhausen identified E—the Elohist narrative—as the Torah's second-oldest source. Its fragmentary nature has caused some scholars to doubt there ever was an E source or a writer in the Northern Kingdom of Israel who produced an alternative view of the origins of Israelite history. E was not an antidote to the Yahwist's history and deliberate focus on Judah. These critics argue the E material is not a separate or unified document of Israel's history created in Samaria but mostly oral traditions that were incorporated and augmented into J's description of Israelite origins.

Arguments regarding P are equally antithetical to key points concerning the Documentary Hypothesis. Based on linguistic analysis, various scholars maintain that some features of the Priestly source originated before the exile. Much of the vocabulary concerning priestly terms and institutions disappears in the postexilic age (Milgrom 1990). Others argue that P was a multigenerational work written over a long period of time and, therefore, cannot be assigned to any single era. Archaeology has supplied some clarification in the matter of P. The discovery of burial tombs in Jerusalem at Ketef Hinnom, which contained jewelry and pottery, shed light on the matter of Priestly writings. Silver amulets uncovered at this site date to the mid-seventh century BCE. They contain verses similar to the Priestly blessing found in Numbers 6:24-26, portions of the biblical text assigned to P. The passages on these amulets make them the oldest copies of the Hebrew Bible and indicate that parts of P were known and used in amulets prior to the exile.

It is not clear whether Priestly writers (P) or later editors of Deuteronomy (D) were responsible for the final form of the Torah. How these sources relate to each other is also not apparent. Furthermore, arguments have surfaced that the date of the Yahwist (J) should be placed in the Persian era (539–333 BCE) and not during the tenth century BCE. Others assert that the J source resembles the works of fifth- and fourth-century BCE Greek historians. And a vocal minority of biblical scholars insists that the Bible has its origins in the Hellenistic era (333–64 BCE). In other words, some scholarly analyses bring Wellhausen's dates for the source later than he argued rather than earlier.

THE DEUTERONOMISTIC HISTORY

A major advance in understanding the composition of the biblical text was the identification of the **Deuteronomistic Historians**, first noted by Martin Noth in 1943 and then developed by Frank Moore Cross and his students. Noth recognized that the books of Deuteronomy through 2 Kings used similar phrasing, language, and theological ideology to that used in Deuteronomy. Noth argued that these books had been edited and compiled in the exile (586–539 BCE) and had major connections to the book of Deuteronomy and that most likely this editor wrote nearly all of the book of Deuteronomy. For Noth, this editor was an author and not just an editor, and Noth designated him the "Deuteronomistic Historian." This author's purpose was to demonstrate that the failure to follow the laws of Yahweh had led to the devastation of Israel by the Assyrians (722 BCE) and to the destruction of the Jerusalem temple and exile of the Judeans by the Babylonians (586 BCE).

Cross added to Noth's theory by suggesting that there were at least two revisions of this material. The first Deuteronomistic Historian wrote most of the book of Deuteronomy in the seventh century BCE as part of King Josiah's monotheistic reform. This material was revised and expanded during the exile by a different editor. The rationale was to explain that God's covenant with Israel was contingent on the people's obedience and opposition to idolatry. For this editor, the Jewish tragedy of exile was based on the people's failure to follow Yahweh and his commandments. The major result of this work on the D source was that the Deuteronomistic Historian was acknowledged as a major writer, the creator, and the editor of a significant portion of the biblical text.

RECENT SCHOLARSHIP AND WELLHAUSEN

Some scholars now argue that it is no longer possible to assign all of the verses of the Torah to one or another of Wellhausen's classical sources of J, E, P, D. It is not surprising that scholars have looked elsewhere for answers related to the dating and authorship of the Torah. However, over the years, so many alternative hypotheses and speculations about revisions and reediting were suggested that this has only increased the frustration experienced by the scholarly community. From the perceptive of some historians, the theory should be discarded.

One approach argues that Genesis and the Moses story in Exodus existed as "two competing concepts" of the origin of Israel and theological philosophies (Schmid 2010). Most likely, Israel's historical traditions begin with the exodus stories. Moreover, Genesis and the patriarchal stories have nothing to do with the exodus and were created separately. Only later did Priestly writers (P) reconcile the accounts with edited material. Originally, there was no single narrative linking the two books. These scholars argue that Genesis was not initially created as an introduction to the book of Exodus. During the pre-exilic era, much of Genesis and Exodus was written and at a later date woven together. These scholars maintain that the Priestly writers constructed a literary and historical connection between Genesis and Exodus.

In contrast to jettisoning Wellhausen's hypothesis, Richard E. Friedman maintains that the J source is indeed a united work, written by one author living in Judah, most likely during the late ninth century BCE. It begins in Genesis with the establishment of the world and ends with the establishment of Solomon's reign in 1 Kings. "It is the first great work of prose" (Friedman 1998, 301).

A new supportive argument for the Documentary Hypothesis comes from Joel Baden. He argues that much of the Torah's material demonstrates a continuity within the traditional four-source hypothesis. The sources comprise distinctive and interlocking claims. They are independent in their historical claims and at the same time contradictory to the historical claims of the other sources. In backing the Documentary Hypothesis, Baden (2012, 246–49) argues for "placing the historical claims of the narrative at the forefront of the analysis, with the style, theme and theology playing only a secondary role."

Another development in understanding the stories of the Torah is through collective memories that have their origin in real events and persons, combined with a variety of mythic elements. Ronald Hendel (2001) has argued that the collective memories that form the book of Exodus are composed of historical truth and fiction, containing "authentic" historical details, folklore, ethnic self-identification, narrative imagination, and ideology.

One way that scholars have tried to bridge scholarly uncertainty and disagreement and provide a more objective basis for dating the written origins of the Torah and Former Prophets is through the study of their language. Avi Hurvitz, for example, has argued that the Priestly source is written in Classical Biblical Hebrew rather than Late Biblical Hebrew and that, thus, it should be dated to the preexilic period rather than to the postexilic period as argued by Wellhausen. A survey of studies of the language of P nevertheless shows that different Hebraists have dated this source to the preexilic, exilic, or postexilic period or to a span of time embracing two or even all three of these periods. Moreover, over the past twenty years or so, there has been an ongoing discussion among Hebraists about the efficacy of language for dating the origins of biblical writings, and in the present moment those scholars seem to be a long way from reaching a consensus on the matter (Tigay 2005, xii).

Notwithstanding scholars' disagreements over exactly how and when the Torah was produced, internal biblical evidence and external analogues such as biblical textual traditions, Mesopotamian literature, and postbiblical Jewish and Christian literature, "whose evolution can be documented by copies from several stages in the course of their development—in other words, on *empirical models*—show that many literary works from ancient Israel and cognate cultures were demonstrably produced in the way critics believe that biblical literature was produced" (Tigay 2005, xii). Furthermore, studies of biblical textual traditions—including the Masoretic Text, the Samaritan Pentateuch, the Septuagint, and especially the Dead Sea Scrolls—demonstrate that the production of the Torah and Former Prophets (and indeed the entire Bible) not only was long and complex, as the empirical models suggest, but also lasted until the final centuries BCE, though in different ways for the Torah and Former Prophets. Eugene Ulrich observes with regard to the Dead Sea Scrolls, "Previously, the Pentateuch was assumed to have been basically complete and static at the time of Ezra, but the scrolls show that it was still developing in substantial ways in the late Second Temple period" (Ulrich 2015, 29). Nonetheless, even empirical models have limitations because they can demonstrate only what in general is reasonable or plausible. They cannot prove specific hypotheses or theories about the Bible's production, especially prior to the time of earliest biblical manuscript evidence—the third century BCE (Person and Rezetko 2016).

Regardless of the Torah's prior editing, the majority of biblical scholars place the *final* compilation of the Torah and the books of the Deuteronomistic History—Joshua, Judges, 1–2 Samuel, and 1–2 Kings—in their present form near the end of the exile (ca. 539 BCE) or during the Persian Period (539–333 BCE). But, in the end, no version of the Documentary Hypothesis addressing the nature of the early biblical texts and their reliability, historical reconstruction, and assessment has found total consensus among biblical scholars. Yet there is no acceptable replacement for Wellhausen's basic theory of multiple authors and sources for the Torah. Wellhausen's model has been revised, but no approach has fully solved the issue of historical writing and the dating of the sources of the Torah. Certainly, history based on folk stories, oral traditions, and myth can retain valuable historical fragments, but numerous revisions over centuries produced under the influence of theology and ideology diminish the prospects for recovering extensive historical information. There is still no agreement among scholars concerning objective criteria for distinguishing factual from fictional accounts in the early sources. Fresh insights into the literary nature of the biblical texts continue to be developed. However, many questions about the sources of early Israel's history cannot be fully answered by present historical and literary methods.

EARLY ARCHAEOLOGY AND THE OPPOSITION TO WELLHAUSEN

At the beginning of the twentieth century, there was a triumphal feeling among many conservative scholars and theologians that archaeology had vindicated the truth of Scripture. Archaeological discoveries had proliferated in the last years of the nineteenth century and the early years of the twentieth century, and some scholars interpreted this new material as demonstrating the Bible's reliability and the errors of Wellhausen's arguments. After all, if Scripture can be shown to be true by archaeological "facts on the ground," then claims that its texts were historically unreliable are irrelevant. Questions of faith motivated conservative scholars and theologians to disparage the Documentary Hypotheses and to defend Scripture and traditional Christian tenets. Conservatives often maintained that no scholar was worthy of undertaking an investigation of Holy Writ until there was some acknowledgment of its divine qualities and its inerrant nature. Moreover, when difficult textual inconsistencies surfaced, it was standard practice for the pious scholar to appeal to the authority and truth of Jesus and the apostles over the analysis of higher criticism. In their oftentimes zealous campaign to attack Wellhausen's theories, many conservatives exploited dubious interpretations of archaeological data to consecrate the biblical text and prove its historical reliability. The purported archaeological evidence was interpreted and integrated into the conservative struggle against Wellhausen's higher criticism. The new data became the bulwark of faith-oriented scholars in the Anglo-American community, where archaeology received its greatest support and promotion. Enemies of the Documentary Hypothesis were adamant that archaeology confirmed and validated the truth of the biblical text, and they utilized archaeological data in their persistent attacks upon the supporters of Wellhausian approaches to biblical criticism.

The conservative response to higher critics was based on the remarkable archaeological discoveries that from the mid-nineteenth century had unearthed the previously shrouded great cities of Babylon, Erech, Nineveh, Nimrud, and Ur. The texts and artifacts from these excavations revealed otherwise unimaginable information that conservative writers claimed verified many episodes of the Hebrew text. Tablets contained the names of Assyrian, Babylonian, and Israelite kings and events mentioned in the Bible. Incredibly, Assyrian and Babylonian cuneiform writings contained flood and creation stories.

The campaign waged by conservative scholars and clergy against higher critics was sustained in part by these new discoveries. First, many of the Tell el-**Amarna Letters**, discovered in 1887 in Egypt, were cuneiform tablets written by many of the kings and princes of Syria and Palestine. These texts depicted the political and social life in Canaan in the fourteenth century BCE and, amazingly, mentioned a group of people called the **Hapiru** (= *apiru*) that many scholars identified as the ancient "Hebrews." Second, while excavating in Egypt in 1883, Edouard Naville believed he had discovered Pithom (Egyptian *pr itm*, "House of Atum"), one of the store-cities erected by the Hebrews during their enslavement in Egypt (Exod 1:11). Third, in 1905–1906, Flinders Petrie believed he had uncovered the other store-city, Ramses, at Tell el-Retabeh. Fourth, by 1900, scholars were aware that the invasion of the Egyptian pharaoh Shishak (Sheshonq I), cited in 1 Kings 14:25 and 2 Chronicles 12:2-12, had been located on a triumphal relief scene at the temple of Amun at Karnak. Fifth, during an excavation in 1896, Petrie recovered the **Merneptah Stele** (1207 BCE), which displayed a victory hymn celebrating the pharaoh's campaign in Canaan—including his boast of destroying a people called "Israel." This was the earliest known reference to Israel in an extrabiblical text. Sixth, French archaeologists digging at Susa in 1901–1902 uncovered the Code of Hammurabi (1792–1750 BCE). At that time, it was the oldest law code in existence and remarkably similar to elements in the Hebrew law code. For many conservative scholars, it confirmed the antiquity of the Mosaic law.

A number of pious Christian scholars—such as Archibald H. Sayce, James Orr, Emil Reich, Albert Clay, Edouard Neville, and Melvin Kyle—praised these archaeological discoveries as confirmation that events depicted in the biblical narrative did indeed occur. Questions of faith motivated conservative scholars and theologians to disparage the Documentary Hypothesis and to defend Scripture's unity and traditional Christian tenets. The new archaeological evidence also encouraged devout scholars to believe they could discredit Wellhausen and his supporters. In the first decades of the twentieth century, a complete validation of the historicity of the biblical record was magnified throughout conservative scholarship. Unfortunately, this was often based on the misuse of archaeological data.

If archaeological finds made an impact among Christian adherents, many major critical scholars—especially those engaged in literary analysis of the Bible—simply ignored the bluster from faith-oriented academics and the archaeological data they touted in support of their claims. Critical scholars were indifferent to the early archaeological excavations in Palestine because of the religious exploitation of archaeology. The search for biblical authenticity in archaeological excavations had spawned unrestrained theories that were incapable of distinguishing fact from fiction. Those modern scholars who actually analyzed the archaeological remains—such as Samuel Rolles Driver, Stanley A. Cook, and George Barton—insisted that higher criticism had not been repudiated by archaeology, and they reiterated, time and again, that any archaeological interpretation inspired by a religious spirit or by direct appeals to Scripture was unacceptable. Driver was particularly incisive. He insisted that no archaeological discovery demonstrated that Moses wrote anything or that Abraham or the other patriarchs ever actually existed, and he insisted that archaeology has not confirmed any "single fact" recorded in the Hebrew

Bible prior to the tenth century BCE. These scholars wrote important studies pertaining to the history and religion of Canaan and ancient Israel, and in their work they often consulted the archaeological evidence. They developed methods for interpreting the archaeological data that were largely free of theological bias and certainly free of conservative theological bias. They and others challenged erroneous claims and warned students that a great deal of archaeological evidence was incomplete and often hypothetical and had not solved the questions of historicity of the Mosaic authorship of the Pentateuch (Elliott 2002).

William F. Albright

William F. Albright's (1891–1971) scholarly work influenced almost every issue related to ancient Near Eastern studies and biblical archaeology. He possessed an astonishing grasp of a wide range of subjects and disciplines, which allowed him to dominate the field of the ancient Near East, biblical studies, and archaeology. Beginning in the 1920s, under the influence of Albright, many North American scholars firmly believed that archaeology had authenticated much of ancient Israel's earliest eras in the Middle Bronze Age (2000–1550 BCE), especially the patriarchal narratives located in Genesis. Albright's archaeological assertions and practices came to be called "biblical archaeology," claiming that archaeology had demonstrated the accuracy of the biblical text. Albright's definition of biblical archaeology encompassed all countries and cultures mentioned in the Bible, from India to Spain to southern Europe to Arabia—an impossible designation of cultures, languages, and history, which no one scholar could master. Albright and his supporters played a key role in biblical scholarship, and not just archaeology, in the United States from the 1920s to the early 1970s (Levy and Freedman 2009).

Albright maintained that archaeology confirmed most of the earlier biblical record of the patriarchs, Moses, and the conquest narratives of Joshua. He asserted that there were parallels between Mesopotamian texts and the patriarchal stories in Genesis. According to Albright, the evidence demonstrated that an ample amount of the text of Genesis is early and should be placed in the Middle Bronze Age. Nomadic customs and migrations, legal and social practices, and many of the patriarchal names found in the book of Genesis had somehow been verified in the archaeological record and Mesopotamian cuneiform records. Albright spent much of his career battling the followers of Wellhausen, who he believed disregarded archaeological evidence in attempt to rewrite biblical history.

Albright was so assured of his victory over Wellhausen's negativity toward the historicity of the biblical record that he could write the following in the 1960s:

> Aside from a few die-hards among older scholars, there is scarcely a single biblical historian who has not been impressed by the rapid accumulation of data supporting the substantial historicity of the patriarchal tradition. (1963, 16)

Albright did not reject the basic source theory of Wellhausen. He agreed that the Pentateuch was based on the documents J, E, P, and D—written or compiled at various dates and representing various interests. But he argued that Wellhausen had ignored the ancient oral traditions, a theme he relentlessly pursued throughout his life. Though Wellhausen maintained that Israelite religion evolved over the centuries, Albright attributed monotheism to Moses. Wellhausen's reconstruction of Israelite religion conflicted with Albright's view that the biblical text was mostly reliable and that monotheism could be traced back to Moses (J. E. Wright 2002, 65). Albright also asserted that the alphabet was in existence from the "Patriarchal Age" and that it is certain that the Hebrew alphabet was being used for "everyday purposes" in the fourteenth and thirteenth centuries BCE, demonstrating an early date for historical writing (Albright 1946, 192–93).

Albright's positivistic arguments and methods were dominant for decades and were popular among conservative scholars and theologians who disparaged the Documentary Hypothesis and defended the reliability of Scripture. More importantly, the "Albrightian School" attracted major biblical scholars and archaeologists, including John Bright, Roland de Vaux, Nelson Glueck, Benjamin Mazar, G. Ernest Wright, Ephraim A. Speiser, and Yigael Yadin, among others.

History and the Patriarchs

By the mid-1970s, many of Albright's theories regarding the biblical text and archaeology had been dealt heavy blows. William Dever (1977) surveyed the archaeological data and concluded that there is nothing in the archaeological record to support Albright's interpretation of the Genesis narratives. Thomas L. Thompson and John Van Seters also questioned the premise that the patriarchal narratives were historical. They argued that Albright and his supporters misinterpreted the archaeological and textual evidence and that the Genesis stories could be dated to a number of historical periods.

FIGURE 2-7. *William G. Dever criticized the American style of "biblical archaeology," whose primary aim was proving the Bible.*

The purported archaeological evidence uncovered in a number of texts located in several Mesopotamian excavated sites that allegedly paralleled and illuminated the nomadic customs, patriarchal names, and laws found in the stories of Abraham were illusionary. Thompson and Van Seters argued that Albright and his supporters relied on faulty archaeological interpretations and comparisons and that the Genesis stories were in fact later historical creations. These "ancient stories" were not early histories of Israel but the products of later eras such as the period of the exile (586–539 BCE), or even later, and so they could not provide truly accurate information for earlier periods. In later years, Dever (1993, 25–35) argued that Albright's notions of archaeological data were naive and that he was not "primarily an archaeologist but a historian, for whom archaeology was simply a technical convenient, pragmatic tool." Moreover, he further argued that many of Albright's historical, archaeological, and biblical syntheses had been overturned.

The critiques of Thompson, Van Seters, and Dever were so devastating that, by the 1980s, most biblical scholars had jettisoned the notion that the patriarchal narratives were accurate historical accounts of the beginnings of ancient Israel. Biblical archaeology as practiced by Albright and his disciples had suffered severe setbacks in demonstrating the trustworthiness of the biblical record in its earliest eras. It appears that the only surviving devotees of Albright's method of biblical archaeology "are fundamentalist and evangelical scholars" (Hendel 2006). Only a handful of conservative scholars maintain that there is a defensible case for locating patriarchal traditions in the Middle Bronze Age (Kitchen 2003; Provan and Long 2003).

THE EVIDENCE AND THE EXODUS

Challenges to Wellhausen and his historical interpretations of the biblical text have included the exodus stories. Albright was influential in promoting the historical trustworthiness of the book of Exodus; for him, monotheism began no later than Moses. A number of modern Albrightians contend that the book of Exodus contains credible elements of historical truth that challenge the basic dating of sources in the Documentary Hypothesis and confirm the basic historicity of the biblical text (Kitchen 2003; Hoffmeier 2005). They and other conservative scholars point to the many indirect connections to the exodus story. Semites (Hyksos) ruled Egypt for over 150 years, and large Semitic populations resided in Egypt for hundreds of years. Egyptian texts record Semites as commonly involved in the royal household for centuries. Egypt dominated and controlled Canaan for hundreds of years, and pharaohs regularly campaigned in Canaan and returned with thousands of slaves. Genesis and Exodus contain Egyptian loan words, and the names of major biblical characters such as Moses, Aaron, and Miriam are Egyptian. Many scholars grant the authenticity of Pithom and Rameses, the cities mentioned in Exodus as places where Hebrew slaves toiled. Egyptian papyrus depicts slaves escaping through the Sinai, and certain geographical features of the journeys in the exodus have been identified. Egyptian records mention nomadic peoples located in the Sinai called Shasu who appear to worship a deity named YHW, perhaps the God of the Israelites.

Though many biblical scholars find that the exodus story may include a small genuine core of historical memories, unfortunately, to date, none of this "proof" provides clear evidence to embrace the exodus as historically reliable or that some of these details invalidate Wellhausen's hypothesis. There is no evidence that Moses lived, much less developed monotheism. There is very little indisputable evidence for the sojourn, exodus, or Sinaitic wanderings. Archaeology has not demonstrated the validity of the Exodus account. Carol Meyers argues, "After more than a century of research and massive efforts of generations of archaeologists and Egyptologists, nothing has been recovered that relates directly to the account in the Exodus of an Egyptian sojourn and escape or a large-scale migration through the Sinai" (2005, 5). Israel Finkelstein insists that there are intractable difficulties in dating the exodus to an early period, and, though there may be vague memories of Canaanites entering and expelled from Egypt, the authors of Exodus integrated many geographical and literary details from the seventh century BCE or later. There is simply no archaeological evidence of Israel's sojourn in the Sinai at the supposed time of the exodus in the thirteenth century or any other earlier period (Finkelstein and Silberman 2001, 48–72).

At the beginning of the twentieth century, conservative scholars thought archaeology could serve and protect faith and negate the critical scholarship of Wellhausen and his supporters. Opponents of the Documentary Hypothesis found sustenance in the belief that archaeology confirmed and validated the truth of the biblical text, and they utilized archaeological data in their persistent attacks on biblical criticism. Beginning in the 1920s, under the influence of William Albright, many American biblical scholars insisted that archaeology had validated early Israelite history and nullified the Documentary Hypothesis. The Albrightian School dominated biblical archaeology until the mid-seventies. By the 1980s, however, the synthesis of biblical studies and archaeology as practiced by Albright and his supporters was no longer considered reliable. Furthermore, following the archaeologists, a majority of biblical scholars rejected the concept that the early traditions in the Torah had a reliable historical foundation.

The attempt to use archaeological evidence to support the case for the authenticity of the Torah's narratives has not succeeded. It has not provided the evidence needed for the absolute dating of the sources. Archaeology has in no way overturned Wellhausen's theory. Unless we uncover a palace archive, temple library, or a number of monumental inscriptions related to early Israel, the issue of the historicity of the early biblical text will remain ambiguous. And this is where matters stand. Today most biblical historians concede that while the early biblical accounts from Genesis through Deuteronomy may provide a few authentic memories of early Israelite history, they do not contain the historical information needed to create a dependable history of early Israel.

Suggestions for Further Reading

If you want to know more about how the biblical text we hold in our hands today came into being—whether the King James, the Revised Standard, or the New International Versions, or some other translation—a full discussion appears in the first volume of the *Cambridge History of the Bible*, published in 1963. All three volumes of the *Cambridge History* contain important essays on the history of biblical interpretation. Two smaller introductions to text criticism—as well as to the historical manuscripts and fragments on which that work is based—are worth reading: Ernst Würthwein's *The Text of the Old Testament* and E. R. Brotzman's *Old Testament Textual Criticism: A Practical Introduction*. Informative guides to the Septuagint and its manuscripts were composed by Karen Jobes and Moisés Silva (*Invitation to the Septuagint*) and by Jennifer M. Dines (*The Septuagint*). Paul Flesher and Bruce Chilton wrote the first book-length overview of the Targums in more than a century: *The Targums: A Critical Introduction*. For the Dead Sea Scrolls and their link to the settlement at Khirbet Qumran, check out James VanderKam's *The Dead Sea Scrolls Today* or *The Meaning of the Dead Sea Scrolls* (the latter coauthored with Peter Flint). Translations of the nonbiblical scrolls and fragments from Qumran appear in Geza Vermes' *The Complete Dead Sea Scrolls in English*.

For different perspectives on the study of the Hebrew Bible / Old Testament as the sacred text of Judaism and/or of Christianity, see Nahum Sarna's essay "Bible" in *Encyclopaedia Judaica*, as well as *The Jewish and the Christian Bible* (by Julio Trebolle Barrera) and Jon D. Levenson's *The Hebrew Bible, the Old Testament, and Historical Criticism: Jews and Christians in Biblical Studies*.

For more information about the history of scholarly approaches to the Bible, read Henning Reventlow's and Leo G. Perdue's *History of Biblical Interpretation*; J. W. Rogerson, *Old Testament Criticism in the Nineteenth Century*; or James Barr, *History and Ideology in the Old Testament: Biblical Studies at the End of Millennium*.

The work of Julius Wellhausen that features above is *Prolegomena to the History of Ancient Israel*, a 1957 translation of the German work *Prolegomena zur Geschichte Israels*, published in 1905. Joel S. Baden's work *The Composition of the Pentateuch: Renewing the Documentary Hypothesis* provides an overview of the scholarly debate that Wellhausen's analysis unleashed. William Foxwell Albright's archaeological response, *The Biblical Period from Abraham to Ezra,* appeared in 1963. For a well-researched study of the early history of archaeological research and biblical interpretation, see Mark Elliot's book *Biblical Interpretation Using Archaeological Evidence.*

3

THE WEST'S REDISCOVERY
OF THE HOLY LAND

Victor H. Matthews

European Collectors, Museums, and the Early Explorers, Seventeenth to Eighteenth Centuries

The roots of what would eventually become the science of archaeology are found in the antiquarian and artistic interests of the Italian Renaissance. What differentiated the work of the humanist scholars during the Renaissance from the **Scholastics** of the Middle Ages was their ability to recognize that there was a profound difference between the cultures of the present and those of the past. By studying the past through its literature, art, and architecture, the humanists obtained a perspective on these ancient cultures that in turn gave them the ability to analyze their own culture dispassionately. Rather than trying to revive the cultures of antiquity in their own time, the humanists rejected the need for constant references to the continuity of human behavior and achievement from ancient times to the present. That new perspective not only contributed to a rise among scholars and artists such as the poet Petrarch (1304–1374) and the engineer Giovanni Doni (1318–1389) in the classical heritage of ancient Greece and Rome but also sparked contributions to these efforts by popes and the nobility of Europe. Of particular importance to the spread of the humanist movement was the fact that many of the growing number of scholars of Latin rhetoric and the classics rose to influential government positions in major **city-states** as well as secretaries at the papal court or became tutors and orators in the courts of northern Italy.

The growing interest in classical literature brought on a massive effort to sketch and map out ancient monuments and to search for ancient manuscripts in the monasteries of Europe. These efforts resulted in the emergence of copies of the writings of eminent classical authors—Herodotus, Aristotle, Strabo, and Lucretius—from their preservation in the Islamic world. In addition, the study of the inscriptions found on ancient structures that littered the landscape of Italy and Greece inspired the idea that these monuments could provide an even more direct testimony to the culture and history of antiquity than the literary tradition. In each of these instances, the desire to study these ancient texts sprang from a literary and historical-critical perspective rather than an effort to provide a theological underpinning for Christianity.

Not all of this enthusiasm for things classical can be attributed to scholars and their wealthy patrons. An example of the enterprising activity of fifteenth-century merchants to the search for classical scholarship and its artifactual remains is Cyriacus of Ancona (also known as Ciriaco de' Pizzicolli [1391–1452]), whose commercial journeys for his family's business provided him opportunities to explore the ruins of ancient sites in Italy, Dalmatia, and Turkey and throughout the eastern Mediterranean. What distinguishes him and his work from many merchants of his time, however, is his meticulous recording of his observations and sketches of ancient monuments, such as the triumphal arch of the emperor Trajan at Ancona. From references to his annotations and a few scraps of what has survived of his *Commentaria*, it is possible to suggest that his efforts to preserve the cultural heritage of the ancient world place him in the position of being among the intellectual founders of archaeology.

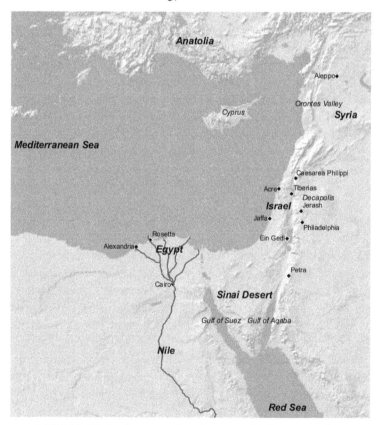

MAP 3-1. *The lands surrounding the eastern Mediterranean Sea.*

As the Renaissance progressed into the fifteenth century, further develop-ments in archaeological techniques were recorded in the monograph published in 1444–1446 by Biondo Flavio entitled *Rome Restored*. This is a study of the topography and the remains of the monumental structures of the ancient city, based on both literary descriptions and his observations of the remains. Being one of the first secular works published on the newly invented printing press in 1471, it became a significant influence on later archaeological treatises and on how architecture and inscriptions were recorded.

Interest in classical antiquity and its physical remains continued into the sixteenth and seventeenth centuries as Italian scholars and travelers from other countries journeyed to long-known sites in Italy and Greece to study their material remains with new techniques and perspectives. The rediscovery and description of classical antiquities led to advances in literary studies and to the development of **antiquarianism**. As had been the case in the previous centuries, the Renaissance popes (Sixtus IV, Julius II, Julius III) and many of the wealthy Italian nobility became art and antiquities collectors—referring to themselves as *dilettanti*, "those who delighted in the arts."

In reviving and studying the material remains of the ancient Mediterra-nean cultures, Renaissance scholars spread the view that these ancient peoples were different but also worthy of study by modern researchers. Thus, it became imperative to train individuals in every aspect of these ancient cultures to observe and record differences between ancient and modern civilizations.

Of course, the growing knowledge of these ancient sites also brought with it a greater desire to acquire examples of ancient art. For example, during the seventeenth century, the Earl of Arundel and the Duke of Buckingham com-peted for antiquities from Greece while King Charles I of England amassed his own collection of artifacts with the assistance of his admirals who were stationed at the Aegean Sea. Along with growing economic competition, these activities contributed to a sense of competitive nationalism, a growth in the development of the field of natural history (especially geology), and the cul-tural shift into the romantic movement.

Indeed, great political changes had come to Italy and the rest of Europe by the beginning of the eighteenth century. These political and economic shifts were sparked by the end of the Wars of Religion that racked the continent from the mid-sixteenth to the mid-seventeenth century, by the colonial explora-tions in the New World with the discovery of new indigenous cultures, by the expansion of commercial activity in India and China that brought an injection of wealth, and by the emergence of new nation-states. As the age of exploration ended, the age of archaeology began in the eighteenth and ninetieth centuries with natural scientists, writers, and artists utilizing their skills on a massive scale to retrieve the remains of extinct animals, lost languages, buried civilizations, and human prehistory on every continent.

Such an expansion of spatial vision and scientific understanding was coupled in the eighteenth century with the assumption among the wealthy elite in Europe that a gentleman's education was not complete without a tour of the ancient sites of Greece and Rome. Well-to-do young men and nobility of Europe fed their appetite for classical learning and the acquisition of finely made objects through a rite of passage known as the "Grand Tour" by traveling to Rome and various cities in Italy and Greece. The eighteenth-century publications of Greek painting and sculpture by Johann Joachim Winckelmann (who served various cardinals and the papal court for decades), particularly his *History of Ancient Art*, were quite influential among travelers and helped usher in the neoclassical period in Europe, with its emphasis on real rather than reproduced artifacts (Marchand 1996, 7–8).

Marvelous collections of Greek and Roman art were assembled by such notables as Sir William Hamilton (1730–1803), the British envoy to the court of Naples. His acquisitions not only adorned his own home, but portions were sold to collectors in England and the British Museum. Another collector was the Earl of Elgin, who contrived with the ruling Turkish authorities in Athens to acquire the incredible architectural marbles from the Parthenon, now known as "the Elgin Marbles." which were shipped to England in 1804. Elgin tried on several occasions to negotiate their sale to the British government. While there was some furor over Elgin's

FIGURE 3-1.
The Pantheon in Rome. Young aristocrats enhancing their classical education on the Grand Tour of Europe. Painting by Giovanni Paolo Panini, 1734.

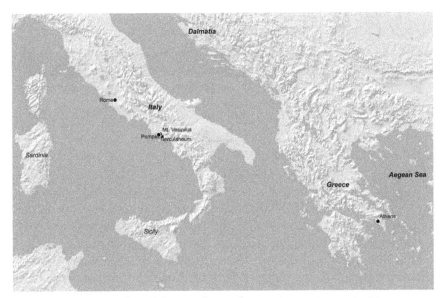

MAP 3-2. *Italy and Greece, where early interest in ancient antiquities dug up from the ground began.*

methods in acquiring what today is considered a Greek national treasure, he persisted with his efforts and eventually took a financial loss selling them to the British Museum.

It was into this cauldron of change and an enthusiasm for things classical that the rediscovery of the ancient cities of Pompeii and Herculaneum precipitated a new generation of treasure seekers and artistic connoisseurs into the hunt for objects to grace their private collections. These two cities were destroyed and buried during the eruption of Mount Vesuvius in 79 CE. Other than the original inhabitants who made some attempt to recover their property at the time, or opportunists who dug indiscriminately through the debris for profit, little effort was made in antiquity to excavate the site. During the Middle Ages, there had been some occasional salvage work. In fact, several Latin inscriptions were recovered but only served as a reminder that an ancient city lay there. In every case, these efforts resulted in the destruction of houses, walls, and artifacts that did not interest the unskilled treasure seekers (De la Bédoyére 2010, 97–98).

Herculaneum was rediscovered in the early 1700s (1738) by workmen digging a well who turned up a fine marble sculpture of Hercules and three female marble figures as well as the remains of the theater. Explorers then dug deep tunnels, sometimes using gunpowder, through the solidified volcanic mud in search of antiquities for wealthy patrons. The work was financed initially by

Emmanuel Maurice de Lorraine, Prince d'Elboeuf, who ordered that all of the statuary that could be removed be brought to the surface without making a record that could establish **provenance** for later researchers. Similar attitudes and methods are evident in the excavations sponsored by the Spanish Bourbon king of the Two Sicilies, Carlos III, who at the behest of his wife, Maria Amalia, financed six years of digging at both Herculaneum and Pompeii during the 1740s and early 1750s.

The excavations were under the direction of Rocque Joaquin de Alcubierre, a military engineer with no knowledge of ancient architecture and an abiding desire to recover as many antiquities worthy of his king's collection as possible. While he did produce records for the king and his prime minister, they were never intended for publication, and little of this information came to light during the first century after the work began. More important to the development of archaeological methods and the preservation of systematic records was the excavation's Swiss-born chief architect Karl Weber. His contributions began with his simple method of following the network of streets he uncovered and excavating the buildings he encountered along the way. In this way, he obtained a greater sense of the city's layout and its architectural features and the functionality of its public and private space. The plans he produced included a catalogue of finds and their precise location, and he called for the publication of complete site plans with drawings and commentary on the objects that were discovered. While he was frustrated by the demands of the Bourbon court to abandon areas that were not producing the rich finds they

FIGURE 3-2. *Herculaneum. Karl Weber excavated Herculaneum systematically and advocated leaving ruins intact (in situ) rather than moving them to a museum.*

craved and to publish only the art according to genre rather than provenance, he still managed to explore and document large sections of the city. Disputes with the various factions in charge of the work prevented his systematically produced plans of temples, the theater, and many private residences from being published in his lifetime, and what remained of them came to light only in the late nineteenth century (Daniel 1976, 153).

One very unfortunate result of the disagreement between those who viewed Herculaneum and Pompeii as simply repositories for ancient art and those, like Weber, who wished to study and recreate the life of these ancient cities was a general impression of chaos and indiscriminate destruction of the sites (Zimmerman 2008, 106). For instance, visitors in the mid-seventeenth century described the massive scar being driven through the city as "strip mining" and noted that the workers simply refilled the rooms that had been stripped of vases, statuary, and other precious items with earth from the next room being excavated (Blix 2009, 13). What could be termed cultural strip-mining of the buried ruins demonstrates the emphasis on aesthetics rather than cultural heritage that characterized this period. The artifacts that were recovered were valued for their artistic qualities, independent of their cultural or historical context, which could be dismissed or neglected by the collectors. Little was actually learned about the artifacts that were recovered, although an initial publication of the finds was produced by the Marquis Venuti in the *Bibliothèque raisonée* in 1751 and 1752.

A similar pattern of unrestricted treasure-hunting occurred at the site of Pompeii when excavations resumed in 1755. Unfortunately, the single-minded and secretive nature of the crews at the site prevented the general public or those on the "Grand Tour" from learning very much about the progress or the artifacts from the dig. Many visitors were given only a perfunctory tour of the site. However, several open letters based on his observations of the shoddy methods being employed were written by the prominent scholar Johann Winckelmann. He had established an extensive circle of distinguished artists (Angelica Kaufmann), writers (James Boswell), and political notables (including Sir William Hamilton and Lord Baltimore), and the weight of their combined criticism had an effect on subsequent excavations.

Public scrutiny and the political influence exercised by Hamilton as the British consul to Naples transformed the work at Herculaneum and Pompeii as it moved into the nineteenth century. Hamilton's interests in volcanology had already drawn him to study Mount Vesuvius, and it was only natural that he would also form an extreme interest in the cities that the eruption had destroyed in the first century, especially after the eruption in 1767. These enthusiasms were accompanied by Hamilton's desire to collect and study Greek-style vases. He was joined by Winckelmann, and together—as

Hamilton collected and Winckelmann catalogued each according to its style and origin—they planned to create a record that promoted interest in classical art and benefited them financially. Although Winckelmann was murdered before it could be completed, their collaboration eventually resulted in a database that would benefit later researchers.

In addition to the standard works of arts, the charred papyri uncovered in the excavations of Herculaneum by Weber were a tantalizing puzzle for epigraphers and linguists. Taken from the Villa dei Papiri, they represented an opportunity to add to our store of knowledge of ancient literature, philosophy, and science. They were in such deplorable condition, however, that most were unreadable or simply fell apart when examined. To assist with their study, Hamilton provided some financial support for the work of Antonio Piaggio, who was the first scholar to successfully unroll one of the scrolls and who eventually spent thirty years (starting in 1753) copying and deciphering their contents. His efforts and techniques were a precursor to the work of the team of scholars who also spent decades reconstructing and preserving the Dead Sea Scrolls. One sign of the significance of the Herculaneum scrolls was their presentation to the then first consul of France, Napoleon Bonaparte, as part of a diplomatic gesture in 1802. They were considered a tie to the glory of ancient Rome and Bonaparte's desire to create a new empire in Europe, as well as a tool he used to legitimize his ambitions.

After these early starts resulted in the recovery of remarkable objects of art that graced private collections and museum exhibits and that served as gifts among the royalty of Europe, the first truly scientific excavations of Pompeii were conducted by Giuseppe Fiorelli in 1860. This former revolutionary, who had struggled to help create an independent Italian nation, transformed the work by opening up new areas using large teams of workers. They were instructed to carry out the careful excavation of each stratum and to preserve features as they were discovered in situ before they were removed. He also founded a "Scuola di Pompei" that was open to scholars throughout Europe who wished to learn and develop archaeological techniques. However, Fiorelli is best known for his development of a technique to fill with plaster the hardened ash husks that contained the remains of animals and humans killed in the volcanic explosion. The result was a tableau of the final agonies of these victims, and the casts quickly captured the imagination of the public (Daniel 1976, 165).

His successor, Michele Ruggiero, took over the directorship in 1875. Among his major achievements was his effort to conserve the remains of buildings and frescos that had previously been excavated—a major problem since they had begun to decay as soon as they had been opened to the elements. His publication of two volumes providing details on the history of the

FIGURE 3-3. *Ruins of Pompeii. The first truly modern scientific excavation of Pompeii was directed by Giuseppe Fiorelli in 1860.*

excavations, the existent archival records, and descriptions (where possible) of the ancient architecture were important to art historians and archaeologists. He also included inventory numbers of the art that had subsequently been placed in royal and private museums. His publications in turn became a major resource for later scholars and excavators in their efforts not only to discover new artifacts but to trace and provide a provenance for what was collected from the site.

Unfortunately, the financial difficulties experienced by the Italian government at the end of the nineteenth century led to the farming out of the excavations at Pompeii to private businessmen who once again treated the site as a private treasure-hunting domain. Victorian-era tourists—attracted by Fiorelli's plaster casts and perhaps urged on by the tragic romance of Edward Bulwer-Lytton's 1834 novel *The Last Days of Pompeii*—continued to flock to the ancient cities, aided by the train line that also took them to the top of Mount Vesuvius to examine its crater. However, what they could see of the ruins of the cities was really quite limited. It was only after 1950 that the site director, Amedeo Maiuri, was able to open up the various excavation areas to create a connected and panoramic view of the cities and its public and private buildings. In conjunction with the construction of a major highway through the region, he arranged for the removal of vast amounts of volcanic slag that became part of the highway's abutments. Their efforts, however, were slowed when in 1959 the workers uncovered a previously unknown section of the ancient city near Murecine. The delay was quickly dealt with by removing sections of the painted walls and other artifacts (including baskets of business documents) and putting them in storage while the uncovered buildings were simply reburied. Road construction then resumed. It was only in 2000 that the buried neighborhood once again came under review when additional lanes were being added to the roadway.

In some ways, the conjunction between personal or governmental interest and the location and excavation of these ancient cities continues into the present. Of course, that is not exclusive to Pompeii and Herculaneum. Many major archaeological finds in Italy, Greece, Turkey, and the nations of the Middle East continue to surface as a result of road construction, private excavations, and happenstance. The lesson from the cities destroyed and held in stasis by the eruption of Mount Vesuvius is that our cultural heritage is ours to preserve. While much has been lost through the cupidity and mismanagement of previous excavations, we can make sure that the information archaeological sites provide for us and future generations is professionally uncovered, studied, and published.

Napoleon's Invasions of Egypt and Palestine and the Decipherment of the Rosetta Stone

It is interesting how personal ambitions, political expediency, and luck led to one of the most remarkable archaeological discoveries of all time—the **Rosetta Stone**. This royal inscription written in two languages and three scripts on behalf of an obscure second-century BCE Ptolemaic king became the key to the decipherment of Egyptian **hieroglyphics**. To better understand how French politics and Napoleon's desire for glory contribute to archaeological history, it is necessary to examine events at the end of the eighteenth century. As France emerged from the excesses of the Reign of Terror, the ruling oligarchy known as the Directory sought for ways to restore the nation's financial and political fortunes. General Napoleon Bonaparte had proven to be a useful tool in protecting France's borders against the incursions of the Austrian Hapsburg rulers and the Russians. His victories in northern Italy and the plundering of its towns and churches had brought badly needed wealth streaming back to Paris. However, his successes also made him a potential political rival to the Directors. They began looking for an expedition for him that would strike a blow at England's monopoly on trade in the Mediterranean and in India and that would remove him, at least temporarily, from Europe. The conquest of Egypt presented an opportunity to accomplish all of these goals (Reid 2002, 34).

FIGURE 3-4. *The Rosetta Stone provided the key to the
decipherment of hieroglyphs. Its three scripts—hieroglyphics,
demotic, and Greek—enabled scholars to recover and read
hieroglyphics and thus unlock Egyptian history and literature.*

More important in the long run for France, however, was gaining control
of the eastern Mediterranean and turning it into a "French lake" for its merchants and challenging the Muslim Ottomans for control of Greece and the
Middle East. A further prize would come from capturing the trade route to
India by way of the Nile and the Red Sea. France had lost many of its New
World colonial holdings in Canada, North America, and the Caribbean to the
British during the French and Indian War of the 1760s. If the French controlled
a route to India via Egypt and blocked the British from using overland routes
through the Middle East, they knew they could invade the British monopoly
on the lucrative trade in India and restore a measure of their former political
and economic influence.

Egypt at the end of the eighteenth century was ruled by an elite corps of
former slaves, the Mamluks, who had been purchased or kidnapped as children from Eastern European villages and trained as devoted Muslims and as
some of the finest cavalry in the world. While still nominally under the political umbrella of the Ottoman Turks, the Mamluks held Egypt as their private

fiefdom, exploiting its wealth and paying little attention to its people or its past heritage. Napoleon and the French strategists saw an opportunity here to "liberate" Arab Egypt from the rule of the tottering **Ottoman Empire** and transform it into a European satellite. This intention held even though France was technically an ally of the Turks. In the face of what seems a contradictory policy, an ideological myth was fabricated to help justify their colonial ambitions. Framing their plans via both humanitarian and logical rhetoric, they stated that they wished to restore a now degenerate and backward Egypt by injecting the ideas, culture, and technology of the European Enlightenment. Exploring its ancient monuments and publishing the results of scientific investigations would also help to reveal Egypt's ancient glory and genius that had been lost for so long and only glimpsed by merchants and travelers over the centuries (Brandt 2010, 42).

In order for their expedition to begin, however, the French plotted to deceive the English about their ultimate intentions. Plans were broadcast on a possible invasion of England along with the staging of vessels, equipment, and men. In the end, a fleet of nearly two hundred vessels was assembled at the French Mediterranean port of Toulon. Only a handful of men, not including the captains of these vessels, were told of their destination. They departed on May 19, 1798. Along the way, they were joined by three additional convoys, swelling the number of ships to nearly four hundred and their company to fifty-five thousand.

Adding to the complexity of this operation, Napoleon recruited a group of approximately 160 French artists and scientists, who were termed "the Commission of Arts and Sciences." These specialists from the fields of astronomy, chemistry, medicine, engineering, botany, geology, and physics represented some of the best minds in France at the time. Some came along enchanted by the images of ancient Egypt circulating at the time among the intellectual community, while the more mature heads saw this as an unprecedented opportunity to study the remains of the ancient culture of Egypt in all of its aspects—collecting, cataloguing, and eventually publishing their findings. For his part, Napoleon envisioned himself as a new Alexander the Great, a conqueror who had also made a point of bringing scientists and philosophers with his army in order to share the benefits of Greek culture (Burleigh 2007).

All of this was a supreme gamble on Napoleon's part. Sailing such a large armada across the Mediterranean to Egypt was hardly a clandestine move. Still, luck was with them when a storm dispersed the British naval blockade of Toulon and the French fleet was able to break free into the Mediterranean. Had they encountered the British fleet commanded by Admiral Horatio Nelson, however, they would have been cut to pieces. In fact, during their journey, they barely escaped being sighted. Nelson arrived in Egypt several days ahead of the French. Not finding them at Alexandria as he had supposed, the English commander took his fleet east and resumed their search. Thus, another piece of fortune favored Napoleon and gave him the opportunity to land his troops with minimal resistance.

Within days the French captured Alexandria. Despite the extreme heat of July in Egypt and the lack of water sources for his men, Napoleon quickly divided his forces and marched south toward the Egyptian capital of Cairo. Some of his smaller vessels were also dispatched down the Nile, carrying heavy artillery. After a grueling march, the soldiers finally arrived in the vicinity of Cairo, where they fought several engagements, culminating in the decisive battle of the Pyramids that broke the resistance of the Mamluks. Although he had taken Cairo, Napoleon now had to govern the new colony and deal with persistent attacks in Upper (southern) Egypt by the remaining Mamluk and tribal leaders. Worse still, however, was the return of the British fleet on August 1 and the battle of Nile that virtually annihilated the French fleet, which had to fight from anchorage in Abuqir Bay (Cole 2007, 208–10).

Although Napoleon remained with his army for another year, his attention remained on expanding his conquests. French troops assaulted and captured the port city of Jaffa (now part of Tel Aviv) but were unable to take the Crusader defenses at the city of Acre. Lacking the ability to reinforce his army, Bonaparte gave up his campaign in Syria. He secretly returned to France in August 1799, leaving a surprised General Kléber in charge of Egypt. Bonaparte felt that more profitable enterprises were available in Europe and within a year was proclaimed first consul (Cole 2007, 243–44).

Over the next two years, the French army in Egypt faced constant attrition from invading British forces, the local Bedouin, and recurrences of disease. In 1801, the survivors were finally forced out of Egypt and given free passage back to France on British and Ottoman ships. Although their efforts were a military and political failure, they still provided the opportunity for the scholars to establish the French Egyptian Institute in Cairo and continue their work in Egypt. During that time they published a journal, *La Décade Egyptienne*, as well as a newspaper, the *Courier de L'Egypte*, which broadcasted information about the French occupation and the activities of the members of the Commission of Arts and Sciences of Egypt. Their most abiding contribution, however, was the production of field reports, reproductions of inscriptions, and scientific observations on plants, animals, and geology in a multivolume work entitled *Déscription de l'Egypte* (1809–1813).

In addition, the drawings of Napoleon, Egyptian cities, and artifacts by Dominique-Vivant Denon, who traveled throughout the Nile Valley, provided an illustrated record of these events that helped to spark continued interest in Egypt and its antiquities. In fact, among the most abiding results of Egyptomania in Europe were changes in fashion, art, and architecture, and unfortunately a nearly insatiable desire for Egyptian antiquities. The market for these items brought many adventurers like Giovanni Battista Belzoni to Egypt, whose techniques more resembled a tomb robber's than an archaeologist's.

The most remarkable discovery by a member of the Commission of Arts and Sciences was made by Pierre Bouchard, an engineer assigned to rebuilding the fortifications at Rosetta on the west bank of the Nile. In July 1799, his men uncovered a black basalt stone nearly a meter in height that contained an inscription commemorating the anniversary of the coronation of the Ptolemaic pharaoh Ptolemy V Philopator in 196 BCE. The fact that it was written in three scripts (Greek, **demotic**, and Egyptian hieroglyphs) is a reflection of the reality that "native" scripts were still important as a means of adding authority, but the pharaoh's court and his people primarily spoke and wrote in Greek. Recognized as a significant artifact, the Rosetta Stone was transported up the Nile to Cairo, where it could be studied by members of the French Institute. Various methods were employed to copy the text. These were sent to the National Institute in Paris in the spring of 1800, where they sparked a growing interest in deciphering the ancient hieroglyphs.

Of course, Egyptian hieroglyphic inscriptions had been known for centuries. The Romans had transported several massive **obelisks**, but the key to understanding their inscriptions had been lost. There is some evidence of early efforts to decipher the texts, such as a Greek translation of the script on one of these obelisks that was discovered in a German monastery in 1414. More important was the copy of Horapollon's *Hieroglyphica*, found in 1419 by the traveler Cristoforo Bundelmonti on the Greek island of Andros. Widely circulated, this text became authoritative during the Renaissance despite the fact that it treated the hieroglyphs as allegorical representations of components of nature (Solé and Valbelle 2002, 17–18).

Another step in the decipherment process was the rediscovery of **Coptic**. Coptic—written with Greek characters and a few borrowed demotic signs (a variant of the hieratic script, a cursive form of hieroglyphics)—replaced Demotic in the third century CE and served as the language of the Alexandrian Church. However, it ceased to be widely used by the end of the first millennium CE, when Arabic became the predominant language after the Islamic conquest. In 1626, Pietro della Valle, an Italian nobleman-adventurer who traveled throughout the Middle East and as far as India, brought back several Coptic manuscripts and Coptic-Arabic dictionaries. These texts became the key for German mathematician and Jesuit Athanasius Kircher's work with both Coptic and Egyptian hieroglyphs. His 1644 publication of *Lingua Aegyptiaca Restitua* contains his speculations on Valle's documents and many others. Unfortunately, he still held to a more metaphysical interpretation of the hieroglyphs, viewing them as symbols of philosophical concepts rather than as a simple means of communication. Other contributions to the early efforts at decipherment of hieroglyphs include the 1761 suggestion by Abbe Barthé-lemy (the curator of the Cabinet royal des médailles in Paris) that the oval cartouches in Egyptian inscriptions contain the names of gods and kings. Another step forward came from the suggestion in 1797 by a Danish scholar, Jörgen Zoëga, that Egyptian script includes phonetic elements and is therefore not an exclusively alphabetic script (see the chart in Solé and Valbelle 2002, 156–59).

While the company of the Commission of Arts and Sciences remained in Cairo, members of the scientific group examined the Rosetta Stone and collected and copied many other hieroglyphic inscriptions. Most important were the efforts of Jean-Joseph Marcel and Louis Rémi Raige, who focused primarily on the mathematical correlation between the Greek text and the Egyptian scripts. Their efforts were hampered by the difference in the number of lines of text (fifty-four in Greek and thirty-two in Egyptian).

In 1801 the French were forced to leave Egypt and to surrender their collection of Egyptian antiquities along with the Rosetta Stone to the victorious English. The French scientists were allowed to keep their notes, drawings, and natural history collections, but the ancient statuaries and the Rosetta Stone landed in the British Museum. Numerous scholars from several countries then went to work producing an authoritative translation of the Greek inscription. It provided remarkable administrative details of the Hellenistic pharaoh's court, but the mystery of the other two Egyptian scripts on the stone remained undecipherable. Although a clear relation between the demotic portion of the text and Coptic characters and some personal and place-names were identified, scholars (including Silvestre de Sacy and Johann David Åkerblad) made little additional progress.

Over the next twenty-five years, a spirited competition arose among scholars to accurately translate the two languages inscribed on the Rosetta Stone. As early as 1810, Jean-Francois Champollion, then just nineteen years old, entered the fray with a presentation to the French Académie delphinale; he theorized that certain hieroglyphic signs were used phonetically to transcribe the Greek foreign names in the inscription. Champollion's main competition in reaching a solution was another remarkable intellect, a practicing physician named Thomas Young, whose eclectic interests ranged from the study of optics to natural philosophy and languages. His enthusiasm for ancient Egyptian culture was increased by his examination of ancient papyri sent to him by the collector Sir William Rouse Boughton in 1814. Like Champollion and other scientists, Young was a natural code breaker; to him, the quest to decipher the hieroglyphs was irresistible (Reid 2002, 41).

During this period, Young corresponded freely with de Sacy and received helpful and frank advice as well as critiques of his findings and posited identifications of various hieroglyphic signs. A summary of his conclusions appeared in an article in the supplement volume of *Encyclopedia Britannica* in 1819. However, de Sacy seemed particularly negative in his response to Champollion's work and successfully blocked his publication of his papers on Coptic grammar in 1815. Champollion was also temporarily out of favor as the Napoleonic era drew to a close and regained his academic position only in 1819. Still, he maintained his studies and even corresponded with Young in his capacity as secretary of external affairs of the British Royal Society. He requested a comparison of the copies made of the Rosetta Stone from the French and the English.

While Young's attentions were often drawn away from work on the hieroglyphs by his medical practice and his role as secretary to both the Royal Society and the Board of Longitude, Champollion continued without interruption in his examination of all of the ancient Egyptian papyri. With this as his database, he concluded in 1821 that both hieratic and demotic script were cursive modifications of the hieroglyphic system. His proposition thus established a clear link between the hieroglyphic and other Egyptian scripts. It also confirmed the importance of including other examples of hieroglyphic inscriptions—such as those copied from the royal temple complex at Karnak—to solve the puzzle, since the Rosetta Stone contained only fourteen broken lines and a small number of personal names. When Champollion was able to identify the signs that comprised the names Ptolemy and Cleopatra in their cartouches, he was able to establish the alphabetic meaning and some of the phonetic values of Egyptian signs that were used to spell Greek and Roman names. He presented his findings on September 27, 1822, to the Académie des inscriptions et belles-lettres, although he held back on his further supposition that the phonetic Egyptian script had been used long before the Hellenistic Period (Meyerson 2004, 247–51).

Champollion followed up his initial publication with *Précis du système hiéroglyphique des anciens Éyptiens* in 1824, in which he explained that the complex signs in this writing system were intended to express both ideas and sounds. His role as the curator of the Louvre's Egyptian collection and the sixteen months of travel he spent in Egypt in 1828–1829 gave Champollion ample opportunity to collect and record additional samples of inscriptions and to test his "alphabetic" system on them. The final result, published after his death by his brother (1836–1841), is his *Grammaire égyptienne*, which contained his complete decipherment method. Still, there was a great deal of criticism by other scholars, although the next major breakthrough by Karl R. Lepsius built on Champollion's system. Lepsius' publication of the bilingual

Canopus Decree (discovered at Tanis in 1866) ended most of the controversy and laid the foundation for modern grammars of Egyptian hieroglyphs such as Alan Gardiner's published in 1927. Furthermore, his massive twelve-volume *Denkmaeler aus Aegypten und Aethiopien* (1849–1859) became the classic reference work for Egypt's monuments during the nineteenth century (Solé and Valbelle 2002, 136–37).

EGYPT'S IMPORTANCE TO THE STUDY OF ANCIENT ISRAEL

One important legacy that emerged from the work on decipherment of Egyptian texts is its contributions to biblical studies and ancient Israelite history and literature. Of course, the intent of modern archaeology is not to prove the veracity of the biblical account. However, when ancient documents or other archaeological finds add insight into what appears in the Bible, then it is possible to flesh out some of the cultural background associated with the stories about ancient Israel.

Egypt has a long history of activity in Syro-Palestine. As a land bridge between Africa and the areas of Mesopotamia and **Anatolia**, this region served as both a trade route and a buffer zone between great empires. One example of Egyptian presence in the land that eventually became Israel is the mid-fourteenth-century BCE correspondence (El Amarna texts) between the pharaohs Amenophis III and Amenophis IV (also called Akhenaten) and their local officials, including the governor of Jerusalem. These texts, however, are written in the international diplomatic language of **Akkadian** and in Mesopotamian cuneiform script. Hieroglyphic inscriptions that assist our reconstruction of ancient Israelite history actually begin with the Merneptah Stele (1207 BCE). This is a royal inscription produced for the pharaoh Merneptah celebrating his victorious campaigning in Canaan, listing various cities and peoples that he claims to have conquered. Among those listed are a people called "Israel." Since the ethnic name Israel appears here for the first time in a nonbiblical text, this provides a beginning date to recognize them as a distinct people. Some scholars think it may figure into the possible dating of the exodus event in the thirteenth century BCE. However, it should be noted that to date no Egyptian text has mentioned Israelite slaves, Moses, or any details about a mass exodus from Egypt.

Perhaps of more importance to our understanding of ancient Israelite culture is a comparison of Egyptian wisdom literature with the themes found in the books of Proverbs, Ecclesiastes, and Job. For example, the Egyptian Book of the Dead, commonly found carved or painted on tomb walls, included segments called declarations of innocence used when the deceased was confronted by the god of the underworld. A similar set of pronouncements appears in Job 31, in which the sufferer tries to clear his name and claims that the typical belief that evil actions rightly justify punishment does not apply in his case since he is innocent and righteous. There is also a rather gloomy dialogue between an Egyptian and his soul (*ka*) over whether he should commit suicide, where the soul responds to his tirade by encouraging him to not worry and to instead enjoy life (compare Eccl 3:12).

Issues of social justice often appear in ancient hieroglyphic texts as well as in the Bible. In the tale of the Eloquent Peasant, written during the Egyptian Middle Kingdom (2133–1786 BCE), the pharaoh listens to a peasant who has been robbed and cheated by a landowner in order to hear his pleas for justice. In his admonishment of current practices and his demand that the pharaoh be a true father to his people, the peasant complains that justice is impossible when judges are not impartial (compare Prov 18:5) and local officials are willing to be bribed (compare Prov 24:23-26).

It is in the writings of the Egyptian sages, however, that we find the closest ties between hieroglyphic texts and biblical wisdom literature. For instance, the Old Kingdom teacher Ptah-hotep (ca. 2500 BCE) instructs his students to abstain from envy and to be humble in their interaction with their patrons (compare Prov 23:1-3 and 15:27). They are also to be trustworthy messengers (see 25:13), and most importantly, they should be willing to take the advice of their teachers and seek wisdom even from the poor and humble (see 2:1-5). Even the literary structure of the New Kingdom, the Wisdom of Amen-em-ope, is copied by the book of Proverbs. Both contain thirty statements of wisdom and advice, and both include contrasts between the "hot-headed" (foolish) and the "cool-headed" (wise) man. There are also commonsense admonitions such as being grateful for what the gods provide (compare 16:8) and not taking counsel from fools (compare 14:7). Legal maxims are also common in these texts, stating that the wise man does not bear false witness (compare 14:5), or steal from the poor (compare 22:22), or remove boundary markers from a field (compare 22:28).

Despite being lost to our understanding for millennia, when the hieroglyphic script was finally deciphered by Champollion and his scholarly successors, the accomplishments of ancient Egypt once again could be studied and appreciated. Furthermore, when scholars and the archaeological authorities of the countries where these antiquities were found realized the importance of preserving our cultural heritage, the age of treasure seekers and collectors was curtailed. Today, although the trade in antiquities continues, the force of law and public opinion has put a premium on learning all we can through careful examination and preservation of the artifacts that emerge from scientific excavations.

Early Explorers, Adventures, Academics, and Visionaries in the Holy Land

A variety of factors contributed to the expansion of archaeological work in Palestine during the nineteenth century. They include the decline of the Ottoman Empire's control over the various areas of the Middle East, possibly accelerated by Napoleon's invasion of Egypt and Syro-Palestine. In addition, the emergence of the Industrial Revolution in Europe and attendant desire to locate sources of raw materials and protect markets for manufactured goods played a part in this expansion, as did a growing wave of missionary work by Christian Evangelical groups (Chapman 1991, 209–11). Archaeology as a science is rooted in antiquarian interests in the past. That interest was fed by the reports of traveler/adventurers like Pietro della Valle (1586–1652), an Italian nobleman who traveled extensively in the Middle East, Persia, and India. His diaries and letters as well as the manuscripts and artifacts that he brought back with him helped to create the climate for exploring and, unfortunately, looting the ancient sites associated with the Bible and the civilizations of the ancient Near East. Travel literature from the nineteenth century continues to embrace the religious-mystical perception of the Holy Land and its major sites, including Jerusalem. These people found it hard to separate their concept of Palestine as a God-sanctified region and its physical reality as the home to a succession of peoples and cultures.

Early efforts to explore the Middle East are also dominated by antiquarianism, which was centered on collecting data and objects rather than the classification of artifacts or scientific analysis of excavations. Initially, the artifacts collected were not typed according to their provenance or stratigraphy within the site where they were found. They were seldom studied as sources of information themselves but were instead treated as objects of art or sources for historical reconstruction without attention to the people who created them or their relation to other, similar finds. That attitude changed with the mid-nineteenth-century creation of organizations like the Palestine Exploration Fund, whose aim was to engage in more systematic research and to ask questions about the materials being discovered within their social context. The records of the PEF contain a rich data set of documents recording geographic surveys of Palestine and its regions and cities as well as the efforts of a number of early explorers. Another organization responsible in part for the growing interest and body of information on the Middle East is the American Board of Commissioners for Foreign Missions, founded in 1810 as the first organized missionary society in the United States. While its scope was international and included Asian and Pacific Islands missionary work, the voluminous letters of the missionaries became fundamental sources for the history of the various places where the board operated.

Politics and Control of the Holy Land, 1800–1860s

Although nominally under the rule of the Ottoman Empire, Syro-Palestine in the first three decades of the nineteenth century was full of turmoil characterized by local tribal uprisings and petty feuds between local sheikhs. Both European and American travelers braved these conditions, many times by flying under the radar and in some cases wearing native dress to avoid being identified as foreigners or to defuse charges of colonial exploitation. In fact, a remarkable group of adventurers and scientists took up the challenge of exploring the Middle East. Their discoveries and records provided a foundation for more systematic efforts in later periods.

In the same year that the Egyptian antiquities discovered by Napoleon's group of scientists were ceded to the British (1801), an English scholar named Edward Daniel Clarke arrived in Egypt and assisted General Hutchinson in determining the most noteworthy of these confiscated objects to be transported to England. An inveterate traveler, Clarke subsequently journeyed throughout Palestine with an entourage of armed guards. While initially determined to seek out sites mentioned in the Bible, Clarke quickly broke with the tradition of following pilgrim routes. He took copious notes on what he encountered and along the way applied scientific principles to the task of site identification, refusing to blindly accept the judgments of local priests or ecclesiastical authority. Although some of his conclusions were flawed, he set the tone for future detailed evaluation of the evidence and the inclusion of various scientific pursuits by explorers, including cataloguing plant life and doing mineralogical studies. In 1810, he published the first volume of his travels and eventually produced five more (Silberman 1982, 18–20).

Another remarkable explorer who traveled through the Middle East in the period just after Napoleon's incursion was the German scholar Ulrich Seetzen. Lacking Clarke's resources, Seetzen realized that he could accomplish very little by traveling as a European explorer. Instead he spent time learning Arabic and adopted the native garb of the regions where he traveled in the guise of Musa el-Hakim. Although he had little money to pursue his many interests, Seetzen soon raised funds by gathering antiquities that he sent back to the Gotha Museum in Germany and to the Russian court of Alexander I. During his travels he copied many Greek, Hebrew, Latin, and Arabic inscriptions; his diaries became an invaluable source of information on landscape features, animals, plants, and the customs of the villagers and sheikhs that he encountered. His drawings and maps provided helpful illustrations of his experiences. Between 1802 and his death in 1811, Seetzen traveled throughout Palestine,

Syria, the Sinai, Egypt, and Arabia. In many cases, he was the first European since the time of the Crusaders to visit or explore sites such as the coast of the Dead Sea, areas of the Upper Galilee, including the site of Caesarea Philippi (Banias), and the ruins of the **Decapolis** cities of Jerash and Philadelphia in Jordan. He even made a pilgrimage to Mecca in his guise as a devout Muslim. Unfortunately, the majority of his diaries and papers were not published until the 1850s. However, a small pamphlet was published describing his travels in Palestine and Jordan, and it at least gave impetus to other explorers.

Among those whose interest was sparked by Seetzen's discoveries was John Burckhardt (1784–1817), a Swiss expatriate who came to England to study and became one of Edward Daniel Clarke's students. His original intent was to explore the interior of the African continent for a new trade route, but he first went to Aleppo in Syria in spring 1809 to study Arabic so that he could work in disguise as an Arab trader. His preparations continued for two more years, during which he traveled extensively from his base in Syria, visiting the site of Caesarea Philippi and the **Golan Heights** region as

FIGURE 3-5. *Petra was built by the Nabateans in the first century BCE. It was originally a center of rock-cut tombs, which the Romans later made into a city.*

well as the Orontes Valley and mountains of Lebanon. In 1812, he traveled south to Tiberias in the Galilee region, and to Nazareth (where he met and influenced Lady Hester Stanhope). Then, in disguise as Sheikh Ibrahim ibn Abdullah, he accompanied an Arab caravan south down the Jordan Valley to the eastern side of the Dead Sea, where he visited Kerak and its Crusader castle. Along the way, he heard from his companions about the ancient city of Petra. This important site had dominated the trade routes from Saudi Arabia to Transjordan during the late Hellenistic and early Roman Empire period, but its location had been lost after the Islamic conquest and the emergence of new powers in the region. Burckhardt, avoiding attacks from Bedouin raiders, eventually found his way there and reopened it to explorers and archaeologists (Chapman 1991, 212).

The next of these nineteenth-century contributors to the exploration of Palestine and its archaeological sites was a well-connected, ambitious romantic, Lady Hester Stanhope. The granddaughter of William Pitt the Elder and niece of William Pitt the Younger, she played hostess for her prime minister uncle until his death. In 1810 she broke her ties with English society and found a new home and a new purpose in the Middle East. One of the most intrepid adventurers of her age, she fearlessly led a caravan across the Syrian Desert to the ancient city of Palmyra and was entertained by sheikhs who had been a danger to other travelers. So remarkable was her appearance and manner that she was given the title of "Star of the Morning" by the Bedouin. Eventually, she established a huge estate in the mountains of Lebanon, where she exercised some influence over that turbulent region's politics.

Among her accomplishments was what could be termed the first focused excavation undertaken in Palestine. Some would say that her interests in archaeology were tinged with personal desire for fame and the prospect (based on an ancient manuscript brought to her by Franciscan monks) of a hoard of gold buried in the ruins of the ancient Philistine city of Ashkelon. While she could not obtain assistance from the British government, Lady Stanhope was able to play on the cupidity of the Ottoman officials. As a result, her expedition included a representative of the Ottoman government as well as the pasha (governor or lord) of the nearby port city of Jaffa, Muhammad Abu Nabbut. With hundreds of hired workers, the excavation quickly turned up a magnificent but headless statue of a Roman emperor. However, this huge artifact proved to be the only major find during several weeks of work. Realizing that even this single artifact might encourage looting of the site and not wanting to be accused of being a "typical" European plunderer of antiquities, she ordered the statue destroyed. Ironically, Abu Nabbut took the opportunity to gather tons of marble and carved building stones from the site to decorate the palaces he was then constructing in Jaffa. Lady Stanhope, disappointed with this attempt and foiled in her dreams of fame, retreated to her Lebanese fortress and to local politics (Silberman 1984).

During the 1820s, American Protestant missionaries (many of them graduates of Andover Seminary in Massachusetts), with the assistance of the American Board of Commissioners for Foreign Missions, attempted to make inroads in Jerusalem and the Holy Land. Their efforts, however, were quickly stopped by the opposition of the pope as well as the Ottoman sultan. Even more damaging to their initial work were the effects of the Greek war for independence, which resulted in the expulsion of the Turks from Greece after 1827 and the capture of Palestine and Syria by the pasha of Egypt, who took advantage of the weakened sultan. Starting in the 1830s, these missionaries redoubled their efforts to convert Muslims and Jews. Among those sent to explore mission possibilities in parts of the Ottoman Empire was the linguist Eli Smith. In 1830–1832, he traveled with Harrison Dwight from Constantinople southeast to Armenia. The record of their journeys both provided valuable information on the people and villages of that area and indicated to the commissioners that further efforts would be worthwhile. On his return to Beirut, Smith and Homan Hallock worked to create an American Arabic typeface that would be adapted to their printing press and used to produce for the first time Arabic-language Bibles, hymnbooks, catechisms, and examples of Arabic literature (Stoddard 2009, 214).

Smith's ability as a translator also assisted his former teacher and traveling companion Edward Robinson during two trips to Palestine. They were a formidable team. Robinson was an extraordinary biblical scholar who is often esteemed as the first American archaeologist and one of the preeminent biblicists of his time. He translated Greek and Hebrew grammars and **lexicons** by German scholars (Georg Winer and Wilhelm Gesenius), in addition to laying the foundation for seminary education that required biblical languages as well as a working knowledge of biblical geography (Dearman 1991, 165–67). But it was Smith's facility with Arabic and his knowledge of the Levant and its people that guided them in their travels.

Initially, Robinson's desire to more critically study the Bible and his travels with Smith were intended to serve the theological agenda of the New England Congregationalists and to prove the literal truth of the biblical account. As part of that pursuit, he and Smith met in Cairo in 1837 with the intent of retracing the route of the exodus, visiting Jerusalem and various sites in Samaria and the Galilee. Their travels on camels and mules were aided to an extent by the strict control exercised by the Egyptian pasha over Palestine and its caravan routes. However, they quickly ceased to be pilgrims bound merely to visit traditional sacred sites. Instead, they viewed scattered ruins and settlement sites with a more trained eye based on their knowledge of the biblical text and the work

FIGURE 3-6. *The Western Wall of Herod's Temple Mount and Robinson's Arch. Robinson realized that the stones protruding out from the Western Wall were part of an original, monumental staircase.*

of the first-century Jewish historian Josephus. Moreover, as they traveled from place to place, Smith would call on the local sheikh and villagers and ask them the names of local hills, streams, valleys, and ruins. In this way they built up a database of place-names that assisted them with making identifications of over one hundred biblical cities and ancient sites through comparison with their modern Arabic names and geographic location (Stoddard 2009, 218).

While Robinson was disappointed with the sorry state of the country, its endemic diseases, and its impoverished villages, he found Jerusalem filled with rich possibilities for discovery. He identified the massive platform upon which the al-Aqsa mosque stood as the foundation of Herod's Temple and noted a number of associated architectural features, including what became known as "Robinson's Arch." The publication of *Biblical Researches in Palestine, Mount Sinai, and Arabia Petraea* (1841) provided critical accounts of Robinson's and Smith's finds and site identifications, a massive amount of detail on the physical geography of the land, and incisive descriptions that benefitted the next wave of scholars and explorers (King 1975).

It should also be noted that the public's interest in the Middle East, its peoples, and its association with the Bible was also increased through the publication of a beautiful set of **lithographs** in 1842 by the British artist David Roberts. Traveling through the Near East in 1839, he sketched in the field 123 lithographs depicting not only holy sites and shrines but the common villagers and pilgrims that he encountered. The romantic character of his portrayals, many times enhanced from his imagination to create a more pleasant or interesting scene, caught the imagination of the public and contributed to the growing desire to know more about a region that Napoleon's invasion had restored to the public consciousness.

During the mid-nineteenth century, European and American scholars were assisted by yet another shift in the political landscape in Syro-Palestine. With the help of his European allies, Sultan Abdülmecid I drove the Egyptian pasha out of the region in 1841, and subsequently European consulates were installed in Jerusalem in order to assist scholars, mapmakers, commercial agents, and explorers to penetrate the country more freely. While the motivation to prove the truth of Bible through exploration remained a high priority for Christians, the desire to navigate and chart a new trade route from Syria to the Gulf of Aqaba and on to the Indian Ocean led to several expeditions down the Jordan River to the Dead Sea. None succeeded until an audacious American navy lieutenant named William Francis Lynch made his attempt in 1848. In addition to making preparations that included collapsible metal boats, specially made harnesses, and a team of well-armed sailors, Lynch also tied his effort to the work of previous American explorers by having his men meet with Edward Robinson at Union Seminary in New York and with Eli Smith in his mission headquarters in Beirut.

To deal with the danger of attack along the way, Lynch hired a local Bedouin chief (Aqil Agha) and his men to accompany them. With their forces divided between the metal boats on the Jordan River and a land force paralleling the river course, the sailors traveled for eight days collecting plant and geological specimens while producing an accurate chart of the river's many twists and turns. In essence their journey demonstrated that the Jordan River could never serve as a commercial link. Despite this daunting reality, Lynch drove his exhausted men to continue their efforts, circumnavigating the Dead Sea, plumbing its depths, and mapping the sources of several freshwater springs like that at Ein Gedi. Sickness prevented the completion of the task of determining the sources of the Jordan River in the Galilee. Lynch's reports and his publication of an account of the expedition added to the continuing interest in exploring the Holy Land and sparked the work of a number of prominent scholars, including Robinson and Smith, during the 1850s (Lewis 1992).

Curiously, the traditional sacred sites in Palestine that Robinson disdained as having no historical value became a new factor in the continuing development of biblical archaeology. The competition between the ecclesiastical leaders of the Greek/Russian Orthodox and the Roman Catholic Churches rose to a fever pitch over who should control and protect Christian shrines such as the Church of the Nativity in Bethlehem. This competition contributed to the Crimean War between Russia and France and France's ally England. When Russia was defeated, the Roman Catholic claims to sacred Christian shrines were strengthened, and France redoubled its efforts to join the teams of scholars engaged in exploring the Holy Land sites.

Most prominent among the French explorers was an artillery officer and amateur archaeologist named Louis Félicien de Saulcy. During a trip to Jerusalem in 1851, he opened excavations among the ruins outside the city known as the Tombs of the Kings and promptly proclaimed them the tombs of ancient Israelite kings. His efforts produced fragments of **sarcophagi** and other artifacts that were subsequently sent to the Louvre and added to his growing fame. Unfortunately, his methods there and in his exploration of the Dead Sea, where he quickly "identified" the location of the destroyed cities of Sodom and Gomorrah, were more like those of tomb raiders than scholars. A subsequent expedition in 1863 produced another sarcophagus that he claimed to be that of Hezekiah's queen but in fact was the tomb of Queen Helene of Adiabene, who lived in the first century CE. Outrage by the Jewish community over the desecration of tombs led to an end to his work, as a remarkable amount of damage had been done to the sites and to the scientific analysis of the artifacts that he quickly carried with him out of the country (Silberman 1982, 66–72).

It is curious that so much effort was put into validating the claims of the traditional sacred sites in Jerusalem. For example, one of the most heated arguments during the 1860s centered on whether the Church of the Holy Sepulcher was indeed the site of the crucifixion and burial of Jesus. Interest in it was sparked by the 1864 publication of *Jerusalem Explored* by an Italian engineer named Ermete Pierotti. (While Pierotti's collection of data, maps, and photographs amassed during his repair of the water system of the Haram ash-Sharif was of great importance, some of it was eventually proven to have been fabricated or overly imaginative. Still, it gave support to the position heralded by the British clergyman George Williams that the massive platform was indeed the vestige of Herod's Temple.)

Of course, the Catholic and Orthodox Church officials in the city derived a great deal of prestige and wealth from pilgrim visitors to the traditional site of the Church of the Holy Sepulcher. As a result, the alternative suggestion by the British merchant and architect James Ferguson that the true site of Jesus' burial was the Dome of the Rock atop the Haram ash-Sharif led to a celebrated scholarly battle as the various proponents engaged in literary salvos in the *London Times*. While Ferguson and Pierotti sparred and garnered a great deal of attention, a more important and long-lasting result was the survey of Jerusalem and the underground cisterns and water system beneath the Haram ash-Sharif that was conducted by Captain Charles Wilson, a member of the Royal Engineers, in 1864.

Unconcerned with previous explorers' desire to engage in biblical archaeology, Wilson's careful topographical survey of the city provided a better sense of the occupational character of Jerusalem in previous periods. In addition, his unprecedented exploration of the underground sewer system that dated back to the time of Herod's construction of the temple platform demonstrated the existence of over eighty feet of occupational deposits in the vicinity of the platform. There were also a number of architectural features that were tied to the temple's entry ways and its role in first-century Jerusalem. With such hard data secured by scientific techniques, the climate was now ripe for the creation of a learned society to sponsor and promote future discoveries. The Palestine Exploration Society, under the royal patronage of Queen Victoria, was established in 1865, with the intention of investigating "the Archaeology, Geography, Geology, and Natural History of Palestine." Of course, it was also intended as a fund-raising agency and an official British institution that could successfully compete with French efforts in the Middle East (Silberman 1992, 82–87).

FIGURE 3-7. *Early twentieth-century photo of Jerusalem from Mt. Scopus.*

The stage was set for a new era in the exploration of the countries and the remains associated with the narratives in the Bible. Biblical archaeology began to slip from the grasp of treasure hunters, fame seekers, and art collectors. Still, it would be several more decades before archaeological excavations would become truly scientific expeditions employing careful and systematic examination of site stratification and artifactual analysis. However, the work of Charles Wilson and the scholarly umbrella of the Palestine Exploration Society and later the American Schools of Oriental Research created a foundation for the next stage in the development of archaeological research and the dissemination of its discoveries.

Suggestions for Further Reading

Pompeii and Herculaneum have captured the imaginations of succeeding generations of Europeans for centuries, and Americans belatedly followed them. Works dealing with the cities and the art, architecture, and other finds discovered within them abound and are too numerous to list. Two books worth reading are Marcel Brion's *Pompeii and Herculaneum: The Glory and the Grief* (1973) and Guy de La Bedoyere's *Cities of Roman Italy* (2010). Students interested in further detail about how the excavations at these sites shaped the nascent field of archaeology could read Göran Blix's *From Paris to Pompeii: French Romanticism and the Culture Politics of Archaeology* (2009) and Christopher Parslow's *Rediscovering Antiquity: Karl Weber and the Excavation of Herculaneum, Pompeii, and Stabiae*, which focuses specifically on Karl Weber and his work.

The impact of Napoleon's invasion of Egypt receives different yet insightful treatments from Nina Burleigh's *Mirage: Napoleon's Scientists and the Unveiling of Egypt*, Juan Cole's *Napoleon's Egypt: Invading the Middle East*, and Donald Reid's *Whose Pharaohs? Archaeology, Museums, and Egyptian National Identity from Napoleon to World War I*. The decipherment of the Rosetta Stone is handled exquisitely in *The Rosetta Stone: The Story of the Decoding of Hieroglyphics* by Robert Solé and Dominique Valbelle.

For the exploration of the Holy Land itself, consult Neil Silberman's engaging study *Digging for God and Country*.

4

"BIBLE LANDS ARCHAEOLOGY" AND "BIBLICAL ARCHAEOLOGY" IN THE NINETEENTH AND EARLY TWENTIETH CENTURIES

Rachel Hallote

This chapter will describe the two different ways that early archaeologists and biblical scholars first explored the physical remains associated with the Bible. The first and more celebrated of the two approaches was known as "Bible lands archaeology." In this approach, archaeologists focused on sites in Mesopotamia (Iraq) that were mentioned in the Bible. Mesopotamia was considered an even more important biblical land than Israel for reasons big and small; not only had Abraham migrated from the city of Ur (in southern Iraq), but more significantly the conquerors of both Israel and Judah were from Mesopotamia. When archaeologists first excavated the palaces of the great Assyrian kings Sargon and Sennacherib—the rulers who had destroyed the monarchy in Samaria and all but ended the dynasty of King David's descendants in Jerusalem—it was considered the first external proof that the Bible was true. Bible lands archaeology ultimately led to some academic disciplines that are still areas of research today: Assyriology (which is the study of the languages of Mesopotamia) and Mesopotamian archaeology.

The second approach to finding physical remains relating to the Bible took place in Ottoman Palestine and was known as "biblical archaeology." This approach focused on the few archaeological remains of Ottoman Palestine that seemed to date to the time of the Old and New Testaments. Unlike Iraq—with its vast ruined cities whose outlines were still easily visible in the nineteenth-century landscape and appealed to "Bible lands" scholars—Ottoman Palestine had very few visible ruins that predated the Greek period. In fact, to many scholars, biblical archaeology did not seem particularly fruitful. Very little of interest was visible on the surface of the ground in Palestine, and the country itself was often difficult to navigate and considered dangerous for travelers. For these reasons, it took much longer—at least half a century longer—for the scholarly community to embrace biblical archaeology, since the archaeology of Iraq (Bible lands) was so much more exciting by comparison. And yet, by the middle of the twentieth century, biblical archaeology had developed into a modern discipline. Today it goes by a variety of names, including the "archaeology of the Levant," "Syro-Palestinian archaeology," and the "archaeology of Canaan and Israel." Sometimes the older term "biblical archaeology" is still used.

We will begin by telling the story of the "archaeology of Bible lands" and then discuss the development of "biblical archaeology."

The Archaeology of Bible Lands

CUNEIFORM AND ITS DECIPHERMENT: NIEBUHR, GROTEFEND, RICH, RAWLINSON, AND HINCKS

Interest in elucidating the Bible was not the only motivation for excavating the mounds of Iraq. Another impetus was Western curiosity about lost languages and cultures. The cultures and writings of ancient Greece and Rome had always been valued and studied in Europe, even during the Middle Ages, when classical texts were still copied in monasteries and emerging universities. Classical antiquity was valued even more highly during the Renaissance and the Enlightenment periods, when proficiency in Greek, Latin, and sometimes even Hebrew (as the language of the Old Testament) was prized. The emphasis on ancient languages, and the possibility of finding and deciphering a new lost ancient language, sent Europeans adventurers to Iraq to find texts.

For centuries, Europeans had been aware of the existence of a wedge-shaped (cuneiform) ancient writing system of the East. Occasionally, some fragments of small-scale inscriptions would reach Europe as exotic souvenirs of Oriental travels. By the seventeenth century, British travelers especially had traveled through Persia (often en route to India for the British East India Company), and some had stopped to see the massive ruins of Persepolis and noted the cuneiform inscriptions visible on the cliffs there. Some inscriptions were even copied and published in England. But it was not until the eighteenth century that serious interest in these inscriptions began, thanks to the travels of German-born Carsten Niebuhr, who, like earlier Western travelers, visited Persepolis.

Niebuhr's story is unusual even in the annals of travelers. While still a young man, Niebuhr, who had already expressed interest in the East and studied Arabic, had the opportunity to join an expedition to the East financed by the king of Denmark, Frederick V. The expedition left Europe in 1761 and headed through Egypt and Arabia to, finally, India. But, one by one, Niebuhr's colleagues all got sick and died, until Niebuhr, the most junior and inexperienced member of the expedition, was left on his own in India. All alone, he made his way back from Bombay to Europe, traveling overland through Persia. It was there that he came across the ruins of Persepolis and noted the inscription carved at the site.

But unlike the few Europeans who had seen this inscription previously, Niebuhr sketched full copies of the cuneiform and brought the images back with him to Europe. Even more remarkably, Niebuhr also made an attempt to figure out what this inscription was. Specifically, he recognized that the inscription was trilingual—that is, contained three distinct versions of cuneiform. The first of these turned out to be Old Persian, the language of the Achaemenid Empire, which ruled Persia in the sixth through fourth centuries BCE. The Achemenids were already well known to Westerners from Greek historical accounts, notably Herodotus' *Persian Wars*. This Old Persian inscription from Persepolis would soon become an important key to decipherment of cuneiform, as forms of Persian were (and are) still known and spoken. The other two languages on the Persepolis inscription turned out to be Akkadian and Sumerian.

In spite of his correct guess that this was a trilingual inscription, Niebuhr could not read it at all. It was another scholar—the German philologist Georg Friedrich Grotefend, a schoolmaster in Gottingen and later Frankfurt who taught Latin and Italian—who was the first to have some success at real decipherment.

Grotefend never traveled to Persian or Iraq himself, but he devoted his career to studying Niebuhr's copies. Grotefend used Greek inscriptions as his starting point, as these often repeated formulaic phrases (specifically "great king" and "king of kings") within their texts. Greek inscriptions would also note dynastic information in their formulas, pointing out when a king was the son of the previous king. Since the names and dynasties of some of the more famous Persian kings were known from Greek history, Grotefend supposed that perhaps these same dynasties might be mentioned in the Persepolis inscription. He also hoped that the Persepolis inscription was formulaic like the Greek ones, and he hoped to find phrases like "king X, son of king Y"—a reasonable hypothesis as one particular word in cuneiform seemed to be repeated many times. He guessed that the often-repeated word might be "king" and also guessed that the well-known names of Xerxes and Darius appeared in these inscriptions. His approach was successful, and he published his largely correct translations in 1802.

Very soon after Grotefend's translations were published, it became clear that the monumental reliefs in Persia were not the only places with inscriptions in cuneiform, as other smaller-scale inscriptions began to trickle into Europe. One collection in particular caught the imagination of scholars—this was the collection of Claudius Rich, who served as the British consul in Egypt and also worked for the British East India Company. Together with his wife, Mary (who kept a detailed journal), Rich traveled throughout the East from 1804 until his death from cholera in 1821. While traveling through northern Iraq near Mosul, Rich had sketched some of the ruins of the mounds of Kuyunjik, which was already known to be Nineveh of the Bible (see below). He also visited Babylon in southern Iraq and brought back cylinder seals inscribed in cuneiform (Sayce 1908, 8–9; Lloyd 1947, 15–72).

After Rich's death, his wife brought his collection of antiquities back to London and ultimately donated it to the British Museum. The artifacts with cuneiform inscriptions were displayed in the museum from 1825 forward, and, while they remained undeciphered, they made the scholarly community aware of the fact that there was much more to be learned in Iraq (not just Persia) about the great biblical civilizations of Assyria and Babylonia. Rich's smaller-scale inscriptions, on top of Niebuhr's accurate copies of the Persepolis inscription and Grotefend's decipherment, allowed other scholars to speculate on how to best approach this civilization.

This is where the story of decipherment—and the study of ancient writing in general—becomes fully dependent on the story of archaeology. The existence of Rich's collection was just the beginning point. In order to decipher the cuneiform, linguists needed more material, and it was only excavations that could bring it to them. Therefore, as we describe the unprecedented deciphering career of Henry Rawlinson, it is necessary to remember that his linguistic work was entirely dependent on the discoveries of the archaeologist Austen Henry Layard, whose excavations at many key sites of Assyria will be outlined in more detail below.

The scholar who made the greatest leaps forward in decipherment was Henry Rawlinson. Rawlinson is largely famous for his successes at decipherment, but he was also an intrepid explorer. Unlike some of the other early figures noted above, Rawlinson's interest in ancient inscriptions stemmed not from a classical education but rather from his army career as an officer with the British East India Company, which sent him to India in 1827. While in India, he distinguished himself by learning several languages, including Persian, which was why in 1833 he was stationed in Persia, where he remained until 1839. In Persia, Rawlinson lived in the village of Kermanshah, close to a high cliff known as Bisutun Rock (often referred to as Behistun), where there was an inscription. In his spare time, he would examine the inscription on the cliff, making the dangerous climb to its top. He understood immediately that he was dealing with a trilingual inscription (written in three different forms of cuneiform) but that only one of them was in the same language as Niebuhr's Persepolis trilingual inscription—this was Old Persian. While he did not know it yet, the other two languages on the rock were Elamite and Babylonian. He painstakingly made copies of all three columns, although the Babylonian inscription was difficult to copy because of where it was positioned on the rock. This caused problems that impeded his deciphering it in later years.

Rawlinson utilized many of the same methodologies as Grotefend, similarly guessing at names of Persian kings that were known from Greek historical material. Throughout this period, he was in touch by letter with the archaeologist Austen Henry Layard, who was actively digging up new inscriptions (see below), as well as with other European scholars. But Rawlinson was largely reluctant to share his unfinished results with the world (and was later criticized for that). Starting in 1839, he began to publish small bits and pieces, but then he was sent back to India, next to Afghanistan, and finally to Baghdad in 1843. All this slowed his decipherment process even more, although, once he was in Baghdad, he made a second trip to Behistun to see the inscription again and make a better copy.

Even Rawlinson's early publications moved the discipline forward. By 1840 he had deciphered the alphabetic symbols of the Old Persian inscriptions and had managed to read all the names and titles of the Persian king Darius. And by the time he returned to England in the 1850s, he had made major strides and began to present his work to scholarly societies. One of Rawlinson's great leaps was to understand that cuneiform was usually (but not always) syllabic in nature. Once he understood this (and with rock inscriptions as well as **bas-reliefs**, inscribed bricks, and later tablets from sites in Assyria at his disposal), he was able to decipher the names of some of the key Assyrian kings, including Sennacherib and Sargon—the very ones mentioned in the Bible. He even found he could read the Assyrian corroborating material regarding the siege of Judah that was discussed in the Bible.

And yet, for all his work, Rawlinson never fully managed to decipher the Babylonian script from Behistun. This was done by one of his competitors, Edward Hincks. Hincks was an Irish minister who never traveled to the Orient and rather relied on copies of inscriptions brought back by others. Hincks had taught himself several languages and had been intrigued by the decipherment of the Rosetta Stone by Champollion in 1823. He had long been working on Niebuhr's Old Persian inscriptions, steadily deciphering parts of them, and then began to work on the inscriptions the archaeologist Layard was sending back from Nimrud and later Kuyunjik.

Thanks to this plethora of material, Hincks figured out some of the more nuanced problems of cuneiform languages. Hincks realized that, unlike the alphabetic Old Persian columns from the Persepolis and Behistun inscriptions, some of the other languages represented were syllabic (a conclusion that Rawlinson had come to as well), and he also understood a further complexity—that a single sign could be read in more than one way, depending on determinatives added into the text. Rawlinson never fully made this leap.

Thus, by the later 1850s, it seemed that cuneiform was largely deciphered, in large part due to the work of Rawlinson and Hincks. This is why, in 1857, the

Royal Asiatic Society of London decided to test the results of these scholars, to see if they were really able to read the texts, or if they had each come up with an independent system that would not correspond to the others. The Royal Asiatic Society chose four scholars to participate: Rawlinson and Hincks as well as two others working on material (Julius Oppert and Henry Talbot). Each man was given a copy of the same text—an eleventh-century Assyrian inscription that no one had worked on previously, and each set about translating it independently. When finished, the translations had small discrepancies but were essentially the same. This proved to the scholars of the Royal Asiatic Society—and to the world—that the languages of Mesopotamia were finally and truly unlocked.

Throughout European scholarly circles, public excitement over the decipherment was enormous, and it was not just because of the linguistic feat. The public reacted with such excitement because the cuneiform languages were seen as a key to finding external proof that the Bible was true—these were the languages and texts of the conquerors of Israel and Judah, and, sooner or later, texts would be found that discussed the Bible directly.

Excavating "Bible Lands" in Iraq: Botta and Layard at Nineveh and Khorsabad

Early in the decipherment process, it became imperative to have as many inscriptions as possible to work with. This need for inscriptions, as well as curiosity about the cities of the biblical conquerors, is what fueled the first archaeological excavations in Iraq.

The birth of archaeology was very much intertwined with the politics and economics of the British Empire in the nineteenth century. We have seen how the collection of Claudius Rich, given to the British Museum, inspired scholars to learn more about Mesopotamian antiquities. Rich was able to put together his collection only because he was stationed in Mosul while working for the British East India Company. Most interestingly, Rich was one of the first Westerners to rediscover ancient Nineveh, the capital of the Assyrians known so well from the Bible.

The city of Mosul, where Rich was stationed, is in northern Iraq at the edge of the Tigris River. Half a century before Rich, Niebuhr had been to Mosul on his journey back to Europe, and he had noted the large ruins that stood across the river from the town and attempted to make a sketch of these. Rich had the opportunity to examine them more closely.

As M. T. Larsen (1994) has pointed out, the locals called the ruins by the name Nuniyeh. These ruins were huge and were enclosed by long mounds that were understood as ancient walls. Within the walls were two distinct mounds. The northern one was sometimes called Calat Nuniyeh (and sometimes Kuyunjik), and the smaller one was sometimes called Nebi Yunis, meaning the burial place of Jonah of the Bible. The few Westerners who had passed through Mosul in the past had understood Kuyunjik to be the ruins of ancient Nineveh—and the name Nineveh was clearly preserved in the name Nuniyeh.

Rich examined the ruins of Nineveh closely, both Kuyunjik and Nebi Yunis, measuring and drawing them accurately, although he never thought to excavate them. His descriptions and drawings and the fairly secure identification of the site gave a head start to the two men whose names are so directly associated with the archaeology of Assyria—Paul Emile Botta and Austen Henry Layard.

Both Botta and Layard began their work in 1843. Botta was a French diplomat stationed in Iraq, and Layard was a young British gentleman traveling through the East, ostensibly en route to a post in India. In Mosul, each became deeply interested in the visible yet unexplored remains of biblical Nineveh.

Botta, who was born in Italy but grew up in France, had studied language and history but also natural history and botany, and he trained as a physician. In 1824, he worked as a ship's physician, and soon thereafter he went to Egypt as a military physician and also traveled elsewhere in the Middle East. Ultimately, his experience led him to a government appointment as French consul at Mosul (Larsen 1994). In Mosul, he saw the mounds of Nuniyeh across the river and understood that the many ceramic remains, bricks, and other markings with cuneiform that he saw throughout the town (and that were often offered for sale by the locals) had originated at Nebi Yunis and Kuyunjik. Finally, in 1842, he tried to investigate Nebi Yunis himself but was hampered by the mosque there, and soon thereafter he decided to excavate Kuyunjik—hoping to find evidence that indeed it was ancient biblical Nineveh.

Botta excavated at Kuyunjik for the better part of a year but found few remains that he considered significant, nothing very large, and no significant inscriptions. He gave up on the mound at that point because he had heard about another mound several miles to the north called Khorsabad. Locals had told him that many inscribed bricks came from Khorsabad, so he went to excavate there instead. As soon as he started, he began to uncover massive architecture—grand Assyrian palaces just below the surface. In later years, it became clear that Khorsabad was ancient Dur Sharrukin (City of Sargon), the capital of the great Assyrian king Sargon II. Botta worked at Khorsabad for many months, in spite of difficulties. The most famous difficulty that he faced was the interference of the local pasha, who thought that Botta's workmen were digging for gold and then began to imprison them to stop any gold removal. This misunderstanding about Western motivations to dig was not uncommon as archaeology took off in Eastern countries.

Although Botta had abandoned Kuyunjik for Khorsabad, it was not abandoned for long. The main Kuyunjik excavations were undertaken by Austen Henry Layard. Trained in London in his uncle's law firm but interested in history, Layard traveled in 1839 to India, where he was meant to have a position as a lawyer. However, Layard's real interests were in seeing the mounds of Assyria and Persia. Thanks to the copious journals and travelogues Layard wrote, we know about his many adventures in the East, including his involvements with warring Bedouin tribes. After several years of traveling, he headed back to Constantinople, hoping to find employment with the British ambassador, Stratford Canning, rather than return to London. Canning hired him as an unofficial advisor. After hearing about Botta's successes at Khorsabad, Canning was willing to send Layard out to excavate a mound himself, but ultimately the British Museum took over the funding of the excavations.

FIGURE 4-1. *Austen Henry Layard excavated ancient Nimrud, an important city in ancient Assyria.*

FIGURE 4-2. *Frontispiece from Layard's 1849 book on his excavations. It depicts the moment when the Winged Bulls were about to be packed for transport.*

The mound Layard explored was called Nimrud by the locals (later identified with ancient Calah). Layard began to uncover Assyrian palaces as soon as he began digging at Nimrud, finding numerous bas-reliefs and a giant guardian figure placed at a doorway, with the body of a bull, wings, and a human head (these figures have since been identified as the protective deities known as *lamassu*, and many were found in Assyrian palaces).

Among the finds Layard made after he had been working at Nimrud for about a year was a large **stele** made of dark stone and covered with inscriptions and carved scenes, which came to be known as the **Black Obelisk** (see Figure 14-8). Of course, when Layard first excavated it, cuneiform was not yet deciphered, but, once the process of decipherment had advanced, it became clear that the Black Obelisk commemorated the victories of King Shalmaneser, a name familiar from the Bible. Phenomenally, one of the scenes on the obelisk actually depicts an individual known by name from the Bible—King Jehu of Israel, well known from the second book of Kings (9–10). On the obelisk, he is shown bowing down before Shalmaneser.

But Layard was not satisfied with digging at Nimrud and was determined to see what the mound of Kuyunjik—ancient Nineveh—could yield, even though Botta had previously abandoned it in frustration. Layard began his work at Kuyunjik in 1849 and worked there through the early 1850s. It was a good decision. Much of what he found at Kuyunjik was tablets, over twenty thousand of them—what turned out to be the huge library of the seventh-century BCE Assyrian king Ashurbanipal, found within his palace. One of the tablets tells about the library itself, explaining that Ashurbanipal wanted to preserve copies of all the great works from all over his empire, so he sent men throughout his lands to collect them; some tablets are copies of older texts that Ashurbanipal had transcribed, while others are originals he took.

More of Ashurbanipal's palace was excavated a few years later by Layard's assistant Horzmund Rassam, a Christian Arab who worked with Layard and directed excavations when Layard could not be present personally. Rassam excavated several now-famous bas-relief scenes that are today displayed in the British Museum. These bas-reliefs include the royal lion hunt sequence, in which the king shoots and kills lions and lionesses that had been caged and then released for his sport, and they also include the Lachish reliefs. The latter depict the capture of the Judahite city of Lachish by Sennacherib (grandfather of Ashurbanipal), a battle described in the Bible, in one of the best biblical parallels known to date. The images include the people of Lachish protecting their city by shooting at the Assyrian army, even as the army approaches the city walls with a battering ram.

Another biblical connection that Rassam's excavations uncovered was a series of tablets now known as the Epic of Gilgamesh. Once deciphered, these

FIGURE 4-3. *Detail of the wall engravings from Sennacherib's Nineveh Palace depicting his siege of Lachish. One of Lachish's towers appears on the right, while a siege machine with a battering ram moves toward the upper left.*

tablets not only told the entire fantastical tale of the hero-king Gilgamesh and his doppelgänger Enkidu but also included an episode (tablet 11) where the story of a great flood is told. This proved to be an earlier version of the flood story that appears in the biblical book of Genesis. Many of the details are the same, even though there are some significant theological differences. This discovery, once translated, fueled the world of biblical studies as well as "Bible lands archaeology."

Both Botta and Layard (who corresponded with each other regularly) encountered the problem of shipping their huge treasures back to Europe—in Botta's case to Paris, and in Layard's to London. Since the blocks of stone weighed several tons each, hundreds of workers placed the reliefs on rollers to maneuver them slowly overland to the bank of the Tigris River. At that point, they were sailed on rafts to a port where a larger French or British ship could meet them. Some of Botta's huge bas-reliefs actually got stuck in the mud en route to the river and were temporarily abandoned. Botta cut others into pieces. Layard did not cut up his.

The Birth of "Biblical Archaeology": Shifting the Focus from Iraq to Ottoman Palestine

It was in the excitement of the earliest explorations of "Bible lands" during the mid-nineteenth century that biblical scholars (often with backgrounds as clergy members) realized that that heart of the biblical world—ancient Israel itself—also needed to be explored. But there were several factors that made this part of the discipline slow to develop. First was the fact that the gigantic mounds of Iraq that were visible to explorers on the ground—and no such mounds existed in Ottoman Palestine. Whatever could be found in Palestine would be smaller and poorer by comparison, they thought. Second, they believed that the landscape of biblical Israel and Judah was already well known, as the Holy Land (and Jerusalem in particular) had been a pilgrimage destination for adventurous European Christians since the early Middle Ages. From the fourth century CE forward, numerous Western travelers wrote detailed accounts of their trips there. Places designated as biblically significant were often marked by churches. Both because Palestine seemed to contain no large ruins and because the sites of biblical interest were supposedly already known, the Holy Land did not seem like a fruitful country for excavation.

But the main reason there was so little interest in archaeological work in Palestine was the fact that most Westerners thought that the land was all but uninhabitable and that its residents were hostile or savage. This image was perpetuated by travelers' accounts, especially those of recent travelers, such as the British explorers Edward Clarke (who traveled in 1801) and James Silk Buckingham (who traveled through in 1815) and the Swiss travelers Ulrich van Seetzen (1802) and John Lewis Burckhardt (1812). Based on the accounts of these well-educated and carefully observant travelers, many Western scholars considered Ottoman Palestine to be desolate as well as dangerous and without good potential for research. These travelers described the dirt and poverty of the cities of Palestine as well as Syria, the dangers of its roads, the violent Bedouin clashes, and the harsh governorship of Jazzar Pasha at the turn of the nineteenth century. Therefore, in the minds of Western biblical scholars as well as the public, there was a fierce disconnect between the ancient land of the Bible and modern Ottoman Palestine. The modern land was not a place worth investigating, as the conditions that existed were so far distant from the image of the ancient biblical land. The only redeeming features of the land were the fact that it was the locus of the core biblical narratives and that it was a good connecting byway to get to places like India or Africa—places where Europeans had colonial holdings.

But because of the excitement of the Mesopotamian discoveries (and in spite of the difficulties of Palestine), a new interest in the antiquities of the

Holy Land emerged gradually among Westerners—what came to be called "biblical archaeology." The path to it had several false starts.

The First Phase of Biblical Exploration, 1830s–1850s

HESTER STANHOPE

As it happened, treasure hunting—not biblical or ancient Near Eastern scholarship—was the impetus for the first excavations ever done in Ottoman Palestine. In 1838, a few years before Botta and Layard began to excavate in Iraq, the British lady traveler Hester Stanhope made a foray into digging, at the site of Ashkelon. Stanhope—who in her youth in London had run the household of her uncle, William Pitt the Younger, during his second term as prime minister (1804–1806)—was traveling through the Ottoman Empire (D. Smith 1968; Silberman 1984). In a misguided attempt to find an appropriate diplomatic gift for the Ottoman sultan, she followed up on a rumor she had heard about buried treasure from the Middle Ages at Ashkelon. She believed that if she found it and presented it to the sultan, it would be a diplomatic coup for herself and for England.

While Stanhope had no real interest in rediscovering the past, she cannot be fully dismissed. Technically, she was the first Westerner to excavate not only in Palestine but in the entirety of the Ottoman Empire, as her excavations actually predated Botta's and Layard's. She was also the first to acquire official permission from the sultan to do so—getting a *firman* (an Ottoman government license) for excavation was a political imperative for all archaeological work to follow. Furthermore, Stanhope was the only woman to become involved with any excavation for many years, doing it all herself, from hiring a team of workers to deciding where on the site to excavate. No other women led archaeological excavations until Kathleen Kenyon.

EDWARD ROBINSON

Slightly over twenty years passed between Stanhope's Ashkelon work and the first real biblical scholarship in Palestine. Edward Robinson is often called the first biblical archaeologist, but in fact he was not an archaeologist at all but a biblical scholar and geographer. As a Bible expert teaching in the United States, Robinson felt hampered by his lack of direct knowledge of biblical geography, and so he traveled to Palestine between his years at Hamilton College and Union Theological Seminary (Williams 1999). His Protestant orientation deeply influenced his approach to the ruins that he examined. Ironically, his first trip in 1838 was during the same year that Stanhope had excavated in Ashkelon, but Robinson approached Palestine scientifically, bringing with him compasses, measuring tapes, and telescopes.

Robinson left two main legacies. The first and greatest is his successful identification of locations of biblical sites. He would talk to local Arabs (via his Arabic-speaking companion Eli Smith) to find out what each site was called, and he realized that the names of many cities mentioned in the Bible or in Greek texts were preserved in Arabic names of contemporary villages. Robinson's second legacy was his noting of a stub of an ancient archway built into the Western Wall of the Temple Mount (just south of the Jewish prayer area), which is now referred to as Robinson's Arch (Robinson and Smith 1856, 285–90). While a friend pointed it out to him initially, Robinson realized something dramatic by looking at the remains of this arch—he understood that the entire Temple Mount, and Jerusalem as a whole, had appeared differently in Roman / New Testament times than it did in his time. This leap of understanding propelled later researchers to excavate in an attempt to see exactly how the city once looked.

The realization that the city looked different than in ancient times propelled forward a long-standing controversy between Catholics and Protestants. Specifically, Protestant scholars disputed the traditional identifications of holy sites, saying that some biblical events could not have happened at the places where they were commemorated. The most famous dispute was over the location of the Church of the Holy Sepulcher, which Protestant scholars thought did not mark the tomb of Jesus after all, which should have been located outside the walls of Jerusalem, according to the text of the Bible itself. This led to numerous scholars trying to find out if the ancient line of the city walls was different from the current Ottoman line.

DE SAULCY AT THE TOMB OF THE KINGS

This type of questioning is what led to the first excavations in Jerusalem, which were undertaken by Louis Félicien de Saulcy, a Frenchman with an interest in antiquities and numismatics. De Saulcy traveled to Palestine in 1850–1851 and came across a burial cave north of Jerusalem's city walls. Because he was predisposed to relate what he saw to the Bible, he incorrectly described the cave as the tomb of the biblical kings of Jerusalem. Because of this misidentification, the burial cave is still known the Tomb of the Kings.

When other scholars disputed de Saulcy's identification, he returned to Palestine twelve years after his initial trip, this time with funding from the French government. He dug in and around the tomb area and uncovered several sarcophagi with inscriptions in Aramaic. He misread the inscriptions in a way that confirmed his original theory about the tombs, still assuming that they were the burials of the kings of Judah (Ben-Arieh 1979, 175; Silberman 1982, 63–72). It is now known that the tombs actually date to the first century

CE and belonged to the family of Helena of Adiabene, a wealthy woman from Iraq who had moved to Jerusalem.

At the time that de Saulcy was excavating, Layard and Botta had already presented the results of their excavations to the public—showing not only that digging was a fruitful approach to the past, but that one could shed light on aspects of biblical history specifically through digging. While de Saulcy was wrong in his interpretations, he was the first to open the possibility that sites in Palestine, like sites in Iraq, could elucidate the Bible.

The Birth of Scientific Methodology in Excavation

Charles Warren and Charles Wilson

It is at this point that we come to what is still considered the most important archaeological work of the nineteenth century—the mapping and excavation work of the British Palestine Exploration Fund. The British had several long-standing connections with the Holy Land already, and archaeology simply evolved out of these. Since the 1840s, there had been a British consul stationed in Jerusalem. One of the longest-serving and most influential of the consuls was James Finn (1846–1863). Finn in fact permanently changed the nature of Jerusalem because, during the hot summer months, he moved his household to a campsite outside the city's Ottoman walls, thereby establishing the first neighborhood in what would become the "new" city. At the same time Finn was in Jerusalem, a British missionary organization—the London Society for Promoting Christianity Among the Jews (also referred to as the London Jews' Society)—began sending missionaries to Jerusalem regularly. Between the consular presence and the missionaries, a small but significant concentration of British citizens lived in Jerusalem as a community. The first archaeological project was actually begun as a result of the needs of this community.

The British missionaries found that the water of Jerusalem was not sanitary by British standards. A decision was made to improve it, and so in 1864 the Jerusalem Water Relief Society was founded in London to accomplish this goal. Consul Finn was on the board of the Water Relief Society and helped to secure the interest and financing of the London philanthropist Angela Burdett-Coutts in the project. The society's first task was to make a full survey of all the water sources in the city. Burdett-Coutts approached the government about employing the Royal Engineers to do this survey (Gibson 2011, 26; Moscrop 2000, 53; Silberman 1984).

The contingent of Royal Engineers came to Jerusalem in the fall of 1864, led by Captain Charles Wilson. While they were exploring the various subterranean water systems, they constantly encountered ancient remains and documented everything they found—all photographed by James McDonald. Images

FIGURE 4-4.
*The frontispiece of
Charles Wilson's survey
of Jerusalem.*

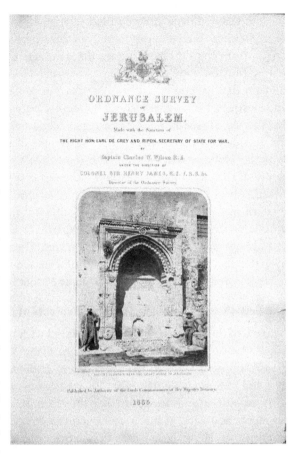

and descriptions of the ancient walls and water systems, some of which were thought to date back to biblical periods, garnered significant public interest in London. After half a year's work, in the spring of 1865, Wilson produced a 1:25,000 map of the city.

The success of the survey inspired several wealthy Londoners— notably George Grove, a well-known music critic who was also interested in the geography of the Bible—to help found a society that would specifically explore the archaeological remains of Palestine. The society was named the Palestine Exploration Fund (PEF). Queen Victoria was an early subscriber, as was Moses Montefiore. The goal of the new organization was to explore the "archaeology, manners and customs, topography, geology . . . of the land of the Bible" (Moscrop 2000, 70).

Because of Wilson's success in mapping Jerusalem, the PEF decided to try to excavate some of the ancient remains. The organization sent Lieutenant Charles Warren, also of the Royal Engineers, to Jerusalem in 1867 with the goal of learning about the history of Jerusalem via archaeological investigation. It was hoped that Warren's excavations could address the pressing problem of the true locations of the holy sites, notably how the Church of the Holy Sepulcher, the traditional location of the tomb of Jesus, related to the walls of the city in the first century CE (see above).

But when Warren arrived in Jerusalem with his small contingent of engineers, he encountered opposition. Even though he had obtained the necessary *firman* from the Ottoman sultan, the members of the local *waqf* (the governing Muslim body of Jerusalem) were suspicious of Warren's motives and thought that his equipment was warlike and could harm the Temple Mount and mosques. Each time Warren began to excavate an area, the city's governor, Izzet Pasha, stopped him. Warren persisted nonetheless, first digging against the outside of the southern wall of the Temple Mount, then moving to a site near the Holy Sepulcher itself, and then back to the unoccupied southern slopes of the city, where he explored the water system and came upon what has since been called Warren's Shaft. Afterward, he moved to the southern and western walls of the Temple Mount. Because of the *waqf*'s objections to his excavations, and because of Warren's experience as a miner, he started to dig less-obtrusive shafts, tunneling underground. During the course of his work, he gathered a tremendous amount of information about early Roman-Period Jerusalem and the structure of the Temple Mount built by Herod.

The British and American Mapping Projects of the 1870s

Because of the difficulties that Warren faced with the *waqf*, and because Jerusalem was so difficult to excavate—since many Muslim and Christian religious structures covered the areas where ancient remains were thought to be—the PEF made a policy shift. They had excelled at mapmaking with Wilson's expedition and decided to map the rest of Palestine properly rather than try more excavating. While a few attempts at excavation were still undertaken (for instance, Henry Maudsley's 1874 excavations in the Mount Zion area were meant to investigate the city's fortifications), the main focus during the 1870s was on map work.

As always, the PEF chose its field man from the ranks of the Royal Engineers, hiring Lieutenant Claude Conder to lead the mapping survey. Conder worked on the map project from 1872 through 1875 and was joined by (then) Captain Horatio Kitchener from 1874 through 1876. Conrad Schick (a German who sometimes worked for the PEF [see below]), Charles Tyrwhitt-Drake, and Charles Clermont-Ganneau were also involved in the survey, especially in the publication phase, which extended through 1878 (Moscrop 2000, 98–99).

Mapping all of Palestine was a large and long project, and, from the beginning, the British recognized that it would take more resources than they had. The organization therefore turned to Americans for help. Although no significant American scholars had explored Palestine since Edward Robinson, biblical scholars in the United States were certainly following the archaeological work going on in both Iraq and Palestine. This is why, when representatives of the PEF traveled to New York to look for funding for their mapping project, they met a group of American scholars who were ready and willing to become involved in the process of exploring the Holy Land.

The American Palestine Exploration Society (APES) was founded in 1870 and was intended as an exact parallel to the British PEF. The founder of the APES was Roswell D. Hitchcock, a protégé of Robinson's at Union Theological Seminary in New York. Hitchcock agreed to collaborate with the British on the mapping project. The plan was that the British would map all of western Palestine (from the Mediterranean to the Jordan River) while the Americans would map eastern Palestine (Transjordan), beginning at the Jordan and moving eastward toward the desert and mountains, much of the area that today is part of the Hashemite Kingdom of Jordan (see Hallote, Cobbing, and Spurr 2012; Cobbing 2005). The two organizations agreed that the resulting map sheets would be published together.

Following the British model, the Americans hired army engineers to head their team—first was Lt. Edgar Steever (who led a group in 1873) and then Col. James C. Lane (a Civil War veteran, who led a group in 1875), overlapping with the British teams. But the British and American teams fared very differently in their projects. The British had state-of-the-art equipment, including prismatic compasses, and were well staffed and adequately funded. Over the course of five years, they were able to complete a properly scaled map of all of western Palestine. The Americans on the other hand were underfunded and lacked proper equipment and, with the exception of the engineers, also lacked staff with proper understanding of the goal of the survey. During their second expedition (which included Rev. Sellah Merrill as the lead archaeologist), almost no mapping was done; rather, the team merely recorded descriptions of the archaeological ruins that were previously known throughout eastern Palestine. The one truly interesting innovation of the American team was the hiring of a professional photographer, Tancrede Dumas, to make a visual record of the archaeological ruins, and one hundred large-scale photographs were produced by the expedition (see Hallote, Cobbing, and Spurr 2012).

When the British tried to combine the American map of the east with their own map of the west, they found it could not be done. The American map sheets of the east lacked detail and did not line up properly with the British map sheets of the west. The PEF rejected the American work and ultimately resurveyed the east itself, sending Conder back to Palestine in 1881. The Americans retreated from archaeological work until the turn of the century.

Steps Backward: The Moabite Stone and the Shapira Forgeries

Although the mapmaking was successful, the story of biblical archaeology in Palestine in the 1860s and 1870s was not always forward moving. Decades passed between Warren's attempts to excavate in Jerusalem and the first real excavations at a tell site. In between, there were several false starts. Two of these were the case of the Moabite Stone and the Shapira forgeries.

The Moabite Stone, sometimes called the **Mesha Stele**, is a large ancient inscription on a stele that came to light in 1868, when it was found by a group of Bedouin who lived in the area of Dhiban in Transjordan. The Bedouin told a German missionary about their find, who made rough sketches of it in its find place and then told the German consul in Jerusalem about it. The consul decided to purchase the stone from the Bedouin on behalf of Prussia.

The stele was made of a large piece of basalt and was covered in writing. Opening with the line "I am Mesha . . . king of Moab," the inscription was dated to the ninth century BCE, based on the style of the letters as well as parallels with the biblical narrative. The text of the stele recounts a rebellion by Moab against Israel—paralleling 2 Kings 3—which tells how Moab was subject to the Kingdom of Israel, until Mesha, the king of Moab, rebelled. Because there are so few long inscriptions in Semitic languages other than Canaanite from the Iron Age, the Moabite Stone is a very important artifact—especially because it offers a close narrative parallel to the biblical text.

When the German consul decided to purchase the artifact, the inscription had not yet been translated. However, the Bedouin who found it had already realized that the stone had value to the Westerners. And, much like the locals in Iraq whom both Layard and Botta had encountered, these Bedouin assumed that the artifact was valuable in and of itself, not for the information it contained. They therefore initially asked a very high price for it and did not allow anyone to make a proper copy of the inscription until they were paid.

When the Germans refused the high price, the Bedouin relented, and an agreement was reached for payment and transport of the stone. However, between Dhiban (where the Bedouin guarded the artifact) and Jerusalem (where the German consulate was located) lived another unrelated Bedouin tribe. This second tribe refused to let the artifact be carried through their territory, probably because they had also realized that it was valuable to Westerners and because they either wanted some of the income it could bring or did not want their rivals to profit from its sale.

As the disputes among the Bedouin intensified, the Germans found that they had competition for the stone from other Westerners—specifically the French. Charles Clermont-Ganneau, a young translator working for the French consulate in Jerusalem, was becoming interested in archaeological exploration (he would later work with the British on their survey of western Palestine). Clermont-Ganneau decided to purchase it himself, on behalf of France. He approached the second group of Bedouin rather than the first, even though their group did not physically own the stone, and asked them to sneak into their rival's territory to secretly make a plaster copy of the inscription.

They did so but were caught by the first tribe in the middle of their work. These Bedouin were now even more certain that the stone contained gold. In order to get to the gold, they broke the stone into small fragments, completely destroying it and the inscription on it.

But this was not the end of the story. The British engineer Charles Warren (see above) was still in Palestine and, shocked at the destruction of the stone, began to purchase the broken fragments from the Bedouin. Meanwhile, Clermont-Ganneau had gotten his plaster copy, and ultimately he and Warren shared their information. Clermont-Ganneau published the inscription first, early in 1870, bringing it to the attention of the world. A reconstruction based on Clermont-Ganneau's copy and Warren's fragments was made and displayed in the Louvre in Paris, where it remains today (Silberman 1982; Allegro 1965).

The Moabite Stone situation made the archaeologically minded community in Jerusalem aware of Moab—a kingdom previously known only through the Bible—as an avenue through which to prove aspects of the Bible true. However, this had some negative effects, as it inspired an antiquities dealer in Jerusalem to manufacture new items and pass them off as Moabite. The antiquities dealer, Moses Shapira, ran a shop in Jerusalem that catered to tourists and pilgrims. Inspired by the idea that Moabite artifacts might be valuable to scholars, Shapira enlisted a local craftsman to make ceramic pieces—mainly pots and figurines—that looked ancient and that he claimed were from Moab. He had success with this in the 1870s—in particular, in the wake of the Moabite Stone discovery. Many of his Moabite forgeries were bought by members of the German community in Jerusalem, as collecting these artifacts (thought to be genuine) seemed like a way of redeeming themselves after losing possession of the Moabite Stone. Many of these forgeries ended up in Berlin museums.

But Shapira sold real artifacts as well as forgeries in his shop. Among the real items were some scrolls, many of which came from Yemen. But Shapira had some other fragmentary scrolls as well, which he claimed had a different provenance: he said they came from the area of the Dead Sea. These scroll fragments were especially interesting, as they contained portions of biblical books. One in particular seemed to contain a version of Deuteronomy that differed slightly from the traditional text.

Some of Shapira's scroll fragments had reached London, where they were on display at the British Museum and were attracting significant attention in advance of being sold at auction. Once again it was Charles Clermont-Ganneau who interfered. Clermont-Ganneau recognized that many of Shapira's ceramic artifacts were forged, and so he declared that these scrolls were forgeries as well, even though he had never examined them directly himself. Clermont-Ganneau's statements completely discredited Shapira, ultimately ruining his career—and he later committed suicide. The auction of the scrolls was derailed, and they sold to a private collector for a pittance and later were likely destroyed in a house fire. Sadly, hindsight has shown that Clermont-Ganneau, in his fervor to catch out Shapira, was probably wrong. The scrolls were probably genuine. They were distinctly similar to the famous Dead Sea Scrolls, found seventy years later.

The Siloam Inscription

One of the aspects of biblical archaeology that was so compelling in its early years (and just as compelling today) is that archaeological finds can sometimes elucidate biblical narratives. We have seen the sort of excitement biblical parallels generated with the Moabite Stone. Another example is the **Siloam Inscription** within the water system of Jerusalem.

In one of the more exciting narratives of the Bible, we hear about King David capturing the city of Jerusalem from the Jebusites, in part by going through the water system, as mentioned briefly in 2 Samuel 5:6-9. Just as exciting and much clearer is another biblical narrative describing events several centuries after King David, when King Hezekiah prepared for war against Assyria. Knowing the Assyrians would attack if he refused to comply with them as his predecessors had done, he preemptively prepared Jerusalem for war. One of the ways he did this was by digging a new water tunnel, presumably to make the water supply of the city more easily accessible from within the fortifications (Finkelstein and Silberman 2001). The event is recounted in 2 Kings 20:20, where we learn that Hezekiah expanded the water system by cutting a tunnel and a pool.

There was never a time when the water system of Jerusalem was not in use, although, over the centuries, different parts of it were added on and other parts were no longer used. The archaeologist Ronny Reich (2011) has meticulously described the way Western archaeologists first explored the water system. In the nineteenth century, two sources of water were known to the locals of the village of Siloam, just to the south of the Old City of Jerusalem. The northern source was a spring (known sometimes as Ein Umm ed-Daraj or as Ein Sitt Maryam) and came to be associated with the Gihon Spring, which is mentioned frequently in the Bible—for instance, in 2 Chronicles 33:14. The southern pool of water was referred to as the Pool of Silwan (Siloam). When Robinson explored Jerusalem in the 1830s, he observed that the two known sources in this area were connected by a long tunnel. This tunnel came to be identified as Hezekiah's tunnel, based on the biblical narrative. Not many decades after Robinson, when Wilson explored it during his water-mapping expedition, and soon thereafter, Warren explored it more thoroughly, climbing through the tunnel completely at great personal risk. Warren noted another subsidiary shaft as well that came to be named for him (Warren's Shaft). One other interesting thing about the tunnel is that the ceiling has two heights, being significantly higher in the north than in the south, as if the two parts were cut from different sides and met in the middle.

But the most interesting piece of archaeological material from this tunnel was found not by any of these explorers but by a local young boy, who was a student in a missionary school. The boy was climbing through the tunnel when he came upon a flat inscribed area within it, and he told his teacher what he had found (Montefiore 2011, 42; Reich 2011, 27).

FIGURE 4-5. *The Siloam Inscription from Hezekiah's tunnel.*

The boy's teacher happened to be Conrad Schick, well known in the growing Western scholarly community of Jerusalem. Born in Germany, Schick was trained as a missionary and sent to Jerusalem to teach, but while there he had fully explored the ruins of the city and become an expert in all things archaeological and architectural. By 1880, Schick was publishing regularly in both British and German academic journals about the archaeology of Jerusalem.

Schick went to explore the newly found inscription himself and, with great difficulty, took a squeeze of it, although it was not fully legible. He also announced the find to the German archaeological organization and sent a copy of it back to Germany. Schick then got a *firman* from the Ottoman government and began excavating in the area (Reich 2011, 27–42).

But Schick's copies were not fully legible due to the lime deposits in the letters. The following year (1881), Henry Archibald Sayce, the British biblical scholar and Assyriologist, made his own copies that were more legible, and Sayce made the first translation. Other copies were made by the Germans, who had sent the scholar Hermann Guthe out to Jerusalem to work with Schick.

Guthe succeeded in removing the lime deposit that covered the inscription, which also made it more legible. The text as translated by Sayce describes the ancient tunneling operation to carve out the tunnel, which consisted of teams working from two directions who ultimately met in the middle. In particular, the inscription describes the moment of meeting, when each team could hear the voices of the other calling through the rock as they approached each other.

But this inscription was almost lost to scholarship. In 1891, probably under instruction from an antiquities dealer, someone snuck into the tunnel and hacked the inscription from the wall and stole it. The slab broke into several fragments when it was stolen, and some of the letters were damaged. Ultimately, it was recovered by the authorities from the home of a Greek Christian. It was then declared the property of the Ottoman government and sent to the Istanbul Museum, where it remains.

The First Decade of Excavations by the Palestine Exploration Fund, 1890–1900

Even through the scandals of the 1860s (Moabite Stone), 1870s (Shapira forgeries), and 1880s (Siloam Inscription theft), the scientific development of archaeology continued in Ottoman Palestine, and it was still largely the British who created a new archaeological methodology for excavating.

Jerusalem was difficult to excavate because it was a living city, with religious and domestic structures blocking all the sites of most archaeological interest. Although the British had tried when they had sent out Warren, and the Germans were trying with the work of Schick and Guthe, it was difficult to find places to dig between modern inhabited areas. But because of the successes of Layard and Botta on the great mounds of Mesopotamia, it was finally apparent that the smaller mounds, or tells (ruins), of Ottoman Palestine were also the remains of cities—the cities of biblical Israel and Judah—and that these should be excavated. By 1889, the British PEF decided to excavate a tell.

The PEF found an excavator for a tell before they chose where to excavate. They hired Sir Flinders Petrie, who had excavated at the Giza pyramid complex in Egypt during the 1880s and thus had already established a reputation as an excellent field archaeologist. During his years in Egypt, Petrie had formulated an excavation methodology that influenced all future excavations. He later published a guide to excavations that included significant portions on archaeological methods as well as the day-to-day practicum of running an excavation project, everything from how to hire and retain a crew of competent fieldmen to how to approach the remains of architecture (Petrie 1904).

Once they hired Petrie, the PEF decided to give him free reign to choose a site to excavate. Petrie consulted with Rev. Henry Archibald Sayce, the biblical scholar and Assyriologist who had translated the Siloam Inscription and who had traveled extensively in Palestine. Sayce suggested that Petrie locate and explore the biblical city of Lachish, so important in 2 Kings 18 and 2 Chronicles 32, where the Assyrian siege of the city is described. The siege of Lachish was among the palace reliefs that Layard excavated at Sennacherib's palace at Nineveh, giving a second accounting of it complete with visual images of the attack from the point of view of the Assyrians, all of which confirmed the biblical narrative.

The PEF applied for the *firman* from the Ottoman government, and in 1890 Petrie set off to Palestine. His first task was to figure out which of the many tells in southern Palestine might be the ruins of ancient Lachish. He surveyed several small archaeological tells that Sayce had suggested and, based on surface finds, determined which mound might be a good candidate—and he proceeded to excavate it for six weeks. This was Tell el-Hesi. (It took another generation before the misidentification was corrected, as Tell el Duweir has since been clearly identified as Lachish, while Tell el-Hesi is a candidate for biblical Eglon.)

While at Hesi, Petrie was able to improve on his understanding of the importance of ceramics. Already in his Egyptian work, he had understood the importance of pottery, specifically the fact that different ceramic styles were used in different time periods. This comparative study of ceramics allowed him to roughly date the tombs he excavated in Egypt, dating them relative to each other in a sequence based on changing pottery styles. The missing piece of this was available at Tell el-Hesi. As a tell, Hesi represented several layers, or strata, of cities all on top of each other—not only did the ceramics change over time, but it was possible to see exactly which preceded the other, as they were "stacked" on top of each other. This had not been readily visible with unconnected tombs and pyramid sites in Egypt, and it took his work at Hesi to clarify it. This pottery sequencing, sometimes known as "ceramic seriation," became a staple of archaeological dating, one that is still the backbone of archaeology today worldwide. While scientific dating methods are constantly being improved, for many decades Petrie's ceramic typologies were able to give a more accurate date than, for instance, ^{14}C dating could for historic periods.

But Petrie disliked Palestine. Not only did he find the archaeology very different from excavating pyramids in Egypt, but he found the comparatively sparse amount of archaeological finds very frustrating. After only a six-week excavation season, Petrie headed back to Egypt, and he did not return to Palestine until several decades later, although in 1905 he worked in the Sinai, at the site of Serabit el-Khadim. The PEF hurried to replace him and quickly hired the American Frederick Jones Bliss as their main fieldman. Bliss was the son of Daniel Bliss, the founder of the Syrian Protestant College in Beirut (now

American University of Beirut). Bliss, who knew Arabic and had already done his own explorations of sites in Lebanon as an independent scholar, knew the landscape of the Middle East and was fluent in Arabic.

Bliss excavated at Hesi between 1890 and 1893, making his own contribution to archaeology by building on Petrie's methodological work. Not only did Bliss grasp Petrie's nascent ceramic typology, but he built on it. Bliss understood that the different strata of a tell reflected layers of occupation that could and should be excavated separately. He recognized at least eleven distinct phases of occupation at Tell el-Hesi, and he even understood that there were subphases within these. Over the course of his years at Hesi, Bliss dug almost the entire northeast quadrant of the tell down to bedrock, then declared the excavations finished.

When Hesi was completed, the PEF thought the time might be right to try Jerusalem again. Bliss' fluency in Arabic and good relationship with the local Ottoman antiquities inspector all made it more likely that Jerusalem would be easier to navigate than in the days of Warren. In fact, Bliss was able to facilitate a particularly difficult process of obtaining a *firman* (Hallote 2006). The Jerusalem excavations (1893–1895) were meant to reinvestigate a problem that Warren had attempted to work on—namely, the ancient line of the walls of Jerusalem. This issue had deep ramifications regarding the real location of the tomb of Jesus—as the Church of the Holy Sepulcher was within the current Ottoman walls of the city. If the Roman-Period walls had a different course, then perhaps the current church location had once been outside the walls. Finding out was the goal of the excavations. Bliss began tracing the ancient wall near Mount Zion, working where Henry Maudsley had worked a decade previously. But he encountered too many obstacles to proceed directly around the city and ended up tunneling, much like Warren had done, and also like Layard had done in the 1850s at Kuyunjik, in order to get closer to the Temple Mount. This meant that he could not learn about the stratigraphy of the area.

In late 1894, in the midst of the Jerusalem project, the PEF hired an architect to join Bliss on the project. Archibald Dickie continued to work alongside Bliss for the duration of the Jerusalem excavations, which ended in 1895. Bliss spent the next two years publishing his material. The PEF sent him back to the field in 1898, for one last long-term excavation project, which lasted until 1900. For this project, the PEF hired R. A. S. Macalister, from Dublin, as an assistant for Bliss. Macalister was a specialist in Celtic archaeology but was willing to learn about Ottoman Palestine.

Over the course of this last project, Bliss and Macalister engaged in major excavations at Tell Zakariyah (Azekah), Tell es-Safi (Gath), Tell el-Judeideh, and Sandaannah (Maresha). The PEF insisted that the excavators split their

FIGURE 4-6. *The tenth-century Gezer Calendar.*

time and resources and excavate each site extremely fast.
Nonetheless, Bliss was able to
publish the findings rather thoroughly in a single large volume.
Due to disagreements with the
PEF and his poor health, the
PEF fired Bliss in 1900 and promoted Macalister to main field
archaeologist.

Macalister was therefore
the field archaeologist who
led the next PEF excavation in
1902–1909 at Tel Gezer. Perhaps the most famous artifact
from Macalister's excavations
is the **Gezer Calendar**, which
is an inscription carved onto a
limestone slab. Epigraphically,
this inscription dates to the
tenth century and describes the
agricultural cycle for planting
and harvesting crops. As part of
the terms of the *firman*, the calendar was kept by the Turks, not the British, and
is still housed in the Istanbul Museum.

Unfortunately, Macalister did not have a good grasp of stratigraphy, and
he misdated Iron Age material to the Maccabean period, describing a large rec-
tilinear structure as a Maccabean castle—misled by the Hellenistic remains
that were also found in the area. In later years (after the site was reexcavated
by an American team in the 1960s and 1970s), it became clear that this "castle" was actually one half of the tenth-century six-chambered gate of the city.
Macalister also famously had trouble distinguishing between the mud-brick
construction material of walls and the debris around them. Macalister briefly
excavated at Jericho as well. When Macalister left the PEF (to return to his
career in Ireland), the PEF hired Duncan Mackenzie, a Scottish scholar who
had worked with Sir Arthur Evans at Knossos on Crete. In 1911, Mackenzie
excavated Beth Shemesh.

The Founding of German Archaeological Organizations, 1877–1914

While the British may have been the star players in early biblical archaeology,
the Germans and French were also heavily involved. German scholars had

already distinguished themselves in terms of biblical scholarship. Julias Well-hausen's *Prolegomena zur Geschichte Israels* (published in 1878 and translated as *Prolegomena to the History of Israel* in 1885) was the culmination of decades of German biblical scholarship (see chapter 2). It is therefore not surprising that there was significant German interest in archaeological exploration of the Holy Land, and, as we have seen, Germans in Palestine such as Guthe and Schick were already becoming involved. This was formalized in 1877 when a group of German scholars founded the archaeological organization the Deutscher Palästina-Verein (German Society for the Exploration of Palestine). The Deutscher Palästina-Verein did not launch an excavation of a tell imme-diately. That did not happen until after the famous visit of Kaiser Wilhelm II to Jerusalem in 1898, which was a visible demonstration of the close politi-cal relationship that Germany had with the Ottoman Empire. It was after this state visit, and after the PEF had already completed a decade of excavation, that the Germans began to excavate.

The first German archaeological expedition to Palestine was to the site of Tell el-Mutesellim, or biblical Megiddo. Megiddo was the locus of several ancient battles—notably the battle of Egyptian pharaoh Thutmose III against the king of the Syrian city of Kadesh (which seems to have been a draw, based on two copies of the treaty that ended it) and the battle of King Josiah of Judah against the Egyptian king Necho. Megiddo is also the predicted site of the bat-tle of Armageddon of the book of Revelation.

Gottlieb Schumacher, who had strong connections to the British PEF, directed the Megiddo excavations between 1903–1905. Schumacher had trained as an engineer in Germany, but by the 1890s he had settled in Haifa with the German Templar community, where he worked for the local Ottoman province, surveying for the railway that would connect Haifa to Damascus. In these years, Schumacher worked collaboratively with the PEF and learned about archaeology. At Megiddo, Schumacher unearthed architectural remains as well as several large stone-built tombs in the center of the tell.

A second, unrelated German archaeology society—the German Orien-tal Society (or Deutsche Orient-Gesellschaft)—was founded in 1898 and was based out of Berlin (Hübner 2011). Its members were initially more interested in sponsoring excavations in Iraq, as the main locus of "Bible lands archaeol-ogy" admired in German academic circles. This is why the Deutsche Orient-Gesellschaft did not initially sponsor work in Ottoman Palestine but rather supported Robert Koldeway's excavations in Babylon, which began in 1899 and continued until the First World War. Although Palestine was never the organization's main focus, they did sponsor the excavations at Taanach from 1902–1904, directed by the Austrian theologian Ernst Sellin, who was on the faculty of the University of Vienna. After Taanach, Sellin continued to work in Palestine, excavating at Jericho in 1907 and 1909 (together with Carl Watzinger, who later helped publish the Deutscher Palästina-Verein's Mutesellim volumes) and then at Shechem in 1913–1914.

It should also be noted that the Germans founded yet another archaeological organization in the same year (1898) as the Deutsche Orient-Gesellschaft. This was the German Protestant Institute of Archaeology (Deutsches Evangelisches Institut für Altertumswissenschaft des Heiligen Landes), which ultimately established a presence in Jerusalem in 1903. One of the early directors of the German Protestant Institute of Archaeology was Albrecht Alt, who led the institution in 1921–1922. Alt is still well known among archaeologists and biblical historians for his theories on the origins of the Israelite settlement. But the German Protestant Institute of Archaeology did not sponsor any excavations, leaving that to the other two German organizations (Hübner 2011, 59–72).

The Founding of the French École Biblique in Jerusalem, 1890

From the time of the Crusades, there had always been a French Catholic presence in Jerusalem. This long-standing interest is why, by the later nineteenth century, French Dominicans were already deeply involved in exploring places in Palestine with the Bible as a reference point. De Saulcy's motivation for exploring the Tomb of the Kings (see above) was an early manifestation of this interest.

But French archaeological involvements really took off in 1889, when the Dominican priest Father Marie-Joseph Lagrange arrived in Jerusalem. Lagrange's approach to the Bible was considered rational and scientific. In 1890, he founded a French archaeological school, the École biblique et archéologique française de Jérusalem—originally called the École pratique d'etudes bibliques (Trimbur 2011, 97). In 1893, just three years after the British had begun to excavate at Tell el-Hesi, Lagrange went to the Sinai Desert, hoping to find material to shed light on the exodus narratives. He returned there in 1896 to explore Roman and Byzantine sites. Also under Lagrange's initiative, the École searched for inscriptions at Petra and went to Gezer in 1899 to do some descriptive surveying work (see Trimbur 2011).

A year after Lagrange arrived at the École, he was joined by Father Louis-Hughes Vincent. Vincent remained associated with the École and with archaeology for the rest of his life and is mainly remembered for work he did in Jerusalem, in the City of David area. Even before Vincent's arrival, LaGrange had made it clear that the French were interested in the City of David. This is why, when a British army captain with no archaeological training began to excavate there, Vincent immediately joined him to make sure the process was done properly. The army captain, Montague Parker, was not associated with the PEF, but despite this he had raised funding for an excavation in the City of David and carried out work between 1909 and 1911. Vincent took charge of the analysis and publication aspects of the project. Vincent's career was extremely long, and one of his students, Roland de Vaux, went on to become one of the better-known archaeologists of the mid-twentieth century. His best-known excavation was at Khirbet Qumran in the 1950s. Another French institution, the Jerusalem branch of Jesuit Pontifical Biblical Institute, was founded in Jerusalem in 1927.

The Founding of the American School of Oriental Research in 1900

At this point, the narrative turns back to the Americans, who had been inactive in Ottoman Palestine since their joint survey with the British in the 1870s. Even in their quiescence, American scholars followed the British work closely, partially because Frederick Jones Bliss was an American whose comings and goings were noted. In fact, it was in the immediate wake of Bliss' work for the British that American biblical scholars once again founded an archaeological organization. In 1900 they founded the American School of Oriental Study and Research (ASOR), based in Jerusalem at the Jaffa Gate, not far from the quarters of the PEF.

One of the foremost goals of ASOR was to have an American-run excavation in Palestine, but for a variety of reasons, especially financial constraints, this did not happen immediately. The first American-run excavation was directed by Harvard University, not by ASOR, and only came about as a second choice for Harvard. The Harvard Assyriologist David Gordon Lyon had hoped to begin an excavation in Iraq, looking to find tablets like some of the larger "Bible lands" excavators had done; however, Lyon's sponsor was the Jewish financier Jacob Schiff, who was interested only in work in Ottoman Palestine—that is, biblical Israel itself. So, in 1907, Lyon traveled to Palestine, where he served for a single year as director of ASOR, using the Jerusalem location as a platform from which to secure a *firman* for the site of Samaria (Hallote 2009). The Samaria excavation revealed a large palace complex, immediately identified with Omri and Ahab of the Bible, as Samaria was their capital city.

The First World War broke out and interrupted ASOR's presence in Jerusalem. Operations resumed in 1920, and, in that year, one of the young scholars to receive a fellowship to ASOR was William F. Albright. Within months of arriving in Jerusalem, Albright was made interim director of the school, and soon thereafter he became full director. In this capacity, he was able to fulfill some of the initiatives begun by his predecessors—notably, beginning the school's first excavations at Tel el-Ful (Gibeah) in 1922 and then the larger-scale excavations at Tell Beit Mirsim in 1926 (Hallote 2011). Although these two excavations were the only fieldwork Albright did in Palestine, his influence on the discipline was enormous. An important aspect of Albright's early career is that, unlike most American biblical scholars, he did not study in Germany and then return to America, but rather he earned his degree at an American university (Johns Hopkins, where he later taught). To be sure, his mentor was German trained (the Assyriologist Paul Haupt), but Albright represents the first homegrown American biblical scholar who refashioned himself as an archaeologist.

By the time the war ended and archaeologists returned to the field, the discipline of "biblical archaeology" was firmly established in Palestine, a country now under British rule. Between the wars, archaeologists of all nationalities continued their excavations at a fast pace. In Iraq, "Bible lands archaeology" also continued, although that particular term was becoming obsolete ("archaeology of the Near East" was more commonly used). The work of some of the better-known biblical archaeologists of the twentieth century, figures such as Kathleen Kenyon and Yohanan Aharoni, was built on the foundations of these earliest scholars, linguists, and archaeologists.

Suggestions for Further Reading

Perhaps the best introductory overview of the rise of interest in the ancient Near East and the early development of archaeology in that region is Neil Silberman's *Digging for God and Country*. Yehoshua Ben-Arieh's *The Rediscovery of the Holy Land in the Nineteenth Century* looks at how the Holy Land emerged from the Ottoman Empire and gained the attention of Westerners in Europe and North America. Rachel Hallote's *Bible, Map, and Spade: The American Palestine Exploration Society, Frederick Jones Bliss, and the Forgotten Story of Early American Biblical Archaeology* details American involvement in biblical archaeology during this period. There are many good books on the history of Jerusalem. Two recent ones worth reading are Simon Montefiore's *Jerusalem: The Biography* (an accessible and enjoyable volume covering the sweep of Jerusalem' history) and Ronny Reich's *Excavating the City of David: Where Jerusalem's History Began* (which provides a look at recent archaeological excavations and what they reveal about Jerusalem's earliest centuries).

5

A CRITIQUE OF BIBLICAL ARCHAEOLOGY
History and Interpretation

William G. Dever

The Hebrew Bible (or Christian "Old Testament") is itself an artifact, a relic from the past. But of course it nowhere speaks of "archaeology," or the modern study of artifacts. Yet from the mid-nineteenth century onward, archaeology has been seen as perhaps the most powerful tool we have ever had for illuminating the Bible and the world that produced it.

This chapter will trace the development of "biblical archaeology" throughout its history and will show how it has been used (and misused) in contributing to our understanding of the history and religion of ancient Israel as well as to the growth of early Judaism and Christianity. Finally, some prospects for the future of both archaeology and biblical studies will be suggested.

A Brief History and Critique of Biblical Archaeology

BEGINNINGS, 1840–1914

Archaeology in the Middle East began in the mid-nineteenth century with the first recovery of impressive, long-lost monuments from Mesopotamia (Iraq) and Egypt. In the Holy Land, however, there were no systematic excavations before the work of the legendary British archaeologist Sir William Flinders Petrie in 1890 at the site of Tell el-Hesi (perhaps biblical "Eglon") near the Gaza Strip. It was Petrie who discovered the two basic archaeological methods that are still used today: (1) stratigraphy and (2) comparative ceramic technology.

Another pioneer, even earlier, was the American biblical scholar Edward Robinson. He was not an archaeologist, but his explorations of the Holy Land in 1837 and again in 1851 (published in 1841 and 1856) produced one of the first modern maps and identified more than two hundred long-lost biblical sites, based largely on the preservation of their ancient names in later Arabic.

Archaeological excavations expanded up until 1914 and the outbreak of World War I. American work began with Frederick Bliss' collaboration with Petrie at Tell el-Hesi in 1893, then with Harvard University's George Andrew Reisner and others at Samaria (1908–1911). In addition, Haverford College excavated at Beth Shemesh in 1911–1912. These were all biblical sites, although the directors and sponsors were not clerics or even necessarily religious in outlook.

In the pre–World War I era, the Germans excavated at Taanach in 1902–1904, at Megiddo in 1903–1905, and at Jericho in 1907–1908. These, too, were prominent biblical sites. Some of the excavators were biblical scholars and clerics, but others were not.

The British carried out the first long-running excavations in this interval at Gezer in 1902–1909 under Robert Alexander Stuart Macalister, for the British Palestine Exploration Fund, which had been founded in 1865. That society was soon complemented by the German Society of the Holy Land (a church-sponsored organization established in 1877) and then the French Dominican École biblique et archéologique in Jerusalem (founded in 1890). Americans got into the act in 1870 with the founding of the American Society of Biblical Archaeology, a significant name change, as we shall see. Then, in 1900, the American Schools of Oriental Research was established and opened a nonsectarian research institute in Jerusalem (now the William Foxwell Albright Institute of Archaeological Research; for its history and related work in the Middle East, see King 1983; Seger 2001).

FIGURE 5-1. *The "Albright," as the Albright Institute for Archaeological Research is affectionately known. This Jerusalem building was constructed as the original home of the American Schools of Oriental Research in the 1920s. It is now named for an early director, the influential archaeologist William F. Albright.*

THE FLOWERING OF "BIBLICAL ARCHAEOLOGY," 1920–1967

Fieldwork resumed in Palestine soon after the war, and until World War II there were numerous large excavation projects in the Holy Land, sponsored at this time principally by the French, German, British, and American societies as well as in-country archaeological institutes. Fieldwork was facilitated enormously by the establishment of the first modern antiquity laws and government authority under the auspices of the newly established British Mandatory Government in Palestine.

The principal excavations can be listed conveniently in chart form:

French: Ai, 1933–1935
German: Shechem, 1926–1934
British: Jerusalem, 1923–1928
    Tell Jemmeh, 1926, 1927 (Arzah)
    Tel el-Farah (S), 1927–1929 (Sharuhen)
    Tell el-Ajjul, 1930–1934
    Samaria, 1930–1935
    Jericho, 1930–1936
    Lachish, 1932–1938
American: Beth Shean, 1921–1928
    Tell el-Ful, 1922, 1923 (Gibeah)
    Megiddo, 1925–1939
    Tell en-Nasbeh, 1927–1935 (Mizpeh)
    Bethel, 1934–1960
    Beth Shemesh, 1928–1933
    Tell Beit Mirsim, 1926–1932

American work in Palestine was now influenced directly or indirectly by the great Orientalist William Foxwell Albright, who was director of the American School in Jerusalem in 1920–1929 and again in 1933–1936 (for the school, see King 1983). It was he, more than any other individual, who was the father of "biblical archaeology," a particularly American phenomenon in many ways. It was characterized from the 1920s to the 1960s by (1) a concentration on biblical sites; (2) a focus on the history and religion of ancient Israel; (3) field projects sponsored mainly by religious institutions, sometimes directed by clerics, both mostly Protestant; and (4) research interests that dwelt with historical (and theological) issues such as the patriarchal era, Moses and the Sinai covenant, the exodus and conquest of Canaan, the rise of "divine kingship," exclusive monotheism, and the uniqueness of ancient Israel. Archaeology related to the New Testament and early Judaism was not a priority.

Albright's protégé, Nelson Glueck, succeeding him as long-time director of ASOR's Jerusalem School (1936–1940; 1942–1947), was unique for that time in being a Jewish rabbi. Well known for his explorations in Transjordan and his excavation of "Solomon's seaport at Ezion-geber" (1938–1940), Glueck was clearly an American-style "biblical archaeologist" and criticized for that just as Albright had been.

The assumption of "biblical archaeology" all along was that the burgeoning archaeological discoveries in the land of the Bible would confirm the essential historicity of the Bible—and thus validate it as the ground of faith. Albright's preoccupation with the Bible was so overarching that he included *all* archaeology of a vast region under the rubric of his "biblical archaeology." As he said in one of his few explicit definitions:

> I shall use the term "biblical archaeology" here to refer to all Bible lands— from India to Spain, and from southern Russia to South Arabia—and to the whole history of those lands from about 10,000 B.C. or even earlier, to the present time. (Albright 1969, 1)

G. Ernest Wright, another of Albright's protégés, became an even more outspoken advocate of the marriage of archaeology and biblical studies. As he put it in his handbook *Biblical Archaeology*:

> To me, at least, biblical archaeology is a special armchair variety of general archaeology, which studies the discoveries of excavators and gleans from them every fact that throws a direct, indirect or even diffused light upon the Bible.... Its central and absorbing interest is the understanding and exposition of the Scriptures. (G. Wright 1947, 74)

Wright began at Bethel with Albright in 1934, but the Second World War intervened. Meanwhile, he became well known as a ceramic expert and then as a vocal spokesman for the "faith and history" movement in biblical theology. From 1956 to 1968, he directed excavations at Shechem, the training ground for a new generation of younger American archaeologists who later launched the well-known Gezer project in Israel (1964–1990; see below). Wright's popular book was entitled *Shechem: The Biography of a Biblical City* (1965). European scholars suspected Wright of fundamentalism. But in Israel from the 1950s onward, the founding fathers of the national school found themselves in sympathy with the "biblical archaeology" of Albright and Wright, although more for nationalist than religious reasons.

The formation of an **Israeli** school was now underway, especially with the epochal project of Yigael Yadin at Hazor (1955–1958). Other Israeli veterans were in the field now, including Benjamin Mazar (Tel Qasile, 1958–1959; Ein Gedi, 1961–1965); and Yohanan Aharoni (Ramat Rahel, 1959–1962). These

FIGURE 5-2. *Late Bronze gates at Shechem.*

FIGURE 5-3. *Tell Hazor became the training ground for many future Israeli archaeologists.*

were mostly biblical sites, but the Israelis did not yet offer any explicit statement of their aims and methods. Yet all the principals noted above obviously considered themselves "biblical archaeologists" in some sense (see further below).

The German, French, and British for their part all along had a mixed "religious-secular" orientation, but American-style biblical theology had never played any significant role in their archaeological fieldwork and research.

The American excavations of this era in the Holy Land, including Shechem, were all in the Jordanian sector of Palestine, partitioned after the creation of the State of Israel in 1948. These are worth noting since all were at biblical sites, directed by biblical scholars and clerics, and sponsored by theological institutions:

> Gibeon—James B. Pritchard, 1956–1962
> Ai—Joseph A. Callaway, 1964–1970
> Taanach—Paul W. Lapp, 1963–1968

The only exception was the excavation at Ashdod in Israel (1962–1972), where Americans had a small role (see below).

During the period up to 1967, the Germans did little or no fieldwork on either side of the border, although the German school in Jerusalem conducted study tours for clergy. The French dug in both the West Bank (Père Roland de Vaux dug at Qumran in 1953–1956 and at Tell el-Farah (N) [Tirzah] in 1946–1960) and in Israel at several prehistoric sites (Jean Perrot, 1952–1962). The British concentrated their efforts on behalf of the school in Jerusalem, first at Jericho under Dame Kathleen Kenyon (1955–1958) and then in Jerusalem (1961–1967) under her direction as well.

This above activity—nearly all the foreign work and schools sequestered in the West Bank, and generally related to a form of "biblical archaeology" that was decidedly Christian—came to an abrupt end with the outbreak of the Six-Day War in 1967. Now the Israeli national school came to prominence, and an era of international competition began.

GROWING PAINS: A REVOLUTION IN METHOD AND THEORY, 1970–1985

At the time of the Six-Day War in 1967, the old American Schools of Oriental Research in East Jerusalem (above) was so moribund that the property was put on the market (Seger 2001, 27–28). On the west side of Jerusalem, however, things were looking up. In 1963, Nelson Glueck opened the Hebrew Union College Biblical and Archaeological School in West Jerusalem, in the Israeli sector. Directed by Wright in 1964–1965, the school in 1964 launched the Gezer project (with Glueck)—the first large American excavation in Israel and the training ground for a younger generation of excavators in Israel and Jordan. Israeli archaeological work was flourishing, expanding soon into the occupied

West Bank. Jerusalem, only sporadically excavated previously, now became the focus of large-scale projects directed at the Western Wall by Benyamin Mazar and in the restored Jewish Quarter by Nahman Avigad. All seemed well for archaeology. But a crisis was brewing.

All archaeological work in the Holy Land up to 1967, in both sectors of former Palestine, had been largely unself-conscious. It had proceeded on assumptions derived from one form or another of traditional "biblical archaeology." What happened in the next decade can be described as our "loss of innocence"—a transformation that was affecting other branches of worldwide archaeology and that brought "biblical archaeology" into the mainstream for the first time in its hundred-year history.

The revolution began almost inconspicuously with a discussion of field methods. American archaeologists were now working in Israel (as at Gezer under W. G. Dever and others from 1964–1973), along with other foreign archaeologists in the former West Bank, together with Israelis who were excavating everywhere and beginning to dominate the discipline. Aharoni and Dever debated excavation techniques, the latter defending the three-dimensional Wheeler-Kenyon (or "baulk-debris") method that British and American excavators had recently adopted (Dever 1973). Lapp also criticized the faulty digging and recording methods of the time. But this early ferment did not yet embrace *theory*—the philosophical (and theological) underpinnings on which the whole enterprise had depended up until that point.

Lectures given by Dever in 1972 at Seabury-Western Seminary in America, followed by several provocative publications in subsequent years, helped to launch a revolution that posed severe challenges to traditional "biblical archaeology" and would eventually transform it (Dever 1974, 1982, 1985).

The principal charges were (1) that "biblical archaeology" was an amateur affair, carried on by nonprofessionals, with poor standards of fieldwork and research; (2) that the agenda was largely theological rather than properly archaeological; and (3) that the whole enterprise was parochial, out of touch with current developments in method and theory elsewhere in worldwide archaeology.

Part of the impetus for the revolution came from the growing acquaintance of younger archaeologists with a movement in America that was called "New Archaeology." The main thrust was an "explicitly scientific approach" that adopted from positivist philosophies of science such novel ideas as borrowing from other disciplines (especially anthropology), explicit research design, hypothesis testing, the formulation of universal and timeless "laws of the cultural process," and a mechanistic concept of history that downplayed the role of ideology and the individual (Dever 1981, with references).

These new ideas were heavily "theoretical"—not in the sense of being impractical, but rather in a way that would fundamentally alter practice if adopted. Americans introduced some aspects of the new theory in projects like the Gezer excavations (see above; 1964–1973) and its offshoots at Tell el-Hesi (1970–1983), at a series of Galilean synagogue sites (1970–), and even in Jordan in the Madaba Plains Project (1968–). The watchwords of the mounting revolution were (1) "specialized," (2) "professional," and (3) "secular" (Dever 1973).

Israeli archaeologists, always more pragmatic, were preoccupied now by their own expanding enterprise (too many field projects even to list). Not until 1995, however, did Israeli archaeologists publish anything significant on theory (Bunimovitz 1995). In Jordan, a national school was slowly emerging, but it remained conventional.

The innovations in American archaeology inspired by the "New Archaeology" and the contemporary critique of "biblical archaeology" in Israel included a more anthropological orientation, multidisciplinary field staffs, and more specific research design. These were not only theoretical advances; they were also necessary adaptations as other developments took place, especially in the increasingly complex field projects that required public rather than private funding and in the introduction of academic summer "field schools" of volunteer students to replace hired native labor.

The latter was introduced at Gezer in 1966 and soon spread to other American projects in Israel and Jordan and eventually to virtually all Israeli excavations. The result was that field projects were now forced to articulate their aims and methods for young student workers who had no commitment to the theological motives of a previous generation of excavators. The "secular revolution" now took hold.

FIGURE 5-4. *The Solomonic gates (Iron II) at Gezer.*
Note the six chambers, three on each side.

"Syro-Palestinian Archaeology" Comes of Age, 1985–2000

The above revolution brought about heated controversies. But, by about 1985, the older-style "biblical archaeology" was dead, and few mourned its passing. In its place was an autonomous, more mature, more comprehensive secular branch of archaeology in Israel and Jordan that came to be styled "Syro-Palestinian" archaeology. This was a name coined by Albright as an alternate term for the discipline in the 1930s, adopted and popularized in the 1970s–1980s by Dever and other American archaeologists. Archaeology was now maturing as a professional discipline, with a scope that went far beyond the concept of conventional "biblical archaeology." Yet the problem of how to integrate the *two* disciplines—archaeology and the Bible—was far from being resolved (see below).

In Israel, new American projects now supplemented those of Gezer and its offshoots (see above), especially large-scale excavations at the Philistine sites of Ekron (Tel Miqne; jointly directed by the Albright's director Seymour Gitin and Hebrew University's Trude Dothan; 1981–1996) and at Ashkelon (directed by Harvard's Lawrence E. Stager; 1985–).

After 1967, the British, French, and German schools in Jerusalem gradually withdrew most of their activities to Jordan. French excavations at Tell Keisan (1971–1979) and Tell Yarmuth (1980–1990) were an exception, as were German excavations at Tel Masos (1972–1975) and Tell Kinneret (1980–). The British essentially boycotted excavations in Jerusalem after Kenyon's final season in 1967. In Jordan the British school's director, Crystal M. Bennett, excavated several sites in Edom: 'Umm el-Biyara (1960–1965), Tawilan (1968–1970; 1982), and Buseirah (Bostra; 1971–1974).

Israeli excavations in the field were numerous in the 1980s, either continuing or beginning projects. Among the more significant were the following:

Dan, 1966–
Jerusalem (many projects, 1968–)
Aphek, 1972–1985
Lachish, 1973–1987
Jokneam, 1977–1988
Tel Qashish, 1979–
Dor, 1980–
Shiloh, 1981–1984
Beth Shean, 1989–1996

By now the Department of Antiquities had metamorphosed into the expanded Israel Antiquities Authority, employing dozens of people. The Israel Museum had opened in 1965 with world-class facilities. There now were flourishing institutes of archaeology at universities in Jerusalem, Tel Aviv, Haifa, and Beersheba (and eventually Bar-Ilan). The Israelis were publishing at a quickened pace, mainly in English. Israeli excavations and publications were increasingly subsidized by American funds, and hundreds of American student volunteers attended the field schools.

Meanwhile, Americans were losing the initiative that they had once had. Only in Jordan did they predominate, where there was less competition. In 1968, the American Schools of Oriental Research opened a sister institute of the Jerusalem school in Amman, Jordan—it was named, for political reasons, the American Center of Oriental Research.

Disciplinary Anxieties, 2000–

By 2000 all the various national schools that we have discussed thus far had matured, but at the same time they had become more diversified. Like "biblical archaeology" previously, the reigning paradigm of "Syro-Palestinian" began to face challenges.

First, with the demise of the colonial era, new indigenous Middle Eastern archaeologies came into their own, with new questions. What role should archaeology play in forging national self-identities? Who owns the past, and how shall we appropriate its lessons? In an era of scarce resources, how can archaeology justify its relevance? Second, in Israel in particular, the political situation changed precipitously after 1967 and then again after the Palestinian intifada began in 1987. American and other foreign involvement in the Middle East now became more problematic. Third, as the cost of mounting the newer, more ambitious field projects soared, excavations and even the institutes of archaeology in Israel faced cutbacks. Fourth, in particular, the old problem of how to relate archaeological data to the Bible, never resolved, became more urgent with the advent of new "revisionist" schools of biblical interpretation, first in Europe but then in America and even Israel. The result was a historiographical crisis.

It has not always been understood that biblical revisionism is a thinly disguised version of a movement called "postmodernism," which arose in Europe some forty years ago, then spread. It is almost impossible to define, because it is a movement, an attitude, whose essence is a resistance to all forms of rational categories of thought. Postmodernism is a wholesale rejection of the Enlightenment ideals of reason and progress; it is essentially a theory of knowledge according to which there is no knowledge.

Some of postmodernism's typical assertions are revealing: (1) "all narratives are texts, and texts refer only to other texts, not to real events"; (2) "texts can be made to mean whatever we need them to mean"; (3) "all claims to knowledge are social constructs, only inventions"; (4) "all meta-narratives should be regarded with suspicion"; (5) "all readings are about race, class, gender, and ultimately politics"; (6) "there are no facts, only interpretations"; and (7) "all history writing is fiction."

The challenge of postmodernism should be obvious. Archaeology in whatever guise—especially "biblical archaeology" and its focus on real events—is all about history and history writing. The nihilism of postmodern thinking makes even the attempt a farce. Yet few archaeologists in our field have taken the postmodern threat seriously, oblivious as always to theoretical developments, especially those in other countries or other fields.

Postmodernism, however, has been widespread for a generation or more, and it has encouraged a certain endless search for novelty rather than certainty—what might be called "contrarianism." Thus, virtually every claim of mainstream archaeology to have discovered new truths is often met with scorn, often by other archaeologists themselves, despite attempts at rational evidence and discourse. For instance, the biblical "united monarchy"—the reigns of Saul, David, and Solomon in the tenth century BCE—is dismissed as fiction because all the archaeological evidence is moved down into the ninth century BCE. There was in fact no Judean state until the eighth century BCE. Revisionist biblical scholars go even further: there was no "ancient Israel," since the Hebrew Bible in its entirety is considered to be nothing but a foundation myth.

This "creeping skepticism" is unfortunate, because we now have a vast source of reliable new information about the Bible and the biblical world, thanks to the progress of archaeology. We know at least ten times as much as we did forty years ago. And this knowledge is now accessible not only to biblical and other scholars but also to general readers. We now have several authoritative topical dictionaries and encyclopedias (ABD; E. Meyers 1996; Sasson 2000). We have a number of up-to-date specifically archaeological encyclopedias, covering hundreds and hundreds of sites (Stern 1993–2008), as well as a superb biblical atlas (Rainey and Notley 2006). There are also several archaeological handbooks and textbooks (A. Mazar 1990; Ben-Tor 1992a; Levy 1995b). Finally, several journals and magazines provide timely, reliable data, such as the *Israel Exploration Journal*; *Tel-Aviv*; *Levant*; the *Bulletin of the American Schools of Oriental Research*; and *Near Eastern Archaeology* (as well as the popular magazine *Biblical Archaeology Review*). There is no longer any excuse for biblical scholars to be uninformed about the archeological revolution that should be transforming our understanding of the Bible.

"Disciplinary anxieties" or not, we will inevitably move on to an archaeology that is more complex, more diverse, more difficult to define. In particular the new "Levantine archaeology"—broadening the inquiry beyond Israel and Jordan, to Syria, Turkey, Cyprus, and elsewhere—may cause a loss of the center, which for most is still ancient Israel and Palestine. There is also a weariness with theory among some younger archaeologists, both in Israel and in America, that has resulted in a call for a "new pragmatism," an emphasis on what works. But without a robust sense of theory to guide and evaluate research, how can we *discern* what works, what is actually relevant? These challenges will undoubtedly be met in the future, because the "archaeological revolution" begun in the 1970s will continue, even if in ways that appear unsettling to the present generation.

Whatever the future may hold, scientific means of analyzing and publishing data will likely take precedence. Already, computer-aided total station mapping is producing far more detailed three-dimensional plans, making the stratigraphy of the site manipulative while being nondestructive. Laboratory analysis of sediments and improved ^{14}C dating—"archaeometrics"—is already yielding more precise data of all kinds. And computers make possible the publication of prompt, better illustrated, and far more detailed information than formerly possible. Science will not save us; but it can facilitate better work.

Meanwhile, the theoretical revolution must continue; without robust theory, we have no way of knowing what we claim to know. We have now moved well beyond the "New Archaeology" of the 1970s–1980s (see above; sometimes called "processual archaeology") to various forms of "post-processualism." This trend reemphasizes the importance of history writing and of the role of ideology and the individual in the process. There is now more emphasis on finding "the meaning of things." Some archaeologists even advocate "reading artifacts" like reading texts, with similar understandings of the vocabulary, grammar, and syntax of material culture (Hodder 1986; Preucel and Mzrowski 2010).

What Archaeology Can and Cannot Do: Some "Case Studies"

In their final years, two veteran "biblical archaeologists" offered us their reflections on a lifetime's devotion to the discipline. In 1970, a year before his death, the venerable French Dominican archaeologist Père Roland de Vaux published a provocative piece entitled "On Wrong and Right Uses of Archaeology." America's doyen, G. Ernest Wright, published an article entitled "What Archaeology Can and Cannot Do" in 1971, before his death in 1974. Both were well-known archeologists as well as churchmen of deep faith and piety.

Both scholars agreed on one thing that critics of biblical archaeology have pointed out since the 1970s: archaeology and theology must initially be pursued entirely independently, in the interest of honest scholarship. Only later, when the data from both sources have been critically evaluated, can there be a search for what have been called "convergences" (Dever 2001). It is in the dialogue *between* two independent disciplines that our best hope for genuine new knowledge lies. However, archaeology cannot "confirm" faith, even when it may produce historical certainty.

To put it simply, archaeology can answer questions like What, Where, When, How, and even Who. It cannot answer the question, What does it *mean*? Archaeology can provide a historical context for events described in the Bible that may (or may not) have happened—that is, a plausible context. But archaeological "proofs" that would validate faith are not obtainable, nor would they be helpful. Faith is faith is faith.

Some case studies of what archaeology has done for biblical studies (in this case, Old Testament or Hebrew Bible) may be helpful.

First, the books of Exodus through Judges tell an extended story of the miraculous escape of many thousands of Hebrew slaves from Egypt; their forty-year wandering in the Sinai wilderness; the giving of the law and the covenant with Israel to Moses at Mount Sinai; and the total conquest of Canaan, the Land of Promise, in a short time under Joshua. Thus, Israel was born. This narrative was taken as conventional history until a generation or so ago in biblical studies and archaeology.

Today, all that has changed. Virtually no trace of the Sinai journeys has been found, despite determined efforts of archaeologists. Of the thirty-one sites the Bible says were taken by the Israelites, actual destructions have been found at only two or three, and these are not necessarily Israelite. Sites like Dhiban, Heshbon, Jericho, and Ai were not even occupied in the late thirteenth century BCE, when we now know that any "exodus-conquest" must be dated. The book of Joshua now looks largely fictitious, while the story of a long drawn-out process of socioeconomic change in the book of Judges seems much more realistic (Dever 2003a and references).

To be sure, there probably was a small exodus group—the biblical "house of Joseph," or the two southern tribes, who later wrote the biblical story and included "all Israel." Here, archaeology has not confirmed the biblical account as expected, to the contrary. Is it still possible to believe that Israel's emergence in the full light of history (which certainly did happen) was miraculous? Perhaps, depending on what one thinks that "miraculous" means.

Second, the exodus tale is a negative case study, at least for conventional history. But there are other cases as well, since Albright's famous "archaeological revolution" has indeed occurred, although not in the way that he anticipated. Nevertheless, there are some success stories.

The social world of the eighth-century BCE prophets, the context in which their message was situated, was scarcely known outside the biblical texts until the beginning of modern archaeology. The ruling elites in Israel are castigated by the prophets for amassing land and wealth by defrauding the poor, for living in conspicuous luxury in "houses of ivory," and for manipulating the currency by dealing in false weights and balances.

All these practices have now been brilliantly illuminated by archaeological discoveries securely dated to the ninth to seventh centuries BCE. At Samaria, the capital of the Northern Kingdom, we have the large and luxurious palace, constructed of costly Phoenician masonry, filled with ivory-inlaid furniture. The dozens of ostraca found at Samaria, written in ink on potsherds, reveal a network of wealthy estate owners, who amassed fortunes no doubt by exploiting peasant farmers and who paid substantial taxes in kind. We even have dozens of small inscribed stone shekel-weights, some of which are oversize, in effect "the butcher's thumb on the scale." Some of the weights bear the name *pîm*, a term that occurs only once in the Hebrew Bible, whose meaning was unknown until the discovery of the actual weights (a *pîm* is about two-thirds of a shekel, the latter supposed to weigh about 11.5 grams).

The abuses of which the prophets complained were real, and so was their world. These biblical accounts may be stories; but they are stories that fit into the eight to sixth centuries BCE, not the imaginary Persian or Hellenistic world of the revisionist's Bible (Dever 2001, 209–11, 221–28, 237–39).

Finally, some case studies are mixed—archaeology neither confirming nor denying the biblical record. For instance, the ideal of the Hebrew Bible is clearly monotheism, the exclusive worship of Yahweh, from Israel's infancy in the desert to the end of the monarchy. Yet archaeology shows beyond doubt that the reality was that polytheism prevailed throughout, not only in folk religion but even in the official cult in Jerusalem. We have hundreds of nude female terra-cotta figurines that in one way or another represent the great Canaanite mother goddess **Asherah**. She is in fact mentioned several times in the Hebrew Bible (sometimes in the guise of her symbol: a tree or a pole). We even have an eighth-century BCE Hebrew inscription from Kuntillet Ajrud that names her in a context of blessing, connected with Yahweh. Thus, she can appear as his consort (Dever 2005).

FIGURE 5-5. *Female terra-cotta figurines that may represent the Canaanite mother goddess Asherah, eighth century BCE.*

All this, and other archaeological evidence, may seem to contradict the biblical depiction of Israelite monotheism. Yet the texts represent the ideal; the biblical writers knew that the reality was quite different. It is their polemics against "idolatry" that prove its widespread existence. Thus, the archaeological data, while perhaps disturbing at first, actually confirm the biblical portrait of biblical religion in actual practice.

Reflections on the Future

Thus far we have looked at what archaeology has and has not done in illustrating the Bible and the biblical world. Now let us turn to what it might contribute in the future.

Many discussions of contemporary archaeology worldwide call for it to justify itself, particularly in an era of diminishing resources—in short, to be "relevant." But relevant to *what*? What is the value of archaeology—the attempt to portray the past—unless we can learn the lessons of that past?

Archaeologists seem recently to be returning to history and history writing as commendable goals—that is the major relevance of the enterprise (Preucel and Mzrowski 2010). In that case, "biblical archaeology," in any guise, should be focused in the future on history rather than theology.

For our understanding of the Hebrew Bible / Old Testament, archaeology's major contribution in the future will probably lie in providing data that will contribute to the writing of newer and more satisfactory histories of ancient Israel. No new history of Israel has been published by American or European biblical scholars in the past generation; and those written earlier are now obsolete. That is because the biblical texts, after two thousand years of interpretation and reinterpretation, have yielded all the information they contain.

The only source of genuinely new information lies in archaeology and the independent witness that it provides. Archaeology will complement and correct the biblical narrative, providing a wealth of more contemporary, more detailed, more varied, more authentic information on *real* life in ancient Israel, not only the lives of the few elites who wrote the Hebrew Bible (Grabbe 2007; Dever, 2012).

For the New Testament and early Christianity, archaeology's potential contribution is less obvious. Many of the fundamental issues in the Old Testament are historical, such as the patriarchal era; the exodus from Egypt and the conquest of Canaan; the rise of the monarchy; and the development of monotheism. By contrast, the fundamental doctrines of the New Testament are more theological than historical, properly speaking. Consider such narratives as those of the virgin birth, the teachings and miracles of Jesus' public ministry, the bodily resurrection from the dead and the ascent into heaven, blood atonement of sin, as well as the descent of the Holy Spirit and the spread of the gospel. None of these essential Christian doctrines is amenable to historical and therefore archaeological investigation, much less verification (for the data, see Reed 2007). What, then, could archaeology contribute?

Archaeology is all about context, not "proof"—establishing a physical and even a psychological setting in which the biblical stories may seem more credible. In this case, context means using archaeological data to reconstruct the historical and cultural environment of the Galilean Jewish community in which Jesus grew to maturity. Recent excavations at Sepphoris, a large Roman-Period site near Nazareth, have done just that. Herodian Jerusalem, the setting of other events in Jesus' life, is now much better known thanks to extensive Israeli excavations since the Six-Day War. For later periods, several early Christian basilicas and monasteries, as well as Jewish synagogues, have been excavated and illuminate the growth of both religious communities and their interaction. However, the most promising region in which to understand the spread of Christianity would be Syria, but it will likely remain off limits to foreign excavations for a long time.

Does any of this recent archaeological evidence validate or even enhance the faith of earnest Christians or Jews? It might, but it might not, depending on how much one's belief is on the historicity of events narrated in the Bible. But archaeology enables one to read these stories with greater understanding, and that is certainly desirable.

"Biblical archaeology" has had a long and checkered history. Today the term is used in several ways. (1) It can be used by amateurs or even professionals to refer to the archaeology of Israel, Jordan, or even Syria, Turkey, and Cyprus (though increasingly the broader term "Levantine" is preferred for this larger region). It may or may not carry some of the theological baggage of an earlier era. (2) It is still used by Israeli archaeologists to refer to the archaeology of the so-called biblical period in Israel—that is, the archaeology of the Bronze and Iron Ages (ca. 3600–600 BCE). That usage, however, is parochial, and it can be confusing. (3) Finally, the term "biblical archaeology" is best used to define not the discipline itself but the dialogue between two disciplines: archaeology and biblical studies. These disciplines have both expanded so enormously and are now so specialized that they must be pursued independently and fully professionally. Yet they are still related, and they can benefit from collaboration in writing new histories of both ancient Israel and the early Jewish/Christian communities.

Conclusion

There are many challenges to be met in facing the future of archaeology in the Middle East, whether pursued by the growing national schools or by foreign scholars. The discipline has now become so varied and so diffuse that it is almost impossible to define any center, such as the concept of "the biblical world." The political instability throughout the region threatens systematic fieldwork, especially that carried out by foreign excavators. A continuing worldwide recession means less support for excavation, conservation of sites, research, and the professional positions needed to place a well-trained younger generation of specialists. Finally, a mass of new information, much of it quantified by scientific means of analysis, must be assimilated and made available not only to scholars in allied disciplines but also to the general public. The latter's fascination continues unabated, and it can and must be satisfied. Perhaps this résumé, while greatly simplified, may help.

Suggestions for Further Reading

Recent studies of biblical archaeology and the changes it underwent as it developed into Syro-Palestinian archaeology combine analyses of its history with critique of its weaknesses and strengths. Two perspectives appear in T. W. Davies' *Shifting Sands: The Rise and Fall of Biblical Archaeology* and R. P. S. Moorey's *A Century of Biblical Archaeology*, while a wide variety of views and studies have been collected by Drinkard, Mattingly, and Miller in *Benchmarks in Time and Culture* and by Hoffmeier and Millard in their *Future of Biblical Archaeology: Reassessing Methodologies and Assumptions*. William Dever follows this shift with several publications over the decades. Two works provide snapshots of his views: *Archaeology and Biblical Studies: Retrospects and Prospects* (1974) and his essay in the *Anchor Bible Dictionary*, "Archaeology, Syro-Palestinian and Biblical" (1992).

The "New Archaeology" of the 1980s was a launching pad for yet further innovation. This can be seen already in I. Hodder's *Reading the Past: Current Approaches to Interpretation in Archaeology* (1986). And explorations and experiments continue into the new century. See the essays in T. E. Levy's *Historical Biblical Archaeology and the Future: The New Pragmatism* and in Preucel and Mzrowski's *Contemporary Archaeology in Theory: The New Pragmatism*.

For more information about American archaeological exploration of ancient Israel, see the history of ASOR in Philip King's *American Archaeology in the Mideast: A History of the American Schools of Oriental Research* and the essays in Joseph Seger's *An ASOR Mosaic: A Centennial History of the American Schools of Oriental Research, 1900–2000*.

II

ISRAEL BEFORE SETTLING IN THE LAND

6

IN THE BEGINNING, ARCHAEOLOGICALLY SPEAKING
Archaeology to the Bronze Ages in Canaan

K. L. Noll

Why Doesn't Genesis Mention *Homo erectus?*

The Bible records nothing about the people to be discussed in this chapter. That is because the documents now contained in the Bible were composed no earlier than the Iron Age, centuries after these people had died (see the chronology chart below, Figure 6-1). It is also because the scribes who created the Bible took no interest in the past, a controversial point that requires additional discussion.

Many researchers (including some authors in this volume) believe that biblical narratives were composed by religious historians—scribes who interpreted the past from a religious point of view—but that belief is not supported by the evidence (Noll 2013b, 66–104, 394–407). Biblical authors were storytellers, poets, and, above all, librarians (Thompson 1992, 389–90). In a few instances, the sources they gathered were reliable historical sources (e.g., 2 Kgs 24:10-12), genuinely ancient poetry (such as Num 21:14-15), and old religious traditions (e.g., Num 6:24-26), but these are rare. In most cases, their sources were not reliable accounts of real people or events but secular folklore (e.g., 1–2 Sam), religious folklore (e.g., Num 24:3-9), and impious or satirical fictions (such as 1 Kgs 12:33–13:32 and 22:2-36). In all cases, the biblical scribes used these sources creatively, never hesitating to modify the details to suit new narrative purposes. Biblical books are *anthologies of narrative and poetry*, not religious history writing (Noll 2007).

Our culture's common assumption that the book of Genesis was intended to be a sacred history is as unfortunate as it is incorrect. The chronological sequence in Genesis looks superficially like a "history," but the ancient scribes invented an artificial chronology as the "filing system" that gave structure to the various stories they gathered for their anthology (Thompson 1987, 156–58). For example, there are two narratives about divine creation, which is odd if the scribes thought they were describing what their god had actually accomplished (P. Davies 1995, 81–94). In the first creation tale (Gen 1:1–2:4a), the humans are created last, after all other creatures (Gen 1:26); however, in the second tale (Gen 2:4b–3:24), a human is created first, before other creatures (Gen 2:4b-7). The first story has male and female created together (Gen 1:27), but the female is a divine afterthought in the second story (Gen 2:18-23). The first story announces that humans were created in the divine image and that fertility was granted as a blessing (Gen 1:27-28), but, in the second tale, fertility is a curse and the humans become similar to their god only through disobedience (Gen 3:5, 16, 22). Contradictory details gathered into one scroll suggest that the scribes were not proclaiming a message about a god but preserving traditional lore perhaps retrieved from originally separate communities (Thompson 1992, 353–72).

It is reasonable to imagine that the scribes would have been puzzled if they had lived to see later generations of readers treat Genesis as a work of sacred authority. Their lack of concern for a religious message is matched by their disregard of narrative coherence. For example, Genesis 6:19 and 7:2 cannot agree on how many animals Noah gathered into his great boat. Cain is able to take a wife even though no females had yet been born in the narrative sequence (Gen 4:17). Names in the genealogical lists are not the names of individuals. In some cases, these names are cities (Gen 11:22-26), ethnic groups (Gen 36:10-30), geographical regions (Gen 10:2-4), or even ancient trade routes (Gen 25:1-4). Figures such as Lamech and Enoch are traced through the lineage of Cain in one chapter but through Cain's brother Seth in another chapter. In fact, the Hebrew names in Genesis 4:17-18 are equivalent to the Hebrew names in Genesis 5:12-27, but several names are spelled differently and placed in a different sequence. In other words, these two lists are variant versions of the same list, possibly gathered from two geographically distinct older sources. That a book like Genesis was designed to be an anthology of folklore, not a religiously authoritative narrative, is unsurprising. In the ancient world, literature was rarely an authoritative element in religious observances or doctrines.

The folktales of the Bible are interesting and sometimes artistic, but they are not a primary source of knowledge about the people of ancient times. The Bible's folklore speculates about people who previously lived in its so-called promised land, people who are given mythological names such as Rephaim, which was a common ancient label for minor gods or deified ancestors (e.g., Deut 2:10-12, 20-23). Speculation of this kind demonstrates that biblical authors were content with folklore and did not try to investigate the thousands of human generations who lived in their land before they were born. Today, pseudoscientific agendas such as "intelligent design creationism" and "theistic evolution" attempt to impose biblical speculation (or, more accurately, to impose *contemporary interpretations* of biblical speculation) on the past, but biological science, archaeological research, and historical investigation provide a more valuable story (Dennett 1995; Pennock 2000; Liverani 2005; Noll 2013b).

FIGURE 6-1. *Archaeological Periods*

ARCHAEOLOGICAL PERIOD	APPROXIMATE DATES
Lower Paleolithic	Prior to about 250,000 years ago
Middle Paleolithic	About 250,000 to 50,000 years ago
Upper Paleolithic	About 50,000 to 20,000 years ago
Epipaleolithic (sometimes called Mesolithic)	About 20,000 to 10,000 years ago (about 18,000 BCE to 8000 BCE)
Pre-Pottery Neolithic	About 8000 BCE to 5500 BCE
Pottery Neolithic	About 5500 BCE to 4500 BCE
Chalcolithic	About 4500 BCE to 3600 BCE
Early Bronze	3600 to 2000 BCE
Middle Bronze	2000 to 1550 BCE
Late Bronze	1550 to 1200 BCE
Iron Age	After 1200 BCE

Paleolithic

Planet Earth is about 4.5 billion years old. If those billions of years could be compressed into twenty-four hours, the species **Homo sapiens sapiens** has walked Earth for fewer than four *seconds*. Among our ancestors prior to the emergence of **Homo sapiens sapiens**, the first to leave Africa was *Homo erectus* just less than two million years ago, or about *thirty-eight seconds* ago in the twenty-four-hour timescale. We are direct evolutionary descendants of *Homo erectus*, but so far our species has survived for only a fraction of the time that *Homo erectus* walked Earth (Mayr 2001, 233–56).

Genome research suggests that the earliest modern humans emerged from Africa about sixty thousand years ago (Li and Durbin 2011). In Palestine, the artifacts seem to corroborate this estimate. Hominid (sometimes written Hominin) remains that are older than sixty thousand years are not yet the modern species called *Homo sapiens sapiens*. For example, a cave in Galilee had been the grave of a hominid skull that is about 350,000 years old and seems to have been an archaic variety of *Homo sapiens*, perhaps an ancestor of **Homo sapiens neanderthalensis** (P. Smith 1998, 60–61, 71–72). However, most of our data from these early millennia are not human remains but stone tools and the stone flakes left behind when tools were made. Often, these stone artifacts are found with butchered animal bones. The bones can tell us a great deal about one aspect of the early human diet, but it is usually in the later prehistoric periods (to be discussed below) that we find the remains of grains and seeds that had been charred during food processing, a kind of evidence that reveals a great deal more about both diet and lifestyle (Rollefson 1993, 88).

During the Middle Paleolithic, *Homo sapiens neanderthalensis* and another variety of archaic *Homo sapiens* began to inhabit the Levant (modern Syria, southern Turkey, Lebanon, Jordan, Palestine, Israel), though there is no evidence (yet) to suggest that they came into contact with one another in this region. The coastal region of the southern Levant was wider than today, and the region from north of Lake Galilee to south of the Dead Sea was covered by a large prehistoric saltwater lake. Also, the climate shifted several times, including periods of ice age and periods of warmer climate and high rainfall. For example, the region northeast of Damascus, Syria, is a desert today, but, during significant portions of the Paleolithic era, the Palmyra basin (as it is called) contained a large freshwater lake that attracted the animals our ancestors hunted for survival (Schroeder 2006, 89).

We find evidence for modern humans, *Homo sapiens sapiens*, in the Levant about 50,000 years ago, the beginning of the Upper Paleolithic (Goring-Morris and Belfer-Cohen 2003). If the average human generation is counted as 20 years, then 50,000 years ago was 2,500 human generations ago. By contrast, the time in which the Bible began to be written was about 600 BCE, or about 130 human generations ago. In other words, the age of Earth and the age of humanity are massive lengths of time. In contrast, the Bible seems quite recent.

Although fire hearths demonstrate that the premodern humans of the Middle Paleolithic sites were capable of technological achievements, the newer encampments in the Upper Paleolithic display a much wider variety of innovations (Gilead 1995, 133–36). People continued to use stone tools, of course, but added tools made from animal bones. Also, these people began to adorn themselves with jewelry made from seashells. They used large grinding stones to prepare vegetal foods and to manufacture an ochre pigment. Nevertheless, the roughly 1,500 human generations that lived through the Upper Paleolithic never settled in one place permanently. Their dwellings seem to have been temporary shelters; charred-grain traces suggest that each occupation was for one season of a year rather than through all the seasons of the year.

Permanent houses emerged late in an era that researchers call the Epipaleolithic (sometimes called the Mesolithic). The early portion of the Epipaleolithic saw the last major ice age, and it was followed by a warmer and increasingly arid climate. The vast prehistoric lake that covered the region from north of Lake Galilee to south of the Dead Sea was receding gradually in the final millennia of this era, so that the region's geography looked much like it does today by about 8000 BCE (Goldberg 1998, 44–45).

During the final two thousand years or so of the Epipaleolithic, a people called the Natufian culture appeared (Weinstein-Evron 2009). These people lived in circular or semicircular houses, apparently year round, and these houses were usually aligned along a slope. They harvested wild cereals, such as wheat. However, we do not find evidence of domesticated strains of wheat among the Natufian; they had not invented farming. Perhaps the Natufian were the first to domesticate wolves, because several dogs have been found buried with their masters in Natufian graves (Valla 1998). Not only did biblical authors know nothing about the Natufian society, but also the artificial biblical chronology puts the creation of the entire universe *after* the Natufian people had ceased to exist, along with their domesticated dogs, sophisticated tools, and everything else they had achieved.

Neolithic

The most significant innovation in human history was the invention of farming, which took place sometime around 8000 BCE. This agricultural revolution is called the New Stone Age, or Neolithic. Modern humans survived two thousand generations or more before inventing farming, and we have lived as farmers for a fraction of that time—about five hundred generations (still assuming about twenty years per generation). Biblical authors were unable to conceive of a time when humans were not farmers, which is why the first human is a gardener in one of the creation stories (Gen 2:15). In fact, the Bible's story compresses many inventions of humanity into the space of a few human generations: shepherds appear in the second human generation (Gen 4:2); city construction during the third (Gen 4:17); the invention of music, the emergence of nomadism, and even the production of metal crafts in the ninth (Gen 4:20-21). One who treats these biblical tales as a reliable historical account of human civilization suffers an impoverished understanding of our collective past because that was not the intent of the scribes who compiled these texts.

Neolithic farmers relied on a handful of crops that have remained basic staples of life into modern times (Grigson 1998). Barley and wheat have been the foundation of this diet, supplemented by lentils and peas. A few fruits and nuts were common as well, such as figs, peaches, almonds, pistachios, and walnuts. Olives were harvested for their oil, which provided fuel for lamps and ointments for medicinal and hygienic needs. Flax was cultivated for making linen cloth. Some agricultural features now common to the region were actually imported from other regions. The grape, for example, was not native but became the basis for the region's most common beverage after it was introduced. Likewise, sheep and goats were not native to the region but became central to the agricultural economy after their introduction. Pigs were a small part of the people's diet in prehistoric times, but pig consumption gradually declined in later eras. The Bible prohibits the consumption of pork (Lev 11:7; Deut 14:8), but that was not an inconvenience to the majority, because few Levantine people ate pork during the Iron Age.

Researchers divide the Neolithic into two unequal parts. The earlier and longer era is called Pre-Pottery Neolithic. Before humans discovered the versatility and convenience of clay, they used plaster that was made from the common limestone of the region. Neolithic people plastered the walls and floors of their homes and made cooking vessels of plaster. In many cases, they fashioned human statues in plaster (K. Tubb 1985). These statues are semiabstract but exquisitely crafted. We are not certain what purpose they served, but artistic similarities to god statues of a much later era (when writing was available to identify the statues as gods) suggest that the Neolithic plaster statues were representations of the gods.

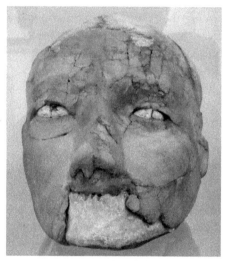

FIGURE 6-2. *Neolithic plastered skull from Jericho.*

During the Pre-Pottery Neolithic, plaster also played a role in funerary practices (Goring-Morris and Horwitz 2007). In some Neolithic communities, selected individuals (sometimes male and sometimes female) were buried under the plaster floors in houses. After sufficient time had passed for the corpse to become dry bones, the plaster floor was broken, and the skull was removed. This skull was covered with plaster, which was carefully molded to resemble human flesh. Sometimes, seashells were added as eyes, and hair was affixed as well. After a time, collections of these skulls were reburied together. Researchers have suggested that this practice might have been a form of religious magic to ward off evil or a commemoration of revered family members (Bonogofsky 2004). A common hypothesis is that this was a form of religion in which ancestral gods were venerated. Ancestor worship is common around the world in most historic periods, particularly but not exclusively among nonliterate cultures, in which a family tomb and associated religious rites function as a deed of property ownership for the living. A variety of biblical passages, as well as Iron Age archaeological discoveries, suggest that ancestral veneration remained common during the centuries in which the Bible was composed. Biblical texts suggest that a few elites disliked the ancestral veneration and tried to outlaw it, but the frustration expressed as sarcasm in some of these biblical passages also suggests that ancestral rites remained popular among the common people (e.g., Lev 19:28; Deut 18:10-11; Isa 8:19-20; 65:4).

The Neolithic agricultural revolution began with the domestication of cereals and continued with the domestication of animals (Bar-Yosef 1998). Ancient trash heaps show a gradual shift in butchered meat, from predominantly wild animals (gazelle, deer, hare, fox) to predominantly domesticated animals (some cattle, but especially sheep and goats). This era also saw a sharp rise in long-distance trade and cultural contacts. The Levant in earlier periods had seen the use of seashell jewelry from the Mediterranean, but the Neolithic sites contain imported seashells of species native to the Red Sea. Also, obsidian from Anatolia (modern Turkey) can be found in the Neolithic communities of the Levant.

Another key innovation of the Neolithic era was the invention of ceramics. This era is called the Pottery Neolithic. Once humans had mastered the craft of firing the clay at high temperatures, often decorating it with an artistic and protective veneer, society had a handy, versatile, and inexpensive resource for food storage, preparation, and consumption. Pottery became so common, and pottery breaks so easily, that it quickly established itself as the ubiquitous roadside trash of the ancient world. This is a great advantage for archaeologists. Not only do archaeologists love trash heaps for their intrinsic worth—helping us to identify common lifestyles, foodways, and daily habits—but the common pottery shards found in any excavation enable us to establish a sequence of chronological phases through which pottery styles changed over time. This enables an archaeologist to date virtually any archaeological excavation to within a century or two, in most cases. For this reason, the study of pottery is one of the most basic tools of archaeological research.

Food storage, preparation, and consumption were the most common uses for ceramics, but many other clay products were produced as well. For example, during the early phase of the Pottery Neolithic, clay figurines depicting humans and animals were produced in great quantity (Freikman and Garfinkel 2009). These objects are highly abstract, but not because the artists lacked skill. The figures display a stylized abstraction that tends to emphasize particular features of the figures, apparently those features that Neolithic people believed to be of primary significance. These figurines might have been toys, but that seems unlikely. They appear to have been serious objects, perhaps of a religious nature. Possibly they depict the gods, or perhaps they depict aspects of human and animal life for which the gods were expected to provide guidance and support.

Chalcolithic

The word *Chalcolithic* means "copper-stone," and it designates the moment when humans discovered metalworking. Copper was the first exploited metal. Combining tin with copper creates a stronger alloy called bronze. Iron was discovered when bronze was the dominant metal, but iron is more difficult to work and only became popular much later. This is why archaeologists divide the metalworking period into three broad categories: Chalcolithic first, then the Bronze era, and the Iron Age after that.

FIGURE 6-3. *Copper scepters from the Nahal Mishmar Cave in the Judean Desert overlooking the Dead Sea. Over four hundred copper items were wrapped in a reed mat in the cave. The find is considered one of the most spectacular collections of copper caches discovered in the Levant from the Chalcolithic period.*

Considerable continuity appears in the material remains from the late Neolithic into the early Chalcolithic, which suggests that the Chalcolithic people were direct descendants of their Neolithic predecessors and that there was no gap in occupation of the land (Levy 1995b). However, the Chalcolithic era saw a significant increase in population, which also led to the exploitation of previously uninhabited marginal zones. For example, the Beersheba Valley, which was not as arid as it is now, supported a vibrant Chalcolithic community that used creative irrigation techniques and survived for about seven hundred years. The largest Chalcolithic community was in the Jordan River Valley, on the eastern side of the river opposite Jericho, at a place known today as Tulei-lat Ghassul. This sprawling village must have been home to at least four thousand people in any generation. The community survived for at least thirty-five human generations, but it vanished before the Chalcolithic era came to an end, and no one knew of these people again until modern archaeology rediscovered them.

Evidence suggests that the social and political structures of the Chalcolithic era were complex and that interregional cooperation took place. In addition to metalworking, Chalcolithic people developed sophisticated crafts, such as the carving of ivory and the working of gold; and this implies an increase in long-distance trade networks so that these luxury items, which are not native to the southern Levant, could be made available. Although the precise nature of Chalcolithic government cannot be known in the absence of writing, clues in the material remains suggest that regions of the Levant had become autonomous entities (archaeologists like to use a word such as "chiefdom"). However, even if each region was politically autonomous, evidence indicates that these regional entities were also somehow integrated or, at least, cooperating with one another. For example, several sites—such as Gilat near Beersheba, and a cave near the Dead Sea called the Nahal Mishmar Cave—appear to have been religious shrines (Levy 2006; Bar-Adon 1980). From the material remains, we can deduce that these religious centers seem to have served local people as well as people coming from quite a distance away (Levy 1995b, 237).

Another indication of interregional cooperation during Chalcolithic times is an extraordinary burial cave discovered recently in the Galilee, called the Peqi'in Cave (Gal, Shalem, and Smithline 2011). Grave goods in this cave enable researchers to identify the cave's transregional importance. People buried in this cave came from many locations, and, based on a comparison of the material remains with the habits of several traditional cultures around the globe, archaeologists believe that these people had been leading citizens of various communities. Once a year (perhaps), a solemn ceremony took place in which that year's deceased were taken for secondary burial in the Peqi'in Cave.

The Chalcolithic era was followed by several centuries in which the southern Levant was only lightly inhabited. This occupational gap separates the Stone Age from the Bronze Age that follows. During the transition from the Chalcolithic into the Early Bronze, the climate shifted toward the higher levels of aridity it has today. Not surprisingly, many of the marginal zones inhabited by Chalcolithic people were uninhabited in the less populated Early Bronze. It is possible that some Early Bronze inhabitants were biological descendants of Chalcolithic people, but archaeologists note several indications of a severe break between these two human civilizations, which suggests that the Bronze era saw a new population entering the region (Gophna 1998, 272; Ahlström 1993, 112–15).

Early Bronze

The folktales about human origins found in Genesis 1–11 never mention the invention of writing, which happened in the Early Bronze era. It is possible but unlikely that the scribes who collected these folktales could not imagine a time when humans did not write. Biblical scribes knew that literacy was a human invention and not an innate human capacity because very few of their contemporaries could read or write. Prior to the expansion of public education in the modern era, the majority of any human population was illiterate. Among the people whom many biblical scholars have labeled "ancient Israel" or "biblical Israel," at least 95 percent were unable to read the scrolls that the biblical scribes were creating. In all likelihood, they were not even aware that the scribes had created these scrolls, because the scribes made no effort to disseminate either the scrolls or their contents among the common people (Noll 2011). The common assumption made by scholars, rabbis, priests, and ministers that biblical documents were intended for public proclamation is incorrect (Noll 2008). In light of the fact that literature was not central to

the lives of most people, it is reasonable to suppose that the authors of Genesis 1–11 did not mention the invention of writing because they did not consider writing that significant.

The invention of writing is the second-most significant human invention, overshadowed only by the invention of farming. Even farming has not exerted the intellectually transforming influence of the written word. In the ancient Near East, writing emerged in two places at roughly the same time. Mesopotamia and Egypt developed

FIGURE 6-4. *Cuneiform tablet. Cuneiform writing was created by the ancient Sumerians of Mesopotamia and was the first (ca. 3200 BCE) and most widespread writing system in the ancient Middle East.*

systems for keeping economic records during the Early Bronze era. As the population in these two harsh environments increased, humans needed to cooperate on a large scale to work the land and produce enough food for everyone. This large-scale labor required large-scale organization, thus stimulating the earliest empires, which provided bureaucrats to oversee production, storage, and distribution. At first, the writing systems were purely practical, designed to keep records and maintain a bureaucracy. After a few centuries, the uses for writing expanded, so that poetry and narrative literatures began to emerge.

The writing systems of Egypt and Mesopotamia were complex (Van De Mieroop 2007, 28–35). The Egyptians created a system of pictures that could be combined in various ways, usually called "hieroglyphs." Mesopotamia created a set of symbols to represent syllables. Their writing system is called "cuneiform," a word that refers to the wedge-shaped symbols pressed into wet clay tablets with a blunt writing tool. Neither hieroglyphs nor cuneiform is an alphabet like the one you are reading now. An alphabet uses symbols to represent single, short sounds rather than entire syllables or words. Therefore, an alphabet requires fewer distinct characters because these characters can be combined in a vast number of arrangements to specify almost any sound humans can make. The invention of an alphabet took place during the Middle Bronze (Rollston 2010, 11). An early alphabet from Syria-Palestine, called Phoenician, spread throughout the Levant and migrated northward to Greece. It evolved into the Greek alphabet as well as into the West Semitic scripts of the Levant (e.g., Ammonite, Aramaic, Hebrew, Moabite). The alphabet you are reading now evolved from Latin, which was a descendant of the Greek alphabet.

Because the Early Bronze is the earliest era in which writing occurs, it marks the beginning of the so-called historical period. Not surprisingly, most ancient history writing was royal propaganda extolling the virtues and accomplishments of kings, whose actual careers were less virtuous and more brutal than their propaganda suggests (Pritchard 1969). Throughout the Early Bronze, the centers of innovation and cultural achievement, as well as military power, were in Egypt and Mesopotamia. The former saw the rise and decline of the famous Old Kingdom of Egypt, with its great pyramids; the latter saw a series of cultures and empires rise and fall, including the ancient Sumerians in southern Mesopotamia, the empire called Agade or Akkad, and the revitalized Sumerian empire known as Ur III (Kuhrt 1995, 19–73, 118–60). The achievements of these Early Bronze kingdoms had faded to ancient memory before Hebrew-speaking people began to write the Bible, but biblical authors knew about some of their architectural monuments. For example, Genesis 11:1-9 is a satirical tale about the "Tower of Babel" that was designed to "explain," with tongue in cheek, the ancient ziggurats of southern Mesopotamia, artificial mountains that housed temples of the gods (Woolley 1954, 125–37).

During the Early Bronze Age, the Levant was a quiet marginal zone wedged between the two emerging imperial regions in Mesopotamia and Egypt. Archaeological finds in Palestine suggest that the northern portions of the region were influenced by trade and cultural contact with Mesopotamia and that the southern portions were influenced by trade and cultural contact with Egypt. The middle centuries of the Early Bronze (roughly from 2700 to 2300 BCE) saw the rise of several Levantine urban centers. We have learned much about the period from archives recovered in a Syrian excavation, where an ancient city called Ebla was a vital part of the international economy—a trade hub for regions to the east, north, and south. The major cities in Early Bronze Palestine collapsed before the end of this era, and biblical texts are silent about them.

Middle Bronze

Shortly after 2000 BCE, the ancient Near East entered into a period of political and cultural renaissance. Egypt's Middle Kingdom began to mine the Sinai Peninsula for turquoise and to establish close diplomatic relations with the cities of Syria and Palestine, a region that was beginning to be called Canaan. In Mesopotamia, large independent cities competed with one another to establish imperial control and trade networks. The southern Mesopotamian cities of Isin and Larsa were early leaders in this competition and were followed by the emergence of the southern empire of Babylon and the northern empire of Assyria (Kuhrt 1995, 74–117, 161–81). Between Egypt and Mesopotamia, the people of Canaan enjoyed a new era of cultural and economic revitalization and occasionally suffered from the military dominance of their more powerful neighbors (Pitard 1998; Bunimovitz 1998).

For the first time, the Levant sustained itself as a significant player in international trade, not only because the coastal cities were vital shipping ports (e.g., Tyre, Ashkelon), but also because the overland trade routes necessarily traveled through the lowland portions of Canaan, connecting Mesopotamia, Anatolia, Egypt, and Arabia (Ilan 1998). The region's cash crops were olive oil and wine as well as the timber produced just to the north in Lebanon. Luxury items from many distant regions also traveled through Canaan, such as exotic animals and skins from Africa, spices from Arabia, gold and silver jewelry and crafts, as well as vital supplies of copper and bronze from Cyprus and elsewhere around the Mediterranean.

The huge cities of Hazor (located north of Lake Galilee) and Ashkelon (on the southern coast) dominated the international trade routes that ran through Canaan. A third vital center of trade was Megiddo, in a fertile valley called

FIGURE 6-5. *The city of Megiddo owes its importance to its strategic location on trade routes. The first settlement remains at Megiddo may date to ca. 7000 BCE.*

the Jezreel. The southern trade was with Egypt primarily, as well as Arabia. The northern trade networks were connected to large cities in Syria and northern Mesopotamia, such as Byblos on the coast, Yamhad (modern Aleppo) in the Syrian interior, and Mari on the Euphrates near the confluence with the Khabur River. Small settlements in the central highlands (such as Shechem) and newly established highland sites (such as Jerusalem) became part of the regional economy as well. But Shechem and Jerusalem were small cities on marginal land, dwarfed by the larger urban centers in the lowlands.

The relationship between the southern Levant, especially its coastal region, and Egypt became more direct in the final century or so of the Middle Bronze. A new ruling class (called the Hyksos) seized power in northern Egypt (Kuhrt 1995, 179–82; Redford 1992, 98–122). The Hyksos originated in Canaan but apparently ruled northern Egypt and the southern Levant simultaneously. At the close of the Middle Bronze, a dynasty from Thebes in the south of Egypt defeated the Hyksos and drove the remnants of these people out of Egypt. Because the story of the Hyksos echoes, vaguely, several biblical stories (the rule of Joseph over Egypt in Genesis and the Israelite exodus under Moses in the book of Exodus), a few historians connect the two, suggesting that the biblical story is a fanciful retelling of the Hyksos era (Redford 1992, 412–13). This claim is not original in the modern era; it was defended two thousand years ago by a Jewish writer named Josephus (*Against Apion* 1.16). The hypothesis that biblical folklore is based on memories of the Hyksos is possible, but not compelling, especially since Hyksos rule was followed by the Egyptian Empire in Canaan, which the Bible knows nothing about.

No biblical stories or poems derive from the Middle Bronze era, but the kind of society that the Bible presupposes included technologies invented in the Middle Bronze (Ilan 1998, 312). Most obviously, the alphabet that biblical scribes used was invented during the Middle Bronze, though the Hebrew dialect of the Bible did not emerge until the Iron Age (Lemaire 2006b, 184–87). Also in this period, horse-drawn chariots appeared in Egypt and the Levant, and biblical scribes take chariots for granted in their stories (e.g., 1 Kgs 1:5; 22:32-35; 2 Kgs 9:21-24). Compound and composite bows increased the range and accuracy of soldiers in the field, and military tactics for siege warfare were improved. These innovations were presupposed by the later biblical authors (e.g., 1 Sam 20:35-38; 2 Sam 1:22; 2 Kgs 16:5; 18:13-37). Also, Middle Bronze cities became better designed to defend against siege warfare. Complex gateways and massive walls sat high above earthen ramparts. Many of these impressive fortifications were ancient ruins by the time biblical authors began to construct the Bible, and these ruins stimulated the scribes' creative imaginations, so that they produced some of the Bible's most memorable fiction (such as Josh 5:13–6:24; see also Num 13:25-33; Deut 3:1-11). However, biblical writers were not able to differentiate between all these Middle Bronze technologies and a variety of innovations from later times, such as Iron Age cavalry (Exod 15:1), Iron Age cities (Gen 26:1, 23), the Iron Age use of domesticated camels (Gen 12:16; 31:17), and the Late Bronze royal title "pharaoh" for the king of Egypt (Gen 12:17; 39:1).

An archive of royal documents from the Middle Bronze city of Mari illustrates two religious elements common to some biblical literature: divine patronage and divine revelation. Every ancient king was selected by a supreme patron god who ruled over humanity and the lesser supernatural beings: minor gods, angels, cherubim, seraphim, etc. (Noll 2013b, 182–214). For example, the kings of Ur III were gods who mediated between their human subjects and the higher gods who placed them on their thrones (Klein 2006, 119–20). The kings of Mari and the Bible also participated in this royal religion. In the Bible, the patron god revealed commandments, and the king was expected to enforce that divine law (Deut 13–25; Pss 45; 72; 110; 132). A patron god communicated warnings and exhortations in two manners. Sometimes, the god communicated through a ritual that scholars call "divination" (e.g., Lev 8:8; 1 Sam 14:37-42; 23:1-13). In other cases, the god spoke through a selected human, called a "prophet," such as Isaiah, Jeremiah, and Ezekiel.

The royal archive at Mari, composed more than one thousand years before the biblical texts, demonstrates that the biblical god followed the same pattern as other ancient patron gods. Like a biblical king such as David (1 Sam 16; Ps 2), the king of Mari was chosen and supported by a patron god (Nissinen 2003, 22). The god judged the conduct of his chosen king. For example, a prophet of the god Adad spoke to the king of Mari, saying, "When a wronged man or wo[man] cries out to you, be there and judge their case" (Nissinen 2003, 19). This prophet suggested that the god will not protect the king's throne if the king fails to bring justice but will support the throne if justice is served. Adad's prophetic message is almost identical to the message of the biblical prophet Jeremiah, who exhorts the king of Judah, saying, "Rescue the victim from the hand of his oppressor; as for the stranger, the fatherless, and the widow, do them no wrong" (Jer 22:3; author's translation). Jeremiah also suggests that the future of the royal throne depends on this commitment to justice.

Many religious scholars try to find distinctive elements in the biblical portrait of the divine, on the questionable assumption that distinctive elements somehow render the biblical god superior to all the other gods and goddesses of the ancient world, but their efforts are in vain. The Bible's god does and says exactly what all the other gods and goddesses did and said. Just as Mari's divine patron threatened enemy kingdoms such as Babylon (Nissinen 2003, 44–47), so also the Bible's god threatened enemies such as Babylon (e.g., Isa 13–14). Just as Mari's royal establishment favored its god as supreme while acknowledging, in the realm of diplomacy, the allegedly "lesser" gods of other kingdoms (Nissinen 2003, 26–27), so also the biblical god accepted the reality of other gods and proclaimed his primacy over them (e.g., Deut 5:7; Ps 82; Jer 48:7, 13; 49:1, 3; 50:2; 51:44; see also Mic 4:5).

The final century or so of the Middle Bronze saw the gradual collapse of many cities in the southern Levant. From the evidence, it does not seem that any single cause stands behind this collapse. Rather, a number of factors influenced specific regions or cities. In some cases, military aggression on neighboring territories was to blame. In other cases, outside factors had repercussions within it. For example, when Babylon conquered Mari on the Euphrates, and when the kingdom of Hatti in Anatolia conquered Yamhad in Syria, this disruption to the north and east sent northern Canaan into an economic depression from which it could not soon recover. Likewise, the Egyptian invasion of southern Canaan, in which the remnants of the Hyksos were defeated, interfered with the lives of the people in that part of the region.

Late Bronze

The key player in Late Bronze Palestine was the Egyptian New Kingdom, which expanded through Palestine and into northern Syria under the aggressive military leadership of Thutmoses III in the fifteenth century BCE (Redford 1992, 192–237; Kuhrt 1995, 185–331). Egypt coveted the entire eastern Mediterranean for strategic reasons as well as raw resources. Any invasion of Egypt from Anatolia or Mesopotamia would have to come through Canaan, and key international trade routes ran through this strategically significant region as well. By maintaining an imperial presence, Egypt was able to exploit copper mines in the Negev Desert south of the Dead Sea as well as the region's cash crops of wine, olive oil, and cedar trees.

Egypt did not rule the Levant directly, but it empowered local city governors—often referred to as "kings"—whose loyalty to the Egyptian emperor was closely monitored. Several hundred letters from the sands of Egypt, known to scholarship as the Amarna archives, shed light on how this imperial system functioned (Moran 1992). The local governors maintained the peace and provided the pharaoh with taxes and slaves. The Amarna archives demonstrate that the local governors did not like each other and often competed with one another, sometimes even fighting wars. The Egyptian imperial government monitored these activities but intervened only if Egyptian interests were threatened. Their policy was a classic example of "divide and conquer." As long as the local governors were at each other's throats, they were unlikely to build an anti-Egyptian coalition or otherwise threaten Egyptian power in the region.

Data from excavations demonstrate that many of the Bible's rituals are Iron Age descendants of common ritual practices from the Late Bronze era (Feder 2010; Pardee 2002). At Ugarit, for example, the new year arrived in early autumn, when grapes were harvested. This festival included a celebration of the new wine and a solemn ritual sacrifice to expiate human sins of the previous year. The Bible has attributed a similar festival, including Rosh Hashanah and Yom Kippur, to Moses in Leviticus 16, 23, and elsewhere (Pardee 2002, 56–58). The Bronze Age city of Emar provides additional examples. In that city, a priestess was anointed to office with holy oil. Ritual meals were followed by the anointing of sacred objects with oil and sacrificial animal blood. These practices are similar to the Bible's commandments for the installation of priests and the consecration of holy objects, found in Exodus 29 and elsewhere (Feder 2010, 110–11; Pitard 1998, 72). Likewise, the Hittite peoples of northern Syria performed rites of purification to cleanse humans of inadvertent sins, like the rites described in Leviticus 4 and elsewhere (Feder 2010, 101–9). These and other similarities between the Bible and Bronze-era rituals suggest that the so-called Torah of Moses is not a set of commandments composed by an individual named Moses but an anthology of ancient priestly lore that reflects the religious culture shared by biblical authors and all the peoples of the Levant.

Near the close of the Late Bronze era, an Egyptian pharaoh mentioned the People of Israel on a huge stone monument (Pritchard 1969, 376–78). This is the first and last known reference to Israel in an Egyptian text. Biblical scholarship frequently advances implausible speculations about this stone monument, but the inscription is useful evidence if viewed cautiously. Pharaoh Merneptah claims to have fought and annihilated Israel around 1207 BCE.

This is useful because it alerts us to the fact that a people called "Israel" were present in Canaan by this early date and, presumably, survived the pharaoh's alleged "annihilation." However, biblical literature knows nothing of Pharaoh Merneptah and assumes that earliest "Israel" never directly encountered Egyptian troops or an Egyptian imperial presence in the region. Ironically, therefore, this earliest extrabiblical evidence for the existence of Israel *also* demonstrates that the biblical authors knew nothing about the early history of their own people and that the biblical tales of origin are unreliable (Noll 2013b, 137–42).

Bronze Age Literature and the Bible

The authors of the Bible knew nothing of the Bronze Age, but they knew something about the literature produced by Middle and Late Bronze societies. How biblical scribes gained access to these Bronze-era literatures is a matter of debate. Researchers agree that the access was not direct. Uncertainty remains, however, concerning whether the indirect access came through contact with Iron Age Mesopotamia (where Bronze-era literature remained in circulation) or contact with Greco-Roman Mesopotamia, in which revised versions and digests of ancient literature were still known (Batto 1992; Gmirkin 2006).

Researchers speculate about the social function and relative popularity enjoyed by the rich assembly of literary texts recovered from ancient Near Eastern excavations. In truth, it is not possible to know how popular the literature was, because we are unable to determine whether the texts were also performed orally before the illiterate masses. Generally speaking, researchers defend one of two scenarios. Some believe the surviving literary texts testify to the religious and political life of the societies in which the literature was found, so that the contents of these texts must have been disseminated publicly. Other researchers, such as myself, suggest that literary texts represent the preserve of educated elites who gathered the raw materials (basic plots and the general characteristics of heroes and gods) from local oral traditions but crafted from those materials new, and much more complex, literary works of art. Assessing the quality and content of the ancient literature that has been discovered, one can argue that much of this literature would not have been valuable (or, in some cases, would not even have been understood) among a vast, uneducated, agrarian population (Noll 2013b, 317–22).

If the two scenarios just outlined represent two poles, many researchers take a position somewhere between them, but all agree that biblical scribes shared the following values and methods with their counterparts throughout the ancient Near East. Compositional custom among all ancient scribes is best described as plagiarism with creative modifications (Van der Toorn 2007; Carr 2005; George 2003, 33–39, 54–70; Dalley 2000, xvi–xvii). That is to say, each scribe inherited the texts of previous scribes and borrowed from those texts liberally. In some cases, a scribe would copy significant portions verbatim. In many cases, a scribe would mix and match texts, or motifs from texts, recycling small or large portions of favorite texts, to produce a new version or an entirely new composition. Even if the scribe chose to copy without creating a new composition, he sometimes introduced large and small revisions to grammar and vocabulary, as well as additions to character speeches, changes to literary themes, or combinations of thematically related stories.

The story of Noah in Genesis 6–9 may be the most famous example of Bronze-era literary masterpieces echoed in the Bible. The Middle Bronze epic of Atrahasis tells of a flood that destroys the world and of the divine selection of a man named Atrahasis to build a boat and preserve life (Foster 1993, 158–201). Even minor details of this story are identical to the biblical version, though the two stories are separated by at least one thousand years. This flood story was popular with many ancient scribes; in a Sumerian version, the hero's name is Ziusudra, and a later Babylonian-Assyrian version involves a hero named Utnapishtim. The latter version of the tale was incorporated into another great poetic epic, called Gilgamesh (George 2003). The Gilgamesh flood story was the first version to be rediscovered by archaeologists in the nineteenth century. Its translation caused a sensation in Victorian England because almost all British people still believed that the Bible had been revealed by a god, and this parallel tale called that belief into question (Damrosch 2007). Although Atrahasis is more significant for biblical comparison, the Epic of Gilgamesh was a first realization that the Bible is an ordinary anthology of ancient literature.

Like the Bible's story of Noah, the tale of the flood in Atrahasis is the second act in the drama, which begins with a story about the creation of humanity (Gen 2:4b–3:24). There are thematic differences, such as the cause of the flood. The biblical version's god was disgusted with unspecified evil actions by humanity (Gen 6:5), but, in the story of Atrahasis, the problem is human overpopulation and noisiness (Foster 1993, 169). Other thematic aspects run parallel. For example, in the tale of Atrahasis, humanity was created to be slaves for the divine, and the human species is made by mixing divine flesh and blood with inert clay (Foster 1993, 165–66). Likewise, the biblical god of Genesis 2 desires a slave to work his garden and fashions a human by mixing divine breath with inert clay.

Like Atrahasis, the biblical tale is not intended to teach a profound religious lesson. Probably, these literatures depend on common religious folklore, but the scribes have made of their raw resources a more creative and ambiguous story. Religious interpreters of Genesis often ignore the plain sense of the text and instead claim that the story presents human rebellion against the god who created a paradise for them (Rom 5). This is a misinterpretation that derives from the false presupposition that the god of the story has the best interests of the humans in mind. In the biblical story, the garden is created for the god, who strolls casually through his paradise (Gen 3:8). The humans are designed to remain slaves who maintain the garden for their divine master (Gen 2:15-17). The humanlike god who walks about is powerful but limited in knowledge. For example, he discovers the idea of male and female by trial and error (Gen 2:18-23). Likewise, this god does not know where his humans are or what they have been doing (Gen 3:9-11). Above all, the author of the tale tries to portray a god who is vindictive and eager to keep humans in a subservient status (Gen 3:13-24), much like the gods of Atrahasis.

Much of the sophisticated literature from the ancient Near East, including a book like Genesis, expresses the philosophical ambivalence toward life that readers encounter in the great literatures of many societies. The general mood in Bronze-era Mesopotamian literature was that life is short and unfair but that humans can hope to maintain their dignity in spite of, as well as with the occasional help of, a capricious divine realm (Foster 1993, 62–63). Like the story of Atrahasis, the story of Genesis presents humans who achieve dignity in spite of the god's imposition of arbitrary limitations (Gen 2:16-17; 4:3-5) and with the god's occasional, and limited, assistance (Gen 3:21; 4:15-16). The humans benefit from the help of a wise supernatural agent who thwarts the god's inhumane plan and compels him to adopt new solutions (in Atrahasis, the god Enki; in Genesis, the shrewd serpent). One can describe this literature as "religious" only in the sense that it wrestles with common human questions about mortality and knowledge (Miles 1995; cf. Batto 1992). It is not religious if the word "religion" refers to the common tendency among humans to imagine infinitely wise supernatural agents who love us, watch over us, and provide guidance with our best interests in mind (Boyer 2001).

I do not suggest that all parts of the Bible lack religious content. Some portions of the Bible reflect common religious beliefs and practices more accurately than does Genesis. Generally speaking, the biblical texts that attempt to define or defend religious beliefs and practices are found not in narrative books but in books such as Leviticus and Deuteronomy (the Torah codes) and poetic compilations such as Psalms, Proverbs, and some portions of the Latter Prophets. Nevertheless, like the narrative portions of the Bible, these sections were gathered by scribes who were not attempting to create religiously useful literature for common people but trying to preserve as much common lore as possible for use by the educated elites who had exclusive access to such literature.

A number of biblical texts echo a popular religious myth about divine warfare, and this provides an example of the extent to which the Bible reflects the influence of the Bronze era. One of our earliest hints of this myth appears in a prophecy from Middle Bronze Mari, in which a god reminds a king that he had secured the king's throne. The god announces, "[T]he weapon[s] with which I fought the Sea I handed you" (Nissinen 2003, 22; M. Smith 1994, 34–35, 108–9). The entity called "Sea" was a god or goddess (its gender varied from one version to another of this myth). The divine Sea was the source of chaos; the heroic patron god subdued that cosmic force of destruction and then gave his divine weapons to the human king of Mari.

Biblical scribes were familiar with this battle myth and used it to affirm the authority of the kings who ruled the city of Jerusalem. In Psalm 89, for example, a section of the poem recalls a prophetic "vision" in which the divine patron of Jerusalem chose David to be king (Ps 89:19-37). One line of this vision announces that the god will set the king's hand on Sea and his right hand on River (Ps 89:25). The words for "Sea" and "River" were alternate names for the god of chaos. For example, in the Late Bronze city of Ugarit, the god who battles the divine patron is both "Prince Sea" and "Judge River" (Parker 1997, 95–96). Like the patron god of Mari, the patron god of Jerusalem promised to give his human king power over this mythic realm of natural chaos.

In at least some versions of the battle myth, the slaughter of Sea and division of its divine body were the first acts in the creation of the earth, the sky (or "heaven"), astronomical bodies, and humans. It is possible that the creation theme was central to all versions of this myth, but some of our excavated texts are damaged or incomplete so that it is not clear that they included the creation motif, which has led to predictable differences of opinion among researchers (M. Smith 1994, 75–87). Biblical versions of the myth usually associate divine warfare with creation. For example, Psalm 89 explicitly connects the divine battle with the foundation of the sky and earth. This psalm's god has no equal among the council of gods because it was he alone who crushed Rahab, the name of the raging sea in this version of the battle myth (Ps 89:5-18).

One version of this myth of cosmic battle derives from a Late Bronze city called Ugarit on the Mediterranean coast, and that version has provided a wealth of detail that sheds light on the Bible (Parker 1997; Wyatt 1998). As noted above, many biblical rituals derive from older rites known to us from the Ugaritic texts. Also, much of the biblical god's personality and actions can be understood by study of the gods described in the Ugaritic archives (Pardee 2002; Watson and Wyatt 1999; cf. Day 2002; Cross 1973).

A variety of divine beings are shared by the Bible and the texts from Ugarit. We noted that the sea-god of chaos bears the dual names Prince Sea and Judge River (Ps 24:2). His reign of chaos is supported by divine monsters named Lotan or Leviathan (the Wriggling One) and Tannin, which means "dragon" (Parker 1997, 111). Biblical authors invoke these monsters as metaphors, and this implies that their intended readers were sufficiently familiar with the common battle myth to make the necessary metaphorical connections (Job 3:8; 7:12; 41:1; Pss 104:26; 148:7; Isa 27:1; Ezek 29:3; 32:2). Another common Ugaritic god is Mot (Death), a fearsome foe who battles both the patron god and his companion goddess Anat (Parker 1997, 138–64). When Anat defeats and destroys Mot, the description is remarkably similar to the Bible's tale about Moses, who discovers the evil golden calf and obliterates it (Parker 1997, 156; Exod 32:20). Also, the prophet Isaiah sneers at people whose religion he does not like by saying that they have made a covenant with the god Mot (Isa 28:14-22). In Isaiah 25:7, the prophet proclaims that his god will defeat Mot, who is described at Ugarit as one who swallows all; but Isaiah's god will "swallow up Death forever."

The Ugaritic champion who defeats these cosmic elements, a god who is virtually identical to the biblical god, is called Haddu (Thunder) or Baal (Lord) or sometimes the Cloud Rider (Parker 1997, 104, 124, 142–43). A few biblical passages hate any god called Baal (Judg 6; 1 Kgs 18), but this fact does not disguise the reality that the god of the Bible is, in almost all respects, identical to Baal. Both are storm gods, military protectors, and providers of fertility (1 Kgs 18; Pss 18; 29; Joel 2:18-27). Both rule a divine council (Job 1–2; Pss 29, 82), defeat the god of chaos (Job 26:5-14; Ps 74:12-17), and even ride on the clouds (Ps 68:4; cf. Ps 18:7-15). Like the Baal of Ugarit's myth (Parker 1997, 110, 129–38), the Bible's god follows his victory over Sea with construction of a temple on a mountain (Exod 15:17; Pss 24, 46, 48, 132; Isa 51:9-11). The biblical mountain associated with Jerusalem is called Zion, but occasionally it is equated with the mountain favored by Ugarit's Baal, a mountain called Zaphon (Job 26:7; Ps 48:2; sometimes translated "north").

A kindly elderly god at Ugarit called "El, the father of years," is also equated with the biblical god (Parker 1997, 127). This god is part of the name "Israel," which is a Hebrew sentence that means "El strives." (The biblical explanation of "Israel" in Gen 32:28 is clever but grammatically

FIGURE 6-6. *An ancient bronze statue of El, the major god in the Canaanite pantheon.*

incorrect.) At Ugarit, **El** is the creator of humanity and lives at the sources of the rivers that water the earth (Parker 1997, 125 and 127). El's goddess, Athirat, proclaims his divine wisdom (Parker 1997, 128–29). Likewise, the Bible presents a creator god who plants his garden at the sources of the rivers and who enjoys the presence of a divine female who proclaims divine wisdom (Gen 2; Prov 8). In Daniel 7:13, after sea monsters have been defeated, "one like a son of man" flies on the clouds and is presented before the "Ancient of Days," who awards him the divine kingdom. This echoes the Ugaritic version of the battle myth, in which Baal receives from the elderly El his right to rule as king after the Cloud Rider has defeated Sea (Parker 1997, 129). These examples can be supplemented but are sufficient to demonstrate that the biblical authors (including the haters of Baal; e.g., Hos 2) routinely conceptualized the god of Jerusalem as identical to the gods that most of Canaan called El and Baal.

The Ugaritic battle myth seems alien to readers of the Bible because it is a story of multiple gods who interact, at times either supporting or opposing one another. By contrast, readers of the Bible permit the agenda to be set by the lonely god of Genesis 1, an anomalous story about a single god who talks only to himself using the royal "we" (Gen 1:26). This has given readers the false impression that the Bible is a monotheistic anthology, so that references to other gods in biblical literature are consciously or unconsciously minimized or rationalized (M. Smith 2001). In reality, the biblical god is an amalgamation of the gods of Canaan, sometimes combining the characteristics of several Canaanite gods (especially El and Baal), and at other times interacting with those gods, as when the biblical god marches from the southern desert with his companion, the god of pestilence, to do battle with Sea/River (Hab 3:3-12). Monotheism is a Greek philosophical concept that was applied to the Hebrew anthology at a late date and has little to do with the contents of the Bible.

Genesis 1 makes an excellent final example of the ways in which biblical authors used their literary heritage. When the background of this biblical chapter is known, its god who invokes the royal "we" does not seem as majestically singular as appeared at first glance. The Bronze-era myth of the divine battle was recycled during the Iron Age as an elaborate ritual text at Babylon. In this version of the tale, the patron god is Marduk, god of Babylon, who battles Tiamat, the sea goddess (Foster 1993, 351–401). Marduk kills Tiamat, slices her body in half, and causes dry land to appear. Half of Tiamat is locked above the sky, which is a solid vault that holds watery chaos back from crashing in on earth, and the other half of Tiamat has become the seas of the world. Then Marduk kills one of Tiamat's divine allies and uses him to fashion humanity. The story is filled with elaborate detail, bizarre divine characters, and gory battle scenes. It concludes with a hymn of praise to Marduk, who absorbs the names of fifty gods, effectively transforming the gods of Babylon into manifestations of the one patron god of that city (Ornan 2009).

There can be little doubt that the author(s) of Genesis 1:1–2:4a used some version of the Babylonian battle myth as a primary source of inspiration (Batto 1992, 75–84). It remains unclear whether this source was identical to the textual versions available from archaeological research or some other source, such as the one known to a Greco-Roman author named Berossus. However, the biblical story begins with watery chaos called *tĕhôm* in Hebrew, which is cognate with Akkadian *ti'āmat.* The sequence of creation is identical to the Babylonian tale. First light emerges. Then the creator god separates the waters so that dry land can appear, and half the waters are bolted above a "firmament," the dome of the sky, while the other half becomes the seas of the world. After dry land has appeared, the lights of the sky and humanity are created. Finally, the divine realm rests. The author(s) of Genesis modified the tale, eliminating details of the battle and adding a few details to creation, but it is the same basic narrative.

Like the Babylonian myth, the story in Genesis 1 has amalgamated all the gods into one god. Genesis did not bother to list fifty divine names that are to be equated with this one god, but the principle of transforming a pantheon of divine specialists into a single divine generalist is the same. All this evidence demonstrates that during the Iron Age, before the Bible as we know it existed, the myth of divine battle was an integral part of Jerusalem's royal religion, as it had been at Bronze-era Mari and Ugarit, and Iron Age Babylon. The fact that biblical authors make frequent use of the myth, often borrowing elements of it to recycle in new literary settings, suggests that they presupposed a local culture that knew the myth well. Because these scribes were not concerned with preserving or defending the common religion of their culture but were intellectuals who revised any sources available to them for any purpose they deemed appropriate, the biblical texts do not describe the religion of ancient Israel or Judah. Rather, they display fragments of the religion that most residents of Iron Age Jerusalem presupposed in their daily lives.

Conclusion

This essay has surveyed more than one million years, several hominid species, the emergence of *Homo sapiens sapiens*, and the evolution of Stone Age and Bronze Age cultures in the Levant. Two points have been emphasized. First, the Bible can tell us nothing about the thousands of generations who inhabited the Near East prior to the Iron Age. Second, the Bible is an authentic and valuable product of a society that had inherited much from preceding generations. For a reader who avoids the mistake of treating the Bible as a religious authority or as a historical narrative, it can be a valuable anthology of literature that sheds light on an ancient, fascinating world.

Suggestions for Further Reading

Charles Darwin's idea of evolution had an enormous impact on how we understand the origin and development of human beings. Daniel Dennett's *Darwin's Dangerous Idea: Evolution and the Meanings of Life* provides a good historical overview of the concept of natural selection—without getting bogged down in biological detail—and the scientific analysis and debate that it has engendered since.

For understanding early civilization as it came about in the Middle East starting in the Bronze Age, see Amélie Kuhrt's *The Ancient Near East c. 3000–330 BC*. These new societies gave rise to numerous literary works. For the Mesopotamian literature, see Benjamin Foster's *Before the Muses: An Anthology of Akkadian Literature*. And for writings from Canaan, read N. Wyatt's *Religious Texts from Ugarit: The Words of Ilimilku and His Colleagues*. Amihai Mazar's work *Archaeology of the Land of the Bible*, vol. 1, *10,000–586 B.C.E.*, brings this discussion of prehistory and history to the land of Israel, and K. L. Noll brings this history down to the period of this book's main focus in his *Canaan and Israel in Antiquity: A Textbook on History and Religion*.

7

ARCHAEOLOGY AND THE CANAANITES

Jill Baker

According to the book of Genesis, "the Canaanites were in the land" when Abram entered it (Gen 12:6). Beyond this short reference, the Hebrew Bible offers limited clues as to the Canaanites' identity, origins, or traditions, despite the fact that they inhabited a wide geographic region. Conversely, the archaeological record provides considerable evidence of their history, culture, and religion. This chapter will examine Canaanite civilization in the Bronze Age with reference to the Hebrew Bible and textual, historical, and archaeological resources. It should be noted that while the texts of the Hebrew Bible were compiled long after the events they record, the Canaanite traditions to which they refer were common practice and custom throughout the Late Bronze and Iron Ages.

The etymology of the word "Canaan"—*kn'n* or vocalized *kĕna'an*—is uncertain, and there are alternative meanings dependent upon the identification of its original root. If its root was Semitic, *kn'n*, it could mean "to bend," "to bow," or "to be subdued." If derived from a non-Semitic root, such as Hurrian *kinaḫḫu*, it may mean "blue cloth": a reference to the blue-dyed cloth the Canaanites, specifically Phoenicians, were known to have produced. Early nonbiblical textual references to Canaan occur in a number of ancient sources, including a text from Mari (eighteenth century BCE) in which the writer refers to *ki-na-aḫ-nu*, when complaining of "thieves and Canaanites" who were causing trouble in Rahisum (Dossin 1973). As a geographic region, the land of Canaan is mentioned in the Story of Idrimi, king of Alalakh (fifteenth century BCE), as the place to which Idrimi was exiled: to "Ammia in the land of Canaan" (Oppenheim 1992, 557). Other texts from Alalakh and Ugarit also mention Canaan and Canaanites; one refers to them as foreign merchants. Early Egyptian references to Canaan appear in a list of spoils by Amenhotep II from his Asian campaign in the late fifteenth century BCE. In the fourteenth century BCE, Canaanite cities are mentioned in the Amarna letters, a collection of diplomatic communications between two pharaohs (Amenhotep III and Akhenaten) and their Canaanite vassal rulers. At the end of the thirteenth century BCE, in the Hymn of Victory (the so-called Israel Stela or Merneptah

Stele [J. A. Wilson 1992, 376–78]), the Egyptian pharaoh Merneptah lists the Canaanite cities he conquered. In Egyptian literature, the Tale of Sinuhe, set in the Twelfth Dynasty (early twentieth century BCE), depicts an official, Sinuhe, who accompanies Prince Senwosret I to Libya. On overhearing a conversation about the recent death of Pharaoh Amenemhat I (founder of the Twelfth Dynasty), Sinuhe flees to Upper Retjenu (Canaan), where he subsequently marries the daughter of Canaanite chief Ammunenshi, battles rebellious tribes, becomes a chief himself, and eventually returns home to Egypt.

While the etymology is far from clear, the land of Canaan and the Canaanites appear to have been known by their contemporaries. The geographical land of Canaan extended the length of the Mediterranean coast of present-day Israel and Lebanon and eastward into southern Syria and the Transjordan, including ancient Phoenicia and Ugarit (Schmitz 1992, 828–31; Tubb 1998). Indeed, the Phoenicians seem to have been Canaanites who developed a strong seagoing tradition.

Canaan and Canaanites in the Hebrew Bible

There are some 160 references to Canaan or the Canaanites in the Hebrew Bible, primarily in the Pentateuch (the first five books of the Hebrew Bible), Joshua, Judges, 1 Kings, 1 Chronicles; in three of the Psalms; and in Isaiah, Obadiah, Zechariah, and Zephaniah. They occur most frequently with reference to genealogies, geographic location, and matters relating to the exodus, conquest and settlement, as well as the covenant and moral conduct.

In Genesis 10, Canaan is identified as a person (Hess 1992): the son of Ham and grandson of Noah. Canaan's eldest son was Sidon, whose descendants were the Hittites, Jebusites, Amorites, Girgashites, Hivites, Arkites, Sinites, Arvadites, Zemarites, and Hamathites. As these clans multiplied, the "Canaanites" increased in number and eventually populated an extensive area, probably extending well north of the Sea of Galilee, in Lebanon, and east of the Jordan River. Throughout the books of Genesis and Exodus, Canaan features prominently as a geographic region and is frequently referred to as "the land of Canaan." However, as a geopolitical unit, "the land of Canaan" that the Israelites were to inhabit later encompassed a considerably smaller area, extending from the Mediterranean Sea eastward to the Dead Sea and Jordan River, and from approximately the Sea of Galilee in the north to the southern end of the Dead Sea and the Negev (Num 33:51, 34:1-12; cf. Gen 10:18-19).

With the geography settled, the biblical record shifts focus to the covenant and conduct, which established the traditions of the Israelites. In the process, numerous Canaanite cultural traditions are briefly mentioned from which the Israelites were specifically prohibited. As the books of Exodus, Leviticus, and Numbers indicate, residing in "the land of Canaan" was an essential element of the Israelites' covenant. They were expected to conduct themselves according to a specific set of laws and customs that were intended to distinguish them from the Canaanites (e.g., Lev 18) while living among them. Paradoxically, it is from this catalogue of prohibitions scattered throughout the Hebrew Bible that we learn about Canaanite religion and culture.

References to the worship of Canaanite deities are numerous (Exod 20:3, 23, 32; Num 25:1-3; Deut 5:7; 6:14; 12:3; 17:3; Josh 24:2; Judg 6:25-28) but consistently incur prohibition for the Israelites. The Canaanites were polytheistic and worshipped multiple deities relating to daily life, nature, and environmental events. These deities were worshipped publicly in temples; at natural sacred places such as hilltops, springs, or ravines; and privately in the household. As an aid to worship, the image of a god could be represented as a pole, stone, statue, or figurine referred to as an idol (Exod 32; Num 25; Deut 27:15; Judg 6:25-28; Hos 4:12-14). Regular sacrifices were offered in the form of incense, animals, and even human children (Lev 18:21; 20:2-5; Deut 18:10; 2 Kgs 21:6; Isa 57:5; Jer 7:31; 19:4-7; 32:35; Ezek 16:20-21; 23:37-39). Both female and male temple prostitutes were not uncommon (1 Kgs 14:24; 15:12; 2 Kgs 23:7). Family-related issues—such as the health and well-being of the family, female fertility, or the safety of infants and children—were the sphere of influence of household deities in the form of a hearth goddess, ancestors, or specific gods who bestowed protection on the family (Gen 31:19-35; Judg 18:14, 18, 20; 2 Kgs 23:24). They were often represented in the form of amulets, paintings, small statues, and other objects that embodied the deity/deities, and they were kept in a shrine within the house (Markoe 2000, 123–24, 131).

In common with most ancient peoples, the Canaanites practiced sorcery, magic, divination, necromancy, astrology, and other esoteric crafts; all of these were distinctly prohibited for the Israelites (Exod 22:18; Lev 19:26, 31; 20:6, 27; Num 23:23; Deut 18:10-11; 1 Sam 28:9; Isa 8:19; 44:25; 47:13; 57:3; Jer 10:2; 27:9; Ezek 22:28; Hos 4:12; Mic 5:12; Nah 3:4; Mal 3:5) because they involved communication with the supernatural world to influence the outcome of a given situation, cast a curse, or seek good fortune. For example, knowledge of future events was generally gained by employing a professional who performed a series of ritual actions, formulaic chants, spells, and incantations in order to connect with the appropriate source and gain the desired information or cause the desired effect. Additionally, the dead were assumed to have powers that could either help or hinder the living and could be consulted by the living regarding matters such as future results, fertility, good fortune, and success in battle (1 Sam 28). The prohibitions found in the Hebrew Bible clearly delineate the magical practices that were acceptable and those that were not. Those practiced and administered by the Canaanites were prohibited; conversely, those practiced and administered by a priest or prophet of

Yahweh were permitted, such as certain forms of magic like dreams and their interpretation (Gen 20:3-6; 31:11; 37; 1 Kgs 3:5, 15; Dan 2; 4; 7) (De Tarragon 1995, 2071–81; Scurlock 1992; Kuemmerlin-McLean 1992).

The Hebrew Bible also provides insights into Canaanite mourning ritual and burial practice. A proper burial was extremely important (Eccl 6:3) and included preparation of the body, which was usually undertaken by the women of the household (Gen 46:4; 50:1; 1 Sam 28:14; 2 Chr 16:14); a period of mourning, which would include fasting, wailing, and feasting (Gen 50:10; Deut 26:14; 2 Sam 3:31; 14:2; Job 30:31; Jer 7:2; 16:5-9; 26:23; 47:5); and burial in a tomb, natural cave, or grave (Gen 23; 35:20; 47:30; 49:30; 50:10-13; Judg 8:32). Mourning for the dead often involved shaving one's head, sitting in dust, wearing sackcloth, tearing one's own flesh, and tattooing (Lev 19:28; 21:5; Deut 14:1-2; Sam 14:2; Ezek 27:31). Laments, music, singing, and dancing were an integral part of the mourning process, and they were usually composed and performed by professional lamenters, who were women (2 Chr 35:25; Jer 9:16-21; Ezek 32:16), although occasionally men were permitted to participate and eulogize (2 Sam 1:17-27). Canaanite funerary customs also appear to have included sacrifices and food offerings to the dead (Deut 26:14; Ezek 24:15-22; Jer 16:1-9). The funerary banquet was likely held in a *beth marzeah*, the exact nature of which remains a subject of debate (Ezek 24:15-22; Jer 16:5-8).

In summary, the Hebrew Bible contains specific information about religious history and moral conduct, and it provides strict guidelines for the worship of Yahweh, while enumerating specific prohibitions clearly intended to set the Israelites apart from their Canaanite neighbors. Equally, the Canaanites had well-established cultural and religious traditions, the details of which are not described in the texts but rather assumed, presumably because they were already familiar to the Israelites. However, many of the missing details may be found in the historical and archaeological records.

Historical Background

While the intricacies of Canaanite culture may not be described in the Hebrew Bible, additional knowledge about them has been obtained through archaeological excavation. Based on this data, much has been learned regarding Canaanite history, political and economic structure, city planning, architecture, religion, literature, art, and daily life. Although the Hebrew Bible frequently portrays the Canaanites as barbaric, their contributions to ancient culture and society should not be underestimated.

While the geopolitical borders of the "land of Canaan" were confined to a relatively small area, its importance in the political and economic arenas was significant. Canaan was part of the Fertile Crescent, an area that stretched from the Tigris and Euphrates in Mesopotamia (present-day Iraq) to Canaan (present-day Israel, Palestine, and western Jordan) and into Egypt, following the Nile. Due to Canaan's climate and fertile soil, numerous edible plants and animals were readily available for consumption. Cultivated plants included grains (e.g., wheat, flax, barley), lentils, chickpeas, and fruits (e.g., dates, figs, olives, grapes), and domesticated animals included sheep, goats, and cattle. Domestic manipulation of resources such as these not only provided a stable food supply but also facilitated mass production of wine, olive oil, textiles, purple dye (murex), and perfume. Similarly, raw materials like salt, tar (bitumen), copper, and iron were mined and either traded as raw commodities or fashioned into tools and weapons. As agriculture and technology became more sophisticated, the raw materials and products became more abundant; greater demand resulted in regional trade. Given the availability of natural and cultivated resources and the topography, Canaan was a highly desirable resource and land bridge that numerous nations sought to control.

Canaan's contact with both Egypt and Mesopotamia is evident in the Early Bronze Age, if not before; however, it is with Egypt that Canaan had the most intimate relationship. Although it is a matter of debate, Egyptian presence in Canaan is considered to have been economic or military or a combination of both; the military may have been deployed to protect foreign economic interests. To further facilitate the movement of commodities and troops, a network of major and minor roadways connected Canaan to points north, south, and east. Two major roads extended north to south: the Via Maris (which paralleled the Mediterranean coastline, extending from Egypt to Lebanon and points north) and the King's Highway (extending from the Red Sea through Heshbon to Damascus and points north). Smaller east-west roads meandered through mountain passes and valleys, connecting the north-south roads and ports with inland destinations.

The so-called first urban revolution—when the first urban centers appeared—is thought to have occurred in the Early Bronze Age. Throughout the Bronze Age, Canaan was comprised of multiple city-states. A city-state is an independent entity that controlled a well-defined geographic region, each with its own ruler (kings or chieftains), government, and administration. A contemporary equivalent would be Vatican City. The Canaanite city-state comprised a walled-in settlement where the king and the administrative and religious institutions were seated and where the upper class lived. Each city-state possessed its own fortifications, palace(s), military, public works, judicial system, temple(s), and religious system. The **hinterland** surrounding these city-states incorporated smaller towns, villages, and farmland where agriculturalists, metalworkers, potters, textile workers, and other artisans worked and lived. Inhabitants of the city and hinterland were interdependent; city dwellers depended on the commodities and goods produced in the hinterland, while dwellers of the hinterland depended on the city as a marketplace and for protection during times of conflict, creating a symbiotic relationship. Although the Canaanite city-states were autonomous and not controlled by a single overarching entity, they were nevertheless bound by widespread traditions and cooperation, although there is evidence to indicate occasional tension between them.

Despite heavy Egyptian presence throughout the centuries, the Canaanites maintained an independent identity, establishing and sustaining deep-seated traditions that distinguished them from their neighbors. Their distinct culture and associated traditions remain identifiable in the archaeological record.

Archaeology of the Canaanites

The most effective method for becoming better acquainted with an ancient people is to study where they lived, how they governed, what they produced, and the possessions they left behind. This involves studying settlement patterns, architecture, industry, political and social structure, religion, and daily life. The Canaanites' unique identity was reflected in their city planning, architecture, technology, ceramic typology, tools and weapons, art, religious customs, and mortuary practices. Carefully studying these components creates a mosaic of Canaanite character and culture.

Settlement Patterns

A settlement pattern is the distribution, location, and nature of urban communities—determined by the proximity of water, fertile soil, other natural resources, access to transportation (roads, sea, and rivers), and defensibility. The location of villages, towns, and cities may be activity specific. For example, they may develop near mineral deposits so that their existence and economy would be devoted to obtaining that mineral. However, once the natural resource was exhausted, or no longer needed, the inhabitants of that settlement would migrate to another location. Conversely, cities located near perennial natural resources or important trade routes often flourished and grew—given a stable population and marketplace. Analysis of the location and size of settlements provides a deeper understanding of ancient industry and its economy.

In Canaan, urban centers flourished during the Neolithic and Chalcolithic periods, and the inhabitants of early cities like Jericho developed a set of characteristics that came to be known as Canaanite, but their distinctiveness was not solidified until the dawn of the Early Bronze Age (the first urban phase). During the Early Bronze Age, major settlements were established in the

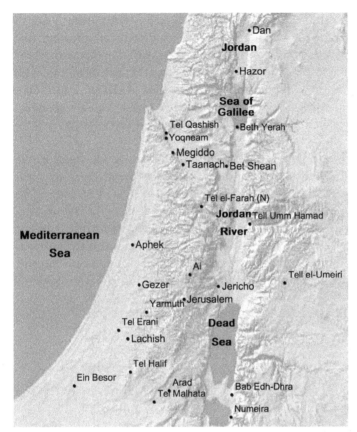

MAP 7-1.
*Map of selected
Early Bronze
Age sites
in Canaan.*

fertile zones in the coastal plains, valleys, and central hills where vital natural resources were present. These were large walled cities surrounded by smaller unwalled villages. The principal industry appears to have been agriculture and associated activities. As the Early Bronze Age progressed, a steady increase in the population and standard of living was evidenced by urban expansion, increased building, and higher-quality goods. However, this expansion was unsustainable and recession followed. Many urban centers were abandoned in the Early Bronze III Period, leading to an unsettled period of about 200 to 250 years called the Intermediate Bronze Age.

During the Middle Bronze Age, beginning about 2000 BCE, numerous fortified coastal sites were established, in addition to fortified cities and forts in the plains and valleys. Many of these were founded on virgin soil, while other established settlements expanded. International exchange and foreign ideas clearly influenced the evolution of Canaanite settlement, city planning, architecture, and culture: existing cities expanded, new ones were developed, and large urban centers became increasingly fortified. Several of these cities were located on or near trade routes—so essential for transporting goods to market—but their heavily fortified nature is also indicative of a growing need to defend themselves against new international threats. Simultaneously, the hinterland, so vital to economic growth and prosperity, was developed with a growing number of well-populated but unwalled settlements surrounding these fortified cities. Their increased number suggests a corresponding increase in the exploitation of fertile zones accompanied by advances in technology and agricultural techniques.

In the Late Bronze Age, settlement patterns shifted again, largely due to the ever-present Egyptians. Smaller hinterland villages became sparsely populated or were deserted, and, at some sites, the Egyptians erected forts during the LB I Period. Many credit this abrupt shift to the expulsion of the Hyksos from Egypt, although primary urban centers and their adjacent towns continued to flourish, especially during the LB II Period. International maritime trade was particularly important during this period, and the coastal cities became bustling centers for both imports and exports. The existence and prosperity of

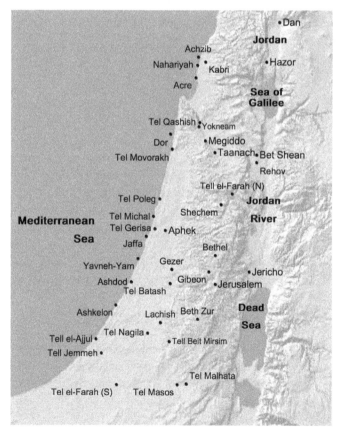

MAP 7-2. *Map of selected Middle Bronze Age sites in Canaan.*

MAP 7-3.
Map of selected
Late Bronze
Age sites
in Canaan.

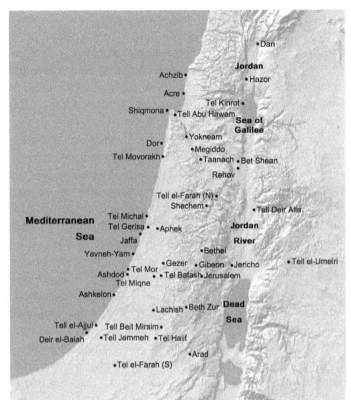

these Canaanite cities was testified to in contemporary Egyptian sources, such as the topographical lists of Thutmose III, the annals of Amenhotep II, and the Amarna letters. Urban centers were clustered in the north from the coastal sites of Acco, Shiqmona, and Dor, inland to Megiddo, Rehov, Beth Shean; in the Galilee from Hazor to Tel Anafah and Kinneret; in the central hills (Tell el-Farah [North], Shechem, Bethel, Jericho, Jerusalem); and in the south from the coastal cities of Jaffa, Tel Mor, Ashdod, Ashkelon, Gaza, Deir el-Balaḥ, inland to Beth Shemesh, Lachish, Debir, Tell Beit Mirsim, and so on. These urban clusters reflect the accessibility of valuable natural resources and fertile agricultural land and the importance of trade routes.

CITY PLANNING

City planning is a deliberate process that determines land use, organizes public and private zones, and systematically arranges streets and structures. Canaanite cities reached their zenith during the Middle Bronze Age, accomplished in part because of technological advances and improved building techniques that facilitated the construction of more substantial defensive systems. Similar advances in civil and social organization provided individual city-states with a centralized authority, administration, a working class, and religious institutions. Royal, sacred, and public buildings were generally located near the city gate, and residential quarters were arranged in blocks, separated by secondary streets farther into the city—a scheme that came to be known as orthogonal town planning. Examples are found at Megiddo, Hazor, Lachish, Gezer, Tell Beit Mirsim, and Shechem.

Throughout the Late Bronze Age, orthogonal planning was the norm, although planners had to reckon with a site's natural topography, particularly if it included a hill or mountain plateau, which could be determining factors in its initial shape. As a result of continuous habitation, occupational debris artificially added to the height of the mound, frequently giving it an irregular trapezoidal shape. These artificial mounds—"tells"—comprised multiple superimposed layers of successive human occupation. Each layer represents a specific period of time, each built on top of the other over several centuries. Consequently, some sites look like a steep hill with an artificial plateau. Compared to those of the previous period, Late Bronze Age fortification systems were inferior. City walls were crudely formed by the exterior walls of adjoining dwellings to create a perimeter ring while a peripheral road was constructed in front of them spanning its circumference, establishing urban boundaries and maintaining their ceremonial function. Orthogonal planning encouraged the construction of political, commercial, sacred, and residential zones through which wound main and secondary streets.

FIGURE 7-1. *Tell Lachish is not a natural hill but results from centuries of human occupation.*

The significance of city planning should not be underestimated, as it reveals the presence of a central authority, division of labor, and social complexity. The type of structures and institutions and their location within the city suggest their importance to the inhabitants and provide invaluable data about these communities.

FORTIFICATIONS

Fortification walls, towers, and gates may be the strongest evidence of urban planning, centralized authority, defense, and exchange of ideas. Although rudimentary walls and gates surrounded earlier settlements, it was during the EB II and III that these became substantial defensive structures. Fortification walls could be 2.5 to 4 meters thick, and they stretched up to 7 to 8 meters in height, with horseshoe-shaped towers placed at regular intervals. Towers measured between 15 and 20 meters long and between 6 and 8 meters wide (Kempinski 1992). An earthen rampart was erected on the exterior side of the wall, creating an imposing steep slope below the wall, rendering siege from below difficult. Entry and exit to the city was through a simple gate that was little more than an opening in the wall, flanked by and defended from two towers, as for example at Tell el-Farah (North).

Although Middle Bronze Age urban defense systems maintained their general purpose, fortification techniques and technology achieved an unprecedented level of complexity and refinement. Borrowing from Syria and Mesopotamia, the Canaanites incorporated earthen ramparts into their defensive system that were very steep, thick earthen mounds that created a massive artificial slope around the city wall. Their purpose was to elevate the vulnerable part of the wall well above ground level and to strengthen its base.

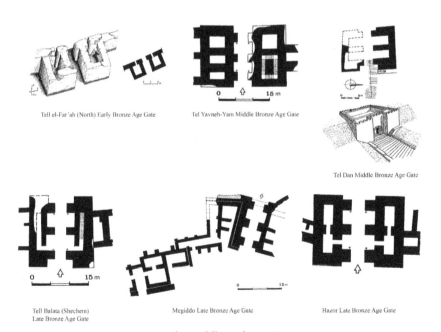

FIGURE 7-2. *Early, Middle, and Late Bronze Age gates.*

To achieve this, a central foundation of stone, brick, and hard-packed earth (measuring ca. 8–10 meters wide and ca. 10 meters high) was constructed, around which a massive quantity of earth was packed. A ditch or fosse could also be located at the foot of the rampart. This formed a solid foundation out of which the city wall extended. Although few have survived, the upper wall could reach great heights. Positioning the foundation well away from the slope prevented invaders from tunneling under the wall and into the city, while the steep slope and great height prevented them from using battering rams or ladders. Towers and gates along the length of the walls provided additional defensive advantage. These city walls, constructed of stone foundations with mud-brick superstructures, were either straight or offset-inset style. Depending on the terrain, the completed shape of these well-fortified cities was roughly round (Dan), rectangular (Hazor), or square (Tel Batash). This system was also used at sites such as Tel Poleg, Jericho, and Shechem. A variation of this defensive structure was the glacis, which employed the same basic construction as the rampart but made use of natural hills or slopes rather than constructing an artificial mound and inner core foundation on flat terrain. The surface of the slope was generally covered with thick lime, making the surface steep, smooth, and slippery (A. Mazar 1992b; Kempinski 1992).

The city gate was one of the most important components of the fortification system. Initially, they were simple structures, but they quickly became more complex and formidable. Most MB IIA gates were straight-axis, flanked by as many as three piers or bent axis, such as at Megiddo. The later part of the MB IIA commonly employed the Syrian gate, named for its presumed place of origin. This design boasted a straight-axis and could have as many as three piers on each side and two chambers that provided access to one or more towers (Yavneh-Yam) or no piers and a barrel vaulted roof (Dan, Ashkelon). The Syrian gate continued to be used during the MB IIB–C and measured some 15–20 meters long by 8–10 meters wide between the chambers and 2.5–3 meters wide between the piers, presumably to allow easy passage for chariots and carts. The piers were outfitted with doors, which could be closed to create smaller inner chambers.

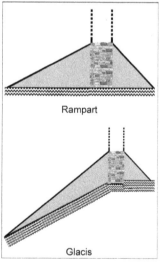

FIGURE 7-3. *Rampart and glacis. Upper: example of a city wall and rampart erected on flat ground. Lower: example of a city wall and glacis, utilizing a natural slope.*

FIGURE 7-4. *Upper: Middle Bronze Age gate at Ashkelon (2006).*
Lower: Late Bronze Age gate at Megiddo (2006).

Although numerous Middle Bronze Age gates remained in use in the Late Bronze Age, their function was less defensive and more civil. Elaborate city walls were razed, allowed to deteriorate, or retained in part for ceremonial purposes, particularly the gate complex. The dominant power, Egypt, likely prohibited Canaanite city-states from possessing elaborate fortification systems in order to reduce the risk of rebellion. Tell Balata, Hazor, and Megiddo offer the best examples.

ROYAL, SACRED, PUBLIC, AND RESIDENTIAL BUILDINGS

As city planning advanced, task-specific zones and buildings developed. For example, early public edifices in the Early Bronze Age included granaries (Beth Yerah) and water systems (Arad). As the sociopolitical nature of Canaanite society became more complex and sophisticated, the division of power, labor, and class became more pronounced. These silent aspects of Canaanite society are reflected in their institutions and in the architectural styles of their civic, sacred, industrial, and domestic structures.

Palaces

Recognizable palaces appeared in the MB IIA at Megiddo and MB IIB–C at Megiddo, Aphek, Hazor, Kabri, Lachish, and Tell el-Ajjul. Referred to as courtyard palaces, these were large, well-built rectangular structures, measuring over one thousand square meters and consisting of large central courtyards surrounded on one or several sides by audience halls, utility rooms, a shrine room, and residential quarters. Their construction included monumental entrances, orthostats, paved courtyards, baths, as well as public and private rooms. The remnants of steps and pillars suggest a second story. Their design resembles those found in Syria at Ugarit, Alalakh, and Ebla. In this phase, palaces were often located near the sacred area, indicative of the intimate

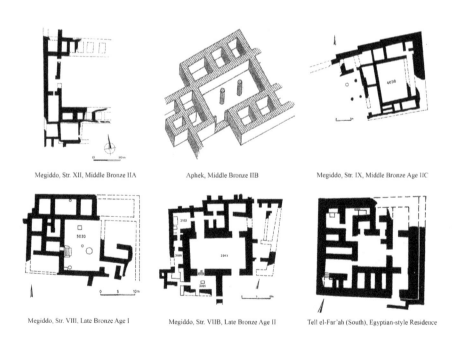

Megiddo, Str. XII, Middle Bronze IIA   Aphek, Middle Bronze IIB   Megiddo, Str. IX, Middle Bronze Age IIC

Megiddo, Str. VIII, Late Bronze Age I   Megiddo, Str. VIIB, Late Bronze Age II   Tell el-Far'ah (South), Egyptian-style Residence

FIGURE 7-5. *Middle and Late Bronze Age palace architecture.*

relationship between state and cult. Toward the end of the Middle Bronze Age and the early Late Bronze Age, palaces were relocated to the gate and city wall area.

Egyptian officials stationed in Canaan appear to have built large structures whose function was likely both administrative and residential. These are often referred to as Egyptian-style residences. Examples are found at Tel el-Farah (S), Deir el-Balaḥ, and Tel Mor. Their recognizable form was square and symmetrical; the entrance was usually located near a corner of the wall; the courtyard was squarish; rooms were either square or long and narrow; and there were one or two pillars in the center of the room, a staircase on the side of the courtyard, very thick mud-brick walls with a mud-brick foundation or no foundation at all, and T-shaped doorjambs and thresholds.

The construction of a palace in a city suggests the presence of a central authority responsible for its organization and oversight. The size and complexity of these structures reflects the importance of the officeholder and the activities that likely occurred within the palace on a daily basis. The location of a palace relative to the temple(s) reflects the degree of relationship between the sacred and secular. Close proximity to religious structures suggests that the civil authority played an important role in the cult, if not controlled it. A location near the city gate would suggest a degree of separation and perhaps emphasize a more military or civil role.

Temples

Temples were perhaps the earliest public edifices, resembling domestic dwellings in size and layout, given that they were home to the deity. Temples included dedicated spaces for cultic activity, for worshippers to gather, and for living and sleeping quarters for the priest(s) and staff. Early Bronze Age temples were of the broad-room style, named for their rectangular shape and entrances revealing the expanse of the room. Although similar in layout, the overall dimensions of Early Bronze Age temples were larger and more monumental than domestic dwellings. The foundation was made of stone, and the superstructure of mud-brick with considerably thicker walls (ca. 1.8 meters thick). The layout generally consisted of a porch with two pillars and a wide entrance into the broad hall. Early Bronze Age temples have been found at Megiddo, Arad, Ein Gedi, Ai, Jericho, and Yarmuth.

In the Middle Bronze Age, temple design adopted the long-room style while retaining separation of zones. The entrance was located on the short wall of a rectangular structure, with the length of the building extending from the entrance, as at Hazor. They were solidly built monumental structures, comprising an entrance chamber, main hall, and inner room referred to as the "holy of holies." The holy of holies contained the cult statue and other objects

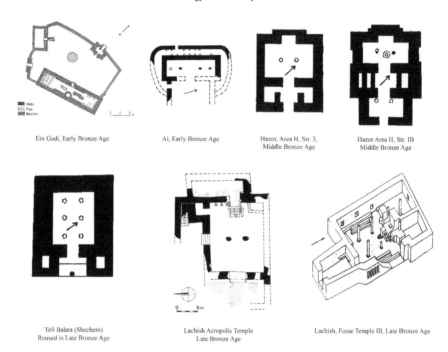

Ein Gedi, Early Bronze Age   Ai, Early Bronze Age   Hazor, Area H, Str. 3,   Hazor Area H, Str. IB
                                                               Middle Bronze Age   Middle Bronze Age

Tell Balata (Shechem)   Lachish Acropolis Temple   Lachish, Fosse Temple III, Late Bronze Age
Reused in Late Bronze Age   Late Bronze Age

FIGURE 7-6. *Bronze Age temple architecture.*

and was normally located on the wall directly opposite the entrance. Worshippers were given access to the antechamber and main hall but not to the holy of holies. This tripartite division is well reflected in temple architecture during this period and was retained throughout the Late Bronze Age. Examples are found at Megiddo, Nahariyah, Hazor, and Tell Balata (Shechem).

In the Late Bronze Age, temple design returned to the broad-room style, although those temples that remained in use from the earlier period, with some exceptions, retained the long-room style. In general, they were monumental, symmetrical, solid structures, most retaining the tripartite division. In rare cases, as at Beth Shean, the temple was approached from an oblique angle, giving added emphasis to the separation of the sacred and secular. Within the hall were pillars, one or more raised platforms, benches, and other installations, which were probably used for seating and displaying cult objects. In some cases, as at Lachish and Beth Shean, the holy of holies was elevated and accessed by steps. Egyptian influence may be observed in the structural features in addition to papyrus-shaped capitals, fluted columns, and interior painted walls. The use of cedar beams imported from Lebanon is evidence of international trade. While most temples shared a common interior style, there were exceptions, as at Tel Mevorakh and the Fosse Temples at Lachish (Figure 7-6). At the Fosse Temples, for example, each of the three superimposed structures comprised an indirect entrance, four wooden pillars, a raised platform, the holy of holies located at the end of the hall, benches, and two rooms adjoining the main hall. Square temples were discovered at Hazor, Mount Gerizim, and Amman (Jordan) comprising a central courtyard around which rooms and passageways were arranged. The actual temple, or holy of holies, was located in a room beyond the courtyard, accessed through a doorway at the corner of the building. The purpose of these particular structures and their dates remains a matter of debate, but they are referenced relative to their possible sacred function. Examples have been found at Beth Shean, Megiddo, Shechem, Lachish, and Hazor (A. Mazar 1992a, 1992b).

Canaanite temples essentially maintained a tripartite division: antechamber, main hall, and holy of holies. This arrangement ensured separation of the sacred from the secular. Temple furnishings included such items as ritual vessels, statues, figurines, lamps, lamp stands, and other cultic objects. Although they were relatively simple structures, their design served to emphasize the separation of the holy from what was considered common.

Domestic Architecture

Early Bronze Age I residential dwellings were usually curvilinear, elliptical, round, or apsidal in shape, consisting of one to three rooms at most. They were constructed with a stone foundation and mud-brick superstructure, and the walls were generally 0.6–0.7 meters in width. These simple dwellings were generally situated in clusters, perhaps reflecting kinship groups.

Dwellings of the EB II–III Period appear to have been better planned and were of two basic types: the "Arad house" and the courtyard house. The "Arad house," named after the site, was broad-room style and generally a one-room unit, though some were partitioned into two. They were constructed on a stone foundation, with mud-brick superstructure, and were probably one story. Benches, platforms, storage bins, postholes, stone slabs, and socles were incorporated around the room's perimeter. Courtyard houses consisted of an open courtyard in front of the dwelling space and usually consisted of one rectangular room. They were also constructed of a stone foundation, with mud-brick superstructure, and were single story. The courtyard served as the focus of household activity and contained the hearth, silo(s), bins, and other installations for food preparation. It probably offered shelter for domestic animals. Dwellings like these are found at Meser (Figure 7-7), Tell el-Farah (North) (EB II), and Tel Qashish (EB III).

During the MB IIA, two basic types of domestic dwelling seem to emerge: village and urban. Village dwellings comprised a courtyard with one or more rooms that were arranged around one or two sides of it and that were directly

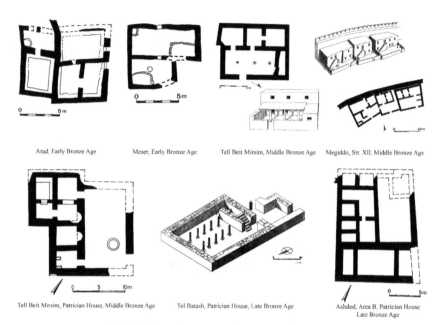

Arad, Early Bronze Age   Meser, Early Bronze Age   Tell Beit Mirsim, Middle Bronze Age   Megiddo, Str. XII, Middle Bronze Age

Tell Beit Mirsim, Patrician House, Middle Bronze Age   Tel Batash, Patrician House, Late Bronze Age   Ashdod, Area B, Patrician House Late Bronze Age

FIGURE 7-7. *Bronze Age domestic architecture.*

accessed from it, since it remained the center of daily activity. The rooms were configured either in clusters or in a straight line and were of equal or varying size depending on their function as living and sleeping quarters. Examples are found at Tell Beit Mirsim and Megiddo (Figure 7-7).

Urban dwellings were modified courtyard houses, of which there were two types: the courtyard house and the patrician's house. The main entrance was from the street into the courtyard, which remained the center of daily activity and could be partially roofed. Rooms were arranged around two sides of the courtyard in linear order, and there was likely a second story. The family probably lived and slept on the second story. Examples are found at Megiddo and Tell Beit Mirsim and measured approximately twelve by seventeen meters. The "patrician house" was a modified courtyard house, though somewhat standardized in plan, and measured approximately eight by ten meters (Figure 7-7). They boasted multiple rooms arranged around a central court, a forecourt, and a second story supported by columns and thick walls. The courtyard and first- and second-story rooms retained their traditional functions. Examples are found at Aphek, Ashdod, Tell el-Ajjul (Building AM), Tell Beit Mirsim, and Megiddo, where a variation of this plan was found in the gate area.

The same basic courtyard-style plan continued to be used for residential dwellings in the Late Bronze Age. They consisted of a central court surrounded by multiple rooms and a second story. The best examples are found at Ashdod (Figure 7-7), Megiddo (houses 3002 and 3003), Hazor, and Tell Beit Mirsim. Their courtyards were uncovered with paved floors that could contain numerous installations, and the dwellings included rooms of varying sizes with floors of beaten earth, plaster, or pavement. They measured approximately fifteen by sixteen meters and were constructed with a stone foundation and mud-brick superstructure. Ceilings were constructed of wooden beams covered by a thick layer of clay. At Tel Batash (Figure 7-7), a slightly different configuration was utilized, with an entrance on the short wall, providing access to a large ground-floor hall (divided by two rows of wooden columns) and access to steps leading to a second floor. During this period, houses were generally arranged in neighborhoods or irregular blocks separated by narrow streets (Megiddo and Hazor) and sometimes shared a wall.

POLITICAL STRUCTURE AND ECONOMY

It has already been mentioned that the Canaanites established numerous independent city-states, each with its own ruler(s). Some Amarna letters, for example, list city-states and their associated ruler: for example, ʿAbdi-Irši, king of Hazor; Biridiya at Megiddo; and Yida at Ashkelon. Other localities had more than one ruler and are listed as corulers, such as at Gezer Adda-Danu, Illi-Milku, and Yapahu. From Ugarit, it is known that there was a royal family, including a king, a queen, princes, and princesses. The king was divinely appointed and officiated at religious ceremonies, underscoring an intimate relationship between the king and El, the principal deity (Schniedewind and Hunt 2007). It may be assumed that rulers in Canaan adopted a similar hierarchy.

The construction and maintenance of monumental fortifications, buildings, public works, and infrastructure emphasize the presence of centralized authority and a nonagrarian working class (e.g., administrators, military personnel, priests, scribes, merchants). For example, at Ugarit, professional scribes produced royal and religious documents that were kept at both the palace and the high priest's home. It may also be assumed there was a military class, and it is known that at Ugarit there was an army and navy whose ranks included both full-time professionals and personnel conscripted from surrounding communities. The professionals, such as chariot warriors, were paid ten shekels each, although occasionally payments were made in the form of land and/or livestock (Schniedewind and Hunt 2007).

The realm of the city-state extended beyond its walls into the rural hinterland, where agriculture, ceramic production, metalworking, textile production, arts and crafts, and related activities were located. The symbiotic relationship between urban center and rural hinterland enabled some city-states to become quite prosperous and command vast territories. Ugarit's fertile rural hinterland accumulated wealth through the development of marketable commodities like grains, olive oil, wine, textiles, purple dye, and other raw materials, which were traded in the vibrant Bronze Age economy. Business transactions included the exchange of in-kind goods and goods for services. For instance, a laborer's remuneration could include a day's or a month's worth of foodstuffs. As Canaanite city-states grew and stabilized, so too did their domestic and international politics and trade networks, maintaining important relationships with Egypt, Syria, Mesopotamia, Cyprus, and the Aegean.

CERAMICS

Pottery production and type is regarded by many as an effective method for identifying communities, activity, and chronological periods. For the ancients, ceramic receptacles provided their packaging, storage, dishes, and ritual vessels and were both commodity specific and function specific. They contained oils, perfumes, unguents, foodstuffs, and drink. Fashioned with strainers, funnels, and lids, they functioned as serving dishes, dining ware, and incense burners. In some cases, the commodity it contained was more highly prized than the vessel itself.

Ceramic types in the archaeological record have long been used to identify people-groups based on the principle that "pots equal people." The general assumption is that a cultural community will produce ceramics with a specific set of characteristics. So, homogeneity among a ceramic corpus is commensurate with cultural uniformity. The appearance of pottery with an altered set of characteristics could therefore, in this scenario, suggest the infiltration of a foreign people-group. But although migratory or invading peoples may carry ceramic traditions with them, not all changes should be attributed to the appearance of new peoples, whether migrants or invaders. Evolving ceramic typologies may also be attributed to local, domestic innovation and external influences such as trading relationships. In the interests of making a holistic interpretation of new ceramic types, a synthesis of all the contributing factors is preferred over a single explanation.

When discovered in the archaeological record, the form and function of vessels may assist in identifying the activities being performed in a particular location. Similarly, as the typology, technology, and technique of ceramic production evolve, recognizable characteristics emerge that offer useful data regarding chronological period, point of origin, and either domestic innovation or foreign influence. For example, numerous storage jars in a room may suggest its use as a storeroom or warehouse, while cooking pots may suggest food preparation.

Canaanite vessels were usually made from local clay sources and were generally pale brown or pale yellow to pinkish in color, with thick walls, bases, rims, and handles. Ceramics were handmade using a coiling technique, or made in sections, or thrown on a mat or wheel. These vessels were then fired in a kiln. Surface decoration consisted of incised banding, glazing, slipping, or painting. Their basic shapes were globular and sometimes included a carination either at the shoulder, at the midsection, or near the base. They tended to be clunky and heavy, not least because the clay source determined the quality of the vessel. Among the vessel types were plates, bowls, mugs, kraters, jugs, juglets, jars, cooking pots, and storage jars. Exterior decoration ranged from red-and-black burnishing and polishing to painted linear designs, such as net patterns and tree of life motifs. Manufacturing techniques, vessel types, and quality developed in response to changing needs and technological advances. Similarly, foreign wares were incorporated into the Canaanites' ceramic corpus as a consequence of their exposure to imported commodities and their packaging, and local imitations of them frequently appeared.

RELIGION

As previously noted, the Canaanites were polytheistic and worshipped several deities. Based on Ugaritic texts and the writer Philo of Byblos (64–141 CE), who documented a great deal of Phoenician history, it is possible to construct the Canaanite pantheon (Tubb 1998). Major deities include El, Asherah, Baal Hadad, and Anat. Wise and compassionate, El was the supreme deity and thus the king and father of the gods, humankind, and all creatures. According to Ugaritic mythology, El seduced two women who become his wives and give birth to Sachar (Dawn) and Shalim (Dusk). Not surprisingly, El of Canaan and Ugarit was associated with the El of the Hebrew Bible, and in Daniel 7 he is depicted as sitting in judgment in his court. Whether El and Yahweh were distinct or a single deity has long been a matter of debate. El's consort, Asherah, was the mother of the gods and creatures and often portrayed as a life-giving tree and referred to as the queen of heaven. She is also credited with having given El an impressive seventy sons.

One of El's sons, Baal Hadad, was the storm god and a symbol of strength and fertility. He brought rain and fruitfulness for abundant crops and was often depicted as a bull or as a human with a raised hand holding a spear. Anat, Baal Hadad's sister and wife, was the goddess of war and love and is also referred to as "virgin Anat." **Astarte** was the third major deity in the Canaanite pantheon, representing fertility, sexuality, and war while also upholding justice and law. She was often depicted on Sidonian coins as riding in a chariot, as standing on the bow of a ship, or as a figurehead for ships. Baal Zaphon, "lord of Mount Zaphon" was another important deity in Ugarit. A storm and warrior deity, he is the patron deity of the ruling dynasty. Other important deities included Shemesh, goddess of the sun; Dagon, god of grain; Yam, god of the sea and river; Mot, god of the underworld (death); and Molech, presumed to be the god of fire and associated with child sacrifice (Lev 18:21; 20:2-5; 2 Kgs 23:10; 2 Chr 28:3; 33:6; Jer 7:31; 19:2-6 [Van der Toorn 1995; Tubb 1998]).

Canaanite gods were dynamic beings, interacting among themselves and with humans. Several Ugaritic texts describe the deities' exploits and actions, revealing their characteristics and attributes. For example, from the Baal Cycle, the function, character, and origin of Baal Hadad are disclosed. Many of these gods are mentioned in the Hebrew Bible because they presented stumbling blocks to the Israelites. Given the attributes of these deities—fertility, war, and death—it is not surprising that the Israelites were seduced into covering all supernatural bases in order to appease pagan deities with practices that were emphatically forbidden by Yahweh's law. The realms over which these gods ruled were intimately interwoven into the fabric of daily life, and individual prosperity depended on affording proper reverence and respect to each deity, making it difficult to venerate only one while ignoring the others.

LITERATURE AND THE ARTS

Aesthetic considerations apart, ancient literature and art were essentially utilitarian vehicles for conveying invaluable information. Literary forms embraced lists of kings, diplomatic correspondence, records, legends, myths, and poetry. The diplomatic texts from Tell el-Amarna in Egypt and legends such as those from Ugarit (including the Legend of King Keret, the Legend of Dan'el, the Tale of Aqhat, and the Baal Cycle) are just a few examples. These king lists and diplomatic texts reveal much about the political and social structure and the state of international relations. Legends, myths, and poetry reveal names and roles of deities and provide insight into religious ritual, mortuary practices, architecture, the landscape, and daily life. Although some of these events may be pure fiction (e.g., the Tale of Sinuhe), the lessons conveyed and contemporary details are invaluable.

The Canaanites made a valuable contribution to the ancient art of writing: the alphabet. During the Middle and Late Bronze Ages, the main writing systems found in the Near East were Egyptian hieroglyphs and Mesopotamian cuneiform. Both of these systems were syllabic, meaning each symbol represented one syllable, which required dozens, even hundreds, of symbols for communication. By the twelfth century BCE, the Phoenicians (i.e., the Canaanites) had developed a twenty-two-letter alphabet, wherein one symbol (i.e., letter) represented a single sound rather than one syllable. This system made written communication more efficient and became the basis for all major alphabets deriving from the Mediterranean region, including Aramaic, Arabic, Greek, Latin, and Hebrew.

The arts included sculpture, stelae, reliefs, figurines, cult and ritual objects, seals, and jewelry, all of which offer details about deities, ritual, dress, flora, fauna, social order, trade, and international contacts. Stone sculpture appeared as early as the Middle Bronze Age. In the Late Bronze Age, stone-carved doorjambs from a temple at Hazor depict a lioness' head, and a basalt slab from Beth Shean depicts a lion fighting with a dog. Smaller stelae and statues depict kings and deities in postures of power. One stele from Tell Shihab depicts a warrior-god holding a spear and wearing a headdress. Reliefs, especially those from Egypt and Mesopotamia, provide invaluable details about a ruler's supremacy, military victories, and divine legitimacy. Figurines were made of clay, stone, or metal—depicting kings, deities, and animals. They were either sculpted or mold-made (a technique common in Byblos) and fashioned as pendants, plaques (probably originally part of friezes), miniatures, or votives, which were often found in temples and homes. Earrings, finger rings, pendants, necklaces, and toggle pins were among popular forms of jewelry and offer further insight into the artistic tradition of the Canaanites and into their customs and practices.

In the ancient world, literature and the arts performed a dual role. Aesthetically, the elegance of the craftsmanship and the materials reflects the nature and beauty of the object. From the perspective of function, the objects are a rich source of information about the political, religious, and personal dimensions of ancient cultures. By successfully incorporating both of these aspects into their art and literature, the Canaanites have provided invaluable information illuminating their culture that survives in the archaeological record.

METALLURGY

The transition from the Neolithic and Chalcolithic periods to the Bronze Age is marked by the ascendancy of metal as the predominant material used for fashioning tools, weapons, and artwork. Bronze proved a much stronger material than those previously used, facilitating the production of new types of weapons, tools, and objects. Objects included figurines and other cultic and symbolic objects. Weapons included battle axes, such as the duckbill axe (MB IIA) and notched axe (MB IIA–B), spearheads, swords, and dagger blades. Tools included plowing blades, sickles, chisels, saws, axes, and needles. Some implements, such as the duckbill axe, were unique to the Canaanites and appear as an identifying marker in Khumhotep II's tomb painting at Beni Hassan.

The production of stronger tools and weapons increased efficiency, offering greater advantage in battle and enabling advances in farming techniques that resulted in more abundant crops.

BURIAL CUSTOMS

Perhaps the most intimate window into the lives of the Canaanites is their burial practice. Burial customs offer details regarding rites, ritual, afterlife scenarios, and family structure as well as ceremony, ceramic typology, and imported goods. Since tombs are relatively undisturbed at the time of discovery, they provide some of the best and most complete examples of pottery, jewelry, weapons, and tools. Large Bronze Age cemeteries have been excavated at Bab edh-Dhra, Jericho, Tell el-Farah (North and South), Tell el-Ajjul, Lachish, Ashkelon, Megiddo, Hazor, and Dan. Bronze Age interments were made in pit graves, dolmens, built tombs, caves, and rock-cut tombs, and there are a few instances of cremation, though this was not the norm. Throughout the Bronze Age, all these methods were employed, but the most common form of grave architecture is found in either natural or human-made cave tombs.

Natural caves or rock-cut chamber tombs could accommodate multiple burials over several generations and contained as few as one or as many as several hundred individuals. These tombs generally consisted of a vertical or horizontal shaft, passageway, doorway, and stone sealing-slab, as well as one or more cave-like chambers, which were oval, circular, rectangular, or square in shape. The walls of these chambers and shafts contained niches for lamps or burials, some of which extended below floor level. Some chambers contained benches or platforms on which the corpse was laid and subfloor pits into which the bones of earlier decayed burials were deposited, enabling repeated use of the same tomb.

Following death, the individual was lowered into the tomb and positioned in a specific location, laying the corpse on either a wooden bier or a reed mat. It is assumed that each tomb was owned by a kinship group and that the occupants were probably related. In some tombs it is possible to observe clusters of burials; corpses were placed on top of, overlapping, or next to specific individuals. These clusters probably represent smaller family groups within the larger clan. Grave goods were situated around the deceased and included essential, status, and personal items. Essential equipment reflects the ritual aspect of the funerary process and comprises ceramics, talismans, burial garments, and toggle pins. Ceramic items contained foodstuffs, given to the deceased at the time of burial, representing their portion of the funerary meal and sustenance for the journey into the afterlife. Status items reveal the individual's position in the community and/or vocation and could include a seal, trade-specific tools, or weapons. Personal items consisted of jewelry, game pieces such as dice, and other favored possessions, reflecting the individual's persona. Once the corpse was situated and grave goods arranged, the tomb door and shaft would be sealed. On the occasion of another burial, the tomb was reopened and the same funerary activities were reenacted. In the event that space was required for the new interment, older burials were pushed aside to make room. This practice accounts for the jumbled mess often found within chamber tombs.

In the ancient world, proper burial was of the utmost importance and included preparation of the body, funeral rites, and burial in a tomb with one's ancestors. This tradition is attested in the Hebrew Bible (Gen 23; 47:29-31; 50). Conversely, a person could be denied a proper burial as punishment for wrongdoing (2 Kgs 9:10; Jer 14:16; 22:19). Burial among one's kinship group was equally important (Gen 47:30; 49:29; Deut 31:16; 2 Sam 7:12; 1 Kgs 1:21). The vocabulary of these passages refers to "being gathered unto" or to "sleeping with" one's fathers, underlining the importance of being buried for eternity with one's kin—hence the importance of surviving family members performing this last act, lest the deceased's ghost haunt them. The belief that the spirits of the dead could perform either benevolent or malevolent acts encouraged the observance of festivals for the dead as a requirement equally important as a proper burial. The associated practice of contacting the ancestors' ghosts for blessings, curses, and foreknowledge of future events was roundly condemned and forbidden by their Israelite neighbors.

Summary

If the Hebrew Bible were the only available source, it could be reasonably concluded that the Canaanites were a thoroughly uncivilized people who were best ignored or at the very least avoided. Such a negative treatment of the Canaanites should not be surprising when considering the texts of the Hebrew Bible, compiled from the perspective of asserting national identity and preserving the purity of Israelite religion. Given these texts and the unique character of the cultic practices and civic customs of the Israelites, refraining from engaging in those of their neighbors was critical to preserving religious and national identity. Condemning Canaanite practices and customs as displeasing to Yahweh, and therefore prohibited, served the purposes of the compilers of the Hebrew Bible. Despite this apparent opposition, it is evident that the Canaanites were a people immersed in their own traditions, accomplished in the arts, skilled craftspeople, and technologically advanced.

The contribution of the Canaanite people to ancient civilization is significant and invaluable. Their defensive fortifications are perhaps the most impressive example, utilizing massive earthworks and monumental, complex gate systems that proved so effective that they were adopted and adapted in later periods throughout Europe and North America (e.g., at Fort Bourtange [Netherlands] and Fort Ticonderoga [New York]). Canaanite civil administration was organized, and their cities were well planned, facilitating the growth of their economy, culture, and society. As entrepreneurs, the Canaanites produced goods that were transported by merchants throughout the Levant and Mediterranean, enabling both the movement of goods and the exchange of ideas.

The land of Canaan functioned as a gateway through which numerous peoples passed. Given the cacophony of cultural expression inundating the Canaanites, it is to their credit that their own cultural identity remained so strong. A section of painted relief in the tomb of Khumhotep II suggests that the Canaanites wore bright, colorful garments (Tomb 3 at Beni Hassan, Egypt; Cohen 2015). Their jewelry reflects skillful craftsmanship in the form of earrings, finger rings, necklaces, pendants, bracelets, belts, and toggle pins—evidence that for the Canaanites outward appearance was an important aspect of daily life. From their funerary practices, it is clear the Canaanites engaged in music and dance and created intriguing literature. Similarly, their funerary practices indicate that the Canaanites were family oriented, taking extreme care in the burial of deceased family members in tombs that would maintain familial relationships even into the next world. For both the Canaanites and other ancient peoples, a person's being did not cease at death, for the spirit lived on in another realm, as reflected by their afterlife scenario.

The Canaanites were a people-group who existed in quiet strength. They seem to have been a practical people, well organized in politics, economy, and society. Despite Egyptian domination, their cultural traditions and identity persisted and survived, often incorporating new ideas into their cultural repertoire. In all, the Canaanites appear to have been not warmongering expansionists but rather a productive and creative people engaged in agriculture, industry, and trade, whose legacy remains an important strand in the fabric of the ancient Near East and Mediterranean world.

Suggestions for Further Reading

Jonathan N. Tubb's *Canaanites* (1998) offers an overview of the Canaanites from the Neolithic and Chalcolithic (ca. 8500–3300 BCE) to the Persian Period (ca. 539–332 BCE). Tubb begins by establishing who the Canaanites were and where they originated, their place in "biblical" and regional history, and their geographical boundaries. These form an important foundation to the overall understanding of the Canaanites. Once the foundation is established, Tubb walks the reader through the birth, life, and eventual absorption of the Canaanites by later governing powers through an examination of their material culture, architecture, pottery, jewelry, weaponry, burial practices, and religion. *Phoenicians*, by G. E. Markoe (2000), describes the Phoenicians' history, economy, religion, language and literature, and westward expansion. Aspects of their culture and material culture resemble those of the Canaanites, which is why it is important to understand who the Phoenicians were and their role in the ancient Near East and wider Mediterranean theaters.

In order to understand the development of the Canaanites, it is important to understand not only their own history but also the events that were unfolding around them. Indeed, much of the Canaanites' later development and eventual assimilation can be best understood when placed in the context of wider historic events. *The History of Ancient Palestine*, by G. W. Ahlström (1993), provides a detailed history of the region, while A. Mazar's *Archaeology of the Land of the Bible, 10,000–586 B.C.E.* (1990) gives a comprehensive description of the archaeology and history of Canaan from the Neolithic Period through the Iron Age. Suzanne Richard's edited volume *Near Eastern Archaeology: A Reader* (2003) comprises a collection of essays discussing various aspects of ancient Near Eastern archaeology, including the Levantine Bronze and Iron Ages, from theoretical, cultural, and technological points of view. Jonathan M. Golden's *Ancient Canaan and Israel: An Introduction* (2009) offers a topical discussion of numerous aspects of Canaanite (and later Israelite) civilization. This work not only updates earlier ones but also introduces the reader to important discussions that persist in the field today.

8

THE BOOK OF GENESIS AND ISRAEL'S ANCESTRAL TRADITIONS

Mark Elliott and J. Edward Wright

The book of Genesis, the first book of the Bible, opens the story of ancient Israel on a cosmic level. The book's title in Hebrew, *bereshit*, is taken from the first word of the book and means "in the beginning." The English title, Genesis, however, is a transliteration of the Greek term meaning "the production or creation of something."

The ancient Israelites—like later Jews—traced their origins back to the founding patriarchs and matriarchs whose stories appear in Genesis 12 to 50. Although the book's author wove these stories together into a flowing narrative to provide an account of the early history of Israel, they are not historical in any modern sense of that term. They are not accounts of "what really happened." Rather, these stories offer a largely religious explanation of who the Israelites are (the people of a particular god), where they came from (Mesopotamians who emigrated to the Levant), and how they came to live where they do (their god gave them the land).

The Patriarchal Founder: Abraham

The story of the people who will bear the name Israel begins with Abram (Gen 11:26), whom God later renamed Abraham (Gen 17:5-6). The ancestors of the twelve tribes of Israel are descendants of Abraham and his spouse Sarah through their son Isaac and his son Jacob (whom God later renamed Israel). Abraham had a personal relationship with God, who promised the patriarch both numerous descendants and a land in which they could live. Abraham and his family originated in southern Mesopotamia at Ur (Gen 11:28; 15:7) and then traveled to Haran (Gen 11:31). It was in Haran where Abraham received God's call to travel to southern Canaan:

> Go from your country and your kindred and your father's house to the land that I will show you. I will make of you a great nation, and I will bless you, and make your name great, so that you will be a blessing. I will bless those who bless you, and the one who curses you I will curse; and in you all the families of the earth shall be blessed. (Gen 12:1-3)

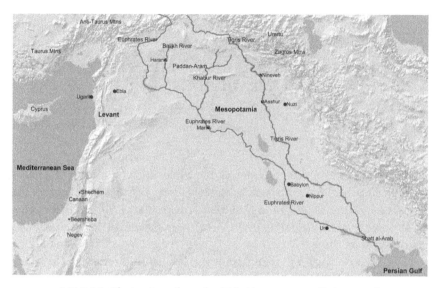

MAP 8-1. *The territory through which Abram supposedly journeyed on his way to Canaan.*

FIGURE 8-1. *Shechem with standing stone in the tower temple. Shechem played an important role in the patriarchal and matriarchal stories. The site was one of the oldest cities in the land of Canaan and was first mentioned in Egyptian texts from the nineteenth century BCE. This temple may date from 1650–1100 BCE. Abraham and Jacob set up altars at Shechem and offered sacrifices.*

The Genesis narratives explain the divine promises and covenants of Yahweh to Abraham as the basis of Israel's claim to the land of Canaan. The movements of the patriarchs and the matriarchs are closely linked to the divine promises. When Abraham entered Canaan with his wife Sarah (originally named Sarai) and his nephew Lot, he traveled first to Shechem in the north and then to the Negev in the south. At Shechem he received a promise of the land (Gen 12:7), built an altar to the LORD in Bethel (Gen 12:8), and eventually fled to Egypt because of famine in the land (Gen 12:10).

Despite this new territory, Haran in northern Mesopotamia retained a strong genealogical connection to Abraham and his descendants. There, Abraham acquired Rebecca as a wife for his son Isaac (Gen 24:4ff.). Likewise, Jacob escaped his bother Esau's rage (Gen 27:43-45) by fleeing to this area, where he met and married Leah and Rachel.

Abraham's confidence in God's protection faltered at times. When entering Egypt, he feared for his life and persuaded his wife Sarah to lie to the pharaoh about their marriage (Gen 12:10-20). Nonetheless, God delivered the family and made Abraham even richer when he returned to the Negev. In the events of Genesis 14, Abraham appears as a fierce warrior of such strength that he was able to defeat a coalition of four kings under the leadership of Chedorlaomer of Elam to rescue his nephew Lot. Later, in a scene with important theological implications, Abraham encountered enigmatic Melchizedek, the king of Salem (i.e., Jerusalem), who blessed him:

> Blessed be Abram by God Most High,
> maker of heaven and earth;
> and blessed be God Most High,
> who has delivered your enemies into your hand. (Gen 14:19-20)

Melchizedek was also a priest of the Canaanite god *El Elyon,* or "God Most High." After receiving Melchizedek's blessing, Abraham invoked his god as "the LORD [*Yahweh*], God Most High [*El-Elyon*], maker of heaven and earth" (Gen 14:22). By this statement, Abraham both recognized the validity of El in the Canaanite cult and acknowledged Yahweh and El as equals, as "God Most High."

Genesis' Abraham narratives focus on the divine promises and who will inherit them after Abraham. The key promises depend upon the matriarchal birth of legitimate heirs. God's promises are passed from Abraham to Isaac to Jacob; all Abraham's covenantal heirs are male. The promises distinguish between the rightful heirs (Isaac and Jacob) and those who are not (Ishmael and Esau). A key figure in these stories is the matriarch (Sarah for Isaac, and Hagar for Ishmael). Both give birth to potential heirs, but only one, Isaac, inherits the divine promises.

MAP 8-2.
*Canaan during the
time of Abraham.*

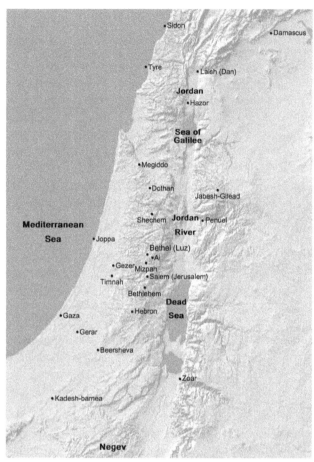

The biblical narratives depict the patriarchs as tent dwellers who ride donkeys and herd sheep and cattle (Gen 12). Other verses refer to the ownership of camels (Gen 12:16; 24:10; for Isaac, see Gen 30:43ff.). Jacob engages in agriculture (Gen 26:12), and his stories are largely situated in the Central Hill Country in Canaan and the Negev, regions where agriculture thrives. At times, the biblical writers portray the patriarchs and matriarchs as behaving contrary to biblical law. For example, Abraham marries his half-sister in opposition to Leviticus 18:9, 11 (Gen 20:12); Jacob marries Leah and Rachel, two sisters, thus violating Leviticus 18:18. Jacob erects sacred stone pillars (Gen 28:18, 22; 35:14) even though Deuteronomy 12:2-3 exhorts the Hebrews to "demolish completely all the places where the nations whom you are about to dispossess served their gods, on the mountain heights, on the hills, and under every leafy tree. Break down their altars, smash their pillars, burn their sacred poles with fire." Moreover, Abraham plants a sacred tree at Beersheba (Gen

21:33), conflicting with Deuteronomy 16:21. Scholars view these acts, which directly contradict Deuteronomistic law, as evidence that these tales arose prior to the time (eighth to seventh century BCE) when those Deuteronomistic religious restrictions were implemented.

Isaac: The Middle Descendant

After a lengthy collection of stories about Abraham and Sarah, the biblical writers briefly recount the life of Abraham's son Isaac. As a token of God's covenant to Abraham, Isaac was their first child, and he was circumcised at the age of eight days. Abraham and Sarah were put to the test by God, who demanded Isaac, their only son, as a human sacrifice (Gen 22). Although a direct threat to the divine promise, it was actually a test of faith. At the last minute, God provided a sacrificial replacement, sparing Isaac and thereby allowing him to continue the line of Abraham's descendants.

FIGURE 8-2. *The Gezer standing stones. R. A. S. Macalister excavated this site in the early twentieth century and interpreted the standing stones as a sacred site, or "high place," used by Canaanites for child sacrifices, since a few burial jars containing the bones of infants were discovered. William Dever disagreed and argued that the stones comprise a standard cultic site.*

Another threat to the divine promise of descendants arose when Isaac could not find a wife. But Abraham sent a servant to his homeland of northern Mesopotamia to secure a wife for him (Gen 24). There the servant found Isaac's future wife, Rebekah, a daughter of Abraham's brother. Rebekah and Isaac, like Abraham and Sarah, had difficulty conceiving a child, but Yahweh intervened and Rebekah eventually became pregnant. This divine intervention kept alive the divine promise to Abraham of descendants (Gen 25:21). But that promise was a bit complicated, for, while still pregnant, Rebekah sought and received a divine oracle about her sons. God told her that she would give birth to twins and that, against all tradition, the younger of the two would be the more prominent and inherit the divine promises (Gen 25:21-27). To ensure this outcome at the right time, Rebekah helped Jacob deceive Isaac into blessing him rather than his older brother Esau. With the blessing secured, Rebekah urged Jacob to flee to her home in Mesopotamia to escape Esau's wrath (Gen 27:41–28:5). Again, Abraham's family found itself in its ancestral homeland in northern Mesopotamia.

Jacob: The Progenitor of the Israelite Tribes

Jacob, like his mother Rebekah, was quick-witted and devious—a trickster who fooled his blind father Isaac into believing that he was actually blessing his older son Esau (Gen 27:1-29). Indeed, Jacob twice outmaneuvered his older brother for their father's blessing but paid a high price for his deception. Esau vowed to kill his brother after the death of their father Isaac (Gen 27:41).

Jacob fled north, stopping at Bethel, where God appeared to him in a dream. He saw angels ascending and descending a stairway that joined heaven and earth, and he heard Yahweh reiterate the same promises of land and numerous descendants that he had made to Abraham and Isaac. In this way, God indicated that Jacob would inherit the Abrahamic promises (Gen 28:12-15). When Jacob awoke from his sleep, he sanctified the site and renamed it Beth El (i.e., Bethel), "the house of El" (Gen 28:16-22). El, the common term in Hebrew for the word "god," is also the personal name for the Canaanite high god worshipped throughout the Levant. The religious practices of Abraham's family generally follow the religious traditions of the Canaanites among whom they lived.

Arriving in northern Mesopotamia, Jacob the trickster was in turn tricked by his uncle Laban into working fourteen years to obtain his wife Rachel (Gen 29:1-30). Desiring Rachel from the moment they met, the penniless Jacob agreed to work seven years as a bride price for her hand. But, in the darkness of their wedding night, Laban substituted the older sister Leah for the younger Rachel, following the custom of marrying the eldest first. Despite this trickery, Jacob's love for Rachel caused him to work a second term of seven years for her hand. The love story is touching, but the outcome of this double marriage and the rivalry between Leah and Rachel led to a pregnancy contest—with Leah, Rachel, and their respective concubines producing children one after the other until Jacob had twelve sons and a daughter (Gen 29:32–30:24). These twelve sons of Jacob (aka Israel) became the forefathers of the "twelve tribes of Israel."

After these years serving Laban, Jacob returned to his family's homeland in Canaan, but not before he managed to trick his uncle Laban in a way that made him enormously wealthy (Gen 30:25–31:55). During his return to

Canaan, Jacob was vexed by his conflict with his brother Esau. Perhaps this conflict was behind a dream he had in which he wrestled with a divine being at the site he called Penuel, "the face of God" (Gen 32:30). The match was a draw and lasted until the next day, when Jacob refused to release this challenger until he bestowed on him both a blessing and a name change: "You shall no longer be called Jacob, but Israel, for you have striven with God and with humans, and have prevailed" (Gen 32:28; compare the story in Gen 35:10). Jacob, now duly impressed, responds that he has "seen God face to face, and yet my life is preserved" (Gen 32:30). The biblical etymology defines Jacob's new name—Israel—as "El strives," but it may also mean "El reigns" (*TDOT* 6:399–401). Despite Jacob's fears of his brother's lingering hatred, Jacob and Esau reunited peacefully; old conflicts were forgotten, and both agreed to live in peace in their own areas. The divine promises to Abraham continued to be realized, although at times they seem to be threatened by neglect, malfeasance, or external menace. The promises made to Abraham in Genesis 12:1-3 come to fulfillment with Abraham's family enjoying a promised land, promised descendants, and promised blessings.

The remaining stories of Genesis revolve around Jacob's children, with Jacob's favorite son, Joseph (Gen 37:3-4), as the central character. In an ironic twist, Jacob was deceived by his sons, who sold his beloved youngest, Joseph, into slavery in Egypt (Gen 37:1-36). Remarkably, Joseph rose from the status of slave to become Pharaoh's most trusted adviser (Gen 39:1–41:56). During a severe famine, Jacob sent his sons to Egypt to buy food. They eventually met an Egyptian official, who, unbeknownst to them, was none other than their younger brother Joseph, whom they had betrayed (Gen 41:57–45:15). Rather than just provide some food supplies, Joseph eventually offered to resettle his father Jacob and all his family in Egypt. To avoid the famine, they made the move to Egypt, where they prospered and multiplied. Jacob died in Egypt, but he made his children promise to return his remains to their ancestral homeland in Canaan. His sons fulfilled that wish by burying him in the cave of Machpelah (Gen 50:1-13).

The Literary and Historical Character of Genesis

The writers of Genesis are unknown because the book reveals no information concerning its authorship. Both Judaism and Christianity have believed that the Torah was the divinely inspired work of Moses, based on biblical passages that claimed "Moses wrote this Torah" (Deut 31:9). During the past two hundred years, however, biblical scholarship has demonstrated that not just one person but rather a combination of authors and editors created Genesis and indeed the entire Torah through a centuries-long process. Julius Wellhausen developed the major theory regarding the composition of the Torah, the "Documentary

Hypothesis" (see chapter 2). The three main sources in Genesis are called J, E, and P: J is short for the "Jahwist" or "Yahwist" source and consists of traditions from the Southern Kingdom of Judah. This source originated in Jerusalem during the ninth century BCE. According to the J source, the deity's name is Yahweh (spelled Jahweh in German). For the Elohist source—designated E—the divine name is Elohim, the standard term for "god." The Elohist source focuses on the religious sites in the Northern Kingdom, Israel. It was composed in Samaria, the capital of Israel, in the eight century. Finally, the P source (Priestly source) originated within the Jerusalem temple priesthood. This source focuses on legal material relating to purity, religious law, and genealogies. This is the latest source, which came into its final form in the exilic or postexilic era (sixth to fifth centuries CE), although it may contain earlier legal traditions.

The basic outline of the Documentary Hypothesis has become broadly accepted among biblical scholars, but its details still attract analysis and discussion. The origins of Genesis apparently derive from a time when Judah (931–586 BCE) and Israel (931–722 BCE) were developing as states. Most of the stories in Genesis began as oral traditions that were eventually written down and then revised a number of times. But it is the consensus of most scholars that the final editing and creation of the text as we know it occurred sometime after the exile to Babylonia in 586 BCE and the return of Judean leadership to Judah during the Persian era, perhaps under Ezra or Nehemiah in the mid-fifth century BCE. Genesis was particularly pertinent to the exiled Judeans, who had no country or king and who were trying to determine their place in the world. They viewed Genesis as explaining their origin, their ancestral land, and their ancestral god.

As the survey above indicates, the biographies of the patriarchs and matriarchs of Israel and their relationship with God are the primary focus of Genesis 12–50. The historicity of these people and the events recounted in Genesis are nearly impossible to demonstrate. Almost all biblical scholars agree these events were written down long after they could have occurred by later authors and editors. Outside of the Bible, Abraham and his descendants are unknown. No character in Genesis appears in any non-biblical, ancient document. Indeed, the majority of biblical scholars remain uncertain whether Genesis 12–50 contains any historical elements that can be located in ancient history or even whether any of the patriarchs or matriarchs actually existed. As J. Alberto Soggin (1985, 29) has commented, "On the historic level, there is no basic objection to supposing that all or some of the patriarchs might have existed . . . or, for that matter, that they may never have existed at all!" William Dever (2001, 98) has emphasized that "after a century of exhaustive investigation, all respectable archaeologists have given up hope of recovering any context that would make Abraham, Isaac, or Jacob credible 'historical figures.'"

Archaeology and the Amorite Hypothesis

The present recognition that no evidence exists that could establish the historical veracity of Genesis's tales was not always the case. Some archaeologists and biblical scholars in the mid-twentieth century rejoiced over the early excavations from Mesopotamia and Palestine and reported connections concerning the biblical narratives. This early research appeared to uncover archaeological data confirming many details of the patriarchal and matriarchal narratives. Led by the American scholar William F. Albright, a leading authority on biblical archaeology in the first two-thirds of the twentieth century, the idea that the patriarchal traditions contained substantial history gained ample support, especially among American archaeologists and biblical scholars. Albright (1963, 5) argued, "As a whole, the picture of Genesis is historical, and there is no reason to doubt the general accuracy of the biographical details and sketches of personalities who make the Patriarchs come alive with a vividness unknown to a single extra-biblical character in the whole vast literature of the ancient Near East."

Albright believed the age of the patriarchs and matriarchs could be situated between the twentieth and sixteenth centuries BCE. Genesis locates the homeland of Abraham and his ancestors in Ur of the Chaldeans (Gen 11:28; 15:7). This site is in southern Mesopotamia, and the British excavations of Ur led by C. Leonard Woolley in the 1920s and 1930s demonstrated that the city was at the height of its prosperity from about 2060 to 1950 BCE, when it was partially destroyed. The city was then restored and, in the seventeenth century, destroyed once again, before disappearing completely from history. Many reports emanating from Woolley (1930, 75, 77) were sprinkled with phrases such as a "private house at Ur in the time of Abraham" or "private houses of Abraham's date." Woolley believed his excavations at Ur verified ancient Hebrew traditions and the historical Abraham. His unabashed support for the historicity of the Genesis narratives most likely appealed to Albright and other traditional Jewish and Christian scholars who were eager for evidence that the biblical stories were accurate. For Albright (1963, 2), the excavations at Ur were evidence "that a date about the third quarter of the twentieth century BCE would suit the historical indications remarkably well."

Despite Woolley's proclamations, there are several sites in the Near East named Ur, and it is not known if any of them can be linked to Abraham. Furthermore, the name "Ur of the Chaldeans" in Genesis is a difficult phrase. The term "Chaldeans" is clearly anachronistic, for it is not attested in nonbiblical sources until the ninth century BCE at the earliest, long after the supposed era of Abraham. The nation known as "Ur of the Chaldeans" existed only after the founding of the Neo-Babylonian Empire in the late seventh

FIGURE 8-3. *Temple of Nannar the Mesopotamian moon god at Ur. Genesis 15:7 states that Abraham was called by God to leave "Ur of the Chaldeans." Historical records know nothing of the Chaldeans before the ninth century, and they did not rule Ur until the seventh century BCE.*

century. The name also appears in Nehemiah 9:7, and in that location it is more reflective of its terminological origins during and after the Judean exile in the sixth century BCE. Remember, that was the time when Judeans living in Babylon engaged in the editing process that produced the biblical texts (discussed above), and they are the ones who knew that the region had only recently been known as Chaldea.

Albright and other scholars sought to associate Abraham and his ancestors with a major migration of nomadic Amorites or *amurru* (westerners) from northern Mesopotamia to Canaan. Amorites are described in Early Bronze Age texts as nomadic peoples living in the upper Euphrates region. These scholars believed that urban society in Canaan collapsed due to several factors: "City after city was destroyed . . . , some with incredible violence, and the Early Bronze Age civilization was brought to an end" (Bright 1981, 44). This incursion of Amorite nomads from the desert in the northeast was regarded as the vanguard of the invasion of Canaan and the sudden breakdown of urban society. According to this theory of Israelite origins, Abraham and his ancestors were situated within this movement as pastoralists involved in the donkey caravan trade. Unfortunately, more recent archeological excavations have shown there was no sudden widespread collapse of Canaanite civilization at the end of the Early Bronze Age, nor was there are any record of a massive Amorite invasion. The dissolution of urban life in Canaan was a process that took place over many decades. Instead, scholars have proposed economic crises, drought, famine, and other long-term societal and environmental disorders as other causes for the decline in Canaan. In addition, most of the population during this phase was indigenous; as Finkelstein pointed out, "The population was descended from the people who had lived in the big cities before" (Finkelstein and Silberman 2001, 321). Archaeological evidence fails to substantiate a great migration from the north. Finally, the proposed explanation of Abraham's movements does not fit the Genesis text, for nowhere does Genesis portray Abraham as part of a substantial invasion, Amorite or otherwise.

Indeed, none of the biblical texts reveal any real awareness of circumstances or events in Canaan prior to Iron Age I. There is no knowledge whatsoever of any destruction of urban life across Canaan in the late Early Bronze Age or at the end of the Middle Bronze Age. Additionally, there is no recognition that Canaan throughout the Late Bronze Age (ca. 1550–1200 BCE) lay under the political control and influence of a powerful Egypt.

Part of the Amorite equation involved the patriarchs' nomadic roots. John Bright (1981, 80, 82), a student of Albright, described the "patriarchs as seminomads, living in tents, wandering up and down Palestine and its borderlands in search of pastureland for their flocks." This depiction "described in Genesis fits" well with the culture and the political milieu of the early second millennium (Bright 1981). Nomads or seminomads living in Canaan were certainly not restricted to a specific era of the second millennium, and referring to the nomadic lifestyle of the patriarchs is too vague to give any historical bearings. Finkelstein contends that Albright's description of the patriarchs' "nomadic lifestyle also proved to be an illusion" (Finkelstein and Silberman 2001, 321). Though the nomadic lifestyle was increasing, much of the population was settled, "living in villages and hamlets" (Finkelstein and Silberman 2001, 321). The reestablishment of Canaanite urban life at the beginning of the second millennium was not due to a great migration of nomads from the north but emerged from the existing Canaanite population.

The basic problem with a search for the historicity of the patriarchs and matriarchs is that the biblical text constitutes our only source of information. The authors of Genesis 12–50 certainly might have material that may ultimately turn out to be in some way "historical," but these writers and editors had no idea of the historical circumstances or accuracy of the folktales, traditions, and stories they used in creating the book of Genesis. Furthermore, some false claims were made by the supporters of Albright based on the belief that Genesis preserved an outline of patriarchal traditions that were firmly anchored in history (see, e.g., Bright 1981, 77).

Names and History

One case for the historicity of the patriarchal and matriarchal narratives came from the archives discovered at Mari in Syria and at Nuzi in northern Iraq. Archaeologists discovered over twenty thousand texts at Mari, the vast majority written in Akkadian. These texts were composed over a period of almost five hundred years, with most dating to the last fifty years of the city's existence. The last inhabitants before the destruction of the city by Hammurabi in 1762 BCE were Semitic. Nuzi, a Hurrian-speaking site, contained over four thousand tablets—mainly from private sources—dating to the fifteenth century and provided a wealth of information on economic, legal, and social customs. The Amorite-speaking peoples mentioned above lived principally in northern Mesopotamia and extended west into Syria. Conservative scholars argued that the personal names of the ancestors of Abraham were typical of Northwest Semitic names from the second millennium. They insisted these names "fit perfectly" into the second millennium in Mesopotamia and Palestine. Albright maintained that "[t]he figures of Abraham, Isaac, Jacob, and Joseph appear to us as real personalities, each one of whom shows traits and qualities that suit his character" (1963, 183). Conservatives agreed that Abram/Abraham, Isaac, and Jacob fit readily into the nomenclature of northern Mesopotamia in the second millennium among the Amorites, and their ancestors Terah, Nahor, Haran, and Serug are personal names that corresponded with place-names in the northern Euphrates region.

However, the patriarchal names fit well not only in the second millennium BCE but also in the first millennium BCE. Haran and Serug are well-known cities that can be dated to the seventh century (Thompson 1974, 305–6). The name Abram has been identified in texts from Ebla, Ugarit, Egypt, and Cyprus (Ahlström et al. 1993, 181). Abram is common among second and first millennia names throughout Syria/Palestine. "There is nothing about Abram that points to the second millennium more than the first" (Van Seters 1975, 41). The name Abraham also spans similar eras. The name Jacob is also easily located throughout the Near East even down to the first century CE, and later. Other significant names—such as Israel and Isaac—can be found in the first millennium.

The discovery of a nomadic tribe named the "Benjaminites" (sons of the south) in the Mari archives led some biblical scholars to argue that the tribes of Mari may have been the ethnic relatives of the Israelite Benjamin. Biblical

Benjamin has always been one of the most obvious links to the people of Mari because Benjamin of Israel matches the exact form and meaning of the earlier Binu Yamina (Fleming 2012, 145–49). However, the Bible appears to preclude any connection with the Mari "Benjaminites" since its narrative of the birth of Benjamin is incompatible with that possibility. The biblical Benjamin was a son of Jacob born in Canaan, not in northern Mesopotamia. Additionally, the biblical writers preserved folktales that relate another name for Benjamin at his birth before Jacob changed it (Gen 35:17-18).

According to Genesis, Abraham is the ancestral patriarch not only of the Israelites but also of other groups: the Arabs through his son Ishmael, the Edomites through his grandson Esau, and the Moabites and Ammonites through his nephew Lot. Indeed, the biblical writers link nearly all the Semitic groups in Canaan to Abraham. This literary creation can hardly be considered an accurate, viable reconstruction of the ethnic groups in Bronze Age Canaan (Ahlström et al. 1993, 184). Names such as Lot, Esau, Laban, and even Abraham are probably the "names of folk heroes" used to express "the political and social ties that Israel has with its neighbors, above all the Arameans" (Thompson 1974, 299). Thus, a reconsideration of the available evidence indicates that while the names of the family of Abraham might be ancient, attempts to connect patriarchal names to specific eras and locations prove to be altogether unreliable. They exist through time and geography across the Near East and cannot serve to substantiate the patriarchs' historicity.

Abraham's Actions and Customs of the Bronze Ages

Some of Albright's followers attempted to place the patriarchs at the beginning of the Late Bronze Age (1550 BCE) based on the cuneiform texts from the second millennium, especially at Nuzi and Mari. These texts ostensibly paralleled many of the social and legal traditions found in Genesis. Though the Nuzi tablets dated much later than Albright's dating of Abraham, Albright declared that it was certain that Nuzi established "the case for the substantial historicity of the tradition of the Patriarchs" (1963, 5). Other scholars thought these texts clearly established the origins of Abraham's ancestors in Mesopotamia and, more importantly, that the patriarchs must be dated to the second millennium (Speiser 1964). As evidence of parallel customs between the patriarchs and Mesopotamian texts, conservative scholars pointed to several stories in Genesis: Abraham and Isaac passing their wives off as their sisters (Gen 12:10-20; 20:1-2; 26:1-11); the childless wife Sarah handing her maid to Abraham, through whom he may have children (Gen 16:1-6; 30:9); Rachel's theft of the household gods (Gen 31:19); the status of inheritance rights of children born to the wife and concubine (Gen 21:9-14); and a person selling his birthright (Gen 25:29-34). However, none of these alleged parallels with Mesopotamian texts actually substantiate the historicity of the Genesis narratives. Critics charged that many of the identified examples of parallel traditions between the biblical narratives and Mesopotamia texts do not exist or have been misinterpreted. More importantly, none of the customs and legal practices depicted in Genesis date exclusively to the second millennium, nor do they verify any historical aspect of the patriarchs and matriarchs. The Nuzi and Mari documents function best as representing the general cultural milieu of the Near East rather than as verifying the historicity of the stories in Genesis 12–50. Many of these practices were so common in the Near East that they covered many cultures and eras dating from the late third millennium into the mid-first millennium BCE (Thompson 1974, 261–97). Cultural and legal affinities between Genesis and evidence from Mesopotamian cities do not prove Genesis' historicity. "In the end, none of the alleged customs demonstrating an early second millennium background for the patriarchal stories seems to have stood up" (Grabbe 2007, 55).

Anachronisms in the Genesis Tales

Scholars have long noticed anachronisms in the patriarchal and matriarchal stories. Many references, geographical incongruities, chronological information, and phrases do not mirror the Bronze Age. Indeed, far too many of the narratives found in Genesis 12–50 better reflect the first millennium BCE, long after the supposed time of Abraham. As mentioned previously, Abraham's migration from "Ur of the *Chaldeans*" (Gen 11:28, 31; 15:7) is improbable in the Early or Middle Bronze Ages since the Chaldeans did not settle in southern Mesopotamia until the first millennium BCE—long after the traditional date for the patriarchal narratives. Another anachronism involves camels, which

FIGURE 8-4. *Camels are mentioned frequently in Genesis 12–50. Yet the domestication of camels did not take place earlier than the tenth century BCE, hundreds of years after the traditional date for the patriarchs.*

are mentioned frequently in Genesis 12–50. The earliest apparent "in situ presence of probably domestic camels in the Levant occurs in the Late Bronze Age levels (late second millennium B.C.) at Tell Jemmeh" (Rosen and Saidel 2010, 75). Furthermore, newer studies by Erez Ben-Yosef and Lidar Sapir-Hen (2013) using radiocarbon dating on the copper-smelting sites in the Aravah Valley concluded that the introduction of domestic camels into the southern Levant and ancient Israel did not take place earlier than the last third of the tenth century BCE. Isaac's encounter with the Philistine Abimelech at Gerar (Gen 26:1-32; and a similar story with Abraham in Gen 20:1-18) is also historically problematic. The Philistines arrived in Canaan only at the beginning of the Iron Age, after 1185 BCE. Gerar has been identified as Tel Haror, and excavations there indicate that it was a small site in the Late Bronze Age and even smaller in the Early Iron Age—certainly not the kingdom attributed to Abimelech in Genesis 20:9. Additionally, Abraham residing "in the land of the Philistines a long time" (Gen 21:34) is impossible until after 1185 BCE, when the Philistines appeared on the scene. Tel Haror was a large fortified settlement in the eighth century and may have been part of an Assyrian military complex (Oren 1993). At this much later date, it would likely have been well known by the writers and editors of the biblical materials. Tel Haror thus provides evidence only in favor of the late date of the narrative, not of the historicity of Abraham.

Genesis' comments about peoples and use of place-names often indicate anachronisms. Genesis 12:6 states, "Abram passed through the land to the place at Shechem, to the Oak of Moreh. At that time, the Canaanites were in the land." This verse challenges the tradition of the Mosaic authorship of the Torah since Moses never knew a time when the Canaanites were not in the land; the comment dates to a later era. Additionally, the reference to the city of Dan in Genesis 14:14 is incompatible with the traditions in Joshua 19:47 and Judges 18:29, which also know the site, but by its original name, Laish. The biblical tradition in Judges 18 describes the migration of Dan and the conquest of Laish, in which the Danites changed the name to Dan, centuries after the biblical Abraham. The town of Beer-sheba is sometimes mentioned in connection with Abraham and his ancestors. The likely location of biblical Beersheba is Tel Beersheba. The first periods of occupation in the area come from the remains of a settlement, which included subterranean dwellings from the Chalcolithic Period. However, it was abandoned until the Iron Age. Excavations in the immediate areas revealed small villages and temporary dwellings dating to the Iron Age, twelfth to tenth centuries BCE. The water system of Tel Beersheba was built concurrently with the first fortified city dating to the Iron Age, twelfth to eleventh centuries BCE. It is unlikely that Beer-Sheba has any connection with an early or late date for a supposed historical Abraham. But it would concur with the Iron Age date of the narrative as it now stands.

Genesis 12:8 and 13:3 connect Abraham to the site of Ai, which is to likely be identified with the site of Khirbet et-Tell. Two archaeologists excavated at Ai—Judith Marquet-Krause in 1933–1936 and Joseph Callaway in 1964–1972—and both concluded that a violent destruction engulfed the site about 2400 BCE. The city was abandoned until a small, unfortified farming village was built on the site around approximately 1220 BCE, and it was abandoned once again in 1050 BCE. If scholars have correctly identified Khirbet et-Tell as biblical Ai, then the city did not exist during any of the traditional eras proposed for Abraham or any patriarch or matriarch (ca. 2200–1200 BCE). More importantly, many biblical scholars perceived the archaeological history of Ai as a severe challenge to the tales of Joshua rather than Abram/ Abraham. The archaeological results did not correspond with the narratives found in the book of Joshua, in which thousands were burned at Ai along with the city (Josh 8:5-28). The traditional date for Joshua's invasion of Canaan has been approximately 1200 BCE. After the excavations failed to substantiate the Joshua narratives, some scholars proposed Ai had been misidentified, but proposed alternative sites have not been accepted by the archaeological community. The majority of scholars, therefore, still maintain that Khirbet et-Tell is the biblical Ai and that any search for other locations was based on the negative archaeological evidence rather than any geographical mistake (Petit 2014, 50–52).

Genesis portrays the Hebrew patriarchs and matriarchs as close relatives of the Arameans in Genesis (Gen 25:20; 31:20). However, the first unquestionable ancient source to mention the Arameans as an influential people is the Assyrian annals of Tiglath-Pilesar I, dating to the end of the twelfth century. Genesis 36:31 mentions "the kings who reigned in the land of Edom, before any king reigned over the Israelites." The author is clearly familiar with a time when Israel was ruled by kings in the first millennium, long after the age of the patriarchs and matriarchs. In the incident of the rape of Dinah (Gen 34:7), the biblical author states that "he had committed an outrage in Israel by lying with Jacob's daughter." By describing this incident as "an outrage *in Israel*" (Gen 34:7), the narrator is speaking of a time when Israel was an organized community or more likely an established state, a political organization that clearly did not exist in the alleged time of the patriarch Jacob.

Conservative scholars have recognized these peculiarities in the biblical text and granted that some narrative features in Genesis may have been created long after the events the book narrates. For many, the anachronisms are generally discounted, and the overall historicity of the patriarchal narratives is valid. Bright (1981, 90) referred to Ur of the Chaldeans as a "natural anachronism."

Albright (1946, 208) argued that the "documentary sources for the history of Israel came from the late thirteenth to the fourth century" and considered them, "in general, remarkably reliable." Of note, he also understood that the "orally transmitted record is superior, but it is peculiarly exposed to the phenomena of refraction and selection of elements suited for epic narrative" (Albright 1963, 5). Speiser (1964, 81), who ignored most of the anachronisms in his book on Genesis, thought them insignificant for dating purposes and claimed that Ur of the Chaldeans was "no more than marginal footnotes to the history of the patriarchs." More recently, Provan, Long, and Longman (2003, 117) recognized some anachronisms as "later glosses" or "simple updating" to the biblical texts. They also seem to hold to the notion that evidence "exists that is consistent with the location of a patriarchal period in the first half of the second millennium" (Provan, Long, and Longman 2003, 116). For Finkelstein, by contrast, anachronisms are crucial in "dating and understanding the meaning and the historical context of the stories of the patriarchs" (Finkelstein and Silberman 2001, 38). The combinations of names, places, and other details are "highly significant," and all indicate "a time of composition many centuries after the time in which the Bible reports the lives of the patriarchs took place" (Finkelstein and Silberman 2001, 38). As is now commonplace in critical biblical scholarship, Finkelstein dates the initial stages of the composition of the patriarchal narratives to the eighth and seventh centuries BCE.

However, it must be noted that not all the evidence is negative. There may well be an early historical memory of Abraham. A tenth-century Egyptian text, the "Karnak Inscription" of the Egyptian pharaoh Shishak, describes an invasion of Canaan in the fifth year of the Judean king Rehoboam (ca. 925 BCE). According to 1 Kings 14:25-28 (see also 2 Chr 12:4), Pharaoh Shishak marched against Jerusalem, and "he took away the treasures of the house of the LORD and the treasures of the King's house; he took everything." The pharaoh's own annals at Karnak list over 150 cities captured during his campaign in Judah and Israel. One captured site holds particular interest; its name is read as either the fort or field of "Abram or Abiram" (Hendel 2005, 48–49). Archaeologists have dated some sites in the Negev to the tenth century, but only a few can be identified in Shishak's annals. However, this inscription is important because it demonstrates the possibility that the name of this site preserves the memory of a patriarch (or someone else) named Abram. Hendel (2005, 50) suggests, "We seem to have credible extra-biblical evidence for the vitality of traditions about Abram in the tenth century BCE."

Nevertheless, in our present state of knowledge, it is hard to imagine that biblical scholars could extract reliable details on the history of Abraham and his ancestors. Even if biblical scholars could establish that the patriarchs and matriarchs were historical figures and were able to pinpoint a specified era in which they lived, there are countless aspects of the stories in Genesis that would remain unresolved. Even if correct, the proposed Amorite origins of Abram's lineage or the existence of Amorite tribal affiliations with Haran and northern Mesopotamia do not prove that the patriarchal stories are historical or allow us to place these stories with any confidence in any century of the second millennium BCE. Other than some general observations, biblical scholars are unable to demonstrate that any of the characters in Genesis said or did anything as specifically portrayed in these narratives. The lack of corroborating evidence serves as a major impediment for biblical scholars trying to reconstruct a viable history of Abraham in Genesis. The real Abraham, therefore, is beyond historical verification.

Canaanite Deities

Modern knowledge of Canaanite religion and deities was extremely limited until 1929 when an archive of cuneiform texts was excavated at the ancient site of Ugarit, modern Ras Shamra, Syria. In addition to their linguistic value, these texts revolutionized the scholarly understanding of Canaanite religion and shed light on the religion of the patriarchs and matriarchs. Dating from the Late Bronze Age, these texts number in the thousands and are written in several languages, including one with affinities to Hebrew; many contain myths and legends about Canaanite gods, mainly El and Baal.

With this new information, it is clear that the authors—the sources—of Genesis knew about the Canaanite gods. Throughout Genesis, the authors of the E and P sources usually call the divine being "El" (the leader of the Canaanite pantheon) or "Elohim" (a plural form of the name applied to a single being), although they use other names and epithets as well. They do not use the name Yahweh until it is revealed to Moses in Exodus 6:2-3: "God also spoke to Moses and said to him: 'I am the LORD [Yahweh]. I appeared to Abraham, Isaac, and Jacob as God Almighty [El Shadday], but by my name 'The LORD' [Yahweh] I did not make myself known to them." The name El Shadday, another divine name, appears five times in the Genesis P source; it comprises the combination of El (the Canaanite god) with the epithet *shaddai*, or "one of the mountain." By contrast, the J source in Genesis regularly uses the name Yahweh for the deity from the time of Adam, beginning in Genesis 4:26: "At that time, people began to invoke the name of the LORD" (i.e., Yahweh).

Of course, elsewhere in the biblical books, the Semitic term "El" simply appears in Hebrew as the generic word for "god," with no reference to the Canaanite god El. But in Genesis and elsewhere in the Torah, it is clear that many of the references to "El" were not simply generic but the name of the Canaanite deity described in Ugaritic texts.

El is linked with other titles in Genesis, such as El Bethel (El of the House of El), El Elyon (El the most high), El Olam (El everlasting), El Roi (El who sees), and "El the god of Abraham." Jacob sets up an altar and calls it "El, the god of Israel" (Gen 33:20). Moreover, many of the attributes of the god El as recorded in the texts at Ugarit—such as the head of the council of gods, an aged, bearded deity, full of compassion, appearing in dreams, and dwelling in tents—are also applied to Yahweh. The Hebrew Bible thus often associates El with Yahweh. Despite this, we should see El and Yahweh as separate deities—at least initially—especially since Yahweh was not a common Canaanite deity. Most scholars recognize Yahweh's origins as from Arabia or Sinai (Day 2002, 15–16; M. Smith 2001, 145). It is important to note that Abraham accepts the blessing from the Canaanite king and priest Melchizedek in the name of El Elyon (God Most High; Gen 14:18-20). In the passage's next verse, Abraham calls the God of Israel "El Most High [El Elyon], creator of heaven and earth" (Gen 14:22).

The lack of Yahweh in the personal names of the patriarchs and matri-archs in Genesis is an indication of the prominence of El and should be seen as evidence for an early El religion in Israelite history. Remarkably, the name Israel (Gen 32:28) contains the element of El in its name. The Bible provides a folk etymology for the name Israel as "he who struggles with El," but the true meaning is unclear. Other names in Genesis follow the pattern, such as Adbeel, Bethuel, Eldaah, Ishmael, Kemuel, Reuel, and others.

In other places in the Torah, El is identified with Yahweh. Exodus 34:6 can be translated as "Yahweh, Yahweh, is El merciful and gracious, slow to anger, and abounding in steadfast love and faithfulness" (translation authors' own). Deuteronomy 32:8-9 preserves a story that depicts Yahweh as a son of Elyon who receives his own nation Israel:

> When the Most High [*elyon*] apportioned the nations,
>   when he divided humankind,
>   he fixed the boundaries of the peoples
>   according to the number of the gods;
> The LORD's [Yahweh's] own portion was his people,
>   Jacob his allotted share.

In Genesis 46:3, the writers likewise associate El with Yahweh: "I am God [El], the God of your father; do not be afraid to go down to Egypt, for I will make of you a great nation there." The writers of Genesis remember a time when their patriarchs and matriarchs worshipped the god El. At first consid-eration, it may appear easy to discount these memories as fictional accounts, a manufactured history. However, Hendel argues that these narratives pre-served Israelite memories of a time when the Canaanite god El was the god of early Israel. The Canaanite god El was supplanted by Baal as head of the Canaanite pantheon sometime in the Late Bronze Age (1400–1200 BCE). The recollection and transmission of these stories cannot be easily dismissed and require an explanation (Hendel 2005, 50–52). Smith recognizes the ancient memories of Israelite traditions and knowledge of Yahweh-El at El cultic sites "such as Shiloh, Shechem, and Jerusalem." However, he also believes that the El cult existed in Israel as late as the first millennium. The use of El epithets in the Priestly source and in E could be important evidence for the worship of El in Iron II Israel (M. Smith 2001, 140–42). Just how these stories were altered and subject to revision, handed down, and preserved by the Israelites shows that the religion of their patriarchs and matriarchs was largely Canaanite.

Joseph

Of all the Genesis narratives, those about Joseph are the longest and most detailed. The Joseph saga (Gen 37–50) is in essence a tale of divine over-sight: no matter what happens, God cares for the fate of his chosen people. Joseph was Jacob's favorite son, and the young Joseph flaunted this before his brothers. Not surprisingly, the brothers' jealousy caused them to hate Joseph (Gen 37:1-11). They devised a scheme to rid themselves of Joseph once and for all; they sold him as a slave to some traders (Gen 37:12-28) and then lied to their father, telling him that Joseph had been devoured by "a savage beast." This news of Joseph's fate broke Jacob's heart (Gen 37:29-35). Meanwhile, Joseph was taken to Egypt (Gen 37:36), where through various trials and tribulations he rose from a lowly slave to one of Egypt's highest officials (Gen 39–41): "The LORD was with Joseph, and he became a successful man" (Gen 39:2). Joseph was first sold as a slave to Pharaoh's captain of the guard, Poti-phar (Gen 39:1), who saw Joseph's potential and exploited it. Joseph was also very handsome, and his looks caught the eye of Potiphar's wife, who tried to seduce him. But Joseph was an honorable man, so he rejected her advances. His rejection enraged her, so she told her husband that Joseph had tried to rape her. This in turn enraged Potiphar, who had Joseph imprisoned (Gen 39:3-20). But, even in prison, "the LORD was with Joseph" (Gen 39:21), and he again rose to a trusted leadership position (Gen 39:22-23). When some of Pharaoh's attendants disappointed him, he had them temporarily imprisoned. They told Joseph about their dreams, and with God's help Joseph interpreted the dreams for them (Gen 40:1-23). Eventually, Pharaoh himself had a vexing dream that required interpretation, so one of Pharaoh's attendants recommended Joseph, the dream interpreter he had met in prison (Gen 41:1-13). Once again, because God supported Joseph, he was able to interpret Pharaoh's dream (Gen 41:14-36). Joseph's wisdom so impressed Pharaoh that he appointed Joseph his second-in-command. Joseph then skillfully led Egypt through a severe famine (Gen 41:37-57). Thus, thanks to Yahweh's favor, according to the biblical tales, Joseph went from a slave to a successful leader.

The famine that plagued Egypt also hit the land of Canaan, where Joseph's family lived. Having learned that Egypt had resources available, Jacob sent his sons there in the hope that they could secure grain for the family (Gen 42:1-5). Little did they know that the Egyptian official in charge was their brother Joseph, the one they had sold into slavery. At first Joseph tested his brothers' goodwill, but he eventually revealed them (Gen 45:4). He told his brothers that his success in Egypt was God's way of caring for the family, and he provided them with the provisions they needed and instructed them to return to Canaan, get Jacob, and return to Egypt, where they could be cared for during the famine (Gen 45:5–47:28). And care for them he did, for Jacob and his family prospered in Egypt: "Thus Israel settled in the land of Egypt, in the region of Goshen. They gained possessions in it, were fruitful and multiplied exceedingly" (Gen 47:27).

The Joseph narrative (Gen 37–50) serves two basic purposes. First, from a strictly literary perspective, this is a transition narrative; it moves the locus of the Israelite story from Canaan to Egypt. In this sense it is a necessary precursor to the exodus narrative; it moves the people into Egypt, from where they will journey under divine guidance to the "promised land" during the exodus. Second, it reinforces the theme of Yahweh's watchful care over his people. Joseph is the favored son, and, through all the twists and turns in his life story, it is apparent that Yahweh is working behind the scenes to bring good out of any misfortune. Joseph is sold as a slave, but he becomes a master because Yahweh is with him. Joseph is accused of rape, but, because his character is without flaw, he becomes a leader even in prison because Yahweh is with him. Mysterious dreams require interpretation, and Joseph provides it because Yahweh is with him. So, although he arrived in Egypt in the worst of ways, he succeeded because Yahweh was with him. In his own words to his brothers, "Even though you intended to do harm to me, God intended it for good, in order to preserve a numerous people, as he is doing today" (Gen 50:20). The narrative informs the reader that Yahweh cares for his people, and that commitment will come into question in succeeding generations. Thus, the carefully crafted literary character of this tale is unmistakable, and its theological import is clear. But is it at all historical?

The historical character of the Joseph story is similar to that of the stories of Abraham and his family in Genesis. As with the early Genesis narratives, biblical scholars need to differentiate between what is actually verifiable evidence as opposed to scholarly reconstructions or theoretical musings. We have no direct evidence for dating Joseph. No Egyptian records confirm the biblical story or mention Jacob or the miraculous deeds of Joseph. This occurrence is surprising since Joseph, next to Pharaoh, is portrayed as the most powerful royal official in all of Egypt. The name of Pharaoh is never specified in the biblical narrative, and Jacob's sons' existence in Egypt is nowhere recorded in Egyptian annals.

The book of 1 Kings (6:1) states that the exodus took place 480 years before Solomon built the Jerusalem temple, and the book of Exodus states that the Israelites lived in Egypt for 430 years (Gen 12:40). Most scholars estimate Solomon built the temple about 960 BCE. Using these figures, one can calculate the date of the Israelite arrival in Egypt at 1870 BCE. Most modern scholars, however, reject these figures and regard them as merely figurative. The biblical authors had no idea of the exact years for the exodus or the Israelite entry into Egypt. For some biblical scholars, the Egyptian background of the Joseph narrative suggests that the main points are plausible for a historical and social reconstruction of the biblical account; for others, the story is simply the authors' fictional imagination (Alter 1981, 177). The Egyptologist Donald Redford (1992, 426–27) perceives that the Joseph narratives contain "various incidental details" that "find some degree of correlation in Egyptian texts." He insists that "a compelling case can be made for a seventh or sixth-century date for the story, regardless of the contentious issue of background details."

According to conservative or traditional scholars, represented by Hoffmeier and Kitchen, genuine historical memories and textual links can be found between the biblical texts and Egyptian sources. The presence of Semites dwelling among Egyptians is well attested in Egyptian records. The Nile Delta was populated by Semites throughout the second millennium. The Hyksos were Semites who ruled Egypt during the Fifteenth Dynasty (ca. 1670–1550 BCE), indicating that Semites could hold even the highest positions in the Egyptian court, even pharaoh. In the succeeding New Kingdom Period, after the Hyksos retreated to Canaan, Semites could be promoted to high positions, and several well-known Semites attained high office. The Syrian Bey in the early thirteenth century had the title "Great Chancellor of the entire land," and Aper-el was vizier to Pharaohs Amenhotep III (1390–1353 BCE) and Akhenaten (1353–1336 BCE). Aper-el is clearly a Semitic name containing the *el* element in his name. His name most likely reflects the Canaanite god El (Hoffmeier 2005, 92–94). A Syrian cupbearer named Ben-Ozen rose to prominence in Merneptah's court (1213–1203 BCE).

Egyptian personal names in the Joseph story may also connect the Joseph traditions to an Egyptian background. Though controversial, the names Potiphar (Joseph's first employer), Asenath (Joseph's wife), Potiperah (his father-in-law), and Zaphenath-paneah (Joseph's given Egyptian name) are Egyptian "beyond doubt" (Kitchen 2003, 345). Kitchen dates three of the names early, but Redford sees their popularity in the seventh and sixth centuries BCE. There are also approximately seventy Egyptian loanwords in the Bible, a remarkable indicator of the contacts between Egypt and the ancient Israelites. According to Genesis 39:4, Joseph was placed in charge (overseer) of the household. A similar expression is found in Egyptian papyri related to Semitic servants. Joseph is sold into slavery for the price of twenty shekels (Gen 37:28), a price that roughly corresponds to the average price of a slave for the early second millennium. Some titles and functions bestowed on Joseph mirror the Egyptian bureaucracy. In Genesis 41:40-43, Pharaoh placed Joseph "in charge of my court," placed his signet ring "on Joseph's hand, had him dressed in robes of fine linen, and put a gold chain about his neck. He had him ride in the chariot of his second-in-command." According to Kitchen, "all this fits both in the Middle [2133–1570/1550 BCE] and New Kingdoms [1550–1070]" and is "authentically Egyptian" (2003, 349). The use of the term "pharaoh," meaning "great house," was never a formal title for the king of Egypt until Thutmose III (ca. 1479–1425 BCE), and then it became commonly used by the Ramesside era (ca. 1300–1100 BCE), as Hoffmeier relates. Until the tenth century BCE, the term "pharaoh" was used alone to identify the king, which is exactly how the Hebrew Bible uses "Pharaoh" throughout Genesis and Exodus. In later periods, the king's personal name was used with the title Pharaoh. After Shishak in the tenth century, the title and the name appear together (Hoffmeier 2005, 87). There are also Egyptian customs concerning dreams and magic found in the Joseph story.

Many of these examples have been debated and disputed for years. Redford (1992, 424–25) admits that some details of the Joseph story "point to Egypt" and "some descriptions have direct application to Egypt." However, the evidence indicates that the "Biblical Joseph story was a novella created sometime during the seventh or sixth century B.C. There is no reason to believe it has any basis in fact" (Redford 1992, 429). Hoffmeier (1997, 97) and Kitchen (2003, 343–52), in contrast, contend that the main points of the Joseph narrative are credible given what is known of Egyptian history and given that the weight of the evidence indirectly affirms the historicity of this narrative and its protagonists.

Dating is essential for the Joseph story. The Joseph narrative may portray a representative vision of Egyptian life, but realistic presentations do not equal historical facts. Even though what the biblical writers thought happened in the past is interesting, it is not a substitute for what the historical record actually contains. For the Joseph traditions to have any historical viability, we need to know something about their creation. When were these stories written down? And by whom? How such a long, complex story of the Joseph narrative could have been preserved accurately in oral tradition is difficult to discern. It is not impossible that some segments of oral tradition can be preserved, such as genealogies. However, most biblical scholars understand the fragile nature of the transmission of oral and written recollections. The narratives change over time and geographical area regardless of storytellers' desire to preserve a tale with perfect accuracy.

Hoffmeier has suggested that scholars should look no further than Moses for the origins of the first written record of the Torah and the exodus. Discarding the past two centuries of the scholarly study of the Torah, Hoffmeier reasons that Moses, who was raised in Pharaoh's court according to biblical tradition (Exod 2), was educated with all the royal children, as was the custom in Egypt's imperial nursery. Moses "was instructed in all the wisdom of the Egyptians" and must have learned the alphabet. This alphabet, or "Proto-Canaanite script," invented by the Canaanites and first known in Egypt, is "attested in Egypt, Sinai, and Canaan throughout the second millennium . . . there is no objective reason to deny Moses the ability to use the Proto-Canaanite script and record laws, itineraries, and historical observations" (Hoffmeier 2005, 180–81). According to Hoffmeier the references in the Torah to Moses and writing indicate "enough evidence has been marshaled to show that there is no doubt that Moses played a crucial role in the recording of the Torah" (Hoffmeier 2005, 181). Hoffmeier is not alone in this observation, as it also appears in other traditional histories of ancient Israel, such as Provan, Long, and Longman's *A Biblical History of Israel* (2003, 58). And recently, several scholars have claimed to have located the name Moses in the Proto-Sinaitic (Proto-Canaanite) script inscribed in the mine complex at Serabit el Khadem in the Sinai. Admittedly, this would be an important discovery, but whether these claims will be sustained is not clear at present.

Frankly, most biblical scholars regard these proposals as a step backward in analyzing the biblical text and reminiscent of biblical fundamentalism. Of course, there may have been a Moses as mentioned in the Torah, but there is no evidence of the biblical Moses outside of the Bible. The name Moses is a sound Egyptian name that fits in the New Kingdom Period (1550–1295 BCE). It stems from the Egyptian verb "give birth," which is an abbreviated form found in the names of Egyptian pharaohs, such as Ahmose (Ah is born), Thutmose, and Ramesses. The name is also found among Egyptians who were simply named Mose. The biblical story has the pharaoh's daughter naming the child Moses because "I drew him out of the water" (Exod 2:10). It is interesting to note that the pharaoh's daughter only named Moses after "the child grew up." What he was called previous to this event is unknown. The Hebrew name Moses or Moshe is exceptionally rare, even unique in the Bible. Grammatically the name actually means "one that draws out." How a pharaoh's daughter understood Hebrew, however, is not explained.

There is certainly no indication that the Proto-Canaanite alphabet was part of the education of Pharaoh's children or that the Egyptians actually used the alphabet. Excluding the finds in the Sinai, few alphabetic inscriptions have ever been found in Egypt. Only a few "very short inscriptions (most containing only a couple of letters) have been found in Canaan dating to the end of the Middle Bronze Age and the Late Bronze Age (1750–1200 BCE). . . . For half of a millennium after its invention, the alphabet was rarely used—at least as far as it is reflected in the archaeological record" (Goldwasser 2010). In our present state of knowledge, all we can say is that it is doubtful that Moses wrote any part of the Torah in the Late Bronze Age or that he even existed.

Egyptian Influence on Ancient Israel

Some evidence suggests Egyptians may have provided aspects of the cultural background for the Joseph narratives. Late Bronze Age Canaan was occupied by Egypt, and Egyptian-style palaces, administrative centers, temples, and more are known at several sites, including Aphek, Ashdod, Beth Shean, Hesi, Jemmeh, Joppa, Tell el-Farah, Tell Masos, Tel Mor, and Ziklag. By the thirteenth and twelfth centuries BCE, a local alphabetic tradition had replaced cuneiform in Canaan, and was possibly influenced by Egyptian scribal traditions (Schniedewind 2013, 57). Egyptian hieratic inscriptions, the cursive form of ancient Egyptian hieroglyphics, have been uncovered in Canaan. The hieratic inscriptions, mainly the numbering system, were found in Canaanite Lachish, Tel Sera, Tel Haror, and Deir el-Balah. The writing dates as late as the reign of Ramesses III (1186–1155 BCE) based on two scarabs uncovered in a "temple estate of Ramesses III" (Goldwasser and Wimmer 1999). Israelite scribes also used hieratic numerals. Paleo-Hebrew script and hieratic numerals have been discovered at a number of sites, such as Arad, Lachish, Kadesh-barnea, Samaria, and perhaps Mesad Hashavyahu in the Iron Age II. It is clear that Judean and Israelite scribes used hieratic numbers at various sites "in Israel and Judea" and "were capable of using a complicated, originally foreign numeric system" (Rollston 2010, 110), requiring some formalized training.

It also appears that the origins of such Hebrew words as "ink" and "papyrus" are Egyptian. The use of ink and papyrus clearly "comes from Egyptian scribal practice and technology" (Schniedewind 2013, 58). A number of Hebrew words are borrowed from Egyptian that relate to the scribal profession—that is, "counting," "scribe's palette," "seal," "signet ring," and the measurements *ephah*, *hin*, and *zeret* (Schniedewind 2013, 59). It is difficult to understand why the Hebrew language contains these Egyptian terms unless the language had been heavily influenced by Egyptian.

There is more specific evidence of the Egyptian impact on early Israelite scribes. The Egyptian word for "scribe" is found in the variant names for David's first scribe, Seraiah (2 Sam 8:17), Sheva (2 Sam 20:25), and Shavsha (1 Chr 18:16). Elihoreph, one of the sons of Shisha (Sheva), is one of Solomon's scribes and has an Egyptian name (1 Kgs 4:3). These scribes, if indeed Egyptian, probably followed Egyptian literary practices and wrote on papyrus; these records have longed since disappeared. It seems reasonable to suggest that the beginning of a scribal guild developed in ancient Israel that was dependent to some extent upon the "Egyptian scribal legacy in Canaan" (Schniedewind 2013, 59). It is possible that these scribal connections are evidence of Egyptian influence upon Judean scribes and scribal practices.

Some scholars maintain that the royal courts of David and Solomon are modeled on the Egyptian bureaucracy. There are a number of biblical references to Solomon's marriage to the daughter of Pharaoh (1 Kgs 3:1; 7:8; 9:16, 24; 11:1), and such alliances by marriage were standard practice in that era. Moreover, Jeroboam I, Israel's first king, was once forced to flee to Egypt. Taking into consideration the problems and reliability of the Bible in recording accurate information regarding this period, these details probably reflect memories connected in one way or another to Egypt. Whether or not Judah was too undeveloped to begin any meaningful scribal activity at this time does not negate the possibility that the Joseph narratives could have been composed in an oral form in the late tenth or early ninth century BCE, before being recorded in writing. Many of the Egyptian royal court traditions could have easily been derived from these connections, as indicated by the scribal and biblical records. There is a distinct possibility that a vague memory of a historical event was recast with a number of details influenced by Egyptian literary archetypes and would be eventually put into writing by the ninth century BCE. Moreover, there is also an oral element to these stories. They were created and

FIGURE 8-5. *The ostracon from Khirbet Qeiyafa dating to the tenth century BCE could be one of the oldest examples of early Canaanite or Hebrew writing. It is one of the longest and earliest examples of the alphabet.*

initially passed on in an oral context. People "memorized" the traditions, and, naturally, they expanded the stories as they retold them. What we have, therefore, is the final product of a long and complex process of transmission, and the goal of the people crafting these traditions was not necessarily the same as that of modern historians. They were transmitting values to their contemporaries, and in this effort they fused their religious ideas with their sense of "Israel" as a collective entity: the one true god was in fact their god, Yahweh.

Conclusion

Albert Einstein is credited with observing that "Memory is deceptive because it is colored by today's events." The biblical authors and editors were focused on serving the needs of their people as they imagined them, not on crafting a complete, detailed, and accurate history. They used their accounts of events to convey values, largely the religious and national values they thought best for their people. Somewhat more suspiciously, however, Yosef Hayim Yerushalmi noted that memory itself is a tricky thing: "Memory is always problematic, usually deceptive, and sometimes treacherous" (1982, 5); that is to say, what people regard as "history" can arise in a multitude of ways, appear in a multitude of forms, and serve a multitude of purposes. Our task is to determine which of these options any given text is trying to achieve. It is that quest that makes the biblical narratives come alive for our generation.

Oftentimes, the quest to prove the historicity of a biblical text such as Genesis is driven by a religious or theological desire to prove the text accurate and reliable. The belief is that if the text is proven to be historically reliable, then it must also be reliable in a religious sense. But as noted with regard to patriarchal narratives, these stories are first and foremost concerned with saying something about Israel as a chosen people, about how it came to be a nation, and why its lifeways (culture, beliefs, etc.) are what they are. But too many discrepancies appear in these narratives to claim that their concerns are remotely historical. The fact that the text as we have it is a product of a long historical evolution attests its vitality and importance to the community, not necessarily its accuracy.

Suggestions for Further Reading

Abraham and his place among Israelite origin stories has become an important topic for analysis by biblical scholars. Three works from different perspectives are Ronald Hendel's *Remembering Abraham: Culture, Memory, and History in the Hebrew Bible* (2005), John Van Seters' *Abraham in History and Tradition* (1975), and Thomas Thompson's *The Historicity of the Patriarchal Narratives: The Quest for the Historical Abraham* (1974). Donald Redford provides an excellent analysis of the history of Egypt and its relationships with Canaan and Israel in *Egypt, Canaan, and Israel in Ancient Times* (1992). The polytheism of the Canaanites and its relationship to the monotheism that arose among the Israelites constitutes an exciting area of study. Both Mark Smith's *The Origins of Biblical Monotheism: Israel's Polytheistic Background and the Ugaritic Texts* (2001) and John Day's *Yahweh and the Gods and Goddesses of Canaan* (2002) provide excellent discussions of this topic. For the discussion of the tribe of Benjamin and its possible relationship to Mari, see Daniel Fleming, "Genesis in History and Tradition" (2004). If you want to know more about the formation of the Torah and the Documentary Hypothesis, consult chapter 2. Also, Richard Friedman's *Who Wrote the Bible?* (1987) gives an engaging description of how the biblical books attained their current form. Several conservative scholars have worked to use academic investigation to address matters of interpretation important to the Christian community. The best of these include K. A. Kitchen's *On the Reliability of the Old Testament* (2003); James Hoffmeier's *Ancient Israel in Sinai: The Evidence for the Authenticity of the Wilderness Tradition* (2005); and Provan, Long, and Longman's *A Biblical History of Israel*, 2nd ed. (2015).

9

ISRAEL IN AND OUT OF EGYPT

J. Edward Wright, Mark Elliott,
and Paul V. M. Flesher

The tale of the Israelites' exodus from Egypt, the establishment of their covenant with God at Mount Sinai, and their subsequent forty-year sojourn in the desert makes a great story. The Torah narrative from Exodus to Deuteronomy provides drama with challenges and triumphs, engaging characters, cliffhanger moments, and final success. Moreover, the story echoes circumstances, events, and international relations of the second millennium BCE. As James Hoffmeier (2007, 226) concludes, it "shows that the main points of Israel in Egypt and the exodus narratives are indeed plausible."

They are plausible because, as W. H. C. Propp (2015, 431–32) points out, so much happened during the Middle and Late Bronze Ages between Egypt and Canaan. Did anyone from Canaan ever govern Egypt? Yes. Did herders from the southern Levant bring themselves and their flocks into Egypt? Yes. Did people or armies of Egyptian origins ever invade Canaan and destroy its cities? Yes. Did Egyptians ever enslave Canaanites? Yes. Were there sacred mountains in the Sinai Desert? Yes. Were there groups of people with names like Israel or Hebrews? Yes. Did large numbers of people settle new territory in Canaan? Yes. Is there any nonbiblical evidence for worshippers of the god Yahweh? Yes, if the name YHW is similar enough. Unfortunately, the evidence for all these "Yes" answers does not lead us to the single collection of tribes known as the Israelites and their activities over a period of forty to forty-five years. Instead, these activities took place over a six-hundred-year period stretching from 1750–1100 BCE and were performed by many different peoples. The events and activities comprise a wonderful background setting for the dramatic exodus story, lending it plausibility but failing to support the historical accuracy of this specific tale.

There are two main problems with trying to identify historical elements in the exodus story. First, archaeological research has uncovered little that would support their historical character. Carol Meyers (2005, 5) observes, "After more than a century of research and massive efforts of generations of archaeologists and Egyptologists, nothing has been recovered that relates directly to the account in the Exodus of an Egyptian sojourn and escape or a large-scale migration through the Sinai."

Second, the exodus story itself seems written to avoid historical specific-ity. There is little direct information in the biblical tale that enables academic historians to answer even the fundamental question of when the exodus took place. The story assigns no names to either pharaoh mentioned or to the pha-raoh's daughter who raised Moses (or to the pharaoh who elevated Joseph at the end of Genesis)—which is a shame, since Egyptologists have detailed knowledge of Egyptian royal chronology. Moses himself appears from nowhere; he is born to Levite parents, but without further pedigree. The bib-lical text indicates his birth date with this vague line: "Now a new king arose over Egypt" (Exod 1:8)—a designation that covers centuries. Not even Moses' name provides a clue. While traditional Jewish exegesis ties the name to the Hebrew verb *mashah*, "to draw out," suggesting his discovery by the pharaoh's daughter, in Egyptian his name is linked to the word for "son of," *mose*, as used in royal names like Thut*mose*s and Ra*mese*s, where the pharaoh is designated the son of a god. That the name Moses lacks such a connection deprives the story of context.

When all is said and done, only the mention of the storage cities of Pithom and Rameses in Exodus 1:11 provides a clue for dating Exodus' opening events (see below). But what about other details in the story? This chapter explores what archaeologists and historians do and do not know about the story of how the Israelites were enslaved in Egypt, gained their freedom, and then spent some years years in the Sinai Desert before entering the land of Canaan. This exploration requires us to understand how the exodus tale was written, to delve into the specifics of what the story actually says, and to bring in the archaeological investigations that have searched for historical evidence to bear on those narrative elements. What we will discover is that much of what we can say is geographical ("Where could this have happened?") but not historical ("Did this happen?").

This chapter begins with a brief précis of the story and identifies how it is related across the books of the Torah. This is followed by a short characteri-zation of where different elements of the story came from and how they were put together. The archaeological survey then begins with the archaeologi-cal background and historical setting of the Middle and Late Bronze periods relevant to the exodus story, including the question of dating when such an event could have taken place. The chapter's main focus will then follow— the exodus story itself. This analysis will highlight events possibly relevant to archaeological evidence.

The Exodus Story

The exodus story appears in the last four books of the Torah and then is completed in the book of Joshua when the Israelites enter Canaan (see the next two chapters for discussion). But it does not make up these books' entire contents. Of the 137 chapters in Exodus, Leviticus, Numbers, and Deuteronomy, only a third of them, some 46 chapters, feature the tale. Even if you add in the eleven chapters in Deuteronomy where Moses recalls the journey and previous events, only 42 percent of the books' contents, less than half, deal with the story. The remainder consists of law codes, instructions for building the ark and the tabernacle and performing worship, other religious instructions, censuses of the people Israel, and descriptions of rituals.

The organization of these four books appears in Figure 9-1. Note how parts of the exodus narrative are distributed across all four books, although only one tale appears in Leviticus. Some elements such as the instructions and the ritual descriptions are tied into the story by casting them as a speech by Moses.

FIGURE 9-1. *Outline of the exodus story,*
from Exodus to Deuteronomy

(1) Exodus	
Exod 1–4	**Moses' early life and call by God**
Exod 5–12	**Moses' struggle with Pharaoh and the exodus from Egypt**
Exod 13–18	**Israel's journey to Mt. Sinai**
Exod 19–20	**Israel at Mt. Sinai**
Exod 21–23	*Covenant Law Code*
Exod 24	**Moses and the seventy elders**
Exod 25–31	Instructions: The Ark, the tabernacle, priestly clothing, etc.
Exod 32–34	**Making the Golden Calf and aftermath**
Exod 35–40	Following instructions: Making the Ark, the tabernacle, priestly clothing, etc.
(2) Leviticus	
Lev 1–7	Instructions: Sacrifice
Lev 8–9	Ritual: Sacrifices consecrating priests and Israel
Lev 10	**Rebellion: Some of Aaron's sons**
Lev 11–15	Instructions: Impurity
Lev 16	Instructions: Day of Atonement
Lev 17–27	*Holiness Law Code*

FIGURE 9-1 *(cont.)*

(3) Numbers

Num 1–4	Census: Of those who left Egypt
Num 5–6	Instructions: Assorted religious rules
Num 7	Ritual: Offerings by all twelve tribes
Num 8–10	Instructions: Assorted religious rules
Num 11–12	**Stories about the quail and Miriam**
Num 13–14	**Spying out Canaan and aftermath**
Num 15	Instructions: Sacrifice
Num 16–17	**Rebellions: Korah and Dathan, then Israel**
Num 18–19	Instructions: Assorted religious rules
Num 20–21	**Deaths of Aaron and Miriam; Confrontations with Edom, Arad, Sihon, and Og**
Num 22–24	**Balaam story**
Num 25	**Phineas story**
Num 26	Census: Of those remaining after forty years
Num 27	**Appointing of Joshua, daughters of Zelophehad**
Num 28–30	Instructions: Assorted religious rules
Num 31	**Battle with Midianites and aftermath**
Num 32	**Reuben and Gad, and Manasseh assigned territory on east side of Jordan**
<u>Num 33</u>	<u>Recap of journey</u>
Num 34–36	Instructions: Delineation of the Land, cities of refuge, and marriage

(4) Deuteronomy

<u>Deut 1–3</u>	<u>Recap of journey and battles</u>
<u>Deut 4–11</u>	<u>Recap of Mt. Sinai (Horeb), Ten Commandments, and following the Torah</u>
Deut 12–26	*Deuteronomic Law Code*
Deut 27–28	Ritual: Blessings and Curses
Deut 29–31	**Exhortation before entering Canaan**
Deut 32	**Moses' condemnation of Israel**
Deut 33	**Moses' blessings on tribes of Israel**
Deut 34	**Moses' death**

KEY

Bold—Exodus Story

Italics—Law Codes

<u>Underline—Recapping of Events</u>

The exodus narrative, once extracted from the accompanying material, divides into three sections. The first section forms the exodus tale proper—that is, the "going out" from Egypt—Exodus 1–20. It begins with the birth of the liberator Moses and then moves to his call by God, his confrontation with the pharaoh, the leaving of Egypt, and the journey to Mount Sinai, where the tale seems to climax as the Israelites receive the Ten Commandments and make a covenant with God. In these chapters, the story runs sequentially and uninterrupted.

The second section consists of a few scattered tales, beginning with a ritual in which Moses and seventy elders hold a sacrifice to ratify the covenant. This is followed by the Israelites making a calf of gold as an idol representing Yahweh and worshipping it, for which God punishes them. After this, there are a few events that happen on the Israelites' journey from Sinai to the land of Canaan, which God intends for them to enter. These chapters run from Exodus 24 to Numbers 12.

FIGURE 9-2. *Bronze calf from Samaria hill country. The calf figurine was most likely a representation of the principal Canaanite deity El and later Baal.*

The third section of the story comprises the two attempts to enter the land of Canaan, separated by forty years (thirty-eight according to Deut 2:14). This section begins with Numbers 13–14, the story of the spies that Moses sends from Kadesh (= Kadesh-barnea) into the land of Canaan to check it out before the Israelites invade. When the spies return, they persuade the Israelites that it is impossible to conquer the land, and so the Israelites cry out against God. God punishes them by decreeing that they will remain in the desert for forty years until the adult Israelites who left Egypt have all died.

Even though this is where the idea of the Israelites' "wandering in the desert" for forty years comes from, they do not actually wander. Instead, they apparently hunker down and remain at Kadesh. The exodus story picks up after four decades, when the Israelites travel south to Ezion-geber at the north end of the Gulf of Eilat on the Red Sea, and then head north toward Canaan to the east of Edom and then down onto the Plains of Moab, just outside the land of Canaan proper. Moses finally dies, in the Pentateuch's last chapter (Deut 34), and so Joshua then leads Israel into the land in the next book, which bears his name.

Sources of the Exodus Story

Why are these four Torah books put together this way? They combine three different versions of the exodus story, originally told by four different groups among later Israelites. A later editor, often called a redactor, combined these tales into a single narrative and included other material as well. Perhaps several editors got involved at different times; it is not clear. This explanation is called the Documentary Hypothesis, and, although scholars debate its details, its general character has remained stable for over a century. We discussed this explanation in chapters 2 and 8, but let us expand on it a bit more.

The Documentary Hypothesis identifies four main sources in the Pentateuch known as J, E, D, and P—as well as a few smaller ones. J and E are the oldest and are distinguished by the name they use for God. In the J material, God is known as Yahweh, or (as the German originators of this analysis termed him) Jahweh—hence "J." (In English translations, Yahweh is usually rendered as "Lord.") The version of the exodus story told by the Yahwist source was probably composed by in the ninth or eighth century BCE. Its theological and political stance favors the tribe of Judah and the Southern Kingdom of Judah, with its capital of Jerusalem, viewing leaders of both the tribe and the kingdom as the legitimate leaders of all the people Israel. The focus on the Judahite Caleb, in Numbers 14, constitutes a good example of J material.

The E version of the story, by contrast, calls God "Elohim," and scholars often refer to its author as the Elohist. (In English translations, Elohim is usually rendered as "God.") The Elohist source represents views from the Northern Kingdom of Israel, not of the royal leadership, but of a group of religious leaders who were opposed to the religious syncretism in that country. They were even against the representation of God by images (such as a calf statue). Written before the kingdom's destruction in 722 BCE, it favors leaders from the northern tribes, such as Ephraim and Manasseh, and especially Joshua, who takes over after Moses' death. At some point, perhaps during King Hezekiah's reign, the two sources were combined; scholars refer to this combination as JE.

The full name of the P version of the exodus story is "the Priestly source." It was written by priests of the Jerusalem temple, probably in the seventh or sixth century BCE. While it contributes to the exodus story, it concentrates on priestly matters of the temple—emphasizing the temple's predecessor (the tabernacle), the worship and sacrifice that took place there, and other priestly rules. Most of the second half of Exodus, all of Leviticus, and key sections of

Numbers belong to this source. It emphasizes the importance of the leadership of Aaron and his descendants, and the subordination of the Levites to them.

D stands for the Deuteronomist, the editor(s)/composer(s) of the book of Deuteronomy. The laws found in Deuteronomy 12–26, the Deuteronomic Code, are essentially unified and usually identified as the book found in the temple during King Josiah's reign, around 622 BCE (2 Kgs 22). The remainder of the book stems from a redactional hand following the code's theology. Nothing from JE or P appears in the book of Deuteronomy.

These sources were brought together by a series of redactors into what we now know as the five books of the Torah. There has been a great deal of scholarly debate on this question, and there is no consensus about when the final, or only, redaction took place. Some scholars place it as early the last years of King Josiah, who died in 609 BCE, while others put it during the Babylonian exile after 597 BCE, and yet others place it after the return from exile beginning in 539 BCE.

However, two points stand out concerning the Torah's sources. First, the various elements of the story of Moses and the exodus were widespread among the Israelites, being told for centuries in two different countries, despite the vicissitudes of war and other challenges. Four communities—represented by the four "sources"—held it as important and told and retold it among themselves. And yet a fifth group, the final redactors, decided that the status of these stories impelled them to recast these several versions as a single tale telling the historical origins of the people Israel's covenant with God and authoritatively linking their social and religious laws to it.

Second, despite the story's importance, the Torah's written material about the exodus is not contemporaneous with the events of the story. At best, there were early tales that were passed down for generations through oral storytelling. Some four centuries or more after the events related by the tales allegedly took place, they began to be written down. The material in the Torah does not represent eyewitness or contemporary accounts but instead at best relates cultural memories as they have been shaped and reshaped by historical circumstances and calamities as major as the rise and fall of not only dynasties but nations.

Israel in Egypt during the Middle and Late Bronze Ages? Biblical Projections and the Historical World

At first glance, positive correlations appear between biblical sources and Egyptian history. The book of 1 Kings (6:1) indicates that the exodus occurred 480 years prior to the fourth year of Solomon's reign. Since Solomon's rule began about 970 BCE, the exodus would have happened about 1450 BCE, roughly a century after the start of the Late Bronze Age. In addition, Genesis

15:13 indicates that the Israelites were enslaved for 400 years, while Exodus 12:40 states they lived in Egypt 430 years. That would place the Israelite migration into Egypt at approximately 1880–1850 BCE. Despite the vagueness of these numbers, several mid-twentieth-century biblical scholars passionately believed these dates fit into what historians knew of Egyptian history. Semites from Canaan began settling in Egypt in large numbers during the nineteenth century BCE. This continued until a Semitic group called the Hyksos (an Egyptian term meaning "foreign rulers") wrested power from native Egyptian kings and ruled northern Egypt from approximately 1670 to 1550 BCE. These Semites were of Canaanite origin, and these events seemed to offer credibility to a story of a movement of Israelites into Egypt under the protection of a people who shared their language and customs. We even know of a Hyksos king named *Y'qb-HR*, or Jacob Har, a familiar Semitic name. The Hyksos capital, Avaris, was located in the Nile Delta, an area that was widely accepted by many as the site of the Israelites' settlement in Egypt.

More than a thousand years later, drawing on a history by the third-century BCE Egyptian writer Manetho, the first-century CE Jewish historian Josephus connected the Israelites with the Hyksos and their expulsion (*Against Apion* 1.73–105, 227–28). Josephus linked the Hyksos and the Israelites' appearance in Egypt to the Joseph story in Genesis and the Hyksos' subsequent expulsion to the exodus. Some biblical scholars followed Josephus' conjectures and argued that if this hypothesis is correct, it provides evidence of the "biblical version of the Hebrews sojourn in Egypt" (Orlinsky 1972, 52). In this view, when the native Egyptians overthrew the hated Hyksos and chased them out of Egypt, the Israelites lost their protectors and became enslaved, along with the remaining Semites in Egypt. Earlier biblical scholars had understood this situation as parallel to the biblical record: "Now a new king arose over Egypt, who did not know Joseph. . . . Therefore they set taskmasters over them to oppress them with forced labor" (Exod 1:8, 11).

However, no archaeological or scriptural evidence links the Hyksos to the Israelite exodus tale, whether as a moment of escape or of enslavement. In fact, the historical and archaeological information we possess in particular militates against an exodus at this time. A fifteenth-century BCE date for the exodus based on a literal reading of 1 Kings contradicts the biblical references portraying the Hebrews as involved in building projects during the period of Ramesses II (1279–1213 BCE)—a name without significant fame until his reign. "They built supply cities, Pithom and Rameses, for Pharaoh" (Exod 1:11). Whatever the historical reliability of this statement, the authors of the book of Exodus place the Israelites in Egypt centuries after the date of the exodus found in 1 Kings. More significantly, a fifteenth-century BCE exodus would place the event during the reigns of some of Egypt's most powerful pharaohs, Thutmose III (1479–1425 BCE) and Amenhotep II (1427–1400 BCE), who repeatedly invaded and controlled Canaan. There is no evidence that either lost control of Canaan to a massive Israelite invasion. Indeed, the book of Joshua's stories of the conquest of Canaan never even presents the Egyptians as opponents in battle.

Semites in Egypt

Throughout the second millennium, a sizable Semitic population lived in Egypt. In addition to the Hyksos, Egyptian scribes wrote of nomadic groups entering Egypt, especially Asiatics (i.e., Canaanites and Syrians). During times of crises, when Egyptian authorities were unable to control their eastern borders and when pastoralists entered the Egyptian delta unopposed, Egyptian scribes recorded "hunger and thirst driving people from Canaan and Sinai to Egypt for relief" (Hoffmeier 1997, 68). Many Egyptian sites located in the delta indicate a strong presence of Semites. Tell el-Daba, Maskhuta, Wadi Tumilat, Tell er-Retaba, Tell el-Yehudiyeh, Inshas, and other sites all contain Canaanite material remains dating to the Middle Bronze Period. There is evidence that Semites introduced sheep into Egypt during the Middle Kingdom (2133–1786 BCE) and that in the New Kingdom (1550–1070 BCE) they were employed as shepherds.

Tell el-Daba, the major city of the Hyksos known as Avaris, has been excavated extensively by Manfred Bietak. In the Hyksos Period, Avaris became one of the biggest settlements in the Near East and Egypt. Though not continuously inhabited, it would become Pi-Rameses, the impressive capital of Pharaoh Ramesses II. The site contains Canaanite pottery, and Canaanite cults were introduced there—especially the northern Syrian storm god Baal Zaphon. "This god was identified with the Egyptian weather god Seth who became, with his Asiatic attributes, the 'Lord of Avaris' and more than 400 years later the 'Father of the fathers' of the Nineteenth Dynasty." Other Canaanite gods found their way into the Egyptian pantheon, such as Astarte and Anat (Bietak and Forstner-Muller 2011).

During the second millennium, especially in the Eighteenth (1550–1295 BCE) and Nineteenth Dynasties (1295–1186 BCE), Semites were depicted in tomb paintings, hieroglyphic, and papyrus records. The tomb at Beni Hassan dated to the Twelfth Dynasty of Pharaoh Sesostris II (ca. 1892 BCE) verifies early contact between Egyptians and Semites. The tomb painting depicts a caravan of people most likely from Canaan visiting the governor. Semites were known to cross the Sinai from Canaan into Egypt regularly, especially traders. Egyptian papyri describe border crossings, incursions, and runaway slaves during the thirteenth century BCE. Although many came as slaves or mercenaries, Semites rose to significant positions in Egyptian society and the royal court. They are found in Egyptian records as scribes, draftsman, butlers, gold-smiths, coppersmiths, musicians, builders, bodyguards of the pharaoh, physi-cians, and king's messengers. We read of Apiru moving a stone at Pi-Rameses. Apiru appear frequently in the Amarna letters and other Egyptian sources as raiders and bandits in Canaan. One Aper-el, a man with a clearly Semitic name (recall that "El" is the word for "god" in Semitic languages), attained the posi-tion of vizier, the most powerful position in the Egyptian royal court. Aper-el served during the Eighteenth Dynasty (1390–1336 BCE) under Amenhotep III and Akhenaten (Redmount 1998, 102). Much later, a Semite (perhaps Syr-ian?) named Bay was influential in placing an Egyptian on the throne during the late Nineteenth Dynasty (1295–1186 BCE).

FIGURE 9-3. *Tomb painting at Beni Hassan depicting a caravan of Semitic metalworkers and traders.*

Canaan and the Pharaohs of the Late Bronze Age

The Egyptian empire reached its height during the reigns of the Eighteenth Dynasty pharaohs, especially under Thutmose III and Amenhotep II. Egyp-tians began to import large numbers of Canaanites to Egypt. Thutmose led seventeen campaigns into Western Asia (i.e., Canaan and Syria) and pushed Egyptian power to the borders of the Euphrates. Egypt eventually controlled much of the Levantine coast. Thutmose fought a crucial battle at the Canaanite city Megiddo in 1482 BCE. He overcame a coalition of Canaanite city-states and captured the city after a siege of seven months. The spoils from the siege are quite impressive. They included 894 chariots, two thousand horses, and another twenty-five thousand animals. Egyptian hegemony over Canaan was secure, and Canaanite city-states became vassals to Egypt who sent tribute to the pharaoh. Thutmose began taking hostages of his defeated enemies, bringing Canaanite children to Egypt, where they were educated and then returning them to their homes as pliant Egyptian subjects. Thutmose's annals are some of the most complete and important in detailing place-names in Canaan (Aharoni 1967, 154–66), listing 119 places he captured. One town is named Jacob-El, perhaps meaning "let El protect." This demonstrates the name was not rare, although no direct connection can be made to the biblical Jacob.

Certainly, the ethnic character of Egypt was changing. Pharaoh Amenhotep II (1427–1400 BCE) claims to have carried off more than eighty-nine thousand people from Canaan to Egypt. Perhaps there is an archaeological correlation; the population in the hill country in Canaan was drastically reduced during this period. Amenhotep III (1390–1353 BCE) records that his temple was filled with "male and female slaves, children of the chiefs of foreign lands of the captivity of His Majesty."

Pharaoh Akhenaten

In the fifth year of his reign, Amenhotep IV (1353–1336 BCE) changed his name to Akhenaten (meaning "Beneficial to Aten") and became one of the most controversial figures in Egyptian history. The pharaoh introduced far-reaching changes in Egyptian architecture and art, but most notable was his remarkable transformation of Egyptian religion. Akhenaten is often viewed as the originator of monotheism because he promoted a revolutionary new cult based on the worship of one deity, Aten, the sun disk. Akhenaten believed he was the only son of Aten, and he made a complete break with the official Amun cult. He began erasing all memories of Amun, one of the most powerful deities in Egypt. Inscriptions and images of Amun and the other gods disappeared from the walls of temples and tombs throughout Egypt. Akhenaten moved his

FIGURE 9-4.
Akhenaten, Nefertiti, and their children worshipping the sun disk Aten above.

capital at Thebes to a new site named Akhetaten (meaning "Horizon of the Aten"), known today as Tell el-Amarna.

The "Hymn to the Aten," attributed to King Akhenaten, is considered the essential account of the Aten religion. This new cult regarded Aten as the sole creator of the universe: "O sole god, like whom there is no other! You create the world according to your desire, being alone." The hymn also refers to "Akhenaten as the god's sole interlocutor, with unique knowledge of the god's plans . . . his earthly delegate" (Dodson 2014, 126). Some scholars note that Akhenaten himself was worshipped by the Egyptians, so his new cult cannot be regarded as true monotheism.

With Akhenaten's death, the exclusive worship of Aten was swept away. Now the pharaoh was mocked and called the heretic king, his legacy and monuments were destroyed, and the old religious cults returned. Though aspects of the worship of Aten persisted for several centuries, the Amarna revolution itself came to a swift end. Even though Akhenaten's monotheistic changes took place less than a century before an Israelite exodus could have happened, there is no indication that their religion was influenced by his activities.

Amarna Letters

The Amarna letters are a collection of cuneiform tablets from a royal archive located in Tell el-Amarna, Akhenaten's capital. The entire corpus numbers 382 tablets. A few letters were written during the last years of Amenhotep III (1390–1353 BCE), but most come from the reign of Akhenaten (1353–1336 BCE). In 1887, peasants digging at Tell el-Amarna discovered several tablets and then sold them on the antiquities market. Today they are scattered across European museums and private collectors. A majority of the tablets are diplomatic letters addressed to Amenhotep, his wife Teye, and Akhenaten. Many of the letters concern arranged marriages, gifts, and accusations against local rulers. Letters come from kings in Canaan, Assyria, Babylonia, Syria, Mitanni, and the Hittites.

The texts written from Canaan have attracted the most scholarly attention, largely because of their potential to shed light on Canaanite and early Israelite history. The Egyptians treated the Canaanites as tribute-paying client states and aimed to control their economic activity. The vassals' letters frequently reflect local turmoil. Canaanite rulers engage in constant rivalries— plundering and fighting with one another and often accusing each other of treachery and disloyalty to the pharaoh. The letters also complain about the lack of Egyptian support in confronting marauding bands who live outside the cities that threatened Canaanite city-states and Egyptian authority. These groups are referred to as *apiru* or *habiru* and are known in Near Eastern texts throughout the second millennium BCE from the Euphrates to the Nile. The term has a derogatory undertone referring to a social class on the fringes of society, frequently identified as mercenaries, slaves, or outlaws. In some letters, Canaanite princes accuse their rivals of joining with the Apiru (even hiring them to attack the loyal supporters of the pharaoh) or claim that the rulers themselves are becoming Apiru (Grabbe 2007, 48). The letters frequently request Egyptian military support to rout these bandits—apparently these pleas were ignored by the Egyptians; the Canaanites were on their own.

When these texts were first discovered, many scholars attempted to link Apiru/Habiru with the Hebrews. However, today few scholars argue for a linguistic connection. Rainey argued that the terms are not related. "There is absolutely nothing to suggest an equation to the biblical Hebrews!" (Rainey and Schniedewind 2014, 33). The Amarna letters represent our most authentic view of Canaan in the fourteenth century BCE. Although many of the letters provide much information about Canaan in the Late Bronze age, no mention of any biblical event or character appears in them.

After the social disruption caused by Akhenaten's religious reform, the main concern for Egypt's new Nineteenth Dynasty was to reestablish its military domination of Canaan and Syria and to resist the Hittites. Given that the reign of Pharaoh Ramesses I (1292–1290 BCE) was so brief, his son Seti I (1290–1279 BCE) must be regarded as the dynasty's true founder. He launched a prodigious building program throughout all of Egypt. The Ramisside royal family had strong ties to the god Seth, who was worshipped in the delta, and Seti associated himself with the worship of this Semitic god; Seti even means "Seth's man" (Aharoni 1967, 176). Seti personally led

FIGURE 9-5. *Seti Stele from Beth Shean.*

the Egyptian army into Canaan and further north. He fought a number of campaigns, of which three were in Canaan and Syria. Although the details of Seti's campaigns are incomplete, many appear on wall reliefs, mostly at the temple of Amun, situated in Karnak, and the steles from Beth Shean. Seti campaigned against the Shasu (for more, see below) in the Sinai and perhaps in Upper Galilee. They are important enough to be depicted in Seti's reliefs. He campaigned extensively in Canaan, conquering Hazor, Yanoam, and Beth Anath. Seti confronted the Hittites and reconquered the strategically important city of Kadesh in Syria. In Seti's topographical list at Karnak, there appears to be a reference to Asher, a possible early indication of an Israelite tribe (Aharoni 1967, 179). In addition, Seti built a small temple near the copper mines in Timnah, north of the Gulf of Eilat. The excavations at Beth Shean uncovered two victory steles of Seti, one depicting the defeat of the Apiru from Mount Yarmath and one the capture of Beth Shean. Although Seti was one of the most powerful pharaohs, he would be overshadowed by Ramesses II.

The End of the Late Bronze Age: Israel in Egypt

The discussion so far indicates no direct or circumstantial evidence of an Israelite exodus during the Middle Bronze Age or the early Late Bronze Age. That leaves the end of the Late Bronze Age, the thirteenth century BCE, as the time that best fits the exodus' setting. As Eric Cline notes, "Assuming that the Exodus did occur as described in the Bible, I am most inclined to place it in or around 1250 B.C. . . . If the Exodus did not take place at all, however, as some have recently suggested, I would prefer to accept Redford, Finkelstein, and Silberman's suggestions that the story was made up in the seventh century B.C." (2007, 90). This does not inspire confidence in the historicity of the exodus story regardless of the date. Nevertheless, many biblical scholars believe the historical core originates in the thirteenth-century period of Ramesses II (1279–1213 BCE). But even if some of the components of the exodus story date to the thirteenth century, these do not on their own verify the historicity of the entire account.

Ramesses II was one the longest-reigning pharaohs in Egyptian history. He carried out the largest building program in ancient Egypt, one that resulted in colossal architecture and detailed sculptures—and needed a large labor force. There is hardly a site in Egypt without a temple or statue from Ramesses II's reign. And as he was the father of many children (over one hundred), all these activities ensured that his fame would be carried well into the future. Ramesses expanded the city of Avaris, now called Pi-Rameses, and made the delta city his principal residence. Because of its strategic location, it soon became an influential economic center and an Egyptian military installation. The delta has always been a home to Semitic influences, and "many foreign deities such as Ba'al, Reshep, Hauron, Anat, and Astarte . . . were worshipped in Piramesse" (Van Dijk 2000, 300). In addition to the evidence of Apiru laboring at Pi-Rameses, his bureaucracy and the army contained a number of foreigners. In his fourth year, Ramesses fought the Hittites at the famous battle of Qadesh (1274 BCE). The Hittites nearly destroyed the Egyptians, but reinforcements late in the battle saved Ramesses and his army. The engagement ended in stalemate—Egyptian annals celebrated Ramesses II's personal bravery and victory, but the Hittites did not relinquish Qadesh. Years later, both sides signed a peace treaty. The Hittite border extended into northern Syria, and Egypt retained tenuous control of Canaan. Ramesses also acknowledged the reign of the Hittite ruler Hattusillis and later married two of his daughters.

As mentioned above, the names of the pharaohs in the exodus story are never mentioned. The most specific historical reference to date the Israelites' exit from Egypt appears in Exodus 1:11: "Therefore they set taskmasters over them to oppress them with forced labor. They built supply cities, Pithom and Rameses, for Pharaoh."

Most scholars agree that Rameses (Pi-Rameses, lit. "house of Rameses") should be located at Qantir, just northeast of Tell el-Daba, which was inhabited from the early thirteenth to the later twelfth century BCE. The first palace was built by Seti I and later expanded by Ramesses II. The city was inhabited by their successors until late in the Twentieth Dynasty (ca. 1130 BCE).

By contrast, there is no agreement on the location of Pithom (Egyptian Pi-Atum, lit. "House of Atum"). Divided opinion identifies Pithom with the sites of Tell er-Retaba or Tell el-Maskhuta. The site of Tell er-Retaba may date to the thirteenth or twelfth century BCE. Its occupation ends in the seventh century BCE as Maskhuta was being built. Maskhuta is problematic. Although it contains building material from the period of Ramesses II and statuary inscribed "Pithom," it was constructed in the seventh century BCE (Finkelstein and Silberman 2001, 63). The blocks, steles, and statues uncovered at Maskhuta must have come from er-Retaba. It is the only major site "that could have produced such material" for building the late seventh-century BCE Maskhuta (Hoffmeier 2005, 61). If the author of the book of Exodus believed the Israelites built Pithom at Tell el-Maskhuta, then the story is clearly a seventh-century BCE invention.

The End of the Late Bronze Age: Israel in Canaan

The first mention of Israel as a people living in Canaan comes from the Merneptah Stelé dated to 1207 BCE. Pharaoh Merneptah (1213–1203 BCE), the successor to the long-lived Ramesses II, was already elderly when he became pharaoh. The stele was discovered during an excavation in 1896 by W. M. Flinders Petrie at Merneptah's mortuary temple in Thebes. On the stele is an inscribed victory hymn celebrating the pharaoh's campaign in Canaan, in which Merneptah boasted of destroying a people called Israel. This is the earliest known reference to Israel in Canaan uncovered in any record. It predates the biblical text by several centuries. Merneptah's claims that relate to Israel are as follows:

> The (foreign) chieftains lie prostrate, saying "Peace." Not one lifts his head among the Nine Bows.
> Libya is captured, while Hatti is pacified.
> Canaan is plundered, Ashkelon is carried off, and Gezer is captured.
> Yenoam is made into non-existence; Israel is wasted, its seed is not; and Hurru is become a widow because of Egypt.
> All lands united themselves in peace. Those who went about are subdued by the king of Upper and Lower Egypt . . . Merneptah. (*COS* 2:41)

In the stele, the terms Ashkelon, Gezer, and Yanoam are specified with the determinative or sign indicating a "city-state." Ashkelon and Gezer sit on the southern Canaanite coast, but Yanoam's location is uncertain. By contrast, "Israel" is identified with the determinative sign representing a "people." Although not identified as a "city-state" per se, Israel was nonetheless an important population group, for Merneptah viewed these people as a major threat. Whether this points to Israel's presence in the highland region of Canaan is another matter. However, it is odd that the biblical record makes no mention of Merneptah's 1209 BCE campaign in Canaan. There was a strong

FIGURE 9-6. *The Merneptah Stele contains the first mention of Israel outside the biblical text.*

Egyptian presence in the Jezreel Valley, Beth Shean, and the southern coastal regions of Canaan. Egyptian artifacts dating to the thirteenth and twelfth centuries BCE have been excavated throughout these areas.

Some scholars have argued that the Israelites were brought to Egypt as captives of Merneptah after his invasion. At this time they may have encountered the nomadic Shasu from Edom. During the end of the Nineteenth Dynasty (ca. 1190), the Semite Bey instigated a revolt and chaos reigned throughout Egypt. The revolt failed but provided the opportunity for groups of Semites including Israelites to escape and return to Canaan, and settle in the Hill Country north of Jerusalem. Soon Egypt hegemony was challenged throughout Canaan, especially by the Philistines. The Israelites believed that God had brought their people out from Egypt, as indicated in Exodus 18:1. (Though not in total agreement, see Knauf and Guillaume 2015, 36.)

Another factor comes into play here. There was a dramatic population increase in the central highlands of Canaan at the end of the Late Bronze Age and the beginning of the Iron Age. It is possible—some scholars would say highly likely—that these new settlers were the people Israel, or at least a "proto-Israel" (see the next chapter). Despite this, the common material culture of these sites—plastered cisterns, terracing, olive orchards, collar-rim jars, cooking pots, four-room houses, storage facilities like silos, and unfortified settlements—has few links to Egypt. The most common house form in these sites is known as the "four-room house," and it is distinctive to them.

Manfred Bietak argues, however, that there is evidence for the four-room house in Egypt at twelfth-century BCE Thebes. Bietak holds that "the builders of this house in Thebes must have been people who were culturally closely related to the Proto-Israelites even though the ethno-genesis of this group had not been completed by that time," for this house type "appears first in what is considered the early settlements of the Proto-Israelites in the Central Hill Country of Canaan at the beginning of Iron Age I, perhaps by the end of the Late Bronze Age." Bietak considers this example "of a Four-Room House in Western Thebes" as circumstantial evidence "for a sojourn in Egypt" and claims it should be dated to the twelfth century BCE (2015, 20). Yet Bietak's theory has not convinced other archaeologists. They see very little archaeological evidence to connect these settlers to anything other than Canaanite culture. The archaeological data cannot support a large influx of refugees fleeing from Egypt.

And Where Does Yahweh Come From?

One further question is that of where the Israelite worship of a god known as Yahweh originates. He does not belong to the Canaanite pantheon or to the gods further north in Syria. Perhaps the answer lies with the nomadic tribes the Egyptians called Shasu. Appearing in Egyptian records from 1500 to 1100 BCE, they receive a negative description, often characterized as "robbers and brigands" (Redford 1992, 278). According to the Egyptians, the Shasu lived in Edom and the Negev, which the records term as the "land of the Shasu," the "Shasu tribes of Edom" (located in Edom or the Negev), and "Seir with the Shasu clans" (in the mountainous regions in Edom). Sometimes, Egyptians allowed Shasu tribes to cross their border to water their cattle in the delta regions of Egypt. Inscriptions from Seti, Ramesses II, and Ramesses III describe clashes against the Shasu throughout Canaan. The annals of Ramesses II record that the Shasu were spies for the Hittites during the battle of Qadesh (1274 BCE).

But the most important point about the Shasu lies in their worship. A papyrus list from the time of Ramesses II mentions "the land of the Shasu of Yhw"— a clear reference to "the name of the Israelite god 'Yahweh'" (Redford 1992, 273). This is our earliest evidence of the worship of Yahweh, and it is important to note that it is established outside of Canaan. Some scholars have wondered whether the "Israel" mentioned in the Merneptah Stele should be associated with the Shasu depicted in the reliefs of Merneptah (Grabbe 2007, 50).

Interestingly, the biblical writers also connect Yahweh's origins to Edom and Seir: "This is the blessing with which Moses, the man of God, blessed the Israelites before his death. He said: The LORD came from Sinai, and dawned from Seir upon us" (Deut 33:1-2); and "LORD, when you went out from Seir, when you marched from the region of Edom" (Judg 5:4). We also have the following from Habakkuk: "God came from Teman, the Holy One from Mount Paran" (Hab 3:3). The geographical term "Teman" means "south," and it is used to designate Edom, both east and west (in the Negev) of the Arabah. Yahweh's links to Teman also appear at Kuntillet Ajrud in northern Sinai. A ninth-century BCE inscription found there further emphasizes Yahweh's southern character: it reads, "I bless you by Yahweh of Teman and by his Asherah" (Knauf and Guillaume 2015).

At this point, there is no way to ascertain whether the Israel mentioned in the Merneptah Stele were worshippers of Yahweh. There is no clear evidence that Israel emerged as a people of Yahweh during their Egyptian subjugation. In fact, the book of Exodus appears to indicate that "El, not Yahweh, was the original God of the Israelites who came out of Egypt. Indeed, Exodus 6:2-3 reflects the notion that Israel's original god was El Shadday" (M. Smith 2001, 147). Of course, the manner by which Yahweh entered Canaan is pure speculation. But we should note that our evidence indicates Yahweh is not a Canaanite god and that the deity belongs to the Shasu further south in Edom. Since the People of Israel grew out of several groups living in Canaan, perhaps some

Shasu had migrated north and contributed their deity to the uniting of these disparate groups in the central Canaanite highlands.

The Exodus Journey: From Egypt to Kadesh

The story of Moses, the Israelites' enslavement in Egypt, and the confrontation between Moses and Pharaoh, in which God fights Pharaoh's hardness of heart with increasingly devastating plagues, is good for high drama, but it provides no direct references for historical investigation. Although there is a small industry of books trying to identify possible natural causes of each plague, these add little to our historical understanding of the events. In that light, our discussion moves from the leaving of Egypt to the journey itself.

TRACKING THE EXODUS

> When Pharaoh let the people go, God did not lead them by way of the land of the Philistines, although that was nearer. . . . God led the people by the roundabout way of the wilderness toward the Red Sea. . . . [T]he LORD went in front of them in a pillar of cloud by day, to lead them along the way, and in a pillar of fire by night, to give them light, so that they might travel by day and by night. Neither the pillar of cloud by day nor the pillar of fire by night left its place in front of the people. (Exod 13:17-22)

The biblical narratives about the exodus describe a fairly straightforward trip from Egypt to the Sinai Peninsula (Exod 12:37; 13:17-20; 14:2; Num 33:1-15). Scholarly efforts at reconstructing the route of the exodus based on the textual and archaeological evidence have produced three standard proposals, although none can be verified. The effort to reconstruct the route is complicated by two factors relating to the historical reliability of the Bible's exodus story. On the one hand, the vast majority of scholars have long doubted the basic historicity of the biblical record in general, regarding it instead as a tendentious account more interested in promoting a theological agenda than in recording history per se (Finkelstein and Silberman 2001). On the other hand, religiously conservative scholars tend to trust the biblical narrative's accuracy above all else. Indeed, their goal is often to prove Scripture right rather than to develop a balanced historical account (see, e.g., Hoffmeier 1997 and Kitchen 2003).

Identifying the location of *yam suph* is actually impossible. The phrase consists of the term for a body of water or sea (*yam*) and a term that appears to be related to the ancient Egyptian terms for "reed" (see Exod 2:3, 5). The various sources use it differently, and, depending on the tale and the source, it could be in (1) the Suez isthmus, (2) Lake Sirbonis, (3) the Gulf of Suez, or (4) the Gulf of Eilat/Aqaba (see Deut 2:1-8).

The place-name *yam suph* appears to have been thoroughly mythologized. That various texts, as well as their later interpreters, locate the event in

FIGURE 9-7. *Sinai Desert.*

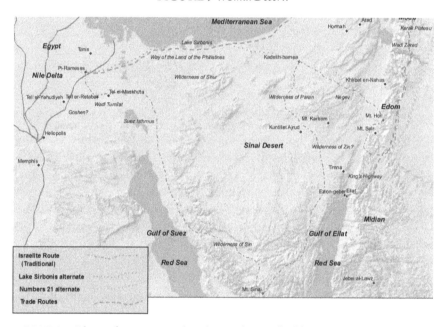

MAP 9-1. *The exodus story says that the Israelites walked from Egypt into the Sinai. These possible routes may fit the exodus story.*

different places is due to the power and ideological importance of the event—God intervened to deliver Israel from its enemies and lead the people to their homeland (Exod 14:30). The quest to identify the physical location of "the" *yam suph* is fruitless because it has become a place of mythic importance, not geographical location. It was a place where a divine act was believed to have taken place, and that place was remembered or used by different authors in different ways.

In the Hebrew Bible, the Hebrew phrase Reed Sea (*yam suph*) is rendered in the early Greek translation called the Septuagint as Red Sea (*thalassa eruthra*). There are a couple of exceptions, however. The Greek text of 1 Kings 9:6, e.g., renders Hebrew *yam suph* in Greek as "the last sea," a geographic reference that refers to a place near Edom on the east side of the Sinai Peninsula (Exod 23:31; Num 14:25; 21:4; 33:10-11; Deut 1:40; 2:1; Judg 11:16).

Although the phrase *yam suph* occurs at the outset of the exodus narrative (Exod 13:18), it does not actually occur in the key story detailing the Israelite crossing and Egyptian defeat (Exod 14), but then it reappears in the celebratory "Song of the Sea" (Exod 15:1-18). The crossing narrative of Exodus 14 refers only to "the sea."

FIGURE 9-8. *DOCUMENTARY SOURCES FOR THE CROSSING OF THE SEA IN EXODUS.*

J: 13:21-22; **14**:5-7, 10b, 13-14, 19b, 20b, 21b, 24, 27b, 30-31; **15**:1-19
E: 13:17-19; **14**:11-12, 19a, 20a, 25; **15**:20-21
P: 13:20; **14**:1-4, 8-9, 10a, 10c, 15-18, 21a, 21c-23, 26-27a, 28-29

In this chapter, the J and E sources provide the majority of the miraculous crossing-story details. They include the guiding/protecting cloud column, the Egyptian pursuit, the wind dividing the sea, and the drowning of the Egyptians at dawn. But this version of the story—as told by the J and E sources (see Figure 9-8)—does not mention any crossing of the sea. The narrative ends with the important point it wishes to demonstrate: "Thus Yahweh saved Israel that day from the Egyptians" (Exod 14:30). The P source, on the other hand, mentions Yahweh's words, his hardening of Pharaoh's heart, Pharaoh's intentions, Moses' hand cleaving the sea, and the Israelites' passage on dry ground between the walls of water. This last event appears especially in 14:28-29. The miraculous event at the *yam suph* became an important community-defining theme in later Judaic cultures (see, e.g., Josh 2:10; 4:23; 24:6; Neh 9:9; Pss 106:7, 9, 22; 136:13, 15; 1 Macc 4:9; Jdt 5:13; Wis 10:18; 19:7).

We should also note the account of this event in the poetic "Song of the Sea" (Exod 15:1-18). This example of early Hebrew poetry is demonstrably the oldest surviving version of the exodus traditions (Cross and Freedman 1975, 31–45), and as such it was composed before and served as a source for the narrative accounts in the previous chapter (Exod 14). Two important points stand out. First, the poem focuses exclusively on Yahweh's tossing the Egyptians into the sea, where they sink like rocks and lead, and it does not mention the dry land crossing. Second, the poem does not mention Israel specifically and instead refers to Yahweh settling "the people" in the vicinity of his divine sanctuary (i.e., Jerusalem). Thus, the textual evidence in the Bible about a miraculous crossing of the sea is not at all uniform.

POSSIBLE ROUTES FOR CROSSING OF THE "RED SEA"

The traditional understanding of the route taken by the Israelites is based on a literal reading of the narrative. The Israelites, oppressed by Pharaoh but now delivered by divine intervention, fled Egypt and came upon a body of water just as the Egyptian army closed in on them (Exod 14:9-10). That body of water has been identified—based primarily on the early Greek and Latin translations of the Hebrew Bible—as the Red Sea, or specifically the northern extension of it, which is today known as the Gulf of Suez. But the Greek and Latin rendering of the designation *yam suph*, however early it may be, is specious. Nonetheless, there is no doubt that it has inspired the religious and popular imagination for millennia.

Although the shortest route to Canaan would have been northeasterly, that is along the "Via Maris" or "Way of Horus," the international coastal highway leading north along the eastern Mediterranean coast (Exod 13:17). Exodus 13:18 makes clear they did not take that direction but turned instead to the southeast to take a more circuitous route via the desert (Exod 13:18). Nonetheless, some scholars have proposed a possible northern route along the Mediterranean coast toward Lake Sirbonis—today known as Lake Bardawil, a lagoon of salty water separated from the Mediterranean Sea by a thin sandbar. Drawing a parallel with the drowning of Persian king Artaxerxes III's army in this same lake in 343 BCE (Diodorus Siculus, *Library* 1.30.4–9; 16.46.5; 20.73.3), Otto Eissfeldt suggested that the Israelites took this coastal route north, and that it was in Lake Sirbonis that the safe crossing of the Israelites and the drowning of the Egyptians took place (Eissfeldt 1932, 30–48; *Harper Atlas* 1987, 56–57). With this scenario, the Israelites' miraculous crossing of water to escape the Egyptians involved either (1) walking along the sandbar and dunes that separate the lake from the Mediterranean Sea or (2) crossing safely through the shallow waters of the lagoon. This approach maintains that such an unremarkable passage was simply exaggerated and presented as a divine intervention in the biblical tale. This northern coastal route, however, is contradicted by the biblical text, which explicitly says that they did not take the more direct Via Maris route northward toward their homeland (Exod 13:17). In addition, Lake Sirbonis is a hypersaline lagoon where reeds do not grow, making any connection between *yam suph* and Lake Sirbonis most unlikely. Furthermore, the presence of Egyptian military outposts along the coastal route would have been an obvious deterrent to people fleeing the pharaoh (Hoffmeier 1999, 183–87). This proposal stems in part from a desire to account for the miracles reported in the Bible, but it creates more problems than it solves.

There is a third possible option for the general route of the exodus. The book of Exodus locates the Israelites in the eastern Nile Delta, in cities such as Ramses, Succoth, and Pithom, far from the more southerly Gulf of Suez. Interestingly, the eastern part of this area has many small lakes and marshlands where reeds can flourish. It is most likely that this is the area where the narrative of the "crossing" is best situated. James Hoffmeier claims that the various marshlands and lakes in the Suez Isthmus to the east of the Nile Delta and between the Mediterranean Sea to the north and the Gulf of Suez to the south could provide the setting for the tale of this miraculous water crossing, although it is impossible to identify the exact place of the "crossing" (1999, 204–12). That does not, however, prove the historicity of the event, as Hoffmeier claims: "In the final analysis, our inability to locate the sea with certainty does not diminish the historicity of the event or its importance for Israel's religious and national history" (1999, 191, 215). To the contrary, Hoffmeier's explanation, which is itself a fine example of a conservative interpretation of the evidence, does not confirm the historicity of the event at all; rather, it simply provides a reasonable context for the setting of the tale—a geographical conclusion rather than a historical one. In the end, "the crossing" is presented as a miraculous event, and such religious claims cannot be proven—or disproven, for that matter.

CROSSING THE SEA ON DRY LAND?

Did the Israelites miraculously cross the sea on dry land? Again, the exodus story has two versions of the "crossing." The narrative account explicitly reports that "the Israelites walked into the sea on dry ground. The water formed a wall for them on their right and left" (Exod 15:22). The Song of the Sea (Exod 15:1b-18) and the Song of Miriam (Exod 15:20-21), however, provide another perspective on the events, and those poetic accounts do not mention a dry land crossing at all. According to these poems, God hurls the Egyptians into the sea, where they sink like rocks or lead (Exod 15:4-5, 10, 21). Since these two poems comprise some of the earliest examples of Hebrew literature, dating perhaps to as early as the twelfth century BCE (see Cross and Freedman 1975, 45–65), the earliest textual evidence about the exodus does not refer to the Israelites crossing a body of water on dry land.

So why add such a feature to the story? The JE narrative accounts of the exodus, written centuries after the poetic accounts, are part of an effort at recounting Israel's early history that has strong theological and nationalist interests. The authors intended to show how the people that would become the nations of Israel and Judah came to reside in the central highlands of Canaan. According to the traditions embedded in the Torah's narratives, Israel's presence in this area is part of God's plan. God called its earliest ancestor,

Abraham, to leave his Mesopotamian homeland and settle here (Gen 12:1-8). Later, Abraham's great grandson Joseph was taken to Egypt by force (Gen 27:25-28) but ultimately rose to a prominent position under Pharaoh. "Pharaoh said to Joseph: Know this, I have given you authority over all the land of Egypt. . . . Then Joseph took control over the land of Egypt" (Gen 41:41, 45). That proved providential as it enabled Joseph to bring his family to Egypt during a time of severe regional famine (Gen 45–46). These modest shepherds would prosper and become a great nation there, just as God said to Abraham's grandson Jacob before he left: "Do not be afraid to go down to Egypt because I will make a great nation of you there. I will go down to Egypt with you, and I promise to bring you out again" (Gen 46:3-4). Abraham's descendants eventually became enslaved there, and with that the prospect of becoming a "great nation" seemed doomed, unless God intervened. And intervene he did!

The exodus story thus presents a national theology of deliverance from slavery to freedom, from a foreign land to a homeland, and from dependence to independence. This tale of deliverance includes many miracles, most of which famously wrought havoc on the oppressing Egyptians: the ten plagues and the drowning in the sea. So, the narrative about this miraculous crossing of the Israelites on dry land is constructed to show God's favor for and protection of the Israelites. Moreover, it fulfills a promise God made to Abraham and his descendants: "I will bless those who bless you, and the one who curses you, I will curse" (Gen 12:3). With the deliverance from Egypt, the hope for nationhood remained alive.

Locating Mount Sinai

Since the Byzantine Period, the site of the biblical Mount Sinai (called Horeb in Deuteronomy) has been identified as Jebel Musa in the southern Sinai Peninsula. Although early Christian monks first made this identification, no archaeological evidence has to date been found to support such a connection. Nonetheless, the monks of St. Catherine's Monastery (founded by Constantine's mother Helena), pilgrims, and countless tourists venerate this site as "the" Mount Sinai of the exodus.

But other sites fit just as well, or perhaps better. One proposal identifies biblical Mount Sinai with Jebel al-Lawz, located in the mountains in the northwestern part of the Arabian Peninsula. Although this proposal has been widely promoted among amateur archaeologists with biblical interests (for a rigorous critique of these efforts, see Hoffmeier 2005, 132–36), the idea of Mount Sinai being located in this area has also attracted scholarly interest (Hendel 2000; Kerkeslager 2000; Shanks 2014). Another biblical scholar, Martin Noth, noted that the "pillar of fire and smoke" suggests volcanic activity, and, since the southern Sinai Peninsula lacks that, he looks elsewhere for Mount Sinai.

FIGURE 9-9. *St. Catherine's Monastery, built in the fourth century CE,*
is the traditional site of Mt. Sinai. However, no archaeological or textual evidence
points to this site as the "mountain of God."

The nearest place would be the mountains of the northwest Arabian Peninsula
(Noth 1962, 156–60). Moreover, as Cross and Hendel have noted, Deuteronomy 33:2 and Judges 5:4-5 appear to locate Mount Sinai in this area (Cross
1998, 45–46, 53–70).

One scholar, Emmanuel Anati, has proposed that Mount Sinai is in fact
Mount Karkom in the southern Negev Desert (Anati 1986, 2015; cf. Finkelstein 1988b). Anati (2015, 450) surveyed and excavated in the area for decades,
and he has identified over 1,300 archaeological sites dating from the Paleolithic to the Iron Age and thousands of rock inscriptions from the Neolithic
to the early Islamic Period. Anati concludes that many of the archaeological
remains (inscriptions, altars, shrines, standing cultic pillars, etc.) found on or
near this mountain plateau (approx. 2,625–2,790 feet above sea level) suggest
that the place served as a holy site for millennia: "People were coming there
to make agreements, to worship, to have pilgrimages. It was a sort of Bronze
Age Mecca where different tribes arrived for centuries" (2015, 453). That long-
standing prominence of the mountain as a cultic site makes it possible that
Mount Karkom might have been the site of biblical Mount Sinai.

Anati's interesting proposal, however, has not been widely accepted
among biblical scholars and archaeologists. Most tellingly, as far as the exodus
story itself is concerned, he has to date not uncovered any Late Bronze Age evidence. This is the major problem for Anati's thesis. In that way, his thesis suffers
from the same lack of archaeological evidence as does Jebel Musa. Undeterred,
he suggests two solutions: that the exodus should be dated earlier or that the

biblical authors were influenced by traditions associated with Mount Karkom when they crafted their "holy mountain" traditions.

So, where is Mount Sinai? The problems that prevent a clear answer to that question are indeed vexing. First of all, the biblical text provides no precise geographical data on its location. Second, there is no clear physical evidence attesting the presence of Israelite migrants at any of these locations. In the end, we must conclude that for the story teller, the biblical tale is about more than a place; it is about the miracle that happened there—God giving Israel its constitution, the Mosaic code. As Ronald Hendel (2000) noted years ago, the curiously unidentified and so unknowable location of the place is part of what makes it special. It is a holy place to which no one can now return, but what Israel received there, the Torah, continues to serve as a sign of and a guide governing God's relationship to the people.

While Mount Sinai may never be identified reliably, several scholars have recently sought to use archaeological remains at sites along the eastern Gulf of Suez as evidence for the route of the exodus (note Hoffmeier 1999). This work typically addresses the names of sites and the presence of some material remains. The literary evidence in the Bible, largely lists of sites, has long been regarded as late additions to the text, meaning that they are not part of any original account of the journey. Such lists have parallels in other ancient Near Eastern writings. But parallels themselves are not evidence that the specific site lists in the Bible are at all historically reliable. They obviously reflect old traditions (Bietak 2015), but they cannot be confirmed as primary evidence of details of the exodus route from Egypt to Sinai. Geography does not equal history. Remember that the Torah draws together several sources of oral traditions and literary compositions. Each reflects the understandings and interests of people who compiled them in different places and at different times between the eighth and fifth centuries BCE. Just because a site from a list or story can be identified does not mean that the Israelites visited it or that events linked to it actually happened. Once identified, a site must be archaeologically investigated for remains from the proper period, and then those remains must be shown relevant to the Exodus story. For the sites in the exodus stories that can be identified, however, they often did not exist at the appropriate time period—as becomes clear in the following discussion.

THE SPIES AND THE FAILURE TO ENTER CANAAN

The final section of the exodus story begins in Numbers 13–14 after the Israelites arrived in Kadesh-barnea (in an area south of Canaan alternatively called the Wilderness of Zin or the Wilderness of Paran), after making a rather direct journey from Mount Sinai. As Deuteronomy 1:2 says, "it takes eleven days to reach Kadesh-barnea from Horeb." Moses' intention at this point is to enter and conquer Canaan. The story of this attempt and its failure is told in Numbers 13–14.

The tale begins with God instructing Moses to send spies into Canaan to determine the lay of the land. Moses chooses twelve spies, one for each tribe except Levi, and sends them out. Interestingly enough, although the text implies they are spying out the entire land of Canaan, the list of towns and villages mentioned in Numbers 13:21-23 gives only locations in the south, the territory of Judah. Forty days later, they return, and all tell how lush and productive the land is. It runs with "milk and honey." But ten of the spies are frightened, saying the Israelites could not possibly conquer the land because the inhabitants are strong and numerous. Not only are they many, but many are giants.

Despite efforts by the Judahite Caleb and the Ephraimite Joshua, the people believe the ten spies about the terrifying inhabitants. In their fear, they seek to appoint a new leader to take them back to Egypt (Num 14:4). God punishes them by forcing them to dwell in the wilderness for forty years rather than entering the land (Num 14:26-35). During this time, all the adults over twenty years of age—who lack faith even though they saw the miracles God performed before they left Egypt—will die. Then God will lead into Canaan those who have grown to adulthood while living under his leadership in the desert.

The Second Attempt to Enter Canaan

The Torah contains no stories directly linked to the punishment of forty years exiled in the desert. If you take Numbers 14 and 20 together—the stories in Numbers 16–17 indicate neither location or time—it seems that the Israelites simply stayed at Kadesh for four decades. Yet Moses' recap of the trip in Deuteronomy 2:14 indicates the Israelites' journey from Kadesh to Wadi Zered, just before they come down into the Jordan Valley, took thirty-eight years— even though Deuteronomy gives no details about where they went and even though the travel time would have been about a month. Whichever version one follows, there are no tales concerning events during the years of punishment.

Despite the incident of the spies being separated from the entrance into Canaan by forty years, the narrative ties the two events together. The last journey begins at Kadesh, with the Israelites' stories of the trip indicating a continuous trip from there to the Plains of Moab. If the trip took forty years, there is no indication where those decades fit or what the Israelites did or where they went. This is true for all three versions of the Israelites' travels found in Numbers and Deuteronomy. The trip from Kadesh to the Plains of Moab in the Jordan Valley is initially described in Numbers 20:1–22:1. The second and third versions come in recapitulations found in Numbers 33 and Deuteronomy 1–3.

MAP 9-2. At
the end of the
forty years of
punishment, the
Israelites walked
from Kadesh-
barnea to the
Plains of Moab.
These routes fit
the narrative.

While the versions contain different details, the main stages of the journey
are clear.

According to Numbers 20–22, the Israelites began their trip in Kadesh
and walked to Mount Hor, where Aaron died. At this point, the king of Arad
attacked them, and the Israelite warriors defeated his army at Hormah. Since
the Edomite king refused them permission to enter Edom, the Israelites then
headed south to the northern tip of the Red Sea at Ezion-geber instead of due
east. From there they traveled northeast, skirting Edom and Moab by passing
through the desert east of it. (According to Deut 2, they go through Edom and
Moab.) The Israelites then came down into Gilead, on the eastern side of the
Jordan Valley, where they conquered Sihon of Heshbon and Og of Bashan to
take control of the territory north of Moab and west of Ammon. They then
camped on the Plains of Moab, east of Jericho and the Jordan River, until the

end of Deuteronomy. So, by Numbers 22:1, the start of the Balaam story, the Israelites' journey is complete. The rest of Numbers and Deuteronomy takes place on the Plains of Moab, and the Israelites remain there until Moses dies in Deuteronomy 34 and Joshua becomes the leader. Joshua takes the Israelites into Canaan in the next book—called, appropriately, Joshua.

Numbers, Deuteronomy, and Archaeology

Archaeological evidence concerning the end of the Israelites' journey is entirely lacking. Most of the sites mentioned in Numbers and Deuteronomy cannot be identified, especially those indicating stops along the journey. In the few sites that archaeologists can identify, they have found no evidence of permanent occupation during the Late Bronze Age, not even near the end when the exodus could have taken place. Although there are more than eighty sites from the Egyptian New Kingdom, including a series of Egyptian fortresses and supply centers cut through the Sinai along the Mediterranean coast, there is no trace of the wandering Israelites in any location in the Sinai Desert.

Archaeologists have identified Kadesh-barnea with Tel el-Qudeirat, located by a spring. Excavations at the site have uncovered three superimposed fortresses, the earliest dated to the tenth century BCE. A number of painted pottery fragments labeled Painted Qurayyah Ware, also known as Midianite

FIGURE 9-10. *The biblical site Kadesh-barnea is usually associated with the Sinai oasis at Tel el-Qudeirat. Though pottery fragments have been dated to the twelfth to eleventh century BCE, at present, archaeology does not confirm the exodus story.*

pottery, were discovered predating the tenth-century BCE fortresses. The pottery was "not found in a secure stratigraphical context" at the site, and there does not appear to be evidence of an occupation level before the tenth century. However, an examination of nearby excavations, especially the copper-mining sites at Khirbet en-Nahas and Timna, has led Singer-Avitz (2010) to date the sherds to the twelfth century BCE. In addition, several seals and seal impressions excavated at Kadesh-barnea identified as most likely Egyptian have been dated to the Late Bronze / Early Iron Age. Singer-Avitz assumes that there was an early (yet undiscovered) settlement at Kadesh-barnea, possibly a way station on the copper-trade route dated to the twelfth century BCE. Unfortunately, a connection from Kadesh-barnea to a massive Exodus is still not plausible. The remains at Ezion-geber, through which the Israelites passed on their way to the Plains of Moab, show it was not even built until the tenth century BCE.

In the area south of Canaan, southern Judah and the Negev, the sites that can be identified were not occupied during the Late Bronze, even when they had been founded in previous centuries. Excavations at Hebron in the Judean Hills show it was occupied during the Early and Middle Bronze Periods but abandoned during the Late Bronze. Only toward the end of Iron I (eleventh century BCE) was it reestablished. Although Arad in the Negev was established in the Early Bronze, it was abandoned sometime around 2650 BCE and not reestablished until Iron I. There was no king there to attack the wandering Israelites or to be defeated by them. Indeed, Hormah, the site of that defeat, was also unoccupied. Excavations at Tel Masos, identified as ancient Hormah, had a fortress during the Middle Bronze era and a settlement during Iron I, but it was empty in the Late Bronze. This repeated lack of evidence militates against the historicity of these elements in the biblical narrative.

Cities mentioned in the exodus story on the east side of the Jordan Valley also were unoccupied during the Late Bronze Age. Heshbon was not established until Iron I, probably as an unfortified village. Dibon, which became the capital of Moab, was established in the Early Bronze but then empty until reoccupied in Iron II. And although Gibeon was founded during the Middle Bronze and then refounded in the Iron Age, it was unoccupied during the Late Bronze era. The only sign of Late Bronze use is the burial of a few bodies in Middle Bronze tombs.

In addition, the Amarna letters reveal that the kingdoms of Edom and Moab did not exist in the Late Bronze Period (and earlier). During that time, each identified town functioned like a small city-state, but no larger-scale countries consisting of multiple cities existed. Edom and Moab as kingdoms did not form until Iron Age II, about the same time as the Kingdom of Israel.

So rather than archaeology providing support for historical elements of the exodus story, excavations to date actually contradict that tale's claims. At Kadesh, there are no remains indicating an Israelite presence, and, at many other sites, from Arad to Heshbon, no remains exist of a people or enemy for Israelites to interact with. It is clear in the end that the geography of the populated locales the Israelites visit or pass through is that of the monarchical period, between the tenth and the seventh centuries BCE. The towns and cities mentioned are those known when the biblical exodus story was being committed to writing, not those of its centuries-earlier setting as claimed by the biblical narratives.

Conclusion: Israel's Cultural Memory

This chapter has shown that the exodus story, as written and preserved in the books of the Torah, does not constitute history per se. It was not composed with the canons of modern historical practice in mind or perhaps even the canons of ancient history writing. While the tale contains general themes and features that parallel known historical events, those events are often separated by centuries or happen to different groups of people. They do not fit together into a single connected tale of what happened to one people in a time frame of less than half a century. When modern scholars are able to isolate information that can be checked against historical knowledge or archaeological discoveries, they do not correspond.

In this light, scholars such as Jan Assmann and Ronald Hendel have argued that asking about factual accuracy is the wrong approach. Instead of investigating the exodus story as history, we should be studying it as cultural memory, or memnohistory, which means the "past as it is remembered" (Assmann 1997, 8–9). The story "may contain traces of historical events and persons, mingled together with mythic motifs, themes, and structures—the stuff that makes the past truly memorable" (Hendel 2001, 621).

Think of it this way: when different groups in Canaan had different experiences, each group and its descendants remembered their past. One group might have remembered slavery. Many groups would have stories about Egyptian oppression, whether in Egypt or in Canaan. Another group could have remembered a strong leader (like Moses), and yet a fourth group remembered pursuit by the Egyptian army, and some people from the Shasu were popularizing the worship of Yahweh (*yahw*). As these groups came together in the land of Canaan and sought a common identity, they shared their memories with each other, and gradually the separate stories became shared memories of a new community and culture.

In the end, these memories—from different peoples and different times— were woven together into a coherent narrative about the common origin of a mixed variety of peoples who came together in Canaan. While the details and emphases shifted from storyteller to storyteller, as we can see in the different sources that make up the Torah, the exodus story became the foundational tale that united the People of Israel. When the Torah's redactors brought these versions together, they shaped them to support the Israelite leaders they knew, presenting the tale of Moses as a myth of national origins in which the Aaronide priests led Israel in God's worship and God supported the Davidic royal line in Jerusalem, his holy city. The people of ancient Israel told and retold this story throughout their history. In both Judaism and Christianity, it became the story of the origin of monotheism and the worship of this one God, celebrated and taught for millennia.

Suggestions for Further Reading

The story of the exodus and the books of the Torah have received much scholarly study over the centuries from a wide variety of perspectives and beliefs. Here we mention a few modern, representative works. Carol Redmount's essay "Bitter Lives in and out of Egypt" provides an important survey of historical research and archaeological investigations. There are many commentaries written on the biblical books of Exodus through Deuteronomy. Those of Carol Meyers and W. H. C. Propp on Exodus are modern standards, while Martin Noth has provided older yet still important studies of Exodus and Numbers, as has G. Von Rad on Deuteronomy. Donald Redford brought his expertise as an Egyptologist to the study of the exodus in 1992 with his still-influential *Egypt, Canaan, and Israel in Ancient Times*. James Hoffmeier, who has excavated Egyptian forts in the Negev, provides a conservative view in his *Israel in Sinai*. To understand more fully the idea of the exodus as cultural memory, see Ronald Hendel's essay "The Exodus in Biblical Memory." Finally, a 2013 conference at the University of California, San Diego, brought together top biblical scholars and archaeologists from around the world to share their knowledge with each other. That has resulted in a collection of essays called *Israel's Exodus in Transdisciplinary Perspective* (edited by Thomas Levy, Thomas Schneider, and William Propp [2015]) that will impact exodus research for decades to come. It deals with topics ranging from straight archaeology and history to belief, cyberarchaeology, interpretation, and cultural memory.

III

ISRAEL SETTLES IN THE LAND OF CANAAN

10

LOOKING FOR THE ISRAELITES
The Archaeology of Iron Age I

J. P. Dessel

Introduction: The Transitional Nature of the Iron Age I in Canaan

The collapse of several of the major political powers of the eastern Mediterranean and Near East at the end of the thirteenth century BCE ushered in a period of great social and cultural transformation in Canaan: the Iron Age I. The Iron Age I is traditionally dated from 1200 to 1000 BCE and understood as a transitional period between the highly cosmopolitan Late Bronze Age II and the rise of an Israelite state in the Iron Age IIA (roughly tenth century BCE; see chapter 13). It is marked by the decline of an urbanized Canaanite society and the emergence, or **ethnogenesis**, of new social groups, most notably the Israelites, but also the Phoenicians, Philistines, Arameans, and others. Following the breakdown of longstanding Bronze Age political and social systems, these new peoples emerged in a political vacuum. The appearance of the Israelites has become a lightning rod in debates on Iron Age I issues. This should come as no surprise: the issue of ethnogenesis—the process by which a culturally bounded group with a distinctive identity emerges from a more diffuse background—is a central, as well as contentious, concern in Iron Age studies of the southern Levant.

The Iron Age I is wedged between two well-documented and more easily defined periods: the Late Bronze Age II and the Iron Age IIA. The Late Bronze Age II was a period of internationalism in which much of the eastern Mediterranean was integrated economically, socially, and culturally (Feldman 2006). Canaan itself was under the imperial control of New Kingdom Egypt (Eighteenth and Nineteenth Dynasties) and organized into a series of small, competitive city-states, each of which had control over an adjacent hinterland. These Canaanite city-states were ruled by dynastic elites that the Egyptians referred to as "princes" and that the biblical texts refer to as "kings." From the Amarna letters, an extensive correspondence between these Canaanite rulers and Eighteenth Dynasty Egyptian pharaohs composed during the fourteenth century BCE, we know quite a bit about the Late Bronze Age political landscape. Canaanite autonomy was limited to local matters, and princes were in a state of seemingly perpetual conflict with their neighbors. While politically not unified, the Canaanites had a common culture going back to the Early Bronze Age. Late Bronze Age Canaanite material culture is marked by relative homogeneity, as seen in the ceramics, architecture, seal-carving, art and iconography, and epigraphic tradition.

Likewise, the sociopolitical landscape of the Iron Age IIA (tenth century BCE) has a unity; it is characterized by a revival of urbanism—but more importantly, by the formation of small independent states. These combine not only several formerly independent city-states but also the rural lands between them. These small regional states—Israel, as well as Ammon, Moab, and Edom—come to define the Iron Age II Period. As in Late Bronze Age Canaan, the material culture assemblage in Iron Age II Israel is relatively homogeneous (though there are some distinctions between the north and south, or what will later become Israel and Judah). Overall, there are broad similarities in the material culture of these southern Levantine states; however, there are also some significant distinctions, especially in ceramic decorative traditions, religious architectural styles, and the mobile arts.

After a brief consideration of chronology and the historical context of the Iron Age I, this chapter will examine four important dynamics in the study of the Iron Age I: cultural continuity, sociocultural disruption, Israelite ethnogenesis, and rural complexity. This will be followed by a discussion of the models used to explain these dynamics. In chapter 11, the biblical material from the books of Joshua, Judges, and 1 Samuel will be analyzed in response to this archaeological information.

Iron Age I Chronology

The Iron Age I is traditionally dated 1200–1000 BCE. The well-rounded precision of these dates stems more from the biblical narratives than archaeological investigation. As with any transitional period, the end points are fluid; for the Iron Age I, a more precise chronological range might be from the late thirteenth century to the early tenth century BCE. The destruction of the Late Bronze city of Hazor, possibly by the Israelites, dates to the mid-thirteenth century—clearly earlier than 1200 BCE. And while Israel's united monarchy belongs to the tenth century, it does not begin precisely in 1000 BCE.

This period is also subdivided into two parts: Iron Age IA (1200–1150 BCE) and Iron Age IB (1150–1000 BCE). The Iron Age IA, while traditionally lasting only fifty years, represents a period of continued Egyptian imperial control over parts of Canaan, especially in the Jordan Valley at Beth Shean, in the Jezreel Valley at Megiddo, as well as along the southern Coastal Plain at the sites of Tel Mor, Tel Sera', Tell el-Farah (South), and as far inland as Lachish

(Tell ed-Duweir). In these areas of Egyptian control and/or influence, there is clear continuity in Canaanite culture.

The Iron Age IA is also the period in which we find the emergence of the Israelites in the Central Hill Country, the destruction of some major Canaanite city-states (and, in some cases, their reconstruction), and the arrival of the Philistines along the southern coastal plain. For these reasons, the sociopolitical landscape of Canaan in the Iron Age IA is particularly dynamic, as it came to be populated by Canaanites, Israelites, Phoenicians, and Philistines, among others.

The Iron Age IB (1150–1000 BCE) is characterized by a reorganization of Canaanite society, the crystallization and expansion of a rural Israelite society, and the flourishing of an urban Philistine society. The end of the period is marked by the foundation of the Israelite state in the early tenth century BCE and changes in the material culture that make the transition to the Iron Age IIA perceptible both archaeologically and historically.

The Historical Brackets: Israelite Ethnogenesis from People to Polity

There are two historical documents that bracket the process of Israelite ethnogenesis and help contextualize the Iron Age I archaeological data. The most important is the Merneptah Stele (also called the Israel Stele), an Egyptian inscription found in Nineteenth Dynasty pharaoh Merneptah's mortuary temple at Thebes. Carved in his seventh year, 1207 BCE, it commemorates Merneptah's victory over the Libyans as well a successful military campaign in Canaan.

> The Princes are prostrate, saying "Shalom" [Peace]!
> Not one is raising his head among the Nine Bows.
> Now that Tehenu [Libya] has come to ruin,
> Hatti is pacified.
> > The Canaan has been plundered into every sort of woe;
> > Ashkelon has been overcome;
> > Gezer has been captured;
> > Yanoam is made nonexistent;
> > *Israel is laid waste, his seed is not;*
> > Hurru is become a widow because of Egypt!
> All lands together, they are pacified! (Adapted from Stager 2001, 93)

This is the earliest historical reference to Israel. In it the word "Israel" is qualified by the Egyptian determinative for people rather than place, distinguishing it from the associated place-names Canaan, Ashkelon, Gezer, and Yanoam. For the Egyptians of the late thirteenth century BCE, the Israelites in Canaan were a recognizable but unrooted social group. Although this reference provides little in the way of details, we can infer that these Israelites may have been tribal and even pastoralists, a well-known component of the Near Eastern landscape in the Bronze and Iron Ages. This invaluable reference inserts Israel into the historical record sometime in the late thirteenth century BCE.

There is one other possible reference to Israel from the reign of Merneptah. Four battle reliefs found on the walls of the Temple of Karnak in Egypt were originally attributed to the reign of Ramesses II but were reassigned by the late Professor Frank Yurco to Merneptah. According to Yurco, one of these reliefs depicts Israelites in a manner similar to Canaanites portrayed in the other three reliefs. Yurco views this damaged scene as a taking place in a hilly countryside against a foe unconnected to fortified cities. He points out that these four battle scenes correspond directly to battles in Canaan referred to in the Merneptah Stele. Yurco's identification is not without problems, but there is growing acceptance of this position among Egyptologists, archaeologists, and biblical scholars.

The next extrabiblical reference to Israel does not appear until the ninth century BCE, beyond the end of the Iron I. This is a stele with an Aramaic inscription from the site of Tel Dan in the far north of ancient Israel (see Figure 14-7). The Dan Stele was erected by Hazael, the king of Aram-Damascus, commemorating his defeat of the nations of both Israel and Judah. In it, the phrase "Beit David" or "house of David" appears; it comprises the only extrabiblical reference to David. This reference to a "house of David" (it is routine in the ancient Near East for states to be referred to by the name of their dynastic founder) strongly supports the contention that a kingdom of Israel, founded by David, existed in the tenth century BCE.

FIGURE 10-1. *Detail from scene of Egyptian pharaoh Merneptah attacking Ashkelon showing defenders praying from the top of a tower. Karnak Temple, Egypt.*

These temporal parameters, the late thirteenth century BCE for the earliest reference to a people Israel, and the ninth century BCE for the earliest reference to the united monarchy of Israel, provide solid beginning and end dates for Israelite ethnogenesis and dates the emergence of the Israelites as a recognizable ethnic or social group to the Iron Age I.

Canaanite Continuity

Several significant sociopolitical processes characterize the Iron Age I. The first is the gradual reordering of Canaanite society. In the geographic boundaries of what will later become Israel, there is a gradual waning of Canaanite society as the Israelites become more dominant toward the end of the Iron Age I. But just as important is the transformation over time of Late Bronze Age Canaanite society into Iron Age Phoenician city-states on the northern coast, in parts of the Upper Galilee, and in Lebanon.

During this Late Bronze Age / Iron Age transition, several sites evidence both destruction and subsequent cultural continuity. Destruction does not necessarily mean a break with the past or that one population replaced another. Cultural continuity from Late Bronze Age Canaanite society into the Iron Age I is most clearly found at urban sites located in the Jezreel and Jordan Valleys, the northern Coastal Plain, and the Akko Plain as well as at a few sites in the Shephelah and Central Hill Country. Some cities were destroyed—perhaps by the Israelites, though not necessarily—and yet in some cases these cities are rebuilt on the same basic Late Bronze Age plan with the same architectural elements and material remains. Continuity in material culture appears likewise in the pottery types and methods of production.

The stratigraphic sequence at Megiddo provides an example of these complex political, social, and cultural machinations at work. The Late Bronze Age city (Stratum VIIB) at Megiddo was destroyed at the end of the thirteenth century BCE, and the site was rebuilt soon thereafter (Stratum VIIA) on the same plan, pointing to the continuity of Canaanite society. Again, the city was destroyed in the mid-twelfth century BCE, after which the resettlement is described as an impoverished squatter phase (Stratum VIB). Megiddo was rebuilt once more in the eleventh century BCE (Stratum VIA) as a dense urban settlement in which Canaanite style pottery and ivories were found, along with collar-rim store jars (henceforth CRSJ), a distinctive type of jar attributed to the Iron I Israelites, and even some Philistine **bichrome** pottery. The presence of Canaanite, Israelite, and Philistine ceramic types allows for a diversity of interpretations as to the ethnic character of eleventh-century BCE Megiddo. Some scholars stress the continuity of Canaanite pottery pointing to a Canaanite population, whereas other scholars believe the appearance of the CRSJ points to an Israelite presence. It is only when the city was again

FIGURE 10-2. *View of Tel Megiddo, looking south.*

destroyed in the early tenth century BCE that Canaanite society at Megiddo finally ends.

Phoenician Ethnogenesis

While Canaanite culture and society contracted over the course of the Iron Age IB, it did not disappear. It remained along the northern coast of Israel (north from Tell Dor) and into the Akko Plain, and, over time, it transformed into Phoenician society. The term "Phoenician" (a Greek term that the Phoenicians themselves never used) initially referred to coastal Canaanites who continued to thrive into the sixth century BCE. In the eleventh century BCE, Phoenician culture expanded north along the Lebanese coast and established itself on Cyprus before pushing west. Regardless of what this term comes to mean in later periods, the roots of Phoenician culture and society lay in Late Bronze Age Canaan. In fact, the emergence of the Phoenicians is another example of ethnogenesis marked by an enigmatic beginning in the Iron Age I. Phoenician culture manifested in ways not unlike early Israelite culture, with distinctive combinations of material remains and ceramic styles. However, perhaps the most consistent Canaanite trait preserved by the Phoenicians is the city-state. Unlike their neighbors to the south, the Israelites, the Phoenicians never formed secondary states with capital cities, and they instead preserved the city-state political arrangement of the Late Bronze Age.

Late Bronze Age City Destructions and Social Change

A second important dynamic of the Iron Age I is the destruction of city-states without any evidence for Canaanite social regeneration. Destruction events provide powerful data for the archaeologist and often provide important chronological information as well as rare insights into "real time" sociopolitical events. However, the identity and motivation of the perpetrators remain elusive, and we are often dependent on specific historical references for that information. The presence of specific types of material culture thought to be Israelite in postdestruction levels (see below) has led some scholars to suggest an Israelite conquest and resettlement. Such is the case at sites such as Bethel (correlating the archaeological evidence with conquest narratives in Joshua) and Taanach. However, the relationship between specific types of material culture and ethnic identity remains a matter of debate.

As already noted, it is important to examine the scale of the destruction and the nature of any subsequent rebuilding at a site. Once a site is destroyed, one of any number of possibilities for its future could arise: the site might be abandoned, it might be resettled on the same plan, it might be rebuilt along a new plan, or it might revert to a lower level of complexity—such as a village.

There is ample archaeological evidence for the destruction of several significant Canaanite cities in early Iron I. These destructions loosely conform to the biblical accounts in that some of the cities listed in Joshua 12:9-24 were destroyed, including Hazor, Megiddo, Lachish, Bethel, and Gezer. However, the archaeological data reveal that these destructions occurred not at the same time but over an extended period between the mid-thirteenth century and mid-twelfth century BCE. This contradicts the notion of a single Israelite campaign led by Joshua as described in the book of Joshua. This is an essential point and cannot be overemphasized: the destructions of Late Bronze Age Canaanite city-states did not all happen at once but rather occurred over the span of almost a century. In addition, these destructions are not unusual; cities in the Bronze and Iron Ages were frequently destroyed, sometimes as often as once a century.

One of the more carefully examined destruction sequences is at Hazor. The destruction of Hazor figures prominently in Joshua 11:10-13, which claims the Israelites burned down the city. Archaeologically, the Late Bronze Age city at Hazor (Stratum XIII) was destroyed in the mid-thirteenth century. After a short gap in occupation, there is a modest resettlement in Stratum XII that in no way resembled the Canaanite city, suggesting to some—including Hazor excavation directors Yigael Yadin and Amnon Ben-Tor—an Israelite conquest of the city. However, the late codirector of the ongoing Hazor excavation project, Sharon Zuckerman, suggested that the destruction is better understood as a reflection of internal political and social deterioration rather than an attack by external forces. As Zuckerman herself noted, the value of her suggestion is twofold: (1) it is an attempt to consider collapse and destruction as a long-term process and not merely an episodic event, and (2) what appears to be clear archaeological evidence for a destruction event has subtle and nuanced elements that must be carefully examined, separately from any text-based sources.

Late thirteenth-century BCE destruction levels have also been excavated at Bethel, Beth Shemesh, Yoqneam, and Gezer. Destruction levels dating a bit later were discovered at Dan (early twelfth century BCE) and Taanach (late twelfth century BCE). What follows these destructions is more difficult to ascertain. It appears that Taanach was abandoned until at least the tenth century BCE, while Yoqneam was also briefly abandoned and then reestablished as a village in the Iron Age I. Gezer is rebuilt in more modest fashion in the Iron Age I, with a significant amount of Philistine cultural influence, but also evidence of at least three destruction episodes in the twelfth century BCE before stabilizing in the eleventh century BCE. Dan and Bethel also revert to a village level at this time, as does Beth Shemesh, which the excavators suggest retains a Canaanite identity as late as the tenth century BCE.

Excursus: Joshua 12, Judges 1, and the Israelite Destruction of Canaanite Cities

There are some significant discrepancies between the archaeology and the biblical text. However, the biblical text itself is by no means consistent in its portrayal of which Canaanite cities Israel conquered. Joshua 12:7-24 provides a list of the kings "whom Joshua and the Israelites defeated." This list includes a number of cities that other biblical passages explicitly indicate were not destroyed. The list in Judges 1 disagrees frequently with the list in Joshua 12. It states that three of the cities in Joshua 12 were not captured: Gezer, Taanach, and Megiddo. Interestingly, even Joshua 16:10 says that Israel "did not . . . drive out the Canaanites who lived in Gezer," and Joshua 17:11-13 indicates the Canaanites remained in Taanach and Megiddo—although they were later driven out.

There are five contradictory statements in the Hebrew Bible concerning how the Israelites took Jerusalem, as the capital of the united monarchy and then of the Kingdom of Judah, from the Jebusites. The Joshua 12 list indicates that Joshua himself successfully led its conquest, but Joshua 15:63 indicates that Judah did not drive the Jebusites from Jerusalem. Judges 1, whose description of the tribe of Judah contains only triumphal attacks, says Judah conquered and burnt Jerusalem (Judg 1:8), even though it was not in their territory. When Judges 1 gets to Benjamin, in whose territory Jerusalem lies, however, the text makes clear that they "did not drive out the Jebusites who lived in Jerusalem; so the Jebusites have lived in Jerusalem among the Benjaminites to this day" (Judg 1:21). And, of course, King David himself makes the first act of his new kingship of the united monarchy the taking of Jerusalem from the Jebusites (2 Sam 5:6-10). The five different biblical passages about Jerusalem are inconsistent about its conquest and even its tribal location. Therefore, disagreement between archaeology and text about Jerusalem, or any other city, should not be surprising.

It has often been overlooked that the account describing Joshua's allotment of the land of Canaan to the Israelites begins with God telling Joshua that the Israelites were not completely successful in driving out the Canaanites. Because of this, God says, "I will myself drive them out from before the Israelites; only allot the land to Israel for an inheritance, as I have commanded you" (Josh 13:6, read vv. 2-6). At various points up to the end of Joshua 19, the narrative of assigning land is interrupted by the admission that Canaanites still dwell in part of it, as in Joshua 15:63, 16:10, and 17:11-13. And we should not forget that the tribe of Dan is driven out of its possession by the Philistines (Judg 17–18), a point that is admitted in Joshua 19:47.

It is clear, then, that the idea the Israelites made a clear sweep of the Canaanites is little more than later religious propaganda. Even the Deuteronomistic Historian recognized Israel's failure in this regard.

Israelite Ethnogenesis

The ways in which archaeological data are or are not suited to assess ethnicity promotes endless discussion among archaeologists. Certainly there are case studies in which the archaeological data—such as pottery, architectural styles, organization of space, mobile arts and iconography, as well as settlement patterns and dietary practices—are clearly associated with discrete social groups or ethnicities. Unfortunately, this kind of direct relationship between material culture and ethnicity is more the exception than the rule. It is ironic that the best example of a specific material culture indicating a specific social group comes from the Philistines. Over time this discrepancy was redressed with the discovery of two distinctive types of material culture that many archaeologists decided identified Iron Age I Israelites: CRSJs and the four-room house (see below). Ever since these linkages were made, there has been an ongoing debate on this question.

The geographic setting of Israelite ethnogenesis is the Central Hill Country, a mountainous region that extends from the southern end of the Jezreel Valley in the north to the Beer Sheva Valley in the south. There were a few well-known Late Bronze Age cities in this region, including Shechem, Shiloh, Bethel, and Jerusalem, but otherwise the highlands were sparsely settled. This changed in the late thirteenth century BCE when a sudden proliferation of hundreds of small village settlements appeared in the Central Hill Country, the Upper Galilee, and parts of Transjordan. In the Central Hill Country alone, there were upward of 250 such villages. The appearance of this wave of village settlements in the Central Hill Country is especially striking as it is

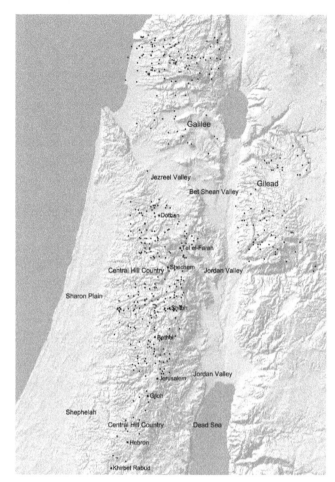

MAP 10-1. *At the end of the Late Bronze Age and the early part of the Iron Age I, hundreds of new, small villages appeared in the Central Hill Country and other hilly regions.*

roughly contemporaneous with the Merneptah Stele and the earliest extrabiblical appearance of the name Israel.

The Material Culture of the New Iron I Villages

The highland villages in these three areas are all very small, usually less than a **hectare** in size, unwalled, and wholly domestic in nature. They are characterized by a simple utilitarian material culture, with a limited range of undecorated ceramic forms. They lack any evidence of public architecture, imported pottery, or prestige items, all of which are typical at Late Bronze Age urban sites. Several aspects of the material culture have come to define these sites and ultimately to serve as the ethnic markers of their inhabitants; these include the CRSJs and four-room houses as well as a high frequency of pits, cisterns, and terraces and, most importantly, the absence of pig bones.

The ceramic assemblage in these villages is, in many ways, a limited version of utilitarian, Late Bronze Age, Canaanite-like ceramic forms, including cooking pots, kraters or deep bowls, bowls, and juglets. A new addition to the assemblage is the CRSJ, a large storage vessel measuring roughly 1.2 meters in height, undecorated, with a distinctive band or collar around the upper shoulder. The CRSJ holds up to eighty liters and was used for the long-term storage of both liquids and dry goods, such as olive oil, wine, grains, and perhaps water. These vessels first appear at the very end of the Late Bronze Age at sites on the coast and in lowland valleys. In the Iron Age I, they appear in great quantities in the Central Hill Country but have a relatively wide distribution, including the Jezreel Valley, the Akko Plain, the Sharon Plain, the Lower Galilee, Central Transjordan, and as far north as Tel Dan. They appear less commonly in the Shephelah and not at all in the Negev, Philistia, the northern part of Lower Galilee, and Upper Galilee.

The four-room house is understood as the typical domestic structure of the period. At the most basic level, these rectangular structures consist of two or three parallel rooms with a perpendicular room spanning the width of the back of the building. The entrance to the structure usually leads to a central courtyard situated in one of the front parallel rooms. Sometimes, the parallel rooms are demarcated by stone pillars. The roof of the four-room house was flat and used as workspace; some had a partial second story used as living space. The chronological and geographic distributions of this house type are more elastic than often surmised. Four-room houses (see Figure

FIGURE 10-3. *A collar-rim storage jar (CRSJ) from Shiloh.*

16-5) have been identified as early as the Late Bronze Age II at Tel Batash in the Shephelah and continue to appear well into the Iron Age II. They are also found outside the Central Hill Country, in lowland valleys, and in Transjordan (see below). It is quite clear that this architectural type was used over a long time and a wide geographical distribution, which calls into question how well the four-room house constitutes a reliable indicator of Israelite culture.

Other features commonly found in the villages in the Central Hill Country are cisterns (plastered for water storage), silos (stone or plastered line for food storage), and agricultural terraces (for highland agriculture). These features are all adaptations made by self-sufficient villages to the environmental requirements of a highland area where water and foodstuffs must be stored for extended periods of time. The value of these features for a successful adaptation to the highland environment is unquestioned; however, the date of the appearance of these adaptions is uncertain, and most scholars now see them as predating the Iron Age I.

Lastly, the issue of foodways or dietary patterns must be considered. Increasingly, archaeologists are looking to foodways to help identify ethnic or social groups, and the relative absence of pig bones in these Central Hill Country villages is notable. Pig bones are found in Iron Age I Philistine sites along the coast, Late Bronze Age Canaanite urban and village sites, Iron Age I Canaanite urban sites, and sites in Transjordan and elsewhere outside of the boundaries of what becomes Israel in the tenth century BCE, but they are absent in the Central Hill Country sites of Iron I. In fact, on Philistine sites, pig bones comprise a significant proportion of the fauna assemblage, suggesting that pork consumption was an important part of the Philistine diet. In Late Bronze Age Canaan sites, there is evidence of a modest degree of pork consumption, though not nearly as high as at the later Philistine sites. Interestingly, pig bones also appear in Iron Age I sites in Transjordan. For many scholars, the distribution of pig bones suggests that the biblical proscription against eating pork was already taking shape or was even in place in the highland villages of the Iron Age I. As foodways and dietary customs are believed to be deeply conservative cultural elements, this becomes some of the strongest pieces of evidence for the emergence of a discrete social group in the Central Hill Country.

Religion: An Indicator of Centralization?

While almost all the architecture in the highland villages is domestic in nature, public cultic architecture appears the Central Hill Country at Mount Ebal and the Bull Site. These sites are reminiscent of the centralized shrines mentioned in Joshua, Judges, and Samuel. Situated just north of Shechem, Mount Ebal is an open-air site surrounded by an enclosure wall encompassing an area of about 1.5 hectares. It has two phases, the earliest dating to the late thirteenth century BCE and a later phase dating to the first half of the twelfth century BCE. The earliest phase is poorly understood and consists of a circular stone installation. Burnt animal bones found in the fill of the later structure are believed to belong to the earlier phase, and the circular stone structure is interpreted as some kind of altar. The discovery of two Egyptian scarabs, one dating to the reign of Ramesses II, is noteworthy and helps date this phase. In the latter phase, the circular installation was reconfigured into a rectangular installation oriented to the cardinal directions and comprised of cross walls that formed internal rectangular cells filled with burnt animal bones (bull,

FIGURE 10-4. *The altar at Mount Ebal.*

sheep, goat, and fallow deer), ash, stones, and sediment. The top of this rectangular installation was covered with a stone pavement that was reached by a stone ramp in the middle of its southern wall. This ramp was part of the founding base for the stone installation and included two courtyard areas delineated by stone walls and ramps.

The excavator of Mount Ebal, Adam Zertal, interpreted this installation as Joshua's altar (Josh 8:30-32; Deut 11:29; 27:4-8). The unusual nature of this structure and a preponderance of burnt bones are significant. The animal bones come from a list of permitted animals that conform to Israelite sacrificial animals and dietary laws. The site is also unconnected to any nearby domestic settlement, suggesting it is a place of pilgrimage and befitting a pastoral society. These data strongly suggest a cultic function for the site, but it goes well beyond the archaeological data to suggest that this altar was actually built by Joshua. Without confirming the absolute historicity of Joshua, and lacking an actual twelfth-century BCE date for the book of Joshua, it is simply impossible to make this kind of correlation.

The Bull Site dates to the twelfth century BCE and is situated on a ridge top located about nine kilometers east of Dothan. The Bull Site consists of an elliptical stone enclosure wall roughly twenty meters in diameter. On the east side of the enclosed area, a large roughly hewn rectangular stone was found standing on its side in front of a stone paved area, suggesting the two features are part of a single installation. Evidence of offerings on the paved area include an amorphous bronze object, bowl sherds, and the fragment of either a model shrine or an offering stand. The hewn rectangular stone is believed to be a standing stone, a well-known element from Levantine cult sites since the Chalcolithic Period. Like Mount Ebal, the Bull Site is unconnected to any domestic settlement, again suggesting it is a pilgrimage site.

The serendipitous discovery of a small bronze bull 17.5 centimeters long and 12.5 centimeters high found on the surface strengthened the interpretation of the site as a biblical "high place." The bull is a well-known image in Canaanite iconography, often used as a symbol of the god Baal (see Figure 9-2). Middle and Late Bronze Age examples of such bronze bulls were found at Ashkelon and Hazor (from a temple) as well as at sites further north in Lebanon and Syria. Such imagery is also found in the Hebrew Bible, most notably in the story of the golden calf in Exodus 32.

Both Mount Ebal and the Bull Site undoubtedly have a cultic association. It also seems likely that they may have served a pastoral or dispersed population. Both are without any good archaeological parallels, which makes the interpretation more difficult. Mount Ebal's biblical pedigree adds to the difficulty in coming to an objective conclusion based only on the archaeological data. Ultimately, a secure ethnic ascription is difficult to pin down; it seems quite possible they are Israelite, but it is by no means certain.

A View East: Transjordan in the Iron Age I

Many of the same archaeological dynamics are also found east of the Jordan River in areas that will become Ammon, Moab, and Edom in the tenth century BCE. What is most striking is the similar settlement pattern. The Transjordan highlands and steppe area were virtually empty in the Late Bronze Age; in the Iron Age I, however, as in the Central Hill Country, there was the sudden appearance of many, perhaps hundreds, of small villages, especially in Gilead (north of Ammon) and Moab. Tall al-Umayri provides one of the best examples of the transition to the Iron Age I in Transjordan. Located on the Madaba Plains in the region of Ammon, Tall al-Umayri has extensive Iron Age I occupation that begins in the late thirteenth to early twelfth century BCE. After the collapse of the Late Bronze II settlement (Stratum 14), there are two strata (13 and 12) separated by an earthquake that necessitated a rebuilding around 1200 BCE that excavator Larry Herr considers transitional Late Bronze II / Iron Age I. Stratum 12 is particularly robust, with an extensive fortification system that includes a dry moat, ramparts, and city wall system that is similar to a casemate-style wall better known in the tenth century BCE. CRSJs are numerous in these levels, and many are found in an incredibly well-preserved four-room house. This house was covered by a significant destruction layer that helped preserve the contents of some of the CRSJs: carbonized barley and vegetables. Next to this four-room house is evidence of a domestic shrine that included a standing stone positioned in front of a stone altar.

The site was destroyed in the mid-twelfth century BCE and abandoned for about fifty years, after which there were two more late Iron Age I strata. Herr tentatively suggests that there is a change of character in the architecture and material culture after the twelfth-century hiatus. It is not at all clear whether or not the inhabitants of Tall al-Umayri can be considered Israelite,

FIGURE 10-5. *Tall al-Umayri, view from northwest.*

even though the same settlement patterns and material culture appear on both sides of the Jordan River. What is clear, however, is that the subsequent political formations that arise following the Iron Age I in Transjordan differ distinctly from Israel.

Rural Complexity

Large urban tell sites and clusters of very small one-period highland villages are not the only settlement types found in the Iron Age I. There are also quite a few examples of long-lived, stable Late Bronze and Iron Age villages, especially in the Lower Galilee of Israel, that might provide some alternative insights into Israelite ethnogenesis in the Iron Age I. At the sites of Tell Ein Zippori and Tell el-Wawiyat, there is clear evidence of cultural continuity from the Late Bronze Age into the Iron Age I. The styles of pottery and architecture, foodways, and iconography demonstrate cultural continuity, and yet these sites are located in the core of what became ancient Israel.

While the Iron I villages further south in the Central Highlands are understood as reflecting a weakly stratified society, the same cannot be said about these multiperiod Galilean villages. Some of the most striking evidence for rural complexity in Iron Age I Canaan is the construction of the large and public Building A found at Tell Ein Zippori. The internal features of Building A—including a bench, roof access, and **ashlar**-like masonry— are frequently associated with public buildings in both the Late Bronze and the Iron Ages. The construction of a large stone silo along with a number of very simple stamped or impressed handles strongly suggests that this building served as a local administrative or small-scale redistribution center. These features provide important insights into the fabric of rural complexity and suggest some level of political organization in the form of large-scale public works. The leaders who built and used Building A are representative

FIGURE 10-6. *The large "Building A" at Tell Ein Zippori indicates a high level of administrative complexity during Iron IA in Galilee.*

of what must have been a pervasive social group found throughout the ancient Near East—village elders or rural elites—a social class also known in Hebrew Bible.

Modeling Israelite Ethnogenesis

Since the 1920s, scholars have endeavored to understand the process of Israelite ethnogenesis—the emergence of the people Israel in the land of Canaan—with increasingly sophisticated and more holistic approaches. Over time this has meant first using archaeology to support the historicity of the biblical narratives, then moving away from a dependence on those same biblical narratives and relying more on archaeological, historical, and environmental data along with a more nuanced consideration of the nature of social identity. These efforts resulted in the development of four main explanatory models that have come to dominate the discipline. All of these models are informed, to varying degrees, by the biblical narratives and an attempt to harmonize them with the archeological and historical records. These models can be divided into two types: "outsider" models that posit the Israelites as a new ethnic group who entered Canaan from the outside, and "insider" models that view the Israelites as emerging from a Canaanite cultural context who ultimately transform themselves into something new and distinctive.

Outsider Models

Outsider models understand the Israelites as newcomers to the land of Canaan, following the basic premise of the conquest and settlement narratives found in Joshua and Judges 1. The two outsider models developed by biblical scholars in the 1920s and 1930s are known as the "Peaceful Infiltration Model" and "the Conquest Model."

The earliest of these models was developed by Albrecht Alt in 1925 with emendations by Martin Noth, his student. The impetus for this model was Alt's discomfort with the depiction of the Israelite settlement found in the conquest narratives in Joshua. He considered the conquest and settlement narratives of Judges 1 as more reliable and set out to demonstrate this.

Alt had a keen interest in historical geography and **ethnography**, having spent some time in Palestine in the 1920s, where he became interested in Bedouin society. By charting the changing geographic boundaries of Canaan from the Late Bronze Age to the Iron Age and incorporating this interest in (Bedouin) pastoralist movements, Alt developed a "Peaceful Infiltration Model."

For Alt, Judges 1 depicts the Canaanite and Israelites battling each other, but also commingling, and eventually they are found living side by side in major Canaanite city-states. As an example of a more peaceful relationship between the two, Alt cited the treaty between Israelite tribes and the Gibeonites in Joshua 9. On the other hand, Alt viewed the conquest narratives of Joshua 1–12 as reflecting a second stage of Israelite expansion when conflict over water and land rights would have occurred.

Alt argued that the earliest penetration of the Israelites into Canaan came in the late thirteenth and early twelfth centuries BCE and formed a long, gradual process in which desert pastoralists moved peacefully from the steppe region to the east (the Transjordanian plateau and highlands) and settled ever closer to established Canaanite city-states. These pastoralists began to settle down for increasingly longer periods of time, eventually becoming sedentary agriculturalists. They moved first into the Jordan Valley and then west into the sparsely occupied Central Hill Country, slowly intermingling with the indigenous Canaanites. Thus, Alt suggests the Israelites emerged from pastoral groups who inhabited the steppe region in Transjordan. This model followed the biblical narratives and was not based on any archaeological or historical data. Most importantly for Alt, the Israelites brought monotheism with them. They adopted some Canaanite cultural traditions but came to dominate them culturally and politically.

When archaeological surveys throughout the southern Levant revealed hundreds of small rural sites dating to the late thirteenth and twelfth centuries BCE, Alt's model seemed to be confirmed. Yohanan Aharoni, whose surveys in the Upper Galilee and northern Negev Desert found many such small Iron Age I villages, was a very strong supporter of this model. And components of this model survive in a variety of incarnations and especially in Israel Finkelstein's Pastoral Canaanite Model.

This Peaceful Infiltration Model is primarily descriptive rather than explanatory; it makes no attempt to explain where the Israelites came from—other than from the east—or why they chose to settle down where they did. The model also never addresses the important question of how Israelite culture became dominant in Canaan.

The second model, called the "Conquest Model," was developed in the 1930s by William Foxwell Albright. For Albright, the discovery of destruction layers at sites with impressive biblical pedigrees—such as Megiddo, Lachish, and Bethel, as well as the discovery of a Late Bronze Age destruction in his own excavations at Tell Beit Mirsim (which he identified as biblical Debir)—supported the biblical narratives found in Joshua 6–12. For the time (the 1930s), Albright should be seen as forward thinking. Albright, who criticized Alt for neglecting the archaeological data, fully integrated the archaeological data into his reading of the biblical narratives. Later, the eminent Israeli archaeologist Yigael Yadin, based on his own work at the site of Hazor in the 1950s, also became a major proponent of the Conquest Model. For many scholars, Yadin's discovery of a major destruction layer ending the Late Bronze Age city spoke volumes in favor of the historicity of the book of Joshua.

According to Joshua, the Canaanite population, at least in the cities, was replaced with an Israelite one. This allowed for a growing acceptance of the notion that any new forms of material culture that appeared after these destruction levels was Israelite. The most important of these ethnic markers were the four-room house and the CRSJ. Albright saw in these two types of material culture evidence of a new people with new cultural traditions. These people were, of course, the Israelites.

There are several problems with the Conquest Model, however. The conquest narratives of Joshua 6–12 clearly depict the Israelite conquest of Canaanite city-states as a single, rapid military campaign. Hewing closely to the conquest narratives in Joshua meant Albright and his supporters needed to date all of the Late Bronze Age destruction levels to roughly the same time. That accorded with the archaeological data known in his time, but, since the 1960s, many of the sites Albright had used to support this model were reexcavated—including Ai, Jericho, Megiddo, Lachish, and Hazor—with more-scientific methods and more-refined analytical tools for dating (such as radiocarbon dating) as well as a more more-refined ceramic typology. Thus, the destruction of Late Bronze Age Hazor was more accurately dated to the mid-thirteenth century BCE, whereas Late Bronze Age Lachish was destroyed in the mid-twelfth century. So while a number of Late Bronze Age city-states claimed to have been destroyed by Joshua—such as Lachish, Hazor, and Bethel—were indeed destroyed, they were not all destroyed at the same time. Even the question of whether or not they were destroyed by the Israelites remains open.

A second problem is that many sites mentioned in conquest narratives were unoccupied in the Late Bronze Age II or the Iron Age IA. This would mean that either there was no Late Bronze Age city for the Israelites to destroy, or there is no evidence of a post-destruction Israelite settlement. Two particularly problematic destruction accounts that figure prominently in Joshua are Ai and Jericho. Based on the biblical description of Ai in Joshua 7–8, the site has been securely identified as et-Tell, just east of Bethel. However, based on the major excavations in 1933–1936 led by J. Marquet Krause and in 1964–1972 by J. Callaway, it became quite clear that the site was uninhabited in the Late Bronze Age. There was, however, an Iron Age I village founded around 1200 BCE on the remains of an earlier city, but one that dated to the Early Bronze Age III (2750–2400 BCE), not the Late Bronze Age. Perhaps the biblical authors left a clue as to why Ai was included among Israelite conquests. The name Ai means "the ruin" in Hebrew. These Early Bronze Age ruins may have inspired the name and ultimately an etiological story of Joshua's conquest of the site.

Jericho is also problematic because of the popularity of the colorful story from Joshua 6 describing its destruction. John Garstang excavated at Jericho from 1930–1936 and concluded the city had been destroyed around 1400 BCE. He posited that an earthquake had destroyed the city wall and that the opportunist Israelites then attacked the city and destroyed it. It all seemed to fit nicely with Joshua's invasion. Kathleen Kenyon, a young archaeologist at London University, reexamined Garstang's data and came to a different conclusion. Unfortunately, there were virtually no Late Bronze Age remains at the site. Jericho had not been inhabited in 1400 BCE, and there were only slight remains during the following century, 1400–1300 BCE. Garstang's city walls actually dated to 2400 BCE—a thousand years earlier. From 1952 to 1958, Kenyon led an excavation at Jericho that reaffirmed her earlier critiques of Garstang. More important, her archaeological techniques and methods revolutionized the field of archaeology in Palestine, and her interpretation of the archaeological data has been attacked by those who want to believe the biblical tale. If the Israelites had visited Jericho in Late Bronze II (1400–1200 BCE), they would have encountered at most a small village. The great walled city of Jericho did not exist then.

Ai and Jericho are not the only sites that appear in the list of Joshua's conquests that lack either Late Bronze Age remains or any evidence of an Iron Age I settlement. Gibeon, Arad, Heshbon, and Dibon are all problematic; none of their archaeological data support the conquest narratives. While some schol-ars dismiss the conquest narratives outright, others, such as Amihai Mazar, suggest they telescope a lengthy process of Canaanite decline and Israelite ascendance that emphasizes the destruction of Canaanite city-states (regard-less of who was really responsible). On the other hand, Israel Finkelstein, as part of his effort to lower the overall Iron Age II chronology, suggests that the conquest narratives were written much later than the events they portray and actually reflect the political realities of seventh-century BCE Judah.

INSIDER MODELS

In the early 1960s, the biblical scholar George Mendenhall questioned the veracity of the biblical narratives concerning Israelite origins, asking whether the Israelites actually migrated from Egypt as the exodus narratives suggest. He argued instead that the Israelites originated from within Canaan itself; they comprised an indigenous group that arose in the wake of social and eco-nomic upheavals in Canaanite society. The "Internal Revolt" Model—or later a "Peasants' Revolt"—proposed that the Israelites were oppressed and disen-franchised peasants who left Canaanite society. These peasants headed for the relatively empty and isolated Central Hill Country, where they established small egalitarian villages.

In the 1970s, Norman Gottwald developed a similar explanation—although with a few significant differences. He portrayed the process as a peas-ants' revolt centered around a group of Yahwists, who changed their world by striking a blow against a hierarchical and materialist Canaanite establishment. Gottwald attached archaeological evidence, especially the recently discovered small villages in the Central Hill Country, to Mendenhall's original ideas. He saw these sites as the loci of new ideas such as social equality and egalitarian-ism, inspired by small group of Yahwists who did in fact come from Egypt.

Gottwald incorporated and expanded Mendenhall's ideas and developed a more sociological, even Marxist, approach. Yahwist ideology spurred changes in religious and political ideology, which were then reflected in the Israelite lifestyle, even in material culture like domestic architectural forms and pot-tery. Mendenhall was highly critical of Gottwald's Marxist agenda, and he believed that Gottwald had seriously misconstrued Israelite society. Menden-hall rejected the notion of an oppressed class of peasants revolting under the banner of a socialist proletarian revolution rather than one of religious free-dom under Yahweh. Like all explanatory models, the Peasants' Revolt Model was a product of its time (the 1960s and 1970s) and reflected the profound social movements of the day.

Unfortunately, neither Mendenhall nor Gottwald had much experi-ence with archaeology, and this model lacked any clear support from the archaeological record or even from the biblical record. One of Mendenhall's main lines of evidence was the enigmatic term *apiru*—which apparently refers to social outcasts, bandits, or propertyless persons—mentioned repeatedly in Middle and Late Bronze Age Near Eastern and Egyptian texts, especially the Amarna letters. Mendenhall connected this term—which can be alternatively transliterated as *abiru*, *hapiru*, and *habiru*—to the name *ivri* ("Hebrew") found in the Hebrew Bible. Mendenhall thus identified the *apiru* with the early Hebrews of the Hebrew Bible. The implication was that the egalitarian, monotheistic Yahwists rebelled against the hierarchical and oppressive Canaanite polytheistic ideology. Unfortunately, such a direct correlation is not that simple; while some texts describe the *apiru* as brigands, other texts present them as prominent citizens of major city-states—members of the establishment in good standing. Furthermore, any linguistic connection between *apiru* and *ivri* has been completely disabused. Without this connection, the Peasant's Revolt Model became more of a theoretical abstract than anything else.

However, the Peasants' Revolt Model made a valuable and long-overdue contribution to the study of Israelite ethnogenesis. The notion that Israelites could have been insiders—Canaanites—decoupled the biblical narratives from the archaeological data. This gave rise to a new way of analyzing evidence of continuity between the Late Bronze Age and Iron Age I.

Israel Finkelstein developed a fourth model, the "Pastoral Canaanite Model"; it is an "insider" proposal even though it builds on Alt's outsider model of peaceful infiltration. Finkelstein based his proposal on the discoveries he made while surveying the Central Hill Country in the 1980s.

This survey uncovered over 250 sites that Finkelstein came to define as Israelite. The appearance of so many contemporaneous small village sites in the Central Hill Country, an area almost uninhabited in the Late Bronze Age, is compelling. The density

FIGURE 10-7. *Fourteenth-century Amarna letter from Labayu of Shechem to Pharaoh Akhenaten.*

of settlement, the speed with which these villages came into being, and the similarity of each site's organization and material remains suggested that they were the result of a coherent settlement episode.

Finkelstein was also influenced by the French historian Fernand Braudel, a major proponent of the Annales school of historiography. Braudel stressed the importance of looking at history with a long-term perspective, *la longue durée*, and with special attention given to the role of the environment. Like Alt, Finkelstein understood these settlements as the result of the process of Late Bronze Age pastoralists settling down. However, for Finkelstein this wave of settlement in the Central Hill Country was neither something new nor a singular event but part of a cyclical, long-term pattern of settlement and abandonment. The core of Finkelstein's argument was that these Iron Age I settlements were part of a long-term historical process based on social and environmental factors.

Finkelstein's survey data led him to identify three waves of settlement, separated by what he refers to as "intervals of social crisis" (Finkelstein 2007, 79). The earliest wave occurred in the Early Bronze Age I, followed by a second settlement wave in the Middle Bronze Age II–III and a final wave of settlement that began with the small highland villages in the late thirteenth century BCE. For Finkelstein, this last wave was different in that Iron Age I villages expanded in the Iron Age II, leading to the formation of the Israelite state and also the end of the settlement/abandonment cycle. Finkelstein interpreted this long-term pattern as the cyclical shift from sedentary agricultural villages in the settlement waves to pastoralism in crisis periods. Thus, he considered the inhabitants of the Iron I highland settlements as indigenous Canaanites who were neither newcomers bent on conquest nor peasants in revolt.

There are two important criticisms of the Pastoral Canaanite Model. First, the dating of when these sites were occupied and for how long is difficult to determine. Of the 250 villages he identified in his surveys, few have been excavated. A precise chronology of when these sites were occupied and for how long requires excavation. Finkelstein suggests that the earliest sites are located in the eastern part of the Central Hill County before spreading west, but, without the excavation of more sites, this is somewhat speculative.

The second area of concern involves the issue of demography, especially the size of the population in the Central Hill Country and where it came from. Most scholars acknowledge that the Late Bronze Age population of Canaan, and specifically that of the Central Hill Country, declined. By the Iron IIA, in the tenth century BCE, the population of what is now ancient Israel and the region of the Central Hill Country was much larger than it had been earlier in the Late Bronze Age. Based on this general pattern, it is assumed that the population in the Central Hill Country (as seen in the appearance of over 250 villages) expanded during the Iron Age I, and the question is how. Finkelstein believes it was solely through the process of sedentarization of a preexisting pastoral population. Others suggest a movement of sedentary Canaanites to the Central Hill Country or new groups of outsiders augmenting the highland population.

One example of nomads settling down during the Iron I Period is the site Izbeth Sartah. Finkelstein pointed to the earliest phase, built in the shape of a large oval courtyard, and it is similar to Bedouin tent encampments known for more than a century ago. This village plan is representative of early Iron villages in the hill country and indicates the first Israelites were once "pastoral nomads undergoing a profound transformation" (Finkelstein and Silberman 2001, 112).

William Dever has challenged Finkelstein's theory. Little of Izbeth Sartah's oval wall was uncovered; thus, it is implausible to imagine that the site's walls should be defined as a typical Bedouin-like tent encampment. The archaeological remains indicate the site was sedentary and more adapted to agriculture and animal breeding rather than nomads settling down. Moreover, Dever points out that many ancient sites—including large urban tells—are oval or circular and have nothing to do with tent dwellers reestablishing themselves (Dever 2003a, 162–63). Similarly, Lawrence Stager doubts that "tent prototypes led to the shape and design of **pillared houses**." It is more likely that four-room houses evolved from the "changes in family structure" rather than the romantic notions of "early Israelite settlement-tent-dwelling nomads who gradually became sedentarized farmers" (1985, 17). In turn, then, it is more likely that hill country villagers grouped together and shared walls in an enclosed pattern based on defensive and security purposes rather than reflecting a nomadic encampment—the villagers were probably protecting themselves from nomads or bandits. Finally, one can hardly imagine that there were enough seminomads in all of Canaan to account for all the new settlers and villages that exploded in the Iron I hill country.

Moving the Models Forward

Ultimately, these models are reductionist in that they present a binary picture of the Late Bronze II / Iron Age I settlement landscape—juxtaposing small, single-period village settlements in the Central Hill Country (or, more generally, the highlands) that are presumably Israelite against large multiperiod urban tell sites in the lowlands that are presumably Canaanite. These two settlement types are the ends of a spectrum, however, with a large variety of settlement types with distinctive occupational histories in between. This spectrum reveals settlement types ranging from small, short-lived, self-sufficient villages to reoccupied tell sites, large villages, and unusual sites with monumental architecture. Canaanites remained viable on tell sites and in long-lived villages for much of the period. Additionally, there is the ethnogenesis of not only the Israelites but also the Phoenicians and even the Arameans, to say nothing of the way the migration and settlement of the Philistines adds another fluid dimension to the sociocultural landscape.

There is a great deal of substantive change, but it is embedded within a matrix of sociocultural continuity. Major urban centers—such as Hazor, Megiddo, Beth Shean, and others—were destroyed at the end of the Late Bronze Age, although clearly these destructions do not reflect a single episode; rather; they occurred over a period from roughly 1250 to 1150 BCE. Likewise, new villages emerged in the Central Hill Country, and the Philistines, an Aegean-based people, were introduced to the area. But these events should not serve as the only defining attributes of the Late Bronze / Iron Age I transition. It is clear that at least some segment of the Canaanite population lived in villages and continued to do so without significant interruption well into the Iron Age. The existence of Iron Age Canaanites is one of the most obvious but also least explored issues of the Iron Age I. This lack of interruption is critical toward understanding the interplay between ethnic and political designations.

Ultimately, it is important to determine where the majority of the population lived: in the cities or villages. If in fact the rural population is as significant as several scholars suspect, the Late Bronze / Iron I transition must be recast, deemphasizing external agents as vehicles of sudden change and supporting models that stress a more gradual social transition.

Suggestions for Further Reading

For readily accessible discussions of the archaeological and biblical evidence concerning the appearance of ancient Israel, see William G. Dever's *Who Were the Early Israelites and Where Did They Come From?*, the relevant chapters in Israel Finkelstein and Neil A. Silberman's *The Bible Unearthed*, and Elizabeth Bloch-Smith's article "Israelite Ethnicity in the Iron Age I: Archaeology Preserves What is Remembered and What is Forgotten in Israel's History." Avraham Faust's *Israel's Ethnogenesis* is the most recent and an indispensable addition to this literature. Lawrence Stager's "Forging an Identity: The Emergence of Ancient Israel" and Israel Finkelstein's "The Great Transformation: The 'Conquest' of the Highland Frontiers and the Rise of the Territorial States" present the key archaeological information in article-length scholarly synopses. Finkelstein presents his initial argument for cyclical settlement of the Central Hill Country in *The Archaeology of Israelite Settlement*. That is supplemented for other regions by a collection of essays edited by I. Finkelstein and N. Naaman, *From Nomadism to Monarchy*. To complement these works, Elizabeth Bloch-Smith and Beth Alpert-Nakhai provide an extensive overview of Canaanite Iron Age I archaeology in "A Landscape Come to Life: The Iron Age I."

11

LOOKING FOR THE ISRAELITES
The Evidence of the Biblical Text

Paul V. M. Flesher

The archaeological evidence of Canaan from the end of the Late Bronze Age to the end of Iron Age I presented by Professor Dessel provides a good fit with the oldest textual evidence of the Israelites prior to the Davidic monarchy. Judges and 1 Samuel relate stories of rural peoples living in the hill country of Canaan while Canaanites and Philistines occupy the cities in the lowlands, such as the Jezreel and Jordan Valleys and the coastal plain. The early tales feature the Central Hill Country—where archaeology has revealed that hundreds of small settlements suddenly appeared at or before the start of the Iron Age I. From the central hill area, the settlers engaged in conflicts with nearby cities and with peoples on the periphery of their settled area. In the stories, the tribes who fight these battles lack hierarchical leadership, just as the archaeology of the villages shows no indication of social or economic differentiation among their inhabitants.

The books of Judges and 1 Samuel tell stories of charismatic leaders, usually military leaders, who arise to conquer an oppressor by leading a continually changing set of allied tribes and occasionally just a single tribe. These "judges"—a title missing from the books themselves but widely used by modern writers—are neither tribal leaders nor government officials; indeed, there is no political organization above that of the tribes. They instead build their leadership by personal charisma, valiant action, or other means; the book of Judges often states that a judge receives divine blessing or anointing in some way (Judg 4:6; 6:14; 11:29; 13). Judges raise their armies from among the people, using approaches from a straightforward call to arms to techniques designed to shame people into coming, such as cutting up a body and sending the pieces to those being called.

In these tales, tribes make ad hoc alliances for the purposes of battle, usually under the leadership of a judge. The tribes involved differ from story to story, and the impression arises that few set alliances bind them. Some tribes only barely exist; for instance, Judges rarely mentions Judah and never Simeon.

Judges portrays tribal alliances as quite fluid. It is only in the last story, where the tribes unite to attack the tribe of Benjamin, that there is any sense of unity—if that is the right word for tribes attacking one of their own (Judg 20:1-2). In 1 Samuel, tribes as tribes largely go unnamed until Saul musters for a battle, and the soldiers of "Judah" are cited separately from those of "Israel" (1 Sam 11:8). Indeed, despite Saul's efforts to unite the tribes, the uncertainty of tribal alliances remains until David becomes king of Israel; before then, we even see David (and Judah?) allying with the Philistine king of Gath against the tribes of Israel (as Baruch Halpern emphasizes in chapter 13).

Three biblical books comprise the textual evidence for Iron Age I, which we shall call the "tribal period": Joshua, Judges, and 1 Samuel. These books—certainly Judges and 1 Samuel—contain stories that may have roots in the tribal period. While they may or may not speak about historical events—we lack corroborating evidence—they apparently reflect the time's social and cultural circumstances. The book of Ruth is also set in the tribal period, but its romantic tale comes neither from the tribal nor the monarchical period but from the postexilic era, more than half a millennium later.

This chapter will begin by describing how Joshua, Judges, and 1 Samuel were composed as part of the Deuteronomistic History and how that process allows us to analyze the books to ascertain the perspective of the Deuteronomistic Historian as well as the social and cultural world of its earliest stories of the Israelite tribes. The main goal will then be to work out the tribes and their territories as well as the dynamics of their relationships (or lack thereof). The climax of this section will be an analysis of the ancient poem in Judges 5 for what it reveals about the tribes and their formation. This will be followed by special attention to the place of the Jezreel Valley and of Hazor during Iron I. Finally, it will conclude with discussions of Benjamin as a northern tribe and of the absence of Judah until late in the tribal period. Although the discussion will be grounded in the texts, it will bring in archaeological evidence as relevant.

The Deuteronomistic History: A Patchwork Quilt of Tales

The relevant biblical books for the period of settlement in the two and a half centuries prior to David are Joshua, Judges, and 1 Samuel. These three books constitute the first half of a series of works called the Deuteronomistic History (DH). The remaining books of the series are 2 Samuel, 1 Kings, and 2 Kings. The six books of the DH took shape in the court of King Josiah of Judah, 640–609 BCE; that is, the work's composition and editing took place some four hundred to six hundred years after the events described in them would have happened.

The literary and historical decipherment of the DH was done by Martin Noth in the first half of the twentieth century. While it has undergone extensive debate and revision in the decades since its initial formulation, the general concept has stood the test of time, in part because of its simplicity. In broad terms, Noth claims the DH was composed in four stages. In stage one, the stories now found in these books were formulated and told orally. In stage two, decades or centuries later, these narratives were written down. Some scholars argue this happened during the reign of King Hezekiah (715–687 BCE), when stories were brought to Jerusalem by refugees from the Assyrian destruction of the Northern Kingdom of Israel in 722 BCE. In stage three, during Josiah's rule, these stories were edited into books close to the form in which we now find them, probably after 622 BCE. The editor who accomplished this task, whether working alone or with coeditors, is known as the Deuteronomistic Historian. In the fourth stage, after the Babylonian destruction of Jerusalem and the exile of many of its residents—and perhaps even after their descendants' return—the DH received its final form, bringing the historical sequence down into the sixth century BCE. Only minor changes were introduced in this stage, the largest being the addition of 2 Kings 23:31 to 25:30, which concerns events after Josiah's death.

The resultant DH is thus like a patchwork quilt and was created largely by the Deuteronomic Historian of Josiah's time. He took the stories from the past and edited them into the six books, stitching them together with his own introductory and concluding observations so that they conveyed the message he intended. The "literary quilt" was sewn from the "patches of stories" that were complete before he started. So while the completed quilt of the DH as a whole presents the interests of Josiah's Deuteronomistic Historian, the patches—the earlier tales—reveal social, religious, and political conditions of an earlier period.

While few academic historians think the tales related in Judges and Samuel are contemporary with their events, many narratives were composed not too long after the events described. We can analyze them and distinguish their early perspective from that of the later Deuteronomic Historian who lived centuries later. Of course, we do not know the precise date when any of the stories were first formulated, but the social and religious circumstances of the tales found in Judges and 1 Samuel seem to reflect a period that had never known an organized monarchy. By contrast, at least half of the book of Joshua (Josh 12–23) consists of lists of locations contemporary to the late monarchical period rather than the tribal period. Furthermore, as J. P. Dessel indicated in chapter 10, the sites of Jericho and Ai were unoccupied at the time that Joshua's Israelites would have arrived, so these tales likewise must reflect a later century, indicating that the book itself probably comes mostly from Josiah's time and contains little early material—unlike Judges and 1 Samuel.

So the stories useful for comparison with the archaeological data are the early tales in Judges and 1 Samuel, and not the material in Joshua. Similarly, the work of the Deuteronomistic editor who sewed together the earlier patches—the stories—that appear in the introductions and conclusions to those stories can be separated from the tales themselves. The remaining stories will then be studied not as revealing history—the course of past events—but rather as evidence for social circumstances and knowledge during the Iron Age I.

Joshua as the Climax of the Torah

The Deuteronomistic Historian composed the book of Joshua in part as the conclusion and climax to the exodus story contained in Exodus, Leviticus, Numbers, and Deuteronomy. With Moses' death, Joshua took over leadership and led Israel to fight and defeat the peoples living in the land of Canaan.

Joshua is thus peopled with the same social groups as the Torah's exodus narrative and reiterates the same territorial divisions. Just as the exodus tale concerns thirteen tribes that are designated as twelve, so Joshua describes the thirteen tribes as twelve—and follows Numbers' practice of naming tribes after the sons and grandsons of Jacob found in Genesis. Moreover, in Joshua, as in the previous four books, the Israelites are called *benei yisrael*, "children of Israel." Finally, in Numbers 32, Moses gave to the tribes of Reuben, Gad, and half of Manasseh land on the east side of the Jordan River. The book of Joshua twice mentions that gift to explain why these tribes did not receive land on the river's west side (Josh 13:8-31; 22:1-9).

The book of Joshua thus portrays the people Israel in the same civil organization seen in the rest of the exodus tale. The twelve/thirteen tribes are unified under the leadership of one man: Moses in the Torah and, in this book, Joshua. Joshua leads them in the conquest of the land of Canaan, and all Israel follows. Once the conquest is finished, Joshua parcels out the land. The tribes do not just randomly take it; it is assigned by the leadership.

The literary organization of the land's distribution is given in Joshua 13–19 in three sections; that is, it comes from three separate sources. Judah is treated in Joshua 14–15, Ephraim and Manasseh in Joshua 16–17, while all the others appear in Joshua 18–19. (Those from the east side of the Jordan were mentioned in Josh 13.) Prominence is given to Judah, although Ephraim and Manasseh take second priority. These sources reflect not Iron Age I but the period of the two kingdoms following Solomon's death, Iron IIB or later. So if we are to find any textual evidence for Israel during Iron I, before David became king, it can be found only in the stories of Judges and 1 Samuel. Joshua's top-down view of the boundaries and divisions of the land of Israel reflects the seventh century BCE, not the eleventh century. In the eleventh century, not only are the tribal locations much less certain, but it is also unclear what tribes work together and get along.

The Earliest Stories in Judges and 1 Samuel 1–15

If the book of Joshua represents the view of the Deuteronomistic Historian, then we can use it to identify the Deuteronomistic Historian's stitching in the quilt of Judges and 1 Samuel. The editorial material that the Deuteronomistic Historian adds into these two books, usually as introduction and conclusions to longer stories, follows Joshua's emphases in three specific ways. First, the Deuteronomistic Historian knows that there are thirteen tribes, which he insists on referring to as twelve. The stories of Judges do not know a consistent number of allied tribes, and they sometimes use different names for them, as we shall see below. Second, the editor's primary interest is in the unified People of Israel, what the Hebrew text calls the *benei yisrael*, "children of Israel." In the book of Judges, for example, when the editor introduces or concludes a tale about a tribe or several tribes, he calls them "children of Israel." Third, the Deuteronomistic editor sometimes reveals knowledge of events, people, or conditions during the later centuries of the monarchical period.

In an archaeological excavation, one must remove the latest layers to reveal the remains of the earlier periods. The same principle applies to literary works. Now that we can identify the elements of the books' final stages—that of the Deuteronomistic Historian—we can separate them out and look only at the earliest stories and other material. While we cannot use these tales to write a history of *events* during the premonarchic period of Iron I, we can use them to get a sense of the *social circumstances* during that time.

There are eight stories in Judges, plus the poem in Judges 5 that constitutes not only the oldest literary element in the book but also one of the oldest literary works of the Hebrew Bible. And, although the book identifies thirteen leaders, only six of them receive a story: judges Ehud (Judg 3:12-30), Deborah (Judg 4, and the poem in Judg 5), Gideon (Judg 6–8), Jephthah (Judg 11–12), and Samson (Judg 13–16)—plus the nonjudge Abimelech (Judg 9). (See Figure 11-1.) There are two stories without judges at the end of the book: Judges 17–18 are about the migration of the tribe Dan to the north, and Judges 19–21 are about the rape and murder done by the men of Gibeah in Benjamin and then, ultimately, the punishment of the entire tribe of Benjamin. These tales were composed independent of each other, but the Deuteronomistic editor placed them together and provided a literary context—an introduction and conclusion—to each one. Even where two passages refer to the same event as at Judges 4 and Judges 5, they clearly differ and function independently.

FIGURE 11-1. ORGANIZATION OF THE BOOK OF JUDGES

A. List of cities conquered and not conquered	Judg 1
B. Judges' theodicy	Judg 2
C. List and tales of Judges and leaders	Judg 3–16
1. Ehud	Judg 3:12-30
2. Deborah	Judg 4–5
3. Gideon	Judg 6–8
4. Abimelech	Judg 9
5. Jephthah	Judg 11–12
6. Samson	Judg 13–16
D. Tales of Israel's decline	Judg 17–21
1. Tribe of Dan migrates north	Judg 17–18
2. Punishment of tribe of Benjamin for rape	Judg 19–21

The six tales of leaders are introduced by Judges 2, which provides a theodicy explaining why judges needed to rescue the people Israel. It is a cyclical response to Israel's apostasy. The cycle is this: (1) the Israelites worship other gods, (2) Yahweh punishes them by allowing non-Israelites to oppress them, (3) the Israelites turn back to God, and (4) God sends a judge to deliver them. Repeat. The stories in Judges exemplify this cycle. In each case, the Deuteronomistic Historian provides a brief introduction relating steps 1 to 3 (e.g., Judg 3:12-15) and then tells an earlier tale of a judge accomplishing step 4 (e.g., Judg 3:16-30).

When we look at 1 Samuel 1–15, which deals with the rise and fall of King Saul, this pattern of editing clearly continues: it consists of nine individual tales stitched together (see Figure 11-2). Each of these circulated independently before being included in the book. That helps account for the two stories of Saul's appointment as king. The poetic Song of Hannah in the second chapter is the oldest. As in Judges, the Deuteronomistic Historian took each independent story and, to continue the quilt analogy, provided literary stitching to connect the narrative patches into a larger work.

Identifying the Tribal and Territorial Core

Both Judges and 1 Samuel 1–15 feature the so-called Tribes of Rachel—those named after her son Benjamin and her grandsons Ephraim and Manasseh

FIGURE 11-2. *Organization of 1 Samuel 1–15*

A. Rise of Samuel	1 Sam 1–3
B. Battle of Ebenezer and loss of the Ark	1 Sam 4–7
C. Samuel and God talk about kingship	1 Sam 8
D. First appointment of Saul as king	1 Sam 9–10
E. Saul's battle for Jabesh-Gilead	1 Sam 11
F. Second appointment of Saul as king	1 Sam 12
G. Saul fights Philistines at Michmash	1 Sam 13
H. Saul's son Jonathan and the battle at Gibeah	1 Sam 14
I. Saul's defeat of the Amalekites	1 Sam 15

(through her son Joseph)—and their interaction with tribes further north and east. These three tribes control the territory from south of the Jezreel Valley to the hills of Benjamin, the northern part of the Central Hill Country. To the north, the three core tribes interact with the tribes of Naphtali, Issachar, Zebulon, and Asher, while to the east the main tribe is called Gilead—although sometimes referred to as Manasseh. The tribe of Judah and its territory, despite its later importance, appears rarely and never in an important role in Judges or in 1 Samuel 1–15. In the opening chapters of 1 Samuel, Judah is absent. It is only in 1 Samuel 11:8 and 15:4, when Saul musters an army, that Judah is mentioned. The location of the tribes participating in the stories in Judges and 1 Samuel is important, for they provide comparison with the archaeological picture.

The clearest indication of the core area—the middle part of the Central Hill Country—comes in the location of shrines important to the tribes. The DH speaks of eight different shrines where Israelites assembled to worship during this time. From north to south, these are Mount Ebal and Mount Gerizim (Manasseh), Shechem (Manasseh), Shiloh (Ephraim), Bethel (Ephraim), and Gilgal, Mizpah, and Ramah (Benjamin). These religious shrines are located in the northern area of the central hills, the tribal areas assigned to Benjamin, Ephraim, and Manasseh.

The books of Judges and 1 Samuel evidence fourteen judges who wield power prior to the rise of King Saul. If we include Abimelech, there are fifteen leaders.

FIGURE 11-3. *The Judges*

Judge	Tribe	Town/Territory	Verses
Othniel	Judah	Hebron?	Judg 3:7-11
Ehud	Benjamin	?	Judg 3:12-30
Shamgar	?	?	Judg 3:31
Deborah	Ephraim	near Bethel	Judg 4–5
Gideon	Abiezer (Manasseh)	Ophrah	Judg 6–8
Abimelech	Manasseh?	Shechem	Judg 9
Tola	Issachar	Shamir in Ephraim	Judg 10:1-2
Jair	Gilead (Manasseh)	Kamon	Judg 10:3-5
Jephthah	Gilead (Manasseh)	Gilead	Judg 10:6-12:7
Ibzan	Zebulon	Bethlehem (Josh 19:15)	Judg 12:8-10
Elon	Zebulun	Aijalon	Judg 12:11-12
Abdon	Ephraim	Pirathon	Judg 12:13-15
Samson	Dan	Timnah	Judg 13–16
Eli	?	Shiloh in Ephraim	1 Sam 1–4
Samuel	Ephraim	Ramah	1 Sam 1–3, 7–8, etc.

There is no immediately obvious pattern indicating which tribes produce judges. Seven tribes have one or two judges, while Ephraim produces three. There are no judges from Reuben, Simeon, Gad, Asher, or Levi.

If we look more closely, however, a pattern emerges. The northern part of the Central Hill Country plays a key role. Six of the fifteen leaders belong to one of the three Rachel tribes located there: Ephraim, Manasseh, and Benjamin. Deborah, Samuel, and Abdon belong to Ephraim; Gideon and Abimelech come from Manasseh; and Ehud belongs to Benjamin. Two more judges make Ephraim's territory their base of operation: Tola and Eli. That means eight—more than half—of the judges are active in this area. In addition, five of the six tales told about judges/leaders involve one of the three core tribes. The northern part of the Central Hill Country and its three tribes thus dominate the narratives of Judges and 1 Samuel 1–15.

Two other areas produce multiple judges. First, Gilead on the east side of the Jordan River produces two: Jair and Jephthah. Jephthah is important enough to receive a two-chapter story in Judges. Second, three judges came

MAP 11-1. *This map shows the location of the Israelite shrines and the towns and tribes associated with individual judges. These indicate the importance of the northern area of the Central Hill Country. Two other tribal areas often worked with judges: Galilee and Gilead. The latter joined with the central region to become the main territory of Saul's kingdom.*

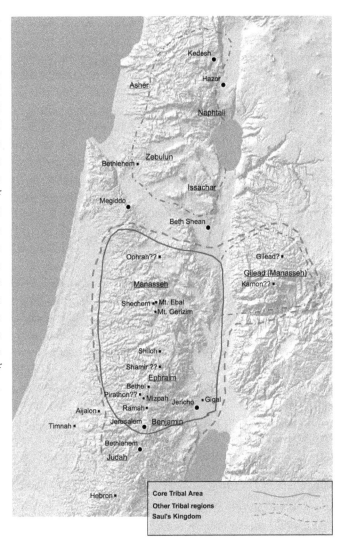

from Upper Galilee: Ibzan, Tola, and Elon, although Elon made his career in the territory of Ephraim. In addition, Deborah's general, Barak, came from Naphtali. By contrast, the tribal area of Judah produced only one judge—Othniel, Caleb's brother—who apparently came from Hebron.

The tribal affiliation and location of judges roughly parallels the most dense areas of the new highland settlements that appeared between 1250 and 1150 BCE. This is a clear result of the archaeological surveys carried in the Central Hill Country (Finkelstein 1988a; Finkelstein and Silberman 2001, 113–18; Stager 2001, 95–96; Dever 2003a, 91–100). From the surveys conducted in these regions, it is clear that the area of Ephraim and Manasseh, and even Benjamin, become heavily settled early on. Both the region of Upper Galilee and the upland territory on the east side of the Jordan River—roughly the area of Gilead—were likewise populated densely in the decades following 1250. (See Map 10-1.) By contrast, the archaeological evidence about the small villages at the start of Iron I places only a few in the hills south of Benjamin— that is, in the region of Judah. This has been documented in the surveys by Avi Ofer, who found few new sites in the Judean Hills at the start of Iron I. It is not until the start of Iron II that Judah experienced significant growth in the number of villages (Ofer 1994, 92–121). Similarly, the Beer Sheva region south of the Judean Hills began with few residents and then gradually increased the number of settlements from the thirteenth to the eleventh centuries. At the start of the tenth century, civilian settlements gave way to military forts (Herzog 1994, 122–49; Finkelstein and Naaman 1994).

Thus, the reason for the focus in Judges and 1 Samuel 1–15 on the tribes whose territories were from Benjamin northward and northeastward reflects the historical reality of the time. These are the areas where settlement occurred. There simply were too few people south of Benjamin for that area to be important. Judges presents not a northern perspective that excludes the south but one shaped by population patterns. The southern population was simply not there to be included. Furthermore, the Deuteronomistic Historian was perfectly capable of injecting his own pro-Judah views. For example, Judah is the leading tribe of conquest in the lists of cities in Judges 1. And, in that chapter, Judah is the only tribe that does not permit non-Israelites to live in the cities they conquer—unlike the other tribes mentioned. If the Deuteronomistic Historian had sensed that Judah was being treated unfairly or inaccurately in the tales of Judges, he could have corrected or rebalanced his work.

What Tribes Do Judges Lead?

If one read only the Deuteronomistic Historian's transitional introductions and conclusions to each of the six judge stories he tells in Judges, one would think that all Israel joins and fights under their leadership. But a closer look at the tribes that actually populate each story indicates nothing could be further from the truth. In three of the stories, the judges muster fighters from the tribes themselves; they do not work through the tribal structure by calling on a tribal chief or elder to organize an army. Sometimes they muster only a single tribe, and at other times they bring together a coalition. The brief story of Ehud is a case in point (Judg 3:12-30). Ehud's liberation of Israel from Moab begins with Ehud using a subterfuge to enter the Moabite palace and slay the king. Ehud then rushes back across the Jordan into Ephraim, sounds a trumpet, and calls together the Ephraimites and leads them in an attack against Moab.

Samson (Judg 13–16) of course leads no one; he is a one-man destruction engine and a tragic figure—selected by God to liberate his people but more dedicated to chasing Philistine women than fulfilling his destiny. Abimelech (Judg 9)—the son of Gideon by a prostitute rather than one of his wives—leads the inhabitants of Shechem, but the only army he raises is a group of "worthless [lit. 'empty'] and reckless fellows" (Judg 9:4) whom he uses to slaughter his seventy half-brothers before killing the Israelites(?) of Shechem when they rebel against him.

Jephthah (Judg 11–12) begins more like Abimelech than Ehud. He too was a prostitute's son and unwelcome at his deceased father's home in in Gilead. He left and gathered together a band of "outlaws" (Judg 11:3 NRSV; lit. "empty men") and raided with them. When the Ammonites attacked Gilead, Jephthah was the only warrior and military leader the elders knew, so they prevailed upon him to lead their defense. In Judges 11, it seems that Jephthah led soldiers only from the tribe of Gilead and did not attempt to muster more from neighboring tribes. But in Judges 12, an army comes from Ephraim demanding to know why Jephthah did not call them to the battle. Jephthah counters that he did summon them, but they did not come (Judg 12:1-3). The dispute ends in a battle between the two forces, which the Gileadites win. The Jephthah tale thus exemplifies what the editor expected: a judge should use his or her own tribe but build on that by summoning soldiers from nearby tribes as well.

The previous tale of Gideon provides both an example of the way a judge should do a muster and an example of what happens when a tribe fails in its duty. When Gideon fights a coalition of Midianites, Amalekites, and other peoples living on the east side of the Jordan, he sounds a trumpet and calls out his clan, the Abiezerites of Manasseh, to follow him. He then sends messages to summon warriors from Manasseh, as well as the tribes of Asher, Zebulun, and Naphtali, which border Manasseh on the north (Judg 6:33-35). After Gideon engages the enemy and triumphs over them, the Midianites and their coalition flee toward Ephraim, Manasseh's southern neighbor. Gideon calls out that tribe's warriors, and they kill two of the enemies' leaders (Judg 7:24-25). The Midianites then run into the territory of Gad, and Gideon asks the Gadite cities of Succoth and Penuel for help. They refuse and are later punished. There are two points here. First, Gideon forms a coalition of five nearby tribes to fight the Midianite coalition. Second, punishment may follow if a tribe refuses the call, especially if it was counted as a fellow tribe. Judges' theodicy from its second chapter's rhetoric expects that all fights are against foreign oppressors, but, at least three times, tribes battle other tribes that the Deuteronomistic editor considers Israelite: Jephthah's fight against Ephraim, Gideon's punishment of Gad, and later, the punishment of Benjamin (Judg 19–21).

The Tribes Who Fought with Deborah

The ancient poem in Judges 5 telling the earliest version of the battle led by the judge Deborah and the general Barak reinforces the notion of a core set of tribes—the Rachel tribes—interacting with an associated group of tribes. This associated group comes from the north. Judges 5 is the oldest passage in Judges and preserves an archaic form of Hebrew earlier than most elements of the DH. This makes it valuable evidence for the social circumstances in the premonarchical period.

The song in Judges 5 praises the tribes that took part in the battle and condemns those who did not respond to the muster. The tribes that responded to the summons and took part in the battle were Ephraim, Benjamin, Machir, Zebulun, Issachar, and Naphtali. These represent the core area of Benjamin, Ephraim, and Manasseh, for Machir is an early designation of Manasseh (more on this below). The tribes that the poem condemns explicitly for failing to show up were Reuben, Gilead, Dan, Asher, and Meroz. Apparently, they did not consider themselves sufficiently tied to the other tribes to support them in their struggle. It is important to differentiate the two levels of the text's editing here. The Deuteronomistic Historian's introduction presenting this tale as about "Israel" (Judg 4:1) portrays the failure of these tribes to join in the fight as despicable, for they are letting the other tribes fight for their benefit. At the level of the story itself, which does not expect the participation of soldiers from all Israelite tribes, this is less of a problem. To be sure, the poem shames them for not showing up, but it castigates them as individual tribes, not as members of the people Israel (C. Meyers 1983, 55–57).

Why might the tribes have failed to come? The poem identifies Gilead as being beyond the Jordan River, which would also account for Reuben, further south on the river's east side. Two other tribes had territories located by the sea, according to both the song and Joshua 19, but failed to drive out the occupants: Dan and Asher. These circumstances made them either difficult to muster or more likely to turn down a muster since they had a closer relationship with non-Israelite peoples.

Several tribes go unmentioned in Judges 5. They are not shamed for failing to appear; the poem simply does not refer to them. This indicates either that they were not associated with the tribes who fought or that they had not yet coalesced into tribes themselves. The missing tribes are Judah, Simeon, Levi, and Gad (see Mayes 1973a, 166–68). Given the later importance of Judah as a kingdom, this is rather surprising, but it fits with the archaeological evidence of Judah having a low population density during most of Iron I. Furthermore, Simeon's territory is placed within Judah's (Josh 19:1), so this observation applies to it as well. It is not until the end of Iron I that the population of the area assigned to these tribes begins to rise. Finally, even in Joshua, Levi is assigned not territory but only scattered cities—a situation that would hinder tribal formation. The tribe of Gad, as we saw in the discussion of Gideon, does not seem to associate itself with the other tribes of Israel.

The variability of the tribal character in Judges 5 is revealed by two names that are not later tribal names: Gilead and Machir. The use of these names and the absence of the name Manasseh suggests an early fluidity in the formation of tribes. Joshua 13–19 cites the thirteen tribal names with which we are familiar and gives the locations in which the tribes are settled by clan. In this later text, Joshua 17:1-2 treats Machir and Gilead as clans within Manasseh. Judges 5 captures an earlier stage in the formation of the tribe of Manasseh, before these two clans have united. The situation with the name of Meroz is probably similar. It is otherwise unknown, but it may be a clan name that later disappears.

So the earliest tales in Judges—as opposed to the editorial layer of the Deuteronomistic Historian—present a fluid and changing association of rural tribes that dwell in the territory ranging from Benjamin north and east. They have loose ties of military and religion but nothing organized above the tribal level. Indeed, some tribes have not yet formed a stable identity, and others do not yet exist. The notion of a unified confederation of twelve/thirteen tribes is part of the story of the rise of the monarchy/monarchies, not their premonarchical history.

Before leaving this topic, we should say something about Martin Noth's 1930s explanation of the emergence of Israel in Canaan as an amphictyony—a Greek concept—in which a group of tribes joined in worship at central shrine (Noth 1960, 85–109). It was not included in the four models presented earlier in chapter 10, because it has no interest in archaeology; indeed, as explained in chapter 2, biblical archaeology saw its goal, in part, as combating what it saw as Noth's dissection of the biblical text.

In Noth's proposal, the people Israel were organized by the covenant ceremony appearing in Joshua 24, which took place early in the tribal period. This event established Israel as an amphictyony around a central shrine—identified as by some as Shechem, Bethel, and/or Gilgal (Noth 1960, 93–95). Noth argued that the sources for the distribution of the land of Canaan in Joshua 13–21 derived from a time after this unifying event but before the formation of the monarchy.

Prior to this covenant ceremony, the tribes that would constitute Israel were independent, unrelated, and shaped by different historical experiences that they remembered in orally told stories. After unification, Noth held, some tribal tales were forgotten, but others came to be applied to the amphictyony as a whole—that is, to the people Israel. Thus, the narrative of the entire exodus experience—from Egypt to Sinai to the forty-year wandering to the conquest—originally consisted of different tales known to different tribes; after the unification, these were melded into a single tale that supposedly happened to the single set of ancestors now believed to be shared by all Israel.

After decades of scholarly analysis, modification, and debate, Noth's Amphictyony Model has been largely rejected like the models discussed earlier in chapter 10 (Mayes 1973b; De Geus 1976). Most of Joshua's sources are considered to be from the monarchic period, many from the time of King Josiah. Rather than tribal unification coming early in the tribal period, it clearly comes late, perhaps not before David's kingship. However, some of Noth's ideas remain useful and have been taken up into other explanations of the appearance of ancient Israel in Canaan.

Hazor and the Jezreel Valley in Judges

The poem in Judges 5 is significantly older than the prose tale of the battle in Judges 4. According to the poem, the tribes fight against the Canaanite kings of Megiddo and Taanach, cities that are situated along the western edge of the Jezreel Valley. According to the poem, the battle took place along the Kishon River, which runs from the southeast to the northwest through the valley, out from the two cities.

Oddly, the later story in Judges 4 makes Hazor into the enemy, which it portrays as the "king of Canaan." Since Barak belongs to the tribe of Naphtali, this makes sense because Hazor is situated in Naphtali's territory (Josh 19:21-26). Barak mustered an army from Naphtali and Zebulon at Kedesh in Naphtali (Judg 4:10), up the mountain north of Hazor and well located for an attack on Hazor—an attack that would entail the army coming down the mountainside to strike at the city. But then the story moves the action to Mount Tabor (an action not part of the poem in Judges 5), a mountain to the south and well situated for an attack on the Jezreel Valley but not for an attack on Hazor. The army comes down from Tabor and fights along the Kishon River, near the enemy general Sisera's town of Harosheth-hagoiim. This makes no military sense; there is no reason to have a battle between two cities—Kedesh and Hazor—in the territories of cities dozens of miles away. Ephraim Stern (1993, 860) argues that the Kedesh referred to lies in the hills west of the Jezreel Valley. Certainly, a confusion of place-names here might explain why Joshua 4 combined an attack on Hazor with a battle in the Jezreel Valley. To understand these two more fully, we shall discuss the Jezreel Valley and Hazor separately.

Deborah and Barak's poem in Judges 5 implies the defeat of Megiddo and Taanach, two ancient cities on the west side of the Jezreel Valley. This battle takes place after the Israelite tribes have settled in the region rather than during the settlement process itself. The residents of Megiddo and Taanach at this time are Canaanites, not Israelites. This should not be a surprise since both Joshua (17:11-12, 16-18) and Judges (1:27) indicate that these cities had not been conquered. Only the list in Joshua 12 (at v. 21) states they were conquered. But this list comes from the period of the monarchy since it also indicates that Jerusalem was conquered—which did not happen until David took it over at the start of his kingship.

The important west-east trade route from the Mediterranean coast to the Jordan Valley runs through the Jezreel Valley. The route begins at Dor on the Mediterranean coast and goes eastward up one of two narrow valleys in the southern end of the Mount Carmel range. These roads cross the Jezreel Valley near Megiddo and Taanach, join, and continue to Beth Shean in the Jordan Valley. Since neither Dor nor Beth Shean was conquered by the Israelites (Josh 17:11-12 and Judg 1:27), this valuable, revenue-producing trade route remained outside Israelite hands well into Iron I (cf. Mayes 1973a, 168–69).

The archaeological record throws an interesting light on this observation. Neither Dor nor Beth Shean came under Israelite control during Iron I, but Taanach and Megiddo were destroyed during the mid- to late twelfth century BCE. Taanach was an unwalled village at the time and was not rebuilt until Iron II. Megiddo suffered massive destruction but was rebuilt in the eleventh century BCE, apparently by Canaanites. So although fighting occurred at a time comparable to the battle referred to in Judges 4 and 5, there is no indication of Israelite conquest. Israelites neither settled at Taanach or Megiddo at the end of the twelfth century or during the eleventh century nor gained control of the trade route.

With regard to Hazor, the DH mentions Hazor in connection with two battles: Judges 4 and Joshua 11:1-15. The Joshua narrative tells of a battle led by Joshua against the king of Hazor—one Jabin, as in Judges 4:2—and kings of other cities in Galilee and elsewhere. Joshua and the Israelite army defeated them and burned Hazor to the ground. That Hazor remained under Israelite control is implied by Joshua 12:19 and 19:36. Nor does Judges 1 mention it as a place the Israelites failed to conquer. The archaeological evidence concerning Hazor indicates that it was destroyed in the latter half of the thirteenth century BCE (Dever 2003a, 67; Yadin 1975, 145), a date appropriate to the time of Joshua and contemporary with the sudden increase in small highland villages. The archaeological remains indicate that Hazor was not resettled except for a small cluster of huts on the area of the former upper city (Yadin and Ben-Tor 1993, 600–601) until Iron II. The archaeology indicates that there was no city at Hazor during Iron I, and thus the inclusion of it in Judges 4 is incorrect (Yadin 1975, 275).

Benjamin between Israel in the North and Judah in the South

The books of Judges and 1 Samuel make it clear that Benjamin is tied to the north and to the northern tribes. It is part of the core tribal area that consists of the northern section of the Central Hill Country, where it, Ephraim, and Manasseh are located. It participates—as supplying either a judge or soldiers—in many battles narrated in Judges and 1 Samuel and is the location of three shared Israelite shrines. And, just to be clear, all of the tribes mentioned in association with Benjamin are in the north. Judah is never linked to Benjamin in the book of Judges.

Judah is not even in the running; it is almost out of the picture, for Judges mentions Judah just three times: first, the judge Othniel, who lives in the Judahite city of Hebron (Judg 3:9-11); second, the concubine raped by the Benjaminites in Judges' final story comes from Bethlehem in Judah (Judg 19:1-2); third, when the assembled tribes decide to attack Benjamin for their crime, Judah is chosen to lead the attack (Judg 20:18), probably because of the dead woman's origin.

It is also worth noting that Saul, Israel's first king, is from Benjamin. His kingdom, as Israel Finkelstein has detailed, extends north from Benjamin to the southern end of the Jezreel Valley and then east into Gilead (Finkelstein 2013, 47–58). It may go south into Judah, but not very far. In fact, when Saul's jealousy leads him to chase David, David hides out in the wild places of Judah. Apart from Hebron, it seems that Judah is only lightly settled at this time (on the cusp of Iron I and Iron II). Furthermore, although 1 Samuel indicates that Saul includes Judah among his followers, the book treats Judah as separate from Israel before the rise of David. When Saul musters men for a battle, 1 Samuel treats Judah separately from Israel. In 1 Samuel 11:8, the muster is numbered as "those from Israel were three hundred thousand and those from Judah seventy thousand." Similarly, 1 Samuel 15:4 reads, "So Saul summoned the people, and numbered them in Telaim, two hundred thousand foot soldiers, and ten thousand soldiers of Judah." In both places, Judah is treated separately from Israel and thus separately from Benjamin.

However, the book of Joshua provides a different picture, for it links the conquest of Benjamin in Joshua 1–9 with the conquest of Judah in Joshua 10, implying a close tie between those two tribes. If we consider the time at which the book of Joshua was created—that is, during the time of the two kingdoms when tribal lands of Benjamin and Judah constitute the sole territory of the Southern Kingdom of Judah—it cannot be accidental that Joshua links the conquest of Benjamin and Judah. Following them, the attack of Joshua 11 on Hazor seems out of place; the conquest of Ephraim and Manasseh is missing. Perhaps the Hazor battle should be seen as an independent event? Perhaps

Joshua 1–10 comprised a Judahite slight against the core tribes of the Northern Kingdom? Whatever the answer, Joshua 1–10 was composed as the story of the conquest of the (post-Solomonic) Kingdom of Judah, with Joshua 11 and the list in Joshua 12 tacked on to imply a larger conquest.

Conclusion

In the end, by carefully analyzing the DH, we can see that it provides two views of early Israel. The first view is easily seen, for it is provided by the editor, the Deuteronomistic Historian. He uses the book of Joshua and repeated editorial remarks and strategies in the books of Judges and 1 Samuel to present the people Israel's occupation of the land as according to God's plan following the exodus from Egypt. The Deuteronomistic Historian's editing uses Judges to show how Israel frequently falls away to follow other Gods. They are conquered by outside powers, from whom a judge liberates them after they begin worshipping Yahweh again. This theological condemnation extends throughout Judges and into 1 Samuel. Indeed, it is not until David reunites all the tribes in 2 Samuel that the people Israel return to the relationship with God they had under Moses and Joshua. This is a theological portrayal that comes from the time of King Josiah, who used the DH to portray himself as the inheritor of David and Solomon and as the first king to lead the pure worship of Yahweh.

The second view lies within the work of the Deuteronomistic Historian, for he did not write the entire work himself but instead used stories and other sources that already existed. Many of the stories in Judges and 1 Samuel had been written long before he started his work, and he included them with only minor editorial changes. From these, it becomes clear that the people identified by the later editor as Israel are actually tribal-based or clan-based associations of people in the Central Hill Country and in the hills east of the Jordan Valley who may have been originally related by contiguous location rather than any other connection. Just as the archaeology indicates the rise of many small villages in this area at the start of Iron 1, the stories suggest a not-quite established character of these peoples, in keeping with the fluid nature of new social formations.

The social picture given by these tales matches the Iron 1 archaeological situation, in that there is little social organization and, apart from the occasional rise of a judge, no government or leadership above that of the tribes. The relationships among the tribes are fluid, apparently changing from event to event. But there seems to be a common core of tribal territory—that of Ephraim, Manasseh, and Benjamin—to which the other tribes relate, whether these are north of the Jezreel Valley or east of the Jordan Valley in Gilead. Within the core area are located all the religious shrines shared by these tribes.

This seems to be the situation throughout Iron I, the tribal period of roughly 1200 to 1000 BCE—down to and including Saul's "kingdom."

The tribe of Judah (as well as that of Simeon) is largely absent from the tales of Judges and 1 Samuel. From the archaeological perspective, this is not surprising, for the population rise in the region of Judah did not keep pace with that from Benjamin northward and eastward. Indeed, it lagged by a century or more. So, at the time of these tales, Judah did not exist because it lacked the population to be involved. It is only at the end of Iron 1, the end of the tribal period, that Judah has sufficient population to become important. (Perhaps this late population rise came from Canaanites fleeing the Philistine invasion. See the next chapter.) And then, of course, with the rise of David in 2 Samuel, Judah becomes the leader of the united tribes and the driving force in the formation of the nation. The book of Joshua reflects this later situation.

In the end, we see two different views of the formation of the people Israel in the DH. On the one hand, the evidence from the earliest stories is that the tribes or clans in rural Canaan acted separately or formed alliances in accordance with their interests. These shifted over time. We lack sufficient data to determine whether these alliances grew in number over time (with perhaps Saul bringing together the largest number of tribes) or whether "unification" did not happen until David imposed it by force of arms. On the other hand, the Deuteronomistic Historian presents the unity of the people Israel as being formed at the beginning. Joshua led the twelve/thirteen tribes in the conquest of the land of Canaan and then parceled out the land to them. The book of Joshua ends with Joshua leading a covenant ceremony at Shechem to emphasize that the people Israel were united in their worship of Yahweh from the beginning.

Suggestions for Further Reading

These are in addition to the readings suggested for chapter 10. For the delineation of the DH by Martin Noth, it is best to go directly to the source. His 1943 ideas were translated into English as *The Deuteronomistic History* in 1981. Noth's proposal that early Israel should be understood as an amphictyony is most easily found in English in his *The History of Israel* (1960, 85–109). Some of the critiques of Noth's amphictyony proposal inform the work of A. D. H. Mayes. See his 1973 articles "Israel in the Pre-monarchy Period" and "The Question of the Israelite Amphictyony." A comprehensive treatment of the scholarly debate was written by C. H. J. De Geus in *The Tribes of Israel*. Yigael Yadin wrote an accessible narrative of the Hazor excavations titled *Hazor: The Rediscovery of a Great Citadel of the Bible*.

12

THE PHILISTINES DURING THE PERIOD
OF THE JUDGES

Ann E. Killebrew

The Philistines, best known in the biblical account as one of premonarchic Israel's most implacable enemies, are among the new peoples that emerge from the ruins of the Late Bronze Age. In the early twelfth century BCE, they first appear as the Peleset (*p-r-s-t*) in ancient New Kingdom Egyptian texts dating to the Twentieth Dynasty, most notably in the account of Ramesses III's year-eight campaign depicted on the walls of his early twelfth-century

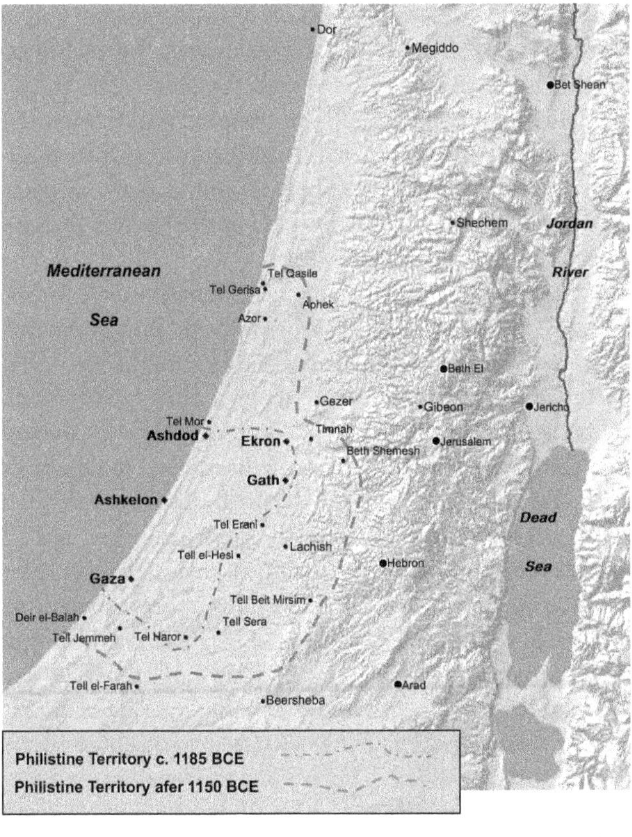

MAP 12-1. *Ancient Philistia and Israel. The line of dots and dashes indicates the area of Philistine first settlement in 1185 BCE, while the line of dashes shows the area of later expansion, following 1150(?) BCE (after Stager 1995).*

BCE mortuary temple at Medinet Habu. Archaeologically, they make their debut during the first half of the twelfth century BCE, where their distinctive Aegean-style material culture serves as an ethnic marker of Philistine presence or influence. The results of excavations during the past half century provide a rich database of primary evidence regarding many aspects of the Philistines. Analyses of both the literary and the archaeological evidence reveal a dynamic process of interaction over time between the Philistines and their neighbors, highlighting customs and traditions that differ dramatically from the preceding Late Bronze Age material culture and the neighboring Iron Age cultures of the southern Levant. Let us begin with the literary evidence.

Hebrew Bible

The biblical account is the starting point for our understanding of the Philistines and any attempts to identify them in the archaeological record. In the Hebrew Bible, where they appear nearly three hundred times, they are portrayed as the quintessential uncircumcised "other" (Dothan and Cohn 1994). Most biblical references to the Philistines (*plištim*) can be grouped into four main periods of contact: the patriarchal, the premonarchic period of the judges, the Israelite kings, and the Babylonian exile and postexilic periods (for detailed discussions, see Ehrlich 1996 and Niesiołowski-Spanò 2016, 89–179). Other biblical references to the Philistines address their origins, geographical boundaries, economy, political and military organization, religion, and language (for a detailed discussion of the biblical Philistines in light of these categories, see Machinist 2000).

The Philistines first appear in Genesis (Gen 21:32-34; 26:1, 8, 14-15) where their encounters with Abraham and Isaac are described. Most scholars consider these verses in Genesis and later in the book of Exodus (Exod 13:17; 15:14; 23:31) as chronologically misplaced and anachronistic. From the biblical point of view, the "five lords of the Philistines" are among the enemies for the "testing of Israel, to know whether Israel would obey the commandments of the LORD" (Judg 3:1-5). The Philistines are most frequently mentioned in the Deuteronomistic History, especially in Judges and 1 Samuel. The former includes accounts of Israel's premonarchic leaders, or judges, who are depicted as sent by God to deliver early Israel from threats, most notably the Philistines. One of these early judges, Shamgar, is credited as having struck down six hundred Philistines with an ox goad (Judg 3:31). The Samson cycle (Judg 13–16) is one of the best-known narratives, illustrating hostile Philistine interactions with Samson, a local Israelite hero (see, e.g., Niditch 1990). Samson's marriage to a Philistine woman and his interactions with two additional women—Delilah and a prostitute (both are usually assumed to be Philistine)—are depicted as the source of his downfall (for a feminist perspective see, e.g., Exum 2012, 120–23).

Though many have legitimately challenged the historicity of the judges, which most scholars assigned to the twelfth and eleventh centuries BCE, there are aspects of the narrative that suggest it may present a "portrait of an age" (Provan, Long, and Longman 2003, 161). Often referred to as the "period of the judges" or Iron Age I, these two centuries can be characterized both biblically and in the material culture record as a time of the initial arrival of the Philistines and their territorial expansion through military victories and domination of their neighbors as portrayed in Judges and 1 Samuel. Their technological superiority over Israel, suggested in 1 Samuel 13:19-21, is also reflected in the material culture. The Philistines resided in large settlements in the southern coastal plain, several of which demonstrate urban characteristics, while early Israel occupied small and modest rural settlements in the hill country.

As described in 1 Samuel, antagonistic relations between these two groups continue during the period of Samuel, the last judge, and into the reign of King Saul. These are best illustrated by the Philistine victories at the battle of Aphek (1 Sam 4:1-10) and against King Saul on Mt. Gilboa (1 Sam 31; Finkelstein and Silberman 2006a, 82–85), as well as their defeats at the battle of Eben-Ezer (1 Sam 7:3-14) and Michmash (1 Sam 14). The biblical account depicts David as the first leader who successfully curtails Philistine expansionist ambitions, foreshadowed in David's defeat of the Philistine hero Goliath (1 Sam 17), resulting in reversing the relationship and balance of power between the Philistines and Israelites (see, e.g., 2 Sam 5). Mention of the Philistines drops noticeably after David, corresponding to a less distinctive archaeological footprint that typifies early Philistine material culture. In the post-Davidic period, most biblical references to the Philistines are confined to prophetic oracles.

The territory of the Philistines, roughly corresponding to Canaan's southernmost coastal plain, is indicated in Joshua 13:2-3. Describing the lands that Joshua did not conquer, the five Philistine lords of Ashdod, Ashkelon, Gaza, Gath, and Ekron are specified. These five cities also appear in 1 Samuel 6:17, suggesting a loosely organized confederation of Philistine city-states often dubbed in modern scholarship the Pentapolis cities. Remarkably, these five settlements are the only excavated sites in the southern coastal plain where the earliest twelfth-century BCE phases of Philistine occupation have been uncovered. Three of these cities—Ashkelon, Ashdod, and Gaza—also appear in association with the Sherden, Tjekker, and Philistines, in the Egyptian listings of the Onomasticon of Amenemope (see below). Philistine expansion eastward toward Judah during the eleventh century BCE is reflected in the story of

Samson and his marriage to a Philistine woman from Timnah (Tel Batash) in Judges 14, a development also confirmed in the archaeological evidence.

In addition to accounts describing Philistine-Israelite interactions, several passages allude to the nonindigenous origins of this group. Jeremiah 47:4 and Amos 9:7 associate the Philistines with Caphtor, usually translated as Crete, or, less often, identified with Cyprus. In the Septuagint, the term "Philistines" is translated in Greek as *allophyloi*, meaning "foreigners" (see, e.g., Septuagint Judg 10:6, 11). In one instance, the Septuagint (Isa 9:11) refers to them as "Hellenes," or Greeks (for a detailed discussion of the biblical references, see Brug 1985, 5–15).

As the uncircumcised "other" (e.g., Judg 14:3; 15:18), unsurprisingly the Philistines are depicted as polytheistic and idolatrous in the biblical text (Judg 10:6; 1 Sam 32:9; 2 Sam 5:21; 1 Chr 10:9; for an overview of the biblical evidence, see Machinist 2000, 59–63). Three deities, which differ from the Canaanite pantheon but are known from other Semitic contexts, are singled out: Dagon (see, e.g., Judg 16:23-31; 1 Sam 5:1-5), Ashtarot (1 Sam 31:10), and Baal Zebub (god of Ekron: 2 Kgs 1:2-3, 6, 16). Of these, Dagon is the most frequently mentioned, with temples at Beth-Dagon (Josh 19:27), Gaza (Judg 16:23), and Ashdod (1 Sam 5:2-7). The capture of the ark of the covenant by the Philistines and its display in Dagon's temple in Ashdod is described in 1 Samuel 5. The next morning, the god's image was found before the ark face down on the floor with his limbs broken off. The limited nature of these extensively redacted biblical references, combined with the lack of corroborating archaeological evidence for the worship of these gods, raises questions regarding the reliability of the accounts for our understanding of the early Philistines. Rather, these passages may reflect later first-millennium BCE Philistine religious practices.

New Kingdom Egyptian Texts

Twelfth-century BCE references to the Peleset (*p-r-s-t*) in New Kingdom Egyptian texts are central to our understanding of the Philistines. The inscriptions, reliefs, and stela from Ramesses III's mortuary temple at Medinet Habu and the Rhetorical Stela at Deir el-Medinah are contemporary with the reign of Twentieth Dynasty pharaoh Ramesses III (ca. 1186–1155 BCE), the last of the New Kingdom "warrior" kings (Kahn 2011). The Papyrus Harris I, also known as the Great Harris Papyrus, refers to events during the reign of Ramesses III but was composed shortly after Ramesses III's death. The Onomasticon of Amenemope, an ancient Egyptian textbook used in scribal schools, dates to the late twelfth / early eleventh centuries BCE (for bibliography, see Adams and Cohen 2013, 645–64).

MEDINET HABU

Ramesses III's three defensive campaigns—two against the Libyans (years five and eleven) and his defeat in year eight of a confederation including the Peleset, Tjekker, Shekelesh, Denyen, and Weshesh—are visually represented in relief and described in an accompanying hieroglyphic text on walls of his mortuary temple at Medinet Habu (O'Connor 2012). These peoples, together with the Lukka and Eqwesh, have been dubbed the "Sea Peoples," a convenient, albeit somewhat misleading, designation invented by modern scholarship that refers to groups described in several New Kingdom Egyptian texts as originating from "islands" (Killebrew and Lehmann 2013, tables 1–2, for a summary). On the northern façade wall of his mortuary temple, Ramesses III portrays and describes two military encounters against a coalition of these "Sea Peoples." The naval battle occurred in the Delta region, followed by a second encounter on land in Djahy—probably best understood as an Egyptian term for Canaan, whose exact location in this context remains unclear.

FIGURE 12-1. *Detail of Ramesses III's naval battle against a coalition of Sea Peoples, north wall at Medinet Habu.*

Though it is difficult to assign specific groups mentioned in the hieroglyphic texts to the individual depictions of Sea Peoples, the Medinet Habu inscriptions and reliefs provide crucial information regarding the appearance of the Philistines and regarding the Sea Peoples' battle tactics and various roles as warriors, captives, or mercenaries. Many Sea People warriors are represented as tall and clean-shaven, as wearing breastplates and short kilts, and as donning what has been interpreted as a feathered headdress. Traditionally, this image has been identified with the Philistines. Comparisons with contemporary depictions of warriors from the Aegean and Cyprus suggest a west Aegean or Cypriot association. However, in another relief on the base of one of the Osirid pillars in the first court, a kneeling captive with a beard and simple headgear is specifically identified in the accompanying hieroglyphic text as a "chief of the Philistines."

FIGURE 12-2. *Detail of captive Philistine chief at the base of the Osirid Column at Medinet Habu.*

A similar bearded figure, also identified as a Philistine, appears on a glazed tile from Ramesses III's palace at Medinet Habu. In Egyptian iconography, these physical features are typical of Levantine peoples, evidence that challenges interpretations of a west Aegean origin for the Philistines (for a general discussion, see Killebrew 2005, 202–4; Dothan 1982, 5–12).

A final consideration is the historical value of these accounts that appear on the walls of Ramesses III's mortuary temple at Medinet Habu. It is tempting to read these texts and reliefs literally and interpret the year-eight battle as an absolute chronological indicator for the appearance of the Philistines in Canaan's southern coastal plain. Egyptologists tend to be more cautious about drawing far-reaching conclusions based on the evidence from Medinet Habu. They warn of the tendency to appropriate the successes of previous pharaohs' campaigns and the propagandistic role of depictions on pharaonic monuments (see, e.g., Cifola 1988). However, in this case, Ramesses III's depictions of the sea and land battles against a coalition of northern groups are unique, lacking a precedent in earlier pharaonic accounts. This would tend to support an element of historicity in this encounter, but year eight should not be taken literally as an absolute date for the arrival of the Philistines, only as a general indicator of their arrival sometime between 1170–1150 BCE (see, e.g., Ben-Dor Evian in press).

RHETORICAL STELAE OF RAMESSES III

Two lesser-known Egyptian inscriptions attributed to Ramesses III refer to the Peleset. The Rhetorical Stela, found in Chapel C at Deir el-Medinah, mention the Peleset together with the Teresh, the latter having sailed(?) "in the midst of the sea." The linking of the Peleset with the Teresh, a group that likely originated from the Anatolian coast, may contain clues to the affiliations and hint at the regional origins of the Philistines. The Southern Rhetorical Stela, erected in the southern wing of the first Pylon at Medinet Habu, dates to Ramesses III's year twelve. In this Medinet Habu text, the pharaoh boasts that he "laid low" the land of the Peleset, though the location of this territory is not clear from the inscription.

PAPYRUS HARRIS I

Composed shortly after the death of Ramesses III by his son Ramesses IV, this forty-two-meter-long papyrus was discovered in a tomb near Medinet Habu and purchased by A. C. Harris in 1855. It contains a detailed list of Ramesses III's benefactions to the gods and temples at Thebes, Memphis, Heliopolis, and elsewhere, and depictions of the king making offerings. The account ends with a historical summary of his thirty-one-year reign, including his military battles with the Sea Peoples, Libyans, and others, and the accession of his son Ramesses IV. In this latter section, Ramesses III boasts that he reduced the Peleset to "ashes." Two other groups—the Sherden and Weshesh, but not the Peleset—are described as being brought as captives to Egypt and settled in Ramesses III's strongholds. Though it has been surmised that reference to his strongholds may refer to Egyptian garrisons in Canaan, location is not stated in the Papyrus Harris I and should not be considered as relevant to the question regarding the mode of Philistine settlement on the southern coastal plain.

FIGURE 12-3. *Papyrus Harris 1: Depiction of Ramesses III.*

ONOMASTICON OF AMENEMOPE

The term "onomasticon" refers to the cataloguing of things arranged according to kinds, such as classes, tribes, and types of human beings. The Onomasticon of Amenemope (or Amenope) is known from numerous copies or fragmentary versions that range in date from the Twentieth through the Twenty-Second Dynasties. In this text, which can be characterized as an instruction or teaching exercise, the Philistines appear in the sequence "Ashkelon, Ashdod, Gaza, Assyria, Shubaru . . . , Sherden, Tjekker, Peleset, Khurma . . ." The appearance of Ashkelon, Ashdod, and Gaza—three of the five cities designated as Philistine in the Hebrew Bible—corroborates their connection with the Philistines and possibly other Sea Peoples.

LUWIAN TEXTS

The 1996 discovery in the Citadel of Aleppo (northern Syria) of an eleventh- or tenth-century BCE relief—which depicts a man clothed in Syrian-style dress accompanied by a Luwian inscription identifying him as Taita, king of Palistin—is transforming our understanding of the Philistines and their origins (see below). The association of Palistin with the same peoples that appear in Egyptian, biblical, and Assyrian texts as the *P-r-s-t*, *Plištim*, and *Pilistu*, respectively, as first suggested by J. D. Hawkins (2009), is now generally accepted. Combined with ninth-century BCE inscriptions recovered from Tayinat, Sheizar, Meharde, and Arsuz that mention a King Taita of Walistin (= Palistin) and the appearance of Iron I Aegean-style material culture at Tayinat in the Amuq Plain that resembles Philistine excavated remains in the southern coastal plain, the suggestion of a northern Philistine group is convincing (for a general discussion, see, e.g., Singer 2012, esp. 461–64).

Textual Evidence for Other Sea Peoples in Canaan

Other ethnonyms associated with the Sea Peoples appear in Egyptian texts as early as the mid-fourteenth-century BCE Amarna letters and continue through the end of the New Kingdom (for a complete list, see Adams and Cohen 2013). Often, these Sea Peoples groups appear in the role of mercenaries. In addition to the Philistines, two groups (the Tjekker/Sikil and Sherden) are associated with possible settlement in the southern Levant. The mention of the Tjekker/Sikil and Sherden in the Onomasticon of Amenemope together with the Philistines and the cities of Ashkelon, Ashdod, and Gaza suggests the presence of these two additional groups in Canaan. A second Egyptian source, the Report of Wenamon, portrays Dor as under Tjekker rule. Discovered in 1890 at al Hibah, Egypt, and found together with a copy of the Onomasticon of Amenemope, this papyrus is the account of Wenamon, a priest of the god Amun at Karnak. The story describes Wenamon's journey to Byblos to procure timber for the construction of a boat for Amun. Along the way, Wenamon is robbed at Dor, a port city ruled by the Tjekker prince Beder. The text, whose historicity is questionable, is dated to either the eleventh or tenth century BCE. Though most scholars consider it to be a work of "historical fiction," it likely reflects political and economic connections between Egypt and the Levant during this period (Sass 2002). In addition to the search for the Tjekker/Sikil at Dor, M. Dothan and A. Zertal have advocated a Sherden presence at Tel Akko and Ahwat respectively (for a recent review and bibliography, see Stern 2012). However, physical evidence is scant, and their proposals regarding the presence of other "Sea Peoples" at these sites remain speculative (for a discussion of the evidence at Dor, see Gilboa 2006–2007; Sharon and Gilboa 2013).

Material Culture of the Philistines

The five cities of the Philistine Pentapolis—Ashdod, Ashkelon, Gaza, Ekron, and Gath—mentioned in Judges 13:3 and 1 Samuel 6:17 serve as the starting point in the search for the Philistines in the archaeological record. In 1899, excavations under the direction of F. Bliss and R. A. S. Macalister commenced at Tell es-Safi, identified as biblical Gath and the home of the Philistine giant Goliath (regarding the history of the search for the Philistines, see Dothan and Dothan 1992). Quickly digging down to bedrock, they uncovered in "pre-Israelite" contexts a handful of "monochrome" Mycenaean-style pottery (decorated in either red or black paint) and "bichrome" sherds with their painted black-and-red motifs. These provided the first glimpse of the Aegean-inspired material culture that was to become the hallmark of the Philistines. Ashkelon, the second Philistine city to be examined, was first explored by D. Mackenzie and then excavated in 1920–1922 by J. Garstang and W. J. Phythian-Adams. Their excavations confirmed Mackenzie's earlier observations of a Philistine presence, situated above the Late Bronze Age settlement. Following his work at Ashkelon in 1922, Phythian-Adams briefly explored Tell Haruba, a mound identified as ancient Gaza of the Philistines, today located within the modern city limits. His excavations uncovered Aegean-style monochrome and bichrome pottery associated with the Philistines. However, difficult conditions precluded extensive work at the site.

The first large-scale excavations at a Philistine site were conducted by M. Dothan at Ashdod. Nine seasons of excavation (1962–1972) revealed a substantial Iron I–II Philistine settlement spanning the twelfth through seventh centuries BCE. The first Philistine town, Stratum XIIIA, was constructed on top of the destruction debris of the Stratum XIIIB transitional Late Bronze / Iron I. This earliest Philistine phase is defined by the appearance of locally produced Mycenaean IIIC (Philistine 1) pottery, accompanied

FIGURE 12-4. *Aerial view of Tell es-Safi/Gath.*

by an assemblage of undecorated Aegean-style vessels. This pottery is a dramatic departure in shape, decoration, and manufacturing techniques from the indigenous Bronze Age assemblages of the Levant (Killebrew 2013). Aegean-style bichrome (Philistine 2) pottery (see Figure 12-6), characterized by its red-and-black painted decoration, develops out of monochrome Philistine 1 pottery (see Figure 12-5) and is the dominant ware at Ashdod during the eleventh century BCE.

FIGURE 12-5. *Philistine monochrome pottery. Also known as Philistine 1.*

Since the early 1980s, a wealth of new information regarding the initial stages of Philistine settlement in the twelfth century BCE has been excavated at Ekron (under the direction of T. Dothan and S. Gitin), Ashkelon (under the direction of L. Stager and D. Master), and Gath (under the direction of A. Maeir). As at Ashdod, the appearance of the distinctive locally produced Aegean-style Mycenaean IIIC pottery marks a clear cultural break with the preceding Late Bronze Age and signifies the arrival of the Philistines at these three sites (Dothan and Zukerman 2004). This cultural break is not only evidenced in the pottery but also reflected in architectural features, cultic practices, cuisine, technology, and industries. Also as at Ashdod, Philistine 2 bichrome pottery stratigraphically follows and stylistically develops out of monochrome Philistine 1 ceramics and, by the eleventh century BCE, becomes the dominant decorated ware.

FIGURE 12-6. *Philistine bichrome pottery. Also known as Philistine 2.*

At the end of the Iron I Period, coinciding with the end of the period of the judges during the transitional eleventh/tenth centuries BCE, red-slipped and burnished pottery supersedes bichrome ware.

The excavations at Ashdod, Ashkelon, Gath, and especially Ekron form the basis for our understanding of early Philistine culture, origins, and initial settlement in the southern coastal plain. The archaeological evidence lends support to the biblical characterization of the Philistine Pentapolis as independently ruled autonomous settlements or "city-states." Later eleventh-century Philistine expansion and influence are indicated by the presence of significant quantities of bichrome pottery at several sites to the north and east of the Pentapolis cities, including Tel Batash (Timnah), Tel Qasile, Azor, Tel Aitun, Tel Beth Shemesh, and Nahal Patish (for archaeological evidence for the Philistines during this time, see Dothan 1982; see also numerous chapters in Oren 2000 and Yasur-Landau 2010).

City Planning and Architectural Features

Of the excavated Philistine sites, Ekron provides the most extensive evidence for early Philistine city planning and material culture. Overpowering the modest ten-acre early twelfth-century BCE village (Stratum VIII) that marks the final Late Bronze Age phase, the initial Philistine settlement (Stratum VII)

FIGURE 12-7. *Aerial view of Tel Miqne-Ekron, looking south.*

expanded rapidly to a fifty-acre fortified urban center, complete with city walls, a new town plan, an elite area in the center of the mound, and an industrial area comprising pottery kilns that produced Philistine 1 and Aegean-style pottery so distinctive of this early Philistine phase. Although there is some debate regarding the urban character of other Pentapolis settlements, this may be due in part to the very limited exposure of the twelfth- and eleventh-century BCE occupation at these other sites.

Residential areas have been excavated at Ashdod, Ekron, and Ashkelon, the latter providing the best example of a twelfth-century BCE Philistine domestic quarter. It comprised several free-standing buildings constructed around an open courtyard dating to the initial phase of Philistine settlement. Departing from Late Bronze Age domestic architectural traditions, the typical Philistine house, termed the "Linear House," includes a main room with a central hearth and pillar, with flanking rooms and a linear access. The best-preserved of these houses at Ashkelon, only partially excavated, included at least five rooms, with benches and a square hearth in the largest of the rooms. The appearance of hearths (round, square, or rectangular) represents the introduction of a new architectural feature to southern Canaan (Maeir and Hitchcock 2011). This unusual feature has been interpreted as a cultic installation situated within a domestic context. Though lacking any exact parallels, it is reminiscent of truncated horns on Cyprus and a plastered installation from Ekron (Master and Aja 2011).

At Ashdod and Ekron, several impressive structures, often interpreted as an elite residential area, display both domestic and cultic features. These imposing buildings at Ekron were uncovered at the center of the mound, though it should be noted that a public function may also be possible. Their architectural features include a large hall or courtyard, often accompanied by columns, flanked by smaller rooms. Rectangular and circular hearths are common elements in these elite structures (Dothan 2003). Rooms with a clearly domestic character excavated at Ashdod also included a hearth and a cache of elite objects, among them figurines, ivories, and jewelry.

CULT AND RELIGION

Archaeological evidence associated with early Philistine cultic practices represents a clear break from Late Bronze indigenous religious practices. Material expressions of an Iron I Philistine cult—best represented at Ekron, Ashkelon, Gath, Tel Qasile, and Nahal Patish—include architecture, installations, ceramic anthropomorphic and zoomorphic figurines, stands and vessels, incised scapulae, and seals (A. Mazar 2000; Ben-Shlomo 2014).

Although the Bible references temples to Dagon, no temples have been found thus far at Ashdod or other Pentapolis sites. Instead, more modest cultic

rooms or buildings, rather than monumental public structures, characterize the earliest stages of Philistine settlement. At both Ashkelon and Ekron,
unusual features such as the plastered horned installation at Ashkelon discussed above have been interpreted as expressions of household cult. Elements
like benches, raised platforms, and unusual objects (including components of
a bronze wheeled stand found in the Ekron "Elite Zone") suggest the presence
of ritual activities in a domestic context.

The appearance of Aegean-style female figurines, and the dearth of male
images, suggest the dominance of a female deity. Ashdoda, embellished with a
bichrome painted decoration, is the most distinctive of these figurines. Named
in honor of the site where it was first discovered, it has often been interpreted
as a stylized female whose neck blends into a couch or chair. Figurines similar to Ashdoda are known from other Philistine sites, including Ekron and
Ashkelon, usually appearing in domestic contexts. These differ both in style
and in concept from Late Bronze Age Canaanite nude female figurines, which
are rendered realistically and are found in public, domestic, and funerary contexts. More recent research emphasizes the ambiguous nature of Ashdoda's
gender. Though Aegean-style in inspiration, this figurine is uniquely Philistine
and lacks close comparisons elsewhere (Press 2012).

Other features of material culture associated with ritual practices include
simple ceramic animal figurines and zoomorphic libation vessels similar to
examples from the Aegean and Cyprus. These zoomorphic figures, especially
depictions of bulls and horses, appear in noteworthy numbers at early Philistine sites and may represent the increasing economic value of these animals
(Ben-Shlomo 2014, 79–83). Incised bovine scapulae have also been recovered
from early Philistine contexts and are often linked to cultic activities. They are
best known from Cyprus, where they have been interpreted as objects used in
scapulomancy (a divination technique based on the natural features of the animal bone) or as bone scrapers or rasps that form part of a musical instrument
(Dothan and Drenka 2010).

Outside the Philistine Pentapolis, structures identified as temples have
been identified at two eleventh-century BCE sites. At Tel Qasile, three superimposed temples (Strata XII–X) represent the development of cult from a modest shrine to a well-developed sanctuary with an entrance room, main hall, and
smaller back room (A. Mazar 2000, 215–22). Finds recovered during excavations by A. Mazar include libation vessels, a lion-headed rhyton, and cylindri-
cal and figurative stands, among other unusual artifacts. A structure similar to
the Qasile Strata XI–X temples was excavated by P. Nahshoni at Nahal Patish,
a small rural site located in the western Negev. Ritual pits (*favissae*) and a rich
collection of cultic vessels support the interpretation that this building served
as a local temple or shrine (Nahshoni and Ziffer 2009). Although both sites

FIGURE 12-8. *Philistine temple at Tel Qasile.*

are associated with Philistine expansionist activities in the region based on the appearance of bichrome decorated Philistine 2 pottery, it remains unclear if their inhabitants were Philistines.

Crafts and Technology

Archaeological excavations have revealed ample evidence for textile and ceramic production at the Philistine Pentapolis. Aegean-style, spool-shaped, unperforated ceramic loom weights, testifying to a break in tradition with Bronze Age weaving practices, are abundant at Ekron, Ashkelon, and Ashdod. Several stone or terracotta basins, originally interpreted as bathtubs, were likely used for scouring or fulling wool (Mazow 2006–2007).

A twelfth-century BCE potters' workshop, complete with kilns used in the manufacture of Philistine 1 pottery, dates to the earliest stage of Philistine settlement at Ekron. The technology employed by the producers of Philistine 1 pottery differs from indigenous traditions in clay selection and preparation, vessel-formation techniques, and firing temperatures. Typologically, this assemblage is also distinguished from the preceding Late Bronze Age pottery in shape and decoration. Although research has tended to emphasize connections with traditions on mainland Greece and the west Aegean, Philistine 1 pottery finds its closest parallels in form, decoration, and technology with Aegean-style twelfth-century BCE assemblages from Cyprus, the east Aegean, and the Cilicia/Amuq regions (for a detailed analysis of Philistine pottery technology, see Killebrew 2013; regarding the later development of Philistine pottery, see Faust 2015).

FIGURE 12-9. *Potter's kiln at Tel Miqne, looking west, Field INE, Area 4.*

Cuisine and Feasting

Cuisine is often considered an ethnic marker for group identity. A significant increase in the number of pig bones characterizes the Philistine arrival at Ekron and other Pentapolis sites. In the earliest Iron I phases at Ekron, pig bones comprise at least 13 percent of the assemblage, a percentage that increases during the course of the twelfth and eleventh centuries BCE, which is a phenomenon typical of other Philistine settlements. This is accompanied by the appearance of a very distinctive Aegean-style cooking jug (Ben-Shlomo et al. 2008) and Aegean-style tablewares, suggesting nonindigenous feasting practices (Faust 2015). The material culture of the Iron I Period thus reflects significant changes in diet and suggests the maintenance of well-defined boundaries during the Iron I Period. The consumption of pork, while uncommon in Late Bronze Age contexts in the Levant, was widespread in the Bronze Age Aegean, Anatolia, and Europe, lending additional support to the view that the Philistine phenomenon represents a significant migration to Philistia in the aftermath of the Bronze Age collapse in the eastern Mediterranean (Killebrew and Lev-Tov 2008; see also Faust and Lev-Tov 2011).

Burial Customs

No cemeteries dating to the twelfth century BCE have been discovered thus far at the Philistine Pentapolis. Earlier research attributed burials in anthropoid coffins—which have been discovered at New Kingdom Egyptian strongholds in Canaan—to the Philistines. However, this identification is based on a very tenuous resemblance between the "feathered" Sea Peoples' headdress depicted on the Medinet Habu reliefs and features that appear on several anthropoid coffin lids. There is no archaeological evidence to support this theory, as these Egyptian-style coffins are found only at sites with an Egyptian presence, prior to the arrival of the Philistines.

The only burials found in twelfth-century BCE Philistine occupation levels are intramural infant and fetus burials recovered from Ekron and Ashkelon (Birney and Doak 2011). Recently, an eleventh- to eighth-century BCE cemetery was uncovered at Ashkelon (Sauter 2016; Master and Aja 2017). Over 211 individuals were interred by means of a variety of burial customs, including individuals in pits or primary burials of multiple individuals in a tomb, with most dating to the tenth century BCE or later. A few cremation burials have also been recovered. Noteworthy is the paucity of grave goods found in the graves. Similar burials dating to the eleventh century BCE were previously excavated at Azor, located southeast of Tel Aviv in the southern coastal plain. Like Ashkelon, this cemetery revealed a large variety of burial customs. These include nonlocal types of funerary practices such as cremation and burials in jars, which the excavator, M. Dothan, suggested are related to the appearance of a new "ethnic group" (see Ben-Shlomo 2008 [who published Dothan's excavations]).

PHILISTINE LANGUAGE

Little physical evidence exists regarding the language spoken by the inhabitants of the Pentapolis. Incised signs and one ostracon recovered from twelfth- to eleventh-century BCE Philistine contexts have been identified as Philistine inscriptions. Most notable are the dozen inscribed jar handles and an ostracon bearing signs that have been identified as derived from Cypro-Minoan script discovered at Ashkelon (Cross and Stager 2006). However, others have challenged this interpretation. In addition to the handful of early inscriptions, non-Semitic names and terms appearing in later Iron Age inscriptions and the biblical narrative have led many scholars to suggest that the Philistines likely spoke non-Semitic languages or even a variety of languages (for the most recent discussion and overview of the epigraphic and linguistic evidence, see Maeir, Davis, and Hitchcock 2016). This debate is likely to be resolved only if a Philistine archive is uncovered in future excavations.

Philistine Origins and Settlement Process in Philistia

The biblical, Egyptian, and archaeological evidence point to nonindigenous origins of the Philistines. From the initial discovery in the early twentieth century of a distinctive Aegean-style material culture associated with the Philistines, archaeologists and historians have proposed various theories

FIGURE 12-10. *Iron I ostracon from Ashkelon.*

regarding the Philistines' arrival in the Levant's southernmost coastal plain. In the past, most of these tended to see the Philistines as a fairly homogenous group originating from a single region and arriving in Philistia by means of large-scale migration. These theories variously propose mainland Greece and the west Aegean, the east Aegean, Illyria via the Balkans, and southeast Anatolia (especially Cilicia) and/or Cyprus as possible places of origin (for a summary and bibliography, see Killebrew 2005, 230–31).

Numerous studies address the question of when the Philistines settled in Canaan's southern coastal plain. The year-eight campaign of Ramesses III is the chronological benchmark for each of the theories. They fall into three general categories: high, middle, and low chronologies. The High Chronology proposes that there were two waves of Philistines, one predating Ramesses III's year-eight battle and the second resulting from his defeat of the coalition of "peoples from the sea." The Middle Chronology, still accepted by many scholars, ties the arrival of the Philistines, represented by the appearance of Philistine 1 (Mycenaean IIIC) pottery to year eight of Ramesses II. The Low Chronology maintains that Philistine migration occurred only after the retreat of New Kingdom Egypt from Canaan during the final years of Ramesses III or shortly thereafter (for a detailed discussion and bibliography, see Killebrew 2005, 232).

A wealth of new evidence from Philistia (especially Ekron, Ashkelon, and Gath), recent discoveries at Tayinat in the Amuq Plain, and several Luwian inscriptions from Aleppo and elsewhere mentioning Taita (king of Palistin) are revising our earlier understanding of the Philistines. Recent excavations at the Pentapolis sites reveal subtle variations expressed in the material culture suggesting that the Philistine phenomenon does not represent a homogeneous movement of peoples and that, rather, each settlement should be considered within its specific context. At Ekron, the closest material culture parallels are to Cyprus, especially Enkomi. Other Pentapolis settlements display closer ties with other regions in the eastern Mediterranean and possibly a more gradual or modest incorporation of Philistine features. Inscriptions referring to King Taita strengthen a Cilicia/Amuq Plain connection to the Philistines and are an indicator of the complex process involved in the transmission of Aegean-style culture to the Levant and movement of peoples.

More-nuanced views that recognize the role of longer-term processes in the transmission of Aegean-style cultural traits and technologies are gaining traction (see, e.g., Hitchcock 2011; Hitchcock and Maeir 2013; Killebrew 2015). In the case of the Philistines, their arrival in Philistia marked the final stop on a complex and multidirectional series of journeys that likely spanned decades and involved interaction with numerous peoples and regions along the way. Regardless of the site-specific details of Philistine settlement at the Pentapolis, their cultural horizon at Ashdod, Ekron, Ashkelon, and Gath represents a case study par excellence of migration in the archaeological record. This is best expressed in the highly visible archaeological break with Late Bronze Age cultural traditions, the Aegean-style ceramic culture, new settlement plans, previously unknown architectural features such as hearths and cultic traditions, new crafts and industries, and the appearance of noteworthy quantities of pig bones and distinct cooking jugs, representing a non-Semitic diet and cuisine. With the rise of Israel and emergence of local polities or kingdoms during the tenth and ninth centuries BCE in the region, the Philistines were weakened politically and militarily. Though retaining their identity as Philistines, over time their material culture lost much of its distinctive character and adopted many of the features of the surrounding cultures (Faust 2013).

Suggestions for Further Reading

The Philistines have been the focus of several in-depth studies and monographs. T. Dothan's 1982 volume *The Philistines and their Material Culture*, though dated, is still a classic review of this topic. A. E. Killebrew's 2005 monograph *Biblical Peoples and Ethnicity: An Archaeological Study of Egyptians, Canaanites, Philistines and Early Israel, 1300–1100 B.C.E.*, contextualizes the Philistines in their broader Iron I context. A more recent, updated synthetic treatment by A. Yasur-Landau entitled *Philistines and Aegean Migration in the Late Bronze Age* appeared in 2010. Specialized studies relating to the Philistines and Sea Peoples appear in E. Oren's 2000 edited book *The Sea Peoples and Their World: A Reassessment* and in A. E. Killebrew and G. Lehmann's 2013 coedited book *The Philistines and Other Sea Peoples in Text and Archaeology*. Two monographs that are more textually focused but that integrate the archaeological evidence include J. F. Brug's 1985 volume *A Literary and Archaeological Study of the Philistines* and Ł. Niesiołowski-Spanò's 2016 contribution *Goliath's Legacy: Philistines and Hebrews in Biblical Times*. For a comprehensive bibliography on the topic, see C. S. Ehrlich's "Philistines" (2015).

IV

THE KINGDOMS OF THE PEOPLE ISRAEL

13

THE UNITED MONARCHY
David between Saul and Solomon

Baruch Halpern

Accounts of David's Israel summon up images of a massive empire as advanced as modern controlling states. That is what the biblical texts have implied to us and to previous generations. But that is not what those texts actually say when understood in their literal sense. Nor does the archaeological evidence fit such broad claims of David's accomplishments.

When comparing biblical passages with relevant archaeological finds, modern historians often choose sides according to their predilections. They fail to consider the gaps between their own cultures and worldviews in comparison with those of the sources. Since an appreciation of any past literature depends on the scholars' historical imagination, as does the degree to which they can reenact a narrator's imagination of characters' imaginations, those gaps impact their re-creation of the past.

With regard to the united monarchy under David and Solomon, when we impose our values and our modern assumptions about the character of a "state" on accounts of it, we distort the picture those accounts portray. The texts do not explicitly make the claims that scholars say they make. Both defenders of the idea that David conquered a vast amount of territory and those who deny a united monarchy ever existed, a persistent but limited group, argue over a scarecrow of their own making. Some scholars liken David to King Arthur, as Philip Davies did in 1992, meaning that his character is at best legendary. Other scholars equate David with Egyptian or Assyrian leaders who built empires. The biblical texts, especially the list of conquests in 2 Samuel 8, are more modest than either set of readers assumes. So conservatives defend an exaggerated view of David's accomplishments, while the revisionists attack the pictures provided by the conservatives rather than those of the actual sources.

The debate's core revolves around the issues of, first, what the biblical texts actually claim and, second, how one measures in the archaeological record the creation of a state—that is, of David's kingdom. Near Eastern archaeology has a history of choosing to excavate monumental public buildings and, by extension, using the presence and character of those buildings as the primary indicator of the power of a central government. Assaults on David's historicity usually begin with the absence of the major fortifications and building projects expected of a powerful empire.

Yet, about such architectural construction, the biblical text is silent. The books of Samuel place David's Israel from Dan to Beersheba; it does not much exceed territory in the central hill ridge of modern Israel. There is also a claim to domination of Ammon, and royal ties, including marriage ties, to Israelite settlement in Gilead. But nothing in the archaeological remains contradicts these claims.

Nor does any text assert that David made inroads into the coastal plain, where the towns of the Philistines lay. In fact, even Gezer, at the debouch of the Ayyalon Pass, remains outside his ambit. His major accomplishment is the conquest and settlement of a capital in Jerusalem. In 2 Samuel, David overcomes Rabbat-Ammon, defeats some Moabites, and installs garrisons in Edom. He also dominates Aramaean and Israelite armies in the field. But David's greatest feat of arms and diplomacy is to conquer Israel.

These claims fit our archaeological evidence. On the one hand, outside of Judah and its close environs, there is little indication of Davidic activity. Possibly, David began a process of reurbanization, especially in the hills, if the results at Tell Ein Zippori can be so interpreted (Dessel 1999). On the other hand, even in Judah, the lack of monumental architecture from David's time (as opposed to Solomon's)—Iron IB/IIA, the first half of the tenth century BCE—has consistently dissuaded informed scholars from thinking of the king as a major player on the international scene, again as the texts suggest.

To understand David, the opportunities and challenges facing him, and his strategies for dealing with them, we need to take a different approach. We need to read the biblical text stripped of the propagandistic picture that has been laid onto it by later readers and scholars and then take the picture that this reading produces and interpret it in the context of the archaeological evidence from recent decades of excavation. The goal is not the hackneyed examination of the truth (or not) of the biblical text. Instead, this chapter's aim is to lay out a picture of how first David (and then Solomon) formed his new state in the context of the military and political forces facing him and to identify the strategies he used in accomplishing that that achievement.

The books of Judges and 1 Samuel emphasize conflicts that the people Israel have with the peoples around them. One of those peoples are the Philistines, who entered the coastal lowlands not long after Israel's appearance along the highland ridge. In many ways, these books present the Philistines as Israel's archetypal enemy. But after Saul turns on David and David's attempts to hide in Judah's rural areas fail, David makes an alliance with Achish, the king of the Philistine city of Gath. After Saul's death, David settles in Hebron, but he apparently retains his alliance with Gath—after all, he and Judah remain at war with Saul's descendants and Israel. Achish is Judah's only ally. This situation is clear from the first chapters of 2 Samuel; readers have just ignored its implications for our understanding of both David's actions related in the books of Samuel and the relevant archaeological remains.

This chapter will begin with a consideration of the geographical character of the Philistine lowlands and the Israelite hill country, as well as developments in the Negev. It will then move to an analysis of Israel's progression in the formation of its state, finally ending by bringing archaeological evidence to bear on David's strategies for forming and securing his new state.

The Philistine Lowlands and the Israelite Highlands: The Time of David

The narratives about David contrast Israelites, who live in the hill country, and Philistines, who inhabit five cities on the coastal plain to the west: Gaza, Ashkelon, Gath, Ashdod, and Ekron. Israel and Philistia are geographically separate. Nevertheless, the heyday of these centers, all excavated, coincides with David's reign. By this time, Philistines had developed outlying settlements to

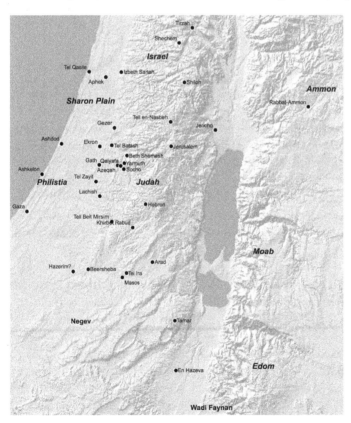

MAP 13-1. *Map of southern Israel showing sites related to the rise of the monarchy and the united Kingdom of Israel under David and Solomon, as well as the five cities of the Philistine Pentapolis.*

the east of their cities. Their settlements differ from contemporary inland villages (i.e., Israelites) in several ways. They differ in the pottery of their table service, which includes painted figural and geometric decorations. They differ in their house types, in the architectural form and location of their shrines, and in their public architecture. The shape of their loom-weights and the areas of their concentration differ as well, suggesting a higher degree of specialization and perhaps the use of textile dyes. So it is natural to conclude that cultural lines were drawn between the Israelites and the Philistines, called "the uncircumcised" in Israelite texts composed about the tenth century BCE.

Philistines also exhibit distinctive foodways. They relied extensively on grain and pig as well as the sacrifice or eating of dogs. Some of the difference in foodstuffs comes from environmental factors: pigs break up soil in grain fields in the lowlands (see Herodotus, *Histories* 2.14), while sheep graze sleepily on upland orchard slopes. Imagine the Philistine flatlands, with pigs rooting and cattle pulling metal-tipped plows. Some sites exhibit elevated cattle numbers without pig (Shiloh stratum V, Izbet Sartah, Masos), but elevated pig numbers appear only at sites with elevated cattle numbers. Iron I Philistine sites exhibit bone remains that are 50–60 percent cattle and pig. Where flat fields had been abandoned due to depleted manpower, as seems to have been the case in the urban areas of Late Bronze II Canaan (Gonen 1984), pigs are particularly valuable for clearing brambles and their roots, even in crusted soil.

Conversely, in the Israelite highlands, the inhabitants raised sheep and goat, with no presence of pig. In fact, sheep consumption increased over time, relative to goat, but they were pastured away from vineyards and orchards. Sheep are less welcome in grain lands before harvest. Goats are problematic where low trees and properly trimmed vines are cultivated, so that the decline in percentage is almost predictable as these developed over time. This was the tradeoff for diminished risk-spreading in the flocks. Cattle were known in the highlands, but, relatively speaking, cattle percentages in Israelite areas reach only to the lower end of the range represented in Philistine sites. On the slopes terraced for olive or grape, cattle are less useful than donkeys for traction and maneuverability when plowing for planting wheat between the trees.

The difference in landscapes and the agricultural and economic strategies needed to exploit them goes a long way toward explaining the hostility between Philistines and Israelites. Philistine ground produced grain in surplus (as the Amarna texts and Judg 15:5 reflect). Specialists may have furnished much of their lamb, certainly later in the Iron Age (Hesse, Fulton, and Wapnish 2011). Israelites, with a more mixed economy, subsisted on the combination of roots, pulses, and grains together with comestibles and goods acquired in trade for cash crops (oil, wine). On some occasions, they also added meat, raised locally, to their cereal gruels. These ecological and agricultural differences joined with others to inhibit collaboration and intermarriage between the two groups. In the Samson cycle (Judg 13–16), thus, although Samson's circumcision does not come up as a factor, the Philistines act like prankster in-laws, and his death results from the escalation of this behavior. Samson's actions, too, seem to fall into this category.

Later, these contrasts partly fell by the wayside. As early as the tenth century BCE, biblical texts tell us, David made common cause with Philistia, and even his son Solomon enjoyed an extradition treaty with Gath (1 Kgs 2:36-44). Likewise, no destruction layer in Philistia should be attributed to Israel, rather than to locals or Egyptians. Indeed, the first evidence for Judahite conquest in Philistia appears at the time of King Hezekiah—at Tel Batash, level III. There remain differences between Israel and Philistia in house forms, settlement organization, hinterland organization, and cult. Yet no text referring to a period after the tenth century BCE characterizes Philistines with the derisive term "uncircumcised," while the differences in both meat consumption and table service disappear in the later Iron IIA.

Consider too the panoramic views at the transition from Iron IB to Iron IIA—the time of David's rise (late eleventh century to early tenth century BCE). Philistine cities were high mounds on the coastal plain. These surveyed the hinterland. This settlement strategy maximized the availability of nearby land for cultivation and enhanced the Philistine ability to control access to their territory. By contrast, people in the denser web of small upland settlements, where the terrain limited visibility, probably crossed boundaries more actively, with commerce based more on proximity than on territorial definitions. The exchange of labor, women, foods, cloth, animals, and perhaps even land was less concentrated but more extensively mediated. These easier contacts and links produced a braided rope of kinship that probably led to increased human capital, which is attested in numbers of settlements. Surplus meant increasing social stratification. In some areas, economic niches formed, as the principle of comparative advantage began to operate, as it had in the decentralized Canaan of the Late Bronze Age. This sometimes led to specialized production, such as honey at tenth-century BCE Tel Rehov and ironworking at Beth Shemesh.

This landscape provides the setting of Saul and David, with their two peoples occupying geographically different regions. Israelites do not live in the Shephelah near the Philistines, and texts only rarely place standing Philistine troops in hill regions of Israel (1 Sam 13:5; 2 Sam 5:17-25; 8:1; 23:14-17). The Pentapolis sites are huge, but few "Philistine" objects reach outlying villages (e.g., Beth Shemesh versus Khirbet Qeiyafa; Tell Beit Mirsim and Khirbet Rabud). In fact, only around 1100 BCE did "sub-Mycenean" settlement extend north to the Yarkon River at Tel Qasile stratum XII or reflect exchange with inland elements—some seventy-five years after their earliest settlement (as Greenberg 1987). In the earliest Philistine phases, nothing physical marks commerce with other local settlements. Later, around 1000 BCE, emissaries left both Philistine pots and Philistine-style sacrifices (puppies in pots, pig bones) as far north as Megiddo in the Jezreel Valley. In the areas identified with Israelite settlement, such remains are scarce. The rarity of textual reference of the two peoples interacting during David's reign should be correlated with the archaeological evidence of Philistine presence only outside Israelite areas.

Saul and the Kingdom of Israel before David

Before we address the impact of David and Solomon, we must consider Saul, who came to the kingship around 1025 BCE. The kingdom of David and Solomon stretched from Dan in the north to the Negev Desert in the south. The polity created by Saul—their predecessor and the "first" Israelite king— was much smaller. Saul's base of support lay in the territory of Benjamin, the stronghold of his own tribe, and it stretched northward. It probably ended around the southern tip of the Jezreel Valley, in the area associated with the northern border of the tribe of Manasseh. Going east, it reached into Gilead in Transjordan, including both Jabesh-Gilead and Mahanaim (Finkelstein 2013, 47–62). He must have held sway over some of northern Judah, but it is clear that Jerusalem was beyond his power despite its nearness. The Judahite territory seems to lack any "national" organization at this time. Saul operates outside this area only on military excursions (see Map 11-1.)

Saul's kingship was based on charisma at first, like that of the judges before him, rather than a standing at the top of a hierarchy. Samuel's conveyance of a divine appointment on him gave him a position but not status. Like the judges, Saul's primary task seemed to be the defense of the people Israel by raising and leading armies on an ad hoc basis (see 1 Sam 11, 13). As his reign continued, Saul organized a permanent standing army—a sign of state formation. And unlike the judges, he was able to pass on his position to his son. Indeed, the transition of power to his son Ishbaal after Saul's death set the stage for a six-year war between Ishbaal and David (2 Sam 3), who then ruled only Judah.

Judah and the Negev under David and Solomon

After David eventually took over Israel as well as Judah, the northern part of his kingdom was largely peaceful. Thanks to David's alliance with Achish, the Israelite-Philistine border to the west was also stable during the period of the united monarchy. But the same cannot be said of the area to the south of Judah and Israel. The unincorporated nature of much of Judah had helped David during Saul's reign. While the books of Samuel assume settlement south of

Judah in the Negev, Judah's center was wilderness. In Samuel, this emptiness is visible in the stories of David hiding from Saul over many months before he flees to the king of Gath (1 Sam 18–26). David moves around Benjamin and central Judah, while various inhabitants inform Saul of his whereabouts. The picture of little central control on movement accords with evidence from archaeological surveys, which have found few settlements of any size in Judah during the eleventh to tenth centuries BCE (Ofer 1993, 1994).

David's alliance with Gath enabled him to address that situation. A few passages in 1 Samuel (27:8-10 and 30:26-29) concentrate on David's activities in southern Judah and the Negev. David's role in the Negev is as a scourge of nomads who by commercial diplomacy wins hearts, cementing assimilation of locals with Judah. Their populations, probably disparate in origin, formed ties as part of Judah, Simeon, and neighboring groups.

The program of desert settlement later expanded under Solomon. This settlement in the Negev appears archaeologically in the installation of garrisons by Solomon. All of these seem to have been eliminated by Pharaoh Shishak (this is the Hebrew name of the Egyptian pharaoh Sheshonq I) around 925 BCE, as in 1 Kings 14. But the landscape of Samuel is that of the tenth century BCE—which suggests the textual claims are close in time to the events being described.

What impelled the Negev settlement and its beneficiaries' identification with Judah was Joab's Edomite campaign. One might imagine it along the lines of a military hunt, as though reflecting colonial clearance of aboriginal populations. Verses 14-16 in 1 Kings 11 describe action against Edom's population by David's general Joab, and 2 Samuel 8:14 describes David's placing of garrisons in Edom, perhaps corresponding to some of the Negev settlements Shishak claims (later) to have destroyed. Two place-names recorded by Shishak even have correlates in our lists from the time of David. David's garrisons enlisted collaborators to expel independents. The settlements' goal was to secure traffic and trade, from which locals gained tolls and sales. Indeed, one component in the names of the sites, Hazer, can be understood as "Rest Area."

On learning of David's and Joab's deaths, according to 1 Kings 11:14-22, an Edomite prince who was allied with Egypt rallied fugitives displaced by Joab's front, perhaps expecting to recruit some of David's agents. His aim, and that of his Egyptian sponsors, was to regain and retain caravan revenues. The failure of this policy of diverting trade dues from Judah to Egypt may underlie Solomon's state marriage to a pharaoh's daughter (probably that of Pharaoh Siamun) in 1 Kings 3:1 and 9:16.

The Negev sites appeared only in the tenth century BCE, then vanished after Shishak's expedition until around 750 BCE. By contrast, settlement increased in the Judean Hills during the ninth to eighth centuries BCE. So the political geography of Saul's and David's narratives in 1 and 2 Samuel best fits an early era. Interpretations of sod and semantics vary and change, but they are most stable when their combination advances the discussion of each. So, again, archaeological remains and text wring sense from one another and reveal the changes on Israel's southern frontier during the life of David and his successors.

State Formation in Antiquity: General Remarks

Perhaps the most common evidence that archaeologists use as indicators of a state and/or a state apparatus in the ancient world is the erection of public buildings and the presence of population density, either in real terms or as a rapid increase over a short period of time. Despite the widespread reliance on such measures, these function better as positive indicators than as negative ones. In other words, while the presence of large public works points toward a state, or at least the ability to engage large amounts of manpower, the absence of such buildings does not indicate the lack of a state. This shortcoming was known even in antiquity; the ancient Greek writer Thucydides discussed the problem. In comparing Sparta with Athens, and in considering Mycenae, Thucydides famously observed that monumentality and density do not necessarily correspond to power. Judging state formation based on archaeological monumentality thus violates a practical historical principle: we must first evaluate what a state was in its own terms before imposing a classification from outside.

What constitutes a West Semitic state? It is an entity that exercises control over its factions, collects revenues, and administers justice. It has a state army. Our texts claim kings are needed to lead the fighting. In 1 Samuel 11, Saul's acclamation as king by the populace takes place when he calls out the military muster to face Ammon. Indeed, the stories of Saul and David emphasize their abilities to raise and lead armies; after them, no biblical narrator needs to revisit the rise or maintenance of a state army.

Raising armies does not necessarily presuppose compulsory taxation. Early Irish kings, for example, marched through territories raising voluntary levees to confront rival clan leaders (Beougher 2007). In such instances, social solidarity, usually based in kinship or nativism, overrides political organization. In Samuel, the source concerned with royal taxation stresses the muster (1 Sam 8; 10:17-27; 11; 12) rather than an organized taxation system. But a standing force and its prospect of spoil justify and facilitate taxation. Both David and Solomon divide the country into districts for taxation and support of the army as well as the court. Lineage representatives, like the tribal heads appointed by David to collect duty, have their loyalties divided between kingly master and their own constituency, and so they serve as little more than mediators. Along the same ideological lines, the texts about David, Ishbaal, Absalom, and David's restoration to the throne all stress, as do the narratives in Samuel, the importance of government by the consent of the citizenry (which is not to be confused with the population at large). In the next generation, Solomon purposely separates the tax districts from traditional tribal areas; this enables him to supplant the tribal elders with more ruthless appointees, who can presumably collect the revenues more efficiently—and serve as rival centers of power. Correspondingly, the electorate for enthroning Solomon consists not of the mustered citizenry, but of the royal guard.

The Kingdom of David and Its Jerusalem Capital: Signs of State Formation

The indications that David's and Solomon's kingdom had a physical presence at best sustain the claim of dominance from Dan to Beersheba. For the time of David, there is relatively little monumental architecture, but there is some. First, Eilat Mazar discovered a public building in Jerusalem that is integrated into the visual counterpart of a pyramid: the "Stepped Stone Structure." The Stepped Stone Structure is essential in evaluating the setting of Jerusalem in the tenth century BCE. This large terraced stone structure is located on the east side of the city and covers the hillside. It has been regarded as the largest

FIGURE 13-1. *The tenth-century(?) BCE Stepped Stone Structure and other excavation areas on the east side of the City of David. Eilat Mazar's "palace" building is above it under the awnings.*

FIGURE 13-2. *A wall of the public building that Eilat Mazar has identified as a "palace" from the eleventh and tenth centuries BCE. It is above the Stepped Stone Structure.*

Iron Age structure in Israel and has been dated as early as the eleventh to the ninth century BCE. Nearly all biblical scholars view the structure as a support platform for a larger building at the top of the City of David. Eilat Mazar suggests that the Stepped Stone Structure was part of the same complex as that public building. The sherds below its floors date to Iron IB, while the pottery from locus 47 shows that the building was in use, in an early phase, during Iron IIA—which is to say, the tenth century BCE: the time of David's rise to power (E. Mazar 2006, 2009).

Some scholars think this building is earlier than David's era, arguing a strict correlation of David's time with Iron IIA culture (A. Mazar 2006, 2010). But expecting late Iron IB sherds in Jerusalem to be earlier in date than Iron IIA in the lowlands is a typological, not sociohistorical, inference. Further, the pottery from the building is roughly contemporary with that of Khirbet Qeiyafa (Singer-Avitz 2010) in western Judah, which archaeologists usually see as guarding the approach to Philistia. Qeiyafa was a planned ring fortress, whose residences/barracks are built into the town wall. It has planning parallels with tenth-century BCE Tell Beit Mirsim and other towns of Judah (Garfinkel and Ganor 2009). Qeiyafa is the border outpost of a central governing authority, probably in Jerusalem. The expansion fits the timeline for David's establishment of a state. An expansion from Jebusite Jerusalem, for which there is no archaeological evidence, is less likely than from David's. Thus, we see the structure found by Eilat Mazar and this fortification of Qeiyafa as an early large-scale construction of the sort enabled by a central state rather than a city-state.

And that is the point. Jerusalem up to this point had been a city-state—that is, an urban center for the surrounding rural farmland—whose origins

FIGURE 13-3. *The oval ring shape of Khirbet Qeiyafa is clearly apparent,*
with excavated buildings clearly constructed against the casemate wall.
Azekah is visible in the back left.

archaeologists have traced back to a village built around 3100 BCE (Reich
2011, 282). The fourteenth-century BCE Amarna letters show that even the
strongest city in Canaan is a city-state, not a multicity country.

And while archaeologist Ronny Reich found remains of a Middle
Bronze II city—including a fortified wall, towers, and water system—there
is no archaeological evidence of a Late Bronze city (i.e., Jebusite Jerusalem).
Instead, it is only the literary evidence of the Amarna letters that indicates the
existence of a Late Bronze Age city. Six of the Amarna letters sent to Pharaoh
Akhenaten were sent by the ruler of Jerusalem (*Urusalim*), Abdi-hepa. In his
letters, Abdi-hepa requests assistance against treacherous Canaanite kings. He
urges Akhenaten to "send the archers against men that commit crimes against
the king." In another letter he begs the pharaoh to recognize the threats posed
by the "Apiru," who "sack the territories of the king." So written evidence and
archaeological evidence do not go hand in hand, neither for Abdi-hepa nor for
David. It is only Eilat Mazar's finds that provide any physical information of
David's Jerusalem.

Second, writing constitutes another indication of state organization in
antiquity, because its use reveals organizational oversight. It is not just the
structure of Qeiyafa's fort but also the presence in it of a long ostracon—likely
a complex exercise—that suggests an administrative function (Misgav, Garfinkel, and Ganor 2009; Yardeni 2009; William 2009; Rollston 2011; Misgav 2011; also note Galil 2009). Another exercise, in the same script, appears

FIGURE 13-4. *The remains of a tower from the Middle Bronze II period found in the City of David area of Jerusalem by Ronny Reich. The picture shows the tower's base and two walls opposite each other, sitting on bedrock. The ladder picture marks the tower's interior.*

at contemporary Izbeth Sartah, just uphill from Aphek (Finkelstein 1986; Demsky 1977). A third inscription has emerged from the public building (or palace) atop Jerusalem's Stepped Stone Structure (E. Mazar, Ben-Shlomo, and Ahituv 2013). All three belong to the same scribal tradition, at closely related times, and indicate the existence of a state-supported administration. In a more Phoenicianizing script, somewhat later, comes an abecedary from Tel Zayit.

Third, pottery can sometimes function as an indicator of state formation. The pottery assemblage at Izbeth Sartah stratum II is later than Qeiyafa's, and it belongs to the time of the almost identical fortification of Tell Beit Mirsim. Izbeth Sartah stratum III and Tell Beit Mirsim stratum A_1 (Iron IIA) contain later ceramic elements in foundational strata before their abandonment or destruction (Iron

FIGURE 13-5. *The ostracon from Khirbet Qeiyafa with an abecedary inscribed on it.*

IIA Judean burnished red slip, absent from Qeiyafa, Beth Shemesh IVA, and the City of David "palace" makeup). This may be an index of contemporaneity *and* differential longevity of the stratum.

So an Iron IB/IIA polity in northern Judah, which could be identified with David, organized at least two Shephelah border forts (Qeiyafa and Beit Mirsim) on a single plan. Their use of writing and the history of their pottery assemblages reveal their link to a coordinating authority.

The situation further south in the Negev is similar. Central planning explains the massing of labor for construction. Marks of specialization and social stratification accompany development in these areas. And Iron IIA witnesses increased distribution of marked elite vessels, funerary goods such as plaque figurines, and distinctions between the quality of a manor house—as at Izbeth Sartah stratum II or at Megiddo stratum VIA—and that of construction for dependents. Intensification in the use of seals, as well as growing conformity in uplands house and ceramic forms, also follows. The pattern is one of increasing social and political integration—which is to say, of imposed external control characteristic of a state. Archaeologically, there is a koine of public works and of elite consumption patterns. Over the course of Iron IIA (tenth century to early ninth century BCE), this spreads, along with the practice of building walls around towns and of placing public spaces in the area adjoining the main city gate—a practice known from lowland, non-Israelite sites of Iron I and even earlier.

Finally, there is the Tell Dan inscription. In an archaeological excavation at Tell Dan in 1993 and 1994, fragments of a stone stele were discovered. The stele was dated to the late ninth century BCE, and the inscription described a victory over Judah and Israel by an Aramean king who scholars conclude was Hazael (842–806 BCE). The king boasted that his victory was helped by the storm god Hadad and explicitly mentioned the "House of David." Most scholars interpret this phrase as a reference to the line of Judahite kings whose founder was King David. Coming just over a century after his reign, the reference to "House of David" is the oldest extrabiblical reference to King David's lineage. The discovery lent credence to David's standing as a historical figure and the founder of the Jerusalem dynasty, even though it adds little to the arguments concerning historicity of the biblical accounts of David's life and the size of his kingdom. The discovery of the stele struck a major blow to the school of minimalists who argued that David was no more historic than King Arthur—a minor leader of a small town or even a fictitious character.

From architecture to writing to the standardizing of pottery styles to evidence of a dynastic identity, the presence of David's Israelite state is clear. It established the foundation for the continuing development of the states that followed.

The Kingdom of Solomon: Signs of State Formation

The period of King Solomon, early Iron IIA, provides more extensive evidence of early Israelite state formation, ranging from large-scale architecture to pottery to military capabilities. First, we look at major building projects. While archaeologists have found little indication of public construction in Jerusalem dated to Solomon's reign, probably due to the extensive reconstruction projects of later centuries, there is significant evidence of building elsewhere that reveals the long arm of state planning and control. At the cities of Hazor, Megiddo, and Gezer, Yigael Yadin recognized that their main city gates each had six chambers behind the outer gate along a single pottery horizon (i.e., at roughly the same time). Yadin observed that 1 Kings 9:15-18 attributes the fortification of these, and three other towns, to Solomon. En Hazeva has another such gate, with pottery from Cyprus; the name of its Roman fort repeats biblical Tamar—and Tamar, the list in Kings claims, was one of Solomon's forts. Its location in the Negev is another story: it was there to protect trade.

Despite scholarly debate, Yadin's correlation of the Hazor, Megiddo, and Gezer gates to Solomon's building projects remains solid. This is indicated in part by the fact that shortly after Pharaoh Shishak's invasion around 925 BCE, gates at these sites changed. They ceased to resemble each other in approach, including the placement of towers with regard to the outer walls, in the numbers of interior gates, and in their drainage plans. Later gates bore resemblance

FIGURE 13-6.
An aerial view of the six-chambered gate at Gezer, three on each side.

to earlier ones, such as those at Lachish, Tel Ira, Ashdod, and others. For the most part, four-chamber gates succeeded six-chamber ones.

Second, the erection of the fortifications in these Solomonic sites that included the six-chamber gates was accompanied by a shift in the character of the populace in these sites. Prior to these architectural changes, these tells held cities. Afterward, they became fortresses. One indication is that none of these tenth-century BCE state forts had much domestic housing. In earlier eras, city-states concentrated human resources on site and subjected them to exit controls: they apparently depended on these to prevent demographic defection—a theme incessant in the Amarna letters of the fourteenth century BCE. Yet after the Solomonic period, in the ninth century BCE, housing for population reappears (probably for the wealthy only) at Hazor and Megiddo. So, suddenly, when the Megiddo and Hazor six-chamber gates were constructed, town

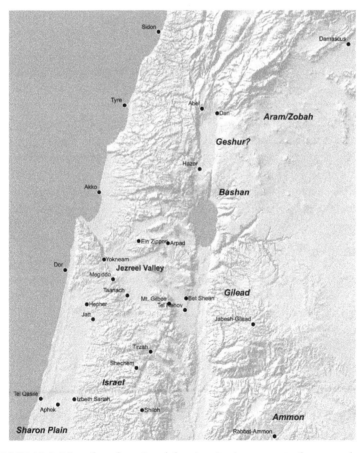

MAP 13-2. *Map of northern Israel showing sites important to the monarchy and the united Kingdom of Israel under David and Solomon.*

dwellers were pushed into the countryside. After a hiatus of five to ten decades, they returned. This smacks of the policy of a larger state incorporating territories that included these centers: the most obvious hypothesis would be Judah and Israel.

Another indication of the shift from city to fortress is that these administrative sites of Hazor, Megiddo, and Gezer lack any temples. In a royal city, the warranty of a state god's presence is symbolically paramount, as can be seen in Jeremiah 7. The temple is the deity's home, and it is the king's defining privilege to maintain it. In microcosm, the temple represents not just the cosmos but the city itself. The absence of formal temples at these sites—versus shrines—reflects a state's removing symbols of local polity, along with the lack of domestic housing, from these sites. The state banished the civilian population to villages. External authority intruded on local practice and overrode towns' internal relations. At the same time, the border sites were fitted with extensive storage facilities, like the gates built on a single general model (Blakely 2002).

Third, another archaeological reflex of an emerging territorial state in Israel is the rapid, widespread distribution of a new pottery type—most evident in the standard table service of burnished red-slipped bowls and related vessels. The Philistine table service had been distinctive since the twelfth century BCE, with its bichrome decoration featuring geometric and animal designs. In the tenth century BCE, the red-slip Israelite counterpart spread widely. Even in the Negev outposts, it probably represented the service of the king. The appeal of this ware was its elite appearance and its ethnic identification. This evidence is comparable to the development in Israel in the next century of related high-fired fine ceramic, when no one disputes its relevance to an Omride state apparatus.

This red-slipped elite ware comes along with evidence of social stratification, and perhaps even administration, as at Qeiyafa and later Izbeth Sartah. Slightly later, it takes architectural expression near the main gate, at Tell en-Nasbeh and Tell Beit Mirsim. Tenth-century BCE settlements also include imported pottery, suggesting that the benefits of secure trade extended, for the first time in about 1,500 years, to trade partners in the south—that is, to Transjordan and to Israel.

Fourth and finally, King Ahab's extensive chariot force did not spring from a void in 853 BCE but instead indicates a long-term development under state auspices. According to the annals of the Assyrian king Shalmaneser III (Kurkh Stele), Ahab of Israel fielded two thousand chariots, or some number dwarfing the numbers supplied by his allies, at the battle of Qarqar in 853. This force required infrastructure. It necessitated the acquisition of horses, the assignment of grazing and training ground, and the acquisition of breeding stock. It needed chariots and the capacity for their manufacture. Such a force also required personnel: trainers, breeders, grooms, drivers, and, finally, tacticians who could integrate the chariot with the infantry and ballistics arms on the field. To all this should be added the costs and time involved in erecting programs to train all of them.

The political element that made this happen is usually overlooked: the crown had to overcome resistance to and resentment of the investment. From 853 BCE, we can project the development of the chariot and army of Ahab well back, probably into the tenth century. Allowing the distinctiveness of Israel's chariotry tradition (Dalley 1985), we must assume that relations with Egypt were such as to enable Ahab and his predecessors to profit as a local ally. Ahab was integral in a web of Levantine alliances; the same holds for the weaker Davidic state Judah. The later reference by Shalmaneser concerning Israel's participation in the battle of Qarqar, attributing thousands of chariots and horses to King Ahab, obscures a gestation period in the development of chariotry capabilities, as the ninth-century BCE Tell Dan Stele makes evident. In other words, the evidence from our earliest Israelite sites and from the empire of the ninth century BCE triangulates on development in the tenth century BCE of organs of controlled exchange. These led to the prosperity of the ninth and eighth centuries BCE. David and particularly Solomon, we can conclude, already had a chariotry force.

The archaeological evidence in Israel from early Iron IIA thus shows a larger administrative footprint that we can attribute to King Solomon's reign rather than to King David's previous organizational work. David began the efforts, but it was Solomon whose exertions provided the most easily recognized archaeological indicators.

Solomon and Jerusalem

The short reference in 1 Kings 9 to Solomon's construction outside of his capital is all well and good, but Solomon built Jerusalem and was known as its temple builder. While repeated destructions and reconstructions over the millennia by kings, generals, emperors, caliphs, and others in authority have apparently removed the remains of Solomon's work—at least where archaeologists have excavated to date—the extensive description of the temple and palace in 1 Kings 6–7 enables us to see how Solomon built in keeping with the architectural styles of his time.

The description of Solomon's temple-palace complex matches material remains of the acropolises at the ninth-century BCE Aramean cities of Sam'al (modern Zincirli) and Kinalua (modern Tel Tayinat) in south-central Turkey. At the latter site, two buildings are conjoined. Each conforms to the architectural plan labeled *bit hilani*, a plan Assyrians copied from the West (the land of Hatti) beginning in the mid-eighth century BCE. This is reminiscent of the claim that Solomon built his own palace in juxtaposition to that of his royal Egyptian bride. Behind these buildings is a tripartite temple, entered on its narrow side, which conforms to the plan reported for Solomon's temple.

Yet another temple, contemporary with Solomon, has been uncovered at Ain Dara in Syria. This one follows the same plan, but with an added feature: carved into the floor is a series of gargantuan footprints depicting the stride of the deity into the temple's *adyton*, or "holy of holies." Reliefs of a striding god, a goddess, a mountain, and theriomorphic humans (lion, bird/eagle, bull) decorate the walls, much like the adornments described in Jerusalem in 1 Kings 6–7. Even the technique of construction associated with Solomon's temple, with wooden beams inset every fourth course, has parallels in Late Bronze architecture—such as the gate of Megiddo strata VIIB–A (late twelfth century BCE)—which do not carry into the late Iron and Persian eras. This was functional not so much for fastening materials to the walls as for absorbing shock. And the description of the clerestory of the temple has parallels to the Phoenician structures known as the "temple of the time," especially on Cyprus.

The description of Solomon's palace in 1 Kings 7 likewise fits the architectural character of others in the region. Palace 1723 at Megiddo, from the same era, exhibits the plan of a *bīt ḥilāni* related to what we would expect of Solomon's palace (Ussishkin 1966). It was arguably the residency of Solomon's governor over the province of Jezreel (see 1 Kgs 4:7-19). Aside from the later finds at Tayinat and Zincirli, mentioned above, the basic layout became a staple of Assyrian royal architecture in the eighth century BCE, especially under Sennacherib: it became the reception suite at the heart of Assyrian, Babylonian, and Persian palaces rather than the palace as a whole. Similarly, the biblical stories of Ehud, of the rape of Tamar, and of Solomon's designation by David presuppose similar, perhaps identical, floor plans.

Solomon's House of the Cedars of Lebanon, as his palace was known, has also attracted parallels from Cyprus. For this building, the temple and the palace, Garfinkel and Mumcuoglu (2013) have shown that there are clear archaeological parallels, including in a model shrine at Qeiyafa. In other words, all aspects of Solomon's Jerusalem building activity in Kings have archaeological parallels from his period and from slightly thereafter.

State Formation: External Recognition

The real test of a state is its integration into a web of other states in the vicinity. States are socially constructed; their organization, large-scale projects, and networked connections may be apparent to them, but their existence as a state ultimately depends on their recognition by fellow states. David's state passes that test—for example, in the enforcement by King Achish of Gath of Shimei's right to extradite fugitive slaves (1 Kgs 2:36-44).

To gauge state recognition in greater depth, we need to understand what a state—in this case a West Semitic state—is. What do the texts reveal? To begin with, kings appear everywhere. Biblical texts mention kings of Moab (in connection with Ehud, David) and multiple kings of Canaan (as in the story of Deborah) and of Ammon (evident in the tales of Jephthah, Saul, and David). We even have a tradition of early kings of Edom in Genesis 36. Naive interpreters assume that a king of Moab or of Edom or Ammon is the king of a territorial state. That may be implied, at least to our modern conceptions, but not explicitly claimed by the texts.

Instead, kings are linked to cities (probably city-states consisting of an urban center with a supporting rural hinterland around it). In the Moabite Stele, Mesha confesses he is a Dibonite, king of a town. Kings of Aram come from Damascus and Arpad. So one king of Aram is the king of Damascus, and one king of Moab is the king of Dibon, and one king of Ammon is the king of Rabbah. Their status as a king is linked to a city. Their territorial status comes from their luck in subjugating neighboring polities and neighboring vassal kings, as David does in 2 Samuel 10:6 and 19. Critical review of the accounts in Samuel-Kings comports with these conclusions.

Foreigners associate King David, as well as the later kings Omri and Ahab, with enemy states. Despite this, neither Omri nor David registers archaeologically. Nor, before them, does Jeroboam or Saul.

In Canaan, kings were almost ubiquitous, as Joshua 13:10-11 has it and Judges 5 attests. But with Israel, we so let the text dominate our imagination as to exclude the imaginable. How can we envision anew the way Saul and David conduct war realistically? They gather troops in numbers amounting to little more than gangs. Fifty trained Egyptian archers could have repelled any of these forces. In our reports, Saul takes one town (Beeroth), and David takes two (Jerusalem, Rabbat-Ammon), none of them at the time a major fortification.

We do not think of Iron I in terms of an Amarna-like tessellation of administrative units, as we would from a statist perspective, but we should. Indeed Saul's sons-in-law were small state-holders: "kings," as the biblical texts say. Magnates such as Saul enlist other rulers—through marriage or other forms of alliance—and thus obscure their antecedent competition, the ones who "lost in the primary," so to speak. But we have textual hints of hereditary authority, such as that of the minor judges—take, for instance, Yair (Judg 10:3-4; compare to Judg 12:8-9; 12:13-14); or the famous case of Abimelech, son of Gideon/Jerubbaal, cited in connection with Uriah almost as though he were a hero come to a bad end: "Which is better for you," he notoriously asks, "that seventy men, all sons of Jerubbaal, rule over you, or that one man rule over you, and remember that I am your bone and flesh?" (Judg 9:2).

In contrast to Abimelech, neither the sons of Milkilu nor those of Lab'aya in the Amarna letters rule over their **patrilocal** homes, and indeed, from among the sons of Abdi-Ashirta, it is one, Aziru, who emerges as leader. By the same token, David tries to enlist the "men" (1 Sam 11:1; 2 Sam 2:4-5) or inhabitants (1 Sam 31:11) of Jabesh-Gilead. More successfully, he wins the allegiance of Saul's in-laws, and one wonders whether he did not also address the Nimshi and Nimshides of the Beth Shean Valley in the course of his state building. This name, that of Jehu's grandfather (2 Kgs 9:2 v. 1 Kgs 19:16), occurs repeatedly there in the tenth and ninth centuries BCE. Nimshi's status in the text and proportional overrepresentation in writing together intimate that he was a king, and minimally an administrator, perhaps in the region of Rehob.

How many kinglets controlled parts of pre-Saulide Israel and her neighboring territories? Was there a king at Megiddo during Stratum VIA, near the gate? How many kinglets persisted to be co-opted later as kings of small city-states? Libnah's secession from Judah in the mid-ninth century BCE at least suggests that the town and its territory had a king. Indeed, the way 1–2 Samuel speaks of boundaries indicates that the territorial units of towns known to us from the fourteenth-century BCE Amarna letters persisted. Later, the law of Deuteronomy 21:1-9 stipulates assignment of jurisdiction over homicide in rural areas to the nearest settlement, and it requires an actual survey to determine its proximity; this suggests the town's "territory" was no longer a matter of fixed boundaries and that "commons" separated territories (Hoffner 1997, 20).

So West Semitic kings begin as rulers of a city. A few may rise to create an alliance or even a hegemony of cities, which they and their city lead. Saul managed to accomplish this, and David built upon his success. And then Solomon did as well. In some cases, those cities joined "voluntarily" and became part of regional identity—Israel. Others were conquered by force of arms and were instead occupied or otherwise kept separate.

During the tenth century BCE, accumulation and movement of capital in its various forms inevitably caused several states to create webs of connections, not just that of David. We hear of such states: Ammon, with kings at Rabbah, allying with Aram Zoba, then David; Geshur, which very much looks like a city-state with Stier-und-Mond Gott, or Bull with Lunar Crescent icon, in the gate; Maacah, with a king in 2 Samuel 8 but no longer at 2 Samuel 20; Zobah with a king; Hamath in alliance with David; Moab with a king; Edom with kings before Saul; various Aramean kingdoms; Tyre with a king; five Philistine towns with the equivalents of kings; as well as Egypt—though not on the horizon until Solomon—and Sidon and Dor and Akko experiencing the same situation. These are the kings, for what they are worth, of Joshua 13 or of Sareptah or Amalek or other groups. Many of them knew and recognized the kingdom of David.

The Strategy of David's State in the Archaeology of North and South

David's United Monarchy brought together two regions: in Judah, he had developed networks of contact and alliance; and in Israel, the power base of Saul's rival dynasty, he enjoyed little familiarity or trust. Even though joined together, they still required different strategies of governance, hints of which are visible in the archaeological records.

In the north of the new kingdom, David's reign brought about two major changes. The first of these was the end of the Iron I culture and its highly distributed—and not palatial—trading culture at cities like Megiddo, Yoqneam, Dor, Beth Shean, and Jatt. The second was the establishment of the Iron IIA Israelite state with administrative centers at Hazor, Megiddo, and Dor but with no domestic population.

David's new Israelite nation reinvented the old city-states as distributed acropolises, without temples. The new elites now had residences in the capital and homes on the acropolises near the estates they administered—hence, the phenomenon of few named provincial capitals in 1 Kings 4:7-19. The poorer population was rusticated, sent back to the farm, so to speak, leaving David's administrators within the walls and the local native Israelites outside them.

We can see how this took place at Megiddo, beginning with Stratum VIA, which by common accord correlates to a number of Jezreel Valley town horizons and predates David. In this stratum, the distribution of artifacts differs from that encountered in earlier and in later layers. In cuts made by Schumacher, Chicago, and Tel Aviv University and Pennsylvania State University, the relatively broad distribution of "luxury" goods in Stratum VIA, in comparison with their concentration in the northern palace in the preceding Strata IX–VIIA, suggests the operation of more egalitarian marketplaces at the site. Together with the inference that Israelites were represented in its population (Esse 1992), as were Philistine artifacts and practices (especially in Area K), and the absence of a real palace on the site, in conjunction with villas housing domestic industries and engaged in trade for such items as Nile perch, the implication is that during the eleventh century BCE a kind of forerunner of the *pax Salomonica/Israelitica*—which lasted to about 841 BCE—had already crystallized at the site (esp. Harrison 2004; Holladay 1995; Halpern 2001; Hirth 1998). It may have been central, and therefore commanded social as well as tangible resources, in mediating the benefits of trade to the region, where, again, pottery seems to be more or less homogeneous stylistically. The population was not yet dispersed, and the town remained autonomous. But it looks as though an oligarchy, rather than a king supported by an empire, had taken charge.

When does the Megiddo VIA horizon vanish? Not before the battle of Gilboa. Possibly, it happened under Abner and Ishbaal late in the eleventh century BCE, though this seems unlikely. And although attributed to David by some archaeologists, neither he nor Solomon achieved this, or their apologists would have trumpeted the victories. Indeed, the absence of a claim to victory by David at this site is evidence as to the accuracy of contemporary biblical traditions.

Two other scenarios are more likely. The first is that Absalom and his allies destroyed the system of trade around the Jezreel Valley and Sharon, which David had exploited. It is clear that David's policy was to ally with elements in Philistia, particularly Gath, in a trade alliance with the Megiddo VIA horizon towns of the Jezreel Valley that surrounded and rivaled a resistant central hills agricultural state, Israel (Halpern 2001). The second possibility is that a third force intervened: not Ashdod or Tyre, but Pharaoh Siamun. Something baked Megiddo VIA, even if possibly an earthquake; someone removed Dor from the checkerboard, and reduced Taanach and Gezer.

Whatever its source, Megiddo was rebuilt by an ascendant, mature state, with logistics, labor, funds, foreign relations, and supplies. It brought in a sophisticated elite to manage the transformation: a state with multiple distributed acropolises to haul in produce and attract purchasing power from the countryside, to channel markets and trade efficiently. In later phases, these regional centers served as centers of industry (as Rehov IV or Megiddo IVA). This phenomenon, beginning in Iron IIA, presupposes a lengthy prehistory of state formation.

The planning alone for this population redistribution is impressive. Local estate holders were handed a lot of the responsibility, with state backing, especially to put each man under his own fig palm or fig leaf, and perhaps thus create a yeomanry. Not dissimilar is the responsibility delegated at Amarna to Abdi-Ashirta to rebuild Sumur—that is to say, relative to its territories, the new united Israelite monarchy acted in part like a sovereign empire, with an "imperial" center and distributed, semiautonomous regions.

Thus, populations—in the case of Megiddo VIA, a mixed population—were rusticated from the fortresses, which now became purely administrative centers. This situation persisted into the late Iron IIA or the mid-ninth century BCE or a bit later (Halpern 2000). The ruralization was deliberate—depriving renowned towns of their independence and, especially, of a population likely to revolt (i.e., against David or Solomon). The administrators in the fortress, and their dependents, were thus the governing agents. Whether they became (or were to begin with) "Israelite" or "Judean," the principle of administrative towns endured to the Damascene conquest and then was abandoned for the principle of shielding populations behind fortifications (Hazor IX–VIII, Megiddo IVA), probably against threats from Aram, Phoenicia, Assyria, and even Egypt. The initial strategy, however, was a sensible one for expanding from a limited to a more aggressive approach toward exploitation of resources (especially agricultural) and trade. David's strategy thus aimed to neutralize any possible opposition (by placing them outside the fortifications), while at the same time increasing agricultural output and enhancing trade networks.

David used a completely different strategy in the south. His Judea seems to have colluded with Gath (for instance, against Ekron—see Halpern 2001) and with other elements sending Iron IB trade north up the coast (Dor, Jatt), through the Jezreel to Dan, Abel, and up the Beqaa. The conflict that arose between Philistines (i.e., the coastal powers) and Saul—and between David and Saul's dynasty, for that matter—was principally one against a consolidated power defending a closed, self-sufficient autarchy in the Israelite highlands (led by Saul), supported by Transjordanian alliances in Gilead and outlets in Syria. In this light, Knauf's point (1991b) about the import of the Faynan copper supply during this era when the copper supply from Cyprus was disrupted comports precisely with the Iron IB–IIA Negev settlement as a state policy. Faynan

FIGURE 13-7. *An Iron Age workshop at the copper mines of Khirbet en-Nahas in Edom, southeast of the Dead Sea. Copper ore in the valley behind was actively mined and then smelted here in both Iron I and Iron II.*

is located in Jordan some fifty kilometers south of the Dead Sea in what was once biblical Edom. Recent excavations led by Thomas Levy and Muhammad Najjar at Khirbet en-Nahas in Wadi Faynan have uncovered a monumental fortress and one of the largest Iron Age copper-production sites in the ancient world. Radiocarbon dating of the site confirms two major phases of production in the twelfth to eleventh centuries and the tenth to ninth centuries BCE (Levy and Higham 2005). This vast copper-industry complex demonstrates an intricate trade system operated by an organized central authority in Edomite territory. Debates have focused on whether the Edomites were settled as a viable kingdom by the tenth to ninth centuries BCE. Critics of the historicity of the united monarchy have argued that any mention of Edomites was an anachronism, because Edom did not emerge as an organized state until the eight to seventh century BCE. Not all scholars are in agreement with the conclusion regarding Khirbet en-Nahas and the Edomites (Grabbe 2007, 97–98), and the discovery of this mining complex from the eleventh century BCE calls for a reassessment of the formation of the Edomite state as well as the biblical narrative of the united monarchy.

Shishak's excursion into the Negev always suggested a focus on trade rather than subsistence, and, for all we know, he may have made some temporary use of the settlements. Their end phase may be slightly later than we suspect, possibly in the ninth century BCE, if they were exploited as a means to redirect trade Egypt's way.

But the Shephelah is another matter. Beth Shemesh in Iron IIA is one of the provincial acropolises planned under Solomon, whenever it was in fact occupied. But Qeiyafa, a touch earlier, is probably Davidic and surely, as the excavator has it, a Judahite fortress site. It is architecturally of a piece with the tenth-century BCE west gate and tower at Tell Beit Mirsim. The Shephelah was the place where Israel, Judah, Philistia, and old Canaanite towns met.

A proper understanding of Qeiyafa is key to perceiving David's strategy. If Qeiyafa belongs to Judah, as its excavator argues, then it makes no sense for it to be a fortress to guard against Gath, for Judah remained in alliance with Gath until at least Solomon's time. Therefore, Qeiyafa was erected against Saul's Israel; it guards a Davidic link to Gath as well as to Yarmuth and Socho. Even in Solomonic times, there was no embarrassment in reporting pacific relations with Gath and with David's old liege, Achish (as 1 Sam 27 vs. 21:11-16). Fights among the Philistines were more prevalent than we typically guess, furthermore, and Gath required a link to Judah. This was Judah's border, but it was also a weak point, because a Napoleonic coup de main could have severed Gath's alliance with David. In other words, we can imagine David laying down the trade connections that Solomon exploited, should we think in terms of interventions prevented (an attack by Ekron or Ashdod on Gath, for example), and facilitated in the end with such policies as ruralization and revising title to lands otherwise in question. The tenth century BCE looks very much like a relative golden age in the Levant, a revival of localism, a time of the forging of intellectual as well as instinctive bonds.

Maybe that is why David became a national hero.

Conclusion

Assessing the account of David's reign has involved reviewing the whole of the united monarchy plus the periods preceding and succeeding it. At this time, Israel's Canaan underwent a thorough transformation. Elements ensconced in the highlands, partly taking advantage of water resources in an Iron I era of relative drought (Halpern 1983; Langgut, Finkelstein, and Litt 2013), multiplied and succeeded at small-scale farming while forging trade and kinship networks of considerable robustness. The population coalesced—partly with and partly in competition with neighboring groups—into a polity, or group of polities, whose rough identity could be cut across by other social bonds.

While Saul seems to have waged war principally against groups in the highlands, particularly the Hivvites and Gibeonites and elements identified with the Philistines, David adopted a strategy, along with some of his Philistine allies, of combining peripheral or marginalized groups against Israelite nativists linked to Saul.

David's policies prevailed, to the extent of allowing him to construct a capital and state. They did not survive unchallenged, however, as Absalom's revolt indicates. And however poor the historical reliability of the succession narrative that describes David's would-be and actual successors (2 Sam 9–20 and 1 Kgs 1–2), it exemplifies the tenuous human element of state formation.

Furthermore, David's policies did not survive the imposition of central authority on upland populations and the dispersal of lowland populations under Solomon. A nativist movement of the tribes, supported by Shishak's Egypt under Jeroboam, claimed the allegiance of Israelites north of Jerusalem and, by then, probably Canaanites as well.

In the meanwhile, Solomon had installed a massive temple-palace complex on the Jerusalem acropolis. He had divided Israel into provincial units, to a large degree conforming to the relationships among kinship and cultural groups (which are not the same as "tribes"), with lowland provinces being more commercial and productive. The "tribal" provinces were kinship-related districts and toponyms (Mahanaim may stand in for a district), but the valley provinces (the Ayyalon Pass, Hepher/Arubot, the coast of Dor, the Jezreel Valley) were city-based. He evidently lost control of Damascus but retained it over Edom, a situation that persisted through the most intensive phases of the Wadi Faynan exploitation down to about 845 BCE.

Life in the region of Syria, Phoenicia, and Israel was perceived by the biblical writers as turbulent. David tried to introduce his own stability into that world, as did many other adventurers. He had some success.

David's experiment was short-lived. In that time, however, it left marks in architecture and other aspects of material culture, and it engendered a stratification of Israelite society. It also played progenitor to a tradition whose endurance was ultimately greater than that of its individual parts.

Suggestions for Further Reading

This chapter encapsulates many of the arguments and ideas that Baruch Halpern put forward in his book *David's Secret Demons: Messiah, Murderer, Traitor, Spy* (2001). For an approach to David and his heir Solomon that relies more heavily on archaeological research, see Israel Finkelstein and Neil Silberman's *David and Solomon: In Search of the Bible's Sacred Kings and the Roots of Western Tradition* (2006). An alternative perspective appears in Amihai Mazar's "Archaeology and the Biblical Narrative: The Case of the United Monarchy." To learn about the agricultural use of pigs in the Near East, see B. Hess and P. Wapnish's "Can Pig Remains Be Used for Ethnic Diagnosis in the Ancient Near East?" and M. A. Zeder's "The Role of Pigs in Near Eastern Subsistence: A View from the Southern Levant." For an accessible article, with photographs, about Eilat Mazar's excavations above the Milo and her discovery of a "palace," see her article "Did I Find King David's Palace?" With regard to the domestication of agricultural animals, especially the camel, see L. Sapir-Hen and E. Ben-Yosef's essay "The Introduction of Domestic Camels to the Southern Levant: Evidence from the Aravah Valley" (2013). For information about the use of and trade in copper, see E. A. Knauf's "King Solomon's Copper Supply" and Thomas E. Levy, E. Ben-Yosef, and Muhammad Najjar's "New Perspectives on Iron Age Copper Production and Society in the Faynan Region, Jordan."

14

ISRAEL
The Prosperous Northern Kingdom

Randall W. Younker

The Northern Kingdom of Israel refers to the Syro-Palestinian kingdom comprising the ten northern tribes that seceded from the united monarchy of Israel in approximately 931 BCE, after the death of King Solomon (1 Kgs 12:1, 16, 19), leaving behind the Southern Kingdom of Judah (see the next chapter). The Northern Kingdom lasted for approximately 210 years, falling to the Assyrians when they conquered its capital at Samaria in 722 BCE. During this time it was ruled by twenty kings from nine different "houses" or dynasties. The most significant houses were those of Jeroboam I (the founding king of the Northern Kingdom); the House of Omri (which included kings Omri and Ahab); and the House of Jehu (which included Jehu, Jehoahaz, Joash, and Jeroboam II). These were long-reigning dynasties that struggled to maintain Israel's prosperity and independence through a series of wars, treaties, and submissions. The short reigns of six kings (Zachariah, Shallum, Menahem, Pekahiah, Pekah, and Hoshea) oversaw the decline and eventual extinction of the Northern Kingdom. Four of their reigns ended in assassination (Zachariah, Shallum, Pekahiah, and Pekah), while the final king, Hoshea, was captured and deported as a prisoner when Samaria fell to the Assyrians in 722/721 BCE.

The Northern Kingdom of Israel, though a relatively small state within the context of the greater ancient Near East, was comparatively prosperous. There were a number of reasons for this. First, the highlands of Israel enjoyed a productive and rich agrarian economy. Although much of the soil is on slopes and had to be terraced, the region normally enjoyed abundant rainfall. Crops—especially the staple foods cereals, grapes, and olives—were usually bountiful. Israel was more densely populated than Judah in the south; estimates suggest Israel's population was approximately eight hundred thousand, while only two hundred thousand people lived in Judah. Israel's large population was able to work the land and provide a good tax base for the government while also supporting a strong army. However, the greatest factor in Israel's economic prosperity was its geographic location, sitting astride several key major trade routes that connected Mesopotamia, Syria, and Phoenicia with the lucrative trade hub of Aqaba and the Red Sea. As will be shown below, this factor would play

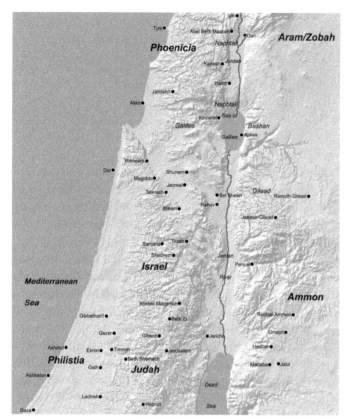

MAP 14-1. *Important cities and towns in the Northern Kingdom of Israel in the centuries after it separated from Judah to the south.*

a key role in enabling Israel to successfully break away from Judah and create a prosperous, independent kingdom. Yet, in the end, the advantages that led to economic prosperity could not resist certain internal challenges that would eat away at Israel's sociopolitical system until it ultimately collapsed before the might of Assyria in 722 BCE.

Biblical Sources for the Northern Kingdom

Our primary source for the history of the Northern Kingdom of Israel is the Hebrew Bible, specifically from what scholars refer to as the Deuteronomistic History (DH) and the Chronicler's History (CH). The DH comprises Joshua, Judges, 1 and 2 Samuel, as well as 1 and 2 Kings, while the CH consists of 1 and 2 Chronicles along with Ezra and Nehemiah. The DH was probably composed in the seventh century BCE and the CH close to the end of the fifth century BCE. The portions of these histories that deal with the Northern Kingdom of Israel and the four-hundred-year history of the divided kingdom include 1 Kings 12:1 to 2 Kings 17:41 with additional information provided in 2 Chronicles 10:1–31:21. The books of Kings feature not just the kings but also the prophets Elijah and Elisha. Additional information about the Northern Kingdom, especially concerning the religious climate of the time, appears in the books of the prophets Amos, Hosea, Jonah, and Nahum. Chronicles clearly adds material not included in the DH, and it has been suggested that much, if not most, of the additional material is propagandistic rather than historical, favoring the Southern Kingdom. While this may be true, recent scholars have argued that Chronicles is not merely negative toward the north but rather invites it to repent, acknowledge the legitimacy of the Jerusalem temple, and rejoin the south.

Linking Archaeology to History

Of course, any proper understanding of the Northern Kingdom of Israel, whether one is interested in its historical/political or cultural/social aspects, requires locating it properly in its historical context. The chronology of the divided kingdom has been worked out to a fairly accurate degree based on a combination of information from the DH and extrabiblical sources from Assyria and Egypt. While there are some differences in details, these differences amount to only a few years. All agree that the Northern Kingdom was founded in the latter part of the tenth century BCE, with most scholars focusing on a date of around 931 BCE; this date is derived from working backward from a synchronism between Israel and Egypt in 853 BCE.

The 931 BCE date overlaps with the reign of the Egyptian pharaoh Sheshonq I, whose twenty-one-year reign is dated by most scholars to approximately 945–924 BCE or 941–920 BCE. Sheshonq I is equated with the biblical Pharaoh Shishak, who is mentioned in two events that occurred just before and after the division of the monarchy in 931 BCE. The first event is described in 1 Kings 11:40, which relates that Shishak gave refuge to the future king of the Northern Kingdom, Jeroboam. The second event is mentioned in 1 Kings 14:25 (recounted with additional details in 2 Chr 12:2-4), which claims that this same Shishak attacked Rehoboam's cities of Judah (including Jerusalem) in the fifth year of the divided kingdom—that is, 926 BCE, just two (or six) years before Shishak's death. The fact that Sheshonq I's Victory Relief at Karnak in Egypt specifically mentions an attack against Israel seems to provide a lock on both the identity of Shishak with Sheshonq I and the general chronology for the latter part of the tenth century BCE.

ARCHAEOLOGICAL DATING OF THE NORTHERN KINGDOM

In recent years a controversy has emerged over this linkage. A small group of scholars has argued for what is called a Low Chronology (see below). Leading the opposition to the Low Chronology are several scholars who argue for what they describe as the Modified Conventional Chronology (MCC) (Frese

FIGURE 14-1. *The wall of the Bubastite Portal at the Karnak Temple. The rows of small figures below and left of Sheshonq's shoulders, each with a cartouche name, represent the 156 Canaanite towns Sheshonq conquered. Many are now missing.*

and Levy 2010; A. Mazar 2005). This chapter follows the position of the MCC because the author finds the arguments of the MCC to be more apropos to both the textual and the archaeological data, including the results of the author's own work in Jordan, which has ties to key events in the history of the Kingdom of Israel (see discussion below). In particular, it adheres to the periodization laid out in 2005 by A. Mazar, as laid out in Figure 14-2.

FIGURE 14-2. *The stages of the Iron Age used in this chapter (as per A. Mazar 2005, 24)*

Iron IA	1200–1140/1130 BCE
Iron IB	1140/1130–ca. 1000/980 BCE
Iron IIA	ca. 1000/980–ca. 840/830 BCE
Iron IIB	ca. 840/830–732/701 BCE
Iron IIC	ca. 732/701–605/586 BCE

As we have already discussed, both biblical sources (DH and CH) and Egyptian sources indicate that the divided monarchy began in the latter part of the tenth century BCE (ca. 931 BCE). The main controversy in correlating the archaeology of the sites with the history of the Northern Kingdom of

Israel as derived from the textual evidence revolves around which dates should be assigned to the stratified material culture assemblages—including pottery, architecture, and so forth—found in archaeological sites. Scholars have correlated the tenth and most of the ninth centuries BCE with the archaeological assemblage called the Iron Age IIA (recently modified by Mazar to 1000–840 BCE). The Iron IIA material culture is characterized by distinctive pottery that prominently features red-slip and irregular hand-burnished wares that displaced the previous Canaanite painted pottery tradition. It is also characterized by new settlement patterns, distinctive monumental architecture (including palaces and fortified six-chambered gates, as at Gezer; see Figures 5-4 and 13-4), and religious art. Historically, the Iron IIA archaeological assemblage corresponds to the historical period from the reigns of David and Solomon (ca. 1000 BCE) to the end of the Omride Dynasty of the Northern Kingdom (ca. 834 BCE).

However, a group of archaeologists, led by Israel Finkelstein (2013), has recently suggested redating this Iron IIA archaeological evidence from the tenth century BCE largely to the ninth century BCE (ca. 920–800 BCE). Similarly, these scholars suggest redating the Iron IIB assemblage to the very end of the ninth and the eighth centuries BCE (ca. 800–720 BCE). The void now left for the tenth century BCE archaeological evidence would be filled by the material previously associated with the Iron I Period (traditionally assigned to the eleventh century BCE, the time of the judges). This Iron I material culture reflects more Canaanite influence, the settlement pattern of small villages with no large cities, and no monumental architecture. This would leave the united kingdom as a small polity, limited to the south (the area that would become Judah), with a relatively impoverished material culture. The rich Iron IIA material culture then becomes that of the divided monarchy.

However, scholars like Baruch Halpern (2005, 2010) have made a series of arguments to the contrary, including linguistic elements in the DH that seem to antedate the seventh century BCE. There are a number of characteristics of the ninth-century BCE polities (Israel and Judah, as well as Ammon and Moab)—such as political structures, social organizational complexities, inscriptions (e.g., Tel Dan Stele, Mesha Stele), linguistic features of the Hebrew text (such as phonology, syntax, orthography, etc.), and historical interactions and developments (with Syria, Assyria, and Egypt)—that presuppose origins for the divided monarchy that reach back into and reflect a tenth-century BCE (united monarchy) setting.

Beyond these issues is the basic problem of redating the Iron Age archaeological assemblages. Several sites with ceramic evidence assigned to the Iron IIA appear to be reliably situated in the tenth century BCE due to the sites' history according to biblical and extrabiblical texts. For example, the destruction of dozens of Iron IIA forts in the Negev is almost certainly the result of Sheshonq I's late tenth-century BCE raid, as is similar destruction in the towns at Arad and Taanach.

The Low Chronology redating encounters a similar problem with regard to the archaeological evidence from Transjordan sites such as Umayri, Hesban, Madaba, and Jalul. By redating the Iron IIA evidence down into the ninth century BCE, this theory conflicts with a unique Transjordan ninth-century BCE Iron IIB archaeological corpus. The issue is even more complicated by the fact that part of the Iron IIB ceramic evidence in the southern part of the Madaba Plains in Jordan includes distinctive Moabite forms that correlate with the Moabite king Mesha's northward move into the Madaba Plains region as recounted in the Mesha Inscription around 840 BCE (see Figure 17-4; A. Mazar 2005; Herr and Bates 2011; Harrison and Barlow 2005). The Iron IIB evidence with distinctive Moabite elements found at these sites is found stratigraphically *above* the Iron IIA evidence. Since it is located above the Iron IIA evidence, it is therefore necessarily later than that material. This forces the Iron IIA back into the early ninth and tenth centuries BCE, just as the supporters of the MCC theory have argued.

A final criticism of the Low Chronology is found in ^{14}C analysis. While Finkelstein has argued that ^{14}C dates support his moving the Iron IIA material culture down to the ninth to eighth century BCE, a recent high-quality series of dates of the Iron I–II strata of Tel Rehov favor the tenth- to ninth-century BCE dates for Iron IIA. Although radiocarbon dating has been enthusiastically embraced by many archaeologists to break the deadlock over the decades-long debates over High and Low Chronology, the latest results are still inconclusive, and interpretations reflect the major antagonists' positions (Finkelstein 2013; A. Mazar 2005). Moreover, Norma Franklin (2005) points out that radiocarbon dating must rest on a secure analysis of stratigraphy, but the stratigraphic record at both Megiddo and Samaria in the Northern Kingdom is unclear. This is important because the Megiddo pottery has been "the cornerstone of Levantine Bronze and Iron Age pottery as we know it today" (Franklin 2005, 313). In addition, Franklin argues that the Samaria building phases were also misidentified. As a result, the stratigraphy and thus dating of these two important Iron Age cities have been seriously misinterpreted (2005, 311). Further, Franklin's surveys have convincingly demonstrated that the palaces at Samaria and Megiddo were constructed by the same builders using the same ashlar stones, the same mason marks, and the same "short cubit" measuring system first used in Egypt during the Twenty-Second Dynasty (ca. 945–712 BCE). The establishment of Omri's Dynasty is documented in the Hebrew Bible and Assyrian records, and the palace at Samaria can be easily dated to sometime after Omri's purchase of the hilltop settlement around 880

BCE. The pertinent strata of Megiddo and Samaria can now be correlated, and archaeologists can establish a firmer archaeological chronology for the ninth century BCE. Still, more work needs to be done with regard to establishing reliable ^{14}C dates for this period.

The Kingdom Divides

With a chronological framework and a corresponding material culture database (Iron IIA) in place, it is now possible to examine the history of the Northern Kingdom of Israel, beginning with its split from the united monarchy (ca. 931 BCE). According to the biblical text, the seeds of the division of the united monarchy of Israel were sown when Solomon appointed Jeroboam, son of Nebat and Zeruah (1 Kgs 11:26), superintendent over all the forced labor working for the house of Joseph. Since this appointment is made within the context of a reference to Solomon's building of the Millo—a major fortification project south of the temple in Jerusalem—it would appear that Jeroboam was in charge of this project; interestingly, the excessive use of forced laborers would be one of the complaints that the northern tribes would have against Solomon's son Rehoboam (1 Kgs 12:4). Jeroboam, a member of the tribe of Ephraim, was a northerner and would have been in the awkward position of superintending the forced labor of his own people. This raises the question as to whether Jeroboam resented this appointment. Thus, when the prophet Ahijah told Jeroboam that he would become leader of the ten northern tribes, the prophet may have been confirming an ambition that Jeroboam was already nurturing. Whatever the case, 1 Kings 11:27 suggests that, after receiving Ahijah's prophecy, Jeroboam began taking steps to assure its fulfillment. Solomon soon learned about Jeroboam's conspiracy, forcing the young rebel to flee to Egypt, where he was given asylum by Pharaoh Sheshonq I / Shishak (1 Kgs 11:40).

While Jeroboam was in exile in Egypt, Solomon died and his son Rehoboam assumed the throne of Israel; his convocation was to be held in Shechem. However, the ten northern tribes were unwilling to accept Rehoboam's rule without certain reformations of royal policy. The attendees included Jeroboam, who had returned from exile in Egypt (1 Kgs 12:1-3). Jeroboam and the leaders of the northern tribes presented their demands to Rehoboam as a precondition for their allegiance. Rehoboam rejected these demands out of hand and instead vowed to enforce his father's unpopular policies even more heavily (1 Kgs 12:5-14). This led the ten northern tribes to repudiate their loyalty to Rehoboam and switch their allegiance to Jeroboam (1 Kgs 12:16).

Sheshonq in Israel

At this point it might be interesting to entertain a growing hypothesis about Sheshonq I / Shishak's involvement in the land of Israel: perhaps the Egyptian pharaoh actually conducted *two* separate campaigns into this country. This would potentially solve the various chronological and geographical discrepancies between the biblical and Karnak accounts (Dodson 2012, 87–93). In this "two-campaign" scenario, the Karnak account describes the first campaign, which is focused more on the north—in the new territory of the Northern Kingdom—possibly to provide support in buttressing key cities in support of his protégé Jeroboam I during the latter's first year of reign. The second campaign is found in the biblical account and describes a campaign against Rehoboam that is limited to forty cities in Judah, culminating in the capture of Jerusalem, five years after the division of the united kingdom. The textual evidence does not provide a clear picture; however, it is quite likely that some surrendered without a fight and avoided any destruction, while others were subjected to some destruction before the city was conquered.

The archaeology seems to confirm this mixed picture. Five cities explicitly mentioned by Sheshonq I include Taanach, Shunem (modern Solem/Sulam), Rehov, Mahanaim (Khirbet Mahneh?), and Megiddo. Of these five, the location of Mahanaim is uncertain, and Shunem has been subjected to only a few exploratory probes, one of which revealed some Iron Age pottery. However, Taanach, Rehov, and Megiddo have been subject to extensive excavations that revealed ceramic evidence associated with some destruction that the excavators would date to this period (see below). Moreover, a victory stele of Sheshonq I was recovered from Megiddo (unfortunately not in situ) that testifies to his presence there. Jeroboam I's move from Shechem to Penuel in Transjordan (1 Kgs 12:25) was probably intended to secure the east flank of his new kingdom, taking advantage of Sheshonq I's first invasion. With a loyal vassal (or ally) controlling these northern cities, Sheshonq I was able to secure control over prized Phoenician trade routes that ran from Phoenicia through the Northern Kingdom and down the Jordan Valley to the Gulf of Eilat on the Red Sea.

Whether Sheshonq I conducted two campaigns into Palestine (in 931 and 925 BCE) or only one (in 925 BCE), many archaeologists argue that evidence of his campaign(s) can be detected at sites mentioned in the Karnak Relief, including Taanach. Scholars such as Lawrence Stager associate Taanach Stratum IIB with the city that was attacked by Shishak (Stager 2003: 63–74; A. Mazar 2005, 2010). Since the strata below and above IIB are rather ephemeral, Stratum IIB is really the only possible occupation of the early Iron II Period that would fit the city that Shishak would have attacked. A. Mazar thus argues that this stratum should serve as an anchor for the tenth century BCE, early Iron IIA (ca. 980–921 BCE). He also notes that the pottery from this stratum matches that of Megiddo Stratum VA–IVB, which has been traditionally associated with Solomon and the latter part of the tenth century BCE. As you can see, the evidence from multiple sites is converging.

The House of Jeroboam I and Archaeology

Having secured his new kingdom, Jeroboam set about strengthening and rebuilding it. According to 1 Kings 12:31-33, Jeroboam began his reign by taking steps to ensure that Israel would not reverse its decision and reunite with Judah. He did this by establishing two new temples, one on the new kingdom's northern border at Dan and a second on the southern border at Bethel. Archaeologists have identified the former but not the latter; Bethel's location remains a matter of controversy. And, while there is no extrabiblical inscriptional evidence relating directly to King Jeroboam I, the biblical texts mention a number of important building projects at sites that have been investigated by archaeologists, including Dan and Shechem (1 Kgs 12:1, 25-33; 2 Chr 10:1).

At Dan, excavator Avraham Biran (1994) found a cultic place for religious rituals as part of the Iron IIA settlement, which he suggested was built by Jeroboam I. Specifically, on the north side of the tell, Biran's team found a structure more than eight meters wide and of indeterminate length built of large ashlar blocks and decorated with marginal drafts. The structure had the appearance of a large podium and was identified as a "high place," or **bamah** in Hebrew. The excavators suggested that a temple stood on this podium, although no traces of a building were preserved. However, found in association with the podium were three large *pithoi* (storage jars) bearing the reliefs of writhing snakes, a storage jar containing seven spouted lamps, incense stands decorated in relief and painted, faience statuettes, a plastered installation that may have served as part of a water ritual, and a clay bathtub. This structure, its associated objects and ceramics, along with an upper gatehouse and possible casemate wall, were assigned to Tel Dan Stratum IVA (Iron IIA).

The pottery found in association with the structure and objects included storage jars, jugs, juglets, and a variety of bowls that can be dated to the end of the tenth century BCE and beginning of the ninth (Iron Age IIA). This "High Chronology" is supported by ^{14}C data as well. Thus, Stratum IVA appears to correspond nicely to the textual data for Jeroboam I. Biran reasonably suggested that this structure was part of a cultic precinct, possibly the one mentioned in 1 Kings 12:31. The establishment of this new cultic site was intended to break the Israelites' ties to the temple at Jerusalem and help secure the viability of the new Northern Kingdom.

The second site that Jeroboam rebuilt is Shechem (1 Kgs 12:25). Ted Campbell's (2002) analysis of the Shechem excavations indicates that the city that Jeroboam built (or rebuilt) should be identified with Stratum IX. Although the pottery for this stratum has yet to be fully published, Campbell argues that the ceramic remains (Iron IIA) associated with this stratum provide a construction date near the end of the tenth century BCE, probably just after the destruction of the unfortified Stratum X settlement by Pharaoh Shishak—that is to say, Campbell believes Stratum IX is tangible evidence of Jeroboam I's rebuilding (I Kgs 12:25), contrary to Finkelstein. Campbell describes this city as an organized and fortified city that was occupied for at least a century.

According to the biblical account, Jeroboam was succeeded by his son Nadab, who ruled for only one year (911–910 BCE) before he was deposed in a military coup led by Baasha. To rid himself of potential rivals, Baasha killed all the remaining relatives of Jeroboam I (1 Kgs 15:27, 28, 30; 14:10, 11). For most of his twenty-three-year reign (ca. 910–887 BCE), Baasha was at war with King Asa of Judah. Baasha's lack of support in Israel is reflected in his condemnation by the prophet Jehu, who predicted the downfall of Baasha's dynasty (1 Kgs 15:16-21; 2 Chr 16:1-6). Ultimately, Baasha was unable to establish a stable kingdom, and his son Elah was on the throne for only a short time (887–886 BCE) before being assassinated by Zimri, commander of the chariotry (1 Kgs 16:6, 8-10).

King Omri of Israel and the House of Omri

The Omride Dynasty represents the zenith of the Northern Kingdom in terms of strength, wealth, accomplishments, and fame. To many outside powers, the Northern Kingdom was known during Omri's time and for years afterward as the "Kingdom of Omri" (see below). The sources for Omri in the Hebrew Bible include 1 Kings 16:15-28 (which provides his basic biography); 1 Kings 16:29-30 and 2 Kings 8:26 (= 2 Chr 22:2), which are filiation formulas with Ahab; and Micah 6:16, which offers a brief negative retrospect on these rulers.

Omri also appears in many ancient Near Eastern sources, including a direct reference in the Mesha Inscription (lines 4–8) and references in several Assyrian inscriptions where he is implicitly acknowledged as the founder of a dynasty of Israel. These references include several inscriptions by Shalmaneser III that refer to "Jehu (the man) of Bit Humri" (i.e., the house of Omri): the famous Black Obelisk, the Calah Bull Annals, the Marble Slab Annals, and the Kurba'il Statue. In addition, an inscription by Adad-nirari III (811–783 BCE) known as the Calah Orthostat Slab refers to Israel as the land of Humri, and Tiglath-Pileser III referred to the border and land of Humria (Israel). In a number of inscriptions, Sargon II claimed to have conquered Samaria and plundered the entire land of "Bit-Humria" (Israel). It is thus clear that the neighboring kingdoms knew well the house of Omri.

According to the DH (1 Kgs 16:15-21), Omri, a "commander of the army," was stationed with his troops at Gibbethon when word reached him and the army that Zimri had murdered King Elah. When news of the king's assassination spread among the troops, they proclaimed their commander Omri as the new king and quickly set out behind him to Tirzah. After beating back a couple of challengers, Omri eventually emerged as sole ruler by 880 BCE. Omri quickly set about consolidating and expanding his hold on power while also establishing a sound economy for his kingdom. He eliminated military threats by forming key alliances, including ending the war with Judah by arranging the marriage of his (grand?)daughter Athaliah to Jehoram, heir to the throne of Judah (2 Kgs 8:18, 26). This alliance effectively isolated Aram (Syria), eliminating, at least for the time being, the threat on Israel's northeast border. Omri further isolated Aram while simultaneously improving Israel's economic prospects by making an alliance with Phoenicia through the marriage of his son Ahab to Jezebel, the daughter of King Ethbaal of Sidon. He enhanced both Israel's security and trade relations by retaking Moab and securing the King's Highway, another vital trade route that connected Phoenicia and Israel with routes into Arabia and beyond. All of these actions created a new era of peace and prosperity for the Northern Kingdom and displayed Omri's keen political acumen. Omri's successful achievements are evident in both the rich material culture of Israel during this time and the extrabiblical records of Israel's political neighbors, especially those of Assyria. The fact that Israel would continue to be known as the "land of Omri" after the king's death only reinforces the lasting success of Omri's policies.

While securing his hold on power during his first six years on the throne, Omri maintained his capital at Tirzah (Tell el-Farah [North]) (1 Kgs 16:23). After he accomplished this task, however, Omri purchased a prominent hill in the center of the country from a man named Shemer for two talents of silver (six thousand silver shekels) and built his new capital—Samaria—on it (1 Kgs 16:24).

The site of ancient Samaria is important for the chronology and history of the Northern Kingdom because it allows the possibility of correlating the textual accounts with the archaeological material. A verse in 1 Kings (16:24) indicates that there was no city at Samaria prior to Omri's founding of the site as his new capital city. This means that the first major construction at the site was that ordered by Omri while he was still reigning from Tirzah (ca. 886–879 BCE). We can thus assume that construction of the new capital began shortly after Omri's accession in 886 BCE.

The archaeology of Samaria comports well with the textual evidence. The earliest evidence of occupation at Samaria consists of a small settlement represented by rock-cut installations (probably grain pits, wine presses, olive presses, and jar sockets), several modest walls, and eleventh–tenth century BCE pottery that has been interpreted as the agricultural estate owned by Shemer (Stager 1990; Tappy 1992, 1:96–97, 1:213–14). Building Phase I is thought to be the city that Omri built. It consists of an ashlar block wall (inner wall) about five meters wide that created an enclosure measuring about 5,840

FIGURE 14-3. *The hill of Samaria where Omri built his capital.*

feet. Within this enclosure was a large building that is commonly interpreted as a palace. Archaeological investigations at Samaria, thus, appear to dovetail closely with the biblical text.

In 875 BCE, five years after establishing his new capital at Samaria, Omri died. Omri's impressive accomplishments—the defeat of Zimri and Tibni, conquest of Moab, dominance over Ammon, forming of key alliances, and creation of a new, impressive capital—all combined to establish the reputation of Omri that so impressed neighboring kings.

The Reign of Ahab, King of Israel

Omri was succeeded by his son, Ahab (ca. 875–852 BCE). Ahab continued his father's successful policies, building the kingdom's economic and military strength, pursuing an ambitious building program, and enriching the kingdom's social and material culture. There is also little doubt that Ahab's marriage to Jezebel, and the marriage of his daughter Athaliah to the king of Judah (2 Kgs 8:18, 26), helped maintain good relations with both Phoenicia and Judah. These connections, along with Israel's natural advantages, especially in agriculture and trade, ensured both security and economic prosperity. Good alliances, natural resources, and control of key north-south trade routes brought great wealth to Ahab and Israel. This is reflected in the extensive building activities that occurred throughout Israel at this time, which are attested both textually (1 Kgs 22:39) and archaeologically.

Even though the Hebrew Bible portrays Ahab in a negative light (1 Kgs 16:30), Ahab's reign represents the apex of power, influence, and affluence of the Northern Kingdom of Israel. This view of Ahab can be seen in extra-biblical sources such as the Qarqar Stele of Assyrian king Shalmaneser III, which lists Ahab as a leader in the anti-Assyrian coalition in the battle of Qarqar in 853 BCE. The material culture excavated in later Iron IIA strata at numerous major sites in the north—including Samaria, Jezreel, Hazor, Dan, and Megiddo—confirms this characterization of Ahab's reign. A. Mazar has correctly noted that excavations of these cities and towns have revealed "a flourishing kingdom with a complex and dense hierarchical settlement system, immense population growth, expanding international trade relations, a flourishing artistic tradition and the increasing use of writing" (Finkelstein and Mazar 2007, 163).

SAMARIA

The capital city of Samaria displays this prosperity. Ahab's additions to Samaria are designated as Building Phase II (second half of Iron IIA) by most archaeologists. Ahab reinforced and expanded the walls of Omri's palace and added a casemate wall (a structure that consists of two parallel walls that are partitioned by cross walls), essentially forming a series of chambers that enclosed an enlarged rectangular acropolis. A pool (ca. ten by five meters) was built against the casemate wall in the northwest corner of this royal enclosure; some have suggested that this was the "pool of Samaria" in which Ahab's chariot was washed after his body was brought back from the battle of Ramoth-Gilead (1 Kgs 22:38). The royal acropolis was apparently entered through a gate complex protected by a large tower that was located along the eastern side of the platform. Of special note are the numerous ivory plaques and fragments of plaques that were found in various rooms and spaces within the ruins of the royal residence. The ivories have attracted special attention by scholars because of their uniqueness in Israel and their beauty. The first group of ivories was found on the floor of Ahab's courtyard north of where the "Ostraca House" would

FIGURE 14-4. *A sphinx carved in ivory found in the Iron II Samaria palace. According to the book of Kings, Ahab's palace was known for its use of precious ivory.*

later be built, probably during the time of Jeroboam II (see below). An alabaster jar with the name of the Egyptian pharaoh Osorkon II (914–874 BCE) incised on it provides a rough chronological link for dating the ivories. The ivories are undoubtedly of Phoenician origin and represent the high artistic attainment that was enjoyed by the upper levels of society in the Northern Kingdom. They also evoke connections with biblical texts such as 1 Kings 22:39, which describes the "ivory house" that Ahab built, and Amos 6:4, in which the prophet reproves the luxury of the wealthy of Samaria as evidenced by their "ivory beds."

Jezreel

The biblical text describes another royal palace from Ahab's time in the city of Jezreel (1 Kgs 18:45; 2 Kgs 9:16). Jezreel does not appear in any ancient written sources prior to the Iron Age and is not mentioned in the list of cities conquered by Sheshonq I, suggesting the city was either not important or abandoned during that time. However, it appears as an important site during the time of Ahab and the location of his winter capital (1 Kgs 21:2). During Ahab's time, Jezreel was surrounded by a wall (1 Kgs 21:23) and had a city gate (2 Kgs 10:8), a tower (2 Kgs 9:17), as well as an upper story with windows (2 Kgs 9:32). The city survived at least until the time of Jehu (2 Kgs 9:30–10:11).

Jezreel was excavated between 1990 and 1996 by David Ussishkin and John Woodhead (1992, 1994, 1997). The dominant Iron Age feature at the site is a 289-by-157-meter rectangular enclosure within a casemate wall; judging from the pottery found within them, some of the casemate rooms had been used as domestic quarters. Two towers were excavated at the northeast and southeast corners of the enclosure; the remains of the southeast tower included part of the mud-brick superstructure that was apparently burned at the time the Omride city was destroyed. Although no palace has been found as of yet, the remains of two public buildings were located within the closure. Jezreel apparently had a palace during the reign of King Ahab and his infamous wife Jezebel. In the well-known episode in 1 Kings 18, after the prophet Elijah defeated 450 of Jezebel's prophets of the god Baal and ended the drought, he raced King Ahab back to Jezreel in a torrential rainstorm. Jezreel is also the location of Naboth's vineyard, for which he was murdered (1 Kgs 21). When Jehu overthrew Ahab's sons to claim the throne for himself, he had Jezebel killed by being thrown out of an upper window of the Jezreel palace (2 Kgs 9:30-37).

The excavators interpreted Jezreel as having been constructed shortly after the time of Omri's accession to the throne of Israel. The excavators further suggested that Jezreel served primarily as a military complex during the Omride period, perhaps as a base for cavalry and/or chariot units. They also noted that the fields located near Jezreel could have provided grain for horses

FIGURE 14-5. *The remains of the southeast tower at Tel Jezreel—
built in the ninth or eighth century BCE.*

in antiquity. The site continued to serve the Omrides until it was destroyed near the end of the ninth century BCE, probably by Hazael, king of Damascus (Ussishkin 2007, 301).

Finkelstein has argued that the pottery from the last destruction of Jezreel is similar to the pottery from the "Solomonic" Stratum VA–IVB at Megiddo and that, since the biblical text indicates that Jezreel was destroyed toward the end of the ninth century BCE (ca. 840–830 BCE), Megiddo Stratum VA–IVB should be redated from the tenth to the ninth century BCE.

However, other scholars have noted that Jezreel's dating is based primarily on the biblical references as there were few clean loci for ceramic dating (ancient robbing, pits, recent bulldozing), making it difficult, if not impossible, to identify clean loci with ceramics that can date the compound (Ben-Tor 2000). Most archaeologists also acknowledge that there was some sort of settlement at Jezreel *prior* to the building of the casemate enclosure. This has led Finkelstein's opponents to argue that Jezreel's ceramics—that is, the Iron IIA ceramics—span both the tenth and ninth centuries BCE (see A. Mazar 2005, 19).

DAN

Dan is not specifically connected with Ahab in the textual sources; however, its association with Ahab is implied by 1 Kings 16:31, where Ahab is said to have continued the sins of Jeroboam, the king who established Dan as an important worship center rivaling Jerusalem. According to Biran (1994, 184), the sacred precinct (Area T) was rebuilt by Ahab following the destruction by Ben-Hadad. A massive nineteen-square-meter ashlar limestone structure referred to as Bamah B (Stratum III, ca. 860–850 BCE) was constructed. The ashlars were laid in the header-stretcher fashion on the three sides that would have been seen by the public, and their exposed surfaces were dressed, exhibiting bossing; this style is common in royal building of the ninth and eighth centuries BCE. A thick yellow travertine floor (the "yellow floor") was built around Bamah B; it included a large courtyard to the south of the *bamah*. In this courtyard was found a large square limestone horned altar and an Astarte figurine. The Bamah B complex is dated to the time of Ahab based on early ninth-century BCE pottery found beneath the yellow floor. The floor and the *bamah* are therefore estimated to have been built in the mid-ninth century BCE (ca. 860–850 BCE), the time of Ahab. The gate complex and city wall along the southern side of the city were also built at this time.

FIGURE 14-6. *The large podium (*bamah*) of the Israelite temple ("high place") at Dan. The Iron Age II podium—dated to the time of Ahab—once held the temple, and the sacrifices would have taken place before it.*

HAZOR

Hazor Stratum VIII exhibits extensive building activity that has been ascribed to Ahab (mid-ninth century BCE; Yadin and Ben-Tor 1993, 605–6). A large pillared storehouse and granary were exposed on the eastern end of the Upper City, showing the importance of Hazor for food administration. A large rectangular "citadel" was excavated—measuring twenty-one by twenty-five meters, with external walls that were two meters thick—on the western end of the city. The interior of the citadel was divided into long rooms with subdivisions that created many spaces. Proto-Aeolic capitals and a large lintel were found in the gate area of the citadel, indicating the monumental nature of the building and its importance. On the south side of the Upper City was a large public water system reached by a staircase cut out of the bedrock. The monumental public works of Hazor VIII are a testament to the wealth, power, and prestige of Israel during the time of Ahab and harmonize with the significant role Ahab played among Syro-Palestinian polities during the ninth century BCE as noted in Assyrian sources such as the Kurkh monolith of Shalmaneser III.

MEGIDDO

The same can be said of Megiddo Stratum IVA. Megiddo IVA (Iron IIB) represents the city during the reign of Ahab. According to the excavators, it was significantly more elaborate than the earlier city. This phase saw the construction of a chariot city with a large complex of horse stables and with a new city wall that measured 820 meters long and was fortified with offsets and insets. A public building (Building 338) called the "Governor's Residence" was built in the eastern part of the city between two stable complexes. Five proto-Ionic capitals were found in secondary use in this level. A new water system (925 BCE) was dug above the spring. Again, the evidence from Megiddo IVA (if dated correctly) testifies to the wealth and power of Ahab.

AHAB'S MILITARY MIGHT

The evidence from sites such as Dan Stratum III, Hazor Stratum VIII, and Megiddo Stratum IVA, described above, testifies to the wealth and abundant manpower that allowed Ahab to create one of the most potent military powers in the region. He defeated the Syrians twice in battle: the first time was when the Aramaean king Ben-Hadad II, along with thirty-two allies, attacked Samaria (1 Kgs 20:1-21) and Ahab successfully repulsed them; the second time was the battle of Aphek (1 Kgs 20:22-30), when Ahab actually captured Ben-Hadad II. By contrast, the Mesha Stele relates that Moab, one of Israel's Transjordan colonies, later pulled away from Israel's dominance. This was the first step in what would be Israel's eventual loss of its Transjordan territories (below).

When the Assyrian king Shalmaneser III invaded the western states in his sixth year (853 BCE), Ahab joined the so-termed twelve-state coalition (actually, only eleven) led by Damascus to resist the Assyrians. Shalmaneser III's inscriptions show that Ahab's army was the strongest of the coalition with 2,000 chariots—more than half of the coalition's total of 3,940—and 10,000 foot soldiers. This battle, which is not mentioned in the Hebrew Bible, took place at Qarqar on the Orontes River in Syria. Ultimately, the battle was a draw, and the Assyrians withdrew from the west. The details of this battle are recorded on the famous Qarqar Stele found in 1861 at Kurkh. The date of the battle in 853 BCE is firmly established and provides one of the chronological anchors for synchronizing biblical history with ancient Near Eastern history.

The Fall of Ahab

With the common threat of Assyria averted, Ahab resumed his conflict with Syria by attacking Ramoth-Gilead in northeast Transjordan, just south of the traditional Syrian border. The Arameans had occupied this Israelite city, and Ahab was determined to reclaim it (1 Kgs 22:3). However, success eluded Ahab, and he was fatally wounded in the battle (1 Kgs 22:2-36). His body was returned to Samaria, where it is said the dogs licked the blood from his chariot (1 Kgs 22:38). Ahab was succeeded by his two sons, first Ahaziah (who ruled for only two years) and then Joram (also known as Jehoram).

At this point it is important to note that, during the rule of Omri and Ahab, Israel's ties with the Phoenicians increased its economic prosperity. However, the wealth that was generated was apparently not evenly distributed among the population. Wealth was concentrated within the hands of a few, leading to significant economic stratification and widespread discontent with the royal family among the general population. This dissatisfaction was increased by the royal family's support for the Baal worship of their Phoenician allies.

Israel's fortunes took a turn for the worse when Edom rebelled against Judah, effectively closing off the Transjordanian King's Highway and the lucrative trade that had benefitted both Judah and Israel (2 Chr 8:20-22). This made the economic disparities in Israel even more keenly felt among the broader population, creating a situation ripe for revolution. On top of this, increased military adventures by Israel's king required heavy expenditures on the army and military equipment (e.g., chariots) that cut even more deeply into Israel's economy. It was within this context that King Jehoram of Israel undertook yet another campaign against Ramoth-Gilead in an attempt to recover the city from the Arameans, who were now probably under the command of the recent usurper Hazael (2 Kgs 8:9-15, 28-29; 9:1-15).

King Jehu of Israel: His Coup and His Reign

It is at this time that Jehu first appears on the historical stage as a high-ranking officer in the Israelite army as it was encamped near Ramoth-Gilead. After receiving a prophetic endorsement and the support of his men, Jehu killed both King Jehoram/Joram and his nephew King Ahaziah of Judah. Jehu then killed Joram's mother, the famous Queen Jezebel, and wiped out all of Ahab's descendants to ensure the end of the house of Omri. The killing of Jezebel (2 Kgs

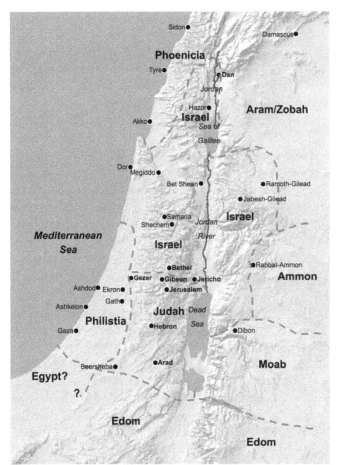

MAP 14-2.
The approximate boundaries of Israel, Judah, and the countries around them.

9:30-37) and Joram (2 Kgs 9:11-26), of course, effectively broke the alliance with the Phoenicians; similarly, the killing of Ahaziah of Judah (2 Kgs 9:27) destroyed Israel's relations with Judah. This meant that Israel, under Jehu, was now essentially isolated.

Based on Assyrian sources, Jehu's coup dates to ca. 842 BCE, shortly after Hazael usurped the throne of Damascus as described in 2 Kings 8:7-15 (Halpern 2010, 270). In fact, some have suggested that Jehu was in collusion with Syria to overthrow the Omrides, meaning that Jehu was Hazael's vassal. Jehu had to know that by killing Joram, Jezebel, and Ahaziah, he would be in conflict with Phoenicia and Judah, not to mention possible supporters of the Omride Dynasty still living in Israel. This would be difficult enough to overcome alone. The last thing Jehu would have wanted was to have Syria under Hazael attacking him as well; therefore, making a deal with Hazael at this point would have made strategic sense. It is likely that such a deal would have required Jehu to become a vassal of Hazael for the latter's support against the Omrides. In return, Jehu ceded Transjordan. The Hebrew Bible notes that Hazael took "from Jordan eastward, all the land of Gilead, the Gadites and the Reubenites and the Manassites, from Aroer, which is by the valley of the Arnon, even Gilead and Bashan" (2 Kgs 10:32, 33). This essentially amounts to all of Israel's Transjordan holdings.

It was apparently at this same time (ca. 841 BCE) that the Moabite king Mesha moved north into the Madaba Plains region, probably with the approval and support of Hazael (Halpern 2010, 270). Mesha's defeat of Israel enabled Hazael to secure a direct Transjordanian trade route to the Red Sea and from there to Egypt and Arabia, while depriving Israel of access to that trade. In this regard it is interesting to note that the Mesha Inscription does not mention encountering Israelite forces as the Moabites moved north into the Madaba Plains region.

Syria's dominance over Israel is commemorated in the Tel Dan Inscription, which most scholars assign to Hazael. In the inscription, Hazael takes credit for killing Joram (son of Ahab) and Ahaziah (son of Joram of the house of David)—in contrast to 2 Kings' ascription of those deeds to Jehu.

The Assyrian king Shalmaneser III's appearance on the scene was unwelcome to both Hazael and Jehu. Hazael was trapped inside Damascus while the Assyrian army ravaged the Syrian countryside. Jehu could only watch helplessly. Rather than waiting for the Assyrians' inevitable move against Israel, Jehu decided to preempt Shalmaneser III's attack by appearing before the

FIGURE 14-7. *The Tel Dan Inscription. Found at Tel Dan in northern Israel, it references the "house of David" and provides the first nonbiblical evidence of King David.*

Assyrian king, submitting, and paying tribute. This act is famously depicted on the Black Obelisk. Jehu's submission to Shalmaneser III also appears in several other recensions and copies of the Assyrian king's annals for the eighteenth year of his reign as well as in a fragmentary stone inscription from Calah, two bull (lamassi) inscriptions from Nimrud (biblical Calah), the Marble Slab Inscription, and the Kurba'il Statue Inscription. Jehu's submission to Assyria is also noted by the prophet Hosea (Hos 1:4-5). Although Shalmaneser was able to ravage the Syrian countryside, he was unable to breach the defenses of Damascus and was forced to withdraw

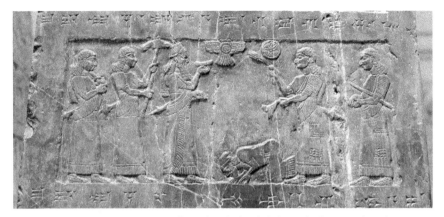

FIGURE 14-8. *A scene from the Black Obelisk in which King Jehu of Israel prostrates himself before King Shalmaneser III.*

with the Syrian capital still intact. This effectively left Jehu to face Aram on his own, the very thing he was hoping to avoid.

Archaeologically, the emergence of Jehu and the rebellion of Mesha can be associated with the Iron IIB archaeological assemblage. Amihai Mazar (2007, 169–70) identifies several ninth-century BCE destructions (ca. 830 BCE) in the Northern Kingdom to attacks by Hazael, king of Damascus, including a massive destruction layer that marks the end of occupation at Tel Rehov in the Beth Shean Valley and the termination of occupation of the royal enclosure at Jezreel. Mesha's move into the Madaba Plains during this same time can be seen in the Iron IIB ceramic horizons at Jalul (Bezer) and Madaba; both are mentioned in the Mesha Inscription.

King Jehoahaz of Israel

Jehoahaz (814–798 BCE) succeeded his father, Jehu, on the throne of Israel and ruled for a total of seventeen years (2 Kgs 10:35; 13:1-9). He inherited a reduced and weakened kingdom as a result of the dominance of Aram-Damascus, first under Hazael and later under his son Ben-Hadad (2 Kgs 10:32-33; 13:7). This is evident in the reduced number of chariots Jehoahaz commanded: only ten, compared with Ahab's two thousand just some fifty years earlier! However, Jehoahaz received relief from the Syrians in the form of a "deliverer" (Hebrew, *moshia'*) (2 Kgs 13:4, 5). There has been some debate over who this deliverer of Israel might have been. However, the majority of scholars (e.g., Cogan and Tadmor 1988) have identified this deliverer with the Assyrian king Adad-nirari III, who invaded Syria in 806/805 BCE and extracted a heavy tribute from the Aramaean kingdom. The king brags:

I marched against the country. . . . I shut up [the] king of Damascus in Damascus, his royal residence. The terror-inspiring glamour of Ashur, overwhelmed him and he seized my feet, assuming the position of a slave of mine. Then I received in his own palace in Damascus, his royal residence, 2,300 talents of silver corresponding to 20 talents of gold, 5,000 talents of iron, garments of linen with multicolored trimmings, a bed inlaid with ivory . . . and countless other objects being his possessions. (*COS* 2:114)

This provided a quiet period for Israel. Jehoahaz died and was buried in Samaria after a relatively peaceful reign. Apart from the Assyrian records, there is little that can be assigned to Jehoahaz archaeologically.

King Jehoash of Israel: The Return of Prosperity

Jehoash (Joash) ruled Israel for sixteen years (ca. 798–782 BCE). He retained Baal worship but admired the prophet Elisha. He conducted several successful campaigns into Transjordan against Ben-Hadad III, reclaiming territory earlier lost by his father Jehoahaz to Hazael. Jehoash also initially had good relations with Amaziah of Judah, but, after the latter insulted a contingent of allied Israelite soldiers by releasing them early, Jehoash was reluctantly drawn into a conflict with Judah at Beth Shemesh. He decisively defeated Amaziah and then looted Jerusalem, destroying part of its wall (2 Kgs 14:13). Jehoash is mentioned in the Tell al-Rimah Stele (797 BCE) as "Joash the Samarian" who paid tribute to Adad-nirari III (810–782 BCE). By staying on good terms with Assyria, Jehoash lived out his reign peacefully and was buried in the royal tombs at Samaria.

King Jeroboam II of Israel: Continued Prosperity

Jehoash was succeeded by his son, Jeroboam II. According to Thiele (1983, 116), Jeroboam II was a coregent with his father for eleven years (793–782 BCE) before assuming sole reign when his father died (782–753 BCE). The stability of his long forty-one-year reign, plus Jeroboam's military successes, provided Israel with perhaps the most prosperous period in the Northern Kingdom's history. Israel's population is estimated to have reached at least 350,000 by some scholars, and archaeological evidence points to a high level of olive oil production and horse breeding, both of which were traded with Mesopotamia and Egypt.

A window into Israel's prosperity during this period is reflected in the Samaria ostraca, which may date to this time (see below). The kingdom's prosperity and resultant social stratification can also be measured by the condemnation of materialism found in the writings of the prophets Hosea, Joel, Jonah, and Amos.

Jeroboam II also achieved military success against Damascus. According to 2 Kings 14:25, Jeroboam II expanded the territory of Israel "from the entrance of Hamath as far as the Sea of Arabah." Archaeological remains thought to be from the period of his reign have been found at the sites of Samaria, Dan, and Megiddo.

SAMARIA

A key find at Samaria from the time of Jeroboam II is a collection of over one hundred ostraca (inscribed sherds), of which sixty-three are legible. The inscriptions document the allocations of oil and wine shipments between the capital and agricultural estates in the Manasseh tribal region. While the meaning of the ostraca is not fully understood, they do give testimony to the agricultural wealth of Israel during the time of Jeroboam II.

FIGURE 14-9. *Three of the 102 "Samaria ostraca" from the time of Jeroboam II. They were written in Paleo-Hebrew script on fragments of broken pottery.*

DAN

Dan witnessed a massive expansion of the high place during the time of Jeroboam II. Renovations included the monumental staircase on the south side of the *bamah*, the horn of a large central altar, a stone altar (with three iron shovels), various rooms adjacent to the sanctuary (including an altar room with two travertine altars), a bronze drinking bowl, a bronze scepter head, an apparent house with an amphora stamped with the inscription *ImmadiYo* (God is with me), as well as the city fortifications of Stratum II.

MEGIDDO

Finkelstein argues that the Stratum IVA city was built by Jeroboam II, while A. Mazar acknowledges that, although this is possible, it is not probable (A. Mazar 2005, 17; Finkelstein and Mazar 2007, 169–70). It is more likely that this stratum of the city was initially built by Ahab and continued in use until it was finally destroyed by Tiglath-Pileser III in 732 BCE. However, the excavators note that several repairs and modifications were made to Megiddo IVA, and, since this city continued in use through the reign of Jeroboam II, it would not be unreasonable to attribute these to Jeroboam's activities. Of interest was the discovery of the "Shema, servant of Jeroboam" seal that some have attributed to Jeroboam II.

King Menahem of Israel

With Jeroboam II's death, the stability that the Northern Kingdom had enjoyed for many years began to disintegrate, ultimately leading to the fall of Israel. Zechariah, Jeroboam II's son, was assassinated at Ibleam by Shallum after a brief reign of only six months (750 BCE), ending the dynasty of Jehu (2 Kgs 15:8-12). Shallum, about whom the text reveals nothing, reigned for only one month at Samaria before he in turn was assassinated by Menahem, son of Gadi, apparently the governor of Tirzah (2 Kgs 15:8-15).

Menahem (ca. 752–742 BCE) took steps to restabilize the kingdom by making an alliance with Assyria. He agreed to pay a heavy tribute of one thousand silver talents (thirty-seven tons!) to Tiglath-Pileser III (known as Pul in the biblical text). In order to raise the funds, Menahem taxed sixty thousand wealthy men fifty shekels each (2 Kgs 15:19, 20). The payment of this tribute is documented in a cuneiform display inscription of Tiglath-Pileser III found at Calah. Menahem brooked no resistance to his rule within his own country. When the city of Tiphsah (Tappuah; LXX Tirzah) refused to acknowledge his kingship, Menahem captured the city, killed all the men, and ripped open all the pregnant women, thus assuring his condemnation as an evil king by the prophet Hosea (Hos 7:1-15; see also 2 Kgs 15:18). Nevertheless, Menahem was able to bring some short-lived stability to the kingdom during his ten-year reign.

The Iran Stela (ca. 737 BCE; Fragment 1, Column IIIA) provides a list of western kings who paid tribute to Tiglath-Pileser III. This list includes "Menahem of Samaria," thereby corroborating the biblical account, in which King Menahem of Israel paid a large tribute to Pul (i.e., Tiglath-Pileser).

PEKAH'S COUP

Menahem was succeeded by his son Pekahiah (ca. 739–737 BCE), who reigned for two years at Samaria. His continuance of the calf worship initiated by Jeroboam I received the condemnation of some of the prophets (2 Kgs 15:22-24). During this time, Pekahiah determined to continue his father's policy of vassalage to the Assyrians. This enraged Pekah, son of Remaliah, one of Pekahiah's military officers, who staged a coup with fifty men of Gilead, assassinated Pekahiah, and assumed the throne, thus ending the "house of Menahem."

The Syro-Ephramite War

Pekah immediately reversed Menahem's policy of alliance with Assyria by joining a new anti-Assyrian coalition with Rezin of Aram. Both of these kings called upon Judah to join the anti-Assyrian coalition. However, King Ahaz of Judah refused, so Rezin and Pekah attacked Judah (735 BCE) with the goal of deposing Ahaz. According to 2 Chronicles 28:6, the conflict initially went against Judah, with 120,000 troops being lost in only one day. Many significant officials were killed, including the king's son; many others were taken away as slaves. On top of this, the Philistines and Edomites also joined against Judah by raiding various towns and village. However, according to 2 Kings 16:5, Rezin and Pekah's campaign ultimately failed, for, although they besieged Jerusalem, they failed to capture it (see also 2 Kgs 15:37; 16:1-6; Isa 6–12).

In the face of the impending destruction of his kingdom, Ahaz appealed to Tiglath-Pileser III to come to Judah's rescue. The Assyrian army arrived in 732 BCE and defeated the Philistines, sacked Damascus, and annexed Aram. Rezin was executed, and the population of Aram was deported.

Tiglath-Pileser III then attacked Israel and "captured Ijon, Abel Beth-Maacah, Janoah, Kedesh, Hazor, Gilead, and Galilee, all the land of Naphtali; and he carried the people captive to Assyria" (2 Kgs 15:29). Israel was annexed to the Assyrian Empire. As for Pekah, 2 Kings 15:29-30 says he was murdered by Hoshea (ca. 732 BCE). The event is also mentioned in two Summary Inscriptions from Kalhu. Thus, both the Hebrew text and Tiglath-Pileser III's records relate Pekah's demise. (See the Hoshea discussion below.)

This 735–733 BCE campaign into northern Israel (Galilee and the Jezreel Valley) is described in Tiglath-Pileser III's records and supported by archaeological evidence in the form of destruction layers from this time at all the major sites in the region that have been excavated, including Dan, Hazor, Beth Shean, Megiddo, Samaria, and Tell el-Farah (N) as well as sites in the south. The destruction at each of these sites marks the end of the Iron IIB material culture horizon.

Assyria's price for saving Ahaz was high. Judah was forced to become a tributary state to Assyria, with Ahaz drawing the required payment from the temple treasure and royal treasury.

The House of Hoshea

Hoshea, an army officer, assumed the throne of Israel after he killed Pekah and was the last king of Israel (732–722 BCE). His usurpation of the throne is described in the Hebrew Bible (2 Kgs 15:30) and by Tiglath-Pileser III: "The House of Omri . . . overthrew their king Pekah, and I placed Hoshea as king over them. I received from them 10 talents of gold, 1000 talents of silver, as their tribute and brought them to Assyria" (*ANET* 284). It can be seen that both Hoshea and Tiglath-Pileser III took credit for the overthrow of Pekah and the elevation of Hoshea. However, the fact that Hoshea had to pay tribute shows who really had the upper hand.

But Hoshea did not like being under Assyria's yoke, and eventually he withheld the expected tribute and made an alliance with the Egyptian pharaoh instead. Shalmaneser responded by attacking Israel and besieging the capital at Samaria for three years; the city finally capitulated in 722 BCE. It seems that Shalmaneser died during or shortly after the fall of the capital, because his successor, Sargon II, took credit for Israel's defeat. Hoshea, along with many of the Israelites, was taken into captivity (2 Kgs 15:30; 17:1-6). Sargon would eventually resettle much of Israel with people from other places he had conquered.

Conclusion

Both archaeological and textual evidence (biblical and extrabiblical) show that, for most of the 210 years of its existence, the Northern Kingdom of Israel thrived, taking advantage of its natural resources, comparatively large population, and unique geopolitical position.

Nevertheless, there were certain elements within Israelite society that, in spite of several fairly long periods of stability, ultimately led to a weakening and eventual collapse of the Northern Kingdom. These include unequal wealth distribution, exacerbated by a heavy tax burden on the average citizen, which led to social stratification as well as challenges from strong neighbors, especially Aram/Syria. This led to political instability, constant overthrow of the government, and unwise political alliances that ultimately led to the collapse of the kingdom. While the prophets ultimately attributed Israel's weakness to unfaithfulness to God, social injustices often formed a major part of the prophetic condemnation. This, combined with Israel's delicate political situation between the Mesopotamian and Egyptian powers, put exceptional burdens on Israel's leaders. Many failed to address those burdens successfully, and over time the kingdom fell prey to overwhelming regional powers.

Suggestions for Further Reading

The two standard works that include the history of Israel and Judah are John Bright's *A History of Israel* and John Hayes and Maxwell Miller's edited volume called *Israelite and Judean History*. These are based primarily on the biblical material. A more up-to-date work that draws heavily upon archaeology excavations is Israel Finkelstein and Neil Silberman's *The Bible Unearthed*. Finkelstein's *The Forgotten Kingdom* is devoted primarily to the understanding of the Northern Kingdom in light of archaeological research. Baruch Halpern's "Archaeology, the Bible and History: The Fall of the House of Omri—and the

Origins of the Israelite State" gives a thought-provoking analysis of that dynasty's impact on the Kingdom of Israel. John Holladay provides a history of Israel and Judah based solely on archaeology in "The Kingdoms of Israel and Judah: Political and Economic Centralization in the Iron IIA–B (ca. 1000–750 BCE)."

15

THE SOUTHERN KINGDOM OF JUDAH
Surrounded by Enemies

Aren M. Maeir

This chapter will survey the archaeological and historical evidence for the Kingdom of Judah from the late tenth century BCE until the destruction of Lachish by the Assyrian king Sennacherib in 701 BCE. Following an introduction on the chronological and regional scope of this survey and the available sources, I will analyze the archaeological remains, and relevant historical and biblical data, in chronological order. Aspects of Judahite material culture will be discussed at the end of the chapter.

Definition of Chronological and Regional Framework

Some scholars follow the general framework laid out in the biblical narrative (primarily in the books of Samuel and Kings), according to which the Kingdom of Israel was first established under the rule of David and Solomon during the united monarchy period and subsequently divided into the Northern and Southern Kingdoms of Israel and Judah during the divided monarchy period (ca. 931 BCE). Others argue that the Kingdom of Israel was the first substantial polity to form while the Kingdom of Judah emerged later, in the ninth century or eighth century BCE, and became a substantial polity only after the fall of the Israelite kingdom to the Assyrians in 722 BCE. This chapter will focus on the archaeological and historical evidence from Judah starting from the late tenth century BCE, using the historically and biblically attested event of Pharaoh Shishak's campaign (ca. 925 BCE) as the beginning of this survey and the destruction of Lachish by Sennacherib (in 701 BCE) as its end.

While there is little doubt regarding the dating and overall historical phasing of the later part of this period (from the mid-eighth century BCE onward), the archaeological and historical understanding of the late tenth through early eighth century BCE is highly debated, and the historical veracity of much of the biblical description is highly contested (see more below). The tension between the biblical descriptions of the chronicles of the Kingdom of Judah during this period and the actual historical corroboration of many of the depicted events should be kept in mind. Thus, while not in any way denying the overall framework of the Judahite Kingdom as reflected in the biblical record, I will try to be sufficiently judicious when connecting events known only from the biblical text with the archaeological remains.

The chronological framework that will be used in the present discussion is as follows: (1) late Iron Age IIA (ca. 925–800 BCE) and (2) Iron IIB (ca. 800–701 BCE).

Sources

There are four sources of information for the period 925–701 BCE: archaeology, the Hebrew Bible, Assyrian sources, and inscriptions found in Judah and the surrounding regions. The archaeological finds make up the primary source for the cultural and historical reconstruction of this period due to the relative lack of inscriptions relating to this period and the debated historicity of the relevant biblical texts. (See below.)

While the biblical narrative supposedly provides a clear historical framework and much detail on the tenth through late eighth century BCE in the Kingdom of Judah, these sources are, in fact, limited in use. While some of the biblical information may be based on actual memories of events and perhaps even limited written sources, the fact that most, if not all, of the biblical sources were first written down only in the late Iron Age (and continuing into the early **Second Temple Period**) limits the historical veracity of much of the details of the biblical text. That said, there are indications that the general historical framework provided in the biblical text can be corroborated using other sources. Early extrabiblical texts relating to this region—such as Pharaoh Shishak's list, the Tel Dan Inscription, and the Mesha Stele described below—indicate the existence of the Judahite Kingdom in the tenth to ninth century BCE. In addition, from the late ninth century BCE on, Assyrian texts provide good comparative frameworks for the biblical chronology and historical framework of the Judahite Kingdom. Thus, while it is clear that the historical picture portrayed in the biblical text is tendentious and heavily colored by ideological interpretations of Judahite history, various details that are found in the biblical text, whether relating to historical events or daily life, may actually reflect Iron Age realities.

Starting in the second half of the ninth century BCE—as the Assyrian Empire expanded toward the Southern Levant—Assyrian texts and in particular royal inscriptions can be used to directly or indirectly glean about the Kingdom of Judah. While ninth-century BCE inscriptions such as Shalmaneser III's Black Obelisk do not mention Judah, there are repeated references to the Kingdom of Judah in the eighth-century BCE inscriptions of Assyrian kings Tiglath-Pileser III, Sargon II, and Sennacherib. Of particular importance are those from the time of Sennacherib (see below).

While it is clear that there was some literacy in Iron Age IIA Judah, it was limited in nature and insufficient to argue for the existence of a state-controlled bureaucracy at the time. Only starting in the ninth century BCE is there substantial evidence for the spread of literacy in Judah, which has clear ramifications for the understanding of the level of societal and state complexity in these cultures. The sequence of development of many of the local languages in the Iron Age Levant can be followed quite clearly, however. The development of Hebrew from a Canaanite-based language to Classical Biblical Hebrew is well known and documented with a sequence of well-dated inscriptions from archaeological contexts. This is important when dealing with questions relating to the dating of various portions of the biblical texts based on linguistic criteria.

Three inscriptions that do not derive from Judah itself are of particular importance. The first is the list of Southern Levantine cities purportedly captured by the Twenty-Second Dynasty pharaoh Shishak that is inscribed on the walls of the temple of Amun at Karnak, Egypt (ca. 925 BCE; see Figure 14-1). This event, which is referred to in 1 Kings 14:25, included the destruction of sites in the northern Negev and areas to the north of Judah, but not cities in Judah itself. Many see this as evidence of two Egyptian objectives in this campaign: to punish the Northern Kingdom of Israel for not remaining loyal to Egypt and to wrest the transportation routes in the northern Negev from the Judahite Kingdom. The fact that Jerusalem and other sites in Judah are not mentioned is seen by some as evidence that the kingdom was not considered a threat to the Egyptians, while others suggest that the lack of reference to Judah in the list indicates the kingdom's minimal status at the time. However, many of the inscriptions are difficult to read, and others have been destroyed. Perhaps mentions of Judah and Jerusalem have been erased (see more discussion in chapter 17).

The second inscription worth noting is the so-called house of David inscription from Tel Dan in northern Israel in which an Aramean king, probably Hazael of Damascus, takes credit for killing the kings of Israel and the house of David (*BYT DWD*) in battle (see Figure 14-7). As this inscription dates to the second half of the ninth century BCE (ca. 840 BCE), it seems to provide the earliest nonbiblical reference to the Kingdom of Judah and the figure David some 150 years or so after the supposed founding of the Judahite Kingdom. Clearly, then, at the time of this inscription, a figure by the name of David was known in the region as having founded the kingdom.

The third inscription of importance is the Mesha Stele, erected by King Mesha of Moab in Transjordan (ca. 830 BCE). In addition to mentioning Ahab, king of Israel, and referring to events alluded to in the Bible, it has been suggested that the house of David is mentioned in this inscription as well. If so, this provided further extrabiblical evidence for the existence of the Kingdom of Judah at the time and of the knowledge and identity of the founding figure: David.

In the Iron IIB and particularly in the Iron IIC, there is a much larger corpus of written material from Judah. There are a few monumental inscriptions from Jerusalem, most notably the Siloam Inscription, which records the late eighth-century BCE construction of the Siloam tunnel (see Figure 4-6). Several inscriptions deriving from contexts later than 701 BCE are also noteworthy. The earliest known fragment of a biblical text, Numbers 6:22-27, or the Priestly Blessing, is inscribed on two silver amulets from the Ketef Hinnom tombs in Jerusalem dated to the very end of the Iron Age IIC (see Figure 18-7). Collections of ostraca (inscribed pottery sherds)—including the corpus from the fortress at Arad dating mainly to the final Iron IIC stratum and the Lachish Letters found in destruction debris of the gate of Lachish Level II, destroyed in 586 BCE by the Babylonians—provide important insights into the Hebrew language in use at the time, the names that were common, and various events (some of which are also mentioned in biblical sources).

Writing is attested in other forms as well, such as numerous seals and seal impressions with either personal names or administrative titles, ceramic vessels and other objects with inscriptions, and several tomb inscriptions. While the inscriptions in the Judahite corpus span the entire Iron II, the many types of inscriptions and different media on which they are written in late Iron IIB and Iron IIC Judah indicates that literacy was quite widespread at the time, that state-level administration and bureaucracy existed, and that this largely literate society could be the source of many of the preexilic biblical texts (Schniedewind 2004).

Chronological and Geographical Development

The Kingdom of Judah was centered on its capital city, Jerusalem. Archaeological evidence attests to its settlement throughout the entire Iron Age II until its destruction by the Babylonians in 586 BCE. The size of the kingdom itself and, in fact, that of its capital Jerusalem fluctuated during this period depending on the geopolitical and economic status of the Kingdom of Judah. Thus, if during some periods its territory covered a limited zone in the central hills only, in other phases of the Iron Age it expanded to the Shephelah, eastern Philistia, the Judean Desert, the northern Negev, and, in certain cases, perhaps even beyond. The definition of the area defined as "Judah" throughout the different stages of the Iron Age depends on a combination of the archaeological evidence for the existence of rich cultural assemblages typical of Judah during specific periods (Kletter 2001) and can most likely be used as evidence for the extent of Judahite cultural and political influence.

FIGURE 15-1. *The City of David south and downhill from the temple platform. This is the area of the ninth-century BCE city. The line of the two curved streets approximates the original shape of this long, narrow hill.*

Late Iron Age IIA (Late Tenth to Mid-Eighth Century BCE)

The exact dating, relative stratigraphy, and cultural affiliation of sites in and around Judah that date to the period between the late tenth and mid-eighth century BCE is far from clear. Nevertheless, various sites clearly fit into this general period, and some of them can be seen as evidence of the initial stages of development of the Kingdom of Judah.

THE JUDEAN HILLS

There appears to have been a tenth-century BCE settlement in Jerusalem (A. Mazar 2010), and royal buildings, palaces, and fortifications can be clearly assigned to this phase. However, there is still no consensus regarding the dating of remains from the late tenth and early ninth centuries BCE in Jerusalem (e.g., Finkelstein 2011). In fact, it is only from the late ninth and early eighth centuries BCE onward that most scholars believe there was a substantial settlement in Jerusalem.

Excavations in the City of David, Jerusalem, have provided evidence of a ninth-century BCE presence, even if the context and significance of these finds are debated. Particularly important are the relatively recent finds from the hewn pool near the Gihon Spring, where a large collection of Iron Age IIA pottery, bullae (clay seals), and fish bones was discovered. While some see this as evidence for the existence of bureaucracy and cultural contacts with Phoenicia in the ninth century BCE (Reich, Shukron, and Lernau 2007), others argue that the context is mixed and includes later, Iron IIB, material as well. Nevertheless, evidence of occupation during this phase is quite clear. Therefore, the argument that Jerusalem was the capital city of the Kingdom of Judah already in the early to late ninth century BCE is somewhat strengthened.

Few sites dating to the late Iron Age IIA have been identified in surveys of the Judean Hills. Faust (2003, 2007a, 2012b) has suggested that the lack of Iron IIA sites in the hill country is to be explained as a purposeful, even forced, abandonment of rural sites during this time and that these inhabitants were moved to the cities of the early Judahite Kingdom. In his opinion, this is evidence of the rise of a strong centralized polity in Jerusalem. This view has been

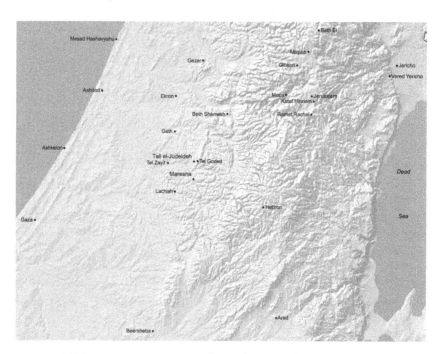

MAP 15-1. *Important sites in the Southern Kingdom of Judah after separating from Israel in the north.*

contested for various reasons (Maeir 2013), and the very fact that there is no evidence for large urban centers during the late tenth and early ninth centuries BCE makes this supposition hard to accept.

Lachish was the second-most important city in Judah after Jerusalem from the Iron IIA until the end of the Iron Age. Levels V (tenth / early ninth century BCE) and IV (ninth / early eighth century BCE) are dated to the Iron IIA, although there is much debate on the placement of these two levels within this timeframe (Ussishkin 2004, 2013). Apparently, Level V was quite limited in character, with just a few domestic structures. The first evidence of a major Judahite settlement is seen in Level IV in an impressive fortification system that includes a gate complex and stone wall, the first stage of the palace on the acropolis, a possible water system, and various private houses.

NEGEV DESERT

Several sites can be connected to the second half of the Iron Age IIA in the Arad and Beersheba Valleys. It appears that already in the late Iron IIA, perhaps even in the first half of the ninth century BCE, the Judahite Kingdom expanded into this region, perhaps in an attempt to control the copper trade routes between Faynan and the Mediterranean (Naaman 2013). The fact that the earliest fortress at Arad dates to the ninth century BCE seems to suggest that only during this phase did the Judahite Kingdom became closely involved in the control of this region (Herzog 2002).

Additional sites have been reported further south. In the Negev Highlands, the so-called Negev Fortresses, dated by some scholars to the early to mid-tenth century BCE (the united kingdom and the reign of Solomon), are seen as evidence of Judahite control of this region at the time. If these sites in fact date to the ninth century BCE (late Iron IIA), it is not clear that they can be connected to sites within the Kingdom of Judah. They might be associated with other groups, such as the Edomites, that were located in the Negev region, or they might be evidence of Judahite expansion into this region at the time.

The very interesting site of Kuntillet Ajrud should also be mentioned. This small site, most likely a caravanserai on the route between the Mediterranean and the Gulf of Aqaba, contained a very important collection of inscriptions, including mention of the Israelite/Judahite deity YHWH (Meshel 2012). Dated by most scholars to the late ninth century BCE, its material culture reflects a late Iron IIA character. Once again, the cultural/ethnic association of this site is debated: it may be Israelite (Meshel 2012, 69), Judahite (Meshel 2012, 68), or even Phoenician (Lemaire 2013). (See Figure 17-6 and discussion.)

The Iron IIB (Eighth Century BCE)

This period is of cardinal importance in the history of the Judahite Kingdom, as it leads up to the reign of Hezekiah, which, although ending with the disastrous consequences of the campaign of Sennacherib (701 BCE), resulted in a substantial expansion of the kingdom and, with it, various social, economic, and intellectual developments.

While the exact date of the transition between the late Iron IIA and the Iron IIB is debated, several events and processes occurring around 800 BCE make this an approximate chronological horizon for this transition. These include the following: (1) the campaigns of Hazael in the second half of the ninth century BCE and, in particular, as far as Judah is concerned, the conquest of Gath, which eliminated the strongest neighbor of the Kingdom of Judah and caused a reshuffling of the geopolitical status of the region; (2) the beginning of a period in which the Assyrian Empire was relatively inactive in the west between the end of Adad-Nirari III's reign and Tiglath-Pileser III, which enabled various polities in the Levant to expand their influence; and (3) a period of apparent expansion and preeminence in the Israelite Kingdom (reign of Jeroboam II 791–753 BCE) and the Judahite Kingdom (reign of Amaziah 796–766 BCE) most likely related to the processes noted above.

Although some scholars question its importance, I believe that the earthquake mentioned in Amos 1:1—"In the days of King Uzziah of Judah and in the days of King Jeroboam son of Joash of Israel, two years before the earthquake"—was a substantial event that left a significant mark on the material culture of the Southern Levant in general and Judah in particular and can be seen as threshold for the transition between the early and late Iron IIB. To start with, there is mention of a substantial earthquake during the mid-eighth century BCE in several biblical texts (Amos 1:1; Zech 14:5; various hints in Isa [Milgrom 1964]). Possible evidence of this earthquake in mid-eighth-century BCE contexts have been noted from quite a few sites in the region of Judah, including Gezer, Tell es-Safi/Gath, Zayit, Tel Sheva, Arad, and perhaps Tel Goded (Gibson 1994). Needless to say, not all destruction levels in the first half of the eighth century BCE should be connected to this, and they might very well relate to other causes; however, the major developments in Judah in the second half of the eighth century BCE may very well have occurred in the aftermath of this earthquake and during the rebuilding of various sites at the time.

Early Iron IIB (ca. 800–760 BCE)

While the second part of the Iron IIB is well attested (see below), evidence of the earlier phase of this period is not as clear; nevertheless, there is enough archaeological data to support the supposition that the Judahite Kingdom expanded during this period.

Above we saw that evidence of substantial activity in Jerusalem, at least during the ninth century BCE if not earlier, can be seen in the City of David. Although it is commonly assumed that Jerusalem expanded only in the late eighth century BCE as a result of the influx of refugees from the fall of the Israelite Kingdom in 722 BCE (Broshi 1974; Finkelstein 2012), a case for the gradual expansion of Jerusalem beginning in the early eighth century BCE can be argued. As Naaman (2007, 2009) points out, the very idea that the Assyrians would enable such a large population of refugees to move from Israel to Judah is highly unlikely. In addition, finds from the Western Hill (modern Jewish Quarter) appear to indicate a gradual rather than a sudden buildup. Finally, there are no finds of a distinctively Israelite character in late eighth-century BCE Judah that would indicate the arrival of Israelite refugees. Therefore, the expansion of Jerusalem from the City of David and the Temple Mount toward the Western Hill was a more gradual process that began in the first half of the eighth century BCE. This part of the city was unfortified until later in the eighth century, and it is possible that some of the rock-cut tombs that have been identified in Silwan east of the City of David (Barkay 2000, 247) date to the late ninth or early eighth century BCE.

Late Iron IIB (ca. 760–701 BCE)

Although the second part of the Iron IIB (ca. 760–701 BCE) is, to a large extent, the continuation of the first part of this period, it is distinguished by the enlarged scale of the relevant archaeological remains. The reason why I suggest differentiating between the two parts of the period, aside from the role of the Uzziah earthquake mentioned above, is that the Neo-Assyrians appeared in full force in the Southern Levant in the second half of this period, conquering the Israelite Kingdom in two consecutive blows: Tiglath-Pileser III captured part of Israel in 733 BCE, and Shalmaneser V and Sargon II captured Samaria and destroyed the rest of the Israelite Kingdom in 722 BCE. While part of the Levant was annexed to the Assyrian Empire, Judah became a vassal state and was incorporated into the Assyrian economic realm. Evidence of this can be seen in the extensive and elaborate development in and around Jerusalem and in regions under Judahite control in the Shephelah and the Negev.

Toward the end of the eighth century BCE and due, perhaps, to an increase of Assyrian pressure on the vassal kingdoms in the Levant, there was a series of revolts against Assyrian rule. In 705 BCE, after the death of Sargon II in battle, King Hezekiah of Judah organized a revolt against the Assyrians along with various other kings from the region. During the early years of this revolt, there was a major flourish of development in Judah witnessed by archaeological

FIGURE 15-2. *The narrow tunnel dug during King Hezekiah's reign to bring water from the Gihon Spring just outside the city walls into Jerusalem proper.*

evidence of the expansion of various cities, the settlement of new areas, the creation of a sophisticated administrative structure, and other aspects.

The second half of the eighth century BCE is one of the most impressive periods in the history of Jerusalem. While a process of expansion of the city may have commenced already in the early eighth century BCE, there is no question that, in the second half of the eighth century BCE, Jerusalem witnessed an extensive expansion both in the city itself and in the surrounding regions. The widespread settlement on the Western Hill and Mount Zion is evidence of this. At some point around this time, perhaps on the eve of Sennacherib's campaign to Jerusalem in 701 BCE and as part of Hezekiah's preparation for the revolt, the western part of the city was surrounded by a robust fortification: the so-called Broad Wall with its associated gate. It is usually assumed that at this time the water system at the base of the City of David was substantially expanded as well, and in particular the so-called Hezekiah's Tunnel. The necropolis of the city expanded as well, and tombs are found around the entire periphery of the expanded cityscape (Barkay 2000).

The finds from Level III at Lachish, located southwest of Jerusalem, indicate that this city was the second-most important in Judah at the time and, according to the biblical text, perhaps the seat of the king's son. Level III at Lachish is the type site for the material culture of the Judahite Kingdom in the late eighth century BCE; this is due both to the extensive excavations and publications of this site and to the fact that this city was destroyed in a terrible conflagration that can be linked to the siege and conquest of Lachish as described in the Assyrian inscriptions and reliefs and the biblical text (Ussishkin 1982).

The large city gate and wall, extensive palace and fort, water system, and other remains are indicative of the importance of the city. As mentioned above, the large assemblage of finds provides an excellent snapshot of contemporaneous material culture in Judah. This includes a large assortment of jars with **LMLK** stamps (which means "belonging to the king"), evidence of the royal Judahite administration at the time. While there is currently a debate on the length of time during which these stamped jars

FIGURE 15-3. *In this relief from the Assyrian king Sennacherib's palace in Nineveh, Lachish's soldiers defend against an approaching battering ram by throwing torches at it. In the lower right, civilians attempt to leave the besieged city.*

FIGURE 15-4. *At Lachish, the road into the city ran along the side of the hill to a gate that stuck out from the city wall, requiring a sharp turn to the right to enter the city.*

were produced and used, it is clear that at least a primary phase of the use of these jars reflects the complex bureaucratic structure of the Judahite monarchy in the late eighth century BCE prior to the Assyrian campaign of 701 BCE (see Figure 15-6). The impressive archaeological evidence of the Assyrian siege of and attack on the site, the population of Lachish's defense, and, in the end, the destruction of the site serve as perhaps the finest example for the dovetailing between the archaeological evidence, the biblical text, and Assyrian texts and reliefs.

A small sanctuary was built at Arad in the northern Negev at this time. The importance of this structure cannot be overstated, as this is one of the few cultic buildings known from Iron Age Israel and Judah. Situated in the northwestern corner of the fortress, it is comprised of an open courtyard with a large altar and two roofed spaces, including a small "holy of holies" with steps, two incense altars, and two *massebot* (standing stones). In and around the structure were found various cult-related objects and installations, including inscriptions relating to known priestly families, dedicatory inscriptions, and other objects. While hardly identical to the biblical description of the Solomonic temple, the tripartite division of the temple and the altars are similar to descriptions of the biblical tabernacle. In the past, this temple was thought to have functioned for a long period before being phased out partially in the late eighth century BCE and finally in the late seventh century BCE. According to new analyses suggested by Herzog (2010), the temple was first erected in Stratum X (early eighth century BCE) and continued to exist in Stratum IX after being refurbished. The temple then went out of use at the end of Stratum

FIGURE 15-5. *The temple area at the Judahite fortress at Tel Arad. The square altar is above the photo's center and the holy of holies is at the upper left.*

IX and the fortress was rebuilt in Stratum VIII. Herzog relates this to King Hezekiah's cultic reforms in the final decades of the eighth century BCE (ca. 715 BCE). This level was destroyed in a conflagration most likely to be related to the 701 BCE Assyrian campaign.

SUMMARY

The role, size, and character of the Judahite Kingdom changed after Assyria's conquest and destruction of the Northern Kingdom of Israel in 722 BCE. In the late eighth and early seventh centuries BCE, Jerusalem became a large and prosperous city with a population many times greater than before. As mentioned above, from the late eighth century onward, Jerusalem was well fortified and possessed a sophisticated complex of water systems that ensured a safe water supply even in a time of siege. At the center of the city was the temple, which, according to biblical tradition, was built by Solomon (1 Kgs 6–8), although its date of construction cannot be determined in the absence of archaeological remains. In any case, the temple during this time was the religio-political focus of the kingdom. It was intimately tied to the legitimacy of the Davidic Dynasty and played a central part in the Judahite Kingdom's ideological and political underpinnings. This would continue until its destruction by the Babylonians in approximately 586 BCE.

The archaeological evidence from the Kingdom of Judah during the late Iron IIB is quite impressive. There was substantial growth in existing sites in the kingdom and expansion into areas that had previously been not as intensively settled—evidence of the social, economic, and political vibrancy of the kingdom during the reigns of Ahaz and Hezekiah. This floruit is best explained by Judah becoming part of the Assyrian world system and international trade networks. These developments most likely are the background for the important cultural and religious developments at the time (e.g., Finkelstein and Silberman 2006b), among others manifested in the apparent cult reformations during Hezekiah's reign, which should be seen, first and foremost, as attempts by Hezekiah to consolidate and control his kingdom.

Judahite Material Culture

SETTLEMENT PATTERN

As with most ancient state-level societies, the settlement pattern in Iron Age II Judah was characterized by a rural-urban continuum (Faust 2012b). This included the capital city, Jerusalem, which from the eighth century BCE onward grew to a large scale (up to ca. fifty hectares in size) and most likely served as the premier city of the kingdom. Under this, there were urban settlements of various sizes: second-tier royal sites (Lachish), administrative sites

(Tel Sheva), medium-size cities (Mizpah, Beth Shemesh), and various smaller-scale cities and towns. These urban entities were spread throughout the regions under Judahite control at different times in the Judean Hills, Shephelah, and northern Negev. Along and side by side with the cities and towns, a dense network of rural sites is known, mainly village sites of various sizes and classes. One can assume that a large percentage of the population of the Judahite Kingdom derived from the rural sector. In addition to the villages, numerous small fortified sites have been identified. These include large forts with a clear administrative function (e.g., Arad) and smaller ones situated in various strategically or economically significant locations.

DIET AND COOKING

The diet in Judah was, by and large, that which was common in the Mediterranean region since late prehistoric period (e.g., Shafer-Elliott 2013). A strong emphasis on local domesticated plants (the so-called Seven Species of the Bible) served as the main components of the diet, along with limited consumption of animal protein. This picture is clearly seen from the archaeobotanical and archaeozoological data from excavations in Iron II Judah. As expected, food consumption was of cardinal importance in the family and public domain, and it most probably played an important role in social cohesion and public cultic practice. Cooking methods used in Judah are relatively well known. The common cooking installation was a clay oven that was used both for baking bread—the staple food—and for cooking foods in cooking pots. The two main types of cooking pots used in Iron II Judah were a larger, more open vessel, which has its roots in Bronze Age cooking vessels well known in the Levant and a smaller, more closed, jug-like vessel, which appears in Judah from the Iron IIB. Finally, it is often noted that there is very little evidence of the consumption of pig in Iron Age II Judah, and it has been suggested that this may be seen as a marker of Judahite/Israelite culture as opposed to the Philistines (Finkelstein 1996; Faust 2012b) and as early evidence of later Jewish dietary restrictions regarding the consumption of pig.

ARCHITECTURE

Various architectural characteristics of the Judahite culture have been noted by archaeologists. Perhaps the best known is the so-called four-room or pillared house, of which many examples are known in numerous Judahite sites dating from the late Iron I until the end of the Iron Age. The ground plan is very fluid and flexible, varying in size, number of rooms, and features. Various explanations of the function and ideology of this house have been suggested, and the fact that it is so common in Judahite contexts clearly indicates that it had specific meaning within the Judahite ethos. That said, claims that these houses are a definitive marker of Judahite ethnicity (e.g., Bunimovitz and Faust 2002, 2003) are hard to accept, as there are Judahite sites without them and as such houses appear outside of Judah in Philistia and Transjordan (e.g., Maeir 2013). Likewise, Faust (2012b) noted that by and large there is a differentiation in the size of urban and rural houses of this type. He suggested that this reflects the different sizes of urban and rural families that lived in these houses. Faust (2001) has pointed out that the entrances of most of these houses are oriented to the west, perhaps indicating a preference dictated by the Judahite cosmological view.

Public architecture can be seen in various urban sites in Judah, including Jerusalem. Fortified towns in Judah often have a wall next to which is built a line of houses, followed by a perimeter street. While in the past it was assumed that a clear chrono-typological differentiation could be shown for the appearance of solid and casemate walls in different phases of the Iron II, based on what is seen from various sites throughout this period, various types of fortifications were used simultaneously at different sites. In fact, solid and casemate fortifications were used simultaneously at various sites at different phases of the Iron II. The city wall is connected to a chambered city gate, which served both as a focus of fortification and as a civic and commercial emphasis. These gates of varying sizes are seen in urban sites of various sizes as well as in smaller forts.

Within the city, there are various public buildings and features. This includes palaces like that seen in Lachish, governors' residences, temples, pillared buildings that probably served various functions (storehouses, stables, workshops), water systems (such as in Jerusalem, Gibeon, Beth Shemesh, Tel Sheva, and Arad), and nonprivate agricultural storage (such as in Gibeon and Moza). An apparent feature of royal architecture in late Iron II Judah is architectural ornamentation using the so-called Proto-Aeolic capital and the decorated balustrade. These decorative elements, though already known from Iron II Israel and Transjordan, appear in typical Judahite form in Jerusalem and Ramat Rahel and in a water system in the Rephaim Valley. In addition to this, one can note public buildings in nonurban contexts and, in particular, palaces (Ramat Rachel) and various fortress-like structures located throughout various parts of the kingdom at various stages, some large (such as Arad, Radum, etc.) and some much smaller and localized.

When one looks at the overall picture of urban planning in Judah, particularly in comparison to neighboring cultures, several issues stand out: (1) the scale of urbanization in Judah is much smaller than in the Israelite Kingdom, save for Jerusalem at the very end of the Iron Age; (2) the display of "ostentatious" architectural features is much less common in Judah, once again save for Jerusalem and Ramat Rahel at the end of the Iron Age, where volute capitals and other features briefly appear; (3) not all Judahite cities appear to have large public structures; and (4) water systems in Judah (except for Jerusalem and Gibeon, which utilized springs or groundwater) were mainly used to collect rainwater. This overview of various urban features stresses the smaller scale of the Kingdom of Judah in comparison to the Kingdom of Israel, but at the same time it shows features expected in a centralized kingdom throughout the entire period surveyed in this chapter.

BURIAL AND TOMBS

Extensive evidence of burials throughout Judah during the Iron IIA–IIC is known, and they provide interesting information on mortuary customs and how these reflect on issues of socioeconomic status, and various hints to the ideological and ritual dimensions of Judahite society (Bloch-Smith 1992). By and large, the most common type of tomb throughout the Kingdom of Judah is the rock-cut burial cave, used in connection with both rural and urban settlements, starting in the ninth century BCE but extensively documented in the eighth and seventh centuries BCE. The so-called bench tomb has been suggested as copying the common four-room house and may reflect conceptions of the afterlife. In general, most of these tombs had rather simple burial offerings. In Jerusalem there are several examples of more lavishly made burials; some are more complex and well-designed examples of the common "bench tomb" (such as at Ketef Hinnom), while others, such as in Silwan, on the ridge to the east of the City of David, are of different types, including monolithic rock-cut tombs such as the so-called Tomb of Pharaoh's Daughter.

WATER SYSTEMS

The water supply, needless to say, was a crucial aspect of daily life in Iron II Judah on the household, urban, and wider societal levels. In particular, public water systems in Iron II Judah are important as they indicate both advanced technological abilities and the central authorities' awareness of the need to invest resources to ensure adequate water supply under all circumstances, including in times of duress. Water systems in urban settings are hardly unique to Judah and are known from other contemporary cultures in the Iron Age Levant, such as in the Kingdom of Israel, Transjordan, and other areas. Nevertheless, several water systems in the Kingdom of Judah are worth noting. Jerusalem has, probably, the most complex and multiphased public water system in the Iron Age Southern Levant. While the exact history of its development is still highly debated (Reich and Shukron 2004), there are several components that most likely date to the Iron II, including the Gihon Channel (which led water from the Gihon Spring along the base of the eastern slope of the City of David) and the Gihon Tunnel (Hezekiah's Tunnel), which led water from the Gihon Spring through an underground artificially hewn channel to the Siloam

Pool on the southwestern side of the City of David. Most scholars believe that this was created by Hezekiah in preparation for the Assyrian siege of Jerusalem in 701 BCE. Other components, such as "Warren's Shaft" and other channels in this system, have been dated to various periods. Whatever the case, it is clear that during the Iron II there was a complex system of water channels and pools to ensure a regular water supply in Jerusalem.

The water system in Gibeon is also a complex system comprised of two distinct parts. The first is a round pool with a spiral staircase that accesses the water table. This is then supplemented by a stepped tunnel that was dug down the side of the site to reach the spring at the base of the site. Both systems enabled safe access to water even when the site was under attack. While the earlier system may date to the Iron IIA, the later one was in use until the late Iron II (Pritchard 1961).

TRADE

Throughout most of the Iron Age II, the Kingdom of Judah had a relatively minor role in trade, on both interregional and international scales. This is seen in the relatively small amounts of imported items found at Judahite sites and the few Judahite items found in other regions. Some of the earliest evidence of interregional trade is found in late Iron IIA Jerusalem, where Phoenician bullae and nonlocal fish bones (including Nile perch) indicate trade contacts with coastal regions (Reich, Shukron, and Lernau 2007). In the late Iron IIB, particularly important evidence of trade is seen at Tel Sheva Stratum II, which as noted above seems to have been an important way station in the Arabian trade. This hints at the role the Judahite Kingdom had in international trade, most likely brought on by the Assyrian economic interests in the Southern Levant. Clear textual evidence of this is seen in the impressive lists of tribute and taxes that Hezekiah gave to the Assyrians, much of which is clearly not local to Judah and could only have been received through trade (see Holladay 2006). During the Iron IIC, evidence of trade is seen in the Judahite sites in the Negev with their contacts with Edomites and other Transjordanian cultures.

At the very end of the Iron Age, there is evidence of trade in agricultural produce between Judah and Ashkelon on the eve of the Babylonian destruction of Ashkelon. Inscriptions noting different types of produce indicate the complex structure and market demands manifested in the agricultural trade at the time. Uniform weights and measures are indicative of this as well. Several late Iron IIC sites also provide evidence of international trade in the form of important timber, possible South Arabian inscriptions, and other finds. Possible evidence of Judahite objects in Egypt has also been noted, perhaps reflecting trade between Judah and Egypt as well (Maeir 2003; Holladay

2004). Nevertheless, when one compares the amounts of imported objects from Judahite sites to those of neighboring cultures such as Philistia, Israel, and Phoenicia, the quantities are quite small. This can be explained either as evidence for the marginality of the Judahite Kingdom during most of the Iron Age or, as recently suggested, as perhaps reflecting an ideology of simplicity and egalitarianism (e.g. Faust 2012b, but see Maeir 2013).

SOCIAL STRUCTURE AND GENDER

The majority of the Israelite and Judahite population belonged to relatively poor social strata, as was the case in most other societies in the ancient Near East. On the other hand, there is evidence, particularly in the large cities but also in some rural forts/farms, of more elevated and well-off portions of society that had more access to prestige items, sophisticated technology, imported items, and other resources. In Iron II Jerusalem in particular, elaborate burial complexes are to be seen as very clear evidence of this. Hints to facets of social inequality can also be seen in the Mesad Hashavyahu ostracon, in which a poor laborer complains of unjust treatment at the hand of an employer or master. In addition to various epigraphic and material evidence of taxation systems in the Judahite Kingdom, clear indications of state- and temple-related bureaucracy are seen, including seals and stamps of various officials, official supplies given out by the kingdom's administration (such as the LMLK storage jars in Iron IIB–IIC), possible depictions of royalty at Ramat Rahel, and apparent evidence of vessels designated for offerings for cultic purposes (e.g., Maeir 2010a). All this indicates the existence of state- and local-level administrative structures side by side with various levels of cultic-related hierarchy.

It can be assumed that, by and large, Judah was an androcentric society as was the case in all ancient Near Eastern societies. While examples of women who attained high levels are known from the textual, epigraphic, and even archaeological evidence, this is by far the exception and not the rule. As with most ancient societies, the public space was dominated by males; in the private, domestic realm, however, women had a central and even dominant role (Meyers 2013).

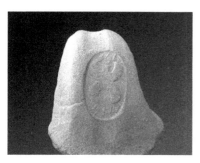

FIGURE 15-6. *The LMLK stamps on jar handles from several sites indicate the royal ability to collect taxes directly from harvests.*

ADMINISTRATION AND BUREAUCRACY

While there is relatively little extrabiblical textual evidence of the administrative and bureaucratic structure of the

Judahite Kingdom, some information can be gleaned from both the archaeological remains and the limited textual and epigraphic evidence. The existence of settlement hierarchy along with apparent administrative structures is indicative of this. The large palace/fort at Lachish, which was first built in the late Iron IIA, is paramount. The various forts and/or estates may very well be part of the royal Judahite administration (Faust 2012b; but see Maeir 2013). Impressive evidence of Iron IIB–C centers for the collection of agricultural produce—most probably from taxes, and meant for state-controlled redistribution and perhaps inter-regional trade—have been found at Gibeon (for wine) and at Moza (for grains). Most likely, other such centers for similar or other types of centralized state-controlled activities existed in other portions of the kingdom. The existence of a complex bureaucratic and tax system in the Iron IIB and IIC is seen through the epigraphic evidence. From the late eighth century BCE onward, there is evidence of a royal system of supply, as seen in the LMLK jars. In addition, there is evidence of other levels of bureaucratic control in the names of officials appearing on the LMLK jars, fiscal bullae, and local-level stamped (e.g., Barkay 1992; Shai, Ben-Shlomo, and Maeir 2012) and inscribed vessel handles. The close governmental control reflected in some of the Arad and Lachish Letters is additional evidence of the kingdom's administrative structure. Finally, the uniform system of weights and measures is seen in the well-known marked weights of Iron IIB–IIC Judah and perhaps in the uniform measures of volume reflected in inscriptions and volumetric studies of Iron II vessels. This said, it has been recently argued (Maeir and Shai 2016) that some of the archaeological evidence suggested as relating to central governmental control of the kingdom, from Jerusalem, may in fact reflect more regionally oriented sub-divisions. This might very well be connected to a kinship based, patronage structure, in which the king in Jerusalem ruled the kingdom through a complex web of relations with local leaders throughout the kingdom.

POTTERY

The pottery assemblage of Iron II Judah is for the most part quite distinct from other neighboring cultures, and this enables it to be used as one of the characteristics for delineating the cultural and political borders of the kingdom throughout the Iron IIA–IIC. Several characteristic features can be noted. In the late Iron IIA, pottery, if decorated, commonly had red-slip and hand-burnished decoration. In the Iron IIB and IIC, wheel burnishing is the most common decoration. While local and even domestic pottery production existed in Iron Age Judah, evidence of central, perhaps royal, ceramic production facilities is known. This is particularly the case for the large storage jars known in Judah from the late Iron IIA until the end of the Iron IIC used as part of the royal Judahite administration, particularly those with LMLK and other official stamps. It has been shown that these jars were produced in the region of the Shephelah, most probably in a centralized production facility. Most interestingly, there is very little decorated pottery and imported pottery in Judah. It has been suggested that this may reflect an ideology of simplicity at the time.

WEAPONS AND WARFARE

There is a wide data set of information on the crucial role that ongoing military confrontations played in the annals of the Judahite Kingdom throughout the Iron Age. In the biblical and other texts, there are many descriptions of warfare-related events, both on local scales—between groups within the kingdom, and between the Judahite Kingdom and other Levantine polities such as the Israelite Kingdom, the Philistines, and the Transjordanian kingdoms—and on the international scale against the much stronger armies of the Assyrian and Babylonian Empires. Archaeologically, evidence of warfare and weapons in the Kingdom of Judah is seen in various ways (Yadin 1963).

As mentioned above, there are many Iron II sites with various types of fortifications, including larger urban fortifications and smaller fortresses. These fortified sites undoubtedly reflect the threats of military confrontations (whether local or foreign), the need to broadcast power, and the logistical, engineering, and planning abilities of the Judahite Kingdom at different stages. Various components can be noted, most of which are hardly unique to the Judahite Kingdom and appear in other regions of the Southern Levant as well: chambered gates (including complex gate structures), casemate or solid walls with towers and/or buttresses, sloping glacis, and more.

There is also some evidence of some of the weaponry used in Iron IIB–C Judah. This includes swords, especially the well-preserved example from Vered Yericho, and depictions of Judahite swords in the Assyrian reliefs; archers depicted on seals and in Assyrian reliefs; arrows, whether local leaf-shaped types made of iron, bronze, or bone or the so-called bronze trilobate "Scythian Arrowheads" usually seen as evidence of Mesopotamian weaponry; knives, daggers, and spearheads of various types; sling stones; and helmets, shields, and other equipment as depicted in Assyrian reliefs of Judahite soldiers in the Assyrian army.

Evidence of the siege and conquest of cities is also known. While these events undoubtedly occurred more than once in Iron II Judah, as various destruction levels seem to indicate and textual evidence implies (Eph'al 2008), the primary evidence in Judah is undoubtedly that of the Assyrian siege and conquest of Lachish Stratum III in 701 BCE. This event is well documented in the Assyrian texts and reliefs and in archaeological evidence from the site and its surroundings. These sources provide unique and ample evidence of the methods, weaponry, tactics, and effectiveness of the Assyrian army as well as the unsuccessful efforts of the defenders to thwart these actions (Ussishkin 1982, 2004, 2014).

DIFFERENCE BETWEEN THE JUDAHITE AND ISRAELITE CULTURES

In most of the literature, the term "Israelite" refers to the Israelite (Northern Kingdom) and Judahite (Southern Kingdom) jointly. While in fact the Israelites and Judahites shared many characteristics that differentiated them from other ethnic or cultural groups, the archaeological evidence indicates subtle and, at times, not-so-subtle differences in culture between the Northern and Southern Kingdoms. Whether or not one accepts the historicity of a united kingdom as the initial stage of the development of the monarchy in Israel and Judah, during the ninth and eighth centuries BCE, many material and cultural indicators seem to indicate that, though closely related, these two kingdoms and cultures were also quite different (e.g., Finkelstein 1999; Gelander 2011; Fleming 2012). For example, very different concepts of kingship and city planning and fortifications are seen in the two kingdoms. Likewise, distinctive northern and southern dialects, iconography, and religious practices, not to mention different founding figures—David (Judah) and Omri (Israel) as the founding dynastic figures in Assyrian and Aramaean royal inscriptions, and Judah versus house of Joseph/Ephraim as eponymic fathers in the biblical text—all indicate major differences. Even the custom of abstinence from pork, which many see as a sine qua non attribute of all Israelite and Judahite sites, may indicate differences between the two cultures, as pig seems to have been consumed at Israelite sites (Maeir, Hitchcock, Horwitz 2013; Sapir-Hen et al. 2013).

Thus, while these two kingdoms/cultures should be viewed as closely related entities, it is only in the later Iron Age, with the collapse of the Northern Kingdom, that these two identities were, at least semantically, "combined." If so, many of the worldviews portrayed in the biblical text may in fact be those of the Judahites or, in some cases, a post–Iron Age Judean culture and less reflective of a very similar Northern Kingdom. It is probably more reasonable to suggest that the two kingdoms/cultures were similar in the same manner as the various Aramean kingdoms and cultures of contemporary Syria.

Suggestions for Further Reading

For decades, advanced students in biblical history have been studying J. M. Miller and John Hayes' *A History of Ancient Israel and Judah*. It was updated with a second edition in 2006 and remains the most expert sifting and synthesis of the Old Testament for historical analysis. Complement this with A. Faust's *The Archaeology of Israelite Society in Iron Age II* (2012; but see Maeir 2013), and you will acquire significant detail about the biblical and archaeological perspectives of Israel and Judah. The question remains, of course, of how to put that information into a single coherent picture. The debate between Israel Finkelstein and Amihai Mazar in *The Quest for the Historical Israel: Debating Archaeology and the History of Early Israel* (2007) shows how two experts at the top of the field put together quite different interpretations of essentially the same information. The place of the religiously central city of Jerusalem within this history is vigorously examined in Andrew Vaughn and Anne Killebrew's collection of essays titled *Jerusalem in Bible and Archaeology: The First Temple Period* (2003). And, finally, a surprising amount of our knowledge about Israelite culture during this period comes from graves. Elizabeth Bloch-Smith's study of those finds provides an insightful analysis in *Judahite Burial Practices and Beliefs about the Dead* (1992).

16

DAILY LIFE IN IRON AGE ISRAEL AND JUDAH

Jennie Ebeling

This chapter describes aspects of daily life in Israel and Judah during the Iron Age (ca. 1200–586 BCE). Utilizing the Hebrew Bible as well as other sources of evidence, I will identify and describe some of the activities that occupied the majority of the women and men who lived in Iron Age Israel and Judah on a daily basis. This will reveal patterns of daily life that will provide information about the dynamics of the household, gender roles, life-cycle events, subsistence strategies, religious practices, and more and will permit a holistic understanding of the realities and concerns of the average person. It is important to note that lifeways varied both chronologically and geographically during this dynamic six-hundred-year period; for the purposes of this chapter, however, I will create a general impression of the more important daily life activities during the Iron Age using the available sources.

Since modern life knows such different realities from those experienced by people who lived in the Middle East some three thousand years ago, it can be difficult to relate to their daily concerns. We must imagine, however, that certain cycles governed many aspects of life. Since the economic basis of society was farming, the annual agricultural cycle was of primary importance; this is suggested by one of the earliest known Hebrew inscriptions, the Gezer Calendar. This small limestone tablet dated to the tenth century BCE and found at Gezer, northwest of Jerusalem, refers to various agricultural activities and their positions in the ancient calendar. Harvests were celebrated with festivals that transformed into some of the major Jewish holidays still celebrated today. Likewise, life-cycle events like childbirth, coming of age, marriage, and death were important within the context of the family and larger community and celebrated with family gatherings, ritual activities, and feasts (Ebeling 2010). These cycles provide context for the daily life activities described in this chapter and help us appreciate some of the meaning behind ancient Israelite traditions, some of which continue to be celebrated today.

Sources

All available sources of evidence should be consulted in order to create the most complete and accurate reconstruction of daily life activities possible. The primary sources available for daily life in ancient Israel and Judah are the Hebrew Bible, archaeological remains from Israel, the Palestinian Authority (West Bank), and surrounding regions, artistic sources, and ethnographic information from contemporary Middle Eastern societies. Other sources from the larger Near Eastern and eastern Mediterranean world, such as inscriptions and art from neighboring Egypt, also inform our understanding of daily life activities, but they must be used with caution and thus appear in only a limited way in this chapter.

Hebrew Bible and Other Texts

As the primary textual source of information about ancient Israel and Judah, the Hebrew Bible offers a number of insights into aspects of everyday life. However, there are a number of limitations to using the Hebrew Bible to reconstruct domestic activities that must be considered. First of all, the primary intent of the biblical writers was theological. Even though bits and pieces of daily life come through, the writers did not intend to provide a thorough account of the culture and traditions of the Israelites. Second, the biblical text was composed largely by elite urban men about elite urban men such as kings, priests, and prophets. Thus, the concerns of the majority of the population, the peasants who lived in nonurban areas, were perhaps unfamiliar to the writers and were not discussed in detail. The biblical text also is largely unconcerned with female issues. Although there are important female characters throughout the text, they are exceptional and probably do not reflect the realities of most of the female population. Therefore, although we will look to the Hebrew Bible as a source, we must use it carefully and in tandem with other sources of information about the lives of the ancient Israelites. Thousands of extrabiblical inscriptions from Israel and Judah also inform on aspects of daily life.

Archaeology

During more than a century of scientific archaeological excavations in the region, archaeologists have unearthed abundant material remains of daily life activities from the Iron Age. In the past, archaeologists tended to focus on monumental remains of temples, palaces, and other examples of elite architecture, while archaeologists today are focusing their attention on the remains of households. Household archaeology is an effort to reconstruct activities in domestic structures using the artifacts and installations of daily life associated with them; such studies also allow for investigation into the utilization of space and into the presence of gendered activities, if certain spaces can be identified with female or male activities (Yasur-Landau, Ebeling, and Mazow 2011). Physical evidence for such activities as food preparation, for example, includes imperishable items like pottery vessels, grinding tools, and ovens, as well as the occasional remains of food itself. The bias of preservation due to variable climate limits our understanding, however, and many look to food remains from Egypt—where organic material preserves very well—for information about the ancient diet. Material from Egypt and other places where artifacts from antiquity preserve well can be helpful for reconstructing similar items that may have existed in ancient Israel, but this information does not provide direct evidence for the existence of materials that we might know about only from texts like the Hebrew Bible.

ART

Artistic representations can be useful in illustrating ancient daily life activities, but they are rather limited in Iron Age contexts in Israel and Judah because of the tendency toward aniconism. Most are in the form of small clay figurines depicting females or animals, especially horses. Figurines in the form of a nude female with a pillar-shaped body and heavy breasts (known as Judean Pillar Figurines) are found in abundance in Iron Age Judah in many different contexts, including houses, tombs, streets, and elsewhere (Darby 2014). A large number of broken Pillar Figurines were found along with various cult objects in Jerusalem Cave I, located several hundred yards from the Temple Mount. Many scholars believe that these figurines cannot represent human women and must instead represent a goddess; since they emphasize the breasts, it is possible that believed that they were amulets representing a goddess like the Canaanite goddess Asherah, who may have protected pregnant and lactating women and young children. These figurines thus provide information about women's and men's concerns and highlight the dangers that accompanied childbirth and early life.

FIGURE 16-1. *Judean Pillar Figurines from eighth-century BCE Jerusalem.*

Small clay figurines from Israel's northern neighbor, Phoenicia, depict pregnant women and women playing hand drums and performing various daily life activities like kneading dough and bathing, and they may illustrate ways of life in Israel as well. The only clear representations of women from Judah are found on the walls of the palace of the Neo-Assyrian king Sennacherib in Nineveh in northern Mesopotamia. In scenes of the siege of Lachish in Judah by Sennacherib in 701 BCE, men, women, and children are shown being led away from the city and likely deported to other parts of the Neo-Assyrian Empire (Ussishkin 1982). Despite the Assyrian perspective of these images, they depict what might have been the typical dress of Judahites during the eighth century BCE and show, for example, women and girls with covered heads and bare feet. In addition, Egyptian three-dimensional models and tomb paintings, many of them from earlier periods, provide insights into various aspects of daily life in the broader region.

Ethnography

Archaeologists working in the region use ethnographic information from traditional Middle Eastern societies to help interpret artifacts and installations that they uncover. There is a great deal of information recorded by anthropologists and others who observed traditional daily life activities in Palestine, Egypt, and other parts of the region in the nineteenth and twentieth centuries; some of the early archaeologists working in this region believed that observable lifeways illustrated life in biblical times, and they used their own ethnographic observations to understand aspects of ancient daily life. Although it is now understood that the ways of life in the modern Middle East are not identical to those three thousand years earlier, analogies between the two can provide useful models against which the archaeological evidence can be tested. Ethnographic information is particularly helpful for reconstructing daily life activities like baking, cooking, and pottery making.

Family and Household

According to the Hebrew Bible, the ancient Israelite family was large and complex and characterized as an extended family household, or, in Hebrew, a *bet av*. Members of an extended family household consisted of the male head and his nuclear family, possibly widowed parents, unmarried children, married sons along with their wives and children, and unrelated persons who might fall under the senior male's protection. Although many believe that ancient Israelite society was a **patriarchy**—a system in which men had authority over the household as well as over political, social, economic, and religious institutions—this idea has been challenged (Meyers 2012, 194). It may be more appropriate to consider ancient Israel as a **heterarchy** instead. Unlike hierarchical systems like patriarchy, heterarchy allows different elements to be ranked in different ways. Thus, within a household, a woman might hold a lot of power and authority, while in other aspects of society a woman might be ranked in a different way. Israelite women therefore no longer must be considered to have been subordinate to men in nearly all areas of life regardless of age, class, and other differentiators. As attested in the Hebrew Bible, women were involved in important family decisions, and their contributions to the functioning of the household were critical and are demonstrated in the textual and archaeological remains.

The marriage pattern in ancient Israel was patrilocal, meaning that a young woman left her birth home to live in her new husband's family's house. One might imagine that this created a potentially difficult situation for a girl who had to leave her birth family at a young age. Inheritance, an important theme in the biblical text, was usually **patrilineal**, or transferred through the male line. An exception is seen in the story of Zelophehad, who had five daughters who were allowed to inherit their father's property if they married men from their own tribe (Num 27:1-11). However, there are also passages in which men take another wife or attempt to have a son through other means (a female slave or a prostitute) in order to have a son who can inherit property.

The archaeological correlates of the extended family's daily life activities can be found in the Israelite four-room house, a characteristic house type during the Iron Age (Bunimovitz and Faust 2002). The four-room house developed in the context of the central highland villages occupied during the Early Iron Age as an adaptation to the challenges of the environment and an expression of the egalitarianism that is believed to have characterized proto-Israelite society. Unlike earlier house types, in which access to certain rooms could be restricted, all rooms on the ground floor of the four-room house could be accessed through a common central courtyard. In addition to reflecting an egalitarian ethos, this pattern might have facilitated purity concerns and/or reinforced the values of the community. Regardless, the four-room house met the needs of extended families that were reliant on **agro-pastoralism** for their survival.

Demography and Life Cycle

From our twenty-first-century vantage point, the ancient Israelite lifespan was short. The analysis of ancient human skeletons shows that the average age of death for men was between thirty and forty years, while women lived to between age twenty and thirty. Much of this is due to the very high mortality rate for infants and young children: perhaps 50 percent of the population died by age five. Women lived statistically shorter lives than men because of the risk of dying from complications of childbirth, and many people likely suffered from malnutrition and disease. Understanding the short lifespan of the ancient Israelites provides context and perhaps special meaning to the life cycle events celebrated in ancient Israel and described in the Hebrew Bible, including coming of age, marriage, childbirth, and death.

Israelite girls probably reached physical maturity by age twelve or thirteen and boys a few years after. Celebrations surrounding the coming of age are not well understood, although a hint to a ritual performed by young women can be found in the story of Jephthah's daughter (Judg 11:30-40). Jephthah promised Yahweh a burnt offering of the first person to come out of his house when he returned home after success in battle with the Ammonites. When he returns home, his daughter is the first to come out to meet him and thus must be sacrificed in fulfillment of her father's vow. Before she is killed, she spends two months in the mountains with her companions "to bewail my virginity" (Judg 11:37). In Judges 11:40, an annual event is described in which all of the young women in Israel went to the mountains to lament the death of Jephthah's daughter. This might have been a female initiation rite before marriage in ancient Israel. There is no biblical evidence for the celebration of male puberty.

Marriage was the norm in ancient Israel, and a monogamous marriage was ideal. Young women were likely married soon after their first menstruation, while men married when they were at least a few years older. It was critical that young women be virgins when they married, although this was not required of men. Marriage was a social contract in ancient Israel, and there was no legal aspect to it; we thus have few details about traditions surrounding marriage in the Hebrew Bible. According to patrilocal marriage practices, a young woman would leave the authority of her father and her father's house and enter her new husband's house under the authority of her new husband. This was more than just a partnership between two individuals: it created or reinforced bonds between members of the same kinship group. The young husband's family paid a bride price to compensate for the loss of her contributions to her birth household. The bride's family may have given a dowry in the form of land, money, jewelry, or other gifts to the new husband's family. Exchanging gifts was important for strengthening relationships between the two families.

The primary concern of all people in ancient Israel was having children, and we might imagine that women were pregnant or nursing for most of their lives, starting soon after marriage at a young age. According to Deuteronomy 24:5, a newlywed man was exempted from military duties for one year so that the couple could be together, presumably to conceive a child. Children were a source of pride in ancient societies, and boys especially were desired as they preserved the family land inheritance while also providing farm labor. Boys were trained in agricultural tasks and shepherding along with more specialized jobs, like metalworking, from a young age. Likewise, girls would have made important contributions to the household at an early age, when they likely began learning the basic daily life activities like food preparation, textile production, and caring for young children that occupied women for many hours each day.

Women typically gave birth at home, assisted by a midwife, female members of the family, or experienced female members of the community, such as the women of the neighborhood who assisted Ruth (Ruth 4:13-17). That midwives played important roles in ancient Israel is shown in such passages as Exodus 1:15-21, which describes the midwives Shiphrah and Puah, who were credited with saving the Israelites after refusing to kill all firstborn sons as decreed by the pharaoh. Midwives also provided emotional support to laboring women, such as Rachel, who was reassured by her midwife (Gen 35:17). Small amulets like figurines and beads may have been used during childbirth, along with birth rituals, like bathing, rubbing with salt, and swaddling in cloth strips immediately after the cord was cut (Ezek 16:4). Rubbing the baby with salt might have been a purification rite required by the polluting blood of childbirth. Barrenness was feared in ancient Israel and was sometimes viewed as a divine punishment. Mothers were honored in ancient Israel, and a lack of children deprived women of the highest status a woman could typically achieve.

Archaeology provides a great deal of information about burial practices, and biblical descriptions allow us to reconstruct some of the events that surrounded death (Bloch-Smith 1992). During the Iron Age, cemeteries were typically located close to a settlement, although not within a city's walls, and internments include rock-cut tombs, pits, and more complex built tombs. Larger tombs might have been conceived as houses for the dead where generations of family members were buried. Individuals might be laid out on benches and their remains pushed aside or gathered up and disposed of elsewhere in the tomb complex to accommodate the recently deceased; this might provide physical evidence for the biblical concept of being gathered to one's ancestors after death (Gen 25:8). Jewelry and other items of adornment are often associated with excavated skeletons, and grave goods (like pottery vessels) were often interred with the dead; these might have been gifts to the dead or intended for use in the afterlife. They also might have contained the remains of feasts that accompanied death. Although necromancy—asking the dead for advice—was apparently outlawed in ancient Israel, its first king, Saul, visits a witch in order to consult the spirit of Samuel for information about his battles with the Philistines (1 Sam 28). This reflects the importance of the dead, particularly deceased ancestors, in the lives of the ancient Israelites.

Agro-pastoralism as the Basis of the Israelite Economy

The basis of the economy in ancient Israel and Judah was agro-pastoralism, meaning the majority of the population participated in farming and herding, and all able-bodied family members participated in these critical daily life activities to ensure that there would be enough food for the extended family year round. Barley and wheat are first on the list of the Seven Species—based on Deuteronomy 8:8—for which the land of Israel is known. And cereal grains, grapes, and olives formed the so-called Mediterranean Triad mentioned in such places as Hosea 2:8, where Yahweh identifies "the grain, the wine, and the oil" as the gifts he lavished on Israel. Thus, cereal grains, grapes, and olives probably accounted for the majority of Israelite land under cultivation during the Iron Age (MacDonald 2008, 19). Sheep and goats, as well as cattle and draft animals, were commonly kept and relied upon at various times of year. Although this mixed economy was relied upon by most Israelites, there was always a nomadic or seminomadic population in the region with a pastoralist means of subsistence.

AGRICULTURAL CALENDAR

As described above, the agricultural cycle was fundamentally important to all areas of Israelite life, and sources like the Gezer Calendar and the biblical text inform on seasonal events. The three most important harvests were marked by celebrations that later became major religious festivals in the Jewish calendar. Fields and terraces were plowed, and cereals (primarily barley and wheat) were sown from October through December; legumes were sown later, from December through February, during the rainy season. Barley was harvested in April, and its completion was celebrated with the *matzot* festival, which later became *pesah*, or Passover. This was the first ingathering of the fruit of the Israelites' agricultural labor in the calendar year (Borowski 2003, 36). *Hag haqassir*—the feast of the harvest—was celebrated seven weeks after *matzot* to celebrate the wheat harvest (approximately early June); it was later known as *shevuot* (weeks). Grapes began ripening with the start of summer and were harvested in June and July, while other fruits—such as pomegranates, figs, and dates—were picked through July and August. This third major harvest was celebrated by *asif*, or "ingathering," in September or October with the olive harvest. *Asif* later became *sukkot* ("booths" or "tabernacles") (Borowski 2003, 28). Although it is difficult to identify clear evidence for ancient cultivation near archaeological sites, the remains of tools that were used in some of these activities are sometimes found, including flint and iron sickle blades and iron plowshares.

CEREALS

We can appreciate the complexity of subsistence agriculture through a closer look at the harvest and processing of the primary staple food: cereal grains. Barley and wheat were highly valuable and consumed in the form of bread and other baked goods, parched grains, stews, beer, and more. After barley and wheat were harvested in late spring, the stalks were cut and gathered and carried to a threshing floor somewhere outside the settlement close to the fields where they were threshed to separate the grains from the stalks and chaff. After winnowing, or throwing the remaining material into the air to allow the heavier grains to fall to the ground, the cereal was cleaned using sieves to remove foreign matter and taken back to the settlement. If they were not to be consumed immediately, cereal grains were stored in jars, pits, and silos in and around domestic areas. Grain could then be used year round to make a variety of edibles and beer any time of year (see further below).

GRAPES AND OLIVES

Wine produced from grapes and other fruits and olive oil were also important dietary staples as well as export products; they played important roles in Israelite religion and culture as well. Grapes and olives grow particularly well in the rocky, well-watered soils of the central highland areas of Israel and in other areas as well. Their importance is shown in Deuteronomy 8:8, where grapes are

FIGURE 16-2.
Palestinian women and men harvesting olives.

mentioned next after barley and wheat among the plants with which the land of Israel was blessed. During grape-harvest season, families may have relocated to stone watchtowers in the vineyards to protect the valuable grape crop (Isa 5:1-7). All available family members probably participated in this annual activity. To harvest, clusters of ripened fruit were cut from the vine with knives and placed carefully into baskets. They were then carried to winery installations cut from bedrock. These were often located close to vineyards so that grapes would not have to be transported far; portable presses made of clay are also known. Grapes were trod in large vats, and the expressed juice flowed into attached rock-cut vats for primary fermentation; secondary fermentation was accomplished in pottery storage jars in cool places like caves and cisterns. Wine could be stored for months or years and was exported to neighboring markets and beyond; industrial-scale wine production was established in the eighth and seventh centuries BCE during the height of the Neo-Assyrian Empire (MacDonald 2008, 23), and the Assyrian kings highly valued this export product and are depicted in art with cups of wine. Unlike beer, which could be made any time of year, wine was a more expensive, high-status beverage in ancient Israel because it could be produced only once per year. Nine types of wine are mentioned in the Hebrew Bible, and it was required in temple rituals.

The olive harvest involved beating the olive trees when the fruit ripened (Deut 24:20) so that the olives would fall to the ground to be collected by all available family members. The olives would then be placed in baskets and sacks and transported to a nearby olive press. Fixed olive presses in stone were located near olive groves; portable presses are also known, and olives could have been pressed using mortar and pestle for small amounts of oil. The precious olive oil was used in cooking, as a base for perfumes, to light lamps, for cleaning the body, and more. Olive oil has a special place in the Israelite cult for anointing kings, as when Saul is anointed by Samuel with olive oil (Judg 9:8), and for lighting lamps in the tabernacle and Jerusalem temple. Olive wood was also used to make architectural features in the temple. Like wine making, olive oil production was a major industry in Israel during the Iron Age, and olive oil was exported in large quantities.

PASTORALISM AND ANIMAL HUSBANDRY

A variety of animals were kept by the ancient Israelites, although archaeological excavations reveal more sheep and goat bones than the remains of any other animal. Sheep and goats provided milk that could be consumed immediately or preserved as cheese or butter; wool and hair that was used to produced clothing and other textiles as well as tents; and meat that was consumed occasionally, primarily at feasts and other special occasions. According to the biblical text, both boys and girls were entrusted with shepherding the flocks. Other animals, including cows, were kept for the milk, meat, and hide they provided. In addition, donkeys were commonly used for overland transport, and bulls or oxen were used to pull plows and wagons. Horses were elite animals that may have been used primarily for military purposes to pull chariots (Borowski 2003, 30). A variety of wild animals were hunted and eaten in ancient Israel, as demonstrated by the remains of butchered animals in archaeological contexts, and a variety of fresh and saltwater fish were also consumed.

Household Activities

In addition to farming activities and pastoralism, a number of activities took place in the context of the Israelite household and are understood primarily from the archaeological remains of excavated houses. Evidence for food production, spinning and weaving, and other activities is found in the artifacts and installations within houses and courtyards, and biblical, artistic, and ethnographic data help archaeologists reconstruct some of these activities. Recent interest in household archaeology has led to the reconstruction of specific Iron Age houses in order to identify activity areas where specific tasks were carried out. Although, as described above, all family members participated in agricultural activities and animal husbandry, women in particular are closely associated with household economic activities; therefore, attempts have been made to identify the presence of women in specific household spaces where cooking, textile production, and other activities were carried out.

Identifying Gendered Activities

Past scholars often assumed that the division of labor between the sexes in nineteenth- and twentieth-century Europe and North America held true for ancient Israel. Therefore, it was assumed that women were closely associated with, or even restricted to, the house and primarily responsible for raising children and performing mundane tasks of daily life, while men were more involved in public life and activities outside the home. The biblical and ethnographic sources reveal that few if any activities were performed exclusively by men or women other than the biologically determined activities of childbearing and breastfeeding. However, these sources suggest that women were more closely associated with the preparation of food and textiles for family consumption in the household in particular, although men later professionalized these activities when the products were made available on the commercial market.

Since the textual evidence is far from complete and the archaeological remains do not speak for themselves, we must look to other sources of evidence to determine which activities were performed by members of which sex. For example, ethnographic evidence from around the world suggests that women are the primary makers of pottery vessels used at home—such as cooking pots, storage jars, plates, cups and more—while men are often responsible for making pottery vessels that are sold in markets. Ethnographic studies also suggest that certain kinds of food-preparation activities—like making bread—are typically women's work, while cooking meat is more often associated with men. We need to keep in mind, however, that these gender roles are not absolutes: the biblical writers describe men grinding grain and baking bread in several passages, for example. Although archaeologists of late have focused on identifying gendered spaces in houses, we will focus here on assessing the remains of specific activities and identifying any activity areas that reveal patterned behavior in Israelite four-room houses. After describing the evidence for some of the more important household activities, we will look at several eighth- to seventh-century BCE houses in Judah as case studies.

FOOD PREPARATION

The biblical text describes some of the tools and installations that were used to transform wheat and barley into edibles, and there are abundant archaeological correlates of these activities; as mentioned above, many are made of imperishable materials, and we thus have plentiful evidence of these activities in ancient households. Numerous passages refer to baking bread and cakes as one of the most important food-preparation activities undertaken by Israelite women on a daily basis (Gen 19:3; Lev 26:26; 1 Sam 8:13; 2 Sam 13:8; 1 Kgs 17:2-3; Isa 44:15) even after commercial, probably male-run, bakeries existed in Jerusalem. Bread was so vital that the Hebrew term—*lehem*—was sometimes used to denote food generally in the biblical text. Before cereals were to be consumed, they were pulverized or ground to a finer texture using ground stone tools. Grinding stones, including mobile handstones and lower grinding slabs, were used along with mortars, pestles, and other tools to grind grains to a finer texture. Grinding equipment is found in abundance at archae-

ological sites and attests to the place of cereal-based foods in the Israelite diet (Ebeling and Rowan 2004). Likewise, clay

FIGURE 16-3. *A statue depicting a servant woman grinding grain with a grinding slab and handstone from Old Kingdom Egypt.*

ovens used for baking bread and cooking other foods are found in houses and associated outdoor spaces. Bread was made by mixing ground flour with water and yeast, if desired, and could baked in an oven, in the embers of a fire, and in other ways. Less processed grain could be added to soups and stews.

Beer was an offshoot of bread production in ancient Israel and is evidenced primarily by archaeological remains. If beer was desired, cereal grains were kept moist for a few days until they germinated. The germinated grains could then be heated so that they malted, and then they were added to water and yeast, or the germinated grains could be ground up and baked into malted bread cakes that were then crumbled and added to water in ceramic jars. Yeast was then added, or airborne yeast spores would ferment the liquid. Various fruits and spices could be added to improve the taste, or it could be drunk as it was within several days; it could not be stored for long periods of time like wine, and thus it had to be consumed quickly. Beer would have provided more calories than consuming grains as bread, and the small amount of alcohol killed off bacteria and made the beer safer to drink than water (Ebeling and Homan 2008, 52–53). Evidence for beer is in the form of distinctive pottery vessels like beer or side-spouted sieve jugs with a filter spout, stoppers placed on top of beer jars that would allow gases produced during fermentation to escape, and straw-tip strainers used to strain the dregs. The biblical term *sekar* is mentioned several times in parallel with wine (1 Sam 1:12-14; Num 6:1-4) and therefore most likely refers to beer (Ebeling and Homan 2008, 48).

Evidence for the storage of liquids, like wine and oil, is seen in large storage jars that are found in houses. In the courtyard house at Megiddo, for example, jars were found in areas that might have functioned as storage rooms (Gadot and Yasur-Landau 2006, 2:588–89). Direct evidence for women associated with food production comes from the gruesome remains of the courtyard house. The house was destroyed by fire, and the remains of seven or eight people were found inside. The only skeleton whose sex could be determined was a woman between thirty and forty who died in the courtyard near artifacts and installations used for food preparation and consumption; it is possible that this woman was caught in the house's collapse while cooking (Gadot and Yasur-Landau 2006, 2:595). Less evidence is available for other foods processed, consumed, and/or stored in the home; occasional evidence of actual food remains bears witness to various fruits, vegetables, and legumes as well as animals consumed.

Spinning and Weaving

Evidence for spinning and weaving is found in a number of Iron Age houses (Cassuto 2008). In the absence of the actual fabric, which rarely survives, textile production is identified in households by tools and other remains made from less perishable materials. Clothing was made at home in ancient Israel, and various other woven items (including rugs, bedding, blankets, curtains, and more) were likely made as well. Spindle whorls were used when spinning wool and other fibers; examples in stone and other materials evidence this activity. Clay loom weights, which were used to weight the warp threads of the horizontal warp-weighted loom, are often found in clusters since a number of them were used for a single loom. Spinning thread and weaving cloth were activities that were strongly associated with women in the ancient world, and the biblical evidence suggests that this was the case in ancient Israel and Judah as well. In Proverbs

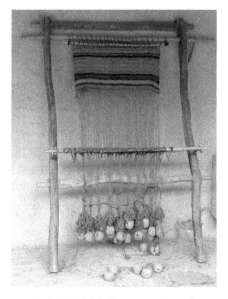

FIGURE 16-4. *Reconstruction of a vertical warp-weighted loom with clay loom weights.*

31, the largest number of specific tasks performed by the high-status woman described refers to making cloth, and activities related to food provisioning are a close second. This demonstrates that these activities were strongly associated with women and valued in ancient Israelite society.

In Iron Age houses, evidence for spinning is sometimes found in the same context as food-preparation activities. This can be seen, for example, in the Early Iron Age courtyard house at Megiddo (Gadot and Yasur-Landau 2006, 2:590). Physical evidence for spinning and weaving coupled with the remains of food-processing activities may strengthen the case for female activity areas in certain household spaces.

OTHER HOUSEHOLD CRAFTS AND TECHNOLOGIES

Archaeologists find an abundance of pottery vessels and sherds in household contexts and study aspects of their manufacture, decoration, trade, use in daily life activities, and more; in fact, we know more about ancient Israelite pottery than any other Iron Age craft or technology. As discussed by Maeir (chapter 15), centralized pottery production in Judah is evidenced by LMLK jars, and it is clear that pottery was produced for commercial use, probably by men, as described in several biblical passages (1 Chr 4:23; Jer 18:2-4). However, within the domestic context, undecorated utilitarian pottery like cooking pots, storage jars, and serving containers of various types was likely made by those who used them on a regular basis for cooking, serving, and storing various foods and liquids. Ethnographic sources show that women are the primary potters in traditional societies and that pottery-making knowledge is often passed down through the female line, and it is likely that women made pottery in Israelite houses for domestic use. Pottery manufacture in the household leaves little trace, and in fact the only clear evidence for pottery production is the rare discovery of stone potters' wheels and kilns.

Unlike food preparation, spinning and weaving, and pottery production, which are strongly associated with women at the household level, metalworking is more closely associated with men in antiquity. The Hebrew Bible preserves the tradition that the neighboring Philistines possessed ironworking knowledge while the early Israelites did not, although, by monarchical times, Israelites were making items out of bronze and iron as well as silver and gold (Borowski 2003, 34–35). There is relatively sparse evidence for metalworking in the Israelite household because it does not preserve as well as ceramic and stone, it was often recycled, and it may have been a more specialized activity that took place outside the home. However, repairing and sharpening tools used in agricultural activities was probably often accomplished in the household, as suggested by the finds from four-room houses at Tel Halif (see below).

Basketry, leatherworking, and similar industries leave fewer traces because of the preservation conditions in this region, but we can assume that many articles made of these and other organic materials were used because they are described in the biblical text and occasionally preserved in the archaeological record. Closely related to textile production, basket making was probably a common household activity, and items woven from plant stalks were likely used as baskets, mats, and more. Occasional direct evidence for these items preserved in desert sites and in the form of impressions on the base of pottery vessels that were built on woven mats. Leather was likely used to make articles of clothing as well as bags and other containers such as wine and water skins and churns. The ethnographic data indicate that both basketry and leatherworking are more closely associated with females than males. Recognizing that such perishable items were common in ancient Israel highlights the bias of preservation toward stone and ceramic artifacts in the archaeological record.

Case Study: Four-Room Houses at Tel Halif

Two relatively well-preserved four-room houses from eighth- to seventh-century BCE Tel Halif—located in Judah northeast of Beersheba—reveal information about daily life activities and the use of space in domestic dwellings. Tel Halif was abandoned before it was destroyed by fire in the context of the Neo-Assyrian campaign in 701 BCE, and destruction debris sealed this fortified Iron Age settlement and the finds within the houses. The area with the houses, Field IV, was resettled after the destruction of the site, and the later levels covered and effectively sealed the predestruction remains as well. The two houses described here contained a large amount of pottery and other artifacts as well as animal bones and plant remains that inform on the diet and plant species at that time; both have been reconstructed in detail in other publications (Hardin 2010; Shafer-Elliot 2013). The following discussion is intended to summarize the contents and use of spaces within the houses in order to give an impression of the abundant material that is available for understanding daily life activities in Iron Age sites.

House F7 (Northern Building)

This house measured 11–12 by 9.5 meters and had three long rooms in the front of the house and a divided broad room in the back; although it is damaged, it is believed that the entrance to the house was from one of the long rooms. Two of the long rooms are believed to have been unroofed spaces, while the third

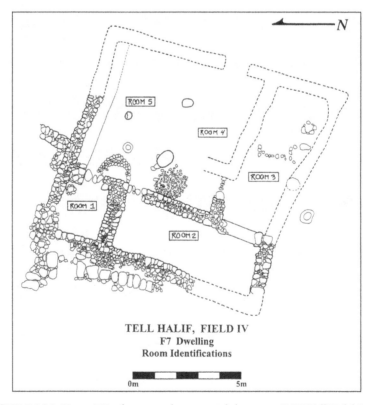

TELL HALIF, FIELD IV
F7 Dwelling
Room Identifications

0m   5m

FIGURE 16-5. *House F7, a four-room house at eighth-century BCE Tell Halif, Israel.*

long room and the broad rooms were believed to have been roofed. One of the long rooms, Room 4, was paved with stones and reconstructed as a stable. An area just to its north appears to have been associated with wine production, as twelve large jars (including three that tested positive for wine) as well as a funnel, a strainer, and fermentation stoppers were found in this space. Objects associated with food production were located in the adjacent long room, Room 5: it contained a limestone mortar embedded in the ground (which was probably used to crush cereal grains); other ground stone tools; an oven; a hearth; many pottery vessels; sheep, goat, cattle, and fish bones; as well as cereal and legume remains and eggshells. In the third long room, evidence for textile production was identified, including a small assemblage of loom weights and a spindle whorl. Artifacts and installations in the two broad rooms in the rear of the house evidence the storage of food serving and consumption vessels as well as household cultic activity in the form of two standing stones, the head of a female pillar figurine, and a ceramic cult stand (Hardin 2010).

SOUTHERN BUILDING

The southern building had long rooms in the front and a broad room in the back; it is believed to have had a second floor as well. The smaller side rooms were used for storing food and tools, while the large broad room was divided with a low wall and used for various activities, including food preparation. Household animals were stabled in one of the large long rooms that had a cobblestone floor, and the central long room was a family room. Storage in Room 5 included such remains as a loom weight, a plow point, and a flaked stone tool along with a cooking vessel and numerous sherds from other vessels; it could be that this was a workroom for weaving and used for storing tools (Shafer-Elliot 2013, 85). Room 6 was the rest of the broad room in the back. It had an oven and lots of pottery as well as a loom weight, a figurine fragment, animal bones, and more; due to the presence of the oven, it has been interpreted as a food-preparation area (Shafer-Elliot 2013, 85–86). Bowls, a jug, and most of the cooking pots recovered in the house were found in Room 2, the second of the three long rooms, providing evidence for the consumption of food. No evidence of a cooking installation was preserved in this space, but oven fragments were identified, possibly indicating a poorly preserved oven. Of course, cooking pots might have been used for serving foods, and this may strengthen the case that it was a communal living room space (Shafer-Elliot 2013, 82–83). The careful excavation, analysis, and reconstruction of these and other houses demonstrate how much can be learned about daily life activities from the archaeological remains.

Other Occupations

MEN

Although agro-pastoralism was the basis of the Iron Age economy, a variety of other professions are attested in the Hebrew Bible that were available to a more restricted segment of the population. These include government jobs like scribes, tax collectors, and more; participation in overland and maritime trade; specialized production jobs like carpenters, masons, and perhaps metalworkers; and priests and other religious specialists. Although most of the evidence for these occupations is found in the biblical text, extrabiblical inscriptions (including ostraca, seals, and seal impressions) provide information about individuals who held various occupations. For example, seals and seal impressions belonging to servants, scribes, priests, doctors, officials, and others are known, while ostraca—inscribed pot sherds—from Samaria in Israel and from Arad and Lachish in Judah inform on bureaucratic and other activities (Borowski 2003, 102–4).

WOMEN

Although many of these positions were restricted to men, notable biblical women illustrate female involvement in political and cultic activities, health care, mercantile activities, and more. At the top of the social pyramid was the queen mother, who held great importance in Israelite and Judahite society. Jezebel, the wife of Israel's most powerful king, Ahab, apparently made decisions that ultimately affected the fate of her husband's line. Her daughter Athaliah ruled Judah after the death of her husband, King Jehoram. In the context of Early Iron Age Israel, the period of the Judges, Deborah is described as a judge and warrior, and Jael is responsible for killing Sisera, general of the Canaanite army (Judg 4). Female prophets are also known as well as wise women who communicated with the dead, such as the witch from En Dor who roused the spirit of Samuel for King Saul. Women also played an important role in health care as midwives, as described above, and healers. Proverbs 31 describes a woman who owns property and sells goods at the market, and we can assume that Israelite women participated in these activities as well.

Domestic Cult

As the description of the four-room houses at Tel Halif suggests, households preserve the remains of everyday religious practices. Although it was condemned by the prophets and the biblical writers, the Israelites worshipped various gods and goddesses outside of the Jerusalem temple and other sanctioned holy sites in the Iron Age. Although there are many motivations for prayer and religious practice, many analysts believe that everyday religious practices revolved around family concerns: venerating various deities as well as ancestors in order to preserve the family; ensure fertility of family members, flocks, and the land; and protect family members, especially vulnerable young children and pregnant women. Since these were the concerns of both women and men, it is likely that all participated in domestic rituals primarily intended to protect the family. The archaeological correlates of these activities include so-called cult corners like that in Tel Halif containing such items as stone altars, clay incense burners, and figurines. These and other specialized cultic objects are often found in association with artifacts and installations related to cooking and other daily life activities, suggesting that women played important roles in household rituals (Albertz and Schmitt 2012, 225). In addition, small protective items, or amulets, are abundant in archaeological contexts, and ethnographic data help inform on how these items might have functioned in the Iron Age (Ebeling 2010).

Conclusion

This overview of what is known about daily life activities in Iron Age Israel and Judah allows for an appreciation of the tasks that occupied most people on a regular basis and the difficult conditions in which most of the population existed. The biblical text provides interesting information about a number of daily life activities but describes very few of them in detail. Artistic representations and ethnographic accounts from the Middle East help flesh out the picture, and archaeological excavations provide abundant remains of the everyday activities that occupied women and men in ancient Israel and Judah. The recent emergence of household archaeology and, with it, interest in learning more about the lives of the majority of the population in ancient Israel allows new opportunities to investigate aspects of ancient daily life. Current and future studies are certain to shed further light on the lives of those who lived in biblical times.

Suggestions for Further Reading

Two recent books that draw upon both biblical and archaeological evidence to reconstruct life in biblical times—that is, Iron Age Israel and Judah—are Philip J. King and Lawrence E. Stager's *Life in Biblical Israel* (2001) and Oded Borowski's *Daily Life in Biblical Times* (2003). King and Stager's encyclopedic work is richly illustrated and covers a wide range of topics, while Borowski's is a more focused text. Interestingly, both provide narratives that follow a day in the life of a family in ancient Israel: King and Stager include a short vignette called "A Day in Micah's Household" based on Judges 17–18, while Borowski devotes an entire chapter to "A Day in the Life of the Ahuzam Family" set in late eighth- or early seventh-century BCE Judah. Jennie Ebeling's *Women's Lives in*

Biblical Times (2010) includes a short fictional account of an Israelite woman "from cradle to grave" at the beginning of each chapter to introduce topics that follow the female life cycle as well as the yearly agricultural cycle. Unlike King and Stager, and Borowski, who give little specific attention to women's lives, Ebeling's work focuses almost solely on the daily life experiences of girls and women and integrates relevant ethnographic sources from the region into her discussion. In *The Lives of Ordinary People in Ancient Israel* (2012), William G. Dever reconstructs life in eighth-century BCE Judah using only archaeological information to demonstrate how much can be understood about the period without relying on the Hebrew Bible as a source. This approach reveals a different perspective on topics covered in the other "daily life" books. Finally, Cynthia Shafer-Elliott's *Food in Ancient Judah* (2013) offers an in-depth study of food and its preparation in Iron Age Judah. In addition to analyzing biblical narratives that focus on food preparation, Shafer-Elliott uses the archaeological remains and ancient Near Eastern sources to reconstruct these fundamental daily life activities.

17

ISRAEL AND JUDAH UNDER ASSYRIA'S THUMB

J. Edward Wright and Mark Elliott

The ancient Israelites and Judeans were quite familiar with the Assyrian Empire, but that familiarity came at great cost—the Assyrian conquest and domination of the region. From the mid-ninth century BCE, Israel was frequently engaged with Assyria, from fighting to vassalage, until finally succumbing to Assyrian conquest and destruction in 722 BCE. Judah was only slightly better off; it managed to avoid destruction of its capital Jerusalem in 701 BCE, but it too endured vassalage and the depredations of the Assyrian army until that empire was conquered by the Babylonian Empire in 605 BCE. This chapter focuses on the worst era of Assyrian depredations, from the destruction of the Northern Kingdom of Israel through Judah's brief rebellion under Hezekiah and its vassalage under Manasseh, to its moment of independence and religious renewal under Josiah.

Our primary textual sources for this era of Israelite and Judean history are the Assyrian kings' own records and the Bible. As Rachel Hallote put it in chapter 4, the finds of Bible lands archaeology illuminate events mentioned in the biblical text. The Assyrian records include annals recording the activities—mostly military—of the Assyrian kings, engraved pictures on palace walls, and numerous inscriptions in a variety of forms, including stelae. The biblical material comes from its sweeping histories—the scribal archival material from Jerusalem and Samaria edited by Deuteronomistic Historians (DH) and the Chronicler's History (CH)—which feature not only the progression of the two countries' kings but also two notable prophets: Elijah and Elisha. In addition, many of Israel's prophets are active during this time; the books containing the sermons, oracles, and visions of Isaiah, Jeremiah, Ezekiel, and other prophets provide a wealth of information. Since both kinds of written material record actual events that took place in space and time and involved real people living in real situations, it is not surprising that the inscriptions from the archaeological record often intersect with the biblical evidence. Sometimes the inscriptions parallel the biblical record, while at other times they serve as a corrective to what is claimed in a written source.

Archaeological excavations provide a third body of evidence for this chapter's focus. The remains of people's lives, their villages, and their cities not only reveal the social setting for people and events described in the written record but also provide details for and correctives to the other two bodies of data. These three types of data provide us with an extensive, impressive, and illuminating wealth of evidence. Indeed, with the archaeological excavations, the inscriptions, and the biblical writings, we know more about the ninth through the seventh centuries BCE—and know it more reliably—than almost any other period of Israelite history.

To be sure, this evidence may be overlapping, but each type provides complementary rather than duplicative material. First, the archaeological excavations set the stage for the historical events by telling us about the lived character of the people in Israel and Judah, but reveal surprisingly little about the events themselves. Second, the inscriptions and other information from the Assyrian kings expose their preoccupations and the accomplishments they claim to have achieved—against Israel and Judah, these are usually military achievements or diplomatic triumphs. Third, speaking from the receiving end of Assyrian aggression, the biblical writings focus on understanding Israel's setbacks, as well as its short-lived successes, in light of its people's special relationship to God. Assyrian actions inspire theological explanations.

This chapter begins by explaining the nature of the biblical evidence and then draws upon archaeological excavations to lay out the setting for the Assyrian Empire's belligerence and invasions. The chapter will then feature the events and impact of Assyrian aggression on Israel and Judah, drawing upon the biblical text and Assyrian inscriptions.

Understanding the Biblical Sources

It is important to remember, when reading the Hebrew Bible, that the histories of the Kingdoms of Israel and Judah as contained in the Bible are the products of southern, that is Judean, scribes. They created a Judean-oriented history of both Judah *and* Israel: it reflects the socioreligious perspectives of the Judean scribes who assembled the materials and edited them into their final form. That religious perspective was a rigidly monotheistic version of Yahwism. The story of the waxing and waning of Israel's adherence to that form of Yahwism, as we described it in chapter 11, appears in the DH—that is, in the books of Joshua, Judges, 1–2 Samuel, and 1–2 Kings. This Judean history incorporated earlier written tales and records as well as oral traditions, but it took several centuries to reach the form in which we now have it. It probably originated in the eighth century BCE and then was elaborated, expanded, and reshaped at the end of the seventh century BCE before being completed during or following the exile of the sixth century BCE.

The DH adheres to a monotheistic theology based upon the book of Deuteronomy. In the books of Kings, it judges every king by his adherence to this strict Yahwistic monotheism. The kings of Judah comprise a mixed lot, with three kings receiving approval, Asa, Hezekiah and Josiah, and all the others receiving condemnation. But for the historians of the books of Kings, every Israelite king was wicked: they "did evil in the eyes of Yahweh," as the Deuteronomistic Historians labeled kings and others who were not strict Yahwists.

But it should be remembered that this Judean ideology was just one of what must have been a wide variety of religious perspectives. Surely not all ancient Israelites subscribed to this assessment or considered their kings evil because they failed to follow these strict religious protocols. Just imagine—had we the good fortune to possess a copy of an Iron Age Levantine history from the palace in Israel—a northern perspective; it would read much differently from what we now have in the Bible. The strict Only-Yahweh perspective was just one of many religious viewpoints in ancient Israel and Judah. Indeed, many scholars think that few outside Jerusalem's temple priesthood held it—the Deuteronomistic version of history was a "minority report."

Even so, this strict monotheism became the dominant perspective of the Hebrew Bible. The CH, written after the Babylonian destruction of Jerusalem and the subsequent exile, doubles down on the Only-Yahweh theology. Similarly, the books of Ezra–Nehemiah tell of attempts to shape the Israelite returnees into a religious society following this Yahwistic monotheism. But these works were composed long after the Assyrian Empire's dominance. If we want more contemporary literary evidence, we must turn to the prophetic literature.

The Prophets of Israel and Judah

The biblical prophets stand out as steadfast leaders who claim to speak for God as they decry injustice and promote ethical behavior and the practice of God's will among elites and commoners alike. This is especially true of the writing prophets such as Amos, Hosea, Isaiah, Jeremiah, Ezekiel, and others. Prophets are professionals who specialize in a form of divination—that is, obtaining information from the gods to benefit people. Across the ancient Near East, such "specialists" were central to the proper functioning of society (Blenkinsopp 1995, 115–65). These peoples believed that the gods communicated to humans through a variety of means: consulting the dead (necromancy), the appearances or movements of the stars (astrology), the appearance of organs taken from sacrificial animals (extispicy), the casting of lots or dice (cleromancy), the interpretation of dreams (oneiromancy), and even the chance flight of birds (augury). Ancient Israelites were like their neighbors in many respects with regard to these types of "divination," even though strict Deuteronomistic Yahwism forbade such divinatory practices (Deut 18:10-13; Jer 27:9-10).

The true Yahwistic prophet, by contrast, was called by Yahweh in either a visionary or an auditory experience (Isa 6; Jer 1; Ezek 1). The Yahwistic prophet speaks in the name of Yahweh: "Thus says Yahweh" (e.g., Isa 38:1; Jer 2:2, 5; 13:12-13; Ezek 11:16). Moreover, a Deuteronomistic prophet's words are always fulfilled; indeed, it is the realization of the prophetic statements that authenticates a legitimate prophet of Yahweh (Deut 18:22). The supreme example of a true Yahwistic prophet is Moses, the man who led the people out of Egypt and received the divine commandments from Yahweh on Mount Sinai. Moses exhorted his people to obey all Yahweh's commandments whether he was with them or not:

> You must be always faithful to Yahweh your god. These nations, which you are about to expel, heed soothsayers and diviners, but Yahweh your god does not permit you to do so. Yahweh your god will raise up for you a prophet like me from among your own people, and him you must heed. Just as you asked of Yahweh your god at Horeb [Sinai] on the day of assembly when you said: "If I hear the voice of Yahweh my god any more, or even see again this great fire, I may die." Then Yahweh said to me: "They are correct in what they have said. I will raise up for them a prophet like you from among their people. I will put my words in his mouth, and he will say to them everything that I command him. Anyone who does not heed my words that he speaks in my name, I will hold accountable. But the prophet who presumes to speak a word in my name which I have not commanded him to speak or the one who speaks in the name of other gods, that prophet must die." Now should you say to yourself, "how can we know a word that Yahweh has not spoken?" Should the prophet speak in the name of Yahweh, but the thing does not occur or come true, it is a thing that Yahweh has not spoken. The prophet has spoken presumptuously, so you should not fear him. (Deut 18:13-22, translation by Wright)

Like Moses, therefore, the true prophet is personally commissioned by Yahweh, directly informed by Yahweh, and always loyal to Yahweh's commandments. Any prophet who deviated from that model was a "false prophet," and such prophets were to be avoided or even put to death (Deut 13:1-5).

The biblical materials contain both extended narratives about prophets and whole books containing prophetic sermons, visions, and social criticisms. The narratives about Elijah the prophet (1 Kgs 17–19; 21; and 2 Kgs 1–2) put the prophetic ministry into a clear social context. Elijah lived in the mid-ninth century BCE during the Omride Dynasty in Israel. His work as a prophet exemplifies the kind of prophet who is the social conscience of the community. The Omride era was largely characterized by internal and, to an extent, external peace and security. The book of 1 Kings portrays Elijah as concerned with proper religion and social justice. As a strict Yahwist, Elijah criticizes the regime and its promotion of the worship of the god Baal and the goddess Asherah, and this criticism brought him into direct personal conflict with the royal house, notably King Ahab and Queen Jezebel. He speaks as a committed Yahwistic prophet in the line of Moses, and proposes a contest to determine who is the true god: Yahweh or Baal (1 Kgs 17–19). In that contest, Yahweh miraculously intervenes on behalf of Elijah, and Baal is exposed as impotent, proving that Yahweh is the only true god and that Elijah is his appointed prophet. Thus, Elijah rescued the people from an oppressive leader and religious syncretism just as Moses rescued the people from oppression in Egypt.

The prophets Amos and Hosea, on the other hand, are literary prophets of the eighth century BCE, whose oracles speak to Israel in the decades before its destruction by the Assyrian Empire. The books named after them contain sermons, visions, and oracles, many of which include sharp social criticisms. Amos, although born in Judah, functioned as a prophet in Israel. Hosea, a native Israelite, was a contemporary of Amos and, like his Judean counterpart, focused his prophetic denunciations on the Northern Kingdom. Their books contain criticisms of Israelite society for its religious infidelity to Yahweh, but the works lack the personal and narrative detail found in the narratives of Elijah; these "prophetic books" are simply collections of the sayings and actions attributed to the prophets.

Despite this, the books provide a peek inside Israel's diverse religious culture. As prophets in the tradition of Moses, they called out Israel's leaders and people for disobeying Yahweh's commands. Such disobedience left the Israelites exposed to Yahweh's wrath. Nonetheless, the prophets noted that the opportunity for repentance remained available, and they encouraged the people to repent, worship Yahweh only, and follow his cultic and social commandments. Their views, however, were clearly a minority opinion in the Northern Kingdom. True, Yahweh was worshipped there in some form, but the overall religious climate was broader than what strict Yahwistic Deuteronomists could tolerate. The Israelites in the north worshipped Baal, Asherah, and other gods in addition to Yahweh or instead of Yahweh. The books of prophets like Amos and Hosea reveal the cosmopolitan and competitive religious climate of the Northern Kingdom, precisely the climate that the DH likewise sought to combat. As we will see, the archaeological record attests the diverse nature of religious life, but it speaks without the socioreligious bias of monotheism.

Isaiah of Jerusalem, Second Isaiah, and Third Isaiah

For Judah, lying to the south of Israel, the biblical book of Isaiah presents itself as a collection of oracles given during the hegemony of Assyria. While traditional scholarship has long identified this person as an inhabitant of Jerusalem in the eighth century BCE, a close reading of the text indicates it derives from more than one author—that is to say, it is a composite text written, compiled, and edited over many decades by multiple people. Although the actual number of contributors may be as high as six, a scholarly consensus has emerged that there are "three Isaiahs"—blandly labeled First, Second, and Third Isaiah. Each part of the book dates to a different period and presents different views.

First Isaiah (chapters 1–39) is often also called the historical Isaiah or Isaiah of Jerusalem. This person was a prophet who lived in Jerusalem from the mid-eighth to the early seventh century BCE. First Isaiah apparently contains written versions of proclamations originally uttered orally by the prophet. It ends in chapters 36–39 by reprising 2 Kings 18:30–20:19 in an apparent attempt to situate Isaiah in the historical context of Assyrian domination of the region.

Second Isaiah (chapters 40–55) has its own theological perspectives and language and is thought to have been composed well after the death of Isaiah of Jerusalem. Israel's enemy is no longer Assyria but the Babylonian Empire. Indeed, Second Isaiah is set in Babylon, and he encourages the exiled Judeans to return to Judah. This section of the book of Isaiah was thus written after the fall of Jerusalem to the Babylonians in 586 BCE and before the conquest of Babylon by Cyrus the Great of Persia (539 BCE). The author (or perhaps authors) may have been an actual disciple of the historical Isaiah of Jerusalem and clearly agreed with the religious ideology of the prophet.

Third Isaiah (chapters 56–66) is a collection of anonymous oracles that scholars have dated anywhere from the sixth to the third century BCE, although many scholars prefer dates in the late sixth and fifth centuries. The difficulty in dating this portion of the book stems from the fact that the material lacks any clear historical allusion. In that regard, Third Isaiah lacks the Assyrian connections evident in First Isaiah and the Babylonian connections in Second Isaiah. It is First Isaiah, then, that will provide us with data concerning the interaction of Judah and Assyria. The other two Isaiahs will make their appearance in later chapters.

Near Eastern Sources

Near Eastern kings were nothing if not vain. They chronicled their cultural achievements—notably the erection of buildings—and military victories to promote their legacy. What likely began as mere records were eventually collated and edited into marvelous accounts of what the kings did for their god and their people. These annals are the primary sources for ancient Near Eastern history, though at times they are problematic; however, in many instances they are remarkable for their historical accuracy. This written evidence is found on clay tablets, the walls of temples and palaces, stelae, prisms, and cylinders. While the accounts deal with historical events, they are clearly propagandistic. Not intended as a mere catalogue of events, they keenly promote each king's reputation. They recount how the kings served their national god and achieved great things with that god's help. Thus, Sennacherib of Assyria claims that Ashur gave him "unrivaled kingship," and he conquered the world in Ashur's name (Prism I:1–19). Likewise, Cyrus of Persia claimed that Marduk, the Babylonian god, called him from among all humans to conquer Babylon and take the kingship from the inept Babylonian king Nabonidus (Cyrus Cylinder 10–15). So while we will use these works as historical evidence, we must keep in mind that their purpose is to convey not mere historical information but the greatness of the kings whose deeds they extol—some real and some exaggerated or even imagined.

Eighth- and Seventh-Century BCE Israel and Judah: An Archaeological Portrait

In the eighth century BCE, the largest cities in the Northern Kingdom of Israel were fortified by massive walls and sophisticated gates. If we follow William Dever (2012, 72), who holds that "a city is a site ten acres or more with a population of 1000 or more," the most important of these—such as Megiddo, Hazor, Dan, and Gezer—contained administrative buildings, bureaucracies, storehouses or stables, impressive water systems, and probably military garrisons. Cities were built on top of the ruins of preceding urban areas, and the city planners reused or rebuilt many of the original structures. The city walls were either casemate or solid walls, frequently using the header/stretcher pattern. Here, rectangular blocks were laid alternatingly with their narrow end or long side facing out. City gates often had multiple chambers with two, four, or even six rooms in the gate complex. Some walls contained towers and a glacis. Israelite and Judean homes were often built in the four-room house (or pillared house) style (Dever 2012, 50–115). Finkelstein holds that the population of the Northern Kingdom of Israel "was the most densely populated settled region in the entire Levant" (Finkelstein and Silberman 2001, 208). Still it must be remembered that most of Judah and Israel's population lived in rural settlements, even though cities in Israel and Judah required a large, skilled, and organized workforce.

Many villages were established on hilltops of approximately one hectare (approx. 2.47 acres) surrounded by a boundary wall. The residents most likely lived in pillared houses, the dominant house type in Israel and Judah. Few public buildings have been uncovered in these small settlements (Faust 2012b, 132). The major economic pursuits in villages were olive oil and wine production. Olive trees flourished on the terraced hillsides in the Central Hill Country. Olive presses were ubiquitous because olive oil was an essential product that affected all aspects of Israelite life. It was used in perfumes, cosmetics, foods, cooking, medicines, fuel for lamps, and religious rituals. At the Philistine site of Ekron (Tel Miqne), archaeologists have discovered over a hundred olive presses, which may have produced up to a thousand tons of refined oil annually. With such a high level of production, Ekron would have been one of the foremost olive-processing sites in the Levant.

Until the end of the eighth century BCE, the largest settlements and the largest construction projects mentioned in the Bible were in Israel (1 Kgs 9:15)—namely, Hazor, Megiddo, and Gezer. The Northern Kingdom of Israel was larger, richer, and less isolated internationally than its southern neighbor Judah. Canaanites/Phoenicians may have been a considerable component of its population. Yet we have few items that could be classified as luxury. According to Faust, "Real luxury items are rare in the archaeological record" (2012b, 119). Pottery, which is abundant in the archaeological record, is not an independent indicator of wealth but must be seen in context with other evidence,

FIGURE 17-1. *Tel Megiddo. One of the great cities in the Kingdom of Israel, dating from the Chalcolithic period (6400–3600 BCE) and covering about thirteen acres. Archaeologists have discovered approximately twenty-six levels of occupation. Megiddo contained administrative buildings, bureaucracies, a large granary, stables, impressive water systems, and probably military garrisons.*

most reliably architecture (2012b, 126). In Judah, there were fewer economic differences between social classes, although Jerusalem and Lachish are exceptions. Tombs are another reliable indicator of economic status. Family tombs in Israel and Judah indicate social stratification. These countries regularly differentiate among large family tombs, small family tombs, and individual trench graves as indicators of wealth and social status.

Villages preserved family, social, and economic frameworks. In some villages, archaeologists have discovered industrial zones, which indicate that these villages were inhabited by multiple families and had a degree of specialization. By the eighth century BCE, tribes no longer constituted the primary social classification. The elemental structure within Israelite and Judean societies was established on a kinship framework, and this is reflected in an agricultural social order. The basic family unit in Israelite society was the *bet av*, literally "father's house," an extended family of related people. A unique archaeological feature of the Iron Age that represents this extended family was the pillared house (Dever 2012, 150). Depending on the square footage, the homes could support up to fifteen people and include several generations (see chapter 10 for further discussion).

Most archaeologists think there was additional living space on a second floor. Some excavated houses reveal steps that led to a second floor for sleeping quarters. The ground-floor rooms offered shelter for animals and could be used for storage. Cooking, weaving, and other work took place in the courtyard, where there was light. Grinding grain was a daily occurrence and was so crucial that Deuteronomy 24:6 prohibits taking a grinding stone as a pledge: "No one shall take as a pledge a millstone or an upper millstone for that is tantamount to taking a life as a pledge." The abundant archaeological evidence clearly shows that the pillared-courtyard house was the foremost house style in eighth-century BCE Judah and Israel, appearing in cities, villages, and farms. In fact, it is such a telling marker of Israelite and Judean identity that Faust maintains that if a site contains no pillared-courtyard houses, it is legitimate to question whether Israelites or Judeans actually lived there. Interestingly, it is not found in the Persian era.

The Rise of Writing and Literacy

The epigraphic material from eighth- and seventh-century BCE Israel and Judah is extensive and includes ostraca, seals and seal impressions (bullae), over a thousand jar handles, as well as writing on weights and measures, vases, and cult objects. Literacy was not the sole possession of a few priests and scribes, as revealed by ostraca collections, bullae, and stone and tomb inscriptions. These inscriptions were written and read by professional scribes, messengers, tax collectors, traders, masons, army commanders, and bureaucrats

(Schniedewind 2013). Archaeologists have uncovered writing in isolated fortresses, tombs, and trading sites. This is all the more impressive since the standard writing material, papyrus, has rarely survived.

Broken pottery pieces called ostraca were often used for writing purposes and inscribed in carbon ink. Major collections of inscribed ostraca come from Arad, Samaria, and Lachish. Wooden tablets were also used throughout the Middle East; the writing was done with a stylus, and the tablets were often coated with wax or plaster. Seals or seal impressions have survived in ample numbers. Seals were used by people as a form of signature or personal identification. Seal impressions, or "bullae," were created by attaching a dollop of wet clay to a rolled papyrus scroll secured by a string. The seal was then pressed into the soft clay so that the insignia of the signer was visible on the outside. These impressions are valuable for understanding the evolution of the Hebrew alphabet and script. They also provide scholars with a number of seals inscribed with the names of kings (such as Hezekiah and Ahaz) and their officials. The seal of one such official, "Shema servant of Jeroboam," dating to the period of Jeroboam II was found at Megiddo. Most of the inscribed seals and bullae uncovered in professional archaeological excavations originate in Jerusalem and were found near pottery dating from the eighth century BCE. It seems that the custom of inscribing names to seals in Jerusalem may have originated during the eighth century (Reich 2011, 219; Avigad 1997).

FIGURE 17-2. *Samaria ostraca. Over one hundred inscribed potsherds have been discovered at Samaria, the northern capital of Israel. Most of the ostraca were discovered in 1910 during Reisner's expedition. Most scholars date the Hebrew writing to the eighth century BCE. The ostraca are records of wine and oil deliveries.*

Two unusual bullae need to be noted. They are from the same seal of Baruch ben Neriah, the prophet Jeremiah's scribe, and have been the focus of scholarly and legal battles. The bullae do not come from controlled excavations, so they lack any archaeological context. They read, "Belonging to Berekyahu, the son of Neriyahu, the scribe." This title is found in Jeremiah 36:32, which reads, "Baruch, the son of Neriyahu." The initial excitement over these "discoveries" has been diminished by the fact that experts in this area regard these two bullae as modern forgeries (Goren and Arie 2014). The majority of our surviving seals and seal impressions have not been excavated in controlled circumstances. Rather, they come to scholars' attention through antiquity dealers and private collectors. Archaeologists and scholars have long been alarmed at the damage caused by the illegal looting of archaeological sites and the trade in archaeological artifacts. Items stolen from sites lack a clear archaeological context and so contribute little to our understanding of the past. Moreover, mixed in with looted artifacts can be fakes that distort the historical record and that are sold to unsuspecting collectors, as is clearly the case with the Baruch bullae. These fakes can end up in museums, where they mislead the public, and they can also contaminate scholarship. In the effort to stop the antiquities trade, nations have passed laws to protect their cultural heritage, and, in 1970, UNESCO passed the international "Convention on the Means of Prohibiting and Preventing the Illicit Import, Export and Transfer of Ownership of Cultural Property." These various national and international laws are key to stopping the illicit trade in antiquities, as is the effort to educate the public about the harm caused by the private purchase of antiquities. The widespread fascination with the past is laudable, but the public interest in "owning" a part of the past sadly enables the illegal trade in authentic and fake antiquities to thrive. It must also be remembered that today the profits from much of this trade fund oppressive governments and international terrorism.

Inscriptions come in many other forms. More than a million clay tablets have been found throughout the ancient Near East. Soft clay was fashioned into a flat tablet that could be held in one hand, inscribed with a pointed stick (cuneiform), and either dried in the sun or fired in kiln. Stones may have been plastered with lime and had writing applied with a brush (Deut 27:2-8). Chiseling on stone was another form of writing, such as that found in Siloam tunnel (see below). Some scribes wrote with a stylus on wooden tablets that were often coated with wax or plaster. The use of papyrus was very common in Egypt, but any moisture rapidly deteriorates papyrus, so it has rarely survived from ancient Israel.

The Last Days of Israel

Chapter 14 ended with the Assyrian conquest and destruction of the Northern Kingdom of Israel and its capital Samaria—a process that took ten years.
A few years after the death of Tiglath-Pileser III, Israel rebelled against its
Assyrian overlord. Tiglath-Pileser III's son, Shalmaneser V (727–722 BCE),
reigned only briefly and failed to contain the rebellion. He was succeeded
on the throne—perhaps via a coup—by Sargon II (722–705 BCE). The
revolt in the western provinces brought Sargon II to the Levantine states,
including Israel and its capital Samaria. He laid siege to Samaria, and the
city fell shortly thereafter (722 BCE), bringing the Kingdom of Israel to an
end. Sargon also attacked Ashdod, Ashkelon, Ekron, Beth-Dagon, Joppa,
Azor, and others. When Sargon conquered the city of Samaria, he claimed to
have deported over twenty-seven thousand inhabitants and then restored it
"greater than before," repopulating the city with "people of lands conquered
by my two hands" (*COS* 2:295–96). Samaria became an Assyrian province
ruled by a governor.

Despite Sargon's boasts, evidence of Samaria's destruction is difficult to find.
The years of siege and the conquest of Samaria left little clear physical evidence
of destruction. There are few traces of Sargon's rebuilding of the city; moreover,
"archaeologists have recovered only a few remains from the entire Assyrian occupation" (Tappy 2006, 67).
Samaria was a small, rocky
hilltop site; it was never
a major populated city. It
"served only as a royal city;
it never became home to
large numbers of the king's

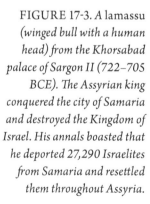

FIGURE 17-3. *A* lamassu
*(winged bull with a human
head) from the Khorsabad
palace of Sargon II (722–705
BCE). The Assyrian king
conquered the city of Samaria
and destroyed the Kingdom of
Israel. His annals boasted that
he deported 27,290 Israelites
from Samaria and resettled
them throughout Assyria.*

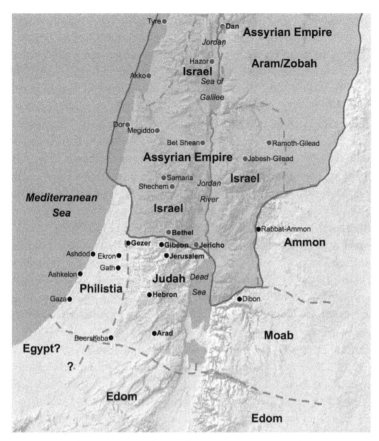

MAP 17-1. *The westernmost limits of the Assyrian Empire after conquering Israel in 722 BCE.*

subjects" (Tappy 2006). Sargon's claim of over twenty-seven thousand deportees from the city of Samaria is simply not reliable, for, even including the surrounding countryside, the boast is simply too far-fetched.

There are few remains of the Omride palace, which occupied about 2,400 square feet on the highest point of the large acropolis. Only the palace area of Samaria has been excavated down to the bedrock. Stager and Franklin have made the claim that Omri purchased the site from Shemer as his "new capital for its economic potential" (Franklin 2006). Shemer's property (1 Kgs 16:23-24) was not a small family farm or enterprise but rather a major commercial enterprise with more than one hundred bell-shaped storage pits and with cisterns with an amazing capacity—350,000 liters, likely for olive oil, a valuable industry that in part funded the development of Omri's kingdom. The populace in the agricultural highlands surrounding Samaria was engaged in impressive olive oil manufacturing. Archaeologists have noted a number of olive presses cut into the bedrock located throughout the area. Franklin discovered large rock-cut tombs beneath the palace, and it may be that these were burial places for the kings of the Northern Kingdom.

Near the palace area, there was an administrative building that scholars have named the "Ostraca House" in honor of the 102 ostraca or inscribed pottery sherds excavated from the fill in the floor of the building. The ostraca were part of an accounting system that recorded shipments of oil and wine sent to the king either as tax payments or as support for royal officials. These ostraca, which provide essential information about the Hebrew dialect spoken in Israel in the eighth century BCE, reveal important information on surrounding geography, land ownership, and women's rights to own land. The ostraca have been attributed mostly to the era of Jeroboam II (791–750 BCE).

Working just north of the palace, archaeologists discovered a hoard of over five hundred exquisite ivories and ivory fragments. With regard to these ivories, it is important to note that 1 Kings 22:39 mentions Ahab's ivory palace, and Amos offers strong admonition against "those who feel secure on Mount Samaria . . . who lie on beds of ivory" (Amos 6:1, 4). These luxurious ivories are considered one of the most important discoveries from the Iron Age in Israel. They contain images of winged sphinxes, lions, bulls, and human figures. For the most part, the motifs are apparently Egyptian and produced by Phoenician artisans, but some of the ivory plaques are inscribed with Hebrew letters. It seems likely that these ivories were inlays that once adorned furniture in the palace or the homes of elites, and they clearly illustrate Amos' social criticisms.

The Assyrians recorded their campaigns in Israel and the west in a number of annals and on bas-reliefs that decorated palace walls. Cities in Israel and Transjordan portrayed on Assyrian reliefs are Ashtaroth (Transjordan), Ekron, Gibbethon, Gezer, and Lachish. The Assyrians left traces of their presence, and thereby their dominion, in the region in many forms. Stelae recounting their exploits have been uncovered in Samaria and Tell Hadid. Several seals and bullae bearing Assyrian deities have also been found in sites across Israel and Judah. These are items used typically in business transactions, and some contain the titles of their owners. One, uncovered in the excavations at the coastal site of Dor, reads "overseer of the palace." Moreover, the excavations at Gezer have produced Assyrian cuneiform contracts.

The Assyrians rebuilt provincial capitals at Megiddo, Samaria, and Dor as well as a number of trading stations along the Via Maris on the coast. New city layouts, which appear to follow Mesopotamian patterns, have been attributed to the Assyrians. Examples of this include Assyrian administrative buildings clustered around courtyards at Megiddo, Gezer, and Dor. The layout of Assyrian-era Megiddo has the streets designed in an orthogonal street pattern,

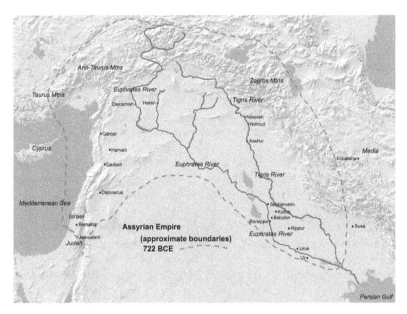

MAP 17-2. *The boundaries of the Assyrian Empire in 722 BCE.*

and its new palaces appear to have been built according to Assyrian models. Moreover, Assyrian house plans and other architectural features have been identified at a few sites, such as Ashdod along the coast. In many diverse ways, therefore, the Assyrian hegemony left a physical imprint on the region.

2 Kings 17: The Fall of the Northern Kingdom

Looking at the Levant during the Assyrian era, we can see how strategic the region was to the empire. It was important for its natural resources, the trade that went through it, and the buffer it provided on the Egyptian border. Assyria was determined to control the region for these reasons. But the history of this era from the Judean perspective looked rather different. According to 2 Kings 17, the Assyrians conquered this area, and specifically Israel, because of the religious failures of the Israelites.

In 722 BCE, Shalmaneser and then Sargon II besieged Samaria and conquered it. The Assyrians, in accord with their standard policy, deported a significant part of the population and then repopulated the region with people they had conquered and deported from their native lands. The Deuteronomistic Historians were unambiguous in their account of the fall and exile of the Northern Kingdom of Israel; 2 Kings 17 recounts the Israelites, evils that led to their downfall. The list of their sins is purposefully built on the proscribed cultic activities mentioned in Deuteronomy 18:

This occurred because the people of Israel sinned against Yahweh their god, the one who brought them up from land of Egypt, from under the hand of Pharaoh king of Egypt. They feared other gods and followed the customs of the nations that Yahweh expelled before the people of Israel, and the customs that the kings of Israel had introduced. The people of Israel secretly did things that were wrong against Yahweh their god. They built for themselves *bamot* in all their towns, from watchtower to fortified city. They erected pillars and sacred poles on every high hill and under every green tree. There they made offerings on all the *bamot*, just as the nations did that Yahweh exiled before them. They did evil things that enraged Yahweh. They served idols about which Yahweh said to them "you must not do this." Yahweh had warned Israel and Judah by every prophet and every seer, saying "Turn away from your evil ways! Keep my commandments and my statutes in accord with all the Torah that I commanded your ancestors and that I sent to you by my servants the prophets." But they did not listen and were stubborn just as their ancestors were stubborn and did not believe Yahweh their god. They rejected his statutes, his covenant that he made with their ancestors, and his testimonies by which he warned them. They pursued false gods and became false. They followed the nations around them, which Yahweh commanded them not to do. They forsook all the commandments of Yahweh their god, and they made for themselves two cast images of calves and an Asherah. They worshipped all the hosts of heaven and served Baal. They passed their sons and daughters through fire, practiced divination and augury, and they committed themselves to do evil in the eyes of Yahweh, which provoked him to anger. So, Yahweh was enraged with Israel and expelled them from his sight. All that was left was the tribe of Judah alone. (2 Kgs 17:7-18, translation by Wright)

So, according to the Deuteronomistic Historians who edited the book of Kings, Sargon's conquest of Israel was not the product of Assyrian foreign policy but rather the product of Yahweh's anger with the Israelites for their religious infidelities.

Israelite Flight to Judah

Despite the testimony of Sargon and the Bible, it seems that the majority of Israelites were not in fact deported. Although we cannot identify specific numbers with confidence, the population of Judah in the eighth century BCE increased massively, from approximately 40,000 to 120,000 (Cline 2007, 178). The growth of Jerusalem at precisely this time and the number of new settlements in Judah are striking. These factors indicate large numbers of displaced Israelites fled southward.

Although not attacked, Jerusalem was not spared from the effects of the Assyrian destruction of Israel. The city experienced a period of enormous growth in the latter half of the eighth century BCE. Expanding from the small hillside City of David, which was probably no more than fifteen acres,

Jerusalem increased to over one hundred acres and became the largest city in Judah. Scholars estimate that the city increased from about one thousand residents to about ten to twelve thousand. Many of these refugees included large numbers of Judeans fleeing from Assyrian incursions during Sennacherib's invasion in 701 BCE. The consequences of this growth were that the population of Jerusalem was now a mix of native Judeans, displaced Israelites, and others. Small changes in the city's eastern wall indicated that some fortified areas were added for Jerusalemites to build their homes (Reich 2011, 313). However, the expansion of the city was primarily to the west since the steep eastern slope prevented significant eastward expansion.

Nahman Avigad's excavations (1969–1983) in the Jewish Quarter of the Old City exposed a new quarter in the city that was fortified by a large wall that ran over 380 feet. The wall became known as the "broad wall," measuring about seven meters thick and eight meters high, and running in a northeast-southwest direction across the Western Hill of Jerusalem. Figurines, stamped jar handles, shreds, and other material dated to the eighth century BCE were found in this area.

FIGURE 17-4. *In the 1970s, Israeli archaeologist Professor Nahman Avigad, excavating in Jerusalem, uncovered part of a city wall called the "broad wall," built during the reign of King Hezekiah (715–687 BCE). The wall was most likely constructed to accommodate the increase in the population of Jerusalem. Other scholars argue it was built in an attempt to fortify the city against the approaching Assyrian invasion led by Sennacherib in 701 BCE.*

Avigad's excavations also uncovered what was likely a gatehouse. The structure showed evidence of burning, and in the debris Avigad found arrowheads from the Babylonian invasion and destruction of Jerusalem in 586 BCE. These and other discoveries during subsequent excavations all confirmed that the Iron Age city was prominent and incorporated a large part of the Western Hill.

Jerusalem was not the only area to experience a population increase. There was a substantial population rise at the end of the eighth century BCE in all areas of Judah. Important Judahite cities such as Beersheba, Tell Beit Mirsim, and Lachish expanded and became well-planned cities featuring storehouses, water systems, gates, fortified walls, and stables (Finkelstein and Silberman 2006b, 264).

As with Jerusalem, the population surge in Judah cannot be explained by natural population growth alone. The Assyrian invasions altered the state of Judah. Within a few decades in the late eighth century, the population nearly doubled, and Judah was transformed into a complex state. As with Jerusalem, the overall population of Judah included a large number of northern Israelite refugees, and some scholars speculate that as much as half of the population of Judah may have been Israelites. The increase of Israelites in Judah must have been a major issue for the Judeans, and, although the archaeological evidence is clear, the biblical texts never mention this massive population increase.

The Deuteronomistic Historian Remembers the Reign of Hezekiah

King Hezekiah is remembered in the Bible as one of the best kings in the long history of Israel and Judah. He is credited with initiating a major religious reform in 2 Kings 18:3-6:

> He did what was right in the eyes of Yahweh just as his ancestor David had done. He tore down the *bamot*, broke down the pillars, and cut down the Asherah poles. He broke in pieces the bronze serpent that Moses had made, for until those days the people of Israel had been making offerings to it; it was called Nehushtan. He trusted in Yahweh the God of Israel. And after him there was no one like him among all the kings of Judah, or among those who were before him. He was devoted to Yahweh and did not depart from following him but kept the commandments that Yahweh commanded Moses. And Yahweh was with him, and wherever he went he prospered. (Translation by Wright)

It has been difficult to determine the details of Hezekiah's reform, to ascertain when it started, and to judge its overall effectiveness. It is interesting to note that the Assyrian envoy Rab-Shakeh, sent by Sennacherib to Jerusalem to urge the Jerusalemites to surrender, commented on the king's attempted reforms. Though our earliest source is the book of Kings, the Chronicler's account of the reform is markedly longer and more extensive. The Chronicler begins the reform in Hezekiah's first year as king (2 Chr 29:3). Whether the Chronicler had other independent source material is impossible to say.

The religious reform of Hezekiah may be reflected in the dismantling or destruction of a number of cultic sites in the south: the Arad temple, the large horned altar of ashlar blocks at Beersheba, and a sanctuary at Lachish that contained a stone altar and cult vessels. Moreover, in the 2016 excavations at the Lachish gateway sanctuary excavators uncovered a toilet that had been placed in the area, an unmistakable attempt to "defile" this non-Yahwistic site. All these cultic sites appear to have been in use during the eighth century BCE, but all three were "dismantled or fell into disuse" by the invasion of Sennacherib in 701 BCE (Finkelstein and Silberman 2006a, 273). It is difficult not to relate the abandonment and defilement of these cultic activities to the reforms instituted by Hezekiah mentioned in the biblical text (1 Kgs 18:3-4).

Sennacherib's Invasion of 701 BCE

In 701 BCE, Sennacherib (704–681 BCE) moved against Judah and its king Hezekiah. His records tell us about his campaign against Judah:

> As for Hezekiah, the Judean, I besieged forty-six of his fortified walled cities and surrounding smaller towns, which were without number. Using packed-down ramps and applying battering rams, infantry attacks by mines, breeches, and siege machines, I conquered (them). I took out 200,150 people, young and old, male and female, horses, mules, donkeys, camels, cattle, and sheep, without number, and counted them as spoil. He himself, I locked up within Jerusalem, his royal city, like a bird in a cage. I surrounded him with earthworks, and made it unthinkable for him to exit by the city gate. His cities which I had despoiled I cut off from his land and gave them to Mitinti, king of Ashdod, Padi, king of Ekron and Silli-bel, king of Gaza, and thus diminished his land. (*COS* 2:303)

Despite warnings from the prophet Isaiah, Hezekiah joined a coalition headed by Egypt (Twenty-Fifth Kushite Dynasty) against the Assyrian king. The Assyrians invaded Judah and claimed to have destroyed forty-six cities and villages. Sennacherib singled out one of those cities, Lachish, for special treatment. Lachish is located in the southern Shephelah approximately forty-five miles southwest of Jerusalem, and it occupies over thirty-one acres on the summit of its tel. Sennacherib graphically depicted his conquest of Lachish in commemorative reliefs carved on stone panels in a room of his palace in Nineveh. The enormous reliefs indicate that the attack on Lachish must have been one of

Sennacherib's greatest military victories. These reliefs were carved in surprising detail on the walls of Sennacherib's palace, and it is not difficult to imagine that these images made a frightening and lasting impression on visitors to the palace as they viewed the scenes of soldiers, bowmen, and lancers marching on the city (see Figure 4-3). These reliefs also portray five siege engines on the ramps at Lachish with battering rams and earthen ramparts erected against the city walls. The Judean defenders on the walls of Lachish hurl stones and burning torches down upon the siege engines and the attacking Assyrian soldiers. Ladders are thrown up against the walls of the city, and Assyrian soldiers use their shields to protect their bowmen and sling throwers as they advance on the city. To one side, Sennacherib sits on his throne, inspecting his spoils as the surviving defeated Judeans are led off into exile. The Assyrian artists revel in the cruelty. Prisoners were impaled on long spikes; others were stretched on the ground while their skin was flayed. Soldiers carry away the spoils of war booty as Judean women follow an oxen-drawn cart, perhaps filled with their possessions and children. It is an altogether frightful depiction of utter conquest.

FIGURE 17-5. *Aerial view of Tel Lachish. The city of Lachish was besieged and conquered by Assyrian king Sennacherib in 701 BCE. After the destruction of Lachish, the surviving population was deported and resettled to regions in the kingdom of Assyria. Sennacherib would now move on Jerusalem.*

The excavations at Lachish were led by J. L. Starkey, L. G. Harding, and O. Tufnell from 1932–1938 and by David Ussishkin from 1973–1987. Level III of the city was violently destroyed, leading Ussishkin to connect that level to the Assyrian invasion. The city was entirely burned; the "destruction was complete and the city was abandoned." The debris of conquest was visible over the entire site. Evidence of a siege ramp was uncovered on the southwest corner of the tel, the area most vulnerable to an attack. The siege ramp, the only Assyrian one ever found, was built with approximately thirteen thousand to nineteen thousand tons of field stones and "coated with a layer of stones and mortar." The defenders built a counter ramp opposite the Assyrian ramp to impede the breach of the wall, but to no avail. Archaeologists discovered a number of military items that further verify the Assyrian attack: Assyrian helmets, equipment for horses, scales of armor, sling stones, fragments of an iron chain, and arrowheads. Stones and arrowheads were discovered at the gate. A mass burial cave at the base of the tel containing the remains of perhaps 1,500 people attests the horrifying results of the siege (Ussishkin 1993b, 908).

Lachish is also essential for the study of a distinctive Judean stamped storage jar type, known as LMLK jars. The handles of these jars are impressed with the word *lmlk* or *lamelech*, "belonging to the king," and they have been found in excavations throughout Judah. More examples of these stamped handles were uncovered at Lachish than at any other site, and these were located in the strata destroyed by the Assyrians. In addition to the writing, two images may appear on the handles: winged solar discs and/or a four-winged scarab beetle. Moreover, the jar handles contain one of four different geographical names, most likely cities: Hebron, Socah, Ziph, and an otherwise unidentified place by the name of MMST. (See Figure 15-6.) Since none of the stamped jars have been excavated in any other level at Lachish, the scholarly consensus is that the jars date to the reign of King Hezekiah (715–687 BCE) and were readied for the Sennacherib invasion in 701 BCE. The jars appear to have been allocated throughout Judah in preparation for the Assyrian invasion.

After the destruction, Sennacherib turned his attention to Jerusalem: "In the fourteenth year of King Hezekiah, King Sennacherib of Assyria came up against all the fortified cities of Judah and captured them. The king of Assyria sent the Rab-Shakeh from Lachish to King Hezekiah at Jerusalem, with a great army" (Isa 36:1-2). Sennacherib also described the event: "As for Hezekiah, the Judean, I besieged forty-six of his fortified walled cities and surrounding smaller towns. . . . He himself, I locked up within Jerusalem, his royal city, like a bird in a cage. I surrounded him with earthworks, and made it unthinkable for him to exit by the city gate" (*COS* 2.303). Hezekiah must have prepared for the expected siege of Jerusalem. The book of 2 Kings reports that the king "made the pool and the conduit and brought water into the city" (20:20). The book of 2 Chronicles, a later account of Judean history, is more specific:

> When Hezekiah saw that Sennacherib had come and intended to fight against Jerusalem, he planned with his officers and his warriors to stop the flow of the springs that were outside the city; and they helped him. A great many people were gathered, and they stopped all the springs and the wadi

that flowed through the land, saying, "Why should the Assyrian kings come and find water in abundance?" ... This same Hezekiah closed the upper outlet of the waters of Gihon and directed them down to the west side of the city of David. Hezekiah prospered in all his works. (32:2-4, 30)

Reich's excavations in the City of David have demonstrated that the Siloam Channel was not the first water system. An earlier water system of towers, a large cut rock-pool, and the famous Warren shaft system have now been dated to the Middle Bronze Age. Many scholars previously believed that the residents of Jerusalem lowered their jars and retrieved water from the springs below through a shaft. However, we now know that the MB residents of Jerusalem used Warren's shaft system—a tunneled area named after the British explorer Charles Warren, who rediscovered it in the nineteenth century—to collect water from the rock-cut pool. The shaft was not connected to the later tunnel or cut in the Iron Age. The shaft Warren identified was a natural karstic fissure in the limestone and unknown to the inhabitants of MB II Jerusalem. The outside towers most likely protected the springs. It should be noted that the towers' stones are quite large; stones this size would not appear again until the building projects of Herod the Great in the first century BCE.

At the time of Hezekiah, the principal water source of Jerusalem was a rock-cut trench covered with large stones that ran along the eastern slope of the hillside of the City of David. This system could be reflected in the verses of Isaiah 8:5: "Because this people has refused the waters of Shiloah [Siloam] that flow gently. . . ." If the account in 2 Chronicles 32 cited above is correct, it preserves a tradition that Hezekiah gathered the people and they stopped "the flow of the springs that were outside the city . . . , and they stopped all the springs and the wadi that flowed through the land" (2 Chr 32:3-4). Though very few scholars now attribute the building of the tunnel to Hezekiah, the tunnel known as Siloam, or Hezekiah's Tunnel, was carved into the bedrock underneath the city. The tunnel is S-shaped, running 583 yards with a slight gradient that allows for a constant flow of water from north to south. Though most scholars have argued that the work crews started from both ends and met at about 234 yards from the northern entrance, as described in the Siloam Inscription, Reich argues that different parts of the tunnel were started at different times. The chisel marks indicate that the workers changed direction a number of times. Though the bends in the tunnel have been explained as attempts to join older channels, we are not entirely sure how this project was accomplished (Reich 2011, 193–205). It is nonetheless clear that the tunnel project was masterfully planned and successfully executed.

Near the end of the southern entrance to the tunnel, a young boy in 1880 discovered the famous Siloam Inscription. Carved into the wall about twenty-five feet from the southern part of the tunnel, it describes the meeting of two teams of workmen meeting in the middle of the tunnel. Shortly after the discovery, thieves removed it by chiseling the inscription out of the wall. At that time the region was part of the Ottoman Empire, so Turkish officials confiscated the inscription and took it to Istanbul, where it still resides. The inscription reads as follows:

> [The day of] the breach. This is the record of how the tunnel was breached. While [the excavators were wielding] their pickaxes, each man toward his co-worker, and while there were yet three cubits for the brea[ch,] a voice [was hea]rd each man calling to his co-worker; because there was a cavity in the rock (extending) from the south to [the north]. So on the day of the breach, the excavators struck, each man to meet his co-worker, pick-axe against pick-[a]xe. Then the water flowed from the spring to the pool, a distance of one thousand and two hundred cubits. One hundred cubits was the height of the rock above the heads of the excavat[ors]. (*COS* 2:145–46)

From the outset, most biblical scholars linked the inscription with the biblical text describing Hezekiah's preparation for the expected siege by Sennacherib. However, Reich indicates that nowhere in the biblical text do we find the word "dig" or "digging," and the Siloam Inscription mentions neither a king (Reich 2011, 316) nor a deity. He also argues that the tunnel was built before the Assyrian invasion, perhaps during late ninth or eighth century BCE. The implication is that Hezekiah's tunnel does not date to the time of King Hezekiah at all. Most assuredly, the debate on the date of the tunnel will continue, but our earliest tradition in the book of Kings states unambiguously: "The rest of the deeds of Hezekiah, all his power, how he made the pool and the conduit and brought water into the city, are they not written in the Book of the Annals of the Kings of Judah?" (2 Kgs 20:20). Scholars will need to explain the meaning of "how he made the pool and the conduit and brought water into the city." Just what are the biblical writers referring to? What exactly did Hezekiah "make," and how did he bring "water into the city"? (See Figure 4-5.)

It needs to be noted that during the Assyrian invasion under Sennacherib in 701 BCE, Jerusalem was not destroyed. Sennacherib claims to have seriously reduced Hezekiah's power and resources as well as exacted tribute:

> I imposed dues and gifts for my lordship upon him, in addition to the former tribute, their yearly payment. He, Hezekiah, was overwhelmed by the awesome splendor of my lordship, and he sent me after my departure to Nineveh, my royal city, his elite troops (and) his best soldiers, which he had brought in as reinforcements to strengthen Jerusalem, with 30 talents of gold, 800 talents of silver, choice antimony, large blocks of carnelian, beds (inlaid) with ivory, armchairs (inlaid) with ivory, elephant hides, ivory, ebony-wood,

boxwood, multicolored garments, garments of linen, wool (dyed) red-purple, vessels of copper, iron, bronze and tin, chariots, siege shields, lances, armor, daggers for the best, bows and arrows, countless trappings and implements of war, together with his daughters, his palace women, his male and female singers. He (also) dispatched his messenger to deliver the tribute and to do obeisance. (*COS* 2:303)

The book of 2 Kings likewise attests that Hezekiah was forced to pay a hefty tribute: "I have done wrong. Turn away from me and whatever you impose on me I will bear." The king of Assyria demanded of King Hezekiah of Judah three hundred talents of silver and thirty talents of gold (2 Kgs 18:14). There is some dispute over whether Hezekiah paid a second ransom because the biblical account continues with the arrival of Sennacherib's envoy, the Rab-Shakeh. This Assyrian official taunts and threatens Hezekiah and the Judeans with exile and the destruction of Jerusalem. Hezekiah consults Isaiah, and the prophet reassures Hezekiah that he has nothing to fear and that Yahweh will deliver the city, for it is he, Yahweh, who controls all events. The Bible reports that the Assyrians withdrew from Jerusalem as the angel of the lord slew 185,000 troops in the camp of Sennacherib in a single night. The king had no choice but to return home (2 Kgs 19).

Sennacherib's invasion of Judah in 701 BCE was certainly devastating. Destruction layers are evident throughout Judah, especially in the Shephelah, Judah's richest and most populated area. The region never regained its former status after the Assyrian attack, and the land was transferred to Philistia. Years later it remained "sparsely inhabited," never fully recovering its demographic strength (Finkelstein 2013, 201, 263). The scholarly consensus is that Judah suffered a major catastrophe. However, Faust maintains that Sennacherib's invasion should be reexamined, and he argues that the revival of Judah was much quicker than has been supposed. The Shephelah region was the only area that did not recover in the Kingdom of Judah. The Assyrians did not devastate the entire kingdom and probably marched through some areas rapidly, which allowed many inhabitants to return and rebuild. Jerusalem, too, was largely spared, apart from the heavy tribute. The population in and around Jerusalem increased to a point that was nearly equal to the rest of Judah. As Sennacherib marched through southern Judah, refugees fled into the region of Jerusalem. In the seventh century BCE, many settlements in Judah experienced a population increase, and new ones were established in the area as well. Many of those areas devastated by the Assyrians recovered over a short period of time. Excluding the Shephelah region, "[a]lmost all the excavated sites in the regions that were part of the kingdom of Judah in the seventh century, i.e., Jerusalem and its surroundings, the region of Benjamin, the highlands of Judea, the Judean Desert, and the Negev, were probably more densely settled at the time [seventh century BCE] than during the eight century" (Faust 2008, 188). Where there is sufficient information, it is clear that the population density of Judah in the seventh century BCE exceeded that of the eighth century BCE.

Deportations to and from Assyria

The mass deportation of population groups from conquered nations and population exchange with foreign elements were policies used by many Assyrian kings. This transplanting of influential citizens weakened the elites' ability to instigate any widespread resistance movements. The deportations of the populace of the Israelite Northern Kingdom took place when Tiglath-Pileser III, Shalmaneser V, and Sargon II campaigned against Israel between 733 and 720 BCE. The Assyrians recorded approximately forty thousand Israelites being deported. Though the accuracy of these numbers is questionable, it is still a small percentage of the residents of the Kingdom of Israel since the entire population of Israel may have been as high as 350,000 inhabitants (Finkelstein and Silberman 2001, 208). How many exiles actually survived the grueling forced march of hundreds of miles into Assyria is unknowable.

Assyrian administrative expertise in organizing their massive empire is indeed impressive. Nonetheless, the challenge of providing for the masses being exiled to Assyria would have been daunting, and the number of survivors of this ordeal must have been relatively small. The supply requirements of a large invading army would be staggering: hundreds of tons of food, water, and forage for animals every day. When thousands or tens of thousands of deportees are added to that, humane treatment could not be accorded to all. Only those whom the Assyrians recognized could benefit their kingdom, such as charioteers or the Judean elite, could have survived months marching in the desert. King Tiglath-Pileser was once informed that six thousand captives would not survive because of a lack of grain and that three thousand of them should be sent to another official to be settled. Tiglath-Pileser insisted that the Assyrian official take care of his captives: "Seven times over you shall not be careless; for that you would die. If there is anyone sick among the captives whom they bring to you, you shall gather (them) together from among (the group). However many there are, they shall transport (them), (and) place them in your presence until they are fit" (Younger 2003). Yet we can hardly imagine anything but a brutal environment for most of the deportees. The logistical aspects of deportation were overwhelming, and survival was negligible. Nevertheless, the inhabitants of Israel were deported and eventually came to be known as the "Ten Lost Tribes," people who were never to be heard from again.

Our earliest biblical source, the book of Kings, does not indicate exactly where Tiglath-Pileser sent these first deportees. The pertinent biblical passage states: "In the days of King Pekah of Israel, King Tiglath-Pileser of Assyria came and captured Ijon, Abel Beth-Maacah, Janoah, Kedesh, Hazor, Gilead, and Galilee, all the land of Naphtali. He carried the people captive to Assyria" (2 Kgs 15:29). A much later source in 1 Chronicles 5:26 states, although this may just echo 2 Kings 17:6, that the Assyrian king "brought them to Halah, Habor, Hara, and the river of Gozan." In his reliefs from Nimrud (Calah), Tiglath-Pileser III claims he exiled Bit Humria (Omri-Land or Israel): "I carried off [to] Assyria the land of Bit-Humria (Israel) . . . all of its people . . . their [possessions] and [I car]ried them [to Assyria]" (COS 2:288; cf. 2:291, 2:293). Another fragmentary inscription of Tiglath-Pileser lists 13,520 as the total number of deportees exiled from his Galilee campaign (Cogan and Tadmor 1988, 175; cf. COS 2:286). Archaeologists have noted a large drop in Galilee's population to a low number that remained constant until the Maccabean conquest and repopulation of the area in the first century BCE (Gal 1992). It appears that Tiglath-Pileser did not settle other peoples in this area of ancient Israel.

In 725 BCE, Shalmaneser V besieged Samaria and likely conquered it in 722 BCE. No Assyrian historical record from the reign of Shalmaneser V has survived; thus, scholars are unsure of the historical details of the fall of Samaria. The biblical text is undeniably brief here. His successor, Sargon II, came to power and immediately responded to a rebellion in Samaria/Palestine in 720 BCE. The revolt in Samaria was unsuccessful, and Sargon II may have had to reconquer the city. Perhaps there were even two deportations, but that is pure conjecture. Sargon II reports: "I besieged and conquered Samarina. I took as booty 27,290 people who lived there. I gathered 50 chariots from them. I taught the rest (of the deportees) their skills" (COS 2:296). The biblical text addressing this event reads: "In the ninth year of Hoshea, the king of Assyria conquered Samaria and he exiled the Israelites to Assyria. He settled them in Halah, on the Habor, the river of Gozan, and in the cities of the Medes" (2 Kgs 17:6).

In place of the Israelite deportees, Sargon II settled residents of other defeated nations in the Assyrian province of Samaria. "I counted as spoil 27,280 people. . . . I settled the rest of them in the midst of Assyria. I repopulated Samerina [i.e., Samaria] more than before. I brought into it people from countries conquered by my hands" (COS 2:295–96). The biblical narrative recounts exiles from Babylon, Cuthah, Avva, Hamath, and Sepharvaim (2 Kgs 17:24) as well as Hena and Ivvah (2 Kgs 18:34). However, the archaeological footprint of these people is nearly invisible. Ephraim Stern observed, "Almost nothing has been uncovered that can be attributed to the countries of the different groups of deportees who are said to have come from the Iranian plateau or Elam" (2009, 45). At present, our evidence is limited. We do have several cuneiform records from Gezer and nearby Tel Hadid that contain the names of thirty-six people. Only one name is Hebrew, "Netanyahu from Gezer"; the rest are Akkadian and Aramean names, indicating that these people were likely not Israelites.

Sargon II was not finished. He would campaign two more times in the southern Levant (716–715 BCE and 712–711 BCE). During his 716 BCE campaign, Sargon II subjugated the western Sinai area and settled four Arabian tribes in Samaria/Samarina (*COS* 2:293). This incident is not recorded in the biblical text, and we cannot say much about these tribes. Moreover, it appears Judah was connected with the revolt of Ashdod in 712 BCE, and in that regard Sargon declares that he conquered and despoiled Azekah, a city in the Shephelah that belonged to Hezekiah (*COS* 2:304).

The book of 2 Kings is not the only biblical source recording deportations of foreign people to Samaria. Ezra 4:2 presents a record of the descendants of these foreign deportees who ask to help Zerubbabel and the Judeans with the postexilic reconstruction of the temple: "Let us build with you, for we worship your God as you do, and we have been sacrificing to him ever since the days of King Esar-haddon of Assyria who brought us here." And, in a later verse, we encounter other foreign deportees writing to King Artaxerxes of Persia. The letter is said to represent "the Persians, the people of Erech, the Babylonians, the people of Susa, that is, the Elamites, and the rest of the nations whom the great and noble Osnappar [Ashurbanipal] deported and settled in the cities of Samaria and in the rest of the province Beyond the River" (Ezra 4:9-10; see Younger 2003). Thus, centuries later, people living in the region of Samaria thought that their ancestors had been transplanted to northern Israel from elsewhere in Mesopotamia during the era of Assyrian dominance.

The last major Assyrian deportation came in the aftermath of Sennacherib's 701 BCE Levantine campaigns. His invasion began with a march into Phoenicia, where a number of cities surrendered or reaffirmed their vassal status to the mighty Assyrian king; among these were Sidon, Byblos, Tyre, Acco, Ashdod, and Ashkelon. As for Judah, Sennacherib claims to have conquered "forty-six of his fortified walled cities and surrounding smaller towns, which were without number," and to have seized "200,150 people, young and old, male and female, horses, mules, donkeys, camels, cattle, and sheep without number, and counted them as spoil" (*COS* 2:303). This is an impossible number even for the entirety of the campaign, much less so for Judah alone. Finkelstein reckons that, at the end of eighth century BCE, "the Kingdom of Judah did not count much more than 100,000 souls" (Finkelstein and Silberman 2001, 208).

Sennacherib continues by noting the following about King Hezekiah of Judah: "His cities which I despoiled I cut off from his land and gave them to Mitinti, king of Ashdod, Padi, king of Ekron and Silli-bel, king of Gaza, and thus diminished his land" (*COS* 2:303). Totally vanquished, Hezekiah had to submit. In the end, he appears to have sent an enormous tribute of gold, silver, and many other valuables along with "his daughters, his palace women, his male and female singers" to Nineveh, the only location mentioned for Sennacherib's captives (*COS* 2:303).

Mesopotamian sources testify to the presence of Israelite exiles throughout the Assyrian Empire. Assyrian records dated to the seventh century BCE indicate that Samarians served among the troops of the Assyrian king. Tiglath-Pileser's army had a unit consisting of deportees, and its commander was known as the "commander of deportees" (Younger 2003). Another Assyrian text documents a large number of West Semitic names among Sargon's army, perhaps as many as 20 percent. It is significant that in Sargon's annals he boasts of forming "a contingent of 50 chariots" from the 27,290 inhabitants of Samarina/Samaria that the Assyrian king claims to have deported (*COS* 2:296). These Samarian charioteers must have had a reputation as superb fighters to have been included in the army of the mighty Sargon II. Scholars have noted a small number of Samarian deportees, with perhaps as many as thirteen serving "as chief officers in Sargon's charioteer forces according to the Nimrud horse lists" (Cantrell 2011, 136). Among Sargon II's documents, we find an Assyrian administrator named Nādbiyau (biblical Nedabiah), who served as a "chariot driver," and a person named Paqaha, a name that is identical to that of Pekah the Israelite king. Moreover, an Assyrian inscription uncovered in Gozan includes several Hebrew names, many of which appear also in biblical texts: Hosea, Dinah, Elisha, Haggai, Hananel, and Menahem. Other Israelite or Yahwistic names in this text include one of Sennacherib's commanders and one of King Ashurbanipal's bodyguards. Hebrew names with this "Yah" element may indicate the worship of the Israelite god Yahweh (Younger 2003).

Assyrian documents attested the presence of exiles in three of the four locations described in 2 Kings 17:6 and 18:11 as the final destination of those Israelites deported by the Assyrians: Halah, Habor, and Gozan. No mention exists of Israelites residing in "the cities of Media." However, scholars have reassessed these texts and now recognize an obvious reference to Israelites in Media. Inscriptions dated from Tiglath-Pileser to Sargon II mention a Hilqia Iua and a Gil-Iau as officials in the Assyrian bureaucracy, the first clear evidence of Israelites living in Media.

Perhaps the most enigmatic of all the Assyrian officials who engaged with the Judeans was the "Rab-Shakeh." The Assyrian "Rab-Shakeh" appeared at the walls of Jerusalem leading a contingent of Sennacherib's army during his campaign in Judah in 701 BCE (2 Kgs 18–19; Isa 36). Who was this Rab-Shakeh? The title Rab-Shakeh, or "chief cupbearer," was an important position in Assyria. As the king's cupbearer, he had achieved a high status within the ranks of the Assyrian bureaucracy. Perhaps he had once lived in Samaria and had been deported there as a young man. The story suggests that such a person must have known the language of Assyria's subjects and enemies, for in this story he appears capable in both Hebrew and Aramaic. The "cup-bearer" is depicted in Assyrian palace reliefs as the king's attendant and was clearly a high-ranking military official, and in that official capacity the Rab-Shakeh was in Jerusalem to deliver Sennacherib's demand Hezekiah's immediate surrender. In the midst of this official's gloomy speech that described Judah's reliance on its ally Egypt as a "splintered reed staff" and that included a taunting bet on Judah's ability to produce two thousand horsemen, Hezekiah's officials asked Sennacherib's representative to speak to them in Aramaic and not "in the language of Judah within the hearing of the people who are on the wall" (2 Kgs 18:26). For maximum effect, Rab-Shakeh continued his threats in Hebrew for all to hear: Hezekiah cannot save them. Yahweh cannot save them. The Assyrian siege will be unrelenting and unpleasant. He even asserted that the people's anticipated exile would not be all that bad, as Assyria would resettle the deportees in a land as good as Judah. Rab-Shakeh withdrew, and we are not sure he returned when Sennacherib sent a second delegation. Of course, the historical reliability of this event is important. What Rab-Shakeh actually said and what parts of the narrative were added by the Deuteronomistic editors has been debated by scholars for decades. Nonetheless, Rab-Shakeh's oration in 2 Kings made a strong impression both on those at the wall who may have heard his threatening rhetoric and on those who read this gripping story.

King Manasseh and the Failure of Hezekiah's Reforms

The narrative about King Manasseh in 2 Kings 21 denounces Manasseh as the most wicked king of all in ancient Judah. This condemnation focuses on his religious behavior. It must be remembered that this denunciation was written by editors who had a strident commitment to a strict version of Deuteronomistic Yahwism that left no room whatsoever for the worship of other gods. Manasseh, the passage notes, promoted the worship of other gods as well as the worship of Yahweh in forms and places not allowed by Deuteronomistic Yahwism. In other words, his religious practices ran directly counter to his father Hezekiah's reforms and the religious program adopted by the editors of the DH.

Why did Manasseh do it? Was he simply a heretic at heart, or are there other explanations? Some scholars have proposed that Manasseh's religious program was driven by the Assyrians as part of a policy to solidify their domination of the region. Locals were expected to adhere, at least to an extent, to Assyrian religious customs. Thus, Manasseh was simply trying to placate his Assyrian overlords.

This explanation overlooks some key biblical and archaeological evidence. The biblical texts were written, edited, and transmitted by people with strict monotheistic ideas: they sought to promote the worship of Yahweh only, only in Jerusalem, and only according to the dictates of the Jerusalem priesthood. That ideology is especially clear in the books of "the Deuteronomistic History" (Joshua, Judges, Samuel, and Kings). But did everyone in ancient Judah accept that ideology? Biblical and archaeological evidence suggests not. The biblical documents are replete with denunciations of aberrant religious practices, from the worship of "false gods" to false prophets (Jer 14:14; Ezek 13:9) and renegade priests (Judg 17–18). Why would those activities be so frequently decried if they were not going on routinely? And if they were popular, then the people doing them surely thought they were doing the right thing. Viewing it differently, one could imagine that the people whose religious practices offended the Deuteronomists were in turn offended by the religious practices of the Deuteronomists. This kind of reading between the lines and against the grain of the text yields a different perspective on people like Manasseh and their religious practices. Thus, Manasseh's religious program may have been driven by populist interests; this is what the people wanted. As described in 2 Kings 21, what Manasseh is charged with doing is largely what the Northern Kingdom of Israel was charged with doing, a form of infidelity to Yahweh that enraged Yahweh and thereby brought about Israel's downfall in 722 BCE.

The presence of many religious beliefs and perspectives also stems from the archaeological record. As has been discussed in other chapters, archaeology has yielded abundant data to support the fact that Israelites and Judahites possessed a diverse and robust religious marketplace of ideas and practices. The numerous Asherah figurines attest the prominence of this goddess. The temple at Arad and the large horned altar at Beersheba attest to local cultic practices far away from Jerusalem. Moreover, special places within private residences where figurines were found attest family practices apart from a temple. Inscriptions such as those found at Kuntillet Ajrud and Khirbet el Qom indicate that Hebrew speakers imagined that Yahweh had a wife, Asherah. Obviously, one could worship Yahweh alone, but Yahweh could also be worshipped along with other gods and goddesses such as Baal and/or Asherah. In fact, one need not worship Yahweh at all to remain part of the Judean community.

Throughout ancient Judah and Israel, furthermore, archaeologists have uncovered cultic high places (*bamot*) or open-air sanctuaries for sacrifice, stone and ceramic altars, offering stands, household shrines, standing stones, images of female goddesses, faience figurines, terra-cotta model temples, and alternative temple worship outside of Jerusalem. All these items are reminiscent of Canaanite religious practices. Yahweh and other deities were worshipped outside Jerusalem without official priestly guidance (Dever 2005, 110–69).

Nonetheless, the biblical editors promoted a strict form of monotheistic Yahwism, and that ideology is inextricably woven into the biblical fabric. So devoted to this ideology were they that they went so far as to redeem even Manasseh. The Deuteronomistic account in 2 Kings 21 views him as an unrepentant reprobate, but the Chronicler's account of Manasseh (2 Chr 33) is a good example of how the Chronicler used and altered his biblical sources. The Chronicler took the information in 2 Kings 21 and added one important feature. He reimagined Manasseh as a model for a repentant sinner! The Chronicler has added a paragraph that completely rewrites Manasseh's life story.

> Yahweh spoke to Manasseh and to his people, but they paid no heed. So Yahweh brought against them the commanders of the army of the Assyrian king. They took Manasseh captive in leg-irons, bound him in handcuffs, and brought him to Babylon. In his distress he sought the favor of Yahweh his god and became deeply humbled before the god of his ancestors. He prayed to him, and God accepted his prayer, heard his plea, and returned him to Jerusalem and his kingdom. Then Manasseh knew that Yahweh alone was god. (2 Chr 33:10-13, translation by Wright)

The account goes on to detail the righteous things that Manasseh did after he repented from his evil ways. Needless to say, the account in 2 Kings 21 knows nothing of this repentant Manasseh. For the Deuteronomistic author(s), Manasseh was irredeemably corrupt. So why did the Chronicler deviate so markedly from his source in 2 Kings here? Either this historian had sources about Manasseh that the Deuteronomistic Historian lacked or ignored, or he invented the tale out of whole cloth in an effort to provide an example for Persian-era Judeans who had returned to Jerusalem after the exile. Like Manasseh, they had been taken into exile because of sin, at least according to the Deuteronomistic ideology. While living in exile, they repented of their evil ways and prayed for restoration, again, just like Manasseh in the Chronicler's account. Now that they were back in Jerusalem, like Manasseh they too should follow the prescripts of strict Deuteronomistic Yahwism. Thus, the Chronicler appears as concerned not so much with history per se as with making a theological point. As the saying goes, "The pen is mightier than the sword," and, in this case, casting Manasseh in an entirely different light, the pen of the Chronicler has had the last word.

Kuntillet Ajrud

The famous inscriptions at Kuntillet Ajrud have changed our understanding of Israelite religion. They may provide direct evidence of other Israelites following polytheistic practices. Kuntillet Ajrud in the Sinai Peninsula was excavated in the late 1970s. Its inscriptions and illustrations were uncovered in two buildings and have been dated to the eighth century BCE, although some argue for an earlier date in the ninth century. The Hebrew inscriptions found at this site were inscribed on storage jars, plastered walls, and stone bowls. The site's location at the junction of several important ancient trading routes in the northern Sinai suggests that it was a caravanserai or wayside shrine.

The discoveries at Kuntillet Ajrud have no parallels in any contemporaneous sites excavated in Israel (Meshel 2012, 66). For a desert site, its water resources are insufficient. There are no accommodations for travelers and little evidence of trading goods. The pottery is not local, and it dates from the ninth to the eighth century BCE. The storage jars were mostly produced in Jerusalem and the south, but some of the smaller vessels and cooking-pot forms originated in northern Israel. There are several abecedaries (alphabet and writing practice texts) all written on *pithoi*, but the absence of any written sherds and the remote location appear to rule out the possibility that this was a scribal school. There were numerous textile finds, the most of any Israelite site in the Iron Age. Some were mixed weaves of linen and wool, a violation of a biblical prohibition (Lev 19:19; Deut 22:11). Ze'ev Meshel, the director of the excavation, argues that the inhabitants were a group of priests and Levites who offered services and religious blessing to travelers. The storage vessels were marked with the Hebrew letters *alef* and *yod*, which scholars believe are abbreviations for offerings and tithes that were collected in Israel to supply the needs of priests. However, apart from four bowls that are inscribed with blessings for their owners, Meshel recognizes that the site has no evidence of "cultic practices such as burning of incense, pouring of libations, sacrifices . . . no traces of any objects, or vessels that would have been used for such activities, such as altars, incense burners, idols or figurines" (2012, 68). The inscriptions include over twenty personal names containing a Yahwistic suffix of the type commonly used in Israel and Judah (2012, 128–29). A wall painting at Ajrud depicts a painted figure dressed in long clothing, seated in a high-back chair, and holding what appears to be a lotus, features that suggest someone of high rank. Similar scenes have been located on Canaanite and Phoenician works. One inscription is addressed "to Yaheli and to Yoasa [Joash]" and includes a blessing that reads, "I bless you by YHWH of Shomron [Samaria] and by his Asherah."

The inscriptions refer to a number of deities found in the Hebrew Bible: Yahweh, El, Baal, and Asherah. On a wall inscription, Yahweh is addressed as "To Yahweh of Teman and to his Asherah." Several large storage jars are also inscribed with the names Yahweh and Asherah. These inscriptions are translated as "I bless you by Yahweh of Samaria and by his Asherah" and "Yahweh of Teman and his Asherah." Some scholars have insisted these inscriptions cannot refer to the personal name of a goddess by the use of a possessive pronominal suffix ("his Asherah"). Though this grammatical construction is known in Ugaritic, it is not standard biblical Hebrew. For many biblical scholars, the inscriptions are not a reference to the actual Canaanite goddess Asherah, rather to a symbolic image. Perhaps, but one would not be surprised to find that travelers or traders wrote inscriptions in ungrammatical Hebrew. More importantly, the high goddess is a common feature in ancient Levantine religions, so it is not at all surprising to find her linked to Yahweh in the inscriptions from Kuntillet Ajrud.

The storage jars also contain illustrations of a variety of flora and fauna—horses, a boar, lions, perhaps a bull, a palm tree that many scholars interpret as a fertility symbol, two ibexes, and a cow suckling her calf. Dever interprets these drawings as part of "syncretistic folk religion" (Dever 2001, 265). However, the most astonishing scene on this storage jar involves two grotesque, human-like images and a seated female figure playing a lyre. Most scholars see a resemblance in the two figures to the Egyptian deity Bes. Amulets with depictions of Bes have been uncovered throughout eighth- and seventh-century BCE tombs in Judea. When first published, both Ajrud figures appeared to have male genitalia between their legs. Some scholars insisted, however, that the Bes figures are displaying tails from the skins of animals and that this depiction is not Yahweh and his Asherah. The episode has produced a number of bizarre and tortured comments on the nature of Bes' sexuality. However, further analysis of the original has now revealed that one of the figures has nothing between its legs. Of course, the entire discussion on Ajrud will dramatically change since it is now obvious that these "Bes figures" are indeed male and female, a goddess and a god drawn on the *pithoi*. Some scholars maintain that Asherah was a fertility goddess and not merely a pole or a cultic object and that she was a consort of Yahweh. Following Dever, the seated female figure playing a lyre might be Asherah. Her chair is a "lion throne," and in the Ancient Near East lion thrones were typically associated with "deities or kings—never with ordinary human beings" (Dever 2005, 165).

Are these drawings connected to the inscriptions, or should the two be treated separately? Some scholars think the two were created at the same time by the same person, while others claim that the inscription was added later by someone other than the artist. Nevertheless, whether the inscription was written before or after the illustrations is a distinction without a difference. One cannot imagine an individual writing a blessing to Yahweh and his Asherah over the top of the illustrations that most scholars identify as deities without associating the inscription with the drawing in some way.

Hadley insists that, even if Asherah is not depicted in this scene, the image of Asherah is contained in the other illustrations on the storage jar. Asherah should be located in the likeness of a palm tree, regarded as the "tree of life,"

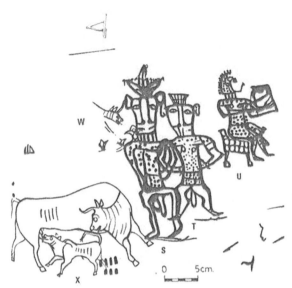

FIGURE 17-6. *Kuntillet Ajrud. When the drawing was first published, both Ajrud figures appeared to have tails or male genitalia between their legs. New analysis has now revealed that one of the figures has nothing between its legs. The drawing and the inscription from Kuntillet Ajrud establish the possibility that the Canaanite goddess Asherah was Yahweh's consort.*

an association that most scholars connect with a deity. The "sacred pole" of the Bible is quite possibly a symbolic tree (Deut 16:21). Thus, the sacred tree flanked by ibexes may well represent Asherah (Hadley 2008).

Admittedly, these inscriptions mentioning Yahweh and Asherah in a small fort, trading post, or even shrine, out in the vast emptiness of the Sinai Desert, do not inspire much confidence as an example of "popular folk religion." However, another contemporaneous eighth-century inscription from the site of Khirbet el-Qom, located several miles west of Hebron, also includes a Yahwistic blessing: "Blessed be Uriyahu by Yahweh, for from his enemies he has saved him by his Asherah." Nearly all scholars agree that the reading "by his Asherah" in the el-Qom inscription is "certain—and identical to that at Ajrud" (Dever 2001, 186). Considering the paucity of nonbiblical inscriptions mentioning Yahweh, the discovery of the el-Qom inscription makes these blessings even more remarkable. In this regard one should also take note of the thousands of terra-cotta fertility goddesses, dating from the preexilic period, that archaeologists have discovered all over ancient Israel and Judah, even in Jerusalem. Often they depict a nude female, occasionally clutching an infant or tambourine, with large hips and breasts, exaggerated pubic triangles, and expanded stomachs signifying pregnancy. Dever identifies the figurines with the "popular Iron Age goddess Asherah" (2012, 280).

Moreover, a cult stand from Taanach discovered in 1902 and dating to 950–800 BCE provides some additional context to the Kuntillet Ajrud material. This cult stand depicts a naked female figure, perhaps representative of a fertility goddess, on one of its four ornamented tiers. On the bottom panel, she is holding the ears of two lions; and, on the second tier, winged sphinxes with female faces are seen wearing the typical wig of the Egyptian goddess Hathor. Lions are on the third tier, and between them are two goats eating at the tree of life, again an image often connected with Asherah. The top panel depicts a winged sun disk over a horse or a calf. Many of these images are clearly representative of deities. The goats or ibexes depicted nibbling on a tree, the naked lady, and calves are all known throughout the Near East as symbols of fertility. The sun disk is also a popular image of the divine. At a minimum, these images can be identified with female and male deities who are most likely identified with Baal or Yahweh and Asherah or another female goddess (Zevit 2001, 324). In light of these discoveries, it is now abundantly clear that Israelite religion was not strictly monotheistic. The Hebrew Bible is replete with texts that reflect a polytheistic background (for instance, Gen 6:1-4; 14:18-22; 31:42; 33:18-20; 31:42; 35:6-7; Exod 6:3; Deut 10:17; 32:8-9; 1 Sam 3:1). For many Israelites and Judahites, Yahweh and his Asherah were certainly regarded as a divine couple.

Ketef Hinnom

Excavations conducted by Israeli archaeologist Gabriel Barkay between 1975 and 1996 in the Hinnom Valley in Jerusalem led to the discovery of two tiny silver amulets in a burial cave called Ketef Hinnom, on the western side of the Hinnom Valley. This is the only burial tomb from "First Temple Period Jerusalem ever discovered with its contents intact" (Barkay 2009). Written in ancient Hebrew script reliably dated to the seventh century BCE, the diminutive sheets of silver constitute the earliest known fragments of a biblical text. The contents of the tomb revealed more than a thousand artifacts. Excavators uncovered a burial bench with stone headrests for the deceased. The human remains may have numbered ninety-five individuals. The tomb contained forty-five iron arrowheads and one bronze arrowhead. Other items in the tomb were "needles, cosmetic kohl sticks, and bronze buttons, as well as a knife and an iron chisel, and a small cream-colored glass" bottle, very rare for this time period. An exceptional coin minted in Cos, an island in the Aegean, was found dating to the sixth century BCE, the earliest ever excavated in Israel. The tomb held an astonishing amount of pottery that included more than 250 intact vessels. They included "wine decanters, juglets, perfume bottles and oil lamps" that dated from the seventh to the fifth centuries BCE. Barkay noted that the "jewelry from this repository is unequalled in Jerusalem excavations" (2009).

Among all these objects, the most significant discovery at Ketef Hinnom was the text on the two silver amulets. It took years to unroll these tiny amulets and decipher the text. The first word recognized on the amulets was YHWH, the Tetragrammaton, the four Hebrew letters transliterated and understood as the Hebrew name of God. Years later, with the use of "fiber-optic light and computer imaging, as well as advanced photography" (Barkay 2009), a new version of the text was produced. The two amulets on thin sheets of silver contain the earliest known fragments of a version of the priestly blessing found in Numbers 6:24-26:

> May Yahweh bless you,
>   and keep you.
> May Yahweh make his face shine upon you,
>   and be gracious to you.
> May Yahweh life up his countenance upon you,
>   and give you peace.

The larger of the two Ketef Hinnom amulet reads: "May YHWH bles[s] you and [may he] keep you. [May] YHWH make [his face] shine." It is also inscribed with the words "the covenant" and Yahweh's "graciousness to those who love him," a clear recitation of Deuteronomy 7:9. The smaller of these amulets reads: "May YHWH bless you, keep you. May YHWH make his face shine upon you and grant you p[ea]ce" (Barkay 2009). What you can see is that this eighth-century BCE inscription attests a fixed form for this blessing that appears in the Bible. It does not prove the date of the composition of the book of Numbers or anything asserted in the book, but it attests that this blessing was known and used with the exact words now found in the Bible (see Figure 18-7).

Josiah's Reform and the Deuteronomistic History

King Josiah of Judah was only eight years old when he became king of Judah after his father Amon had been assassinated in a palace coup in 640 BCE. The biblical text does not mention the reason behind this conspiracy, but we learn that the "people of the land" (*am haaretz*) killed Amon's assassins. They then installed Amon's young son (and Manasseh's grandson) Josiah as king of Judah.

In surprising detail, 2 Kings 22–23 depicts one of the most remarkable events in the religious history of Judaism. In 626 BCE, when he had reached twenty-two years of age, King Josiah ordered repairs to the temple, and, during these repairs, the workers discovered the long-lost book of the Torah. The high priest Hilkiah passed the information to the king's secretary Shaphan, who in turn informed Josiah that the priest Hilkiah had given him this unanticipated book. "Shaphan then read it aloud to the king" (2 Kgs 22:10). The king tore his clothes in a display of mourning and immediately requested an inquiry "concerning the words of this book that has been found" (2 Kgs 22:13). The prophetess Huldah verified the book but pronounced an unpleasant verdict from Yahweh: because the people had abandoned the LORD, he would "bring a disaster on this place and on its inhabitants" (2 Kgs 22:16). However, the king's appropriate display of grief guaranteed that he would go to his grave in peace and that he would not see the coming catastrophe. Huldah's prophecy suitably impressed Josiah, who immediately assembled all the people of Judah. The king read the book to them and led all the people in reestablishing a covenant to follow Yahweh and keep his commandments, his decrees, and his statutes (2 Kgs 23:3). Renewing this covenant seems inconceivable given the fact that the temple was home to a variety of deities and altars dedicated to foreign gods. However, at the time of Josiah, the sole worship of Yahweh alone was not the norm among the Israelites. Most people were apparently not strict monotheists.

The discovery of this book, whether by chance or design, motivated Josiah to embark on a massive reform throughout all of Judah to cleanse the nation of the polytheism. Only the worship of Yahweh would be tolerated, and sacrifices to him would be offered only at the Jerusalem temple. It is possible that Josiah also began a campaign to expand the borders of Judah, coupled with his religious reform. Any expansion of Judah was dependent upon the decline of the Assyrian Empire. Although it is hard to determine when Assyrian power over Judah came to an end, perhaps a decline took place after the death of Ashurbanipal in 627 BCE. Rival claimants to the throne weakened Assyria internally, and Babylon broke away and achieved independence. By the time of Josiah's reform, the Assyrian Empire was collapsing. Egypt and Babylonia then vied to become the major power in the Levant.

Josiah moved quickly and engaged in a series of acts commonly designated by biblical scholars as "Josiah's Reform" (2 Kgs 23:1-24). The statue of Asherah was taken from the temple and burned along with the vessels for her, Baal, and the host of heaven. Asherah, Baal, and the host of heaven had been worshipped since the days of Ahaz and Manasseh. Josiah deposed the idolatrous priests and destroyed their sanctuaries and high places (*bamot*). The houses of the cultic prostitutes that were located near the temple were likewise destroyed. The women who wove garments for Asherah (2 Kgs 23:7) were barred from the temple. Josiah also ordered that all the high places (*bamot*) throughout the land be destroyed. Josiah also put an end to the Topheth "so that no one would make a son or a daughter pass through fire as an offering to Molech" (2 Kgs 23:10). Horses and chariots dedicated to the sun and located near the entrance to the temple were destroyed. And, remarkably, Josiah destroyed the high places east of Jerusalem that Solomon himself had built in honor of Astarte, Chemosh, and Milcom (2 Kgs 23:13). How these altars survived three hundred years in the shadow of the Jerusalem temple is difficult to understand. Josiah also smashed the pillars and sacred poles "and covered the sites with human bones." He destroyed the altar at Bethel erected by Jeroboam, for Bethel and Dan had been established as national religious centers for the Kingdom of Israel, an abomination to the Lord. Finally, Josiah is said to have removed the shrines throughout the northern territory of the former Kingdom of Israel and slaughtered their priests.

On his return to Jerusalem, Josiah celebrated the Passover as depicted in the book of the covenant. According to the writers of 2 Kings 23:22, "No such Passover had been kept since the days of the judges who judged Israel, even during all the days of the kings of Israel and of the kings of Judah; but in the eighteenth year of King Josiah this Passover was kept to the Lord in Jerusalem." Yet it is difficult to believe that the Passover had not been celebrated for over four hundred years, since it clearly contradicts 2 Chronicles 30, which includes a Passover celebration during the reign of Hezekiah, although the historical accuracy of these verses in 2 Chronicles is highly debated. As for the verse in 2 Kings, one wonders if "no such Passover" excludes any Passover? Was there really no celebration of Passover or simply one not chronicled? Nevertheless, the authors of 2 Kings sanctify Josiah's reforms with this astonishing attribute: "Before him there was no king like him, who turned to the Lord with all his heart, with all his soul, and with all his might, according to all the law of Moses; nor did any like him arise after him" (23:25). The biblical record certainly depicts him as a resolute reformer.

According to 2 Chronicles 34:3, the reform began years earlier than recorded in 2 Kings, even before the "book of the law" was discovered. The Chronicler depends on Kings as a source, but he may also have had access to other annalistic materials that assisted his work. Whether the reform began in Josiah's twelfth or eighteenth year is impossible to say, but, whichever account is accurate, Josiah was king for some years while the temple was full of pagan gods and vessels. Nevertheless, the contents of the book of the Torah guided the reform movement. Josiah eradicated foreign gods from the temple, eliminated foreign altars in Jerusalem, and destroyed sanctuaries throughout Judah and the former land of Israel. More importantly, he designated the worship of only Yahweh, only in the Jerusalem temple, and only according to the protocols of the priests in Jerusalem.

The impetus for Josiah's reform is evident: the author of 2 Kings tells us Josiah was determined "to perform the words of this covenant that were written in this book" (23:3). Since the early nineteenth century, the vast majority of biblical scholars have followed De Wette's case that most of Josiah's reforms were based on an early version of the book of Deuteronomy (Cogan and Tadmor 1988, 294). Many of the reforms and acts Josiah undertook were done as commanded in Deuteronomy.

Note the directives in Deuteronomy that are fulfilled by Josiah:

Do not worship the "other gods" (Deut 17:3; see 2 Kgs 23:5).

Do not allow cultic prostitutes to serve in the temple of Yahweh (Deut 23:18; see 2 Kgs 23:7).

Do not imitate other nations who burn their sons and their daughters in the fire to their gods (Deut 12:31; see 2 Kgs 23:10).

Destroy the sacred altars, sacred pillars, sacred poles, and idols of other gods (Deut 7:5; see 2 Kgs 23:14).

Do not consult those who practice magic or the cult of the dead (Deut 18:10-11: see 2 Kgs 23:24).

Israel must keep all the commandments and worship Yahweh alone (Deut 6:2, 4; 13:4).

Curses and destruction will envelop the people if they do not obey the LORD (Deut 28:16-68).

The destruction of the cultic sites throughout the north and south gave the religious hierarchy full control of the Jerusalem temple. This is consistent with Deuteronomy's command to "[t]ake care that you do not offer your burnt-offerings at any place you happen to see. But only at the place that the LORD will choose in one of your tribes—there you shall offer your burnt-offerings and there you shall do everything I command you" (12:12-13). Though some polytheistic practices continued, archaeological evidence demonstrates that open-air sanctuaries began to disappear at the time of Josiah's reform. Judean Pillar Figurines had been widespread in Judah during the eighth and seventh centuries BCE. The majority, which may number over a thousand, have been located in Jerusalem and its surroundings areas. It appears that figurines were manufactured in Jerusalem for distribution throughout Judah. Most of these figurines appear to have been intentionally broken, perhaps destroyed as part of Josiah's reform. Outside of tombs, complete figurines are rare in the archaeological record. However, a few figurines have appeared in the archaeological record of Judah following the destruction of Jerusalem in 586 BCE, suggesting their continued importance to at least some people's religious identity.

Remarkably, no biblical passage indicates the book of the Torah had been misplaced, or stored in the temple, or missing for hundreds of years. At the beginning of the reform, there is no mention that Moses had authored this text. Only when the reform is completed do we encounter the phrase "according to all the law of Moses" (2 Kgs 23:25). The book's mysterious appearance and staging only serve as a vehicle to energize a massive reorientation of Judah's religious system. It is obvious that some form of Deuteronomy was written during the reign of Josiah to influence and instruct the young king to purge Judah of all non-Yahwistic cults. It is not coincidental that the book was discovered by the high priest Hilkiah, read to the king by Shaphan the secretary, and authenticated by the prophetess Huldah. These were all prominent court officials with the ability and knowledge to craft or edit a document to influence the actions of the king. There can be little doubt that members of the royal court were involved in writing substantial portions of Deuteronomy. They had much to gain. These officials would have increased their prestige and power by centralizing the religious cult in Jerusalem. A reasonable conclusion is that they are eyewitnesses to Josiah's reform and are the primary authors of his actions as described in 2 Kings 22–23.

Josiah's End and the End of Assyria

The members of Josiah's court who authored the DH finished their history in 2 Kings before Josiah's violent death at Megiddo—now recorded in 2 Kings 23:29-30. Josiah's death in battle contradicts the peaceful death predicted for Josiah by Huldah. The failure to remove this inconsistency indicates that a later editor was responsible for recording Josiah's demise. The last chapter of 2 Kings 25:27-30 leads us to another editor. The chapter ends noting the release of King Jehoiachin of Judah in the thirty-seventh year of the exile in captivity in Babylon, which dates to approximately 560 BCE. This important remark is the last recorded historical footnote in 2 Kings. Most scholars recognize there might be at least two major redactions of the book of Kings, one edited during the reform of Josiah and one edited during the exile celebrating the release of King Jehoiachin.

The (Neo-)Assyrian Empire dominated the Near East for almost three centuries (ca. 900–612 BCE), but Assyrian power was eventually broken by their longtime rival and neighbor to the south, Babylonia. The end came quickly. Under King Nabopolassar, the Babylonians began their return to regional prominence. He created alliances that enabled him to challenge and ultimately conquer the Assyrians. Moving from south to north, in 612 BCE Nabopolassar captured the Assyrian capital of Nineveh. But the Assyrians and their last king, Ashur-uballit II (612–609 BCE), fled to the west and established their headquarters in the town of Haran. Lacking the resources to counter Nabopolassar, Ashur-uballit II called on his ally in Egypt, Pharaoh Necho II, for support. As Necho and his forces were marching northward along the Via Maris, King Josiah of Judah marshaled his army and engaged the Egyptians in battle at Megiddo. Vastly overpowered, the Judeans were defeated, and Josiah was killed (2 Kgs 23:29-30; 2 Chr 35:20-24). The combined Egyptian and Assyrian forces, however, were not enough to stop the Babylonian advance across northern Mesopotamia and into the Levant. Haran fell to the Babylonians in 609 BCE, but the Assyrians continued to fight. Due to advanced age, Nabopolassar passed leadership of his forces over to his son and successor, Nebuchadnezzar II, and, at the famous battle of Carchemish in 605 BCE, Nebuchadnezzar soundly defeated the remaining Assyrian forces and their Egyptian allies. Babylonia's rise to hegemony in the Near East was complete.

Conclusion

The DH is an extensive history of Israel and Judah from the time of Moses to the fall of Judah to the Babylonians. It begins with book of Deuteronomy, which records and promotes the religious and social values of the strict Yahwists living in and near Jerusalem. Tracing the origins of the Deuteronomistic Historians is challenging. These historians have been identified as the authors and editors of the books of Joshua, Judges, 1–2 Samuel, and 1–2 Kings. Though the book of Deuteronomy may contain ancient laws, they can hardly be from the time of Moses or even the judges. These books passed through many stages, perhaps beginning as early as Hezekiah (715–687 BCE) and extending to the priests and scribes in the reign of Josiah. It then appears that, during the Babylonian exile, editors updated the histories of the kings from the earlier works, and then yet further editing took place in the Persian Period. Since parts of these books mention the exile and even the return from the exile, those sections could not have been written before 586 and 539 BCE.

Some scholars believe that the beginnings of the Deuteronomistic Historians are found among the refugees from the Northern Kingdom prior to the destruction of Israel by Sargon II in 722 BCE. They brought their history and legal traditions in written form, linked with the eighth-century BCE northern prophetic movements (especially Amos and Hosea), and joined other scribal and priestly groups in Jerusalem. Here they urged King Hezekiah to enact a religious reform in Judah.

During the reign of King Manasseh, the reforms of his father, Hezekiah, were discontinued, and the reform movement foundered. Manasseh's religious program was severely criticized by the biblical writers, condemning him as an idolater who killed his religious opponents and brought God's wrath upon the nation (2 Kgs 21). The supporters of cultic reform returned to power during the reign of Josiah, who was the quintessential model of the righteous king committed to Yahweh: "Before him there was no king like him, who turned to the LORD with all his heart, with all his soul, and with all his might, according to all the law of Moses; nor did any like him arise after him" (2 Kgs 23:25). The language and phrases that are replicated in the book of Deuteronomy and in Josiah's reform in 2 Kings 22–23 point to an explicit connection between the Deuteronomistic Historians and the circle of court officials during the reign of Josiah. Furthermore, the prophecy of Josiah as fulfillment of Israel's history found in 1 Kings 13:1-3 clearly puts him and his court authors front and center.

Several of the sources used by the Deuteronomistic Historians are clearly stated. The "History of the Kings of Israel" and "History of the Kings of Judah" are mentioned numerous times throughout the books of Kings, and are all similar to modern bibliographical notes (Cogan 2001, 90). Also mentioned is "The Book of the Deeds of Solomon" (1 Kgs 11:41). Other sources include material from prophets such as Elijah, Elisha, and Micaiah, among others. Another source to be considered would be temple records (Cogan 2001, 92–94). This "history of Israel and Judah" was largely completed in the Babylonian exile, although it surely went through several revisions before it obtained its largely canonical form during or shortly after the exile.

The DH creates a masterful historical narrative based on the theological principle that Yahweh ultimately rewards the righteous and punishes the wicked. The reign of every king and one queen is assessed on the basis of his or her fidelity to the basics of Deuteronomistic ideology: the strict worship of only Yahweh, only in Jerusalem, and only according to the cultic practices approved by the Yahwistic priests in Jerusalem. Only three kings from Judah—Asa, Hezekiah, and Josiah—walked in the ways of the LORD and are compared to King David, the prototypical good king. More importantly, only Hezekiah and Josiah are universally acclaimed for their loyalty to Yahweh, and both undertook major religious reforms. In contrast, the Deuteronomistic Historians judged all the kings of Israel negatively for following the "way of Jeroboam son of Nebat, and in the sins that he caused Israel to commit, provoking the LORD, the God of Israel" (1 Kgs 16:26).

The Deuteronomistic worldview is succinctly stated in the blessings and curses listed in Deuteronomy 27–28: "If you will indeed obey Yahweh your God by diligently observing all his commandments, . . . all these blessings will come upon you" (28:1-2). "But, if you do not obey Yahweh your God by diligently observing all his commandments . . . , all these curses will come upon you" (28:15).

The DH ends with what the strict Deuteronomistic Yahwists predicted all along: disobedience would bring Yahweh's punishment, and that punishment came in the form of the Babylonian exile.

Suggestions for Further Reading

The phenomenon of prophecy in ancient Israel provides a fascinating set of questions. Marvin Sweeney's book *The Prophetic Literature* provides an introduction to all the prophets in the Old Testament and aims to help the introductory student make sense of their actions and speeches. Robert Wilson's *Prophecy and Society in Ancient Israel* takes a sociological approach to Israelite prophecy, placing it in comparative perspective with divine intermediation in other religions. Joseph Blenkinsopp's *Isaiah 1–39* provides a scholarly but quite understandable commentary to First Isaiah in the context of the Assyrian Empire and its threat to Judah. Alison Joseph's *Portrait of the Kings* looks at the DH and the books of Kings to investigate how the author(s) used David and Jeroboam as literary prototypes for their discussion of each king. Marvin Sweeney's *King Josiah of Judah* looks at this important king who was responsible for the DH in the light of that work and of the prophetic books. Mordechai Cogan and Hayim Tadmor's *II Kings: A New Translation with Introduction and Commentary* offers a careful scholarly analysis of the entire text, giving a highly coherent explanation of the two kingdoms of Israel and Judah. For more general works on this period, consult William Dever's *The Lives of Ordinary People in Ancient Israel*, a thoughtful introductory work that helps students understand the daily life of the average Israelite during the Iron Age. Ephraim Stern's *Archaeology of the Land of the Bible*, vol. 2, *The Assyrian, Babylonian, and Persian Periods (732–332 BCE)*, provides a solid overview of the intersection of history, archaeology, and the biblical information in this period.

18

THE RELIGIONS OF THE PEOPLE ISRAEL
AND THEIR NEIGHBORS

Richard S. Hess

Many of us think we understand the concept of religion. The Bible is a religious book; however, not everything in the Bible is necessarily religious. When archaeology is factored in, it may be difficult to distinguish what is religious and what is not. For example, many passages of the Bible describe various religious practices involving the worship of idols (and mocks them; e.g., Isa 44:1-23). But how do we recognize an idol in the archaeological record? Is the term "idol" even a good one to use? For example, Babylonian texts detailing rituals used in the production of images of gods and goddesses suggest a complicated understanding of the process as well as of the result that appears and receives the offerings of worshippers (Walker and Dick 2001).

The Hebrew Bible forbids these images in the worship of Israel's God. Indeed, the first part of the laws, commonly called the Ten Commandments, explicitly forbids the creation of any image that might be worshipped (Exod 20:2-6; Deut 5:6-10). Thus, the foundation of the Bible's version of orthodox worship resides in strict monotheism and the prohibition of idols. What the Bible remembers as essential to orthodox worship of Yahweh, Israel's deity, is the denial of the worship of other gods and of the worship of divine images. In fact, the expression "other gods" occurs sixty-three times in the Hebrew Bible (primarily in Deuteronomy, Judges, 1 and 2 Kings, and Jeremiah). This indicates how serious a threat these groups were to the Bible's own belief in the worship of Yahweh alone.

The Traditional Interpretation

Therefore, it is unsurprising that in the past century the religious world of ancient Israel has often been perceived as hosting a conflict between the gods of non-Israelite nations and Yahweh (1 Kgs 11:33; 2 Kgs 23:13) or between the local superstitions (Baals) and the national god Yahweh (Hos 2). The story of the struggle between Elijah and the prophets of Baal and Asherah on Mount Carmel (1 Kgs 18) illustrates the victory of the worship of Israel's one true God over the so-called "false gods" imported from foreign nations. Since the concern was for rain to end a drought, it was natural for people to regard Baal

FIGURE 18-1. *Baal figurine from Ugarit. Baal supplanted El as the head of the Canaanite pantheon in the southern Levant. The Bible mentions Baal worship from the earliest period of Israel's existence.*

as the god of the thunderstorm. The association of Baal and Asherah here and elsewhere in the Bible (Judg 3:7; 6:25-30; 2 Kgs 23:4; 2 Chr 33:3-4) suggests a relationship between this god and goddess as the chief couple of the Canaanite pantheon in the southern Levant.

The biblical scholar Martin Noth (1981) understood this interpretation as being a scholar's editorial message of the story of Israel (especially as found in the so-called Deuteronomistic History—Joshua, Judges, 1 and 2 Samuel, and 1 and 2 Kings) during the final years of the monarchy, supported further by an editor writing during the exile. These descriptions were either composed or embellished in order to explain the failure of Israel

FIGURE 18-2. *Temple at Tel Tayinat, located in southeastern Turkey. The temple is similar in size and style to the Solomonic temple depicted in the book of Kings.*

to worship Yahweh alone. Further, this worship of other gods and goddesses, especially as recounted in 1 and 2 Kings, explains the fall of the Northern Kingdom of Israel in 722 BCE, followed by the destruction of the Southern Kingdom of Judah in 586 BCE. Baal and Asherah became the chief opponents of Yahweh and of the success of these kingdoms as understood by the later editors of the Bible, "the Deuteronomists."

Archaeological discoveries also appear to confirm this interpretation of the religious landscape; certain architectural remains of temples could fit into the scheme as outlined by the Bible. Many three-room "long room" temples discovered to the north at sites such as Tayinat and Ain Dara share architectural features with the temple of Solomon (1 Kgs 5–8), also built by a Phoenician architect (Hurowitz 2011). The structure of a court with a sacred building and an inner holy chamber seems to parallel one south of Jerusalem at Tel Arad (Hess 2007b, 303–4).

FIGURE 18-3. *Bronze calf and shrine from Ashkelon. It is regarded as representative of the Canaanite deities El and, later, Baal.*

In the corner of the Israelite fort, there appears to be a sacred place for worship that the excavator and others associated with "Solomon's" temple in Jerusalem. Furthermore, the altar of field stones in the outer court reminded the excavators both of sacred structures of field stones occurring further south in the Negev and of the biblical requirements for using uncut stone to create such an altar (Exod 20:24-26). To the north at Tel Dan, the excavators uncovered a large area at the top of the tell that would have served as a sacred spot during the monarchy for King Jeroboam's golden calf figurine as well as a huge altar (if the size of the sole remaining "horn" of the altar is an accurate reference) positioned in front of the image (1 Kgs 12:25-33; Hess 2007b, 301–2).

To the south in the modern (Israeli) Negev, the copper-rich and well-mined Timna Valley reveals a "high place" set against a cliff where the miners would have worshipped (Hess 2007b, 202–3). Dating from approximately 1200 BCE, around the time of the supposed Israelite exodus from Egypt, this cult center contains a site with an altar for animal sacrifice along with the remains of a drain. The excavation uncovered significant remains of red-and-yellow cloth suggestive of a tent. If this evidence is so, it would be the only remaining example of a tent sanctuary similar to those used by Israel in its wilderness wanderings (Exod 25–31, 35–40). The discovery of a bronze image of a snake also invited comparison with the religious experience of Israel in its travels through this region (Num 21). Later comparisons have also been made between the camp of Israel with the tabernacle of Yahweh in its midst and the thirteenth-century BCE war camp of the Egyptian army with the tent of the pharaoh in its midst (as found portrayed on the wall of the southern Egyptian temple of Abu Simbel; Kitchen 1993).

Furthermore, the story of the golden calf in Exodus 32 gained new meaning with the discovery of a room by the gate of eighteenth-century BCE Ashkelon. In the room was a small calf made of bronze with silver-plated head and feet. Like the calf made by Israel at Sinai and the two by Jeroboam at Dan and Bethel, this earlier version seems fashioned to protect the people of the community (Hess 2007b, 155–57).

Archaeologists have located many other cult centers in the large Canaanite cities of Israel. In some cases, such as Hazor in the north, there is evidence of what could be identified as divine images that were mutilated during destruction of the site in the thirteenth century BCE—which some have associated with the Israelite attack and burning mentioned in Joshua 11 (Ben-Tor and Rubiato 1999, 35–39), while others have argued for an invasion by some other group. In other cities, such as Megiddo, a great circular altar was found from a thousand years earlier. At Gezer, large standing stones (representing deities) were found at the sacred site on the highest part of the mound. In the hill country, ancient Shechem revealed a "fortress" temple (*migdal*) with a large standing stone and an altar. While some saw no connection with the biblical record, L. E. Stager identified it with the contemporary temple mentioned in Judges 9. Other Canaanite temples have been excavated at different sites, such as Lachish, where the picture was one of a strong and thriving Canaanite religion that could challenge the worship of the God of Israel.

In addition to temple and cult shrines, other material finds reveal elements of the worship of other gods and goddesses (Hess 2007b, 297–98, 301). For instance, excavators discovered many figurines and other cultic objects at the site of Jerusalem Cave 1 outside the walls and east of the houses of the City of David. Images of horses and riders, dozens of other animals and birds, miniature altars and couches, an offering stand and a miniature (model) shrine, and female figures were placed here in the latter part of the independent kingship of Judah (eighth and seventh centuries BCE). Similar objects were found in a cave about half a mile southeast of the city gate of the Northern Kingdom's capital at Samaria. Pieces of an altar with four horns were recovered from parts of a building in Beersheba. A temple found in the fosse below the tell of the city of Lachish included a piece of gold foil inscribed with the picture of a nude goddess standing atop a horse (Ussishkin 1993b, 898–905), among other important discoveries. Variously identified as Asherah or Astarte (both mentioned in the Bible), this female figure may have appeared again in a tenth-century BCE cult stand from Taanach, a city southeast of Megiddo (Hess 2007b, 321–24). This image can be found on the lowest of four panels decorating the front of the stand, a nude female figure flanked by a pair of lions. Two panels above the female is a tree with an ibex on either side and another pair of lions positioned as on the lower panel, indicating the connection of the female goddess with the lions and the tree.

The Moabite Stele, composed by King Mesha (2 Kgs 3:4) in the ninth century BCE, refers to Chemosh, the god worshipped by the Moabites in the Bible (Num 21:29; Judg 11:24; 1 Kgs 11:7, 33; 2 Kgs 23:13; Jer 48:7, 13, 46. Hess 2007b, 275–76). This same text notes Israel's god Yahweh, whose religious items Mesha took for himself when he destroyed Israelite towns. This early mention of Yahweh suggests his (exclusive) association with Israel. The same name of this god appears in blessings written as part of letters exchanged

between the fortress commanders at Lachish and at Arad and their military leader, perhaps in Jerusalem (Hess 2007b, 283). Yahweh was the only figure used to bless the recipient in these texts from approximately 600 BCE. Some have determined that this first mention of Yahweh in the Israelite area proves that Yahweh first appeared as a deity in the Northern Kingdom of Israel in the ninth century BCE (e.g., Thompson 1992, 411–12, 423).

FIGURE 18-4. *The Mesha Stele (aka Moabite Stone), which mentions Yahweh as god of Israel, as well as Chemosh the god of the Moabites.*

MAP 18-1. *Sites important in the discussion of ancient Israelite religion.*

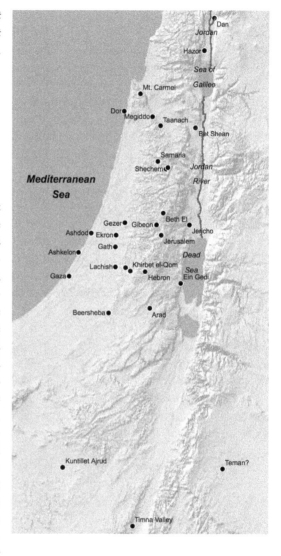

Evidence of Yahwistic worship appears in the numerous personal names on seals and seal impressions excavated in Judah in the eighth and seventh centuries BCE (and on into the early sixth century). These names are compounded with Yahweh, and we find many of the same examples of compound names in the biblical text (Hess 2007a). This suggests the prominence of the public and official worship of Yahweh. It also provides proof that Yahweh was worshipped as the chief deity in the late Judean state. The one exception is the eighth-century BCE ostraca from the Northern Kingdom's capital, Samaria. The dozens of receipts of wine and oil from estates in the region included many with personal names, with Yahweh constituting part of many of these names. However, unlike the virtually exclusive use of Yahweh in the Judean names, these included a number of personal names compounded with the divine element Baal. We also know that Baal could be taken to mean "lord, master." However, its regular use as the name of the god Baal could explain its appearance here in about 15 percent of the personal names in the Samaria ostraca. This may indicate a rise in the prominence of Baal worship in the Northern Kingdom during the first half of the eighth century BCE, the era of Jeroboam II. According to the biblical record, prophets during this time such as Amos and Hosea warned people against worshipping this false god. Evidence for greater emphasis on the deity Baal may have support in the personal names outside the Bible in addition to the messages of these prophets in the Bible.

Albertz and Schmitt present an alternative view (2012, 245–386, 482–89). Their analysis does not distinguish between personal names from earlier centuries in Israelite history and those from later periods. Rather, they conclude that the gods and goddesses represented in the personal names were similar in their distribution to other nearby states (such as Moab, Ammon, Edom, etc.).

In this survey of the traditional interpretation of Israelite religion as a monotheistic belief in Yahweh versus the worship of Baal within Israel and of other gods outside of the land, one major element remains. This source is found in textual evidence located farther from the homeland of Israel itself. In particular, there was a cultural continuity with Israel, the inhabitants of Canaan, and those people living in what is modern Lebanon, Jordan, and western and northern Syria. The most important feature that identifies this commonality is the presence of shared or closely related languages. That language family is West Semitic.

At the end of the nineteenth century, a collection of several hundred cuneiform tablets were discovered in Egypt at Tell el-Amarna (Hess 1986). These included many letters from city leaders in the West Semitic world of the midfourteenth century BCE to the pharaoh. Many of these were cities that became part of Judah and Israel in the following centuries: Hazor, Megiddo, Taanach, Shechem, Lachish, Gezer, Gaza, Jerusalem, and so forth. Yahweh is absent in the personal names and in the overt allusions to deities from this early period. Instead, the city leaders make occasional references to Baal and other deities. In one letter from Shechem, there may be a suggestion of an ancestral deity.

More important were the discoveries of archives from West Semitic cultures to the north of ancient Israel. The site of Mari along the Euphrates (near the modern border between Syria and Iraq) yielded thousands of tablets that continue to be published after many decades of research (Hess 2007b, 83–90). Dating from the eighteenth century BCE, these texts include many related to religious purposes: ritual descriptions, treaties with names of deities as witnesses, prophecies, and others. In one text (Mari A 1968), the god of the thunderstorm speaks through a prophecy. He is referred to as Adad (biblical Hadad; also written as Addu), identical in many ways to the Baal worshipped in regions to the south. Adad promises to restore the king to his throne, referring to weapons that he gave him as the weapons with which Adad defeated the Sea, which is the name of the deity that Baal defeats in the myths from Ugarit (see below). Thus, the warrior storm god of the West Semitic world fights and defeats a deity that represents the power of the Sea. Echoes of this myth have been found in the Hebrew Bible. Perhaps one of the best examples occurs in Psalms 74:12-14, where the kingship of God is affirmed by his action of splitting open the sea and breaking the heads of the (sea) monster. Ugarit also includes texts that refer to the annual death and rising of the divine Dumuzi, which remained in West Semitic and Greco-Roman myth long after Ezekiel (8:14) saw the women of Jerusalem weeping for his death (as Tammuz). Some prophetic texts describe ecstatic trances not unlike those of Saul (1 Sam 10:10-13; 19:24). These prophets prophesied favorable times for battle and other royal concerns.

In 1928, a farmer in Syria was plowing near the coast close to Ras Shamra (Hess 2007b, 95–112). He uncovered the first remains of Ugarit, an ancient metropolis that formed the center of commerce in the middle of the second millennium BCE and that then ceased to exist a few decades after 1200 BCE. By 1930, excavations on the acropolis of the ancient site yielded tablets of poetry describing the mythic adventures of deities from the Bible: El, Baal, Asherah, Astarte, Anat, and so forth. These finds likely parallel the beliefs of the Canaanites regarding their gods and goddesses. The acropolis has two temples many scholars believe were dedicated to Baal and another important deity, Dagon, who is the god of the Philistines in 1 Samuel 5:2-5. The acropolis also offers an ideal vantage point for viewing the legendary home of El, Mount Zaphon. In the Psalms (see Ps 48:2), this mountain is identified with Mount Zion.

While El is the chief god, he is older and not as involved in the battles and activities of the younger gods. Instead, they approach him for his permission and endorsement. His wife Asherah is mother of the gods. Following this couple are the chief gods and goddesses, such as Baal, Anat, and Astarte. Astarte may have been the consort of Baal, but Anat, a goddess of war, seems to have had a special relationship with him. Baal is the chief character in the longest poetic drama recorded on the tablets at Ugarit, sometimes called the Baal cycle. Although only partially preserved, the narrative describes three major events: First, Baal defeats the Sea and, like Adad at Mari, becomes a hero. He becomes a leader for the gods and goddesses and, in the second event, holds a banquet for them and builds a temple for his personal dwelling. In the third and final part of the Baal cycle, the god is killed by the god of death, Mot, who in turn is attacked by Anat. In the end, however, Baal seems alive and well again.

Some scholars insist that the Old Testament attests to the depravity of Canaanite practices (Gen 15:16; Lev 18:3-30), with its myths suggesting drunkenness and debauchery among the deities at Ugarit. For instance, one myth seems to describe how El procreates through his "daughter," Dawn and

Dusk (*CAT* 1.23). The text has strong and crude sexual imagery; however, this is not its focus (Hess 2013). The concern is more the inability of the chief human character to procreate and thus produce an heir, a concern involving prayers and sacrifices to the divine world (see Abraham and Sarah in Gen 12–22).

Among the ritual texts, one has been identified as a special sacrificial recitation for the purposing of national reconciliation or atonement (see Lev 16). This text indicates an awareness of other nations and discusses their relations. It also addresses the concern for moral failing through the incorrect performance of rituals. Another text describes a ritual for a dead king that connects the spirit of the recently deceased with those of his predecessors. *CAT* 1.119 contains a prayer to Baal to drive the enemy from the gate of the city, resembling biblical prayers to Yahweh such as the laments of Psalms and prayers of Judean kings (2 Kgs 18–19 [= Isa 36–37]; 2 Chr 20).

The sacrificial texts at Ugarit contain many names of sacrifices (burnt offering, "wave" offering, peace/fellowship offering) that resemble those found in the texts of Leviticus 1–7 and elsewhere. They use similar words to describe altars, priests, special cultic functionaries, and the tent of meeting (= tabernacle).

Ancient biblical texts undoubtedly borrowed terms and ideas from widespread West Semitic traditions. However, their context in the Bible is decidedly monotheistic, thus being profoundly different from the polytheism of the ancient world of Mari, of Ugarit, and of all the cities and places of pre-Israelite Canaan.

But is there really a difference? Scholars who followed the work of Albrecht Alt (1989 [1912]) found evidence of traces of polytheism among Israel's ancestors in many biblical passages. This evidence involved a later rewriting of what originally was an amalgamation of names of Canaanite city deities and tribal deities. These scholars further maintain that only later in its history did Israel adopt monotheism. This view promotes a strong continuity of polytheistic religion between these texts and artifacts and Israel itself.

These descriptions would have been almost entirely unknown to students of Israelite religion in the middle of the twentieth century and as late as the 1970s. However, by the end of that decade, a dramatic change took place in the archaeological and textual evidence as well as in their assessment. It is to that change and its effect on the study of ancient Israelite religion that we now turn.

The Challenges of the Last Forty Years

Challenge to the Yahweh vs. Baal Paradigm

The death of William F. Albright in 1971 represented the passing of a generation of scholars who had dominated the field in America, Europe, and Israel.

In their place arose a new generation of archaeologists and biblical scholars who rejected many of the connections between the two disciplines that earlier generations had made. While some connections remained, assumptions about matters such as patriarchal customs and their context in the Mari and Nuzi archives of the second millennium BCE, the widespread destruction of the cities (during the thirteenth century BCE) mentioned in Joshua 12, and the existence of a great Israelite empire under David and Solomon (ca. 1000 BCE) were questioned (Finkelstein and Silberman 2001; Thompson 1974; Van Seters 1975).

In the field of religion, doubts were raised concerning the assumption that there was an early monotheistic belief among the Israelites. While Alt (and others) had earlier challenged this thought, those who followed him began to push the date of emerging monotheism later and later. It had long been assumed that the Akhenaten revolution in fourteenth-century BCE Egypt provided a prototype (some popular works had even argued for a genetic connection) of the Israelite belief in a single deity that could be traced to its beginning.

Everything began to change with the 1978 discovery of Hebrew inscriptions at a site in the northeastern Sinai Desert called Kuntillet Ajrud (Meshel 2012). Excavators found what they identified as a caravanserai dating from approximately 800 BCE. In a bench-lined room inside the entrance, they discovered inscriptions on the walls and on decorated pottery that were presumably votive offerings. Many of these inscriptions expressed blessings and praise to deities, some often translated as "I bless you to Yahweh and (his) Asherah." Yahweh was sometimes identified as Yahweh of Samaria and Yahweh of Teman, places known from the Bible and other texts. These readings also confirmed a similar text identified as a tomb inscription at the Judean site of Khirbet el-Qom. Another blessing dating to around the same time as those from Kuntillet Ajrud includes a reference to blessing by Yahweh and (his) Asherah (Hess 2007b, 283–90).

The discovery and reporting of these texts formed a dramatic change in the evaluation of Israelite religion and its relationship with the surrounding environment. Already the idea of an early "Moses" figure and unique religion had been largely discarded in favor of (1) a prophetic religion introduced during the monarchy (Lang 1983), or (2) a revolution toward monotheism and a single place of worship under King Josiah near the end of the seventh century BCE (Römer 2005), or (3) an exilic/postexilic emergence of a belief in one god, as seen in the writings of Second Isaiah (Isa 40–55; Niehr 2010). The Kuntillet Ajrud evidence now demonstrated that there were no longer two poles: Canaanite polytheism and Israelite monotheism. Instead, there was a continuum where Israel and Judah were dominated by the concept of Yahweh having a consort and being comparable to the chief gods of the other nations that preceded (e.g., Ugarit) and were contemporary with Israel (e.g., Ammon, Moab, and Edom). Like El and Asherah at Ugarit, Yahweh and Asherah in Israel formed the chief divine couple, whom the worshipper could invoke to bless others. Yahweh was localized as a deity, associated with Samaria, or recognized as lord over the southern desert of Teman. While this blessing at one site could act as a local manifestation of an obscure religious cult, the same could not be argued with its appearance at both Kuntillet Ajrud and Khirbet el-Qom.

This understanding has led to attempts to identify pictures of Yahweh and Asherah in various expressions of art. For example, one of the inscriptions at Kuntillet Ajrud appears on a piece of a large broken pot. The same piece contains drawings of three figures. Many scholars want to see these as Yahweh, Asherah, and a lyre player in the background. Even when art historian Pirḥa Beck objected that the two "gods" were actually Egyptian-style Bes figures common throughout the region, some still insisted upon manifestations of Yahweh and Asherah in the form of Bes (Beck 1982; Hess 2007b, 319–21). Another supposed portrayal of Yahweh and Asherah was identified on sherds discovered by Macalister's excavation in Jerusalem. One sherd contained two humanoid figures scratched on it and was identified as portraying Yahweh and Asherah (Gilmour 2009). While possible, it remains difficult to prove the identity of the schematic figures.

Also important was the pictorial representation on the earlier (tenth-century BCE) Taanach cult stand (Hess 2007b, 321–24). As noted, the first and third (counting from the bottom) panels of the stand seem to portray the naked human figure of the goddess Asherah and her symbol, the tree. Both images on the panels are flanked by lions carved on the front and side. But what about the remaining two panels? The second scene is an empty hole opening to the back of the cult stand. There is no evidence of anything broken off that was originally present; the rim around the void has no breaks or rough spots on the terra-cotta frame that would indicate a break. Like the lions for the Asherah figure, two sphinx-like carvings flank the emptiness. The sphinx can be interpreted as the cherubim of the Bible. The fourth panel at the top of the stand portrays either a horse figure or, less likely, a calf. Over the horse figure "shines" a sun disk with wings, a symbol of the divine. The second panel may portray the invisible deity who is not represented by any image—that is, Yahweh in the most holy place of the temple with cherubim on either side. If there is a pattern to the panels, the identification of the horse representation on the fourth panel should correspond to the deity Yahweh on the second panel, just as the symbol of Asherah on the third panel corresponds to the human-like figure of Asherah on the first panel. In that case, the horse may represent an animal ridden to battle and victory by Yahweh (Hab 3:8). Here then would

FIGURE 18-5.
Taanach cult stand depicting Asherah on the bottom register.

be a pictorial combination of the textual evidence where Yahweh and Asherah represent the premiere divine couple receiving worship from the Israelites.

This interpretation is by no means the only one possible, especially for the second and fourth panels. The calf or horse may depict Baal or other deities, while the empty second panel could reflect another matter unrelated to the fourth panel. Indeed, there may be more than two deities represented on this stand.

Nevertheless, this evidence led to the reevaluation of assumptions about "orthodox" Yahwism in the period of the monarchy. Consider the case of the sanctuary in the fortress at Arad that was thought by the excavator to resemble the biblical temple of Solomon. The two incense altars at the stairs to the niche in the back of the shrine with the two standing stones in the "Most Holy" place could imply that two deities were venerated in this sanctuary (Zevit 2001, 309–10). Were they Yahweh and Asherah? Even biblical texts such as 1 Kings 18 were understood in a different light.

If these reflect an event from the period of the monarchy, then the figure of Asherah might not necessarily have been the consort of Baal. Rather, the texts would relate to whoever won the conflict on Mount Carmel (Zevit 2001, 652). If Baal were the supreme male deity in Israel, then Asherah would be his consort; however, if Yahweh won, Asherah would join him.

Thus, the traditional interpretation of the Bible—that either Yahweh alone was worshipped or that Baal was worshipped—yields to a more complex understanding of ancient Israel. Many Israelites seem to have believed that Yahweh was part of a pantheon that resembled others across the West Semitic world. The question on Mount Carmel was the major religious question of ancient Israel and Judah. But it was not whether Yahweh alone should be worshipped. Instead, the issue was the identity of the "chief god": Yahweh, Baal, or another deity entirely (M. Smith 2003).

While these discoveries were being made, epigraphers began to shed new light on the goddess. At Ugarit, hundreds of texts were uncovered in ongoing excavations, including a song to Astarte (Pardee 2007). In the first two lines, the poetic parallelism clearly identifies the goddess with a lion. Aside from

FIGURE 18-6. *Israelite sanctuary at Arad patterned after the tripartite (three-room) temple in Jerusalem. Note incense altars and standing stones are located at the back of the temple in the inner chamber or "holy of holies."*

assumptions made from the fourteenth-century BCE title "Lady of the Lions," this was their first explicit connection. Some scholars had already recognized it due to textual corruptions or blendings of the two goddesses during Israel's history; the relationship between Asherah and Astarte overlapped and may have even been interchangeable with one another in the Hebrew Bible (Hess 2007b, 322).

In addition to alternative interpretations of the Kuntillet Ajrud evidence, some have found reason to question the existence of Asherah during the monarchy (M. Smith 2003). Others doubt any significant historical value to the biblical record itself (Niehr 2010). They believe the entire history of the kings of Israel and Judah was rewritten during the exile (Römer 2005, 154, n. 109) and is thus of no value in portraying the religious history of Israel during the monarchy.

Another major aspect of Canaanite religion has been challenged with research asserting that there is no evidence of sacred prostitution or sympathetic magic (Hess 2007b, 332–35). Scholars had previously assumed that the sexual immorality so closely connected with idolatry in the Bible (e.g., Ezek 16; Hos 4:10-14) was in fact a means by which the Israelites and Canaanites sought to encourage fertility in the soil. Thus, the engagement with prostitutes was an enactment of the storm god Baal bringing fruitfulness to "mother" earth by raining upon the land. In retrospect this seems to have been an attempt to theologize the practice of engaging in extramarital sex. However, there is no evidence for such an explanation as applied to this custom. While Ishtar in Mesopotamia and Asherah/Astarte in the West Semitic world may have been a personification of sex, with engagement in sex with prostitutes at high places or other cult sites being a form of worship, there is also no evidence that this was used as sympathetic magic (Lambert 1992). Probably more went on than merely the wild parties suggested by some, but this falls short of a complete lack of connection with worship of the goddess of sex.

CHALLENGE TO THE POSTEXILIC ORIGINS OF THE PRIESTLY MATERIALS

While this new evidence and the emerging critiques focused on the old model of an overly simplistic Baal (and Asherah) versus Yahweh paradigm, other evidence regarding the Hebrew Bible's religious texts struck at further assumptions regarding the reconstruction of the religious world and history of ancient Israel—the full sense of which has yet to work its way into critical biblical scholarship.

In 1878, Julius Wellhausen published his *Prolegomena zur Geschichte Israels* (translated into English as *Prolegomena to the History of Israel*). Scholars a century prior had developed a model for the construction of the Pentateuch that portrayed different parts of the first five books of the Bible as having been written at different times. It was Wellhausen's insight to redate the composition of the Priestly materials to the period after the exile (Hess 2007b, 45–59). He argued that the priestly material—including Genesis 1, most of Leviticus, and other materials in the first five books of the Bible—should be dated to the period following the exile (539 BCE) and to the return of Jewish refugees to Judah in the late sixth and the fifth centuries BCE. Wellhausen maintained that this literature was created at that time to justify the power of the priesthood and the Levites as they oversaw the reconstruction of the temple, performed the sacrifices, and governed under the Persian administration; since there was no king in Jerusalem, the priest became the leader.

Such a reconstruction sometimes assumed that the complex rites of sacrifice found in Leviticus and elsewhere stood at the end of a long period of evolution; that is to say, Israelite religion evolved from the simplicity of early Israel's stories about their direct interactions with God to a religious system involving intermediaries and rituals that in essence increasingly blocked direct access to God. The postexilic dating for the formation of the Priestly literature served as a benchmark of critical studies of the Pentateuch for more than a century. This reconstruction of Israelite religion was based in large measure on a bigoted view of Judaism: the vibrant, diverse, liberating religion of Israel's early ancestors was reduced during the exilic period to a legal system that was eventually to become rabbinic Judaism. This anti-Semitism characterized much scholarship on biblical religion by non-Jews in the nineteenth and early twentieth centuries.

In what follows, challenges to Wellhausen's reconstruction will be noted, especially as they have appeared in the discoveries of texts related to the priestly and other religious practices found in the Pentateuch.

Perhaps the most important discovery in this area is that of the oldest biblical text ever found (Barkay et al. 2003). The Hebrew Bible was written on scrolls of papyrus and vellum that would not have survived in climates such as Jerusalem. Drier areas such as Egypt, however, preserved papyri for thousands of years. The same is true of the Dead Sea area where scrolls of the Bible have been discovered dating to the second century BCE (i.e., the "Dead Sea Scrolls"). In 1979, the excavation of several tombs from approximately 600 BCE on the western side of the Hinnom Valley, just to the west of Jerusalem, led to the accidental discovery of two small silver scrolls, which would outlast any made of papyrus. On each of the tiny scrolls was scratched a part of the blessing of Aaron as found in Numbers 6:24-26. Based on the style of their script, these texts can be securely dated to the middle or early part of the seventh century BCE, rendering them the oldest biblical texts ever found. The blessing of Aaron was generally recognized as a form of a Priestly text found in Numbers 6:24-26. Thus, this archaeological artifact directly contradicts Wellhausen and suggests that at least some of the priestly material was known long before the exile.

Other scholars had already begun questioning whether or not the priestly material of Leviticus, with its rituals and sacrifices, showed evidence of a preexilic origin (Milgrom 1991). For example, in the second millennium BCE, the Hittites had rites of blood atonement for sin that had concepts similar to

FIGURE 18-7. *One of the amulets from Ketef Hinnom.*
Dated to the seventh century BCE, the amulets contain part of the blessing of
Aaron as found in Numbers 6:24-26; therefore, the inscriptions are the oldest
biblical texts ever found.

the first millennium BCE Israelite sin and guilt offerings and rituals described in Leviticus 1–7 and 16–17 (Feder 2011). This evidence suggests that complex priestly rituals existed long before the Israelites emerged as a people in the southern Levant.

However, the most dramatic discovery was a group of cuneiform texts at Tell Meskene, located upriver from Mari along a bluff overlooking the Euphrates in modern Syria. Hundreds of cuneiform tablets from the royal archives and other sources were promptly published in the 1980s, though serious study drawing implications for the literature was reserved for the following decades. The site was identified as ancient Emar, a city known from the Mari archives. The date of the tablets was determined as the thirteenth century BCE.

While most of the contemporary cult-related texts from Ugarit contain lists of deities and details about what sacrifices were delegated to which gods, the material from Emar includes lengthy descriptions of how the rituals were performed (Hess 2007b, 112–22). For the first time, these provided parallels with biblical ritual texts found in Leviticus. For example, Emar text 369 contains the ritual for the consecration of the high priestess of the storm god followed by a series of sacrifices extending for one week. We may compare this with the seven-day festival for the consecration of the priest of Yahweh followed by sacrifices (Exod 28; Lev 8–9). Of greater importance is the anointing with oil that forms a key part of the consecration in both texts. Before the discovery of Emar 369, the only ceremony known that involved anointing with oil was one that established a king. Assuming that the biblical texts were postexilic, scholars reinterpreted the anointing ritual as a substitution for the installation of the high priest in place of the king. Thus, the priest was anointed as a king as if **Yehud** had been an independent state. However, with the discovery of the thirteenth-century BCE Emar text, it became clear that anointing a priest as a means of installation was a custom dating to this early period (Fleming 1998); this now establishes the anointing of priests as an early West Semitic custom, whenever one chooses to date the Levitical ritual.

A second ritual text, Emar 373, describes the *zukru* festival. No identical festival occurs in the Bible. However, the root of the name *zukru* is *zkr*, "to remember, invoke." This verbal root describes the Passover in Exodus 12:14 (see also Lev 23:24). There are numerous similarities between these festivals, which is an important issue in scholarly analysis of the Passover. A popular view asserts that the roasting of the lamb in the Passover ritual originated among pastoralists as a sacrifice that formed part of a spring ritual in seeking divine favor when moving from one set of pasture lands to another. The unleavened barley bread in the feast that immediately followed originated separately among villagers in thanksgiving for their harvest. Only in the late seventh century BCE did Josiah integrate the two and attach them both to the memory of the exodus from Egypt. The *zukru* festival belies this reconstruction. Like the Passover, it takes place well into the first month of the year and on the fifteenth day, and, like the Feast of Unleavened Bread, it lasts for seven days. Not only is twilight a critical time (as with the Passover), but the foods are similar. Roasted lambs, sheep, and special barley bread form part of the offerings that are also consumed. Thus, in the thirteenth century BCE, a West Semitic ritual resembling Passover was celebrated at Emar.

In this context it is perhaps worthwhile to discuss the biblical account of the reform of Josiah as described in 2 Kings 22–23. In 1805, the German scholar De Wette proposed that the "Book of the Law" discovered by King Josiah initiating the reform of Judah (ca. 622 BCE) was in fact the book of Deuteronomy. Since that time, many scholars have argued that this book was actually written at the time of Josiah and designed to justify political and religious innovations benefitting the king and securing his reign. This continues to be a popular critical position. Others have argued that Josiah's "reforms" were largely the work of a later postexilic writer who wished to superimpose monotheism on this preexilic king. (For more on this discussion, see the section entitled "Monotheism, Polytheism, and the Beliefs of Ancient Israel" below.) In any case, the Emar evidence does not conclusively prove any one interpretation of the biblical evidence; it only suggests that scholars cannot make the facile claim that rituals like the Passover and the Feast of Unleavened Bread could not predate the seventh century BCE.

We have only been able to consider a small number of the cultic parallels that are emerging with the study of this new archive. Arguably for religious purposes, the Emar texts are just as important to our understanding of the cultic background to biblical rituals as anything found at Ugarit. This is not to diminish the value of the Ugaritic texts, but it does suggest that, in addition to Ugarit and the traditions behind the Pentateuch, Emar forms a "third leg" in supporting the "stool" that describes the religion of this region around 1200 BCE.

Ultimately, the certainty of the postexilic dating for the origins of many of the practices in the so-called Priestly literature has been challenged by new data. The Syrian archives and the new texts they have yielded have changed our understanding of West Semitic religious rituals, especially those of the second millennium BCE.

CHALLENGE TO THE BIBLICAL PRIORITY IN THE RECONSTRUCTION
OF EARLY ISRAELITE RELIGION

If the "Yahweh and (his) Asherah" inscriptions have pulled Israelite religious research away from the contrast between Yahweh and Baal, and if further research into the archives of the second millennium BCE West Semitic world has challenged assumptions about many Israelite religious customs, then the assumptions concerning the priority of the Hebrew Bible as a primary source for our understanding of ancient Israelite religious practices and beliefs needs to be reexamined as well.

A minority of scholars have argued that the biblical text provides an ancient and authentic picture of ancient Israel's religious customs whose closest parallels are at Mari, at Emar, and in other second-millennium BCE cuneiform sources in the region. However, the Kuntillet Ajrud texts have certainly shed light on an area that was ignored in the biblical text, have attested the presence of Israelite religious practice that included Yahweh alongside other gods and goddesses, and perhaps have even brought a goddess such as Asherah to an equal level with Yahweh. If this was unacceptable to "orthodox" Yahwism as described in the Bible, the evidence suggests that many believed it regardless. So why then was it not condemned with any explicit description in the prophets? Prophetic texts such as Amos, Hosea, Isaiah, and Micah are relatively quick to condemn such practices in the eighth and early seventh centuries BCE in both the Northern Kingdom of Israel and the Southern Kingdom of Judah. Why is there no mention of Yahweh and Asherah together (Hess 2007b, 287–89)?

Some interpret this as evidence that the Asherah of these inscriptions was not a goddess but rather a cult object connected with Yahweh (Keel and Uehlinger 1998). Others suggest that the goddess Asherah did not even exist during the monarchy but was written into the text by later scribes who wished to vilify ancient Israel in its polytheism and justify Yahweh's judgments against it (M. Smith 2003, 26–28). Many, if not most, scholars remain convinced that the inscriptions suggest a belief that Yahweh did indeed have a consort.

Is there evidence for Yahweh and Asherah as a divine couple in the Bible? The Bible contains narratives that locate images of Asherah in temple contexts (2 Kgs 21–23). Nonetheless, apart from grammatical gender, the Bible does not make any sexual allusion to Yahweh as a male deity. This is unrelated to the few feminine similes or metaphors associated with the deity (e.g., Isa 42:14; 46:3; 49:14-15). Yahweh is not understood in any texts of the Bible as taking on male sexual characteristics of any sort. This may pertain to the numerous legal, narrative, and prophetic warnings against sexual sin and the comparisons between adultery and sexual license, on the one hand, and idolatry and the abandonment of Yahweh's covenant, on the other (see, e.g., Ezek 16; Hos 1–4). The result was the blatant absence of a connection of Yahweh with any consort such as Asherah, even in the indictments against Israel for its abandonment of the worship of Yahweh alone.

If that explanation is correct (and admittedly this is only one possible explanation), it does not detract from the need to examine the full range of archaeological and extrabiblical texts to reconstruct the most accurate picture of ancient Israelite religion. The Bible is not privileged in this research, because it seeks to portray only one strand of religious life and contrast it with select strands of what it regards as perversions.

The resulting image of ancient Israelite religious practice is incomplete. In fact, it is now apparent that there was no uniform religion practiced by all of Israel at all times. Instead, the image is one of varieties of religious practices influenced by outside cults as well as by indigenous beliefs and practices. This is true on an individual level (e.g., personal names and naming), a family level (e.g., sacrifices and burial customs [see below]), and a state level (e.g., temples and priestly rituals). The result is no longer a single Israelite religion but multiple Israelite religions at all levels of society. It is within the ferment of such diversity and change that we must turn to our final and most important topic: Where do we stand in terms of understanding the picture of monotheism in ancient Israel?

Monotheism, Polytheism, and the Beliefs of Ancient Israel

With our survey of the textual and archaeological evidence, we have observed some of the primary shifts in the study of Israelite religions over the past few decades. Perhaps the most striking shift is the recent tradition of adding an *s* to the end of the term "Israelite religion." And that leads us to the critical issue of the emergence of monotheism. The term itself is loaded with unhelpful connotations that presuppose a philosophical definition inherited from later Greek thought. Perhaps it is better to follow the contours of the biblical text and refer to this faith as exclusive belief in only one God—namely, Yahweh. In so doing, however, we also recognize that the interpretation of the biblical text itself is in dispute. As noted earlier, there remains a vigorous debate about the time of the emergence of monotheism in Israel. Thus, the biblical texts that might be understood as indicating the exclusive worship of Yahweh alone are dated according to theories about when and how religious ideas evolve.

The result is that the material remains and the extrabiblical textual evidence play an important role in answering the critical question of the origin of belief in a single deity. There remain problems here, as well. First, the biblical text does not claim that preexilic Israel possessed an exclusive belief in a single deity. The indictments of the prophets and the narratives that describe the early period are unified in their view that belief in a single deity was always in competition with other beliefs accepting additional deities. Therefore, one would expect to find witness to other deities and tendencies toward syncretism, as already noted in the Kuntillet Ajrud and Khirbet el-Qom texts, as well as the Taanach cult stand. A second area of difficulty in the material culture is the aniconic nature of the worship of Yahweh. The texts emphasize the absence of any form representing Yahweh (Exod 20:4-5; Deut 4:12, 15; 5:8-10). Therefore, we may not expect to find the normal cultic images that characterize much (though not all) of the worship of other gods and goddesses in the West Semitic world. The Taanach cult stand's second panel, if it is indeed the representation of Yahweh without an image, is unique in such a presentation; formlessness is difficult to represent as a form—or, to put it another way, the nonimage or absence of an image is Yahweh's image.

If we set aside the Bible as a primary source for historical reconstruction and turn to consider the remaining archaeological material, we find evidence that runs along two lines. There is evidence for the worship of images and deities other than Yahweh, but there is also a second strand of evidence pointing toward a unique emphasis on the worship of Yahweh.

We may review the evidence in a chronological manner. Israel's existence is first attested on the Merneptah Stele from approximately 1207 BCE (Hess 2007b, 210–16). There it is identified as a people located among the towns of Ashkelon, Gezer, and Yanoam. This would place it in the hill country of southern Canaan, where a significant increase in the villages and their population around 1200 BCE has also been observed.

Mt. Ebal is located in this Central Hill Country and is one of the earliest sites that does not conform to archaeological expectations. On the basis of pottery and scarabs, the Mount Ebal site can be dated between 1250 and 1150 BCE, the only one on the mountain from the second millennium BCE (R. Hawkins 2012). It had at least two phases of occupation. The earliest seems to have been primarily a circular stone structure containing ash and bones. The latter construction shows evidence of a field stone structure built over an earlier structure, which the excavator identified as an altar with a ramp and veranda. While some have suggested a domestic residence or a watchtower, neither the animal-bone distribution, the implements, nor the location of the site supports these interpretations. More than 2,800 animal bones attest to mostly sheep and cattle, with a smaller percentage of fallow deer and miscellaneous bones. There are no figurines such as might be found at earlier and contemporary cultic installations. If this is an altar, it is indeed anomalous compared to other altars in southern Canaan. Some archaeologists argue that this site may have been a cult center (with several buildings and courtyards surrounded by a low wall) built according to requirements of the altar in Exodus 20:23-26. Joshua 8:30-35 (cf. Josh 24) suggests that early Israel worshipped Yahweh alone at an altar on Mount Ebal. Does this somehow reflect an ancient tradition of a cultic site on this mountain, or is it merely a later development with which the structure on Mount Ebal has no relevance? Scholars cling to both sides of this debate.

The Mount Ebal site brings us to the period of Iron Age I (ca. 1200–1000 BCE), which begins with a sudden explosion of hundreds of village settlements in the Central Hill Country (Finkelstein 1988a). The region possesses many villages with houses of similar design (see chapter 10). Only a little has been discovered indicating an elite group, larger government building, palaces, and temples. Additionally, the society so far excavated is largely devoid of images, figurines, and other paraphernalia typically used in temples found in the fortified Canaanite cities of the lowlands. Therefore, the Mount Ebal site is exceptional if it does indeed have an altar; it otherwise conforms to the mostly aniconic culture of the surrounding villages.

The single significant exception to this trend is the Bull Site, located about four miles east of Dothan (Hess 2007b, 34, 236, 248). There, an oval-shaped space distinguished from the surrounding village by a small stone wall reveals a paved area with a standing stone and a bronze image of a bull. The "zebu" (hump-back) style of the bull parallels one at the city of Hazor and other places farther north of the Central Hill Country, all from the earlier period of the Late Bronze Age. It seems to have been imported and possibly used as a divine image by peoples before 1200 BCE. Perhaps some early Israelites also worshipped it as an image of Yahweh, or maybe other peoples from the north worshipped it (e.g., Girgashites, Hittites, Hivites, etc.—as in Gen 15:18-21; Deut 7:1; Josh 3:10; 24:11; Neh 9:8). We do not know. Like Mount Ebal, the Bull Site is anomalous for the Central Hill Country of Iron Age I. However, if there is an altar at Mount Ebal, the absence of images suggests a different set of beliefs and form of worship from that found at the Bull Site. Thus, we may have evidence for two strands of worship appearing at the beginning of Israel's attested existence in the highlands of southern Canaan.

As we transition into Iron Age II, the monarchic period, we have already noted many elements earlier in this chapter. The Mesha Stele identifies only Yahweh as the God of Israel, which is consistent with Yahwist monotheism but could also relate to the concept of Yahweh as the national god and head of a pantheon in Israel. The two incense altars and two stelae found in the Arad sanctuary's Most Holy place may represent the worship of two deities. However, if this sanctuary was also used (perhaps at different times) for the aniconic worship of Yahweh alone, the resulting materials found there likely would not look any different. One of the incense altars would have served that purpose, while the second altar could have been introduced when a change took place in religious policy. The sanctuary at Dan has revealed no obvious image for worship, although there were cultic paraphernalia (including the "Dancer at Dan"; see Biran 1994) consistent with the worship of a god other than aniconic Yahweh. The tenth-century BCE Taanach cult stand provides evidence of the honoring of multiple deities in this old Canaanite city.

Religion is closely related to the treatment and cult of the dead (Bloch-Smith 1992). An examination of hundreds of burials in Judean territory during the time of the monarchy revealed that every excavated burial possessed evidence of utensils that could be used for eating and drinking. It is difficult to determine if this describes some sort of consultation or connection with the dead or simply a means of respecting the deceased. These practices were forbidden in the Deuteronomic law (Deut 18:11; 26:14), even as Saul outlawed consultations in 1 Samuel 28 while performing them himself. Possibly already in Isaiah 26:14 and more clearly in Daniel 12:2 (a text from the Hellenistic Period), there was an expectation of some sort of physical resurrection. However, the biblical texts offer little about life beyond death, other than that it continues in some form. Wealthy families possessed tombs in which the body was laid out on a bench until decomposition left nothing but the bones to be collected with those of ancestors in the same tomb. This style of tomb dominated the latter part of the Judean kingdom. However, it too does not shed much light on belief in the afterlife beyond its association with one's ancestors (e.g., Gen 49:29).

During the last century of the Kingdom of Judah, the development of a distinctive art form emerged: a pillar-based female upper body and head made of clay and possessing pronounced breasts (Hess 2007b, 308–11). More than eight hundred of these forms have been identified, far more than the horse-and-rider figurines and other images from Jerusalem Cave 1 (see the section entitled "The Traditional Interpretation" above). They occur only within the perimeter of the kingdom but are found throughout Judah; however, they do not appear after 586 BCE. Archaeologists find them especially in homes and domestic contexts. The number and distribution of the figurines make it difficult to believe that this was an "opposition cult," or one otherwise unknown and uncontrolled by the state. This has led some to conclude that the Pillar Figurines represent a goddess and were an alternative to the exclusively male worship at the temple (Dever 2005).

In the view of other scholars, the mass production of several distinct types of these figurines as well as the cheapness of their clay composition works against the theory of the image of a deity. Instead, they may have provided some sort of good luck charm to encourage healthy births or to encourage lactation. Alternatively, these could be physical symbols of prayers for the same concerns. Certainty about their use is not possible at this point.

A review of contemporary extrabiblical texts mentioning Israel and Judah and their deities reveals important trends. The Mesha Stele from the ninth century BCE is actually a Moabite text. However, it is unique as an outside witness to the religious concerns of the Northern Kingdom of Israel. The text of Mesha mentions only Yahweh as god of Israel, without any mention of the image of God when Mesha describes the destruction of an Israelite town.

The mention of Yahweh and (his) Asherah at Kuntillet Ajrud and Khirbet el-Qom has already been noted. The inscriptions at the two sites form the only mention of Yahweh in association with other gods and goddesses. They originate from perhaps the same period as the Jerusalem pomegranate (ca. 800 BCE), which is likely the head of an ornate staff. Although the authenticity of the text on this small piece of art has been contested, the antiquity of the patina over the inscribed letters is without question (Hess 2007b, 276–78). The text is best read as "Belonging to the Temple of Yahweh, holy to the priests." This suggests the existence of a temple to Yahweh alone.

Of the many hundreds of seals and seal impressions (bullae) uncovered in excavations, not one of these ancient means of identification names a deity other than Yahweh. One in particular occurs on the seal of "Miqneyahu, servant of Yahweh" (Hess 2007b, 282).

The inscription found in a cave at Ein Gedi on the west coast of the Dead Sea has been dated to approximately 700 BCE on the basis of the letter forms (Aḥituv 2008, 236–39). It proclaims Yahweh alone as blessed and as ruler of the nations and also describes Yahweh as "my lord." Around the same time at Khirbet Beit Lei near Lachish (though some would date it later, ca. 600 BCE), an inscription on a burial cave declares Yahweh's sovereignty over Jerusalem and probably over Judah (Aḥituv 2008, 233–36). The writer also requests Yahweh's absolution from sin.

Among the already mentioned ostraca from Lachish, number 5 requests that Yahweh bring news of peace and well-being (Aḥituv 2008, 76–79). Lines 7–9 are especially interesting as they request, "May Yahweh show you a successful harvest today." Here Yahweh alone is mentioned as the god of fertility in the harvest; the text mentions neither the storm god Baal nor a fertility goddess such as Asherah.

In the section above entitled "The Traditional Interpretation," we mentioned the two silver scrolls found in a burial cave near Jerusalem, dated by their script to the early or middle seventh century BCE. These texts record the blessing of Aaron from Numbers 6:24-26, where Yahweh alone is the source of light, grace, and peace. The texts mention Yahweh in association with the covenant, with his covenantal love (*hesed* in Hebrew), as the Rock and one who helps and as the one who delivers from "the evil" (Aḥituv 2008, 49–55). These texts suggest that a form of the blessing found in Numbers 6 had become a common blessing.

By far the largest number of texts throughout Judah and beyond—from all periods between the ninth century BCE and the destruction of Jerusalem in 586 BCE—identify only Yahweh as a deity. Yahweh blesses others and is the source of fertility and fruitfulness. Yahweh delivers from evil, has covenantal loyalty, is a Rock, and offers help. Yahweh alone receives appeals for blessing, for absolution, and for his reign over Jerusalem and possibly Judah. While the Kuntillet Ajrud and (to a lesser extent) Khirbet el-Qom inscriptions associate Yahweh with Asherah and also mention Baal, Yahweh remains prominent, while elsewhere Yahweh is the sole deity. After the seventh century BCE, only Yahweh is mentioned in all the Judahite inscriptions.

The record of the personal names provides one other source (Hess 2007b, 269–74). The names of Israelites and Judeans, like those of their neighbors, often contained the names of deities that formed part of the personal names (referred to as a theophoric element). These combinations indicate a divine source to whom the parents might have appealed for assistance (perhaps in the birth of the child) and to whom they might have given thanks and praise. Thus, the personal names demonstrate the religious beliefs that the parents or other namers wished to make known through the name given to the child. More than seventeen hundred different names have been identified on seals, bullae, and ostraca. Some of these are identical to those names found in the Bible from the same time period, while others are previously unattested names. Some names do not include any deity. However, a general estimate suggests that about 46 percent of all such Hebrew names from before the exile include a form of Yahweh. About 6 percent include El, a name that could designate a specific god, as at Ugarit; but in biblical literature and thus in these names, it may also form a kind of title for an unspecified deity, perhaps Yahweh. Less than 1 percent of these Hebrew names mention any non-Yahweh deity as part of the name, including those names compounded with Baal, as noted from the Samaria ostraca of the early eighth century BCE. During this period, prophets in the Northern Kingdom, such as Amos and Hosea, condemned the people for worshiping Baal.

The names constructed with Yahweh omit any reference to sexual or reproductive matters. Some scholars maintain that no consort of Yahweh is implied in these names, nor is there any request for the vengeance or harming of another person, unlike some names from surrounding and earlier West Semitic cultures.

The dominance of Yahweh in theophoric Hebrew personal names is noteworthy. This almost exclusive reference to Yahweh is much more prominent among the ancient Israelites than the incorporation of national deities into personal names in surrounding nations such as Ammon, Moab, and Phoenicia. Yahweh becomes absolutely exclusive in the names dating from the final decades of Judah's existence, more than the earlier period. This trend is unique and suggests that, along with the inscriptional material, something special was going on in Israel.

Albertz and Schmitt (2012) have examined the theophoric elements in these personal names and concluded that they are similar to those in the neighboring kingdoms of Moab, Ammon, and Edom. Thus, there is nothing distinctive about the prominence of Yahweh; it is not exclusive in Israel and Judah. The arguments of this alternative position are complex and supported with much evidence and research. An important difference between this view and that of the preceding paragraph is that the exclusive reference to Yahweh appears in the later names (seventh and early sixth centuries BCE); but the study of Albertz and Schmitt does not distinguish changes in Israelite naming patterns over the centuries of the monarchy.

There are three general positions that have been taken regarding the religion of ancient Israel and the belief in a single god, Yahweh. Some argue that belief in one deity was a pervading and virtually exclusive position by the end of the preexilic period (Tigay 1986). Others maintain that belief in Yahweh did not exist to any extent until the time of Josiah (Römer 2005) or the postexilic period (e.g., Niehr 2010). Between these two poles lies a third view that sees evidence for two tracks. Throughout much of its history, Israel and Judah included those who regarded Yahweh as a chief deity in a pantheon. However, a significant collection of extrabiblical evidence suggests that at least some people recognized Yahweh alone.

Suggestions for Further Reading

The history of religion among the ancient Israelites is a large topic with many important shifts and changes. Two recent works provide accessible surveys and discussions of important aspects: Richard Hess' (this chapter's author) *Israelite Religions: An Archaeological and Biblical Survey* (2007) and Ziony Zevit's *The Religions of Ancient Israel: A Synthesis of Parallactic Approaches* (2001). The latter provides helpful information about the archaeological evidence relevant to the religion of ancient Israel and found in the land during the Iron Age. The variety and diversity of beliefs among the ancient Israelites are featured in *Religious Diversity in Ancient Israel and Judah* (2010), a collection of essays edited by Francesca Stavrakopoulou and John Barton. Many of the essays argue that the Israelites and Judahites did not limit their belief to a single deity prior to the exile.

William Dever's *Did God Have a Wife? Archaeology and Folk Religion in Ancient Israel* (2005) presents a readable introduction to Israelite religion, arguing for Asherah as the goddess of Judean women before the exile. The altar on Mount Ebal and the interpretive controversy surrounding it receive a useful survey in Ralph K. Hawkins' *The Iron Age Structure on Mt. Ebal: Excavation and Interpretation* (2012). To learn more about how the finds at Mari shape our understanding of the Hebrew Bible (especially Gen 12–36), read Daniel Fleming's essay "Abraham in History and Tradition: The Syrian Background of Israel's Ancestors" (2004). An important survey of the evidence for family and popular Israelite religion is Rainer Albertz and Rüdiger Schmitt's *Family and Household Religion in Ancient Israel and the Levant* (2012). Finally, the most useful and accurate reading, translation, and interpretation of virtually all Hebrew and Iron Age West Semitic inscriptions relevant to Israelite religion has been assembled by Shmuel Aḥituv in *Echoes from the Past: Hebrew and Cognate Inscriptions from the Biblical Period* (2008).

V

JUDAH AS A PROVINCE

FROM THE BABYLONIANS TO THE PERSIANS

19

DESTRUCTION AND EXILE
Israel and the Babylonian Empire

Bob Becking

A quick look at the Wikipedia page "Babylonian captivity" offers its readers the traditional view on this decisive and incisive period in the history of ancient Israel. According to this view, the exile was a phase in Jewish history when they were captives in Babylon. Some dates are given: the exile started with a three-stage deportation—597, 587, and 582 BCE—and it ended with the conquest of Babylon by the Persian king Cyrus the Great in 538 BCE. The Persian king then gave permission for return to the area around Jerusalem and the rebuilding of the devastated temple.

First, I would like to remark that the label "Jewish" in this period is an anachronism based on a claimed tradition. Historically speaking, Judaism arose out of the ancient Yahwistic religion only after the conquest of Alexander the Great. The traditional Jewish view that the life and customs of the exiles in Babylon already were a form of Judaism—including synagogues—cannot be reinforced by existing evidence.

Second, and more important, is the fact that recent research and new evidence have changed the concept of exile as well as the historical view on that period. In this chapter, the results of that change will be displayed in a more or less thematic order.

Babylon and Israel

Before the exilic period, there was not much contact between Babylon and Israel, since they were at the opposite ends of the Fertile Crescent. The narrative on the Tower of Babylon in Genesis 11 is a legend set in the dawn of civilization. No historical data can be drawn from this text. Abram is said to have migrated from Ur of the Chaldeans to the promised land (Gen 11:31). This is an obvious anachronism, since this Aramaic-speaking tribe only entered the stage of history in the eighth century BCE (Dietrich 1970). Abram's origin in Babylon should be read instead as a claimed tradition that functioned as a sign of hope for return to the exiles living under Chaldean rule in Babylon. After the conquest of Samaria by the Assyrians in 722 BCE, Babylon came into the orbit of Israel as a result of the Neo-Assyrian deportation politics that brought people from "Babylon, Cuthah, Avva, Hamath, and Sepharvaim, and placed them in the cities of Samaria" (2 Kgs 17:24).

During the reign of King Hezekiah of Judah, the Babylonian ruler Merodach-Baladan sent diplomats to visit to Jerusalem, offering an anti-Assyrian alliance. The prophet Isaiah warned the Judahite king to be reticent because "[d]ays are coming when all that is in your house, and that which your ancestors have stored up until this day, shall be carried to Babylon" (2 Kgs 20:17), a clear indicator of the exile. Although a Babylonian king, Marduk Apla Iddina II, is known to have ruled at the end of the eighth century BCE, it should be noted that the story in 2 Kings 20 is molded after the conquest of Jerusalem. It was eventually the decline of the Neo-Assyrian Empire that enabled the Chaldeans to create their own Neo-Babylonian Empire, which after some time also influenced the history of Israel.

The Rise of Babylon and Its Conquest of Assyria

Babylon's rise to power was in part triggered by the brute and rigid measures taken by the Neo-Assyrian king Sennacherib in his eighth campaign. After a siege of fifteen months, the Assyrian army conquered the city of Babylon in 689 BCE. Sennacherib devastated the city, flooded it with water, and brutally massacred many people (Sennacherib Taylor Prism v:17–vi:34). This conquest became a scar on the national identity of the Babylonians.

The traumatic events in 689 BCE functioned as a catalyst that led to the formation of a Babylonian national identity that would function as the basis of the Neo-Babylonian Empire. During the seventh century BCE, several wars between Assyria and Babylonia took place; the most well known is the war between the two brothers Ashurbanipal and Shamash-shumu-ukin (652–648 BCE). In the power vacuum after the death of Ashurbanipal (630 BCE), the Chaldean sheikh Nabopolassar took advantage and rose to power. He exploited the growing "national" identity of the Babylonians and joined forces with the urban elite. They installed him as king of Babylonia in 626 BCE, and he spent the first ten years of his reign ridding the Babylonian area from Assyrian influence. In 616 BCE, Nabopolassar started campaigning directly against Assyria and joined forces with Kyaxares, the king of the Medes. The joint forces of Media and Babylon ultimately conquered Assyria, and the capital city, Nineveh, fell in 612 BCE. The "Nabopolassar Epic" presents the destruction of Nineveh as an ultimate revenge for the devastation of Babylon in 689 BCE. In 610 BCE, the last Assyrian stronghold, Harran, fell. The Egyptians came to the Assyrians' defense, but the Babylonian army under Crown Prince Nebuchadnezzar soundly defeated them in the famous battle of Carchemish (605 BCE), bringing Assyria to an end and elevating Babylonia to the major power in the region.

FIGURE 19-1. *The restored Adad Gate at Nineveh.*
One of the fifteen gates of the city.

Judah under the Babylonians

After the decisive victory at Carchemish, Nebuchadnezzar learned of the death of his father, Nabopolassar. He returned to Babylon and was quickly acknowledged as king by all. He centralized power in the city of Babylon and restored the city as never before. As a result of the treaty with the Medes, he had to

FIGURE 19-2.
Babylon in 1932.
Note the mud-
brick construction
of the walls.

give Media influence over parts of the Assyrian mainland. Nebuchadnezzar, however, gained power over the areas conquered in the Levant. The conquest of Jerusalem and the beginning of the deportation of exiles to Babylon was the outcome of a historical process in which the Babylonians wanted to strengthen their control over the area near the Egyptian border, while in the meantime some political factions in Jerusalem overestimated their own military strength as well as the ability of Egypt to provide meaningful help.

BABYLON'S CONQUEST OF JUDAH

Written evidence for the conquest of Jerusalem is to be found in the Hebrew Bible and in a fragment in a Babylonian Chronicle. In 2 Kings 24:1-2, we read:

> In his days King Nebuchadnezzar of Babylon came up; Jehoiakim became his servant for three years; then he turned and rebelled against him. The LORD sent against him bands of the Chaldeans, bands of the Arameans, bands of the Moabites, and bands of the Ammonites; he sent them against Judah to destroy it, according to the word of the LORD that he spoke by his servants the prophets.

The narrator in the book of Kings continues with a few more theological remarks: in them, the siege of Jerusalem is construed as a result of transgressions against YHWH. At just this time, King Jehoiakim of Judah died and was succeeded by his son Jehoiachin.

> Jehoiachin was eighteen years old when he began to reign; he reigned three months in Jerusalem. His mother's name was Nehushta daughter of Elnathan of Jerusalem. He did what was evil in the sight of the LORD, just as his father had done.
>
> At that time the servants of King Nebuchadnezzar of Babylon came up to Jerusalem, and the city was besieged. King Nebuchadnezzar of Babylon came to the city, while his servants were besieging it; King Jehoiachin of Judah gave himself up to the king of Babylon, himself, his mother, his servants, his officers, and his palace officials. The king of Babylon took him prisoner in the eighth year of his reign. (2 Kgs 24:8-12)

This report has a counterpart in a Babylonian Chronicle:

> (11) The seventh year:
>   In the months Kislev the king of Akkad mustered his army and marched to Hattu.
> (12) He campaigned ag[ainst] the city of Judah and on the second day of the month Adar he captured the city and seized the king.
> (13) A king of his own [choice] he appointed in the city.
>   He took a vast tribute and took it to Babylon.

As has generally been accepted, the two Judahite kings referred to in this inscription are Jehoiachin and Zedekiah. This historical note connects the first year of Jehoiachin's imprisonment with Nebuchadnezzar's seventh regnal year in the Babylonian system of counting years—that is, sometime between spring 598 and spring 597 BCE (Parker and Dubberstein 1946, 27). A second conquest is mentioned only in the book of Kings:

> And in the ninth year of his reign, in the tenth month, on the tenth day of the month, King Nebuchadnezzar of Babylon came with all his army against Jerusalem, and laid siege to it; they built siege-works against it all round. So the city was besieged until the eleventh year of King Zedekiah. On the ninth day of the fourth month the famine became so severe in the city that there was no food for the people of the land. Then a breach was made in the city wall; the king with all the soldiers fled by night by the way of the gate between the two walls, by the king's garden, though the Chaldeans were all round the city. They went in the direction of the Arabah. But the army of the Chaldeans pursued the king, and overtook him in the plains of Jericho; all his army was scattered, deserting him. Then they captured the king and brought him up to the king of Babylon at Riblah, who passed sentence on him. They slaughtered the sons of Zedekiah before his eyes, then put out the eyes of Zedekiah; they bound him in fetters and took him to Babylon. (2 Kgs 25:1-7)

The absence of a remark on this event in Babylonian inscriptions cannot function as an argument against its historicity, especially since it is well known that the accounts in the Babylonian Chronicles are rather fragmentary.

A quick calculation makes clear that over ten years passed between the first and the second conquest of Jerusalem. Oded Lipschits has developed an intriguing theory on the delay in the Babylonian consolidation of their Judahite conquest (2005, 36–133). In his view, the Babylonians were not very much interested in economically and administratively consolidating their Levantine conquests. Lipschits assumes that the Babylonians suffered from a lack of administrative knowledge and skills to control the whole western territory. Therefore, Judah could remain a vassal under Zedekiah, despite the revolt of Jehoiachin. The Babylonians generally turned the territory of a vassal into a province after a rebellion. According to Lipschits, Babylonian politics changed dramatically as a result of the acts of the Egyptian kings Psammetichus II and Hofra (Apres), who challenged Babylonian power with military pinpricks.

In reaction, the Babylonians would have intensified their control over the western part of the empire. They also would have changed their attitude toward disloyal vassals into some sort of zero-tolerance politics. This shift would eventually lead to the conquest of Jerusalem in 587/586 BCE.

Lipschits offers an interesting example that accounts for a greater part of the existing evidence and is generally more convincing than the remarks of some minimalists who state that the absence of evidence in Babylonian sources for a conquest in 587/586 BCE makes the report in 2 Kings 25 nonhistorical.

Archaeology has revealed a few (but interesting) pieces of evidence for the destruction of the city by the Babylonians. On the side of the defenders stands a fortified tower, whose remains were uncovered in 1975. The tower is a massive six-meter-high construction that shows signs of attacks and remains of a fire. In the direct vicinity of this defensive tower, four bronze arrowheads were found. Since these arrowheads can be classified by their triple-winged form as of Scythian origin, they give evidence of a Scythian presence in the Babylonian army (Avigad 1980). The prophet Jeremiah knew of Scythians, although he refers to them as "Ashkenaz" (Jer 51:27). Another piece of evidence of the Babylonian attack and conquest can be seen in the destruction of residential houses in Jerusalem by fire (Shiloh 1984, 18–19).

Interesting evidence on the march of Nebuchadnezzar's army to Jerusalem is to be found in the Lachish Letters. This is a group of ostraca with inscriptions written in Paleo-Hebrew script uncovered near the city gate of Lachish. They date from the period just before the conquest of Jerusalem (Torczyner 1938). They contain letters written by a certain Hoshaiah to Jaush, the officer in command at Lachish. Hoshaiah most probably was in charge of a nearby military post. He communicated to Jaush on the military situation at the threshold of Judah. The Babylonian army is not mentioned as such, but between the lines the conflict is apparent. One of the letters, however, refers to Chonia, the son of Elnathan, who was on a mission to Egypt for help:

> Your servant, Hosayahu, sent to inform my lord, Yaush: May YHWH cause my lord to hear tidings of peace and tidings of good. And now, open the ear of your servant concerning the letter which you sent to your servant last evening because the heart of your servant is ill since your sending it to your servant. And inasmuch as my lord said "Don't you know how to read a letter?" As YHWH lives if anyone has ever tried to read me a letter! And as for every letter that comes to me, if I read it. And furthermore, I will grant it as nothing. And to your servant it has been reported saying: The commander of the army Konyahu son of Elnatan, has gone down to go to Egypt and he sent to commandeer Hodawyahu son of Ahiyahu and his men from here. And as for the letter of Tobiyahu, the servant of the king, which came to Sallum, the son of Yaddua, from the prophet, saying, "Be on guard!" your ser[va]nt is sending it to my lord. (Torczyner 1938)

Another letter refers to the cities of Lachish and Azekah:

And let it be known to my master that we will be looking for the signals from Lachish, according to the instructions which he has given, for no signals from Azekah have been seen.

The absence of a fire signal from Azekah—a Judahite city not far from Lachish—might indicate that Azekah had already been conquered by the Babylonians. Jeremiah 34:7 indicates that during the siege of Jerusalem in 586, the cities of Lachish and Azekah were the only strongholds still under Judahite control. All in all, the Lachish letters communicate a sense of anxiety connected to the forthcoming conquest of Judah and Jerusalem. This can be connected with the result of archaeological excavations throughout Judah that indicate that the great majority of the seventh century cities and fortifications in Judah and Philistia have been were destroyed at the end of the Iron Age, a fact that agrees with the textual accounts of Babylon's conquests in this area (Faust 2012a, 21–32).

FIGURE 19-3. *The Lachish Letters were a group of letters written on ostraca (potsherds) uncovered in a burnt layer in the guardroom by the gate of the Judean city of Lachish. The letters point to the last days of the city during the invasion of Judah by the Babylonians in 586 BCE.*

ISSUE OF THE EMPTY LAND

A historical myth is a social construction of the past that functions within the value system of a community or society and serves some ideologies within that society. Our world is full of historical myths. It is the task of serious journalism to deconstruct them, as it is the task of serious historical research to unmask them.

In the traditional historiography of the Babylonian exile, the "myth of the empty land" has been a standard fabric. The idea is based on a note in the book of Chronicles:

He took into exile in Babylon those who had escaped from the sword, and they became servants to him and to his sons until the establishment of the kingdom of Persia, to fulfill the word of the LORD by the mouth of Jeremiah, until the land had made up for its sabbaths. All the days that it lay desolate it kept sabbath, to fulfill seventy years. (2 Chr 36:20-21)

According to this text, the land of Judah was laid waste and was sparsely inhabited for seventy years as a punishment for not keeping the commandment to give the land a sabbatical every seventh year (see Lev 25:1-12). The myth of the empty land assumed that during the Babylonian Period the territory of the former Kingdom of Judah was uninhabited. Everyone important had been exiled with the court to Babylonia. In 597 BCE, Nebuchadnezzar had emptied Jerusalem:

> He carried away all Jerusalem, all the officials, all the warriors, ten thousand captives, all the artisans and the smiths; no one remained, except the poorest people of the land. He carried away Jehoiachin to Babylon; the king's mother, the king's wives, his officials, and the elite of the land, he took into captivity from Jerusalem to Babylon. (2 Kgs 24:14-15)

Nevertheless there were still persons living in Jerusalem, so that after the second conquest

> Nebuzaradan the captain of the guard carried into exile the rest of the people who were left in the city and the deserters who had defected to the king of Babylon—all the rest of the population. But the captain of the guard left some of the poorest people of the land to be vine-dressers and tillers of the soil. (2 Kgs 25:11-12)

These reports in the book of Kings gave rise to the idea that only a few socially unimportant persons (at least in the eyes of the editors) were left in the land. Thus, the textual tradition is itself clear that some people remained in the land.

Hans Barstad has deconstructed this view and unmasked it as a historical myth. His analysis of the textual data and the archaeological evidence showed that "the land was not empty." The territory of the former Kingdom of Judah remained inhabited, and these surviving groups have contributed more to the emergence of the Hebrew Bible than generally assumed (Barstad 1996; 2008, 90–134). His view is mainly based on an evaluation of archaeological data that indicate a continuity of activities in the territory under consideration.

His view has been challenged, for instance by David Vanderhooft. Central to his challenge is a dispute on the dating of the archaeological evidence. Vanderhooft (1999) stresses that the dating of the archaeological evidence on which Barstad builds his thesis should be treated with great care. Bustenay Oded (2003) defends the thesis of radical discontinuity between the late monarchic and the Babylonian periods in Judah. His argument, however, is far from convincing. Lisbeth Fried (2003) agrees with Barstad that Judah was not a space empty of people during the "exilic" period, but she modifies his thesis by arguing that Judah was empty of its God. Despite these remarks, Barstad's view is still valid, although it is in need of modification: although life in the rural areas continued, the land as such was devastated (Faust 2012a).

EVIDENCE OF ARCHAEOLOGY

The more general archaeological observations are of great importance. It is remarkable that, during the Babylonian Period, the number of inhabitants in the area of Bethel and Mizpah was quite constant, while the habitation of Jerusalem appears to have dropped significantly. About thirty years ago, Kochavi (1972) argued that archaeological data hinted at an approximately 25 percent increase in the population of Judah/Yehud at the beginning of the Persian Period. His estimates, however, are now obsolete due to new findings and surveys. More recent estimates based on the new data seem to be more accurate. It should be noted, however, that all estimates are quite rough since such calculations are made using uncertain and vague parameters. Scholars reckon with different numbers—for instance, the number of people that would have lived *per dunam*. Nevertheless, all recent estimates of demographic changes in Judah/Yehud show a comparable pattern (Carter 1999; Lipschits 2005, 185–271; Faust 2012a, 119–48):

- A decrease of the population is observable from the late monarchic or Iron IIC Period to the Babylonian or Iron III Period. A concentration of the population in the Bethel-Mizpah area is visible, indicating that "those who remained in the land" concentrated in the northern part of the former Kingdom of Judah.
- A clear continuity between the Neo-Babylonian and the Persian I Periods is also discernible. This implies that the land of Judah was not empty during the so-called exilic period and that a considerable part of the population of Judah/Yehud in the Persian I Period consisted of the descendants of those who remained in the land.
- The population of Judah/Yehud in Persian I has been estimated at 13,350 persons (Carter 1999, 201), which is about 30 percent of the 42,000 persons implied in the list of returnees in Ezra 2 and Nehemiah 7. It is not easy to decide how many of these 13,350 persons should be construed as returning exiles. The archaeological record, however, can give a few clues. The number of "New P sites"—that is, sites that were inhabited for the first time in the Persian I Period—in the various environmental niches of Yehud is 27 percent. Considering that not all returnees settled in new sites and that some of the descendants of those who remained in the land moved to these

new sites, the number of returnees in Persian I might be estimated at 4,000 persons at a maximum.

• Assuming that 4,000 persons is the correct number, it should be noted that their return most probably took place during various waves of movement during Persian I, a fact that comports well with the narratives in Ezra and Nehemiah.

• Carter and Hoglund have observed an increase in population in Judah/ Yehud during the Persian II Period. Carter estimates the population of Yehud in this period at 20,650 persons. This increase, of course, could have been the result of a natural expansion of the population. The scale of the increase, however, is such that it is more probable to suggest an influx from outside. Hoglund makes a connection with general political measures of the Persian Empire. In the middle of the fifth century BCE, the Persians seem to have stimulated trade affairs in and with Yehud, leading to new returnees and an increase of the population (Hoglund 1992a, esp. 57–59, 63–64; 1992b). He even argues that the missions of Ezra and Nehemiah should be construed as "an effort on the part of the Achaemenid Empire to create a web of economic and social relationships that would tie the community [in Yehud] more completely into the imperial system" (Hoglund 1992b, 244). This influx roughly coincides with the appearance of Nehemiah on the scene in Jerusalem and its vicinity.

The general picture that emerges is that of a demographic decrease in the early sixth century BCE, followed by a very slow increase during the Persian Period. From the archaeological data, a "return to Zion" is not testified. The evidence available supports Barstad's view and besides cannot be connected to a theory of mass return in the sixth century BCE. It hints toward the direction of the assumption of a process of waves of return that lasted for over a century.

Babylonian Chronicles

These chronicles relate the activities of the Neo-Babylonian kings. Although the available cuneiform tablets date to the Seleucid Period, it is safe to assume that the originals were composed in the Persian Period (Grayson 1975a, 69–114; Gerber 2000; Albertz 2001, 47). Unfortunately, the tablets are often broken and fragmentary. Entries for the years 594–558, 556, 552–550, and 544–540 BCE are absent entirely. In line with their genre, these chronicles relate only events that were important from the point of view of the Babylonian court. The fact that Babylonian Chronicle V mentions the conquest of Jerusalem indicates that this event was important enough to be recalled.

Excavations in Babylon

The German architect Robert Koldewey (1855–1925) achieved world fame with his excavation of Babylon. His innovation was the application of a method by which he could identify excavated mud bricks and thus reconstruct several buildings that otherwise would have gone unnoticed. Among Koldewey's finds were the outer and the inner walls of the city, which provided a robust defense to the city. Perhaps the most famous feature of these walls is the so-called Ishtar Gate. This was the eighth gate in the outer wall of the city and gave entrance to a magnificent roadway that led to the center of the city. The construction is made of blue glazed bricks.

FIGURE 19-4. *The modern reconstruction of the Ishtar Gate in the Pergamon Museum in Berlin. Ishtar was the Mesopotamian goddess of love.*

The roadway functioned as a processional way in the yearly *akitu*, or New Year Festival. Part of this processional way has been reconstructed and is on display in the Pergamon Museum in Berlin. Other parts of the buildings are scattered over various museums all over the world. Koldewey also found the foundation of the Etemenanki temple. This Sumerian temple's name can best be rendered as "the house of the connection between heaven and earth." According to the description in a late Babylonian cuneiform text, the temple must have been ninety-one meters high. Herodotus (*Histories* 1.181) gives a

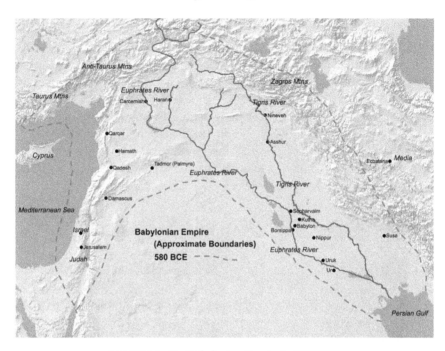

MAP 19-1. *The Babylonian Empire in 580 BCE.*

hyperbolic description of a sacred precinct for Jupiter Belus that can be identified with the Etemenanki. The building plan of the Etemenanki is comparable
to the ancient Sumerian *ziggurat* temples. A cuneiform text of uncertain provenance contains an inscription on the construction of the building and next
to it an image of the tower. The Etemenanki has often been identified with the
Tower of Babel as mentioned in Genesis 11.

Until the excavations by Koldewey, another notable feature of ancient
Babylon—the Hanging Gardens of Babylon—was only part of a legendary
tale according to which a Babylonian king made a beautiful mountain in the
midst of his city for his homesick wife, who had come from the mountainous
area of the Medes. The oldest reflex of this legend is found in the writings of the
Babylonian priest Berossus (around 300 BCE). Berossus' view is known from a
quotation in Josephus' *Contra Apion* 1.19:

> In this palace he erected very high walks, supported by stone pillars; and by
> planting what was called a pensile paradise, and replenishing it with all sorts
> of trees, he rendered the prospect an exact resemblance of a mountainous
> country. This he did to gratify his queen, because she had been brought up in
> Media, and was fond of a mountainous situation. (Whiston 2015)

His contemporary Diodorus Siculus was the first to use the depiction "Hanging Gardens" in a tradition that—as he claimed—went back to the fifth-century BCE Greek historian Ctesias. Ctesias, however, does not refer to these gardens in his known writings (Dalley 1994). Koldewey's excavations in Babylon uncovered, in the northeastern part of the city, a structure that contained various features mentioned in the legendary texts on the Hanging Gardens. Koldewey identified this structure with the Hanging Gardens, but his identification has been contested for two reasons: (1) the location of this structure did not concur with the tradition that locates the hanging gardens on the banks of the Euphrates; (2) in this structure, many administrative cuneiform inscriptions were found, which indicates that the building was used as a storeroom (Finkel and Seymour 2008).

Apart from discoveries of monumental architecture, there are a host of textual artifacts that have been uncovered in Mesopotamia. Of importance to our topic, excavations at Babylon have uncovered a variety of so-called assignment lists. These texts list names of prisoners at the Babylonian court who were allowed rations of food. One of these documents refers to [*Ia*]-'*ú-kinu*/*Ia-ku-ú-ki-nu* = **Yahu-kin*—in biblical terms, Jehoiachin (Hebrew, *Yahuyakin*)—his five sons, and some other Judahites as regular receivers of portions of food from the Babylonian king, as becomes clear from the following passage:

(a)   To Ya'u-kin, king [of the land of Yaudu].
(b)   1/2 (PI) for Ya'ukinu, king of the land of Ya[hu-du]
        2 1/2 sila for the fi[ve] sons of the king of the land of Yahudu
        4 sila for eight men, Judeans [each] 1/2 [sila]
(c)   1/2 (PI) for Ya'u[-kinu]
        2 1/2 sila for the five sons . . .
        1/2 (PI) for Yaku-kinu, son of the king of the land of Yakudu
        2 1/2 sila for the five sons of the king of Yakudu by the hand
        of Kanama.
(d)   . . . Ya]'u-kinu, king of the land of Yahudu [. . . the five sons of the
        king] of the land of Yahudu by the hand of Kanama.

The lists under consideration are dated to the thirteenth year of King Nebuchadnezzar, which is 592 BCE. These documents provide direct nonbiblical evidence that the Babylonian court maintained Jehoiachin during his exile, or imprisonment. The texts do not, however, even hint at some sort of release or amnesty as is narrated in the book of Kings (2 Kgs 25:27-30). Moreover, these assignment lists make clear that the Babylonians adopted a custom known from Assyrian inscriptions. These earlier inscriptions make clear that according to the Assyrian worldview, prisoners at the court had a right to live. Food and even women had to be given to them. The assignment lists reveal that the

Judahite royal family and its entourage were imprisoned at the Babylonian court, but at the same time they were well cared for.

Several cuneiform documents of great importance have surfaced recently (Joannès and Lemaire 1999). The first document is dated to the seventh year of Cyrus (532 BCE) and is a receipt for one shekel of silver. This shekel was the payment of the *ilku* tax by Bunanitu (the widow of Achiqar, the governor) to Abda-Yahu. Both *Ab-da-ia-hu-ú* (i.e., Abda-Yahu) and his father *Ba-rak-ka-ia-ma* have clear Judahite names. The document was written in URU *ša* ᴾ*na-šar*, "the City-of-Nashar," i.e., "'Eagleton,' most probably in the vicinity of Borsippa" (Pearce 2006).

One document is of great importance for the construction of the history of the exile. This document refers to the sale of a bovine by Hara, the daughter of Talimu and "Nerî-Jahu, the son of Achiqam." The transaction took place in *al Ya-hu-du*, "the city of Judah/Yehud," in Babylonia, in 498 BCE (Lambert 2007). The designation "the city of Judah" reflects the politics of the Neo-Babylonians to bring deportees together in specific ethnic groups. The cities in which these persons were settled were often named after their area of origin. There exists evidence for a number of exiled communities outside of the boundaries of Judah, such as Ashkelon, Gaza, Neirab, Qadesh, Qedar, and Tyre.

The most important conclusion that can be drawn from these texts is the fact that, obviously, not all the descendants of the exiled Judahites immediately returned to Jerusalem after the conquest of Babylon by Cyrus. The inscriptions as a whole indicate the following:

(1) The exiled Judahites remained a separate ethnic group in Babylonia, at least for the majority of them.
(2) Many of them were settled in newly reclaimed agricultural areas.
(3) A group descending from Judahite exiles enjoyed a modicum of prosperity and self-governance.
(4) After the conquest of Babylon by Cyrus, not all descendants of these exiles returned to Yehud.

It is a remarkable fact that these texts attest that the Judahites and their descendants acted in various roles in transactions that were important enough to be registered. They are not only listed among the witnesses but also mentioned as buyers and sellers of goods and properties. Before we arrive at some preliminary conclusions, it should be noted "that all of the transactions are in the context of work done as obligations to royal lands. These are not the transactions of entirely free people working in a true capitalistic market economy" (Pearce 2011). Next to that, it becomes clear that both "Eagleton" and "New Yehud" were newly established locations that were of importance for the production of food for the increasing population in the Babylonian Empire and later Persian

Empire. This feature does not tally with the traditional image of exile and the myth of the unified mass return.

The book of Jeremiah contains a letter intended for the exiles living in Babylonia. This letter appears to be a response to questions asked by the exiles about the organization of their lives in Babylon:

> Build houses and live in them; plant gardens and eat what they produce. Take wives and have sons and daughters; take wives for your sons, and give your daughters in marriage, that they may bear sons and daughters; multiply there, and do not decrease. But seek the welfare of the city where I have sent you into exile, and pray to the LORD on its behalf, for in its welfare you will find your welfare. (Jer 29:5-7)

In its present literary context, the letter is connected to exiles of the first wave—that is, after the first conquest of Jerusalem by the Babylonians in 597 BCE. Traditionally, the letter has been construed as addressed to Judahites living in the city of Babylon. From a historical point of view, its contents could be widened to a larger period. The words of Jeremiah can easily be applied to the life of exiled Judahites in "Eagleton," "New Yehud," or elsewhere in Babylonia.

Two additional archaeological discoveries deserve attention in this context. In 1996, Joseph Naveh published a Persian-Period jar handle with a seal impression that had been found in Tel Ḥarasim, near Kibbutz Kfar Menachem, in the Shephelah (Naveh 1996, 44–47). This find was of no major importance, since a variety of seal impressions have been found from the Persian Period. The inscription on the seal is quite standard:

לחננו יהוד
Belonging to Ḥananu Yehud

What is astonishing is the fact that over one hundred years ago a very similar, if not identical, seal impression on a Persian-Period jar handle had been unearthed during German excavations in Babylon. That seal impression had not been published, but Naveh printed a nice photograph for his readers, supplied to him by the Vorderasiatisches Museum in Berlin. Both seal impressions have the same inscription. It is only due to the wear and tear of the ages that both impressions cannot completely be compared. It could be argued that the impressions were made by the same seal. If so, then this identification has an interesting implication: it hints at the existence of commercial contacts between Yehud and Babylon during the Persian Period. The jars most probably contained wine or olive oil imported from Yehud. It is likely, therefore, that well-to-do Babylonian or Yehudite families in Babylon occasionally enlivened their banquets with a *Grand Cru Shephelah*(!).

The Role of the Deuteronomistic Historians and Editors of the Biblical Text

As Rainer Albertz has argued convincingly, the Hebrew Bible contains a set of views on exile and destruction: the book of Kings construes the exile as the (provisional) end of history; the book of Jeremiah sees it as a spoiled chance for salvation; and the book of Chronicles interprets the exile as a period of Sabbath rest for the land (2001, 14–22). Let us focus first on the views expressed in the final chapter of the book of Kings. This biblical book ends with two narratives that inform the reader on historical events as well as on the religious assessment of these events: the assassination of Gedaliah and the amnesty for Jehoiachin.

The book of 2 Kings (25:22-26) narrates the murder of Gedaliah, who was appointed governor over those Judahites who remained in the land by the Babylonians after the destruction of Jerusalem in 587 BCE. This narrative has a parallel in the book of Jeremiah (Jer 40:7–41:15). The report in the book of Jeremiah has more details than the much shorter note in the book of Kings (2 Kgs 25:22-26). The Jeremiah account contains the following additional details:

(1) Jeremiah identifies the names of the various persons who assumably were involved in the incident. The account in Kings identifies only the main characters.

(2) The book narrates a temporary migration of Judahites to the territories of Ammon, Edom, and Moab. This detail is missing entirely from Kings.

(3) The author of the book of Jeremiah informs its readers about the political background of the assassination. About Jehohanan, the son of Kareah, it is narrated that he, together with a group of leaders, would have warned Gedaliah about his forthcoming fate: "'Are you at all aware that Baalis king of the Ammonites has sent Ishmael son of Nethaniah to take your life?' But Gedaliah son of Ahikam would not believe them" (Jer 40:14).

(4) Finally, Jeremiah reports the slaughter of a group of mourning pilgrims on their way to Jerusalem by Ishmael (Jer 41:4-8).

Strangely enough, a remark on the Gedaliah incident is absent from 2 Chronicles. A reference in Josephus, *Antiquities*, remarks that the deportation of a group of Ammonites in the twenty-third year of Nebuchadnezzar should be construed as the Babylonian answer to the assassination of Gedaliah:

> And when they were there, God signified to the prophet that the king of Babylon was about making an expedition against the Egyptians, and commanded him to foretell to the people that Egypt should be taken, and the king of Babylon should slay some of them and, should take others captive,

and bring them to Babylon; which things came to pass accordingly; for on the fifth year after the destruction of Jerusalem, which was the twenty-third of the reign of Nebuchadnezzar, he made an expedition against Coelesyria; and when he had possessed himself of it, he made war against the Ammonites and Moabites; and when he had brought all these nations under subjection, he fell upon Egypt, in order to overthrow it; and he slew the king that then reigned and set up another; and he took those Jews that were there captives, and led them away to Babylon. (Josephus, *Jewish Antiquities* 10.180–182 [Whiston 2015])

Josephus, however, composed his *Antiquities* in the first century CE and can therefore not be taken as a reliable primary source. This text simply states what Josephus understood based on the information available to him six hundred years after the fact.

It is interesting to note that the three personal names—*Gdlyhw* (Gedaliah), *Yšmʼʼl* (Ishmael), and *Bʼlyšʼ* (Baalisha)—all occur in contemporary epigraphic sources. From a historiographic point of view, two problems are involved:

(1) The problem of identification and the probability of a certain proposal. Since various persons are known with the same name, it is not prima facie clear that the individuals referred to in the seals and inscriptions are identical with the biblical persons.

(2) "A name is not a story." This slogan refers to the fact that although the presence of a name indicates the historicity of that person, the stories narrated about him or her—for instance, in the Hebrew Bible—are not by implication historical.

The book of Kings, in its present form, ends with a note on the release from prison of the exiled Judahite king Jehoiachin (2 Kgs 25:27-30). He had been king in Jerusalem for three months, unfortunately during Nebuchadnezzar's siege and conquest of the city. This event took place in the seventh year of the Babylonian king. His release can thus be dated in the spring of the year 561 BCE. The book of 2 Kings (25:27) relates that the release from prison took place during the accession-year of Evil-Merodakh. The expression refers to "the period preceding the first full regnal year of a king," and it is parallel to "the beginning of his reign." Both are equivalents of Akkadian, "year in which the king started to reign." In sum, the data on the regnal and other years underscore the plausibility of the release from prison of Jehoiachin in spring 561 BCE.

The book of Kings contains an interesting detail with regard to the date of Jehoiachin's release. In the narrative world of the book of Kings, it is dated on the twenty-seventh day of the twelfth month of the accession year of Evil-Merodakh (2 Kgs 25:27). It should be noted that this is only a few days before the (spring) New Year Festival in the reign of Evil-Merodakh. It is of great importance to remark that the spring equinox was an appropriate time for rearrangements in the royal administration. Court dignitaries who had acted favorably were promoted; others were demoted. In the Babylonian creation epic *Enuma Elish*, it is narrated that Marduk—the head of the Babylonian pantheon—granted amnesty to a group of deities that had rebelled against him. *Enuma Elish* is not only a narrative text on the beginnings of the universe; it also proffers a clear connection between this creation epic and royal ideology. The deeds and doings of the gods function as a mirror for the behavior of kings and court. Just as Marduk granted amnesty to his former enemies, a Babylonian king was incited to release his imprisoned enemies. The epic theme of amnesty was an invitation to the king to play it out in real life. Together with the assignments lists, the amnesty for Jehoiachin hints at a slightly more positive image of the Judean exile. Albertz' assumption—that, in the eyes of the authors of the book of Kings, the exile was the end of history—can only be seen as correct when the adjective "provisional" is added. The exile in the Deuteronomistic view is a dark hole deserved by the illicit acts of kings and community; it was by means construed as the end of history.

Life in the Exile

In the texts from āl-Yāhūdu and Našar, a few hints on life in the Babylonian exile can be found, and these lead to the following observation. Pearce (2006) notes that, in three documents from the corpus under consideration, Yehudites are indicated with the professional title *šušānu*, a word that is not easily translated. It refers to a class of semifree agrarians who worked at "estates of the crown," who had an obligation for statute labor and who had to pay taxes on the yield of their acres. Documents from the Murashu Archive indicate that the title of *šušānu* was often given to persons belonging to a group of professional, institutional, or ethnic coherence (Stolper 1985, 79–82). Next to that, a *dēkû* is mentioned in another set of texts. A *dēkû* was some sort of local administrator who, empowered by a governor of a larger territory, was responsible for jurisdiction and taxes in his realm of power. Both words, *šušānu* and *dēkû*, imply the existence of a *hatru*, some kind of "guild" of semifree men. This would imply that, in the area of Borsippa during the Babylonian Period and on into the Persian era, a group of people descending from Judahite exiles lived at an acceptable level of prosperity and were organized in their own, albeit limited, organization.

Baruch Seal

Baruch ben Neriah was the scribal assistant of the prophet Jeremiah, and some scholars maintain that Baruch might even have been the scribe responsible

for composing the book of Jeremiah (see J. Wright 2003, 1–39). Such a conclusion is based largely on Jeremiah 36:18, which recounts how Baruch wrote
in a scroll the prophecies of Jeremiah as dictated to him: "He uttered all these
words to me, and I wrote them in ink in the scroll." Since that scroll was subsequently burnt by King Jehoiakim, Baruch had to write a second edition of that
scroll on the same day. Like Jeremiah, Baruch was an eyewitness of the devastation of Jerusalem, and together with the prophet he took refuge in Egypt
(Jer 43:4-7).

In 1975, an unprovenanced clay bulla with a seal inscription containing
Baruch's name became known (Avigad 1978). Since this bulla was not found
as part of a professional excavation, it is difficult to decide whether or not it
should be construed as a forgery.

(1) [belonging] to Berachyahu	לברכיהו
(2) son of Neriyahu	בנריהו
(3) the scribe	הספר

A second unprovenanced clay bulla, found in 1996, was stamped with the
same seal. Some scholars think that this second impression establishes the
authenticity of the first bulla as well as of the historicity of Baruch. The fingerprint on the second bulla is sometimes even construed as the fingerprint of the
scribe himself (Shanks 1996). There is an emerging scholarly consensus, however, that these two bullae are in fact forgeries (Goren and Erie 2014). Even if
these bullae were authentic (and although they are often cited as proof of the
existence of Jeremiah's scribe Baruch), it should be noted that the bullae only
actually attest the existence of the name—again, and only *if* they are authentic,
something that now seems most unlikely.

Nabonidus and Cyrus

Nabonidus was the fifth—and last—king of the Neo-Babylonian Empire. He
ruled from 556 to 539 BCE. He became king after a coup d'état by his son
Belshazzar, who dethroned Labaši-Marduk. Nabonidus was not as militarily or
politically strong as his predecessors, but he did take a great interest in building
projects, science, and religion. He built and restored temples of the moon god
Sin but also of Assyrian divinities such as Šãmaš and Ishtar. His veneration of
the moon god Sin in the northern city of Haran alienated him from the politically important Marduk priests of the Esağila temple in Babylon. For unclear
reasons, he spent many years in the Arabian oasis of Tayma. But, in the final
years of his life, he returned to Babylon, where he defended the city against the
Persian king Cyrus, albeit in vain. After his death, a negative image arose. He

was depicted as madly ill and as leading Babylon astray. This view can be found in several texts: the Cyrus Cylinder, the Verse Account of Nabonidus, several Greek depictions of his reign, the book of Daniel, a text from Qumran entitled "The Prayer of Nabonidus" (4QprNab), and many later legends.

Cyrus II the Great (Hebrew, *Kôreš*, Old-Persian *Kurvauš*, meaning "in the likeness of the Sun") became king of Persia in 559 BCE, albeit as a vassal of the Medes. He eventually formed an alliance with the Medes and started a great march that led to important conquests across the Near East. In 539 BCE, he conquered the city of Babylon, ending the political rule of Nabonidus and the Neo-Babylonian dynasty. Cyrus' rule ultimately extended to the Mediterranean, and his Persian Empire was in many respects the first world empire. Cyrus died in 530 BCE during a battle with the Scythian tribe of the Massagetai in Iran (Herodotus, *Histories* 1.201–214).

The Cyrus Cylinder was discovered in 1879 and is widely regarded as extrabiblical evidence for the historicity of the decree of Cyrus as presented in Ezra 1. The inscription has been interpreted as showing a liberal policy of respect toward other religions. The inscription was thought to indicate that Cyrus' policy toward the descendants of the Judahite exiles was not unique but fitted the pattern of his rule. Amelia Kuhrt, however, has made clear that the inscription is of a propagandistic and stereotypical nature. The text reflects the worldview of the Marduk priests of the Esaĝila temple at Babylon as becomes clear from the following passage:

> From Babylon to Aššur and from Susa, Agade, Ešnunna, Zamban, Me-Turnu, Der, as far as the region of Gutium, the sacred centres on the other side of the Tigris, whose sanctuaries had been abandoned for a long time, I returned the images of the gods, who had resided there [i.e., in Babylon], to their places and I let them dwell in eternal abodes. I gathered all their inhabitants and returned to them their dwellings. In addition, at the command of Marduk, the great lord, I settled in their habitations, in pleasing abodes, the gods of Sumer and Akkad, whom Nabonidus, to the anger of the lord of the gods, had brought into Babylon. (Cyrus Cylinder 30–33)

The priests of Marduk present Cyrus as a "good prince" replacing the "bad prince" Nabonidus. The return of divine images and people related in Cyrus Cylinder 30–33, if not mere propaganda, refers to measures taken on a local scale. It concerns divine images from cities surrounding Babylon that were brought back to the shrines from where they were exiled by Nabonidus. This passage has nothing to do specifically with Judahites, Jews, or Jerusalem (Kuhrt 1983).

FIGURE 19-5. *Cyrus Cylinder. King Cyrus of Persia proclaims in the first person that the chief Babylonian god Marduk chose him to conquer the great city of Babylon and return (the images of) gods taken by the Babylonians to their temples across the Near East.*

Murashu Archive

The Murashu Archive contains records of the financial dealings of three generations of bankers and brokers working in the town of Nippur in southern Mesopotamia during the second half of the fifth century BCE. These texts were found at the end of the nineteenth century and were edited by A. T. Clay (1912). The more than eight hundred cuneiform tablets from this archive contain legal and business documents that provide insight into the activities of this "firm." Their main activity was the renting of fields. From the archive, it becomes clear that they had business connections with the Persian crown and court, with local officials in Nippur, but also with commoners of the city. Next to renting fields, they earned money by supplying agricultural implements, seeds, tools, and animals. These documents attest that "Murashu and Sons" conducted business with about one hundred families, some of whose members had personal names with a Yahwistic-theophoric element—that is, they had apparently Jewish names. For instance, line 2 of text 185 from Murashu contains the Israelite name *Abî-Jahô*, the father of *Šabbatay*. Many other examples indicate the presence of a Judean, Judahite, or "Jewish" community in southern Babylonia. Members of this community, although not belonging to the richer echelons of the society at Nippur, were free to conduct business transactions. The cuneiform tablets indicate that these people were integrated into the Babylonian and Persian society. From a methodical point of view, it would be incorrect to make a one-to-one connection between the Judahites deported by Nebuchadnezzar and the persons in the Murashu Archive with a Yahwistic-theophoric element in their names, construing the latter as descendants of the former. There might have been a connection with the Yehudites mentioned in the texts from āl-Yāhūdu and Našar. What the documents show is that, about a century after the conquest of Babylon by Cyrus the Great, persons—likely Jewish—with a Yahwistic-theophoric element in their names were still living in Mesopotamia.

Summary

The archaeological and textual evidence available to us is naturally fragmentary, and that enables us to craft a similarly fragmentary history of the exilic period. Too many pieces of the puzzle are missing to make a coherent and unified portrait possible. A few things, nevertheless, are apparent:

(1) The land of Judah did not lie desolate during the Babylonian Period.
(2) Mizpah and Bethel most probably functioned as administrative and religious centers for the people who remained.
(3) Many exiled Judahites were settled in agricultural areas in order to supply the urbanized areas of Babylon with food.
(4) The exiled Judahites reached an acceptable standard of living and were free to conduct business in Babylon.
(5) The exiled Judahites presumably were free to continue to practice their religion in modes they thought appropriate.
(6) The return from exile should not be construed as a massive, unified event; the descendants of the exiled Judahites returned in waves, and many remained in Babylonia.

It cannot be denied that the conquest of Jerusalem, the burning of the temple, and the end of the Davidic Dynasty caused pain and sorrow. This pain is acutely depicted in several psalms (e.g., Pss 74, 79, 137) and in the books of Ezekiel and Lamentations. Nonetheless, this traditional depiction of the exilic period is not entirely accurate. The Judahite exiles were able to make lives for themselves in the cities to which they were deported, and the people who remained in the land of Israel likewise found a way to cope with the reality of the destruction of their central temple, the toppling of their king, and the imposition of foreign rule. They not only coped with these painful facts and sought to make the best of their current circumstances. They also looked forward to better times.

Suggestions for Further Reading

It was the army of the Babylonian Empire (Neo-Babylonian Empire, to be exact) that captured Jerusalem, sent its residents into exile, and later destroyed it. With that in mind, it is important to understand this empire well. To assist that task, read Finkel and Seymour's *Babylon* (2008), H. W. F. Saggs' *The Babylonians—A Survey of the Ancient Civilization of the Tigris-Euphrates Valley* (1999), and D. J. Wiseman's *Nebuchadrezzar and Babylon* (1985).

Following the emphases of the biblical books, most research has been into the fate and circumstances of the exiles, who were forced to leave for Babylonia (2 Kings and Ezekiel) or who fled the land for Egypt (Jeremiah), and who then returned—at least some of them and some of their descendants. J. Ahn and J. Middlemas' edited work *By the Irrigation Canals of Babylon* brings together a number of essays aiming to take a new look at these traditional circumstances. In her early book *The Troubles of a Templeless Judah*, J. Middlemas tried to go further, pointing out that the Judeans' problem was better characterized as being without a temple than being in exile—especially since, as she holds, most Judeans did not leave the land. In 2003, O. Lipschits and J. Blenkinsopp brought together a collection of essays in which scholars approach this question from a variety of angles: *Judah and the Judaeans in the Neo-Babylonian Period*. In 2005, Lipschits provided his own position in *The Fall and Rise of Jerusalem: Judah under Babylonian Rule*.

The question of who resided in the land of Judah during the sixth century BCE continues to be controversial. In 1996, H. M. Barstad argued, in his *The Myth of the Empty Land*, that the archaeological remains indicated that large numbers of Judeans did remain in and around Jerusalem. Some fifteen years later, in his *Judah in the Neo-Babylonian Period: The Archaeology of Desolation* (2012), A. Faust interpreted the archaeological evidence as indicating the exact opposite, that the land of Judah had been largely depopulated—even though E. Farisani had come down on Barstad's side in his essay "The Israelites in Palestine during the Babylonian Exile" (2008). E. P. Stern provides a dispassionate look at the same archaeological evidence in *Archaeology of the Land of the Bible*, vol. 2, *Assyrian, Babylonian, and Persian Periods (732–332 B.C.E.)*.

20

PERSIA AND YEHUD

Charles David Isbell

The Political Context and the Biblical Narrative

The period of exile in Babylonia marks a watershed in biblical history, the era during which an international religion was birthed out of a parochial and nationalistic womb, the moment when Judaism began to be formed from Israelite Yahwism. What happened to Judah was not a unique phenomenon in the ancient world. Numerous other nations had been born, flourished for a brief period, worshipped ancestral or tribal gods, and then been defeated by a more powerful neighbor, usually a much larger empire. Such an occurrence had an understandable consequence: the defeated people acknowledged the superiority of the deity of the conquerors and lost their culture and national identity along with their religious beliefs.

It would have been understandable for the conquered and exiled citizens of Judah to turn away from the god they believed had defeated Egypt, sustained them in the desert, and conquered the land of Canaan, but who had just lost a decisive battle against the Babylonian god Marduk, a defeat that appeared to confirm Marduk's superiority. The national paradigms of history and culture had been horribly shattered. Promises believed to have been made to Abraham, Moses, and David had once been demonstrably fulfilled—a people with their own land, a sizable population, a king with an army at his disposal to defend the nation, and a temple symbolizing divine presence in the world. But these were gone forever, and no reasonable person could have dreamed of their reclamation. Tellingly, the prophet Jeremiah sent a letter to his exiled compatriots, urging them to become good citizens in Babylonia—to buy property, build homes, plant gardens, and arrange marriages for their children (Jer 29:1-8). Also significant in this regard is the statement to an anti-Babylonian group by Gedaliah, whom the Babylonians appointed as governor of Judah: "Live in the land, serve the king of Babylon, and it shall be well with you" (2 Kgs 25:24).

However, the prophets and spiritual leaders of the Jews who were hauled into exile did not accept the option normally chosen by defeated nations. Instead, they searched for answers to their fate by turning inward, unwilling to abandon traditional ideas about their relationship to God. Their theology of "covenant" and "election" needed to be reexamined alongside equally compelling ideas about the divine imperative for justice.

After the Babylonian destruction, the biblical text depicted Judean society in ruins and on the verge of collapse. Jeremiah stated that only the poorest in the land had not been exiled to Babylon (Jer 40:7) and that "there are only a few of us left out of many" (Jer 42:2). According to Chronicles, the land lay desolate for seventy years (2 Chr 36:20-21). The prophets Ezekiel, Jeremiah, and Second Isaiah all recall the devastation of Jerusalem and the cities of Judah. From the first deportation of Judah in 597 BCE to the return of the exiles in 538 BCE, the biblical writers give the impression that most of the cities and villages in Judah remained destroyed and desolate. Though agreeing with the premise that Judah had suffered from the devastation of the Babylonian invasion, some scholars argue that Judah's population remained basically intact and continued to function. Judah was not shattered and abandoned. The theory is called the "myth of the empty land" (Barstad 1996). The event was not the calamity represented by the biblical writers. The former territory of the Kingdom of Judah was still inhabited by large numbers of survivors, who even contributed to the emergence of the Hebrew Bible. True, Jerusalem and some of the surrounding areas, especially the Shephelah, had been decimated, but there was no collapse of Judean society. Moreover, it would not be beneficial to the economic interests of the Babylonian Empire to destroy Judah. Life in Judah existed as it had before with virtually no changes resulting from the Babylonian invasion. Other scholars, many of whom are archaeologists, have argued that there was a cultural continuity from the Iron Age through the Persian Period. They recognize the harsh Babylonian destruction of the Kingdom of Judah and do not minimize the destructions of the large urban centers, but they maintain that there were Judeans living in the northern mountains and that the area of Benjamin and the rural areas had suffered little damage and recovered quickly. As examples, they point to recent surveys that indicate that sites in the northern hills of Judah—such as Bethel, Gibeon, Moza, Mizpah (which served as the administrative center of Judah), and Tell el-Full—were intact. Moreover, excavations at Ramat Rahel, south of Jerusalem, demonstrated that the site was not destroyed by the Babylonians. It may have been an administrative center during both the Neo-Babylonian and the Persian Periods. It was simply against Babylon's interest to totally destroy Judah. Defending the continuity of the people of Judah, these scholars believe that only a small minority of Judeans were exiled, most of the population lived scattered in the rural areas, and there was little change from former times.

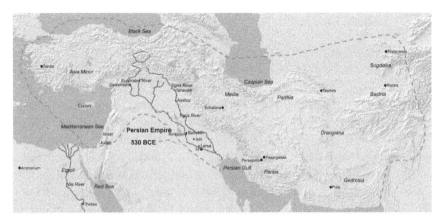

MAP 20-1. *The boundaries of the Persian Empire in 530 BCE.*

Another approach is that of Abraham Faust, who returns to the older models of massive devastation and desolation of nearly all of Judah caused by the Babylonians. Faust argues that much of the urban and rural areas of Judah were destroyed by the Babylonians. Archaeological surveys and excavations demonstrate dramatic reductions in settlements, fortresses, and populations of nearly all the large urban centers; thus, nearly every major sixth-century BCE site experienced a decline or was uninhabited until the later Persian Period. The population decline of Judah was so severe that it recovered only at the end of the Persian era. Those Judeans who survived were scattered over large areas, mostly abandoning the large cities. Faust claims that "no clear-cut archaeological assemblages dated to the sixth century have been identified in Judah, and this makes the attempts to date sites to this period very problematic" (2012a, 11). The lack of international trade exacerbated economic conditions and indicates Judah was in an economically depressed state. Economic prosperity from the seventh century BCE only recovered in the Hellenistic Period. By the Persian era, Judean social practices such as burial practices and domestic architecture such as the four-room house had disappeared. Faust believes that rather than life continuing as before, Judea after the Babylonian invasion was devastated.

At present it is not all that clear whether there is a middle ground concerning the "myth of the empty land" and the traumatic events of the exile. Scholars are unsure of the extent of the war, famine, disease, exile, economic instability, and social and political turmoil that followed the Babylonian invasion. Of course, the debates will continue as scholars wrestle with the interpretation of the biblical texts, historical research on the Neo-Babylonian era, and archaeological evidence.

How and why did Judah re-create itself in response to defeat at the hands of Babylonia? The prophetic traditions remembered the career of Elijah and his fight to the death against syncretism with Baalism (1 Kgs 18); the messages of Amos excoriating people for injustice and specifying unjust behavior as the root cause of political calamity; the anguished warnings of Jeremiah about the inevitability of punishment as the consequence of the people's failure to comply with the standards of the Sinaitic covenant. Before the exile, few heeded these and similar prophetic messages (see 2 Chr 36:16). But the intergenerational prophetic guild had honored, studied, and transmitted those warnings, and it is probable that copies of prophetic writings were among the ideas that claimed the attention of the exiles in Babylonia (Isbell 2009). For the Hebrew Bible's final editors, the exile furnished the proof of everything the prophets of the past had threatened. The prophets had been correct! There was a link between the moral character of the nation and its survival and prosperity. Yahweh did indeed punish his own people for their sins.

But disobedience resulting in divine punishment was only part of the prophetic message. And the messages of virtually every prophet had included a second part that contained the germ of a crucial idea in exilic thought, a concept that made possible the reformulation of Yahwism and that led ultimately to early Judaism. If the prophets had been correct in their announcement of punishment, then it must be asked whether they had also been correct in their messages of restoration and hope. Even the frightfully negative Amos had agreed that after the people of God had been torn apart by Yahweh as a lion ravages a defenseless sheep, "two legs, or a piece of an ear" (Amos 3:12) could be snatched to safety. Isaiah had indeed threatened disaster, but he had also promised that the destruction would not be total and that a "remnant" would remain. Symbolically, Isaiah had named one of his own children Maher-Shalal-Hash-Baz, the ominous meaning of which was "swift is the booty, speedy is the prey" (Isa 8:1-4). But, to another son, he had given the equally symbolic name of She'ar Yashuv, "a remnant will return" (Isa 7:3).

In addition to his letter noted above advising the exiles to settle down, purchase land, and lead normal lives as good citizens in Babylonia, Jeremiah had also promised that exile would end after seventy years, after which restoration would begin (Jer 29:10). And while advising others to settle into normal life in Babylonia, Jeremiah had purchased land in his home town (Anathoth), ordering that the purchase deed be sealed in a jar for preservation in the public record, evidence of his unshakeable confidence that Jews would someday return from Babylonia and once again own land in Judah (Jer 32:6-15).

If, therefore, the prophets were correct about restoration, as they had been about punishment, the moral imperative to maintain a life of faithfulness to Yahweh and all the demands made at Sinai remained in force! Even in abject defeat and humiliation, the Jews in Babylonia could not afford to abandon the core truths of the past (see Ps 37:5). Stories about a deity who freed, sustained, blessed, and guided his people and who demanded ethical and moral behavior in exchange were still valid and must continue to be taught and inculcated into life. Restoration apart from faithfulness to Yahweh could not be achieved. Sitting in Babylonia, the exiles learned for the first time that they had been wrong, smugly and dangerously wrong. The prophets had been correct. Ignored in Judah, they came to be respected in Babylonia. The task at hand was to create in Babylonia the kind of society that had never been created in Judah.

Cyrus the Persian "Messiah"

The prophetic messages and thus the dreams of Judeans who had been exiled in Babylonia received both an emotional lift and political validation from the actions of a Median prince known as Cyrus of Anshan, son of Cambyses I. Seizing the throne of Media in 550 BCE, Cyrus immediately demonstrated his military genius with successful campaigns that brought the entire region north and south of Babylonia under his control (including Assyria, Mesopotamia, Syria, Armenia, and Cappadocia). The new empire took the name Persia, from the Old Persian *parsa*, the modern province of Fars. Cyrus also quickly subjugated the kingdoms of Lydia and Ionia (including major Greek cities on the coast of Asia Minor). While these campaigns were still in progress, Cyrus initiated a propaganda assault aimed at Nabonidus, the king of Babylonia. Babylonian policies of ruthless destruction, heartless deportation of people from their homelands, and forced integration of conquered peoples into Babylonian life had all contributed to a negative view of Nabonidus within his own country, and the propaganda campaign of Cyrus against the Babylonian king was so successful that when the Persian army entered Babylon on October 12, 539 BCE, the majority of the city surrendered immediately and peacefully.

With the capture of the capital city of Babylon, control of the vast Babylonian Empire came into the hands of Cyrus. Conscious of his historical legacy, Cyrus, a devotee of Zoroaster, publicly declared himself the restorer of the Babylonian god Marduk(!), and he accepted accolades from the citizens of Babylonia for bringing their nation back to worship of their ancestral deity. Further declaring himself "King of the World," Cyrus issued a decree that offered the official Persian version of the defeat of Babylon and enunciated the Persian policies regarding the administration of the empire thereby obtained. The decree of Cyrus has been preserved on the famous Cyrus Cylinder, a clay barrel containing an Akkadian inscription describing the overthrow of Nabonidus and Babylon. This cylinder was found in the foundation of a Babylonian temple in 1879. Three things stand out in this decree. First, Cyrus contrasted the lowly origins of Nabonidus with his own aristocratic family and presented himself as the legitimate successor of the ancient kings of Babylonia.

Second, the decree presents a clear statement of Cyrus' foreign policy and its radical shift from the harsh Assyrian and Babylonian policies. With propagandistic fervor, the decree recounts a description of the fact that, when Cyrus entered the proud city of Babylon some seventeen days after it had surrendered, he proceeded to stand in front of the statue of Marduk, grasping the statue by its hands and announcing publicly his intention to allow Babylonian customs and culture to remain largely undisturbed. These actions contributed to his reception as a liberator rather than a foreign conqueror.

Third, although it lacks specific reference to Jews, to the Jerusalem temple, or to Judah, the decree refers to several "cities on the other side of the Tigris," along with their sanctuaries that had long been in ruins and the cultic images that once had been housed in those sanctuaries. In particular, the decree notes that the policy of Cyrus was to repatriate inhabitants of these unnamed cities to their homelands. While the book of Ezra (Ezra 1:1-4; 6:3-5; see also 2 Chr 36:22-23) cites the decree of Cyrus as specifically applicable to Jerusalem (even leaving the impression that it applied *only* to Judah), the wording of the decree itself indicates that this portrayal of Persian authorization allowing exiles from Judah to return to their homeland and its capital city, Jerusalem, is neither impossible nor implausible. Such a repatriation of exiles accords well with the overall policies of Cyrus in the governance of his empire.

The policies put into effect by Cyrus made good sense politically and economically as well as militarily. Vast territories that the Babylonians had conquered in a manner similar to their conquest of Jerusalem and Judah had been

FIGURE 20-1. *Mausoleum of Cyrus. With the capture of the capital city of Babylon, control of the vast Babylonian Empire came into the hands of Cyrus (576–530 BCE).*

stripped of their most-prominent and best-educated citizens (see 2 Kgs 25:12) and then allowed to sit idly with the passing of the years. These territories contained few people with administrative skills, organizational ability, or leadership experience. Cyrus recognized a fact that had been overlooked by the Babylonians—such barren territory would offer neither a deterrent to Egypt should it decide to march into the Levantine buffer zone that led to Mesopotamia nor competent local allies to aid the Persian army should it seek to mount an invasion of Egypt. The new Persian policy also ended the nearly complete absence of revenue from the outlying areas. It was essential for the Persians to authorize a return to these territories of people who cared about the land and who had the leadership and administrative skills to oversee its growth and development. But progress was slow. Judah lacked the economic infrastructure and population to support itself. Growth was faster in the coastal regions, whose economy was stimulated by international trade. Yet in Jerusalem during the Persian Period, the city remained smaller than in the reign of David. Thus, the decision to allow repatriated peoples to worship their own deities along with Persian financial support to rebuild the demolished sanctuaries of those deities was not the main focus of Persian foreign policy but merely the by-product of an empirical program that was more efficient than what the Babylonians had installed.

The biblical versions of a portion of the edict perceived as pertaining to Judah are contained in three separate versions in the Bible: two in Hebrew (Ezra 1:2-4; 2 Chr 36:23) and a truncated third reference in Aramaic, the lingua franca of both the Persian Empire and the Jews (Ezra 6:3-5). These biblical accounts mention three critical provisions that are consistent with the general policy attested on the Cyrus Cylinder itself: (1) the intention of the emperor to restore a conquered city and rebuild its ruined temple; (2) the decision to underwrite the rebuilding project financially; and (3) the determination to restore the sacred objects that had been stolen from the temple at the time of its fall. These three are then applied specifically to Jerusalem and the temple of Solomon that the Babylonians had destroyed.

The Hebrew form in Ezra appears to reflect an oral version by which the news might have been delivered to the Jews initially, while the Aramaic version has the literary characteristics of a formal letter or an official document. According to the Hebrew version, Cyrus derived his authority to rule over the entire world directly from Yahweh, not Marduk as in the Cyrus Cylinder. The biblical text also specified that Cyrus' commission from Yahweh included orders to rebuild the temple in Jerusalem. However, it was Marduk and not Yahweh who bestowed this great victory. Cyrus informs us, "Marduk, the great lord, was well pleased with my deeds. . . . I gathered all their (former) inhabitants and returned (to them) their habitations" (*ANET* 315–16).

Cyrus further claims to have resettled all the gods in their sacred cities, which was customary Persian policy for all conquered peoples. Perhaps the religious officials in each of these cities viewed their own god as the moving cause behind the decision of Cyrus. The emperor, for his part, must have been pleased that so many deities had backed his quest for power, and he apparently regarded himself as the patron of virtually all the gods in the known world.

The success of Cyrus and the belief that his policies included Judah also prompted a message from Isaiah of Babylon to the exiles from Judah. This "Second Isaiah" identified Cyrus as an emissary of Yahweh who had been sent to conquer those who had destroyed Judah. In a poem of critical significance (Isa 44:28–45:8), the prophet hailed Cyrus as the "shepherd" and "messiah" of Yahweh(!) and argued that his military success had come not from Marduk but because he was acting as an agent of the God of Israel. While the decree of Cyrus described Marduk "going at his [Cyrus'] side like a real friend," Yahweh claims in Second Isaiah: "I will go before you [Cyrus]" (Isa 45:2). Where the decree notes that "[Marduk] pronounced the name of Cyrus [i.e., created him] and proclaimed him ruler of the entire world," the prophet has Yahweh proclaim: "I call you by your name, I surname you, though you do not know me" (Isa 45:4).

In this way, the prophet interpreted the political and military victories of the human king Cyrus as proof of the activity of the divine king Yahweh on behalf of his people. As a further consequence of Cyrus' victory, Second Isaiah rhapsodized that the Persian monarch would free Judean captives from exile and rebuild Jerusalem (Isa 45:13). Such an announcement is not surprising. The foreign affairs acumen of earlier prophets like Elijah and Elisha, Amos, Isaiah, and Jeremiah shows that Isaiah of Babylonia could have been capable of understanding the international developments of his day. He would have noted the tolerant policy of Cyrus toward people whom he had conquered before seizing control of Babylonia, and he might even have longed for Cyrus to topple Nabonidus and institute his liberal Persian policies for Judah. Seen through the prophetic lens of Isaiah of Babylon, the foreign policies of Cyrus were ordained by Yahweh specifically for Judah and Jerusalem, and the coming to power of Cyrus could be understood to have triggered the actualization of the prophetic promise of restoration and repatriation: a second chance to be the people of Yahweh, a second chance to worship in the rebuilt temple, a second chance to dwell in the holy city of Jerusalem.

The "Persian Period" in Biblical Narrative

The conquest of Babylon led to the "Persian Period" (539–332 BCE) of biblical literature. The Babylonian destruction of Judah was complete. The country was largely devastated. The coastal cities of Akko, Dor, Jaffa, Ashkelon, and Gaza were mostly populated by Phoenicians. Judah was a part of a strategically important but struggling Persian province. Determining the reestablishment of Judah as a functioning state after the exile is virtually impossible. The country lacked the economic conditions to thrive. The population was insufficient, and there was no proper administrative infrastructure (Stern 2001, 580–81).

After the defeat of the Babylonians in 539 BCE, the Persian Empire became the largest empire in the ancient Middle East. It was organized into enormous administrative provinces known as *satrapies*, each ruled by independent governors. The Persians controlled a diverse empire that extended from Greece to India and Egypt. Judah belonged to the satrapy called *'Ever Naharaim*, "Beyond the River," which extended from the Euphrates to the Mediterranean. The Persians were known for their tolerant domestic policies, and they promoted local customs and rule wherever possible, as long as they did not conflict directly with Persian policies. Though the high officials, royal guard, and standing army were recruited from among Persians and Medes, non-Iranians could occupy high posts. They built an extraordinary highway,

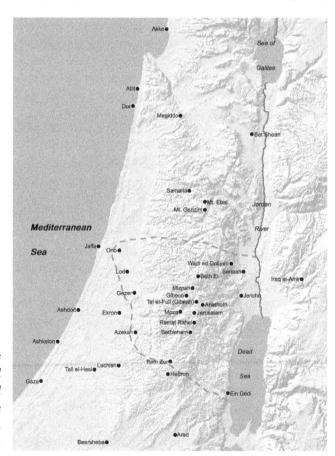

MAP 20-2. *The boundaries and towns of Yehud (Judea) at the end of the sixth century BCE.*

the "Royal Road," which ran from the Persian capital of Susa to the Aegean Sea, and on it riders on horseback carried messages back and forth from station to station. The Greek historian Herodotus was duly impressed and wrote that "neither snow nor rain nor dark of night will keep these swift messengers from the accomplishment of their appointed rounds." The royal riders could travel the entire 1,500-mile route in nine days.

The power and majesty of Persia furnished a new context for the composition of biblical literature like Isaiah 40–66 and the books of Malachi, Haggai, Zechariah, Ezra-Nehemiah, and Esther. These books do not cover the entire Persian Period fully or equally, but they offer sketches of selected events. For example, shortly after the decree of Cyrus, a delegation of exiled Judeans was sent to Jerusalem by the Persian authorities. The delegation was headed by Sheshbazzar (note the Babylonian name), who was given custody of the vessels of the Jerusalem temple—said to be the ones that had been carted off to Babylon by Nebuchadnezzar (Ezra 1:7-8). Because he is titled "*the* [not merely *a*] prince of Judah" (Ezra 1:8) and designated as the man appointed by Cyrus as "governor," Sheshbazzar appears to have been an important person, perhaps even a Davidide (the grandson of Jehoiakim if he was identical with the Shenazzar mentioned in 1 Chr 3:18). Since the texts of Ezra-Nehemiah, Haggai, and Zechariah offer contradictory perceptions of the founding and rebuilding of the Jerusalem temple, some reconstruction of the process is necessary. The following reconstruction seems likely.

Sheshbazzar, appointed as the first governor of Judah by Cyrus (538 BCE), initiated but did not complete the process of restoring the temple (Ezra 3). No explanation is given as to why the work of Sheshbazzar was halted. Without noting that Sheshbazzar had been replaced, the text of Ezra simply states that Zerubbabel (another Judean leader with a Babylonian name), apparently the head of a second wave of returning exiles (see Ezra 2:2-70), was in charge of the initiation of the temple project and that he was faced with opposition from "the enemies of Judah" (Ezra 4:1), who requested that they be allowed to join in the rebuilding. Their claim to be worshippers of the deity of Israel and the Jews and their memory of having been transplanted by Esarhaddon of Assyria have been taken to mean that these "enemies" were Samaritans, although Assyrian deportees could well have originated in a variety of countries other than the former kingdom of Samaria (defeated by Assyria in 722 BCE).

Ezra 4:5 states that this opposition continued "throughout the reign of Cyrus king of Persia, and until the reign of King Darius of Persia," and Haggai 1:1 places the restarting of the temple rebuilding in the second year of Darius, or 520 BCE. Along with his priestly counterpart Joshua (Ezra 3:8; 5:2), Zerubbabel, the leader of the second return, restarted the rebuilding project (Ezra 5:2). He faced additional opposition, this time from a group led by Tattenai, a governor from one of the provinces in the satrapy of "Beyond the River." Asked by Tattenai by whose authority they were proceeding, the Jews responded by citing the decree of Cyrus (Ezra 5:15). Refusing to accept this answer, Tattenai and his associates sent a letter of complaint to King Darius (on which see further below). It is noteworthy that Tattenai did not have the authority to stop the temple project, work on which continued until the answer arrived from Darius (Tattenai's letter is quoted in Ezra 5:6-17).

After a search of the Persian archives uncovered the decree of Cyrus, Darius wrote in support of the rebuilding project and warned Tattenai and his associates to keep their distance. He then issued his own decree authorizing payment for the work from the Persian treasury and threatening death by impalement to anyone who violated his edict (Ezra 6:1-12). The messages preserved in the book of Haggai are portrayed as having served to encourage Zerubbabel as he led the project of rebuilding to its completion by the year 515 BCE.

Written several decades after the rebuilding project, the narrative of Ezra-Nehemiah conflates the efforts of Sheshbazzar and Zerubbabel into a single event (compare Ezra 1:8 with 2:1-2). This has the result of presenting both stages of the rebuilding project as a simple, unified response to the decree of Cyrus, and it led earlier scholars to toy with the theory that Sheshbazzar and Zerubbabel were the same person. Both names are given the title "governor" (Ezra 5:14; Hag 1:1), both are placed by the text of Ezra during the reign of Cyrus (1:11; 2:2), and both are said to have initiated the project of temple restoration (Hag 1; Zech 4:9; cf. Ezra 5:14 with 3:2, 8; and 5:2). However, the books of Haggai and Zechariah clearly place Zerubbabel during the time of Darius I (522–486 BCE), while Ezra 4:7 depicts events involving Zerubbabel during the reign of King Artaxerxes (465–424 BCE), before placing him in the second year of Darius I (520 BCE). The mention of Darius in Ezra 4:5 indicates the correct time frame for the delegation headed by Zerubbabel.

Judean Religion in the Persian Era

Judean religion underwent significant changes during the Persian era. Some of these changes were due to the historical vicissitudes endured by the people of Judah/Yehud as they endured Babylonian, Persian, and Greek domination. Religious ideas evolve as people use religion to explain their lives. People who have experienced domination long for a deliverer, and that longed-for deliverer can be imaged as an inspiring king or even a divinely sent messiah. Some forms of religious change take place due to foreign influence. For over a century, scholars have debated the extent and nature of Persian influence on Judaic religion during the Persian Period. Some scholars identify virtually all innovations as foreign imports, while others take a more nuanced approach that explains apparently new ideas as the product of the fruitful interaction between longstanding Judaic traditions and newly encountered foreign ideas. For example, Judaic texts from this period indicate a growing interest in a vibrant afterlife, a theme that resembles depictions of the afterlife in Persian Zoroastrianism. Likewise, Zoroastrianism imagines history as a dualistic struggle between the forces of good and evil, a struggle that will see the eventual triumph of good. These themes, thought to come directly from Persian Zoroastrianism, appear prominently in late biblical and nonbiblical texts such as Zechariah, Daniel, and sections of the nonbiblical book of 1 Enoch. In these texts, however, these themes appear in distinctly Judaic garb. Thus, it is clear that religious ideas among Jews were quite diverse during this era. Some people could maintain longstanding traditional views of religion, others might have adopted other religions altogether, while yet others found ways to express their Judaic ideas in forms and with vocabulary that were popular in this era. The Persian Period, therefore, can be understood as setting the stage for the growth of Jewish cultural diversity and religious sectarianism in the following centuries. Jews employed a wide range of adaptive strategies in an effort to express what they imagined as the most appropriate ways to honor their past, while at the same time addressing the pressing social, political, and religious issues of their day (Stone 2011).

Biblical Prophets of the Persian Period

Mention has already been made of the great unnamed exilic prophet, dubbed "Second Isaiah" in testimony to his probable membership in an "Isaiah School," whose pronouncements about the Persian Cyrus date him clearly to the time after 538 BCE. Three additional prophets also came to prominence during this era—Haggai, Zechariah, and Malachi.

HAGGAI

We have noted the demise of the Babylonian Empire and examined the famous decree of Cyrus, the Persian monarch named by Second Isaiah as the messiah. We have also seen from the book of Ezra that, pursuant to the edict of Cyrus, a number of Babylonian Jews, led by Sheshbazzar, returned to Jerusalem and laid the foundations for a second temple in 538 BCE. After starting the project with great optimism, a period of some eighteen years passed before construction continued. It was Haggai the prophet who provided the inspiration that prompted work to recommence. Working closely with the political leader named Zerubbabel and the priest named Joshua, Haggai articulated a vision of the temple restored to the condition that would make it a suitable place to which God might return on "the day of Yahweh." For Haggai, that day would be the time when gentile rule of the world would end and the throne of Yahweh alone would be established forever in Zion.

The structure of the book of Haggai is clear, consisting of four messages by the prophet. The first message (chapter one) is dated to the first day of the sixth month, in the second year of the reign of Darius, king of Persia, or mid-August 520 BCE. Haggai noted the hardships the people faced and opined that the blessings of God were being withheld because God's house stood desolate (Hag 1:9). If the people would obey the call of God to rebuild his house, their own lives would be blessed in return. The prophetic word from Yahweh was clear: "I am with you" (Hag 1:13). So stirring was the initial message that work on the temple was begun again within three short weeks. But less than one month later, it was necessary for Haggai to preach a second sermon proclaiming the promise of Yahweh that "the latter splendor of this house will be greater than the former" (Hag 2:9).

Two months after his second message, Haggai came preaching again. In his third message (Hag 2:10-19), Haggai made the technical point that something ritually unclean has more power to contaminate than something ritually clean has to purify (Hag 2:11-13). He argued that people who are unclean must realize that everything they do and all the gifts they bring to God are also technically unacceptable, probably implying that the unwillingness of the people to work on the temple had tainted their service. However, when Haggai refers to "this people" (Hag 2:14), he may be referring to the Samaritans, in which case he was counseling that their offer to help with the project should be rejected because they were ritually unacceptable.

Haggai's fourth message (Hag 2:20-23) was delivered on the same day as the third. This final message proclaimed that gentile domination would soon end (Hag 2:21-22) and that Zerubbabel, a descendant of David, would someday become the chosen ruler of God (Hag 2:23). This would be comforting news. Along with his younger contemporary Zechariah, Haggai lived to see the temple rebuilt and dedicated in 515 BCE. This central shrine would be the center of Jewish worship for almost six hundred years, until its destruction by the Romans in 70 CE.

ZECHARIAH

The world and local conditions that pertained to the career of Haggai were the same for his contemporary Zechariah as well. The connection between the two prophets is noted in Ezra 5:1, while Ezra 6:14 credits the successful rebuilding of the temple to "the prophesying of the prophet Haggai, and Zechariah." The specific contribution of Zechariah was the proclamation of a coming world kingdom in which Jew and gentile alike would be drawn to the worship of Yahweh. His call to rebuild the temple was seen as a necessary prelude to that happy state of affairs. This is evident from the four messages dispersed throughout the first eight chapters of the book of Zechariah. These messages call the people to repent of their misdeeds (Zech 1:1-6), to obey God's commands (Zech 7:1-7), to practice social justice (Zech 7:8-14), and to live in expectation of the coming messianic era. This is a summary of great ideas from earlier prophets, concluding that true justice, covenantal faithfulness, and compassion must replace oppression of widows and orphans, resident aliens, and the poor (Zech 8:1-23). The ultimate promise is that, one future day, people from every country and language will "seize the skirt of a Jewish man and say, 'Let us go with you, for we have heard that God is with you'" (Zech 8:23).

"Second Zechariah"

Scholars have long known that the book of Zechariah is not a unified composition by a single author. The compositional, literary, and thematic differences between chapters 1–8 and 9–14 indicate that the book consists of two independent units. These two compositions are generally referred to as First and Second Zechariah. The apocalyptic visions of "Second Zechariah" (chapters 9–14) reflect the prevailing demographic conditions in Yehud: concern about an ingathering and return of dispersed Jews (Zech 9:11-17), the repopulation of a new and greater Israel (Zech 9:1-10), and the complete repopulation of Jerusalem (Zech 14) all appear to reflect Jewish feelings during the first fifty years of the fifth century BCE.

Malachi

Biblical narratives are silent about the years between the completion of the temple (515 BCE) and the career of Malachi, and the conditions of life in Jerusalem and Judah do not furnish the background to another biblical narrative for almost sixty years after the completion of the temple rebuilding project. This silence is broken by the book of Malachi. Following the careers of Haggai and Zechariah, four factors contributed to continued strife and uneasiness among Jews during the era when Jews were returning to Jerusalem and rebuilding the temple. First, not everyone in Babylonia wanted to return to Jerusalem. Life in Babylonia had not been physically difficult, and many Judeans experienced material success. Most of the exiles in Babylonia had never seen Jerusalem; others had left it as small children. Virtually their entire way of life had become Babylonian. Their language was not Hebrew but Aramaic, a language used throughout the empire. Babylonia was home, and why would they leave "home" for an unfamiliar place?

Second, those who did return encountered a difficult situation: the temple was in ruins, the city walls were down, and the former glory of Jerusalem was gone. Even when the temple was rebuilt, older people who remembered the splendor of the original structure built by Solomon wept because the rebuilt model was so markedly inferior (Ezra 3:12).

Third, the agricultural situation was difficult and totally unlike the nutrient-rich alluvial plains they knew in Babylon. The Judean soil is rocky and sandy, yielding only modest produce even in good years. The hills required terracing to preserve both soil and moisture. And throughout the time of their exile, only a sparse population remained to care for the land. Thus, nature and neglect produced an agricultural challenge.

Fourth, according to Nehemiah 7:4, only a few years after Malachi, the shortage of people, scarcity of livable houses, and large size of the city to be repopulated added to a general attitude of discouragement.

Given these circumstances, it is not surprising that Malachi's audience was shocked when the prophet spoke of divine love for them. They must have wondered why life in the "holy land" continued to be so hard and filled with problems. The question posed by Malachi was right on point: "Where is the God of justice?" (Mal 2:17).

The date of the book is clear from several internal clues. Since the rebuilt temple was already in use, the prophet was preaching after 515 BCE. Since there was no official legislation against religiously mixed marriages, his ministry must precede approximately 458 BCE, when Ezra arrived to enforce religious injunctions against intermarriage. Thus, there is broad scholarly agreement for dating the book of Malachi around 460 BCE.

The identity of the book's author is not as easy to determine as its date of composition. The Hebrew word "Malachi" is not a proper name but a designation taken from Mal 3:1: "my messenger." This implies that the book of "My Messenger" is an anonymous piece of prophetic literature. In addition to the superscription (Mal 1:1) and the "conclusion" (Mal 3:22-24; English 4:4-6), there are six messages in the book, each one framed exhibiting the three steps outlined above.

The point of the first message (Mal 1:2-5) is simple: God's love for his people is certain. Thus, complaints that "God does not love us" are groundless, no matter how bad the living conditions might be. The second message (Mal 1:6–2:9) lays the blame for the present hardships in part on the priests for their failure to provide moral and spiritual leadership by word and deed. Malachi's third message (Mal 2:10-16) targets the citizens of Judah for their intermarriage and divorce, factors that would have been key influences on family life. The prophet's fourth message (Mal 2:17–3:5) addresses the vexing issue of theodicy: How could God allow the wicked to prosper while the righteous suffer? "Malachi" notes that God would right this apparent wrong through an (angelic) agent (*mal'akh*) who would achieve justice by destroying the wicked worshippers and purifying those who worshipped God properly. The fifth message (Mal 3:6-12) reinforces the idea that God is not capricious— not likely to change from one moment to the next: "I Yahweh never change."

The people who disobey God should expect him to punish them in full compliance with the covenant. Malachi's sixth message (Mal 3:13-21; English 3:13-4:3) returns to the theological incongruence in the fact that proud people are happy, wicked people acquire great wealth, and arrogant people who defy God are spared punishment. To this charge, the prophet replied that God keeps a "book of remembrance." Persian kings often recorded the names of various people who did things that were beneficial to society but were not rewarded immediately. These records were reviewed periodically by the king, who gave out appropriate rewards to those listed, a custom described in Esther 2:21-23 and 6:1-11. Surely God would do no less than a Persian ruler! At the moment of his choosing, God would consult his "book" and act swiftly to dispense appropriate rewards or punishments.

The "Conclusion" to the book (Mal 3:22-24; English 4:4-6) summarizes the essence of the prophetic teachings contained in the six messages. People must follow the "Torah of Moses" and await "Elijah" to herald "the great and terrible day of the LORD." In sum, the prophet was calling for a life based on God's commandments, faith in a God who will act to ensure justice, and hope for a future day of divine intervention in human history. The book of Malachi, therefore, records one of the theologically driven perspectives on life in Yehud during the Persian Period.

Recently, an extraordinary collection of 103 cuneiform tablets has surfaced documenting the deported Judean community that had been uprooted and exiled to Babylon. Dating to the sixth and fifth centuries BCE, they provide important new information on the social and economic life of the exiled Jewish community. One of the villages named in the tablets is Al-Yahudu, or "village of the Judeans." The tablets contain the locations and the dates of the lives of exiled Jews in Babylonia and Persia, providing scholars with unparalleled documentation. Residents have been identified as Jews with names such as Barīkyah, Hananyah, Yahu-zēra-iqīša, Zakaryah, Ahīqām, Nēriyah, and Haggay (Abraham 2011). The documents mostly comprise administrative texts that date to the period of 572–484 BCE, and they show that Jews were active in local businesses (Pearce and Wunsch 2014). The tablets record the residents engaging in trade, including the selling of slaves, leasing of homes, and purchasing of livestock. The tablets also provide important information on a number of settlements located between the Euphrates and Tigris rivers where Jews were settled on crown land and were required to pay rent and to carry out a duty of service. On some tablets, ancient Hebraic letters appear beside the Akkadian cuneiform.

Before the Al-Yahudu texts came to light, scholars had only few details of Judean life in the Babylonian and the Persian Empires. These documents indicate that some Judean exiles were integrated in a short period of time and thrived and lived normal lives. From the initial studies of the cuneiform texts, it appears that, within a few years after the trauma of the destruction of Jerusalem and the exile, some Jews were able to live in harmony in Babylon: owning property, engaging in mercantile activities, learning the local language and legal customs in a relatively short time, and adjusting to life in Babylonian society.

The integration of Jews parallels that of non-Jews, as the Murashu Archive shows. This collection of administrative texts reveals the activities of a family business in southern Babylonia during this period (see chapter 18).

Ezra and Nehemiah

Following the narrative in Ezra 1–6, in which the efforts of Sheshbazzar and Zerubbabel are recounted, the book of Ezra focuses on its title character, "a scribe skilled in the law of Moses" (Ezra 7:6). The return of Ezra to Jerusalem is set in the seventh year of Artaxerxes (458 BCE). In the biblical account, Ezra arrived in Jerusalem armed with a copy of "the wisdom of your God" (Ezra 7:25) as well as a decree from the king that granted him authority to spend money from the Persian treasury for the temple (Ezra 7:20-22) and to excuse Jewish religious professionals from taxes (Ezra 7:24). The decree further authorized Ezra to teach Jewish law and to judge the citizenry both by its statutes and in accordance with Persian law: "All who will not obey the law of your God *and the law of the king*, let judgment be strictly executed on them, whether for death or for banishment or for confiscation of their goods or for imprisonment" (Ezra 7:26).

The narrative raises three questions. The first question involves the terms "The Teaching/Law of Moses" (Ezra 7:6), "The Teaching/Law of Yahweh" (Ezra 7:10), "The Law of your God" (Ezra 7:14; 7:26), and "the laws of your

FIGURE 20-2. *Darius the Great (522–486 BCE) built the palace complex at Persepolis around 518 BCE. The city became one of the four capitals of the empire and the center of the vast Persian (Achaemenian) Empire.*

God" (Ezra 7:25). This law is further identified in Nehemiah 8:1 as "The book of the law of Moses" given to Israel at the express command of Yahweh. There is no hint that Ezra wrote or even compiled it but a clear supposition that he had brought it with him from Babylon. Thus, Ezra is a Jewish official who was sent by the Persians to lead the people of Yehud. Both the religious and the civic law he brought came from Persia. Although the biblical text offers no hint about the extent of Ezra's document, many scholars have concluded that it was either in large part or nearly all of the Pentateuch (Genesis, Exodus, Leviticus, Numbers, and Deuteronomy) in its current form.

The second question is whether a Jewish "scribe" who held no office or position in the Persian government would be granted almost unlimited authority to requisition funds from the Persian treasury and to administer both Jewish and Persian law. The third question derives from the fact that Jewish men had married foreign (non-Jewish) wives, a discovery that shocked and dismayed Ezra when he first learned of it (Ezra 9:3). Why, if he had absolute authority to enforce Jewish law, was the reaction of Ezra to mourn and make a list naming all the men who had married non-Judeans but not to force the dissolution of those marriages? In fact, chapters 9 and 10 of Ezra portray a religious leader who accuses his congregation of wrongdoing (Ezra 9:10), demands confession and orders the illegal marriages to be dissolved (Ezra 9:11), and exacts agreement from his listeners (Ezra 9:12). The book ends with a detailed list of 113 men who *voluntarily* divorced their non-Jewish wives, and it adds an explanation: "All these had married foreign women and they sent them away with their children" (Ezra 10:44).

Aside from the voluntary action noted above, the words of Ezra produced no further definitive action, and it was only with the arrival of the political leader Nehemiah in 444 BCE (the twentieth year of Artaxerxes) that additional measures were undertaken. Alerted by his brother of conditions in Jerusalem (Neh 1:1-3), Nehemiah, then serving as an important official in the Persian court (see below), sought permission from Artaxerxes to visit and inspect the city, receiving not only royal permission but royal appointment as provincial governor (a post Ezra lacked), letters of safe passage, materials for the rebuilding of the city walls, and an army escort (Neh 2:1-10), a security measure Ezra had lacked (Ezra 9:22). The physical conditions Nehemiah found were appalling (Neh 2:11-18). Many returnees had been forced to mortgage their possessions to afford food during a time of famine (Neh 5:3). Others had to borrow money just to pay taxes (Neh 5:4), resulting in internal dissension among the returnees. Although Nehemiah notes that they were "brothers," equal members of the covenantal society of Yehud, wealthier citizens had evidently seized opportunities to lend money at usurious interest to those who were poorer (Neh 5:4-8).

Nehemiah was a man of action, and he began by rebuilding the city walls, work that was especially difficult. Rubble was so thick that work was deemed impossible by some (Neh 4:10). Non-Judean opposition to the work was open and flagrant (Neh 4:1-3, 7-8). Work had to be done in shifts, with half of the men standing guard while the other half worked (Neh 4:16-18). Despite repeated attempts by his enemies (see below) to lure him into a trap (Neh 6:1-4) and then their false claims that he was disloyal to Persia and planning to announce himself as king in Jerusalem (Neh 6:5-9), Nehemiah pushed the repair work to completion in fifty-two days (Neh 6:15). However, our knowledge concerning Jerusalem during the Persian Period is sparse. Jerusalem had greatly diminished in size. Archaeological studies indicate that, during the Persian era, much of the city of Jerusalem outside the walls of the City of David was abandoned and a large amount was damaged and destroyed. Nehemiah's attempts at settling the areas outside the City of David were unsuccessful. Moreover, large regions of the walled city remained uninhabited (Ussishkin 2006, 162–64). The rebuilding of the walls of Jerusalem by Nehemiah and his cohorts were most likely on the eastern slope of the City of David. Archaeologists recognize that the archaeological remains of Jerusalem from the Persian Period are meager. Only a few shards, stamps, and remnants of walls have been uncovered. The data reveal a very small settlement located in the "City of David hill only" (Reich 2011, 319–20).

After a stay of twelve years in Jerusalem, Nehemiah returned to King Artaxerxes. How long he remained is difficult to determine, but, upon his return to Jerusalem, Nehemiah succeeded in carrying out important religious reforms. Not only did he expel from the temple one of the persons (Tobiah) who had opposed his earlier work on the city walls (see Neh 6:17-19; 13:6-9), he also reinstituted the payment of dues owed to the Levites (Neh 13:10-12) and appropriate observance of the Sabbath (Neh 13:15-22). Significantly, he also abolished all mixed marriages, against which Ezra had preached with only limited success (Neh 13:23-28).

The "Province" of Judah

The scarcity of archaeological evidence about the events described in Ezra-Nehemiah raises questions about both the status of Ezra and Nehemiah and the political status of Judah within the Persian Empire. In the book of Ezra, the Hebrew term *medinah* ("province" in Ezra 2:1) and the Aramaic phrase *yehud medinta* ("Jewish province" in Ezra 5:8) occur. This designation in both languages indicates the assumption that Judah was a separate administrative unit with its own autonomous internal rule.

Jews assimilated in varying degrees to Persian culture. The people of Judah proper had complex interactions with the Persian political and economic administration. Exiled and expatriate Jews living in Persia found ways to preserve their ethnicity, cultural heritage, and religion in and outside of their traditional territorial state. However, for the Persians, Yehud/Judah was an inconsequential province within a vast satrapy in an enormous empire. Jerusalem was a small town, and most Persian kings paid little heed to Jewish concerns. The Jerusalem temple was rebuilt under the tutelage of the Persian bureaucrats. Notable leaders such as Ezra and Nehemiah emigrated from the Persian capital to Jerusalem. In many respects, the roots of early Judaism began to emerge during this period. While under Persian hegemony, the people of Yehud began the process of creating the collection of writings that would become their "scriptures."

The Akkadian loanword *pehah* (governor) is used both in Hebrew and in Aramaic to designate the top official in a Persian province. Three Jewish individuals are titled *pehah* in the Bible. In Ezra 5:14, Sheshbazzar is described as having been appointed *pehah* by Cyrus as part of his initial decree regarding repatriation (538 BCE). Twenty years later, the prophet Haggai twice (Hag 1:1, 14) refers to Zerubbabel as the "governor of Judah" (*pehat yehudah*). Almost one hundred years later still, the book of Nehemiah twice refers to its title character similarly, once with a suffixed form, "their governor" (*peham* in Neh 5:14), and once as "*the* governor" (*ha-pehah* in Neh 12:26).

Despite these biblical references, some scholars have maintained that Judah was not a separate province but merely a small region subordinated to the province of Samaria (see North 1992, 5:89–90). Apart from the designation of Sheshbazzar and Zerubbabel as "governor," the Bible offers no clue to the status of Judah before the mid-fifth century BCE. But from the time of Nehemiah, the biblical depiction of Judah as a separate province is strengthened by multiple factors. There is no evidence in the extrabiblical sources that Judah was subordinated to Samaria, and Persian sources speak of Judah using the same description found in the Bible: *Yehud Medinta/Medinata* or simply Yehud. Indeed, although "Samaritan[s]" is/are mentioned several times in the Ezra-Nehemiah narratives, the complaint is not that they are already overlords of Judah but simply that they are seeking to achieve dominance over Judah. The opposition of Sanballat the Samaritan was surely based upon his fear that a strong governor in Judah would threaten his own authority and further dilute his influence with the Persian rulers. The contacts between Sanballat and Nehemiah are depicted in Scripture as a struggle between equals, with Nehemiah able to gain the upper hand on multiple occasions.

Nehemiah 2:7 recounts the request of Nehemiah for letters from Artaxerxes I (465–424 BCE) guaranteeing safe passage to Jerusalem through the territories of governors of *'ever ha-nahar*. If the phrase *'ever ha-nahar* is a proper noun naming a larger administrative unit (satrapy), "Beyond the River," then *paḥavot ʿever ha-nahar* would describe multiple leaders (governors) of the smaller units (provinces) within the satrapy. News of these letters made Sanballat angry, but there is no indication that he or any other official appealed to Persia on the grounds that he was the satrap whose authority extended to Judah. Nor is there any indication that people from the province of Samaria had settled in Judah, which surely would have been the case were Judah part of that province or merely an annex to a larger Samaritan satrapy.

In addition to the three men named in Scripture, five men titled "governor" (*peḥah*) have now been identified from extrabiblical sources, including a large cache of bullae, seals, coins, and wine jars used in the collection of taxes. The large number of seal impressions found at Ramat Rahel inscribed with the names of the province's governors and other officials indicates the city may have been the residence of the governor of Yehud. Located just to the south of Jerusalem, Ramat Rahel had an impressive palace complex, and it may have been one of the residences of the kings of Judah. The site also contained a notable garden that flourished during the Persian Period, and scholars suggest that the trees were imported from Persia. In particular it may be noted that Persian administrative structure assigned responsibility for the collection of taxes either to the satrap or to the governor of a province. Numerous wine jars stamped with the name *yhd/yhwd* (Judah) and/or the name of the "governor" attest the official sanction that set them apart from regular commercial use and dedicated them to the collection and payment of taxes.

In addition to control over taxes and their collection, the right to mint coins has always been a prerogative of the central governing authority. Here the evidence is somewhat difficult to interpret. While the Persian government exerted a major influence on governmental and military organization, economic life, and taxation, the material culture of Judah appears not to have been significantly impacted. This period also witnessed the gradual appearance of the province name (Yehud) in Aramaic on coins that at times included the name of the governor, also in Aramaic.

FIGURE 20-3. *The Yehud coin. The controversial Yehud coin has been a subject of much debate. Scholars are divided whether the seated figure is Yahweh or a Persian god or official.*

During the fourth century BCE, Athenian coinage became commonplace on the international trade scene, and as a consequence Greek coins have been uncovered in nearly every excavated Persian-era site in Israel (Meshorer 2001, 19). Toward the middle of the fourth century BCE, a number of local governors began to mint their own coins, and so, too, did the Jews of Jerusalem. The use of Greek coins is evident in even early Persian Periods. These coins have been located throughout Judah. The first Judean coins, dated about 350 BCE, include images of owls in an effort to imitate Athenian coinage, but these coins also contain Hebrew inscriptions, such as YHD (Yehud), the Persian-Aramaic name for the Persian province of Judah. Other minted Judean coins had depictions of bearded males, various types of helmets, crowns, women's heads, falcons, the Jewish shofar, and an ear representing "the god's ear" (Stern 2001, 565). A major Jewish symbol often depicted in these coins is the lily, characteristic of Jewish art in Jerusalem and a frequent design used in the architecture of the temple. The lily design has been uncovered in many First Temple–era cities such as Hazor, Megiddo, and Samaria in their proto-Ionic and Aeolian capitals (Meshorer 2001, 9). Although Jerusalem and other sites minted many coins, the principal coinage for Judah and Samaria during the fifth and fourth centuries BCE came from Phoenicia in Sidon and Tyre.

Other signs of Greek influence on the material culture of Levant steadily increased, and Greek scholars as well as mercenaries and traders began to visit the area in growing numbers. Even before the Alexandrian conquests, Greek culture was penetrating the Near East. Greek pottery has turned up in nearly all Judean sites dated to the Persian Period. Local potters imitated Greek styles, and evidence of trade in Greek goods appears at Persian-era sites in Judah. Archaeologists have identified Greek perfume oil flasks, drinking goblets, bowls, and large amphora. The archaeological evidence indicates that Greek traders lived in a number of coastal cities in southern Levant, and Greek tombs have been uncovered in Tell el-Hesi and Atlit (Meyers and Chancey 2012, 1–5). As the Hellenistic Period dawned, it appeared as the completion of a cultural process that had been underway for a long time.

The discovery of governors over Judah in addition to the three named in the Bible sets in context the testimony of Nehemiah regarding "former governors before me" (Neh 5:15), indicating a situation that obtained immediately before his arrival rather than referring to either Sheshbazzar or Zerubbabel of earlier times. Nehemiah is not complaining about Samaritan governors. Instead, he clearly indicts Jewish leaders with his accusation that those who are maltreating the citizens of Jerusalem are doing so to "brothers" (Neh 5:7). The beleaguered people themselves had voiced complaint to Nehemiah about "their Jewish kin" (Neh 5:1), and Nehemiah remonstrates with the offenders by warning them about "the taunts of the nations" (Neh 5:9) who are the true enemy. Clearly, the biblical narrative portrays an internal Jewish dispute and offers no hint that the Samaritan governor is the one abusing the Jews in Jerusalem about taxes, usurious loans, or hungry children.

In this regard, the claim from Robert North that Nehemiah held no genuine civil office from Persia is quite surprising. Setting aside for the moment the significance of his title as "the Governor," it is useful to examine the title he held in the Persian court before he arrived in Jerusalem: "cupbearer." The meaning of the word itself (*mašqeh*—"one who gives [something] to drink") may be taken to imply a low-level position, requiring someone who was loyal and could be trusted to serve drink to the ruler but not necessarily a person of high authority. However, two examples indicate that the position was far more than that of a loyal butler or waiter/server. First, in Assyria, the "cupbearer" was an extremely high official who had administrative, military, and/ or diplomatic responsibilities. This is illustrated in the biblical narratives by the prominent role played by the "Rab-Shaqeh" (the chief cupbearer) in the siege of Jerusalem led by Sennacherib in 701 BCE (see 2 Kgs 18–19 = Isa 36–37). Second, the Hellenistic-era book of Tobit (1:21-22) notes that the cupbearer Ahikar, who had exercised "authority over the entire administration" as "keeper of the signet and in charge of administration of the accounts under King Sennacherib of Assyria," was reappointed to the same position by Esarhaddon. It is thus not surprising that a "cupbearer" would be appointed to an office as high as "governor" of a Persian province.

The Opponents of Nehemiah

The opponents of Nehemiah included leaders of three provinces. Sanballat is listed as "the governor of Samaria" (*paḥat šamrin*) in a letter sent from the Jews of the Elephantine fortress on the Nile to the governor of Judah (*CAP* 30.29; Porten 1996b, 19:29). He appears as the most vocal and determined opponent of Nehemiah. Geshem the Arab was apparently in charge of the north Arabian confederacy that controlled trade routes over which myrrh and frankincense were shipped. Fear that he might lose revenue from this trade to a strong governor in Jerusalem may well have been the source of his opposition to Nehemiah. Tobiah the Ammonite referred to in Nehemiah 2:10, inter alia, apparently served as the governor of the province of Ammon in Transjordan; his grandson, also named Tobiah, held the title "governor" (see Josephus, *Antiquities* 12.160ff.). This family created a locally powerful dynasty in Transjordan that was eventually centered at the Hellenistic-era palace of Iraq el-Amir (Qasr el 'Abd), located in the hills approximately twelve miles southwest of Amman, Jordan.

A combination of the opposition groups represented by Sanballat, Tobiah, and Geshem may be designated by the generic phrase "people of the land" as people whose political interests were the opposite of those pursued by "the people of Yehud" (Ezra 4:4). In some texts, the phrase denotes those who opposed the restoration of the Jerusalem temple. In others, it refers broadly to a mixed population encountered in the area by the returning Judean exiles, "foreigners" with whom Jews should not have social intercourse or marry (Ezra 9:1, 2; 10:2, 11).

In short, the harsh reality was that returning Judean exiles were not the only group of people who wanted official recognition from the Persian government to serve as the leaders of the rebuilding of Jerusalem and its environs. Opposition groups led by the governors of Samaria (Sanballat), Ammon (Tobiah), and Edom (Geshem the Arab) viewed the efforts of the returning exiles as a threat to their own authority in the region and attempted to define the activities of the group led by Nehemiah as an act of rebellion against Persian authority with the aim of setting up an independent Judean kingdom (see Neh 2:9, 19; 4:7; 6:1-7). These opponents regarded the Jews coming from Babylonia as foreign immigrants rather than natives returning to their homeland. But from the time of Cyrus and Sheshbazzar in 538 BCE, formal Persian backing to head the province of Judah was consistently given to the Babylonian Jews rather than to a local governor of any other province.

Samaritans

No biblical narrative material describes the period between the time of Nehemiah and the advent of the Greek Empire in 332 BCE. But several external sources furnish important information shedding light on these final one hundred years of the Persian Period. In particular, the references to the "Samaritans" noted often in the books of Ezra and Nehemiah should be clarified. And it is noteworthy that the arguments between the Samaritans and the Jews did not begin in the mid-fifth century BCE with Sanballat and Nehemiah. According to the Bible, the Samaritans were a mixed group of people consisting of Israelites who had not been exiled by the Assyrians in 722 BCE (when the Northern Kingdom was destroyed) and individuals of a variety of nationalities who were resettled by the Assyrians in the conquered Northern Kingdom. The ethnically mixed group exhibited a religious mixture as well, adopting some old northern traditions along with other religious practices of those who had been resettled from outside Samaria. When certain unspecified "enemies of Judah and Benjamin" approached Zerubbabel with an offer to participate in the rebuilding of the temple, they claimed that they too were worshippers of the God of Judah and had been "since the days of King Esar-haddon of Assyria (681–669 BCE), who brought us here" (Ezra 4:2). Their offer was refused by Zerubbabel and the other leaders with the blunt declaration that the Judeans would complete the rebuilding alone (Ezra 4:3). Naturally, such a refusal ensured that those whose offer of assistance was rebuffed would continue to oppose the project. In fact, according to Ezra, they wrote directly to Artaxerxes, warning that, if they were successful in rebuilding their temple, the returned Jews would refuse to pay taxes, bringing "harm to the kingdom" (Ezra 4:13). Heeding their warning, Artaxerxes wrote back with an order to halt the project of rebuilding (4:22), a work stoppage that lasted until the second year of Darius.

Inspired by the preaching of Haggai and Zechariah (Ezra 5:1), Zerubbabel restarted work on the temple, prompting yet another letter to the Persian court, this time from Tattenai, governor of "Beyond-the-River" and other provincial officials. This epistle cited the claim of the returned Jews that their right to rebuild was based on the decree of Cyrus, and they asked that the new king (Darius) search the records to see if their claim could be substantiated (Ezra 6:6-17). The record search turned up the decree of Cyrus and prompted the order from Darius that the Jerusalem temple project be completed without hindrance (Ezra 6:1-15).

In a letter written by Yedoniah, the leader of the Jewish military colony in Elephantine (ca. 408 BCE), two sons are named who appear to have been designated as cogovernors of Samaria (*CAP* 30.29). The letter is part of about one hundred papyrus documents written in Aramaic. These "Elephantine Papyri," discovered at Elephantine Island opposite Aswan, also include numerous ostraca and reveal a Jewish colony that had been influenced by Egyptian culture and religion but that was clearly tied to the larger Persian Empire administratively. In fact, the Elephantine Jews appear to have been established in a military colony charged by the Persian Empire with the defense of its interests in the upper Nile region. Such a link between Jews and Persians explains why Yedoniah, the community leader (high priest?) of the colony, would write to the Persian governor of Yehud (Judah), Bagohi, asking

FIGURE 20-4. *Elephantine Island. The "Elephantine Papyri" were discovered at Elephantine Island. Jews established a military colony on the island as part of the Persian Empire.*

for assistance to rebuild the Yahu temple that had been destroyed by Egyptian priests of the god Khnum. But the letter appears to seek assistance also from Delaiah and Shelemiah, and it is fascinating that they did not oppose the rebuilding of the Elephantine temple as their father had the one in Jerusalem. Clearly, then, the split between Samaritans and Judeans was not yet complete at this date.

The Elephantine documents span the century from 496 to 399 BCE, and they are thus roughly contemporaneous with the careers of Ezra and Nehemiah. These important texts offer no compelling evidence to show that Judah was merely part of the province of Samaria. The fact that numerous duplicates were sent to the governors of both Judah and Samaria indicates that they were separate provinces, each with its own governor. Apparently the ambition of the Samaritan governors recounted in the biblical accounts was to expand their own province to include Jerusalem/Judah rather than to assert authority they held from the Persian court. Further, the texts from Elephantine reveal a Jewish community that was heavily influenced by pagan religion, as the occurrence of names like Anat, Anat-Bethel, Anat-YHW, Herem-Bethel, and Eshem-Bethel attests. This level of syncretism, which exceeded that of the Jews who had been exiled into Babylonia, doubtless explains why no role was accorded to Egyptian-exiled Jews in the reconstruction of Yehud during the Persian Period.

Archaeological data suggests that the region of Samaria did not suffer destruction from the Neo-Babylonian campaigns as did Judah. In fact, the Persian Period witnessed an unprecedented expansion in many of the areas of the territory of Samaria. Site surveys demonstrate that most of the territory of Samaria witnessed substantial population increases during the Persian era. Samaria was wealthier and larger than Jerusalem, and it seems in many ways to have become the Persian administrative capital of the region. The Judean establishment was not dealing with a depopulated province. Samarian leadership was an important force and posed difficult challenges for Jerusalem's elite (Knoppers 2006, 268–80).

The split between the Samaritans claiming to be worshippers of Yahweh and the Judeans was finalized with the erection of a separate temple on Mt. Gerizim by the Samaritans in the latter half of the fourth century BCE. But this final step was in some respects part of a longer tradition of conflict that may be in part rooted in the ancient dispute between north and south that had led to the division of the Davidic kingdom at the death of Solomon in 922 BCE. It is probable that northerners opposed the centralization of sacrificial worship in Jerusalem during the reign of Solomon and that this opposition resulted in the establishment of sanctuaries at Dan and Bethel by Jeroboam.

This sense of opposition to the centralization of worship may also have contributed to the attempts by fifth-century BCE Samaritan leaders to hinder the reconstruction of the Jerusalem temple.

The Samaria Papyri discovered in the Wadi ed-Daliyeh offer further evidence of the fate of the Samaritan province as the biblical Persian Period came to a close. This wadi or dry stream bed east of Samaria winds down to the Jordan Valley. In one of the caves a few miles north of Jericho, numerous fragments of fourth-century BCE manuscripts have been recovered, along with clay seals, coins, some pottery, and some jewelry. Several of the fragments include the names of Samaritan community leaders on written contracts of marriage, sales, loans, and slave purchases. Four factors contribute to the importance of the Samaria Papyri. First, they are a significant cache of legal documents from Samaria itself. Second, they furnish an example of the dialect of Aramaic as it was used in the late fourth century BCE. Third, they are accompanied by several bullae or seal impressions that are inscribed with scenes from Greek mythology, a clear indication of the Greek influence in the area even before the conquests of Alexander. Fourth, they include one seal inscribed with the name of Sanballat, governor of Samaria. This name, presumably indicating the grandson of the Sanballat who opposed Nehemiah, shows the continuing dominance of the Sanballat family in Samaritan politics.

The time of the arrival of Samaritans in the caves that line the Wadi ed-Daliyeh and the reason for the survival of their papyri are set by the date of the attempted Samaritan revolt against the forces of Alexander in 331 BCE. After burning to death the Greek prefect in Syria, Andromachus, they were forced to flee; and having fled to the cave known as Mughâret 'Abū Shinjeh (roughly eight miles north of ancient Jericho), they were overtaken by Macedonian forces and massacred inside the cave itself.

The earliest affair involving opposition from the Greeks who were destined to oust Persia from the role as master of the Levant in 332 BCE was a series of wars between Greece and Persia that began late in the sixth century and ended in 449 BCE. Persia did not lose much of its holdings during this period, but the local populations were thrown into turmoil by the uncertainty of the outcome of the struggle between the two superpowers. The Babylonians succeeded in breaking away from Persian hegemony in 481 BCE, and the Egyptians, supported by Greek troops, made an unsuccessful attempt to follow suit. When the series of wars ended, Persian military control over local areas was tightened, and a number of fortresses were constructed along the trade routes linking Egypt with Mesopotamia.

But Persian control of the area, weakened by the growing Greek influence noted above, ended with the military conquests of Alexander the Great. Judah came under a new master and began the process of adjusting to the Greek methods of administration and empire management as well direct engagement with all things Hellenistic.

Suggestions for Further Reading

Since the events discussed in this chapter take place in the context of the Persian Empire, it behooves us to gain an understanding of that empire. The classic work on Persia is A. T. Olmstead's *History of the Persian Empire*, while Matt Waters has provided a newer portrayal in his *Ancient Persia: A Concise History of the Achaemenid Empire, 550–330 BCE* (2014). A close look at the key figure in these events—the Persian emperor Cyrus, who set into motion the return from exile—appears in *The Cyrus Cylinder: The King of Persia's Proclamation from Ancient Babylon*, by Irving Finkel.

The only contemporary narrative about the events in Yehud (Judea) following the return of the exiles' descendants at the end of the sixth century BCE appears in the books of Ezra and Nehemiah. These two short books have been provided a detailed, step-by-step commentary by Jacob Myers in *Ezra-Nehemiah* (1965) and H. G. M. Williamson in *Ezra, Nehemiah* (1985). The period's archaeological discoveries are characterized in E. P. Stern's *Archaeology of the Land of the Bible*, vol. 2, *The Assyrian, Babylonian, and Persian Periods (732–332 B.C.E.)*.

Diana Edelman provides an analysis of Jerusalem after the return in her *The Origins of the "Second" Temple: Persian Imperial Policy and the Rebuilding of Jerusalem*. Charles Carter takes a different approach to the same set of questions in his *The Emergence of Yehud in the Persian Period: A Social and Demographic Study*. The first volume of Lester Grabbe's *A History of the Jews and Judaism in the Second Temple Period* (2006) gives a more methodical picture of the time and the scholarly approaches to its analysis.

GLOSSARY

Agro-pastoralism—The basis of the ancient Near Eastern economy: agriculture and sheep/goat herding.

Akkadian—Ancient Semitic language spoken and written in Mesopotamia from the third through first millennium BCE; usually written in cuneiform script.

Amarna Letters—Fourteenth-century BCE archive found in New Kingdom Egypt containing letters from Near Eastern kings and rulers of Canaanite city-states.

Ammon, Ammonites—Northernmost of the three Transjordanian kingdoms in the Iron Age.

Anatolia—Asia Minor; ancient Turkey.

Antiquarianism—The collection of ancient or historical objects for their own sake and without attention to or study of the context in which they were found—a common practice prior to the development of the field and methods of archaeology.

Apiru, Habiru, Hapiru—Term designating a social group outside of societal and legal norms. Described in the Amarna letters as raiders and bandits in Canaan and elsewhere in the Near East.

Apocalyptic Literature—From apocalypse, "uncovered" (Greek). A work or passage revealing the secrets of God's plan for the future or the secrets of heavenly space.

Apocrypha—"Hidden things" (Greek). A collection of Jewish religious texts of the Hellenistic and Roman Periods that are part of the canons of Roman Catholic and Orthodox churches but not the Jewish or Protestant. See also "Deuterocanonical."

Arabah, Aravah—Area south of the Jordan Rift Valley and the Dead Sea.

Aramaic—A common Semitic language of the Near East in the first millennium BCE and CE; initially spread throughout the lands of the Assyrian Empire by Tiglath-Pileser III.

Arameans—Ancient Aramaic-speaking people in northern Syria and Babylonia in the late second and early first millennia BCE. Aramaic originated with them.

Archaeology—The study of past cultures through the analysis of their material remains.

Archaeozoology—Study of animal bones found in the archaeological record.

Artifact—Any object made, used, or altered by humans.

Asherah—Canaanite fertility goddess and consort of El in the Ugaritic texts. Strongly condemned by the biblical writers, she is associated with high places and poles/trees and was sometimes worshipped alongside Yahweh in ancient Israel.

Ashlar—Large cut-stone blocks laid horizontally in large buildings and walls.

Assyrian Empire, Assyria, Assyrians—The Neo-Assyrian empire that originated in northern Mesopotamia and was the most powerful state in the Near East ca. 911–612 BCE.

Astarte—Canaanite goddess who was also worshipped in ancient Israel.

Baal, Ba'al—Canaanite storm god who was a rival to Yahweh and strongly condemned by the biblical authors.

Babylonian Empire, Babylonians—The Neo-Babylonian empire that originated in central-southern Mesopotamia and conquered the Neo-Assyrian capital of Nineveh in 612 BCE. After the defeat of the Neo-Assyrians, it was the dominant power in the Near East until its own defeat by the Persian king Cyrus the Great in 539 BCE.

Babylonian Exile—Period following the conquest of Jerusalem in 597 BCE and the deportation of the Judean upper classes to Babylon. The exile ended in 538 BCE when Cyrus the Great conquered Babylon and allowed the Jews to return to Judah.

Balk, Baulk—Vertical section of earth that preserves stratigraphy in an archaeological unit such as a square.

Bamah, Bamot—"High place" (Heb). An open-air cultic site or platform.

Bas-Relief—A sculptural technique in which the sculpted shapes are slightly higher than the flat background to give a three-dimensional effect.

Bet Av—"House of the Father" (Heb). A joint family household that was the smallest social unit in ancient Israel.

Beqaa Valley, Biqa' Valley—A large, fertile valley in eastern Lebanon.

Bichrome Ware—Philistine and later Phoenician pottery characterized by a decorated motif of geometric and floral designs in two colors, usually black and red.

Black Obelisk—Stela inscribed by the Assyrian king Shalmaneser III depicting the earliest image of an Israelite king (Jehu).

Bulla/Bullae—The clay impression of a stamp used to seal a rolled document written on papyrus or other flexible material.

Burnish—Rubbing the surface of a ceramic vessel before it is completely dry to create a shiny appearance.

Canaan, Canaanites—The Southern Levant; the name of the Land of Israel and its inhabitants before the Israelite conquest.

Canon—An official list of texts that make up the Hebrew Bible.

Casemate—A defensive wall that is actually two thin, parallel walls that can be divided into rooms or filled in with rubble to create a single, stronger wall.

Catchment—Water that is captured by diverting rainwater runoff along walls or channels into basins or cisterns.

Central Hill Country—The highlands of Palestine stretching from south of the Jezreel Valley to north of Arad, roughly equivalent to today's West Bank and Jerusalem.

Cisjordan—Land west of the Jordan River, often termed Land of Canaan, Land of Israel, or Palestine.

Cistern—Lined pit used to store water, food, and other items.

City-State—A city with its surrounding territory that forms an independent state.

Codex—A set of rectangular sheets of papyrus or parchment that were bound on one side.

Coptic—Language of the Coptic Christians; the final stage of the ancient Egyptian language.

Covenant—A contract or agreement used in the Hebrew Bible often for a relationship between Yahweh and the Israelites.

Cult—The religious practices of a people.

Cuneiform—A syllabic writing system invented in southern Mesopotamia in the late fourth millennium BCE. Using wedge-shaped writing on clay tablets, it was one of the earliest writing systems.

Dead Sea Scrolls—Collection of texts found in caves on the western shore of the Dead Sea containing some of the earliest manuscripts of books included in the Hebrew Bible.

Decapolis—A group of ten Greek cities on the east side of the Jordan Valley, opposite northern Israel.

Demotic—"Popular" (Greek). Refers to an ancient Egyptian script.

Deuterocanonical—Books and passages in the Catholic Old Testament that do not appear in the Hebrew Bible. See also "Apocrypha."

Deuteronomistic Historian(s)—A group of priests and scribes who edited the books of Joshua through 2 Kings. Perhaps influenced by the reforms of Hezekiah in the eighth century BCE, the movement ended in the exile. Their major period of productivity was during the reforms of King Josiah in the seventh century BCE. Some scholars think they wrote the core of Deuteronomy, chapters 12–26.

Documentary Hypothesis—A theory formulated by Julius Wellhausen, who argued that the Torah/Pentateuch was not written by Moses but rather composed of four primary literary sources that were designated with the letters J, E, D, and P. The finished work was thus the product of many writers and editors.

Edom, Edomites—Southernmost of the three Transjordanian kingdoms in the Iron Age.

Egypt, Egyptians—Modern country and ancient land in the northeast corner of Africa. Featured prominently in the Hebrew Bible, especially in Exodus, the Egyptian Empire extended its control into the southern Levant during the Late Bronze Age and exerted considerable power and influence on the rest of the ancient Near East.

El—"God" (Heb). Main Canaanite god according to the Ugaritic texts; it also one of the names for God in the Hebrew Bible.

Elohim—One of the names for God in the Hebrew Bible. Grammatically, it is a plural form for the singular word for "god" in Hebrew, *El*. Usually rendered as "God" in English translations.

Epigrapher, Epigraphy—One who studies and interprets ancient inscriptions.

Ethnoarchaeology, Ethnoarchaeologist—Ethnographic research on modern societies conducted by an archaeologist examining the link between social behavior and its physical remains.

Ethnogenesis—The early formation and development of a people, such as the Israelites in the Iron Age I Period.

Ethnography, Ethnographic Research—The study of a living people and culture.

Exegesis, Exegete—A knowledgeable explanation or interpretation of a religious text. A person who creates an exegesis.

Faience—Glaze-like "pre-glass" material used for ornaments and figurines in ancient Egypt.

Fertile Crescent—An arc spanning the territory from the Levantine coast northeastward through Syria and then southeast into Iraq that corresponds to the area where plants and animals were first domesticated in the Neolithic Period.

Field—A group of excavation squares or trenches.

Field School—Archaeological program of excavation, laboratory work, lectures, and trips; often worth university credit.

Flotation—Method used to recover plant and other small remains from archaeological contexts.

Form Criticism—A method of biblical studies that isolates certain passages and attempts to trace their origins and history.

Four-Room House, Pillared House—Common Iron Age house plan that typically features four interior rooms.

Gezer Calendar—Tenth-century BCE inscription from Gezer that is an early Hebrew account of seasonal agricultural activities.

GIS (Geographic Information Systems)—A computer system that allows for the production of maps and other graphic displays of geographic data.

Glacis—A solid, sloping mantle created by layering soil and chalk that was part of the defensive systems of Canaanite and Israelite cities. Protected the fort or city from the approach of soldiers or siege engines, as well as tunneling.

Golan Heights—A rocky plateau overlooking the northern Jordan Valley rising to the east and northeast of the Sea of Galilee.

Hectare—A metric unit of square measure, usually used in the measurement of land. One hectare is equivalent to 2.471 acres or 10,000 square meters.

Heterarchy—A system of organization in which the elements are unranked or can be ranked in different ways.

Hieroglyphs, Hieroglyphics—Invented in Egypt in the late fourth millennium BCE, it was one of the earliest writing systems. Consists of pictures used to represent a word, syllable, or sound.

Higher Criticism—Biblical criticism that investigates the origins and composition of the biblical text as a product of human activity.

Hinterland—The area around a city or town, which it controls.

Homo erectus—An extinct hominid species (ancestor of modern humans) that lived ca. 1.9 million to 100,000 years ago and used stone handaxes. The first hominid species to leave Africa.

Homo sapiens neanderthalensis—Our closest extinct human relative, who lived ca. 400,000 to 40,000 years ago.

Homo sapiens sapiens—Anatomically modern humans that evolved ca. 200,000 years ago. There is evidence of their presence in the Levant beginning around 50,000 years ago.

Human Geography—Branch of geography that studies the interplay between people and the environment.

In Situ—"In position" (Latin). Refers to objects located in their original (archaeological) context.

Installation—Nonportable artifact found in an archaeological context, such as an oven or storage bin.

Israel, Israelites—A people formed in the southern Levant from twelve tribes (according to the Hebrew Bible). It also was the name of the northern kingdom during the period of the Israelite monarchy. Israelites comprised the population of the northern kingdom, but the term is used generally to describe most of the population of Israel and Judah during the monarchical period.

Israeli—A citizen of the modern State of Israel.

Jeshimon—A wilderness in Judah between the hill country and Dead Sea.

Judah, Judahites—The southern kingdom during the period of the Israelite monarchy and those who lived in it.

Judea, Judeans—The area surrounding Jerusalem and those who live in it. Usually refers to the time of the Maccabees and later.

Ketuvim—"Writings" (Heb). The third division of the Tanakh, along with the Torah (Pentateuch) and Neviim (Prophets).

Kinneret, Lake Kinneret—"Sea of Galilee" (Heb).

Levant—Land along the eastern coast of the Mediterranean Sea.

Lexicon—The words used in a language.

LiDAR (Light Detection and Ranging)—Aerial reconnaissance technique that allows for the discovery of archaeological sites and features underground.

Lithograph—Printing from a stone or metal plate.

LMLK Jars—Storage jars found mainly at sites in Judah and dating to the late eighth century BCE—marked with a stamp reading "for the king," suggesting the contents were rations, taxes, or tithes.

Locus, Loci—"Place" (Latin). Defined unit(s) or location(s) in an archaeological context.

LXX—An abbreviation for the Septuagint.

Maquis—A dense growth of underbrush and scrub vegetation.

Masoretes—Groups of Jewish scholars responsible for standardizing the biblical text and its vowels between the sixth and tenth centuries CE.

Masoretic Text (MT)—Medieval text of the Hebrew Bible. This is the earliest complete text of the Hebrew Bible in its original languages. The oldest manuscript is from the ninth century CE.

Material Culture—Artifacts and installations found in archaeological contexts.

Matrix—The material that immediately surrounds an artifact, like clay, sand, or sediment.

Merneptah Stele—Late thirteenth-century BCE stela written by the Egyptian pharaoh Merneptah that includes the earliest mention of a people called Israel.

Mesha Stele, Moabite Stone—Ninth-century BCE stela composed by Mesha, king of Moab.

Mesopotamia—Land between the rivers (Euphrates and Tigris) in modern Iraq and Syria; the homeland area of several ancient empires.

Moab, Moabites—The middle of the three Transjordanian kingdoms of the Iron Age.

Negev Desert—Desert south of Judah.

Neviim—"Prophets" (Heb). Comprises the Tanakh along with the Torah (first five books of the Hebrew Bible) and Ketuvim (Writings).

Obelisk—Tall, four-sided monument with a small pyramid on top.

Orthography—Set of conventions for writing a language.

Ossuary—Bone box used for secondary burials in Chalcolithic and Roman Palestine.

Osteology, Osteologists—Study of the human skeletal system; those who study the human skeletal system.

Ostracon, Ostraca—Inscribed pottery sherd.

Ottoman Empire—Empire founded in Anatolia (Turkey) at the end of the thirteenth century CE that controlled much of southeast Europe, the Middle East, the Caucasus, North Africa, and the Horn of Africa; it ended with the establishment of the Republic of Turkey in 1923.

Paleoethnobotany—Study of the relationship between humans and plants in the past.

Palestine—Land west of the Jordan River, equivalent to Cisjordan.

Pastoralism—Sheep and goat herding.

Patriarchy—Male-dominated society.

Patrilineal—Descent reckoned through the father's line.

Patrilocal—Marriage pattern in which a wife moves into her husband's family's house.

Pentateuch—The first five books of the Hebrew Bible: Genesis, Exodus, Leviticus, Numbers, Deuteronomy. Also called the Torah.

Persian Empire, Persia, Persians—Ancient Iran; ethnic group native to Iran. The Persian Empire consisted of a series of imperial dynasties in Iran beginning with Cyrus the Great in 550 BCE.

Philistia, Philistines—Land west of Judah on the Mediterranean coast occupied by the Philistines; a group of migrants and refugees from the Aegean region in the decades after 1200 BCE.

Philology, Philologist—Study of the history of language and the historical study of literary texts; one who studies the history of language.

Phoenicia, Phoenicians—Land north of Israel on the Mediterranean coast occupied by Phoenicians; Iron Age Canaanites who were renowned seafarers.

Pillared House—*See* Four-Room House.

Pottery Reading—The examination of ceramic vessel remains during excavation to help archaeologists determine the date of archaeological contexts.

Provenance—The exact horizontal and vertical location of an object in an archaeological context; also the origin and history of ownership of an archaeological object.

Pseudepigrapha—"Falsely attributed" (Greek). Ancient noncanonical writings attributed to biblical figures, such as the Book of Enoch.

Realia—Artifacts and other materials that illustrate ancient daily life.

Qumran—The site on the northwestern shore of the Dead Sea near where the Dead Sea Scrolls were discovered. It served as the center of the Jewish Essene movement in the first centuries BCE and CE.

Rosetta Stone—Bilingual inscription in three scripts (Egyptian, Demotic, and Greek) on a second-century BCE stele that enabled Egyptian hieroglyphs to be deciphered.

Samaritans—A Jewish sect descended from the northern Israelites who follow preexilic religious traditions and practices.

Sarcophagus/Sarcophagi—Stone coffin(s) either displayed or buried and associated with the Egyptians, Greeks, and Romans.

Scholastics (of the Middle Ages)—Academics of medieval universities in Europe who taught scholasticism, a method of critical thought.

Seal—An inscribed stamp usually made of stone that was used to mark ownership in clay or wax.

Second Temple Period—The period after the return of the exiles to Israel in the late sixth century BCE and after a new Jerusalem temple was built to replace the First Temple destroyed by the Babylonians.

Section—Vertical record of material excavated in a square, usually seen in the balk/baulk.

Septuagint—Greek translation(s) of the Hebrew Bible, first made in the third century BCE.

Shephelah—"Low-lying" (Heb). Refers to the north-south strip of low hills in the land of Israel between the Mediterranean coast and central highlands.

Sherd—Broken piece of ceramic vessel.

Siloam Inscription—The only monumental inscription from Judah, it describes the cutting of a tunnel under the City of David in Jerusalem that allowed access to the water of the Gihon Spring outside the city; probably from the late eighth century BCE.

Sitz im Leben—"Situation in life" (German). Refers to the original sociocultural context in which a text was created.

Slip—Thin layer of clay applied to the outside of a ceramic vessel as decoration.

Sondage—Trench or other relatively small excavation unit.

Square—The five-by-five-meter square is the standard excavation unit used in Israel and Jordan.

Steppe—A large, treeless, grassy plain.

Stela, Stele, Stelae—Standing stone(s).

Stratum, Strata, Stratigraphy—Level/levels. The layers of occupation at an archaeological site. The Law of Superposition states that layers on the bottom are older than layers at the top.

Tanakh—The Hebrew Bible in Jewish tradition; an acronym of Torah (first five books), Neviim (Prophets), and Ketuvim (Writings).

Targum—A translation of the Hebrew biblical text into Aramaic. The term traditionally refers to translation texts composed during the rabbinic period but has also been applied to translations found among the Dead Sea Scrolls. In Rabbinic Judaism, it can also refer to the oral act of translating, whether into Aramaic or into another language.

Tel, Tell, Tall, Tepe—An artificial mound formed over centuries and millennia by continued occupation on the ruins of earlier settlements.

Terrace—A leveled surface. In the Iron Age I, terraces were constructed and used around hilltop settlements to grow crops.

Text Criticism—Study of ancient manuscripts to determine the original wording.

Top Plan—Plan of an archaeological square, field, or site from above.

Toponym, Toponymy—A place-name; regular and specific use of place-names.

Torah—"Teaching" (Heb). The first five books of the Hebrew Bible. Comprises the Tanakh along with Neviim (Prophets) and Ketuvim (Writings). Also called the Pentateuch.

Transjordan—Land east of the Jordan River.

Ugarit—Late Bronze Age site on the Syrian coastline in the northern Levant.

Ugaritic Literature—Cuneiform documents discovered at Ugarit, including texts that shed light on Canaanite religion.

Vulgate—"Common" (Latin). Jerome's fourth- to fifth-century CE Latin translation of the Bible.

Wadi—"Stream bed" (Arabic).

Yahweh, YHWH—One of the names for God in the Hebrew Bible. Usually rendered as "LORD" in English translations.

Yehud—Judah during the Persian Period.

BIBLIOGRAPHY

Abou-Assaf, A. 1983. "Ein Relief der kriegerischen Göttin Ištar." *Damaszener Mitteilungen* 1:7–8.

———. 1990. *Der Tempel von 'Ain Dārā*. Damaszener Forschungen 3. Mainz: Zabern.

———. 1993. "Der Tempel von 'Ain Dārā in Nordsyrien." *Antike Welt* 24:155–71.

———. 1994. "Zwei neue Stelenfragmente aus Ain Dara." Pages 1–5 in *Beiträge zur altorientalischen Archäologie und Altertumskunde*. Edited by Fs. B. Hrouda, P. Calmeyer, K. Hecker, L. Jakob-Rost, and C. B. F. Walker. Wiesbaden: Harrassowitz.

———. 1996. "Die Kleinfunde aus 'Ain Dārā." *Damaszener Mitteilungen* 9:47–111.

Abraham, Kathleen. 2011. "The Reconstruction of Jewish Communities in the Persian Empire: The Āl-Yahūdu Clay Tablets." Pages 261–64 in *Light and Shadows—The Catalog—The Story of Iran and the Jews*. Edited by Hagai Segev and Asaf Schor. Tel Aviv: Beit Hatfutsot.

Ackroyd, Peter R., Christopher Francis Evans, G. W. H. Lampe, and S. L. Greenslade, eds. 1963–1970. *The Cambridge History of the Bible*. 3 vols. Cambridge: Cambridge University Press.

Adams, M., and M. Cohen. 2013. "The 'Sea Peoples' in Primary Sources." Pages 645–64 in *The Philistines and Other Sea Peoples in Text and Archaeology*. Edited by A. E. Killebrew and G. Lehmann. Atlanta: SBL Press.

Adler, R., et al., eds. 1985. *Atlas of Israel: Cartography, Physical and Human Geography*. 3rd ed. Tel Aviv: Survey of Israel.

Aharoni, Yohanan. 1967. *The Land of the Bible: A Historical Geography*. Translated by A. Rainey. Philadelphia: Westminster.

Aharoni, Y., and Michael Avi-Yonah. 1980. *The Macmillan Bible Atlas*. Rev. ed. New York: Macmillan; London: Collier Macmillan. Fourth printing.

Aharoni, Y., M. Avi-Yonah, A. Rainey, and Z. Safrai. 1993. *The Macmillan Bible Atlas*. 3rd ed. New York: Macmillan.

Aḥituv, Shmuel. 2008. *Echoes from the Past: Hebrew and Cognate Inscriptions from the Biblical Period*. Jerusalem: Carta.

Ahlström, Gösta W. 1986. *Who Were the Israelites?* Winona Lake, Ind.: Eisenbrauns.

———. 1993. *The History of Ancient Palestine from the Palaeolithic Period to Alexander's Conquest*. With a contribution by Gary O. Rollefson. Edited by Diana Edelman. Sheffield: JSOT Press.

Ahlström, Gösta W., Gary Orin Rollefson, and Diana Vikander Edelman. 1993. *The History of Ancient Palestine from the Paleolithic Period to Alexander's Conquest.* Sheffield: JSOT Press.

Ahn, J., and J. Middlemas, eds. 2012. *By the Irrigation Canals of Babylon: Approaches to the Study of the Exile.* LHB/OTS 526. New York: T&T Clark.

Albertz, Rainer. 2001. *Die Exilszeit: 6. Jahrhundert v. Chr.* Biblische Enzyklopädie 7. Stuttgart: Kohlhammer Verlag.

———. 2012. "More or Less than a Myth: Reality and Significance of Exile for the Political, Social, and Religious History of Judah." Pages 20–33 in Ahn and Middlemass, 2012.

Albertz, Rainer, and Rüdiger Schmitt. 2012. *Family and Household Religion in Ancient Israel and the Levant.* Winona Lake, Ind.: Eisenbrauns.

Albright, William Foxwell. 1946. *From the Stone Age to Christianity: Monotheism and the Historical Process.* Baltimore: Johns Hopkins University Press.

———. 1963. *The Biblical Period from Abraham to Ezra.* New York: Harper & Row.

———. 1969. "The Impact of Archaeology on Biblical Studies." Pages 1–4 in *New Directions in Biblical Archaeology.* Edited by D. N. Freedman and J. C. Greenfield. Garden City, N.Y.: Doubleday.

Alexander, P. S. 1996. "Early Jewish Geography." *ABD* 2: 977–87.

Allegro, John. 1965. *The Shapira Affair.* Garden City, N.Y.: Doubleday.

Alt, Albrecht. 1989. "The Gods of the Fathers." Pages 1–77 in *Essays on Old Testament History and Religion.* Translated by R. A. Wilson. The Biblical Seminar. Sheffield: JSOT Press. Reprinted and translated from *Der Gott der Väter.* BWANT III Folge, Heft 12. Stuttgart: W. Kohlhamer, 1912.

Alter, Robert. 1981. *The Art of Biblical Narrative.* New York: Basic Books.

Amiran, D. H. K., et al., eds. 1970. *Atlas of Israel.* 2nd ed. Jerusalem: Survey of Israel.

Anati, Emmanuel. 1985. "Has Mt. Sinai Been Found?" *BAR* 11 (4): 42–57.

———. 1986. *The Mountain of God: Har Karkom.* New York: Rizzoli.

———. 2003. "Where Is Mt. Sinai?" *Bible and Interpretation,* October. http://www .bibleinterp.com/articles/Anati_Mount_Sinai.shtml.

———. 2013. *Is Har Karkom the Biblical Mount Sinai?* Capodiponte: Atelier Editions.

———. 2015. "Har Karkom: Archaeological Discoveries in a Holy Mountain in the Desert of Exodus." Pages 449–56 in Levy et al. 2015.

Ashbel, D. 1971. "Israel, Land of (Geographical Survey)—Climate." Pages 131–36 in vol. 9 of *Encyclopædia Judaica.* New York: Macmillan.

Assmann, Jan. 1997. *Moses the Egyptian: The Memory of Egypt in Western Monotheism.* Cambridge, Mass.: Harvard University Press.

Aster, S. Z. 2003. "What Was Doeg the Edomite's Title?" *JBL* 122:353–61.

Aufrecht, W. 1989. *A Corpus of Ammonite Inscriptions.* Lewiston, N.Y.: Edwin Mellen.

Avigad, Nahman. 1976. *Bullae and Seals from a Post-exilic Judean Archive.* Jerusalem: Institute of Archaeology, the Hebrew University of Jerusalem.

———. 1978. "Baruch the Scribe and Jerahmeel the King's Son." *Israel Exploration Journal* 28:52–56.

———. 1980. *The Upper City of Jerusalem.* Jerusalem: Shiqmona (in Hebrew).

———. 1983. *Discovering Jerusalem.* Nashville: Nelson.

———. 1997. *Corpus of West Semitic Stamp Seals.* Revised and completed by Benjamin Sass. Jerusalem: Israel Academy of Sciences and Humanities, Israel Exploration Society, and the Institute of Archaeology, Hebrew University of Jerusalem.

Avioz, M. 2011. "The Names Mephibosheth and Ishbosheth Reconsidered." *Journal of the Ancient Near Eastern Society* 32:11–20.

Babcock, Bryan. 2014. *A Study of the West Semitic Ritual Calendars in Leviticus 23 and the Akkadian Text Emar 446.* BBRSup 9. Winona Lake, Ind.: Eisenbrauns.

Baden, Joel S. 2012. *The Composition of the Pentateuch: Renewing the Documentary Hypothesis.* New Haven: Yale University Press.

Baines, J., and J. Malek. 2000. *Cultural Atlas of Ancient Egypt.* Rev. ed. Oxfordshire: Andromeda Oxford.

Baly, D. 1974. *The Geography of the Bible: A Study in Historical Geography.* London: Lutterworth.

———. 1987. *Basic Biblical Geography.* Philadelphia: Fortress, 1987.

Bar-Adon, Pessah. 1980. *The Cave of the Treasure: The Finds from the Caves in Nahal Mishmar.* Jerusalem: Israel Exploration Society.

Bar-Yosef, Ofer. 1995. "Earliest Food Producers—Pre-Pottery Neolithic (8000–5000 BCE)." Pages 190–204 in Levy 1995a.

Barag, D. 1992 "En-Gedi." *NEAEHL* 2:399–409.

Barkay, Gabriel. 1992. "'The Prancing Horse'—an Official Seal Impression from Judah of the 8th Century B.C.E." *Tel Aviv* 19 (1): 124–29.

———. 2000. "The Necropoli of Jerusalem in the First Temple Period." Pages 233–70 in *The History of Jerusalem: The Biblical Period.* Edited by S. Ahituv and A. Mazar. Jerusalem: Yad Izhak Ben-Zvi (in Hebrew).

———. 2009. "The Riches of Hinnom." *BAR* 35 (4): 22–28, 30–33, 35, 122–26. http://members.bib-arch.org/publication.asp?PubID=BSBA&Volume=35&Issue=4&ArticleID=4.

Barkay, Gabriel, Marilyn J. Lundberg, Andrew G. Vaughn, and Bruce Zuckerman. 2003. "The Challenges of Ketef Hinnom: Using Advanced Technologies to Reclaim the Earliest Biblical Texts and Their Context." *NEA* 66 (4): 162–71.

———. 2004. "The Amulets from Ketef Hinnom: A New Edition and Evaluation." *BASOR* 334:41–71.

Barr, James. 2000. *History and Ideology in the Old Testament: Biblical Studies at the End of a Millennium; The Hensley Henson Lectures for 1997 Delivered to the University of Oxford/ James Barr.* Oxford: Oxford University Press.

Barstad, H. M. 1996. *The Myth of the Empty Land: A Study in the History and Archaeology of Judah During the "Exilic" Period.* Symbolae Osloenses Fasc. Suppl. XXVIII. Oslo: Scandinavian University Press.

———. 2003. "After the 'Myth of the Empty Land': Major Challenges in the Study of Neo-Babylonian Judah." Pages 3–20 in *Judah and the Judaeans in the*

Neo-Babylonian Period. Edited by O. Lipschits and J. Blenkinsopp. Winona Lake, Ind.: Eisenbrauns.

———. 2008. *History and the Hebrew Bible: Studies in Ancient Israelite and Ancient Near Eastern Historiography*. FAT 61. Tübingen: Mohr (Siebeck).

———. 2012. "The City State of Jerusalem in the Neo-Babylonian Empire: Evidence from the Surrounding States." Pages 34–48 in Ahn and Middlemass 2012.

Batto, Bernard F. 1992. *Slaying the Dragon: Mythmaking in the Biblical Tradition*. Louisville: Westminster John Knox.

Beaulieu, P.-A. 1989. *The Reign of Nabonidus, King of Babylon, 556–539 B.C.* New Haven: Yale University Press.

Beck, Pirḥa. 1982. "The Drawings from Ḥorvat Teiman (Kuntillet ʿAjrud)." *Tel Aviv* 9:3–68.

Becking, B. 1992. *The Fall of Samaria: An Historical and Archaeological Study*. SHANE 2. Leiden: Brill.

———. 1999. "The Seal of Baalisha, King of the Ammonites, Some Remarks." *BN* 97:13–17.

———. 2006. " 'We All Returned as One': Critical Notes on the Myth of the Mass Return." Pages 3–18 in Lipschits and Oeming 2006.

———. 2007. *From David to Gedaliah: The Book of Kings as Story and History*. OBO 228. Freiburg: Universitätsverlag & Göttingen: Vandenhoeck & Ruprecht.

———. 2012. "Global Warming and the Babylonian Exile." Pages 49–62 in Ahn and Middlemass 2012.

Ben-Arieh, Yehoshuah. 1979. *The Rediscovery of the Holy Land in the Nineteenth Century*. Jerusalem: Magnes.

Ben-Dor Evian, Shirly. 2017. "Ramesses III and the Sea-Peoples: Towards a New Philistine Paradigm." *Oxford Journal of Archaeology* 36 (3): 267–85.

Ben-Dov, M. 1992. "Middle and Late Bronze Age Dwellings." Pages 99–104 in Kempinski and Reich 1992.

Ben-Shlomo, D. 2008. "The Cemetery of Azor and Early Iron Age Burial Practices." *Levant* 40:29–54.

———. 2014. "Philistine Cult and Household Religion according to the Archaeological Record." Pages 73–102 in *Family and Household Religion: Toward a Synthesis of Old Testament Studies, Archaeology, Epigraphy and Cultural Studies*. Edited by R. Albertz, B. Alpert Nakhai, S. M. Olyan, and R. Schmitt. Winona Lake, Ind.: Eisenbrauns.

Ben-Shlomo, D., I. Shai, A. Zukerman, and A. M. Maeir. 2008. "Cooking Identities: Aegean-Style Cooking Jugs and Cultural Interaction in Iron Age Philistia and Neighboring Regions." *American Journal of Archaeology* 112:225–46.

Ben-Tor, Amnon, ed. 1992a. *Archaeology of Ancient Israel*. New Haven: Yale University Press.

———. 1992b. "Early Bronze Age Dwellings and Installations." Pages 60–67 in Kempinski and Reich 1992.

———. 2000. "Hazor and the Chronology of Northern Israel: A Reply to Israel Finkelstein." *BASOR* 317:9–15.

Ben-Tor, Amnon, and Maria Teresa Rubiato. 1999. "Excavating Hazor Part Two: Did the Israelites Destroy the Canaanite City?" *BAR* 25 (3): 22–39.

Ben-Yosef, E., and Lidar Sapir-Hen. 2013. "The Introduction of Domestic Camels to the Southern Levant: Evidence from the Aravah Valley." *Tel Aviv* 40:278–85. http://archaeology.tau.ac.il/ben-yosef/pub/Pub_PDFs/Sapir-Hen&Ben-Yosef13 _CamelAravah_TelAviv.pdf.

Ben-Yosef, E., R. Shaar, L. Tauxe, and H. Ron. 2012. "A New Chronological Framework for Iron Age Copper Production in Timna (Israel)." *BASOR* 366:1–41.

Beougher, D. 2007. "Brian Boru: King, High King and Emperor of the Irish." PhD diss., Penn State University.

Berger, P.-R. 1975. "Der Kyros-Zylinder mit dem Zusatzfragment BIN II Nr. 32 und die akkadische Personennamen im Danielbuch." *Zeitschrift für Assyriologie* 64:192–234.

Berlin, Adele, Marc Zvi Brettler, and Michael A. Fishbane. 2004. *The Jewish Study Bible*. Oxford: Oxford University Press.

Bietak, Manfred. 2015. "On the Historicity of the Exodus: What Egyptology Today Can Contribute to Assessing the Biblical Account of the Sojourn in Egypt." Pages 17–38 in Levy et al. 2015.

Bietak, Manfred, and Irene Forstner-Müller. 2011. "The Topography of New Kingdom Avaris and Per Ramesses." Pages 23–51 in *Ramesside Studies in Honour of K.A. Kitchen*. Edited by M. Collier and S. Snape. Bolton, UK: Rutherford.

Biran, Avraham. 1994. *Biblical Dan*. Jerusalem: Israel Exploration Society and Hebrew Union College / Jewish Institute of Religion.

Birney, K., and B. R. Doak. 2011. "Funerary Iconography on an Infant Burial Jar from Ashkelon." *Israel Exploration Journal* 61:32–53.

Blakely, Jeffrey A. 2002. "Reconciling Two Maps: Archaeological Evidence for the Kingdoms of David and Solomon." *BASOR* 327:49–54.

Blakely, J., L. Toombs, and K. G. O'Connell, eds. 1980. *The Tell El-Hesi Field Manual: The Joint Archaeological Expedition to Tell El-Hesi*. Vol. 1. Cambridge, Mass.: ASOR.

Blenkinsopp, Joseph. 1995. *Sage, Priest, Prophet: Religious and Intellectual Leadership in Ancient Israel*. Louisville: Westminster John Knox.

———. 1998. "The Judaean Priesthood during the Neo-Babylonian and Achaemenid Periods: A Hypothetical Reconstruction." *CBQ* 60:25–43.

———. 2000. *Isaiah 1–39: A New Translation with Introduction and Commentary*. New York: Doubleday.

———. 2003. "Bethel in the Neo-Babylonian Period." Pages 93–107 in Lipschits and Blenkinsopp 2003.

Blix, Göran. 2009. *From Paris to Pompeii: French Romanticism and the Culture Politics of Archaeology*. Philadelphia: University of Pennsylvania Press.

Bloch-Smith, E. 1992. *Judahite Burial Practices and Beliefs about the Dead.* JSOTSup 123. JSOT/ASOR Monograph Series 7. Sheffield: Sheffield Academic.

———. 2003. "Israelite Ethnicity in Iron Age I: Archaeology Preserves What Is Remembered and What Is Forgotten in Israel's History." *JBL* 122 (3): 401–25.

Bloch-Smith, E., and Alpert-Nakhai, B. 1999. "A Landscape Comes to Life: The Iron Age I." *NEA* 62 (2): 62–92, 101–27.

Bonogofsky, Michelle. 2004. "Including Women and Children: Neolithic Modeled Skulls from Jordan, Israel, Syria, and Turkey." *NEA* 67 (1): 118–19.

Borowski, O. 1987. *Agriculture in Iron Age Israel.* Winona Lake, Ind.: Eisenbrauns.

———. 1998. *Every Living Thing: Daily Use of Animals in Ancient Israel.* Walnut Creek, Calif.: AltaMira.

———. 2003. *Daily Life in Biblical Times.* Atlanta: SBL Press.

Botterweck, G. Johannes, and Helmer Ringgren, eds. 1974–2006. *Theological Dictionary of the Old Testament.* 15 vols. Grand Rapids: Eerdmans.

Bowden, M. J., et al. 1981. "The Effect of Climate Fluctuations on Human Population: Two Hypotheses." Pages 479–513 in *Climate and History: Studies in Past Climates and their Impact on Man.* Edited by T. M. L. Wigley, M. J. Ingram, and G. Farmer. Cambridge: Cambridge University Press.

Boyer, Pascal. 2001. *Religion Explained: The Evolutionary Origins of Religious Thought.* New York: Basic Books.

Brandt, Anthony. 2010. "French Fiasco in Egypt." *Military History* 27:40–47.

Braudel, Fernand. 1972. *The Mediterranean and the Mediterranean World in the Age of Philip II.* New York: Harper & Row.

Brenner, A., ed. 1999. *Judges: A Feminist Companion to the Bible.* The Feminist Companion to the Bible (Second Series) 4. Sheffield: Sheffield Academic.

Brettler, M. Z. 2002. *The Book of Judges.* Old Testament Readings. New York: Routledge.

Brichambaut, G. Perrin de, and C. C. Wallén. 1963. *A Study of Agro-climatology in Semi-arid and Arid Zones of the Near East.* Geneva: World Meteorological Organization.

Bright, John. 1981. *A History of Israel.* Philadelphia: Westminster.

Brisco, T. 1998. *Holman Bible Atlas.* Nashville: Broadman & Holman.

Broshi, M. 1974. "The Expansion of Jerusalem in the Reigns of Hezekiah and Manasseh." *Israel Exploration Journal* 24:21–26.

———. 1978. "Estimating the Population of Ancient Jerusalem." *BAR* 4:10–15.

Brotzman, Ellis R. 1999. *Old Testament Textual Criticism: A Practical Introduction.* Grand Rapids: Baker.

Brug, J. F. 1985. *A Literary and Archaeological Study of the Philistines.* BAR International Series 265. Oxford: B.A.R.

Bunimovitz, Shlomo. 1995a. "How Mute Stones Speak: Interpreting What We Dig Up." *BAR* 21 (2): 58–67, 96.

———. 1995b. "On the Edge of Empires—Late Bronze Age (1500–1200 BCE)." Pages 320–31 in Levy 1995a.

Bunimovitz, Shlomo, and A. Faust 2002. "Ideology in Stone: Understanding the Four Room House." *BAR* 28 (4): 32–41, 59–60.

———. 2003. "Building Identity: The Four-Room House and the Israelite Mind." Pages 411–23 in *Symbiosis, Symbolism, and the Power of the Past: Canaan, Ancient Israel, and Their Neighbors from the Late Bronze Age through Roman Palaestina; Proceedings of the Centennial Symposium W. F. Albright Institute of Archaeological Research and American Schools of Oriental Research, May 29–31, 2000*. Edited by W. G. Dever and S. Gitin. Winona Lake, Ind.: Eisenbrauns.

Bunimovitz, Shlomo, and Z. Lederman. 2009. "The Archaeology of Border Communities: Renewed Excavations at Tel Beth-Shemesh, Part 1: The Iron Age." *Near Eastern Archaeologist* 71:114–42.

Burleigh, Nina. 2007. *Mirage: Napoleon's Scientists and the Unveiling of Egypt*. New York: HarperCollins.

Butzer, K. 1995. "Environmental Change in the Near East and Human Impact on the Land." Pages 123–52 in Sasson 1995.

Campbell, Edward F. 2002. *Shechem III*. Boston: American Schools of Oriental Research.

Cantrell, Deborah O'Daniel. 2011. *The Horsemen of Israel: Horses and Chariotry in Monarchic Israel (Ninth–Eight Centuries B.C.E.)*. History, Archaeology, and Culture of the Levant 1. Winona Lake, Ind.: Eisenbrauns.

Carr, David M. 2005. *Writing on the Tablet of the Heart: Origins of Scripture and Literature*. New York: Oxford University Press.

———. 2011. *The Formation of the Hebrew Bible: A New Reconstruction*. New York: Oxford University Press.

Carter, C. E. 1999. *The Emergence of Yehud in the Persian Period: A Social and Demographic Study*. JSOTSup 294. Sheffield: Sheffield Academic.

Cassuto, D. 2008. "Bringing the Artifacts Home: A Social Interpretation of Loom Weights in Context." Pages 63–77 in Nakhai 2008.

Chapman, Rupert. 1991. "British-Holy Land Archaeology: Nineteenth Century Sources." Pages 208–25 in *With Eyes toward Zion—III: Western Societies and the Holy Land*. Edited by Moshe Davis and Yehoshua Ben-Arieh. New York: Praeger.

Cifola, B. 1988. "Ramses III and the Sea Peoples: A Structural Analysis of the Medinet Habu Inscriptions." *Orientalia* 57:275–306.

Clark, D. 2003. "Bricks, Sweat and Tears: The Human Investment in Constructing a 'Four-Room' House." *NEA* 66 (1–2): 34–43.

Clay, A. T. 1912. *Business Documents of Murashu Sons of Nippur Dated in the Reign of Darius II*. Philadelphia: University of Pennsylvania Museum.

Cline, Eric H. 2007. *From Eden to Exile: Unraveling Mysteries of the Bible*. Washington, D.C.: National Geographic.

Cobbing, Felicity. 2005. "The American Palestine Exploration Society and the Survey of Eastern Palestine." *Palestine Exploration Quarterly* 137:9–21.

Cogan, Mordechai. 2001. *1 Kings: A New Translation with Introduction and Commentary*. New York: Doubleday.

Cogan, Mordechai, and Hayim Tadmor. 1988. *II Kings: A New Translation with Introduction and Commentary*. Garden City, N.Y.: Doubleday.

Cohen, M. E. 2013. "The Language and Culture of 2 Samuel." PhD diss., Penn State University.

Cohen, S. 2015. "Interpretative Uses and Abuses of the Beni Hasan Tomb Painting." *Journal of Near Eastern Studies* 74 (1):19–38.

Cole, Juan. 2007. *Napoleon's Egypt: Invading the Middle East*. New York: Palgrave Macmillan.

Collins, J. 2005. *The Bible after Babel: Historical Criticism in a Postmodern Age*. Grand Rapids: Eerdmans.

Coogan, Michael D. 1976. "More Yahwistic Names in the Murashu Documents." *JSJ* 7:199–200.

———. 2011. *The Oxford Encyclopedia of the Books of the Bible*. New York: Oxford University Press.

Crabtree, P. J. 1989. "Sheep, Horses, Swine and Kine: A Zooarchaeological Perspective on the Anglo-Saxon Settlement of England." *Journal of Field Archaeology* 16:205–13.

Cross, Frank Moore. 1973. *Canaanite Myth and Hebrew Epic: Essays in the History of the Religion of Israel*. Cambridge, Mass.: Harvard University Press.

———. 1998. *From Epic to Canon: History and Literature in Ancient Israel*. Baltimore: Johns Hopkins University Press.

Cross, Frank Moore, and David Noel Freedman. 1975. *Studies in Ancient Yahwistic Poetry*. Missoula, Mont.: Scholars Press.

Cross, Frank Moore, and Lawrence R. Stager. 2006. "Cypro-Minoan Inscriptions Found in Ashkelon." *Israel Exploration Journal* 56 (2): 129–59.

Currid, J. 1984. "The Deforestation of the Foothills of Palestine." *Palestine Exploration Quarterly* 116:1–11.

———. 1999. *Doing Archaeology in the Land of the Bible*. Grand Rapids: Baker Books.

Dalley, Stephanie. 1985. "Foreign Chariotry in the Armies of Tiglath-Pileser III and Sargon II." *Iraq* 47:31–48.

———. 1994. "Nineveh, Babylon and the Hanging Gardens: Cuneiform and Classical Sources Reconciled." *Iraq* 56:45–58.

———. 2000. *Myths from Mesopotamia: Creation, the Flood, Gilgamesh, and Others*. Oxford: Oxford University Press.

Damrosch, David. 2007. *The Buried Book: The Loss and Rediscovery of the Great Epic of Gilgamesh*. New York: Henry Holt.

Dandamaev, M. A. 1984. *Slavery in Babylonia from Nabopolassar to Alexander the Great (626–331 B.C.)*. DeKalb: Northern Illinois University Press.

Daniel, Glyn. 1976. *A Hundred and Fifty Years of Archaeology*. Cambridge, Mass.: Harvard University Press.

Darby, E. 2014. *Interpreting Judean Pillar Figurines: Gender and Empire in Judean Apotropaic Ritual*. Tubingen: Mohr Siebeck.

Davies, Philip R. 1992. *In Search of "Ancient Israel": A Study in Biblical Origins*. Sheffield: Sheffield Academic.

———. 1995. *Whose Bible Is It Anyway?* Sheffield: Sheffield Academic.

Davis, T. W. 2004a. *Shifting Sands: The Rise and Fall of Biblical Archaeology*. New York: Oxford University Press.

———. 2004b. "Theory and Method in Biblical Archaeology." Pages 20–28 in *The Future of Biblical Archaeology*. Edited by J. Hoffmeier and A. Millard. Grand Rapids: Eerdmans.

Day, John. 2002. *Yahweh and the Gods and Goddesses of Canaan*. London: Sheffield Academic.

Dearman, J. Andrew. 1991. "Edward Robinson: Scholar and Presbyterian Educator." *American Presbyterians* 69 (3): 163–74.

De Geus, C. H. J. 1976. *The Tribes of Israel: An Investigation into Some of the Presuppositions of Martin Noth's Amphictyony Hypothesis*. Studia semitica Neerlandica 18. Assen: Von Gorcum.

De la Bédoyère, Guy. 2010. *Cities of Roman Italy: Pompeii, Herculaneum and Ostia*. London: Bristol Classical.

De Miroschedji, P. 1993. "Far'ah, Tell El- (North)." *NEAEHL* 2:433–40.

De Tarragon, J-M. 1995. "Witchcraft, Magic, and Divination in Canaan and Ancient Israel." Pages 2071–81 in vol. 3 of *Civilizations of the Ancient Near East*. Edited by J. M. Sasson. New York: Simon & Schuster Macmillan.

De Vaux, R. 1970. "On the Right and Wrong Uses of Archaeology." Pages 64–80 in *Near Eastern Archaeology in the Twentieth Century*. Edited by J. A. Sanders. New York: Doubleday.

Dennett, Daniel C. 1995. *Darwin's Dangerous Idea: Evolution and the Meanings of Life*. New York: Simon & Schuster.

Dessel, J. P. 1999. "Tell 'Ein Zippori and the Lower Galilee in the Late Bronze and Iron Ages: A Village Perspective." Pages 1–32 in *Galilee through the Centuries*. Edited by E. M. Meyers. Winona Lake, Ind.: Eisenbrauns.

Dever, William G. 1973. "Two Approaches to Archaeological Method: The Architectural and the Stratigraphic." *Eretz-Israel* 11:1–8.

———. 1974. *Archaeology and Biblical Studies: Retrospects and Prospects*. Evanston, Ill.: Seabury Western Theological Seminary.

———. 1977. "Palestine in the Second Millennium B.C.E." Pages 70–120 in *Israelite and Judean History*. Edited by J. H. Hayes and J. M. Miller. Philadelphia: Westminster.

———. 1981. "The Impact of the New Archaeology on Syro-Palestinian Archaeology." *BASOR* 242:15–30.

———. 1982. "Retrospects and Prospects in Biblical Archaeology." *Biblical Archaeology* 45:103–8.

———. 1985. "Syro-Palestinian and Biblical Archaeology." Pages 31–74 in *The Hebrew Bible and Its Modern Interpreters*. Edited by D. Knight and G. M. Tucker. Philadelphia: Fortress.

———. 1992. "Archaeology, Syro-Palestinian and Biblical." *ABD* 1:354–67.

———. 1993. "What Remains of the House That Albright Built?" *Biblical Archaeologist* 56 (1–*Celebrating and Examining W. F. Albright*): 25–35.

———. 2001. *What Did the Biblical Writers Know and When Did They Know It? What Archaeology Can Tell Us about the Reality of Ancient Israel*. Grand Rapids: Eerdmans.

———. 2003a. *Who Were the Early Israelites and Where Did They Come From?* Grand Rapids: Eerdmans.

———. 2003b. "Why It's So Hard to Name Our Field." *Biblical Archaeology Review* 29 (4): 57–61.

———. 2005. *Did God Have a Wife? Archaeology and Folk Religion in Ancient Israel*. Grand Rapids: Eerdmans.

———. 2012. *The Lives of Ordinary People in Ancient Israel*. Grand Rapids: Eerdmans.

———. 2015. "The Exodus and the Bible: What Was Known; What Was Remembered; What Was Forgotten?" Pages 399–408 in Levy et al. 2015.

———. 2017. *Beyond the Texts: An Archaeological Portrait*. Atlanta: SBL Press.

Dever, William G., and D. Lance, eds. 1978. *A Manual of Field Excavation: Handbook for Field Archaeologists*. New York: Hebrew Union College.

Dietrich, Manfried. 1970. *Die Aramäer Südbabyloniens in der Sargonidenzeit (700–648)*. AOAT 7. Kevelaer: Butzon & Bercker.

Dietrich, Manfried, Oswald Loretz, and Joaquín Sanmartín, eds. 2013. *The Cuneiform Alphabetic Texts from Ugarit, Ras Ibn Hani and Other Places*. 3rd enlarged ed. KTU3. AOAT 360/1. Münster: Ugarit Verlag.

Dines, Jennifer M. 2004. *The Septuagint*. London: T&T Clark.

Dodson, Aidan. 2012. *Afterglow of Empire: Egypt from the Fall of the New Kingdom to the Saite Renaissance*. New York: American University of Cairo Press.

———. 2014. *Amarna Sunrise: Egypt from Golden Age to Age of Heresy*. Cairo: American University in Cairo Press.

Dorsey, D. A. 1991. *The Roads and Highways of Ancient Israel*. Baltimore: Johns Hopkins University Press.

Dossin, G. 1973. "Une mention de Cananéens dans une lettre de Mari." *Syria* 50:277–282.

Dothan, T. 1982. *The Philistines and Their Material Culture*. Jerusalem: Israel Exploration Society.

———. 2003. "The Aegean and the Orient: Cultic Interactions." Pages 259–72 in *Hesed Ve-Emet: Studies in Honor of Ernest S. Frerichs*. Edited by J. Magness and S. Gitin. Providence, R.I.: Brown University Press.

Dothan, T., and R. L. Cohn. 1994. "The Philistine as Other: Biblical Rhetoric and Archaeological Reality." Pages 61–73 in *The Other in Jewish Thought and History*. Edited by L. J. Silberstein and R. L. Cohn. New York: New York University Press.

Dothan, T., and M. Dothan. 1992. *People of the Sea: The Search for the Philistines.* New York: Macmillan.

Dothan, T., and A. J. Drenka. 2010. "Incised Scapula in a Cultic Context from Philistine Ekron." Pages 35–56 in *"A Woman of Valor": Jerusalem Ancient Near Eastern Studies in Honor of Joan Goodnick Westenholtz.* Edited by W. Horowitz, U. Gabbay, and F. Vukosavovic. Madrid: Consejo Superior de Investigaciones Cientificas.

Dothan, T., and A. Zukerman. 2004. "A Preliminary Study of the Mycenaean IIIC:1 Pottery Assemblage from Tel Miqne-Ekron and Ashdod." *BASOR* 333:1–54.

Drinkard, J. F., G. L. Mattingly, and J. M. Miller, eds. 1998. *Benchmarks in Time and Culture: Essays in Honor of Joseph A. Callaway.* Atlanta: Scholars Press.

Drower, Margaret S. 1995. *Flinders Petrie: A Life in Archaeology.* Repr., Madison: University of Wisconsin Press. Orig. pub. London: V. Gollancz, 1985.

Ebeling, J. R. 2010. *Women's Lives in Biblical Times.* London: T&T Clark.

Ebeling, J. R., and M. M. Homan. 2008. "Baking and Brewing Beer in the Israelite Household: A Study of Women's Cooking Technology." Pages 45–62 in Nakhai 2008.

Ebeling, J. R., and Y. M. Rowan. 2004. "The Archaeology of the Daily Grind: Ground Stone Tools and Food Production in the Southern Levant." *NEA* 67 (2): 108–17.

Edelman, D. V. 2005. *The Origins of the "Second" Temple: Persian Imperial Policy and the Rebuilding of Jerusalem.* London: Equinox.

Ehrlich, C. S. 1996. *The Philistines in Transition: A History from ca. 1000–730 BCE.* Leiden: Brill.

———. 2015. "Philistines." *Oxford Bibliographies in Biblical Studies.* http://www.oxfordbibliographies.com/view/document/obo-9780195393361/obo-9780195393361-0144.xml.

Eichmann, R., H. Schaudig, and A. Hausleiter. 2006. "Archaeology and Epigraphy at Tayma (Saudi Arabia)." *Arabian Archaeology and Epigraphy* 17:163–76.

Eissfeldt, Otto. 1932. *Baal Zaphon, Zeus Kasios und der Durchzug der Israeliten durchs Meer.* Halle: Niemeyer.

Elliott, Mark. 2002. *Biblical Interpretation Using Archeological Evidence: 1900–1930.* Lewiston, N.Y.: Mellen.

Eph'al, I. 2008. *The City Besieged: Siege and Its Manifestations in the Ancient Near East.* Culture and History of the Ancient Near East 36. Leiden: Brill.

Esse, D. L. 1992. "The Collared Pithos at Megiddo: Ceramic Distribution and Ethnicity." *Journal of Near Eastern Studies* 51:81–103.

Exum, J. C. 2012. "Judges: Encoded Messages to Women." Pages 112–27 in *Feminist Biblical Interpretation: A Compendium of Critical Commentary on the Books of the Bible and Related Literature.* Edited by L. Schottroff and M.-T. Wacker. Grand Rapids: Eerdmans.

Fagan, Brian. 2015. "Did Akhenaten's Monotheism Influence Moses?" *Biblical Archaeology Review* 41 (4): 42–49, 70–71.

Farisani, E. 2008. "The Israelites in Palestine during the Babylonian Exile." *Old Testament Essays* 21:69–88. http://www.scielo.org.za/pdf/ote/v21n1/05.pdf.

Faust, Avraham. 2001. "Doorway Orientation, Settlement Planning and Cosmology in Ancient Israel during Iron Age II." *Oxford Journal of Archaeology* 20:129–55.

———. 2003. "Abandonment, Urbanization, Resettlement and the Formation of the Israelite State." *NEA* 66:147–61.

———. 2006. *Israel's Ethnogenesis*. London: Equinox.

———. 2007a. "Rural Settlements, State Formation, and 'Bible and Archaeology.' " *NEA* 70 (1): 4–9.

———. 2007b. "The Sharon and the Yarkon Basin in the Tenth Century BCE: Ecology, Settlement Patterns and Political Involvement." *Israel Exploration Journal* 57:65–82.

———. 2008. "Settlement and Demography in Seventh-Century Judah and the Extent and Intensity of Sennacherib's Campaign." *Palestine Exploration Quarterly* 140 (3): 168–94.

———. 2012a. *Judah in the Neo-Babylonian Period: The Archaeology of Desolation*. Atlanta: SBL Press.

———. 2012b. *The Archaeology of Israelite Society in Iron Age II*. Winona Lake, Ind.: Eisenbrauns.

———. 2013. "From Regional Power to Peaceful Neighbor: Philistia in the Iron I–II Transition." *Israel Exploration Journal* 63:174–204.

———. 2015. "Pottery and Society in Iron Age Philistia: Feasting, Identity, Economy, and Gender." *BASOR* 373:167–98.

Faust, A., and J. Lev-Tov. 2011. "The Constitution of Philistine Identity: Ethnic Dynamics in 12th–10th Centuries Philistia." *Oxford Journal of Archaeology* 30:13–31.

Feder, Yitzhaq. 2010. "A Levantine Tradition: The Kizzuwatnean Blood Rite and the Biblical Sin Offering." Pages 101–14 in *Pax Hethitica: Studies on the Hittites and Their Neighbours in Honour of Itamar Singer*. Edited by Y. Cohen, A. Gilan, and J. L. Miller. Wiesbaden: Harrassowitz.

———. 2011. *Blood Expiation in Hittite and Biblical Ritual: Origins, Context, and Meaning*. Writings from the Ancient World Supplement Series 2. Atlanta: SBL Press.

Feldman, Marian. 2006. *Diplomacy by Design: Luxury Arts and an "International Style" in the Ancient Near East, 1400–1200 BCE*. Chicago: University of Chicago Press.

Finkel, Irving. 2013. *The Cyrus Cylinder: The King of Persian's Proclamation from Ancient Babylon*.

Finkel, Irving, and M. J. Seymour. 2008. *Babylon*. New York: Oxford University Press.

Finkelstein, Israel. 1986. *'Izbet Ṣartah*. British Archaeological Reports. Oxford: British Archaeological Reports.

———. 1988a. *The Archaeology of the Israelite Settlement*. Jerusalem: Israel Exploration Society.

―――. 1988b. "Raider of the Lost Mountain—An Israeli Archaeologist Looks at the Most Recent Attempt to Locate Mt. Sinai." *BAR* 15 (4): 46–50.

―――. 1995. "The Great Transformation: The 'Conquest' of the Highland Frontiers and the Rise of the Territorial States." Pages 349–65 in *The Archaeology of Society in the Holy Land*. Edited by T. E. Levy. New York: Facts on File.

―――. 1996. "Ethnicity and Origin of the Iron I Settlers in the Highlands of Canaan: Can the Real Israel Stand Up?" *BA* 59:198–212.

―――. 1999. "State Formation in Israel and Judah: A Contrast in Context, a Contrast in Trajectory." *NEA* 62 (1): 35–52.

―――. 2011. "The 'Large Stone Structure' in Jerusalem: Reality versus Yearning." *Zeitschrift des deutschen Palästina Vereins* 127 (1): 1–10.

―――. 2012. "L'Archéologie et l'Histoire de Jérusalem (1000–700 Av. J.-C.)." *Comptes rendus de l'Académie des Inscriptions et Belles-Lettres* 2:827–58.

―――. 2013. *The Forgotten Kingdom: The Archaeology and History of Northern Israel*. Atlanta: SBL Press.

―――. 2015. "The Wilderness Narrative and Itineraries and the Evolution of the Exodus Tradition." Pages 39–54 in Levy et al. 2015.

Finkelstein, Israel, and Amihai Mazar. 2007. *The Quest for the Historical Israel: Debating Archaeology and the History of Early Israel*. Edited by Brian B Schmidt. Atlanta: SBL Press.

Finkelstein, Israel, and N. Naaman, eds. 1994. *From Nomadism to Monarchy*. Washington, D.C.: Yad Izhak Ben Zvi, Israel Exploration Society and Biblical Archaeology Society.

Finkelstein, Israel, and E. Piasetzky. 2011. "The Iron Age Chronology Debate: Is the Gap Narrowing?" *NEA* 74 (1): 50–54.

Finkelstein, Israel, and Neil Asher Silberman. 2001. *The Bible Unearthed: Archaeology's New Vision of Ancient Israel and the Origin of Its Sacred Texts*. New York: Free Press.

―――. 2006a. *David and Solomon: In Search of the Bible's Sacred Kings and the Roots of the Western Tradition*. New York: Free Press.

―――. 2006b. "Temple and Dynasty: Hezekiah, the Remaking of Judah and the Rise of the Pan-Israelite Ideology." *JSOT* 30 (3): 259–85.

Fleming, Daniel E. 1998. "The Biblical Tradition of Anointing Priests." *JBL* 117:401–14.

―――. 2004. "Genesis in History and Tradition: The Syrian Background of Israel's Ancestors, Reprise." Pages 193–232 in *The Future of Biblical Archaeology: Reassessing Methodologies and Assumptions; The Proceedings of a Symposium, August 12–14, 2001 at Trinity International University*. Edited by James K. Hoffmeier and Alan Millard. Grand Rapids: Eerdmans.

―――. 2012. *The Legacy of Israel in Judah's Bible: History, Politics, and the Reinscribing of Tradition*. New York: Cambridge University Press.

Flesher, Paul V. M., and Bruce Chilton. 2011. *The Targums: A Critical Introduction*. Waco, Tex.: Baylor University Press.

Foster, Benjamin R. 1993. *Before the Muses: An Anthology of Akkadian Literature.* Bethesda, Md.: CDL Press.

Franklin, Norma. 2005. "Correlation and Chronology: Samaria and Megiddo Redux." Pages 310–22 in *The Bible and Radiocarbon Dating: Archaeology, Text and Science.* Edited by Thomas E. Levy and Thomas Highman. London: Equinox.

———. 2006. "Revealing Stratum V at Megiddo." *BASOR* 342:95–111.

———. 2013. "Why Was Samaria Made the Capital of the Kingdom of Israel?" *Bible and Interpretation,* September. http://www.bibleinterp.com/opeds/2013/09/fra378013.shtml.

Freikman, Michael, and Yosef Garfinkel. 2009. "The Zoomorphic Figurines from Sha'ar Hagolan: Hunting Magic Practices in the Neolithic Near East." *Levant* 41:5–17.

Frerichs, Ernest S., and Leonard H. Lesko, eds. 1997. *Exodus: The Egyptian Evidence.* Winona Lake, Ind.: Eisenbrauns.

Frese, Daniel A., and Thomas E. Levy. 2010. "The Four Pillars of the Iron Age in Low Chronology." Pages 187–204 in *Historical Biblical Archaeology and the Future: The New Pragmatism.* Edited by Thomas E. Levy and Thomas Higham. Oakville, Conn.: Equinox.

Fried, L. S. 2003. "The Land Lay Desolate: Conquest and Restoration in the Ancient Near East." Pages 21–54 in Lipschits and Blenkinsopp 2003.

Friedman, Richard Elliott. 1987. *Who Wrote the Bible?* New York: Summit Books.

———. 1998. *The Hidden Book in the Bible.* New York: HarperCollins.

Gadot, Y., and A. Yasur-Landau. 2006. "Beyond Finds: Reconstructing Life in the Courtyard Building of Level K-4." Pages 583–600 in vol. 2 of *Megiddo IV: The 1998–2002 Seasons.* Edited by I. Finkelstein, D. Ussishkin, and B. Halpern. Emery and Claire Yass Publications in Archaeology. Tel Aviv: Tel Aviv University.

Gal, Zvi. 1992. *Galilee during the Iron Age.* Translated by Marcia Reines Josephy. Winona Lake, Ind.: Eisenbrauns.

Gal, Zvi, Dina Shalem, and Howard Smithline. 2011. "The Peqi'in Cave: A Chalcolithic Cemetery in Upper Galilee, Israel." *NEA* 74:196–206.

Galil, Gershon. 1996. *The Chronology of the Kings of Israel and Judah.* New York: Brill.

———. 2009. "The Hebrew Inscription from Khirbet Qeiyafa/Neta'im: Script, Language, Literature and History." *Ugarit Forschungen* 41:193–242.

Galor, Katharina, and Gideon Avni, eds. 2011. *Unearthing Jerusalem: 150 Years of Archaeological Research in the Holy City.* Winona Lake, Ind.: Eisenbrauns.

Garfinkel, Y., and S. Ganor. 2009. *Khirbet Qeiyafa.* Vol. 1: *Excavation Report 2007–2008.* Jerusalem: Israel Exploration Society and Institute of Archaeology, Hebrew University.

Garfinkel, Y., and M. Mumcuoglu. 2013. "Triglyphs and Recessed Doorframes." *Israel Exploration Journal* 63:135–63.

Gelander, S. 2011. *From Two Kingdoms to One Nation—Israel and Judah: Studies in Division and Unification.* Studia Semitica Neerlandica 56. Leiden: Brill.

George, A. R. 2003. *The Babylonian Gilgamesh Epic: Introduction, Critical Edition and Cuneiform Texts*. 2 vols. Oxford: Oxford University Press.

Gerber, M. 2000. "A Common Source for the Late Babylonian Chronicles Dealing with the Eighth and Seventh Centuries." *JAOS* 120:553–69.

Gibson, Shimon. 1994. "The Tell Ej-Judeideh (Tel Goded) Excavations: A Reappraisal Based on Archival Records in the Palestine Exploration Fund." *Tel Aviv* 21 (2): 194–234.

———. 2011. "British Archaeological Work in Jerusalem between 1865–1967: An Assessment." Pages 23–57 in Galor and Avni 2011.

Gilboa, Ayelet. 2006–2007. "Fragmenting the Sea Peoples with an Emphasis on Cyprus, Syria and Egypt: A Tel Dor Perspective." Pages 209–44 in *Cyprus, the Sea Peoples and the Eastern Mediterranean: Regional Perspectives of Continuity and Change*. Edited by T. P. Harrison. Special issue of *Scripta Mediterranea* XVII–XVIII.

Gilead, Isaac. 1995. "The Foragers of the Upper Paleolithic Period." Pages 124–40 in Levy 1995a.

Gilmour, Garth. 2009. "An Iron Age II Pictorial Inscription from Jerusalem Illustrating Yahweh and Asherah." *PEQ* 141:87–103.

Gitin, S., Mazar, A., and E. Stern, eds. 1998. *Mediterranean Peoples in Transition, Thirteenth to Early Tenth Centuries BCE*. Jerusalem: Israel Exploration Society.

Glassner, J.-J. 2004. *Mesopotamian Chronicles*. SBL WAW 19. Atlanta: Scholars Press.

Gmirkin, Russell E. 2006. *Berossus and Genesis, Manetho and Exodus: Hellenistic Histories and the Date of the Pentateuch*. New York: T&T Clark.

Goldberg, Paul. 1995. "The Changing Landscape." Pages 40–57 in Levy 1995a.

Golden, Jonathan Michael. 2009. *Ancient Canaan and Israel*. Oxford: Oxford University Press.

Goldwasser, Orly. 2010. "How the Alphabet Was Born from Hieroglyphs." *Biblical Archaeology Review* 36 (2): 36–50, 74.

Goldwasser, Orly, and Stefan Wimmer. 1999. "Hieratic Fragments from Tell el-Far'ah (South)." *BASOR* 313:39–42.

Gonen, R. 1984. "Urban Canaan in the Late Bronze Period." *BASOR* 253:61–73.

Gophna, Ram. 1995. "Early Bronze Age Canaan: Some Spatial and Demographic Observations." Pages 269–380 in Levy 1995a.

Goren, Yuval, and Eran Arie. 2014. "The Authenticity of the Bullae of Berekhyahu Son of Neriyahu the Scribe." *BASOR* 372:147–58.

Goring-Morris, A. Nigel, and Anna Belfer-Cohen, eds. 2003. *More than Meets the Eye: Studies on Upper Palaeolithic Diversity in the Near East*. Oxford: Oxbow Books.

Goring-Morris, Nigel, and Liora Kolska Horwitz. 2007. "Funerals and Feasts during the Pre-pottery Neolithic B of the Near East." *Antiquity* 81:902–19.

Grabbe, Lester L. 2006. *A History of the Jews and Judaism in the Second Temple Period*. Vol. 1, *The Persian Period (539–331 BCE)*. London: Bloomsbury T&T Clark.

———. 2007. *Ancient Israel: What Do We Know and How Do We Know It?* London: T&T Clark.

Grayson, A. K. 1975a. *Assyrian and Babylonian Chronicles*. TCS 5. Locust Valley: J. J. Augustin.

————. 1975b. *Babylonian Historical-Literary Texts*. Toronto: University of Toronto Press.

Greenberg, R. 1987. "New Light on the Iron Age at Tell Beit Mirsim." *BASOR* 265:55–80.

Grelot, P. 1978. "La Prière de Nabonide (4QPrNab)." *Revue de Qumran* 9:483–95

Grigson, Caroline. 1995. "Plough and Pasture in the Early Economy of the Southern Levant." Pages 245–68 in Levy 1995a.

Hacker, Joseph, and Adam Shear. 2011. *The Hebrew Book in Early Modern Italy*. Philadelphia: University of Pennsylvania Press.

Hadley, Judith. 2008. "Evidence of Asherah." *Bible and Interpretation*. Accessed October 22, 2013. http://www.bibleinterp.com/articles/ashart1212.shtml.

Hallo, William W., ed. 1997–2002. *The Context of Scripture*. 3 vols. Leiden: Brill.

Hallote, Rachel. 2006. *Bible, Map and Spade: The American Palestine Exploration Society, Frederick Jones Bliss and the Forgotten Story of Early American Biblical Archaeology*. Piscataway, N.J.: Gorgias.

————. 2009. "Jacob H. Schiff and the Beginning of Biblical Archaeology in the United States." *American Jewish History* 95 (3): 225–47.

————. 2011. "Before Albright: Charles Torrey, James Montgomery, and American 'Biblical' Archaeology 1907–1922." *NEA* 74 (3): 156–69.

Hallote, Rachel, Felicity Cobbing, and Jeffery B. Spurr. 2012. *The Photographs of the American Palestine Exploration Society*. Annual of the American Schools of Oriental Research 66. Boston: ASOR.

Halpern, Baruch. 1978. "The Rise of Abimelek ben-Jerubbaal." *Hebrew Annual Review* 2:79–100.

————. 1983. *The Emergence of Israel in Canaan*. SBMS 29. Atlanta: Scholars Press.

————. 2000. "Centre and Sentry: Megiddo's Role in Transit, Administration and Trade." Pages 535–75 in *Megiddo III: The 1992–1996 Seasons*. Edited by I. Finkelstein, D. Ussishkin, and B. Halpern. Sonia and Marco Nadler Institute of Archaeology Monographs 18. Tel Aviv: Institute of Archaeology, Tel Aviv University.

————. 2001. *David's Secret Demons: Messiah, Murderer, Traitor, Spy*. Grand Rapids: Eerdmans.

————. 2005. "David Did It, Others Did Not: The Creation of Ancient Israel." Pages 422–38 in *The Bible and Radiocarbon Dating: Archaeology, Text and Science*. Edited by Thomas E. Levy and Thomas Higham. Oakville, Conn.: Equinox.

————. 2010. "Archaeology, the Bible and History: The Fall of the House of Omri—and the Origins of the Israelite State." Pages 275–77 in *Historical Biblical Archaeology and the Future: The New Pragmatism*. Edited by Thomas E. Levy and Thomas Higham. Oakville, Conn.: Equinox.

Hardin, J. W. 2010. *Lahav II: Households and the Use of Domestic Space at Iron II Tell Halif: An Archaeology of Destruction*. Winona Lake, Ind.: Eisenbrauns.

Harris, Judith. 2007. *Pompeii Awakened: A Story of Rediscovery*. London: I. B. Tauris.

Harrison, Timothy P. 2004. *Megiddo III: Final Report on the Stratum VI Excavations*. Oriental Institute Publications 127. Chicago: University of Chicago.

Harrison, Timothy P., and Celeste Barlow. 2005. "Mesha, the Mishor, and the Chronology of Iron Age Madaba." Pages 179–92 in *The Bible and Radiocarbon Dating: Archaeology, Text and Science*. Edited by Thomas E. Levy and Thomas Higham. Oakville, Conn.: Equinox.

Hawkins, J. D. 2009. "Cilicia, the Amuq, and Aleppo: New Light in a Dark Age." *NEA* 72:164–73.

Hawkins, Ralph K. 2012. *The Iron Age Structure on Mt. Ebal: Excavation and Interpretation*. BBRSup 6. Winona Lake, Ind.: Eisenbrauns.

Hayajneh, H. 2001. "First Evidence of Nabonidus in the Ancient North Arabian Inscriptions from the Region of Taymā." *Proceedings of the Seminar for Arabian Studies* 31:81–95.

Hayes, John H., and J. Maxwell Miller, eds. 1977. *Israelite and Judean History*. Philadelphia: Westminster.

Hendel, Ronald S. 1989. "Sacrifice as a Cultural System: The Ritual Symbolism of Exodus 24, 3-8." *Zeitschrift für die Alttestamentliche Wissenschaft* 101:366–90.

———. 2000. "Where Is Mount Sinai?" *BibRev* 16 (3): 8.

———. 2001. "The Exodus in Biblical Memory." *JBL* 120 (4): 601–22.

———. 2005. *Remembering Abraham: Culture, Memory, and History in the Hebrew Bible*. Oxford: Oxford University Press.

———. 2006. "Is There a Biblical Archaeology." *BAR* 32 (4): 20.

———. 2011. "Cultural Memory and the Hebrew Bible." *Bible and Interpretation*, July. http://www.bibleinterp.com/opeds/hen358016.shtml.

———. 2015. "The Exodus as Cultural Memory: Egyptian Bondage and the Song of the Sea." Pages 65–80 in Levy et al. 2015.

Herr, L. G. 1985. "The Servant of Baalis." *BA* 48:169–72.

Herr, Larry, and Robert Bates. 2011. "The Iron IIB Pottery from a Stratum 8 House at Tall al-'Umayri, Jordan." Pages 18–32 in *Eretz Israel (Ben Tor Volume)*. Jerusalem: Israel Exploration Society.

Herzog, Z. 1997. *Archaeology of the City*. Tel Aviv University Sonia and Marco Nadler Institute of Archaeology Monograph Series Number 13. Tel Aviv: Sonia and Marco Nadler Institute of Archaeology, Tel Aviv University.

———. 2002. "The Fortress Mound at Tel Arad: An Interim Report." *Tel Aviv* 29 (1): 3–109.

———. 2010. "Perspectives on Southern Israel's Cult Centralization: Arad and Beer-Sheba." Pages 169–99 in *One God—One Cult—One Nation: Archaeological and Biblical Perspectives*. Edited by R. G. Kratz and H. Spieckermann. BZAW 405. Berlin: de Gruyter.

Hess, Richard S. 1986. "Divine Names in the Amarna Correspondence." *UF* 18:149–68.

———. 1992. "Canaan (Person)." *ABD* 1:828.

———. 2007a. "Aspects of Israelite Personal Names and Pre-exilic Israelite Religion." Pages 301–13 in *New Seals and Inscriptions, Hebrew, Idumean and Cuneiform*. Edited by Meir Lubetski. Hebrew Bible Monographs 8. Sheffield: Sheffield Phoenix.

———. 2007b. *Israelite Religions: An Archaeological and Biblical Survey*. Grand Rapids: Baker.

———. 2010. "Names in Genesis 1–11." *Bible and Interpretation*, February. http://www.bibleinterp.com/articles/hess357903.shtml.

———. 2013. "'Because of the Wickedness of These Nations' (Deut 9:4-5): The Canaanites—Ethical or Not?" Pages 17–38 in *For Our Good Always: Studies on the Message and Influence of Deuteronomy in Honor of Daniel I. Block*. Edited by Jason S. DeRouchie, Jason Gile, and Kenneth J. Turner. Winona Lake, Ind.: Eisenbrauns.

Hesse, B. 1990. "Pig Lovers and Pig Haters: Patterns of Palestinian Pork Production." *Journal of Ethnobiology* 10:195–225.

Hesse, B., and P. Wapnish. 1997. "Can Pig Remains Be Used for Ethnic Diagnosis in the Ancient Near East?" Pages 238–70 in *The Archaeology of Israel: Constructing the Past, Interpreting the Present*. Edited by N. A. Silverman and B. D. Small. JSOTSup 237. Sheffield: Sheffield Academic.

Hesse, B., D. N. Fulton, and P. Wapnish. 2011. "Animal Remains." Pages 615–43 in *Ashkelon 3: The Seventh Century B.C.E.* Edited by L. E. Stager, D. M. Master, and J. D. Schloen. Winona Lake, Ind.: Eisenbrauns.

Hirth, K. G. 1998. "The Distributional Approach. A New Way to Identify Marketplace Exchange in the Archaeological Record." *Current Anthropology* 39:451–76.

Hitchcock, L. A. 2011. "'Transculturalism' as a Model for Examining Migration to Cyprus and Philistia at the End of the Bronze Age." *Ancient West and East* 10:267–80.

Hitchcock, L. A., and A. M. Maeir. 2013. "Beyond Creolization and Hybridity: Entangled and Transcultural Identities in Philistia." *Archaeological Review from Cambridge* 28:43–65.

Hodder, I. 1986. *Reading the Past: Current Approaches to Interpretation in Archaeology*. Cambridge: Cambridge University Press.

Hoffmeier, James K. 1997. *Israel in Egypt: The Evidence for the Authenticity of the Exodus Tradition*. New York: Oxford University Press.

———. 2005. *Ancient Israel in Sinai: The Evidence for the Authenticity of the Wilderness Tradition*. New York: Oxford University Press.

———. 2007. "What Is the Biblical Date for the Exodus? A Response to Bryant Wood." *Journal of the Evangelical Theological Society* 50 (2): 225–47.

Hoffmeier, James K., and A. Millard, eds. 2004. *The Future of Biblical Archaeology*. Grand Rapids: Eerdmans.

Hoffner, H. A. 1997. *The Law of the Hittites*. Leiden: Brill.

Hoglund, K. G. 1992a. "The Achaemenid Context." Pages 54–72 in *Second Temple Studies*. Vol. 1, *Persian Period*. Edited by P. R. Davies. JSOTSup 117. Sheffield: Sheffield Academic.

———. 1992b. *Achaemenid Imperial Administration in Syria-Palestine and the Missions of Ezra and Nehemiah*. SBLDS 125. Atlanta: Scholars Press.

———. 2002. "The Material Culture of the Persian Period." Pages 14–18 in *Second Temple Studies III: Studies in Politics, Class and Material Culture*. Edited by P. R. Davies and J. M. Halliga. JSOTSup 340. London: Continuum.

Holladay, J. S., Jr. 1995. "The Kingdoms of Israel and Judah: Political and Economic Centralization in the Iron IIA–B (ca. 1000–750 BCE)." Pages 368–98 in Levy 1995a.

———. 2004. "Judaeans (and Phoenicians) in Egypt in the Late Seventh to Sixth Centuries B.C." Pages 405–37 in *Egypt, Israel, and the Ancient Mediterranean World: Studies in Honor of Donald B. Redford*. Edited by G. Knoppers and A. Hirsch. Probleme der Ägyptologie 20. Leiden: Brill.

———. 2006. "Hezekiah's Tribute, Long-Distance Trade, and the Wealth of Nations Ca. 1000–600 BC: A New Perspective ('Poor Little [Agrarian] Judah' at the End of the 8th Century BC: Dropping the First Shoe)." Pages 309–31 in *Confronting the Past: Archaeological and Historical Essays on Ancient Israel in Honor of W. G. Dever*. Edited by S. Gitin, J. E. Wright, and J. Dessel. Winona Lake, Ind.: Eisenbrauns.

Hooke, S. H. 1935. "A Scarab and Sealing from Tell Duweir." *PEQ* 67:195–97.

Horn, S. H. 1967. "The Babylonian Chronicle and the Ancient Calendar of the Kingdom of Judah." *AUSS* 5:12–27.

Hübner, Ulrich. 1992. *Die Ammoniter: Untersuchungen zur Geschichte, Kultur und Religion eines transjordanischen Volkes im 1. Jahrtausend v. Chr.* ADPV 16. Wiesbaden: Harrasowitz.

———. 2011. "The German Protestant Institute of Archaeology." Pages 59–72 in Galor and Avni 2011.

Hurowitz, Victor. 2011. "Solomon's Temple in Context." *BAR* 37 (2): 46–57, 77–78.

Ilan, David. 1995. "The Dawn of Internationalism—The Middle Bronze Age." Pages 297–319 in Levy 1995a.

Isbell, Charles D. 1980. *Malachi: A Study Guide Commentary*. Grand Rapids: Zondervan.

———. 2009. "The *Limmûdîm* in the Book of Isaiah." *JSOT* 34 (1): 99–109.

Joannès, F., and A. Lemaire. 1999. "Trois tablettes cunéiformes à onomastique ouest-sémitique." *Transeuphratène* 17:17–34.

Jobes, Karen H., and Moisés Silva. 2000. *Invitation to the Septuagint*. Grand Rapids: Baker Academic.

Joffe, A. 2002. "The Rise of Secondary States in the Iron Age Levant." *Journal of the Social and Economic History of the Orient* 45 (4): 425–67.

Johnston, Philip S. 2002. *Shades of Sheol: Death and Afterlife in the Old Testament*. Downers Grove, Ill.: InterVarsity.

Joseph, Alison L. 2015. *Portrait of the Kings: The Davidic Prototype in Deuteronomistic Poetics*. Minneapolis: Fortress.

Kahn, D. 2011. "The Campaign of Ramesses III against Philistia." *Journal of Ancient Egyptian Interconnections* 3 (4): 1–11.

Keel, Othmar, and Christoph Uelinger. 1998. *Gods, Goddesses, and Images of God in Ancient Israel*. Translated by Thomas H. Trapp. Minneapolis: Fortress.

Keller, M. 1970. "The Great Jewish Drink Mystery." *British Journal of Addiction to Alcohol & Other Drugs* 64:287–96.

Kempinski, A. 1992. "Middle and Late Bronze Age Fortifications." Pages 127–42 in Kempinski and Reich 1992.

Kempinski, A., and R. Reich, eds. 1992. *The Architecture of Ancient Israel: From the Prehistoric to the Persian Periods; In Memory of Immanuel Dunayevski*. Jerusalem: Israel Exploration Society.

Kerkeslager, Allen. 2000. "Mt. Sinai—In Arabia?" *BibRev* 16 (2): 32–39, 52.

Killebrew, Anne E. 2005. *Biblical Peoples and Ethnicity: An Archaeological Study of Egyptians, Canaanites, Philistines and Early Israel, 1300–1100 B.C.E.* SBL Archaeology and Biblical Studies 9. Atlanta: SBL Press.

———. 2013. "Early Philistine Pottery Technology at Tel Miqne-Ekron: Implications for the Late Bronze–Early Iron Age Transition in the Eastern Mediterranean." Pages 77–129 in *The Philistines and Other "Sea Peoples" in Text and Archaeology*. Edited by A. E. Killebrew and G. Lehmann. Atlanta: SBL Press.

———. 2015. "In the Footsteps of the Philistine Potters: Tracking the Dissemination of Technical Knowledge in the Production of Twelfth-Century B.C. Aegean-Style Pottery to the Coastal Southern Levant." Pages 51–61 in *The Distribution of Technological Knowledge in the Production of Ancient Mediterranean Pottery*. Edited by W. Gauß, G. Klebinder-Gauß, and C. von Rueden. Österreichisches Archäologisches Institut Sonderschriften 54. Vienna: Österreichisches Archäologisches Institut.

Killebrew, Anne E., and G. Lehmann. 2013. "Introduction: The World of the Philistines and Other 'Sea Peoples.'" Pages 1–17 in *The Philistines and Other Sea Peoples in Text and Archaeology*. Edited by A. E. Killebrew and G. Lehmann. Atlanta: SBL Press.

Killebrew, Anne E., and J. Lev-Tov. 2008. "Early Iron Age Feasting and Cuisine: An Indicator of Philistine-Aegean Connectivity." Pages 339–46 in *DAIS—The Aegean Feast: Proceedings of the 12th International Aegean Conference, University of Melbourne, Centre for Classics and Archaeology, 25–29 March 2008*. Edited by L. A. Hitchcock, R. Laffineur, and J. Crowley. Aegaeum 29. Liège: Université de Liège, Histoire de l'art et archéologie de la Grèce antique; Austin, Tex.: University of Texas at Austin, Program in Aegean Scripts and Prehistory.

King, Philip J. 1975. "The American Archaeological Heritage in the Near East." *BASOR* 217:55–65.

———. 1983. *American Archaeology in the Mideast: A History of the American Schools of Oriental Research*. Philadelphia: American Schools of Oriental Research.

King, Philip J., and L. E. Stager. 2001. *Life in Biblical Israel*. Louisville: Westminster John Knox.

Kitchen, K. A. 1993. "The Tabernacle—A Bronze Age Artifact." *Eretz-Israel* 24:119*-29*.

———. 2003. *On the Reliability of the Old Testament*. Grand Rapids: W. B. Eerdmans.

Klein, Jacob. 2006. "Sumerian Kingship and the Gods." Pages 115–31 in *Text, Artifact, and Image: Revealing Ancient Israelite Religion*. Edited by G. M. Beckman and T. J. Lewis. Providence, R.I.: Brown Judaic Studies.

Kletter, R. 2001. "Between Archaeology and Theology: The Pillar Figurines from Judah and the Asherah." Pages 179–216 in *Studies in the Archaeology of the Iron Age in Israel and Jordan*. Edited by A. Mazar. JSOTSup 331. Sheffield: Sheffield Academic.

Knauf, E. A. 1988. *Midian*. Wiesbaden: Harrassowitz.

———. 1991a. "Eglon and Ophrah: Two Toponymic Notes on the Book of Judges." *JSOT* 51:25–44.

———. 1991b. "King Solomon's Copper Supply." Pages 167–86 in *Phoenicia and the Bible*. Edited by E. Lipiński. Studia Phoenicia 11. Orientalia Lovaniensa 44. Leuven: Departement Oriëntalistiesk.

Knauf, Axel, and Philippe Guillaume. 2015. *A History of Biblical Israel: the Fate of the Tribes and Kingdoms from Merenptah to Bar Kochba*. London: Equinox.

Knoppers, Gary. 2006. "Revisiting the Samarian Question in the Persian Period." Pages 265–89 in Lipschits and Oeming 2006.

Knowles, M. 2006. *Centrality Practiced: Jerusalem in the Religious Practice of Yehud and the Diaspora in the Persian Period*. SBL Archaeology and Biblical Studies. Atlanta: Scholars Press.

Kochavi, M. 1972. *Judea, Samaria and the Golan: Archaeological Survey, 1967–1968*. Jerusalem: Survey of Israel (in Hebrew).

Koenen, K. 2003. *Bethel: Geschichte, Kult und Theologie*. OBO 192. Freiburg: Universitätsverlag; Göttingen: Vandenhoeck & Ruprecht.

Koldewey, R. 1913. *Das wieder erstehende Babylon*. Leipzig: J. C. Hinrichs.

Krahmalkov, Charles R. 1994. "Exodus Itinerary Confirmed by Egyptian Evidence." *BAR* 20 (5): 54–62.

Kuemmerlin-McLean, J. K. 1992. "Magic (Old Testament)." *ABD* 4:468–71.

Kuhrt, Amélie. 1983. "The Cyrus Cylinder and Achaemenid Imperial Policy." *JSOT* 25:83–97.

———. 1995. *The Ancient Near East c. 3000–330 BC*. 2 vols. London: Routledge.

———. 2003. "Making History: Sargon of Agade and Cyrus the Great of Persia." Pages 347–61 in *A Persian Perspective: Essays in Memory of Heleen Sancisi-Weerdenburg*. Edited by W. Henkelman and A. Kuhrt. Leiden: Nederlands Instituut voor het Nabije Oosten.

Kuklick, Bruce. 1996. *Puritans in Babylon*. Princeton: Princeton University Press.

LaBianca, Ø., and L. Lacelle. 1986. "Chapter 8: Conclusion." Pages 145–46 in vol. 2 of *Environmental Foundations, Hesban*. Edited by Ø. LaBianca and L. Lacelle. Berrien Springs, Mich.: Andrews University Press.

Lambert, W. G. 1992. "Prostitution." Pages 127–57 in *Außenseiter und Randgruppen: Beiträge zu einer Socialgeschichte des Alten Orients*. Edited by V. Haas. Xenia: Kontanzer Althistorische Vorträge und Forschungen 32. Konstanz: Universitätsverlag.

———. 2007. "A Document from a Community of Exiles in Babylonia." Pages 201–5 in *New Seals and Inscriptions, Hebrew, Idumean, and Cuneiform*. Edited by M. Lubetski. Sheffield: Phoenix.

Lang, Bernhard. 1983. *Monotheism and the Prophetic Minority*. Sheffield: Almond.

Langgut, Dafna, Israel Finkelstein, and Thomas Litt. 2013. "Climate and the Late Bronze Collapse: New Evidence from the Southern Levant." *Tel Aviv* 40 (2): 148–75.

Larsen, Mogens Trolle. 1994. *The Conquest of Assyria: Excavations in an Antique Land*. London: Routledge.

Layard, Austen Henry. 1970. *Nineveh and Its Remains*. New York: Praeger.

Lemaire, André. 2006a. "La datation des rois de Byblos Abibaal et Élibaal et les relations entre l'Égypte et le Levant au Xe siècle av. notre ère." *Académie des Inscriptions & Belles-Lettres. Comptes Rendus* (November–December): 1697–1716.

———. 2006b. "Hebrew and Aramaic in the First Millennium B.C.E. in the Light of Epigraphic Evidence (Socio-historical Aspects)." Pages 177–96 in *Biblical Hebrew in Its Northwest Semitic Setting*. Edited by S. Fassberg and A. Hurvitz. Winona Lake, Ind.: Eisenbrauns.

———. 2013. "Remarques sur les inscriptions phéniciennes de Kuntillet 'Ajrud." *Semitica* 55:83–99.

———. 2014. "Fifth- and Fourth-Century Issues: Governorship and Priesthood in Jerusalem." Pages 406–25 in *Ancient Israel's History: An Introduction to Issues and Sources*. Edited by B. T. Arnold and R. S. Hess. Grand Rapids: Baker.

Levenson, Jon Douglas. 1993. *The Hebrew Bible, the Old Testament, and Historical Criticism: Jews and Christians in Biblical Studies*. Louisville: Westminster John Knox.

Levine, Baruch A. 1993. *Numbers 1–20: A New Translation with Introduction and Commentary*. New York: Doubleday.

———. 2000. *Numbers 21–36: A New Translation with Introduction and Commentary*. New York: Doubleday.

Lev-Tov, J. S. E. 2012. "A Preliminary Report on the Late Bronze and Iron Age Faunal Assemblage from Tell es-Safi/Gath." Pages 589–612 in *Tell es-Safi/Gath I: The 1996–2005 Seasons*. Edited by A. M. Maeir. Ägypten und Altes Testament 69. Wiesbaden: Harrassowitz.

Levy, Thomas E., ed. 1995a. *The Archaeology of Society in the Holy Land*. London: Leicester University Press.

———. 1995b. "Cult, Metallurgy and Rank Societies—Chalcolithic Period (ca. 4500–3500 BCE)." Pages 226–44 in Levy 1995a.

―――, ed. 2006. *Archaeology, Anthropology and Cult: The Sanctuary at Gilat, Israel.* London: Equinox.

―――, ed. 2010. *Historical Biblical Archaeology and the Future: The New Pragmatism.* London: Equinox.

Levy, Thomas E., and David Noel Freedman. 2009. "William Foxwell Albright 1891–1971: A Biographical Memoir." *Bible and Interpretation*, February. http://www.bibleinterp.com/articles/albright5.shtml.

Levy, Thomas E., and T. Higham, eds. 2005. *The Bible and Radiocarbon Dating: Archaeology, Text and Science.* London: Equinox.

Levy, Thomas E., E. Ben-Yosef, and M. Najjar. 2012. "New Perspectives on Iron Age Copper Production and Society in the Faynan Region, Jordan." Pages 197–214 in *Eastern Mediterranean Metallurgy and Metalwork in the Second Millennium BC.* Edited by V. Kassianidou and G. Papasavvas. Oxford: Oxbow Books.

Levy, Thomas E., Thomas Schneider, William H. C. Propp, and Brad C. Sparks, eds. 2015. *Israel's Exodus in Transdisciplinary Perspective: Text, Archaeology, Culture, and Geoscience.* Cham, Switzerland: Springer.

Lewis, Jack P. 1992. "William Francis Lynch, Explorer of the Dead Sea." *Near East Archaeological Society Bulletin* 37:2–9.

Li, Heng, and Richard Durbin. 2011. "Inference of Human Population History from Individual Whole-Genome Sequences." *Nature* 475:493–97.

Lipinski, E. 2006. *On the Skirts of Canaan in the Iron Age, Historical and Topographical Researches.* Orientalia Lovaniensia Analecta 153. Leuven: Iutgeverij Peeters en Department Oosterse Studies.

Lipschits, Oded. 2005. *The Fall and Rise of Jerusalem: Judah under Babylonian Rule.* Winona Lake, Ind.: Eisenbrauns.

Lipschits, O., and J. Blenkinsopp, eds. 2003. *Judah and the Judaeans in the Neo-Babylonian Period.* Winona Lake, Ind.: Eisenbrauns.

Lipschits, O., and M. Oeming, eds. 2006. *Judah and the Judaeans in the Persian Period.* Winona Lake, Ind.: Eisenbrauns.

Liverani, Mario. 2001. "The Fall of the Assyrian Empire: Ancient and Modern Interpretations." Pages 374–91 in *Empires: Perspectives from Archaeology and History.* Edited by S. E. Alcock et al. Cambridge: Cambridge University Press.

―――. 2005. *Israel's History and the History of Israel.* London: Equinox.

Lloyd, Seton. 1947. *Foundations in the Dust.* London: Oxford University Press.

MacDonald, N. 2008. *What Did the Ancient Israelites Eat?* Grand Rapids: Eerdmans.

MacGinnis, J. D. A. 1988. "Ctesias and the Fall of Nineveh." *Illinois Classical Studies* 13:37–42.

Machinist, P. 2000. "Biblical Traditions: The Philistines and Israelite History." Pages 53–83 in *The Sea Peoples and Their World: A Reassessment.* Edited by E. D. Oren. University Museum Monograph 108. University Symposium Series 11. Philadelphia: University of Pennsylvania Museum.

Maeir, A. M. 2003. "The Relations between Egypt and the Southern Levant during the Late Iron Age: The Material Evidence from Egypt." *Agypten und Levante* 12:235–46.

―――. 2010a. "'And Brought in the Offerings and the Tithes and the Dedicated Things Faithfully' (II Chron 31:12): On the Meaning and Function of the Late Iron Age Judahite 'Incised Handle Cooking Pot.'" *JAOS* 130:43–62.

―――. 2010b. "Stones, Bones, Texts and Relevance: Or, How I Lost My Fear of Biblical Archaeology and Started Enjoying It." Pages 295–303 in Levy 2010.

―――. 2013. Review of *The Archaeology of Israelite Society* by A. Faust (Winona Lake, Ind.: Eisenbrauns, 2012). *Review of Biblical Literature.*

Maeir, A. M., and L. A. Hitchcock. 2011. "Absence Makes the Hearth Grow Fonder: Searching for the Origins of the Philistine Hearth." *Eretz-Israel* 30:46*–64*.

Maeir, A. M., and I. Shai. 2016. *Reassessing the Character of the Judahite Kingdom: Archaeological Evidence for Non-Centralized, Kinship-Based Components.* Pages 323–40 in *From Sha'Ar Hagolan to Shaaraim: Essays in Honor of Prof. Yosef Garfinkel.* Edited by S. Ganor, I. Kreimerman, K. Streit, and M. Mumcouglu. Jerusalem: Israel Exploration Society.

Maeir, A. M., B. Davis, and L. A. Hitchcock. 2016. "Philistine Names and Terms Once Again: A Recent Perspective." *Journal of Eastern Mediterranean Archaeology and Heritage Studies* 4 (4): 321–40.

Maeir, A. M., L. A. Hitchcock, and L. K. Horwitz. 2013. "On the Constitution and Transformation of Philistine Identity." *Oxford Journal of Archaeology* 32:1–38.

Magness, Jodi. 2012. *The Archaeology of the Holy Land: From the Destruction of Solomon's Temple to the Muslim Conquest.* Cambridge: Cambridge University Press.

Marchand, Suzanne L. 1996. *Down from Olympus: Archaeology and Philhellenism in Germany, 1750–1970.* Princeton: Princeton University Press.

Markoe, G. E. 2000. *Phoenicians.* Berkeley: University of California Press.

Martin, M. A. S., and I. Finkelstein. 2013. "Iron IIA Pottery from the Negev Highlands: Petrographic Investigation and Historical Implications." *Tel Aviv* 40:6–45.

Martin, M. A. S., A. Eliyahu-Behar, M. Anenburg, Y. Goren, and I. Finkelstein. 2013. "Iron IIA Slag-Tempered Pottery in the Negev Highlands, Israel." *Journal of Archaeological Science* 40:3777-92.

Master, D., and A. Aja. 2011. "The House Shrine of Ashkelon." *Israel Exploration Journal* 61:129–45.

Master, D. and A. Aja. 2017. "The Philistine Cemetery at Ashkelon." *BASOR,* 377.

Matthews, Victor H., and Don C. Benjamin. 2006. *Old Testament Parallels: Laws and Stories from the Ancient Near East.* 3rd ed. Mahwah, N.J.: Paulist.

May, J. 1985. *Oxford Bible Atlas.* New York: Oxford University Press.

Mayes, A. D. H. 1973a. "Israel in the Pre-monarchy Period." *Vetus Testamentum* 23 (2): 151–70.

―――. 1973b. "The Question of the Israelite Amphictyony." *Hermathena* 116:53–65.

Mayr, Ernst. 2001. *What Evolution Is.* New York: Basic Books.

Mazar, Amihai. 1990. *Archaeology of the Land of the Bible*. Vol. 1, *10,000–586 B.C.E.* Anchor Bible Reference Library. New York: Doubleday.

———. 1992a. "Temples of the Middle and Late Bronze Ages and the Iron Age." Pages 161–89 in Kempinski and Reich 1992.

———. 1992b. "The Iron Age I." Pages 258–301 in *The Archaeology of Ancient Israel*. Edited by A. Ben-Tor. Translated by R. Greenberg. New Haven: Yale University Press.

———. 2000. "The Temples and Cult of the Philistines." Pages 213–32 in *The Sea Peoples and Their World: A Reassessment*. Edited by E. D. Oren. University Museum Monograph 108. University Symposium Series 11. Philadelphia: University of Pennsylvania Museum.

———. 2003. "Three 10th–9th Century B.C.E. Inscriptions From Tel Rehov." Pages 171–84 in *Saxa loquentur: Studien zur Archäologie Palälastinas/Israels. Fs. V. Fritz. C. G. den Hertog, U. Hübner and S. Münger. eds. Münster: Ugarit-Verlag*. Münster: Ugarit-Verlag.

———. 2005. "The Debate over the Chronology of the Iron Age in the Southern Levant." Pages 15–30 in *The Bible and Radiocarbon Dating: Archaeology, Text and Science*. Edited by Thomas E. Levy and Thomas Higham. Oakville, Conn.: Equinox.

———. 2006. "Jerusalem in the 10th Century B.C.E.: The Glass Half Full." Pages 255–72 in *Essays on Ancient Israel in Its Near Eastern Context: A Tribute to Nadav Na'aman*. Edited by Y. Amit, E. Ben Zvi, I. Finkelstein, and O. Lipschits. Winona Lake, Ind.: Eisenbrauns.

———. 2007. "The Divided Monarchy: Some Comments on Archaeological Issues." Pages 159–79 in *The Quest for the Historical Israel: Debating Archaeology and the History of Early Israel*. Edited by Brian B. Schmidt. Atlanta: SBL Press.

———. 2010. "Archaeology and the Biblical Narrative: The Case of the United Monarchy." Pages 29–58 in *One God—One Cult—One Nation: Archaeological and Biblical Perspectives*. Edited by R. G. Kratz and H. Spieckermann. BZAW 405. Berlin: de Gruyter.

———. 2011. "The Iron Age Chronology Debate: Is the Gap Narrowing? Another Viewpoint." *NEA* 74 (2): 105–11.

Mazar, Eilat. 2006. "Did I Find King David's Palace?" *BAR* 32 (1): 16–27, 70.

———. 2009. *The Palace of King David: Excavations at the Summit of the City of David, Preliminary Report of Seasons 2005–2007*. Jerusalem: Shoham Academic.

Mazar, Eilat, D. Ben-Shlomo, and S. Ahituv. 2013. "An Inscribed Pithos from the Ophel, Jerusalem." *Israel Exploration Journal* 63:39–49.

Mazow, L. B. 2006–2007. "The Industrious Sea Peoples: The Evidence of Aegean-Style Textile Production in Cyprus and the Southern Levant." Pages 291–322 in *Cyprus, the Sea Peoples and the Eastern Mediterranean: Regional Perspectives of Continuity and Change*. Edited by T. P. Harrison. Special issue of *Scripta Mediterranea* XVII–XVIII.

McDonald, Lee Martin, and James A. Sanders. 2002. *The Canon Debate*. Peabody, Mass.: Hendrickson.

McKenzie, Steven L. 2013. *The Oxford Encyclopedia of Biblical Interpretation*. New York: Oxford University Press.

Mein, A. 2001. *Ezekiel and the Ethics of Exile*. Oxford: Oxford University Press.

Meshel, Ze'ev. 2012. *Kuntillet 'Ajrud (Ḥorvat Teman): An Iron Age II Religious Site on the Judah-Sinai Border*. Jerusalem: Israel Exploration Society.

Meshorer, Ya'aḳov. 2001. *A Treasury of Jewish Coins from the Persian Period to Bar Kokhba*. Jerusalem: Yad ben-Zvi.

Mettinger, T. N. D. 1971. *Solomonic State Officials: A Study of the Civil Government Officials of the Israelite Monarchy*. Coniectanea Biblica 5. Lund: Gleerups.

Meyers, Carol L. 1983. "Of Seasons and Soldiers: A Topological Appraisal of the Premonarchic Tribes of Galilee." *BASOR* 252:47–59.

———. 2005. *Exodus*. Cambridge: Cambridge University Press.

———. 2013. *Rediscovering Eve: Ancient Israelite Women in Context*. Oxford: Oxford University Press.

Meyers, Eric M., ed. 1996. *The Oxford Encyclopedia of Archaeology in the Near East*. 5 vols. Oxford: Oxford University Press.

Meyers, Eric M., and M. Chancey. 2012. *Alexander to Constantine: Archaeology of the Land of the Bible*. New Haven: Yale University Press.

Meyerson, Daniel. 2004. *The Linguist and the Emperor*. New York: Ballantine.

Middlemass, J. 2005. *The Troubles of Templeless Judah*. Oxford Theological Monographs. Oxford: Oxford University Press.

Mierse, W. E. 2012. *Temples and Sanctuaries from the Early Iron Age Levant*. Winona Lake, Ind.: Eisenbrauns.

Miles, Jack. 1995. *God: A Biography*. New York: Vintage Books.

Milgrom, Jacob. 1964. "Did Isaiah Prophesy during the Reign of Uzziah?" *Vetus Testamentum* 14 (2): 164–82.

———. 1990. *The JPS Torah Commentary: Numbers*. Philadelphia: Jewish Publication Society.

———. 1991. *Leviticus 1–16: A New Translation with Introduction and Commentary*. Anchor Bible 3A. Garden City, N.Y.: Doubleday.

Misgav, H. 2011. "The Khirbet Qeiyafa Ostracon." *Qadmoniot* 44:13–16.

Misgav, H., Y. Garfinkel, and S. Ganor. 2009. "The Ostracon." Pages 243–57 in *Khirbet Qeiyafa*. Vol. 1, *Excavation Report 2007–2008*. Edited by Y. Garfinkel and S. Ganor. Jerusalem: Israel Exploration Society.

Mittmann, Siegfried. 1970. *Beiträge zur Siedlungsund Territorialgeshchichte des Nördlichen OstJordanlandes*. Wiesbaden: Otto Harrassowitz.

Montefiore, Simon Sebag. 2011. *Jerusalem: The Biography*. New York: Alfred A. Knopf.

Moore, Megan Bishop, and Brad E. Kelle. 2011. *Biblical History and Israel's Past: The Changing Study of the Bible and History*. Grand Rapids: Eerdmans.

Moorey, R. P. S. 1991. *A Century of Biblical Archaeology*. Cambridge: Lutterworth.

Moran, William L. 1992. *The Amarna Letters.* Baltimore: Johns Hopkins University Press.

Moscrop, John. 2000. *Measuring Jerusalem: The Palestine Exploration Fund and British Interests in the Holy Land.* London: Leicester University Press.

Myers, Jacob M. 1965. *Ezra-Nehemiah.* New York: Doubleday.

Mykytiuk, L. J. 2004. *Identifying Biblical Persons in Northwest Semitic Inscriptions of 1200–539 B.C.E.* SBL Academia Biblica 12. Atlanta: Scholars Press.

Naaman, N. 1992. "The Pre-Deuteronomistic Story of King Saul and Its Historical Significance." *Catholic Biblical Quarterly* 54:638–57.

———. 2007. "When and How Did Jerusalem Become a Great City? The Rise of Jerusalem as Judah's Premier City in the Eighth-Seventh Centuries B.C.E." *BASOR* 347:21–56.

———. 2008. "Sojourners and Levites in the Kingdom of Judah in the Seventh Century BCE." *Zeitschrift für Altorientalische und Biblische Rechtsgeschichte* 14:237–79.

———. 2009. "The Growth and Development of Judah and Jerusalem in the Eight Century BCE: A Rejoinder." *Revue Biblique* 116 (3): 321–35.

———. 2013. "The Kingdom of Judah in the 9th Century BCE: Text Analysis versus Archaeological Research." *Tel Aviv* 40:247–76.

Nahshoni, P., and I. Ziffer. 2009. "Caphtor, the Throne of His Dwelling, Memphis, the Land of His Inheritance: The Pattern Book of a Philistine Offering Stand from a Shrine at Nahal Patish." *UF* 41:543–80.

Nakhai, B. A., ed. 2008. *The World of Women in Ancient and Classical Near East.* Newcastle upon Tyne: Cambridge Scholars.

Naveh, J. 1996. "Gleanings of Some Pottery Inscriptions." *Israel Exploration Journal* 46:44–51.

Niditch, S. 1990. "Samson as Culture Hero, Trickster, and Bandit: The Empowerment of the Weak." *Catholic Biblical Quarterly* 52:608–24.

Niehr, Herbert. 2010. "'Israelite' Religion and 'Canaanite' Religion." Pages 22–36 in Stavrakopoulou and Barton 2010.

Niesiołowski-Spanò, Ł. 2016. *Goliath's Legacy: Philistines and Hebrews in Biblical Times.* Philippika: Altertumswissenschaftliche Abhandlungen / Contributions to the Study of Ancient World Cultures 103. Wiesbaden: Harrassowitz.

Nissinen, Martti. 2003. *Prophets and Prophecy in the Ancient Near East.* With contributions by C. L. Seow and Robert K. Ritner. Atlanta: SBL Press.

Noll, K. L. 2007. "Is the Book of Kings Deuteronomistic? And Is It a History?" *Scandinavian Journal of the Old Testament* 21 (1): 49–72.

———. 2008. "Was There Doctrinal Dissemination in Early Yahweh Religion?" *Biblical Interpretation* 16:395–427.

———. 2011. "Did 'Scripturalization' Take Place in Second Temple Judaism?" *Scandinavian Journal of the Old Testament* 25 (2): 201–17.

———. 2013a. "Presumptuous Prophets Participating in a Deuteronomic Debate." Pages 125–42 in *Prophets, Prophecy, and Ancient Israelite Historiography.* Edited by M. Boda and L. W. Beal. Winona Lake, Ind.: Eisenbrauns.

———. 2013b. *Canaan and Israel in Antiquity: A Textbook on History and Religion.* 2nd ed. New York: T&T Clark.

North, Robert. "Palestine, Administration of (Judean Officials)." *ABD* 5:89–98.

Noth, Martin. 1960. *The History of Israel.* 2nd ed. New York: Harper & Row.

———. 1962. *Exodus: A Commentary.* London: SCM.

———. 1968. *Numbers: A Commentary.* Philadelphia: Westminster.

———. 1981. *The Deuteronomistic History.* JSOTSup 15. Sheffield: University of Sheffield.

Novák, M. 2012. "The Temple of ʿAin Dāra in the Context of Imperial and Neo-Hittite Architecture and Art." Pages 41–54 in *Temple Building and Temple Cult: Architecture and Cultic Paraphernalia of Temples in the Levant.* Edited by J. Kamlah. ADPV 41. Wiesbaden: Harrassowitz.

O'Connor, D. 2012. "The Mortuary Temple of Ramesses III at Medinet Habu." Pages 207–70 in *Ramesses III: The Life and Time of Egypt's Last Hero.* Edited by E. Cline and D. O'Connor. Ann Arbor: University of Michigan Press.

Oded, B. 2003. "Where Is the 'Myth of the Empty Land' to Be Found? History versus Myth." Pages 55–74 in Lipschits and Blenkinsopp 2003.

Ofer, Avi. 1993. "The Highlands of Judah during the Biblical Era." PhD diss., Tel Aviv University.

———. 1994. "'All the Hill Country of Judah.' From a Settlement Fringe to a Prosperous Monarchy." Pages 92–121 in *From Nomadism to Monarchy: Archaeological and Historical Aspects of Ancient Israel.* Edited by I. Finkelstein and N. Naaman. Jerusalem: Israel Exploration Society.

Olmstead, A. T. 1959. *History of the Persian Empire.* Chicago: University of Chicago Press.

Oppenheim, L. A. 1992. "Babylonian and Assyrian Historical Texts: The Story of Idrimi, King of Alalakh." Pages 557–58 in *Ancient Near Eastern Texts Relating to the Old Testament.* 3rd ed. with supplement. Edited by J. B. Pritchard. Princeton: Princeton University Press.

Oren, E. D. 1992. "Palaces and Patrician Houses in the Middle and Late Bronze Ages." Pages 105–20 in Kempinski and Reich 1992.

———. 1993. "Haror, Tel." *NEAEHL* 2:580–84.

———, ed. 2000. *The Sea Peoples and Their World: A Reassessment.* University Museum Monograph 108. University Symposium Series 11. Philadelphia: University of Pennsylvania Museum.

Orlinsky, Harry Meyer. 1972. *Understanding the Bible through History and Archaeology.* New York: Ktav.

Ornan, Tallay. 2009. "In the Likeness of Man: Reflections on the Anthropocentric Perception of the Divine in Mesopotamian Art." Pages 93–151 in *What Is a God? Anthropomorphic and Non-anthropomorphic Aspects of Deity in Ancient Mesopotamia.* Edited by B. N. Porter. Winona Lake, Ind.: Eisenbrauns.

Ottosson, M. 1996. "Gilead." *ABD* 2:1020–22.

Pardee, Dennis. 2002. *Ritual and Cult at Ugarit.* Atlanta: SBL Press.

———. 2007. "Preliminary Presentation of a New Ugaritic Song to *Attartu* (RIH 98/02)." Pages 27–39 in *Ugarit at Seventy-Five*. Edited by K. Lawson Younger Jr. Winona Lake, Ind.: Eisenbrauns.

———. 2009. "A New Aramaic Inscription from Zincirli." *BASOR* 356:51–71.

Parker, R. A., and W. H. Dubberstein. 1946. *Babylonian Chronology, 626 B.C.–A.D. 45*. 2nd ed. Studies in Ancient Oriental Civilization 24. Chicago: University of Chicago Press.

Parker, Simon B., ed. 1997. *Ugaritic Narrative Poetry*. Atlanta: Scholars Press.

Parry, M. L. 1978. *Climatic Change, Agriculture and Settlement*. Folkestone, UK: Dawson.

Parslow, Christopher C. 1995. *Rediscovering Antiquity: Karl Weber and the Excavation of Herculaneum, Pompeii, and Stabiae*. Cambridge: Cambridge University Press.

Pearce, L. 2006. "New Evidence for Judaeans in Babylonia." Pages 399–411 in Lipschits and Oeming 2006.

———. 2011. "'Judean': A Special Status in Neo-Babylonian and Achemenid Babylonia?" Pages 267–77 in *Judah and the Judaeans in the Achaemenid Period: Negotiating Identities in an International Context*. Edited by O. Lipschits, G. N. Knoppers, and M. Oeming. Winona Lake, Ind.: Eisenbrauns.

Pearce, L., and C. Wunsch. 2014. *Documents of Judean Exiles and West Semites in Babylonia in the Collection of David Sofer*. CUSAS 28. Potomac, Md.: Capital Decisions.

Pedersén, O. 2005. *Archive und Bibliotheken in Babylon: Die Tontafeln der Grabung Robert Koldeweys 1899–1917*. Abhandlungen der Deutschen Orient-Gesellschaft 25. Wiesbaden: Harrasowitz.

Pennock, Robert T. 2000. *Tower of Babel: The Evidence Against the New Creationism*. Cambridge, Mass.: MIT Press.

Petersen, David L. 1995. *Zechariah 9–14 and Malachi: A Commentary*. Louisville: Westminster John Knox.

Petit, Lucas P. 2014. "An Archeological Historiography of Khirbet Et-Tell and the Ongoing Search of the Biblical City of 'Ai.'" Pages 41–59 in *Archaeology in the Land of "Tells and Ruins": A History of Excavations in the Holy Land Inspired by the Photographs and Accounts of Leo Boer*. Edited by Bart Wagemakers. Oxford: Oxbow Books.

Petrie, William Matthew Flinders. 1904. *Methods and Aims in Archaeology*. New York: Macmillan.

Pfeiffer, C., L. Carlson, and M. Scharlemann. 2003. *Baker's Bible Atlas*. Grand Rapids: Baker Academic.

Pitard, Wayne T. 1998. "Before Israel: Syria-Palestine in the Bronze Age." Pages 32–77 in *The Oxford History of the Biblical World*. Edited by M. D. Coogan. New York: Oxford University Press.

Porten, Bezalel. 1996. *The Elephantine Papyri in English: Three Millennia of Cross-Cultural Continuity and Change*. Leiden: Brill.

Press, M. D. 2012. *Ashkelon 4: The Iron Age Figurines of Ashkelon and Philistia*. Final Reports of the Leon Levy Expedition to Ashkelon 4. Boston: Harvard Semitic Museum.

Preucel, R. W., and S. A. Mzrowski, eds. 2010. *Contemporary Archaeology in Theory: The New Pragmatism*. Oxford: Wiley & Blackwell.

Pritchard, James B. 1961. *The Water System of Gibeon*. Museum Monographs. Philadelphia: University of Pennsylvania Museum.

———, ed. 1969. *Ancient Near Eastern Texts Relating to the Old Testament*. 3rd ed. with supplement. Princeton: Princeton University Press.

———, ed. 1987. *Harper Atlas of the Bible*. New York: Harper & Row.

Propp, William H. C. 1999. *Exodus 1–18: A New Translation with Introduction and Commentary*. Anchor Bible. New York: Doubleday.

———. 2006. *Exodus 19–40: A New Translation with Introduction and Commentary*. Anchor Bible. New York: Doubleday.

———. 2015. "The Exodus and History." Pages 429–36 in Levi et al. 2015.

Provan, I., V. P. Long, and T. Longman III. 2003. *A Biblical History of Israel*. Louisville: Westminster John Knox. Second edition printed in 2015.

Rainey, Anson F., and R. Steven Notley. 2006. *The Sacred Bridge: Carta's Atlas of the Biblical World*. Jerusalem: Carta. Abridged as *Carta's New Century Handbook and Atlas of the Bible*. Jerusalem: Carta.

Rainey, Anson F., and William M. Schniedewind. 2015. *The El-Amarna Correspondence: A New Edition of the Cuneiform Letters from the Site of El-Amarna Based on Collations of All Extant Tablets*. Leiden: Brill.

Raphel, C. N. 1996. "Geography of Palestine." *ABD* 2:964–77.

Rast, Walter E. 1992. *Through the Ages in Palestinian Archaeology: An Introductory Handbook*. Edinburgh: T&T Clark.

Redford, Donald B. 1992. *Egypt, Canaan, and Israel in Ancient Times*. Princeton: Princeton University Press.

Redmount, Carol. 1998. "Bitter Lives in and out of Egypt." Pages 79–121 in *The Oxford History of the Biblical World*. Edited by Michael Coogan. Oxford: Oxford University Press.

———. 2013. "Egyptology and Biblical Interpretation." In *The Oxford Encyclopedia of Biblical Interpretation*. Oxford: Oxford University Press.

Reed, J. L. 2007. *The Harper Collins Visual Guide to the New Testament: What Archaeology Reveals about the First Christians*. New York: Harper One.

Reich, Ronny. 2011. *Excavating the City of David: Where Jerusalem's History Began*. Jerusalem: Israel Exploration Society.

Reich, Ronny, and E. Shukron. 2004. "The History of the Giḥon Spring in Jerusalem." *Levant* 36:211–23.

———. 2011. "The Date of the Siloam Tunnel Reconsidered." *Tel Aviv* 38 (2): 147–57.

Reich, Ronny, E. Shukron, and O. Lernau. 2007. "Recent Discoveries in the City of David, Jerusalem." *Israel Exploration Journal* 57 (3): 153–69.

Reid, Donald M. 2002. *Whose Pharaohs? Archaeology, Museums, and Egyptian National Identity from Napoleon to World War I.* Berkeley: University of California Press.

Renfrew, C., and P. Bahn. 2012. *Archaeology: Theories, Methods and Practice.* 6th ed. New York: Thames & Hudson.

Reventlow, Henning, and Leo G. Perdue. 2009. *History of Biblical Interpretation.* Atlanta: SBL Press.

Richard, Susan, ed. 2003. *Near Eastern Archaeology: A Reader.* Winona Lake, Ind.: Eisenbrauns.

Richter, W. 1963. *Traditionsgeschichtliche Untersuchungen zum Richterbuch.* Bonner Biblische Beiträge 18. Bonn: P. Hanstein.

Roaf, M. 1990. *Cultural Atlas of Mesopotamia and the Ancient Near East.* New York: Facts on File.

Robinson, Edward, and Eli Smith. 1856. *Biblical Researches in Palestine, and in the Adjacent Regions: A Journal of Travels in the Year 1838.* Boston: Crocker & Brewster.

Rogerson, John W. 1985. *Old Testament Criticism in the Nineteenth Century: England and Germany.* Philadelphia: Fortress.

Rollefson, Gary O. 1993. "Prehistoric Time." Pages 72–111 in *The History of Ancient Palestine from the Palaeolithic Period to Alexander's Conquest*, by Gösta W. Ahlström. Edited by Diana Edelman. Sheffield: JSOT Press.

Rollston, Christopher A. 2010. *Writing and Literacy in the World of Ancient Israel: Epigraphic Evidence from the Iron Age.* Atlanta: SBL Press.

———. 2011. "The Khirbet Qeiyafa Ostracon: Methodological Musings and Caveats." *Tel Aviv* 38:67–82.

———. 2013. "Ad Nomen Argumenta: Personal Names as Pejorative Puns in Ancient Texts." Pages 367–86 in *In the Shadow of Bezalel: Aramaic, Biblical and Ancient Near Eastern Studies in Honor of Bezalel Porten.* Edited by A. F. Botta. Culture & History of the Ancient Near East 60. Leiden: Brill.

Römer, Thomas. 2005. *The So-Called Deuteronomistic History: A Sociological, Historical and Literary Introduction.* New York: T&T Clark.

Rosen, Steven A., and Benjamin A. Saidel. 2010. "The Camel and the Tent: An Exploration of Technological Change among Early Pastoralists." *Journal of Near Eastern Studies* 69 (1): 63–77.

Roth, Cecil. 1959. *The Jews in the Renaissance.* Philadelphia: Jewish Publication Society of America.

Rowton, M. B. 1967. "The Woodlands of Western Asia." *JNES* 29:261–67.

Sack, R. H. 2004. *Images of Nebuchadnezzar: The Emergence of a Legend.* Cranbury, N.J.: Associated University Presses.

Saggs, H. W. F. 1982. "Assyrian Prisoners of War and the Right to Live." Pages 85–93 in *Vorträge gehalten auf der 28. Rencontre Assyriologique in Wien 6.–10. Juli 1981.* Edited by H. Hirsch and H. Hunger. AfO Beiheft 19. Horn: Berger.

———. 1999. *The Babylonians—A Survey of the Ancient Civilization of the Tigris-Euphrates Valley.* London: Folio Society.

Sapir-Hen, L., and E. Ben-Yosef. 2013. "The Introduction of Domestic Camels to the Southern Levant: Evidence from the Aravah Valley." *Tel Aviv* 40:277–85.

Sarna, Nahum M., et al. 2007. "Bible." Pages 572–679 in vol. 3 of *Encyclopaedia Judaica*. Edited by Michael Berenbaum and Fred Skolnik. 2nd ed. Detroit: Macmillan Reference USA.

Sass, B. 2002. "Wenamun and His Levant—1075 BC or 925 BC?" *Ägypten und Levante* 12:247–55.

Sasson, J. M., ed. 1995. *Civilizations of the Ancient Near East*. 4 vols. New York: Charles Scribner's Sons.

———, ed. 2000. *Civilizations of the Ancient Near East*. 4 vols. Repr., Peabody, Mass.: Hendrickson.

Sauter, M. 2016. "First-Ever Philistine Cemetery Unearthed at Ashkelon Discovery Brings Us Face to Face with the Israelites' Archenemy." *Bible History Daily*, July 10. http://www.biblicalarchaeology.org/daily/ancient-cultures/ancient-israel/first-ever-philistine-cemetery-unearthed-at-ashkelon/.

Sayce, A. H. 1908. *The Archaeology of Cuneiform Inscriptions*. London: Society for Promoting Christian Knowledge.

Schlegel, William. 2013. *Satellite Bible Atlas*. Israel: Bibleplaces.com.

Schloen, D. 2001. *The House of the Father as Fact and Symbol: Patrimonialism in Ugarit and the Ancient Near East*. Winona Lake, Ind.: Eisenbrauns.

Schmid, Konrad. 2010. "Genesis and the Moses Story." *Bible and Interpretation*, October. http://www.bibleinterp.com/articles/3gen357926.shtml.

Schmitz, P. C. 1992. "Canaan (Place)." *ABD* 1:828–31.

Schniedewind, W. M. 2000. "Sociolinguistic Reflections on the Letter of a 'Literate' Soldier (Lachish 3)." *ZAH* 13:157–67.

———. 2004. *How the Bible Became a Book: Textualization in Ancient Israel*. Cambridge: Cambridge University Press.

———. 2013. *A Social History of Hebrew: Its Origins through the Rabbinic Period*. New Haven: Yale University Press.

Schniedewind, W. M., and J. H. Hunt. 2007. *A Primer on Ugaritic Language, Culture, and Literature*. Cambridge: Cambridge University Press.

Schroeder, Bruce. 2006. "Shelter or Hunting Camp? Accounting for the Presence of a Deeply Stratified Cave Site in the Syrian Steppe." *NEA* 69 (2): 87–96.

Scurlock, J. A. 1992. "Magic (ANE)." *ABD* 4:464–68.

Seger, J. D., ed. 2001. *An ASOR Mosaic: A Centennial History of the American Schools of Oriental Research, 1900–2000*. Boston: American Schools of Oriental Research.

Shafer-Elliott, Cynthia. 2013. *Food in Ancient Judah: Domestic Cooking in the Time of the Hebrew Bible*. Bristol, Conn.: Equinox.

Shai, I., D. Ben-Shlomo, and A. M. Maeir. 2012. "Late Iron Age Judean Cooking Pots with Impressed Handles: A New Class of Stamped Impressions from the Kingdom of Judah." Pages 225–44 in *"Go Out and Study the Land" (Judges 18:2): Archaeological, Historical and Textual Studies in Honor of Hanan Eshel*. Edited by A. M. Maeir, J. Magness, and L. H. Schiffman. JSJSupp 148. Leiden: Brill.

Shanks, Herschel. 1996. "Fingerprint of Jeremiah's Scribe." *BAR* 59 (2): 36–38.

———. 2014. "Where Is Mount Sinai? The Case for Har Karkom and the Case for Saudi Arabia." *BAR* 40 (2): 30–41, 66, 68.

Shapiro, Allen L. 2011. "Judean Pillar Figurines: A Study." Master's thesis, Towson University.

Sharon, I., and A. Gilboa. 2013. "The *SKL* Town: Dor in the Early Iron Age." Pages 393–468 in *The Philistines and Other Sea Peoples in Text and Archaeology*. Edited by A. E. Killebrew and G. Lehmann. Archaeology and Bible Studies 15. Atlanta: SBL Press.

Shiloh, Y. 1980. "Solomon's Gate at Megiddo as Recorded by its Excavator, R. Lamon, Chicago." *Levant* 12:69–76.

———. 1984. *Excavations at the City of David I: Interim Report of the First Five Seasons*. Qedem 19. Jerusalem: Institute of Archaeology, Hebrew University of Jerusalem.

Silberman, Neil A. 1982. *Digging for God and Country: Exploration, Archaeology, and the Secret Struggle for the Holy Land, 1799–1917*. New York: Alfred A. Knopf.

———. 1984. "Restoring the Reputation of Lady Hester Lucy Stanhope: A Little-Known Episode in the Beginnings of Archaeology in the Holy Land." *Biblical Archaeology Review* 10 (4): 68–75.

Singer, I. 2012. "The Philistines in the North and the Kingdom of Taita." Pages 451–71 in *The Ancient Near East in the 12th–10th Centuries BCE: Culture and History; Proceedings of the International Conference Held at the University of Haifa 2–5 May, 2010*. Edited by G. Galil, A. Gilboa, A. M. Maeir, and D. Kahn. Alter Orient und Altes Testament 392. Münster: Ugarit-Verlag.

Singer-Avitz, L. 2010. "The Relative Chronology of Tel Qeiyafa." *Tel-Aviv* 37:79–83.

Skolnik, Fred, and Michael Berenbaum, eds. 2007. *Encyclopaedia Judaica*. 2nd ed. Detroit: Macmillan Reference USA in association with the Keter Pub. House.

Smith, C. 1999. "Delilah: A Suitable Case for (Feminist) Treatment?" Pages 93–116 in *Judges: A Feminist Companion to the Bible*. Edited by A. Brenner. The Feminist Companion to the Bible (Second Series) 4. Sheffield: Sheffield Academic.

Smith, Dorothy. 1968. "Queen Hester." *Huntington Library Quarterly* 31 (2): 153–78.

Smith, Mark S. 1994. *Introduction with Text, Translation and Commentary of KTU 1.1–1.2. Vol. 1 of The Ugaritic Baal Cycle*. Leiden: E. J. Brill.

———. 2001. *The Origins of Biblical Monotheism: Israel's Polytheistic Background and the Ugaritic Texts*. New York: Oxford University Press.

———. 2002. *The Early History of God: Yahweh and the Other Deities in Ancient Israel*. Grand Rapids: Eerdmans. 2nd ed., 2003.

Smith, Patricia. 1995. "People of the Holy Land from Prehistory to the Recent Past." Pages 58–74 in Levy 1995a.

Sneh, A., R. Weinberger, and E. Shalev. 2010. "The Why, How, and When of the Siloam Tunnel Revisited." *BASOR* 359:57–76.

Soden, W. von. 1983. "Kyros und Nabonid: Propaganda und Gegenpropaganda." Pages 61–68 in *Kunst, Kultur und Geschichte der Achämenidenzeit und ihr Fortleben*. Edited by H. Koch and D. N. MacKenzie. Berlin: Dietrich Reimer.

Soggin, J. Alberto. 1985. *A History of Ancient Israel*. Philadelphia: Westminster.

Solé, Robert, and Dominique Valbelle. 2002. *The Rosetta Stone: The Story of the Decoding of Hieroglyphics*. New York: Four Walls Eight Windows.

Speiser, E. A. 1964. *Genesis*. Garden City, N.Y.: Doubleday.

Stager, Lawrence E. 1985. "The Archaeology of the Family in Ancient Israel." *BASOR* 260:1–35.

———. 1990. "Shemer's Estate." *BASOR* 277–278:93–107.

———. 1995. "The Impact of the Sea Peoples in Canaan (1185–1050 BCE)." Pages 332–48 in *The Archaeology of Society in the Holy Land*. Edited by T. E. Levy. New York: Facts on File.

———. 1999. "The Fortress-Temple at Shechem and the 'House of El, Lord of the Covenant.'" Pages 332–48 in *Realia Dei: Essays in Archaeology and Biblical Interpretation in Honor of Edward F. Campbell Jr*. Edited by P. H. Williams Jr. and T. Hiebert. Atlanta: Scholars Press.

———. 2001. "Forging an Identity: The Emergence of Ancient Israel." Pages 90–131 in *The Oxford History of the Biblical World*. Edited by M. D. Coogan. New York: Oxford University Press.

———. 2003. "The Patrimonial Kingdom of Solomon." Pages 63–74 in *Symbiosis, Symbolism, and the Power of the Past: Canaan, Ancient Israel, and their Neighbors from the Late Bronze Age through Roman Palestine*. Edited by W. G. Dever and S. Gitin. Winona Lake, Ind.: Eisenbrauns.

Stavrakopoulou, Francesca, and John Barton, eds. 2010. *Religious Diversity in Ancient Israel and Judah*. New York: T&T Clark.

Stern, Ephraim, ed. 1993–2008. *The New Encyclopedia of Archaeological Excavations in the Holy Land*. 5 vols. Jerusalem: Israel Exploration Society.

———. 1993. "Kedesh, Tel [In Jezreel Valley]." *NEAEHL* 2:860.

———. 2001. *Archaeology of the Land of the Bible*. Vol. 2, *The Assyrian, Babylonian, and Persian Periods (732–332 B.C.E.)*. New York: Doubleday.

———. 2012. "Archaeological Remains of the Northern Sea Peoples along the Sharon and Carmel Coasts and 'Akko and Jezreel Valleys." Pages 473–507 in *The Ancient Near East in the 12th–10th Centuries BCE: Culture and History; Proceedings of the International Conference held at the University of Haifa 2–5 May, 2010*. Edited by G. Galil, A. Gilboa, A. M. Maeir, and D. Kahn. Alter Orient und Altes Testament 392. Münster: Ugarit-Verlag.

Stern, Ephraim, and Amihai Mazar. 2009. *Archaeology of the Land of the Bible*. Anchor Yale Bible Reference Library. New Haven: Yale University Press.

Stoddard, Robert D. 2009. "The Rev. Eli Smith, 1801–1857: Evangelical Orientalist in the Levant." *Theological Review* 30:202–22.

Stolper, M. W. 1985. *Entrepreneurs and Empire: The Murašû Archive, the Murašû Firm, and Persian Rule in Babylonia.* PIHANS 54. Leiden: Nederlands Instituut voor het Nabije Oosten.

Stone, Michael E. 2011. *Ancient Judaism: New Visions and Views.* Grand Rapids: Eerdmans.

Sweeney, Marvin A. 2001. *King Josiah of Judah: The Lost Messiah of Israel.* Oxford: Oxford University Press.

———. 2005. *The Prophetic Literature.* Nashville: Abingdon.

Tamar, K., G. Bar-Oz, S. Bunimovitz, Z. Lederman, and T. Dayan. 2013. "Geography and Economic Preferences as Cultural Markers in a Border Town: The Faunal Remains from Tell Beth-Shemesh, Israel." *International Journal of Osteoarchaeology* 10: 414–25.

Tappy, Ron E. 1992. *The Archaeology of Israelite Samaria.* 2 vols. Atlanta: Scholars Press.

———. 2006. "Samaria." Pages 61–71 in vol. 5 of *The New Interpreter's Dictionary of the Bible.* Nashville: Abingdon.

Thiele, Edwin Richard. 1983. *The Mysterious Numbers of the Hebrew Kings: A Reconstruction of the Chronology of the Kingdoms of Israel and Judah.* Chicago: University of Chicago Press, 1951. Repr., Grand Rapids: Zondervan.

Thompson, Thomas L. 1974. *The Historicity of the Patriarchal Narratives: The Quest for the Historical Abraham.* BZAW 133. Berlin: de Gruyter.

———. 1987. *The Literary Formation of Genesis and Exodus 1–23.* Vol. 1 of *The Origin Tradition of Ancient Israel.* Sheffield: JSOT Press.

———. 1992. *Early History of the Israelite People: From the Written and Archaeological Sources.* SHANE 4. Leiden: Brill.

Tigay, Jeffrey H. 1986. *You Shall Have No Other Gods: Israelite Religion in the Light of Hebrew Inscriptions.* HSS 31. Atlanta: Scholars Press.

Torczyner, H. 1938. *Lachish I: The Lachish Letters.* London: Oxford University Press.

Trebolle Barrera, Julio. 1997. *The Jewish Bible and the Christian Bible: An Introduction to the History of the Bible.* Leiden: Brill.

Trimbur, Dominique. 2011. "The École Biblique et Archéologique Française: A Catholic, French and Archaeological Institution." Pages 95–108 in Galor and Avni 2011.

Tubb, Jonathan N. 1998. *Canaanites.* Peoples of the Past 2. Norman: University of Oklahoma Press.

Tubb, Kathryn Walker. 1985. "Preliminary Report on the 'Ain Ghazal Statues." *Mitteilungen der Deutschen Orient-Gesellschaft* 117:117–34.

Ullendorff, Edward. 1971. "Is Biblical Hebrew a Language?" *BSOAS* 34 (2): 241–55.

Ulrich, Eugene. 2015. *The Dead Sea Scrolls and the Developmental Composition of the Bible.* Boston: Brill.

Ussishkin, David. 1966. "King Solomon's Palace and Building 1723 at Megiddo." *Israel Exploration Journal* 16:174–86.

———. 1980. "Was the 'Solomonic' City Gate at Megiddo Built by King Solomon?" *BASOR* 239:1–18.

———. 1982. *The Conquest of Lachish by Sennacherib*. Publication of the Institute of Archaeology 6. Tel Aviv: Institute of Archaeology.

———. 1993a. *The Village of Silwan: The Necropolis from the Period of the Judean Kingdom*. Jerusalem: Israel Exploration Society.

———. 1993b. "Lachish." *NEAEHL* 3:898–905.

———. 2004. *The Renewed Archaeological Excavations at Lachish (1973–1994)*. Monographs Series of the Institute of Archaeology. Tel Aviv: Tel Aviv University.

———. 2006. "The Borders and De Facto Size of Jerusalem." Pages 147–66 in Lipschits and Oeming 2006.

———. 2007. "Samaria, Jezreel and Megiddo: Royal Centres of Omri and Ahab." Pages 293–309 in *Ahab Agonistes: The Rise and Fall of the Omri Dynasty*. Edited by Lester L. Grabbe. London: T&T Clark.

———. 2013. *Biblical Lachish: A Tale of Construction, Destruction, Excavation and Restoration*. Jerusalem: Israel Exploration Society (in Hebrew).

———. 2014. "Sennacherib's Campaign to Judah: The Archaeological Perspective with an Emphasis on Lachish and Jerusalem." Pages 75–103 in *Sennacherib at the Gates of Jerusalem: Story, History and Historiography*. Edited by I. Kalimi and S. Richardson. Leiden: Brill.

Ussishkin, David, and John Woodhead. 1992. "Excavations at Tel Jezreel 1990–1991: Preliminary Report." *Tel Aviv* 19:3–56.

———. 1994. "Excavations at Tel Jezreel 1990–1991: Second Preliminary Report." *Levant* 26:3–56.

———. 1997. "Excavations at Tel Jezreel 1994–1996: Third Preliminary Report." *Tel Aviv* 24:6–72.

Valla, François. 1995. "The First Settled Societies—Natufian (12,500–10,200 BP)." Pages 169–87 in Levy 1995a.

Van De Mieroop, Marc. 2007. *A History of the Ancient Near East ca. 3000–323 BC*. 2nd ed. Malden, Mass.: Blackwell.

Van der Toorn, Karel. 1995. "Theology, Priests, and Worship in Canaan and Ancient Israel." Pages 2043–58 in vol. 3 of *Civilizations of the Ancient Near East*. Edited by J. M. Sasson. New York: Simon & Schuster Macmillan.

———. 2007. *Scribal Culture and the Making of the Hebrew Bible*. Cambridge, Mass.: Harvard University Press.

Van Dijk, Jacobus. 2000. "The Amarna Period and the Later New Kingdom (c. 1352–1069 BC)." Pages 272–313 in *The Oxford History of the Ancient Egypt*. Edited by Ian Shaw. Oxford: Oxford University Press.

Van Seters, John. 1975. *Abraham in History and Tradition*. London: Yale University Press.

———. 1981. "Histories and Historians of the Ancient Near East." *Orientalia* 50:137–85.

———. 1983. *In Search of History: Historiography in the Ancient World and the Origins of Biblical History*. New Haven: Yale University Press.

Vanderhooft, D. S. 1999. *The Neo-Babylonian Empire and Babylon in the Latter Prophets*. HSM 58. Atlanta: Scholars Press.

———. 2003. "New Evidence Pertaining to the Transition from Neo-Babylonian to Achaemenid Administration in Palestine." Pages 219–35 in *Yahwism after the Exile*. Edited by R. Albertz and B. Becking. Studies in Theology and Religion 5. Assen-Maastricht: Van Gorcum.

———. 2006. "Cyrus II, Liberator or Conqueror? Ancient Historiography Concerning Cyrus in Babylon." Pages 351–72 in Lipschits and Oeming 2006.

VanderKam, James C. 2010. *The Dead Sea Scrolls Today*. Grand Rapids: Eerdmans.

VanderKam, James C., and Peter Flint. 2002. *The Meaning of the Dead Sea Scrolls: Their Significance for Understanding the Bible, Judaism, Jesus and Christianity*. New York: HarperSanFrancisco.

Von Rad, Gerhard. 1966. *Deuteronomy: A Commentary*. Philadelphia: Westminster.

Wagenaar, Jan. 2005. *Origin and Transformation of the Ancient Israelite Festival Calendar*. Beihefte zur Zeitschrift für Altorientalische und Biblische Rechtsgeschichte 6. Wiesbaden: Harrassowitz.

Walker, Christopher, and Michael B. Dick. 2001. *The Induction of the Cult Image in Ancient Mesopotamia: The Mesopotamian Mīs pî Ritual*. State Archives of Assyria Literary Texts 1. Helsinki: Neo-Assyrian Text Corpus Project.

Ward, W., and M. Sharp Joukowsky, eds. 1992. *The Crisis Years: The 12th Century B.C.* Dubuque, Iowa: Kendall Hunt.

Waters, Matthew W. 2014. *Ancient Persia: A Concise History of the Achaemenid Empire, 550–330 BCE*. New York: Cambridge University Press.

Watson, W. G. E., and N. Wyatt, eds. 1999. *Handbook of Ugaritic Studies*. Leiden: Brill.

Webb, B. G. 2012. *The Book of Judges*. The New International Commentary on the Old Testament. Grand Rapids: Eerdmans.

Weidner, E. F. 1939. "Jojachin, König von Juda in Babylonischen Keilschrifttexten." Pages 923–35 in *Mélanges syriens offerts à Monsieur René Dussaud: II*. J.-A. Blanchet et al., eds. Paris: Geuthner.

Weinfeld, Moshe. 1991. *Deuteronomy 1–11: A New Translation with Introduction and Commentary*. Anchor Bible. New York: Doubleday.

Weinstein-Evron, Mina. 2009. *Archaeology in the Archives: Unveiling the Natufian Culture of Mount Carmel*. Leiden: Brill.

Weippert, M. 1971. *The Settlement of the Israelite Tribes in Palestine: A Critical Survey of the Recent Scholarly Debate*. Studies in Biblical Theology, Second Series 21. Naperville, Ill.: Alec R. Allenson.

———. 2010. *Historisches Textbuch zum Alten Testament*. GAT 10. Göttingen: Vandenhoeck & Ruprecht.

Weitzman, S. 2003. "King David's Spin Doctors," review of *King David: A Biography*, by Steven L. McKenzie; *David's Secret Demons: Messiah, Murderer, Traitor, King*, by

Baruch Halpern; *The David Story: A Translation with Commentary of 1 and 2 Samuel*, by Robert Alter; and *1 Samuel*, by David Jobling. *Prooftexts* 23:365–76.

Wellhausen, Julius. 1957. *Prolegomena to the History of Ancient Israel*. Gloucester, Mass.: Peter Smith. Repr., 1973. Translation of *Prolegomena zur Geschichte Israels* (1905).

Whiston, William. 2015. *The Complete Works of Josephus*. Palatine Press. (Original: 1878).

William, S. H. 2009. "The Qeiyafa Ostracon." *Ugarit Forschungen* 41:601–10.

Williams, Jay. 1999. *The Life and Times of Edward Robinson: A Connecticut Yankee in King Solomon's Court*. Missoula, Mont.: Scholars Press.

Williamson, H. G. M. 1985. *Ezra, Nehemiah*. Waco, Tex.: Word Books.

Wilson, J. A. 1992. "Egyptian Hymns and Prayers: Hymn of Victory of Mer-ne-Ptah (the 'Israel Stela')." Pages 376–78 in *Ancient Near Eastern Texts Relating to the Old Testament*. 3rd ed. with supplement. Edited by J. B. Pritchard. Princeton: Princeton University Press.

Wilson, Robert R. 1980. *Prophecy and Society in Ancient Israel*. Philadelphia: Fortress.

Wiseman, D. J. 1985. *Nebuchadrezzar and Babylon: The Schweich Lectures 1983*. Oxford: Oxford University Press.

Woolley, Leonard. 1930. *Digging Up the Past*. London: Ernest Benn.

———. 1954. *Excavations at Ur: A Record of Twelve Years' Work*. London: Ernest Benn.

Wright, G. E. 1947. *Biblical Archaeology*. Philadelphia: Westminster.

———. 1965. *Shechem: The Biography of a Biblical City*. New York: McGraw Hill.

———. 1967. "The Provinces of Solomon." *Eretz Israel* 8:58*–68*.

———. 1971. "What Archaeology Can and Cannot Do." *BA* 34:70–76.

Wright, J. Edward. 2002. "W. F. Albright's Vision of Israelite Religion." *NEA* 65 (1): 63–68.

———. 2003. *Baruch Ben Neriah: From Biblical Scribe to Apocalyptic Seer*. Columbia: University of South Carolina Press.

Würthwein, Ernst. 1979. *The Text of the Old Testament*. Translated by E. F. Rhodes. Grand Rapids: Eerdmans.

Wyatt, N. 1998. *Religious Texts from Ugarit: The Words of Ilimilku and His Colleagues*. Sheffield: Sheffield Academic.

Yadin, Yigael. 1963. *The Art of Warfare in Biblical Lands in the Light of Archaeological Study*. Jerusalem: Jerusalem International.

———. 1972. *Hazor*. Schweich Lectures. London: British Academy.

———. 1975. *Hazor: The Rediscovery of a Great Citadel of the Bible*. New York: Random House.

Yadin, Yigael, and Amnon Ben-Tor. 1993. "Hazor." *NEAEHL* 2:594–606.

Yardeni, A. 2009. "Further Observations on the Ostracon." Pages 259–60 in *Khirbet Qeiyafa*. Vol. 1, *Excavation Report 2007–2008*. Edited by Y. Garfinkel and S. Ganor. Jerusalem: Israel Exploration Society.

Yasur-Landau, A. 2010. *Philistines and Aegean Migration in the Late Bronze Age*. Cambridge: Cambridge University.

Yasur-Landau, A., J. R. Ebeling, and L. B. Mazow, eds. 2011. *Household Archaeology in Ancient Israel and Beyond*. Leiden: Brill.

Yerushalmi, Yosef H. 1982. *Zakhor, Jewish History and Jewish Memory*. Seattle: University of Washington Press.

Yurco, F. 1997. "Merneptah's Canaanite Campaign and Israel's Origins." Pages 27–55 in *Exodus: The Egyptian Evidence*. Edited by E. Frerichs and L. Lesko. Winona Lake, Ind.: Eisenbrauns.

Younger, K. Lawson, Jr. 2003. "Israelites in Exile." *BAR* 29 (6): 36–45, 65–66.

———. 2004. "The Repopulation of Samaria (2 Kings 17:24, 27-31) in the Light of Recent Study." Pages 254–80 in *The Future of Biblical Archaeology: Reassessing Methodologies and Assumptions; The Proceedings of a Symposium, August 12–14, 2001 at Trinity International University*. Edited by James Karl Hoffmeier and A. R. Millard. Grand Rapids: Eerdmans.

Zadok, R. 1979. *The Jews in Babylonia during the Chaldean and Achaemenian Periods According to the Babylonian Sources*. Haifa: University of Haifa.

Zawadzki, S. 1988. *The Fall of Assyria and Median-Babylonian Relations in Light of the Nabopolassar Chronicle*. Delft: Eburon.

Zeder, M. A. 1996. "The Role of Pigs in Near Eastern Subsistence: A View from the Southern Levant." Pages 297–312 in *Retrieving the Past: Essays on Archaeological Research and Mythology*. Edited by Gus W. Van Beek and J. D. Seger. Winona Lake, Ind.: Eisenbrauns.

Zertal, Adam. 1986–1987. "An Early Iron Age Cultic Site on Mount Ebal: Excavation Season 1982–1987." *Tel Aviv* 13–14:105–65.

Zevit, Ziony. 2001. *The Religions of Ancient Israel: A Synthesis of Parallactic Approaches*. New York: Continuum.

Zimmerman, Virginia. 2008. *Excavating Victorians*. Albany: State University of New York Press.

Zohary, M. 1982. *Plants of the Bible*. New York: Cambridge University Press.

Zorn, Jeffrey. 2012. "Is T1 David's Tomb?" *BAR* 38 (6): 44–52, 78.

Zuckerman, S. 2007. "Anatomy of a Destruction: Crisis Architecture, Termination Rituals and the Fall of Canaanite Hazor." *Journal of Mediterranean Archaeology* 20 (1): 3–32.

GAZETTEER

Key: Site name, followed by other site names if relevant. This is then followed by the map number on which the site first appears.

Abel: Also Abel Beit Maacah, Tel Avel Bet Maakha. Map 13-2

Abel Beth Maacah: *See* Abel

Abu Simbel: Map 1-1

Abydos: Also Abdju. Map 1-1

Achzib: Map 7-2

Acre: Also Akko, Acco. Map 3-1

Aegean Sea: Map 3-2

Ai: Map 7-1

Aijalon: Map 11-1

Aijalon Valley: Also Ayalon, Ajalon. Map 1-5

Ain Dara: Map 1-4

Akko: *See* Acre

Aleppo: Map 3-1

Alexandria: Map 3-1

Amarna: Also Akhetaten, Tell el-Amarna. Map 1-1

Ammon: Map 9-2

Ammonium: Also Siwa. Map 20-1

Anathoth: Also Anata. Map 20-2

Anatolia: Also Asia Minor, Turkey. Map 3-1

Anti-Lebanon Mountains. Map 1-4

Anti-Taurus Mountains: Map 1-3

Aphek (#1): Also Tel Afek, Antipatris. Map 7-1

Aphek (#2): Also Tel Ein Gev. Map 14-1

Arad: Map 7-1

Aram-Naharaim: *See* Paddan Aram

Aram/Zobah: Map 13-2

Arpad: Also Horbat Arpad. Map 13-2

Arvad: Map 1-4

Ashdod: Map 7-2

Asher: Map 11-1

Ashkelon: Map 7-2

Ashtaroth: Also Astartu. Map 9-2

Asia Minor: Also Anatolia. Map 3-1

Asshur: Map 1-3

Assyrian Empire: Map 17-2

Aswan: Map 1-1

Athens: Map 3-2

Atlit: Map 20-2

Avaris: Also Pi-Rameses, Tel el Daba. Map 1-1

Azeqah: Also Azekah. Map 13-1

Bab Edh-Dhra: Map 7-1

Babylon: Map 1-3

Bactra: Map 20-1

Bactria: Map 20-1

Balikh River: Map 1-3

Bashan: Map 1-5

Beer-lahai-roi: Unknown.

Beersheba: Also Beer-sheba, Beersheva, Beer Sheva. Map 1-4

Beirut: Map 1-4

Beni Hassan: Map 1-1

Benjamin: Map 11-1

Beqaa Valley: Also Biqaa. Map 1-4

Beth Anath(?): Map 9-2

Beth El: *See* Bethel

Beth Shean: Map 7-1

Beth Shemesh: Map 13-1

Beth Yerah: Map 7-1

Beth Zur: Map 7-2

Italy: Map 3-2
Izbeth Sartah: Map 13-1

Jabesh-Gilead: Also Jabesh, Tall al-Maqlub.
  Map 8-2
Jabneel: Also Yavneel, Yavneh, Yavne. Map
  9-2
Jaffa: Also Joppa. Map 3-1
Jalul: Also Bezer. Map 14-1
Janoah(?): Also Yanoah. Map 14-1
Jatt: Also Arzi, Baqa-Jatt. Map 13-2
Jebel al-Lawz: Map 9-1
Jerash: Map 3-1
Jericho: Map 7-1
Jerusalem: Map 1-4
Jezreel: Map 14-1
Jezreel Valley: Map 1-5
Joppa: See Jaffa
Jordan River: Map 1-4
Judah: Map 13-1
Judean Hills: Map 1-5

Kabri: Map 7-2
Kadesh: See Kadesh-barnea
Kadesh-barnea: Also Tel el-Qudeirat. Map
  9-1
Kamon(?): Also Gilead. Map 11-1
Karnak: See Thebes
Kedesh: Map 11-1
Kerak Plateau: Map 1-4
Ketef Hinnom: Map 15-1
Khabur River: Also Habur. Map 1-3
Khirbet Beit Lei: Also Beth Loya.
  Map 1-5
Khirbet el-Qom. Map 1-5
Khirbet en-Nahas: Also Khirbet en-Naúas.
  Map 9-2
Khirbet Marjameh. Map 14-1
Khirbet Rabud: Also Debir, Kiryat Sepher.
  Map 13-1
Khorsabad: Also Dur Sharrukin.
  Map 1-3
King's Highway: Map 1-4
Kinneret: Also Chinnereth. Map 14-1
Kuntillet Ajrud: Map 1-4
Kutha: Also Cuthah. Map 17-2
Kuyunjik: See Nineveh

Lachish: Map 7-1

Laish: Also Dan. Map 8-2
Lake Galilee: See Sea of Galilee
Lake Sirbonis: Also Lake Bardawil.
  Map 9-1
Larsa: Map 20-1
Lebanon Mountains: Map 1-4
Levant: Map 1-3
Lod: Map 9-2
Lower Egypt: Map 1-1
Lower Galilee: Map 1-5
Luxor: See Thebes
Luz: See Bethel

Madaba: Map 14-1
Mahanaim: Unknown, near Jabesh-Gilead.
  Map 8-2
Manasseh: Map 11-1
Maracanda: Also Samarkand. Map 20-1
Maresha: Also Sandahannah. Map 15-1
Mari: Also Tel Hariri. Map 1-3
Masos: Also Tel Masos. Map 13-1
Media: Map 17-2
Mediterranean Sea: Map 1-2
Megiddo: Map 1-5
Memphis: Map 1-1
Mesad Hashavyahu: Map 15-1
Mesopotamia: Map 1-2
Midian: Map 9-1
Mizpah: Also Mizpeh, Tel en-Nasbeh. Map
  8-2
Moab: Map 9-2
Mosul: Map 1-3
Moza: Map 15-1
Mt. Behistun: Also Bisutun Rock.
  Map 1-3
Mt. Carmel: Map 1-5
Mt. Ebal: Map 1-5
Mt. Gerizim: Map 11-1
Mt. Gilboa: Map 13-2
Mt. Hermon: Map 1-4
Mt. Hor: Map 9-1
Mt. Horeb: See Mt. Sinai
Mt. Karkom: Also Har Karkom. Map 9-1
Mt. Nebo: Also Pisgah. Map 9-2
Mt. Seir: Map 1-4
Mt. Sinai: Also Horeb, Jebel Musa.
  Map 9-1
Mt. Vesuvius: Map 3-2

Mt. Zaphon: Also Jebel Aqra. Map 1-4

Nahariyah: Map 7-2
Naphtali: Map 11-1
Negev, Negev Desert: Map 9-1
Neirab: Map 1-4
Nile: Map 1-1
Nile Delta: Map 1-1
Nimrud: Also Calah, Kalakh. Map 17-2
Nineveh: Map 1-3
Nippur: Map 1-3
Numeira: Map 7-1
Nuzi: Also Gasur. Map 1-3

Ono: Also Kafr Ana, Or Yehuda.
   Map 20-2
Ophrah(?) in Manasseh: Map 11-1
Orontes Valley: Map 3-1

Paddan-Aram: Map 1-3
Parthia: Map 20-1
Pasargadae: Map 20-1
Penuel: Map 8-2
Persepolis: Map 1-3
Persia: Map 17-2
Persian Gulf: Map 1-3
Petra: Map 3-1
Philadelphia: Also Rabbath Ammon,
   Amman. Map 3-1
Philistia: Map 12-1, 13-1
Phoenicia: Map 14-1
Pi-Rameses: Also Tel el Daba, Avaris.
   See Rameses
Pirathon(?) in Ephraim: Map 11-1
Pithom: Also Pi-Atum. *See* Tell er-Ratabah,
   Tell el-Makshuta
Plains of Moab: Map 1-4
Pompeii: Map 3-2

Qadesh: Map 1-4
Qarqar: Map 1-4
Qeiyafa: Also Khirbet Qeiyafa.
   Map 13-1
Qumran: Map 1-5

Rabbat Ammon: Also Ammon, Philadelphia.
   Map 9-2
Ramah: Map 11-1

Ramat Rahel: Also Ramat Rachel, Khirbet
   es-Sallah, Beit Hakerem.
   Map 15-1
Rameses: Also Tell el-Daba, Avaris, Qantir.
   Map 9-1
Ramoth-Gilead: Map 14-1
Ras Shamra: *See* Ugarit
Red Sea: Map 3-1
Rehov: Map 7-2
Rift Valley: Map 1-4
Rome: Map 3-2
Rosetta: Map 3-1

Salem: *See* Jerusalem
Samaria: Map 1-5
Samarian Hills: Map 1-5
Sardinia: Map 3-2
Sardis: Map 20-2
Sea of Galilee: Also Lake Galilee.
   Map 1-4
Sepharvaim: Also Sippar, Abbu Habbah, Tell
   ed-Der. Map 17-2
Shamir(?) in Ephraim: Map 11-1
Sharon Plain: Map 1-5
Shatt al-Arab waterway: Map 1-3
Shechem: Map 1-4
Shephelah: Map 1-5
Shiloh in Ephraim: Map 11-1
Shiqmona: Map 7-3
Shunem: Also Solem, Sulam. Map 14-1
Sicily: Map 3-2
Sidon: Map 1-4
Sinai Desert: Map 1-1
Socho: Also Horvat Sokho. Map 13-1
Sodom: Unknown. Map 8-2
Sogdiana: Map 20-1
Sorek Valley: Map 1-5
Suez Isthmus: Map 9-1
Susa: Map 1-3
Syria: Map 3-1
Syro-Arabian Desert: Map 1-2

Taanach: Map 7-1
Tadmor: Also Palmyra. Map 20-1
Tamar: Also Mezad Tamar. Map 13-1
Tanis: Map 1-1
Taurus Mountains: Map 1-3
Tayinat: Also Tel Tayinat. Map 1-4
Tel Batash: Map 7-2

Tel el-Farah (N): Map 7-1
Tel el-Farah (S): Map 7-2
Tel el-Full: Also Gibeah. Map 20-2
Tel el-Maskhuta: Also Pithom, Makshuta.
    Map 9-1
Tel Erani: Map 7-1
Tel Gerisa: Map 7-2
Tel Goded: Map 15-1
Tel Halif: Map 7-1
Tel Ira: Map 13-1
Tel Kinrot: Map 7-3
Tel Malhata: Map 7-1
Tel Masos: Map 7-2
Tel Mevorakh: Map 7-3
Tel Michal: Map 7-2
Tel Miqne: Map 7-3
Tel Mor: Map 7-3
Tel Movorakh: Map 7-2
Tel Nagila: Map 7-2
Tel Poleg: Map 7-2
Tel Qashish: Map 7-1
Tel Qasile: Map 13-1
Tel Rehov: Map 13-2
Tel Sheva: Also Beersheba. Map 1-4
Tel Zayit: Map 13-1
Tell Abu Hawam: Map 7-3
Tell Beit Mirsim: Map 7-2
Tell Deir Alla: Map 7-3
Tell el-Ajjul: Map 7-2
Tell el-Daba: Also Avaris, Rameses, Qantir.
    See Rameses
Tell el-Farah (N): Also Tirzah. Map 7-2
Tell el-Farah (S): Map 7-3
Tell el-Hesi: Map 20-2
Tell el-Judeideh: Map 15-1
Tell el-Umeiri: Map 7-1
Tell el-Yehudiyeh: Also Leontopolis. Map 9-1
Tell en-Nasbeh: Map 13-1
Tell er-Retaba: Also Pithom. Map 9-1
Tell Jemmeh: Map 7-2
Tell Meskene: Also Emar. Map 1-4
Tell Umm Hamad: Map 7-1
Teman(?): Map 18-1
Tesmes: Also Mashhad. Map 20-1
Thebes: Also Waset, Luxor, Karnak.
    Map 1-1

Tiberias: Map 3-1
Tigris River: Map 1-2
Timnah: Also Tel Batash. Map 9-2
Tirzah: Also Tell el Farah (North), Tappuah,
    Tiphsah. Map 13-2
Transjordan: Map 1-4
Tyre: Map 1-4

Ugarit: Also Ras Shamra. Map 1-3
Umayri: Map 14-1
Upper Egypt: Map 1-1
Upper Galilee: Map 1-5
Ur: Map 1-3
Urartu: Map 1-3
Uruk: Also Erech. Map 17-2

Vered Yericho: Map 15-1

Via Maris: Also International Coastal
    Highway. Map 1-5

Wadi Arnon: Map 1-5
Wadi ed-Daliyeh: Also Wadi Daliyeh, Abu
    Shinjeh. Map 20-2
Wadi Faynan: Map 13-1
Wadi Jabbok: Map 1-4
Wadi Ma'in: Map 1-5
Wadi Tumilat: Map 9-2
Wadi Yarmouk: Map 1-4
Wadi Zered: Map 1-4
Way of the Land of the Philistines: Also Way
    of Horus. Map 9-1
Wilderness of Paran: Map 9-1
Wilderness of Shur: Map 9-1
Wilderness of Sin: Also Wilderness of Sinai.
    Map 9-1
Wilderness of Zin: Map 9-1

Yarmuth: Map 7-1
Yavneh-Yam: Map 7-2
Yoqneam: Map 7-1

Zagros Mtns: Map 1-3
Zebulun: Map 11-1
Zoar: Also Bela, Zoara. Map 8-2

INDEX OF BIBLICAL AND ANCIENT REFERENCES

Other Ancient Texts

GENERAL INDEX

Aaron, 78, 243, 244, 247, 268, 491, 499
Aaronide priests, 272
Abda-Yahu, 518
Abdi-Ashirta, 356, 358
Abdi-hepa, 347
Abdi-Irši, 203
Abdon, 306
Abel/Abel Beth-Maacah 359, 387, 458
Abî-Jahô, 525
Abiezerites of Manasseh, 306, 309
Abimelech, 227, 303, 306, 309, 355, 356
Abisha Scroll, 57
Abner, 358
Abraham/Abram, 8, 9, 15, 21, 52, 61, 64, 65,
    70, 75, 78, 81, 111, 185, 213–24, 227–30,
    263, 264, 318, 485, 501, 505, 529, 213–40
Absalom, 344, 358, 361
Abu Nabbut, Muhammad, 104
Abu Simbel, 480
Abuqir Bay, 95
Acco, 193, 459
Achaemenid Empire, 113, 514, 545, 556
Achaemenids, 113
Achiqam, 518
Achiqar, 518
Achish, 338, 339, 342, 355, 360
Acre, 95
Adad, 175, 483, 484
Adad Gate, 507
Adad-nirari III, 372, 383, 384, 398
Adam, 63, 230
Adar, 508
Adbeel, 231
Addu: see Adad
adyton, 354

Aegean, 204, 321, 322, 329, 330, 331, 333,
    467; artifacts, 332; figurines, 329; pottery,
    325, 326, 328, 330, 331, 334
Aegean Sea, 85, 538
Aegeans, 298
Agade, 171, 524
Agha/Aqil, 107
agro-pastoralism, 417, 419, 430
Ahab, 138, 352, 353, 355, 363, 372–83, 385,
    393, 430, 437, 446
Aharoni, Yohanan, 43, 139, 144, 147, 291
Ahaz, 387, 403, 442, 469
Ahaziah, 380, 381, 382
Ahijah, 369
Ahikam, 520, 544
Ahituv, Shmuel, 502
Ahiyahu, 510
Ahlström, G. W., 211
Ahn, J., 527
Ahuzam, 431
Ahwat, 324
Ai, 143, 153, 199–200, 228, 292–93, 301
Aijalon, 28, 306
Ain Dara, 354, 479
Air, 146
Akhenaten, 99, 185, 234, 250–53, 295, 347,
    486
Akkad, 22, 99, 171, 183, 224, 459, 508, 521,
    524
Akkadian cuneiform, 544
Akkadian language, 548
Akko, 356, 536; Plain, 279–80, 285
Al-Yahudu, 12, 522, 526, 544
Alalakh, 185, 198
Albertz, Rainer, 483, 500–502, 520, 522

CONTRIBUTORS

Gary P. Arbino. Professor of Archaeology and Old Testament Interpretation, Curator of the Marian Eakins Archaeological Collection, Gateway Seminary, Ontario, California

Jill L. Baker. Independent Researcher of Ancient Near Eastern Archaeology, Teaching Fellow, Honors College, Florida International University, Miami

Bob Becking. Professor for Bible, Religion, and Identity, Emeritus, Faculty of Humanities, Universiteit Utrecht, Netherlands

J. P. Dessel. Steinfeld Associate Professor of Jewish History, Department of History, University of Tennessee, Knoxville

William G. Dever. Professor Emeritus, University of Arizona, Tucson

Jennie Ebeling. Associate Professor of Archaeology, Department of Archaeology and Art History, University of Evansville, Evansville, Indiana

Mark Elliott. Adjunct Professor of Judaic Studies, Arizona Center for Judaic Studies, University of Arizona, Tucson

Paul V. M. Flesher. Professor of Religious Studies, University of Wyoming, Laramie

Rachel Hallote. Professor of History, Purchase College, State University of New York, Purchase

Baruch Halpern. Covenant Foundation Professor of Jewish Studies, Department of Religion, University of Georgia, Athens

Richard S. Hess. Earl S. Kalland Professor of Old Testament and Semitic Languages, Denver Seminary, Littleton, Colorado

Charles David Isbell. Professor of Jewish Studies, Louisiana State University, Baton Rouge

Ann E. Killebrew. Associate Professor, Classics and Ancient Mediterranean Studies, Jewish Studies and Anthropology, Pennsylvania State University, University Park

Aren M. Maeir. Professor of Archaeology and Director, Minerva Center for the Relations between Israel and Aram, Department of Land of Israel Studies and Archaeology Bar-Ilan University, Bar-Ilan University, Ramat-Gan, Israel

Victor H. Matthews. Professor of Religious Studies, Dean of the College of Humanities and Public Affairs, Missouri State University, Springfield

K. L. Noll. Professor, Religion Department, Brandon University, Brandon, Manitoba

J. Edward Wright. The J. Edward Wright Endowed Professor of Judaic Studies, Arizona Center for Judaic Studies, University of Arizona, Tucson

Randall W. Younker. Professor of Archaeology and History of Antiquity, Institute of Archaeology, Director, Seventh Day Adventist Theological Seminary, Andrews University, Berrien Springs, Michigan